The Great Radio Sitcoms

Radio Speakers: Narrators, News Junkies, Sports Jockeys, Tattletales, Tipsters, Toastmasters and Coffee Klatch Couples Who Verbalized the Jargon of the Aural Ether from the 1920s to the 1980s—A Biographical Dictionary (2007)

The Daytime Serials of Television, 1946–1960 (2006)

Music Radio: The Great Performers and Programs of the 1920s through Early 1960s (2005)

Mr. Keen, Tracer of Lost Persons: A Complete History and Episode Log of Radio's Most Durable Detective (2004)

Frank and Anne Hummert's Radio Factory: The Programs and Personalities of Broadcasting's Most Prolific Producers (2003)

Radio Crime Fighters: Over 300 Programs from the Golden Age (2002)

Say Goodnight, Gracie: The Last Years of Network Radio (2002)

The Great Radio Audience Participation Shows: Seventeen Programs from the 1940s and 1950s (2001)

The Great Radio Soap Operas (1999)

# The Great Radio Sitcoms

## JIM COX

McFarland & Company, Inc., Publishers
*Jefferson, North Carolina, and London*

*All photographs provided by Photofest.*

LIBRARY OF CONGRESS CATALOGUING-IN-PUBLICATION DATA

Cox, Jim, 1939–
The great radio sitcoms / Jim Cox.
p.    cm.
Includes bibliographical references and index.

**ISBN-13: 978-0-7864-3146-5**
illustrated case binding : 50# alkaline paper ∞

1.  Radio comedies—United States—History and criticism.
I. Title.
PN1991.8.C65C69    2007        79144'617—dc22        2007025482

British Library cataloguing data are available

Cover photograph: Marian and Jim Jordan, later the stars of *Fibber McGee & Molly,*
in a publicity shot from the 1931–1935 show *Smackout*

Manufactured in the United States of America

*McFarland & Company, Inc., Publishers
Box 611, Jefferson, North Carolina 28640
www.mcfarlandpub.com*

*With esteem for my colleagues of the
Audio Studio for the Reading Impaired, Inc.,
Anchorage, Kentucky,
who season noble service with euphoria,
habitually reaffirming
laughter mollifies the soul*

# Acknowledgments

No one poured more time, energy and talent into helping me pull together the detail in these pages than Irene Heinstein, one of the most tireless and determined researchers I know. Her dogged persistence paid off time and time again when I was convinced that the task was little short of impossible. The woman has sources and an uncanny intuition for locating obscure matter that most of us can only envy. Beyond her ability to capture heretofore undisclosed colorful tidbits, on numerous occasions she offered insightful perspectives that allowed me to reach beyond the statistical stuff and move past actual events to comprehend how and why issues of import transpired as they did. Irene is due a profusion of accolades. Without her zealous dedication, this work would be sorely lacking, I assure you. I am manifestly in her debt.

My pal Charles Niren, one of the most gracious fellows I know, came through with transcriptions of the shows I needed that weren't in my personal collection. Every time I asked Charlie for "a couple of episodes" of this and that, I received a half-dozen to a dozen installments of a given series. This, of course, allowed me to better compare a show over longer broadcast timeframes. Charlie has amassed a sizable library of programs, and he invariably shares his wealth. As a beneficiary, I am grateful.

So many more aficionados of OTR (old-time radio) contributed materially to this project by clarifying details and supplying additional trivia. None stands higher than Claire Connelly and Gary Mercer, reliable comrades who have helped me with so many previous books. I am truly grateful once again. In addition, I'm thankful for the contributions of all of the following who responded to specific requests for assistance: Tom Brown, Eddie Carroll, Travis Conner, Doug Douglass, Don Frey, Martin Grams Jr., Ben Kibler, Stuart Lubin, Elizabeth McLeod, Ted Meland, Gregg Oppenheimer, Catherine Passelli, Ron Sayles, David Schwartz, Harlan Stone and Paul Urbahns.

Along the way I enlisted the input of a panel of OTR buffs that helped in determining the final selections of the sitcoms for inclusion herein. Their valuable participation is duly acknowledged with my thanks: Melanie Aultman, Chris Chandler, Doug Douglass, Andrew Godfrey, Ted Kneebone, Ted Meland, Gary Mercer, Elizabeth Minney, Arlene Osborne, Chuck Schaden and Stewart Wright.

As always, I am particularly appreciative of the supportive efforts of a handful of vintage radio and nostalgia periodical journalists who not only encourage me but support all of our collective efforts in preserving and perpetuating old time radio for present and future generations. Among my friends in that arena I am pleased to include Bob Axley, Bob Burchett, Steve Darnall, Jack French, Jay Hickerson, Ken Krug, Patrick Lucanio, Robert Newman and Marilyn Wilt. A quartet of broadcasters I have worked with is also helping to keep OTR alive: Frank Bresee, Tom Heathwood, Walden Hughes and Chuck Schaden. All of these stalwarts encourage authors like me in our collective quest.

The love of my life, Sharon Cox, yields to my obsession with OTR far more than I should expect. I am in love with her even more than I am this compelling passion. I'm surely a lucky man to have her by my side.

Finally, thanks to one and all who read these words. I hope my efforts will prove worthy of keeping the spirit alive.

# Contents

# Introduction

## FUNNY BUSINESS

In his defining, comprehensive trilogy of the history of radio broadcasting in America, author Erik Barnouw (1908–2001) unfortunately all but dismissed the contributions of the radio sitcom.[1] Instead he reminded his readers multiple times that the comedians of vaudeville and musical comedy topped the radio popularity polls from the 1930s (when those numbers were gathered for the first time) through the 1950s. We can find no fault with the tabulations of a consummate scholar like Barnouw; however, overlooking the sitcom may be a disservice to readers and researchers.

It's at least troubling that—with the exception of *Amos 'n' Andy* and an itsy bitsy teeny weenie handful of its aural equivalents, most named only once in three volumes, plus a couple of headliners who branched into narrative plotting—the sitcom is virtually written off, though perhaps inadvertently. From that genre sprang popular fare like *The Adventures of Ozzie and Harriet, The Aldrich Family, Archie Andrews, Baby Snooks, Blondie, Duffy's Tavern, Father Knows Best, The Great Gildersleeve, Our Miss Brooks* and so many more series that found an enduring niche inspired future programs. The casual listing of only a few series of its type leaves unfinished a very important chapter in radio's pervasive story.

Not every authority buys into Barnouw's assessment, however. Writing in a more recent treatise, an erudite university professor named Alfred Balk, who also carries a fertile pen, proclaims: "As in other entertainment, drama's comedy form—situation comedy, or sitcoms—was king."[2]

Applying the colorfully expressive term *sitcom americanus*, media historiographer Gerald Nachman describes the category as follows:

> Situation comedy was a totally new comic form. It ventured beyond crude gag-oriented sketches and involved listeners in middle-class lives not so unlike their own—simple homey incidents inflated into domestic farce....
>
> Radio was the massest of mass entertainment, and its audience mostly middlebrow and increasingly suburban, was amused and flattered at seeing itself reflected in shows that made light of its travails but never questioned the all–American family unit. *The Aldrich Family, A Date with Judy,* and *Vic and Sade* didn't know from divorced parents, single mothers, illegitimate kids, swinging singles, and biracial broods. Radio sitcoms didn't prattle on about the nuclear family because it had not yet been threatened.[3]

Merriam-Webster didn't add *situation comedy* to its dictionaries until 1946, a term that it condensed into *sitcom* in 1964. The linguistic authority delineated the phrase as "a radio or television comedy series that involves a continuing cast of characters in a succession of episodes."

Although some may think of the sitcom as a product of the 1940s or possibly even the 1930s, radio historians have affirmed that the form can be traced to the 1920s. While it wasn't recognized by a descriptive phrase at the time, most authorities agree that the sitcom's origin is a pithy 10-minute nightly exchange of humor—*Sam 'n' Henry*—that Freeman Gosden and Charles Correll launched over Chicago's WGN Radio on January 12, 1926. That was followed by *Amos 'n' Andy* (1928) and *The Rise of the Goldbergs* (1929), which perpetuated the form and solidified it as a new genus within broadcast programming. Those series offered returning figures that functioned in familiar surroundings, traits that were emblematic of sitcoms of considerably later vintage. Notwithstanding the fact that it took Webster (and the country) two more decades to classify the species, the situation comedy or sitcom was up and running well before anybody put a label on it.

Despite limited acclaim for a handful of sitcoms airing in the 1930s, most listeners—as Barnouw correctly pointed out—preferred a comedy-variety mix long associated with stage clowns. This included shows starring a few early radio legends, like Fred Allen, Jack Benny, Eddie Cantor, Jimmy Durante, Jack Pearl, Joe Penner, Rudy Vallee, Ed Wynn and more. According to historiographer Fred MacDonald, *Amos 'n' Andy* was the only spectacularly successful sitcom of the 1930s. When *Amos 'n' Andy* began to wane late in the decade, *Fibber McGee & Molly* emerged as the new leader of the sitcom pack. It ultimately became such a sensation, in fact, that it prompted a cluster of fresh sitcoms to surface at the end of the 1930s and beginning of the 1940s. Subsequently, *The Aldrich Family* and *Blondie* (both with 1939 starts), *Duffy's Tavern*, *A Date with Judy* and *The Great Gildersleeve* (all in 1941) further set the tone for a spate of laugh-filled treasures to come down the pike.

Some of those innovations replaced a handful of vaudevillians-turned-broadcasters who—a decade earlier—transferred their gag-filled routines from sight-oriented to audio-oriented venues. Now many of them were departing, and in their stead Americans were laughing at a nascent craze in domestic-oriented wit. "The key to success with audiences in the 1940s," astute media academic MacDonald attested, "was the development of a fallible, recognizable, sympathetic human character with whom listeners could warmly identify."[4] Thus, audiences were attracted to newly arriving protagonists like Corliss Archer, Archie Andrews, Judy Canova and Chester A. Riley, who were filling up the vacancies in the program itineraries.

In the meantime, to avoid extinction, venerated comedians like George Burns and Gracie Allen shifted their once proud series centered on unconnected skits to a half-hour situation comedy. The revision in 1941 returned them to radio's top 10 performers after they had fallen to one of the lowest rungs on the ratings ladder. A few of their peers similarly adapted or were soon abandoned by listeners. It was a new day in audio comedy, and showmen could hop onto the bandwagon or risk unemployment.

As the end of the 1940s approached, the sitcom blossomed, with a plethora of still more laugh-filled narratives bursting forth in the final three years of the decade. It was kind of a last gasp for network radio, although it was an era in which the medium drew some of its largest audiences and its most loyal fans. Among that sizable deputation of pristine programming, shows like *My Friend Irma* (debuting in 1947); *Junior Miss, Our Miss Brooks, The Phil Harris–Alice Faye Show* and *Life with Luigi* (all in 1948); and *My Favorite Husband* and *Father Knows Best* (both in 1949) were attractive innovations. By the time radio's golden age neared its end a decade later, some 170 sitcoms had played out their mirthful plotlines over three decades (see Appendix A). Collectively, that wasn't a shabby sample of a genus that weathered the ups and downs of broadcasting, obviously increasing prolifically and in popularity as time elapsed.

Characterizing the form, one modern source explained: "Radio situation comedies were middle-class morality tales. The American family was portrayed as a vital institution in which love, trust, and self-confidence were best developed. Altercations resulted from misunderstanding or a lack of trust; disruptions in social harmony were short-lived and trivial; personal weaknesses were often the signs of tolerant characters; and love and respect permeated the narrative."[5] Answer this truthfully: do you still witness those sterling behaviors in the preponderance of sitcoms televised today? (You really don't have to respond.)

MacDonald defines three distinctive species of sitcoms. There were those that had: (1) episodes occurring within a family that lived in its own dwelling (i.e., *The Adventures of Ozzie and Harriet, Father Knows Best, My Favorite Husband, The Great Gildersleeve*); (2) a group of recurring but unrelated figures that maintained a commercial enterprise (i.e., *Duffy's Tavern, Meet Me at Parky's, Smackout*); (3) a distinctive personality as the central character, who was mobile and traveled often to multiple locales (i.e., *The Jack Benny Program, My Friend Irma, Our Miss Brooks, The Judy Canova Show, Life with Luigi*). There were subgroups, too, like a rash of teen-oriented family sitcoms in category 1, such as *The Aldrich Family* and its imitators (*That Brewster Boy, A Date with Judy, Junior Miss, Archie Andrews, Meet Corliss Archer, Harold Teen, Maudie's Diary*, and more, ad infinitum). Another segment of the same consortium could be signified as conversant couples—married duos who devoted much of their airtime to humorous exchanges, without much infringement by others. Examples are *Ethel and Albert, Niles and Prindle* and *Vic and Sade*.

In the early 1950s radio comedies of every stripe were in freefall, spiraling into decline as a form of American entertainment. MacDonald lays the phenomenon almost entirely at the feet of television, which by then had burst onto the scene in many parts of the nation and was quickly replacing radios in the nation's living rooms. "Ironically," says he, "the chief catalyst in this development was a comedian whose radio career had been less than spectacular. Milton Berle had never had a successful radio series."[6] In 1947 Berle was the first "name" comic to jump ship and land a thriving weekly video series. Several other humorists were prompted to abandon the sinking ship by Berle's incredible showing on the small screen. At the very least, a few launched video versions of their long-successful radio features.

Sitcoms followed the same path, some leaving their radio roots behind altogether. *The George Burns and Gracie Allen Show* is typical of those seeking television's potentially greater number of greenbacks. Others, like *Our Miss Brooks*, ran simultaneously in both media. The new trend was ultimately sealing radio's fate. As sponsors pulled the big bucks out of radio and shifted them to the tube, fan loyalties evaporated, too, as legions moved with little hesitation from the avenue that spawned much of early TV. Left behind was an almost empty shell of the nation's initial universal communications tool. "Radio comedy had served its audience faithfully as companion, advisor, model, and entertainer. Its passing into irrelevance in the 1950s signaled the end of a distinct era in the history of American civilization."[7]

Aside from purely subjective observations, eight shows readily stand out from their more than 160 contemporaries as the most enduring (based on airtime in half-hour original and exclusively sitcom formats). In ranking order, they are:[8]

1. *The Jack Benny Program*
2. *Fibber McGee & Molly*
3. *The Aldrich Family*
4. *The Great Gildersleeve*
5. *Baby Snooks*
6. *Blondie*
7. *The Amos 'n' Andy Show*
8. *The Adventures of Ozzie and Harriet*

With few exceptions (Jack Benny, George Burns and Gracie Allen among them), most of the sitcoms weren't headlined by legendary performers whose names brought instant and widespread recognition. The lion's share of such radio fare was usually headlined by individuals with "lesser" monikers like Jim and Marian Jordan, Arthur Lake and Hattie McDaniel.

Hidden still further from widespread detection and adulation were fraternities of

skilled artisans who were called upon for supporting roles in the surfeit of sitcoms airing
from both the East and West coasts. Among
their number was a handful whose voices
could he heard almost incessantly. Some appeared simultaneously in a half-dozen or
more of the situation comedies. Based upon
studies of their documented accomplishments, the most durable of the supporting-
role actors—without regard to their achievements elsewhere in radio—were these, in
order of their number of series:

**Bea Benaderet** (13 series, plus another as co-star); Key Roles: Blanche Morton
on *The George Burns and Gracie Allen Show*,
Bertha Bronson on *Meet Millie*, Millicent
Carstairs on *Fibber McGee & Molly*.

**Gale Gordon** (13 series, plus another
as co-star); Key Roles: Osgood Conklin on
*Our Miss Brooks*, Mayor Charles LaTrivia and
F. Ogden "Foggy" Williams on *Fibber McGee
& Molly*, Rudolph Atterbury on *My Favorite
Husband*, Rumson Bullard on *The Great
Gildersleeve*.

**Hans Conried** (11 series); Key Roles:
Professor Kropotkin on *My Friend Irma*,
Schultz on *Life with Luigi*, Uncle Baxter on
*The Life of Riley*.

**Elvia Allman** (8 series); Key Roles:
Cora Dithers on *Blondie*, Tootsie Sagwell on
*The George Burns and Gracie Allen Show*.

**Arthur Q. Bryan** (8 series); Key Roles:
J. C. Dithers on *Blondie*, Doc Gamble on *Fib-
ber McGee & Molly*, Floyd Munson on *The
Great Gildersleeve*.

**Alan Reed** (7 series); Key Roles:
Lancelot "Daddy" Higgins on *Baby Snooks*,
Clancy on *Duffy's Tavern*, Pasquale on *Life
with Luigi*.

**Lurene Tuttle** (7 series); Key Roles:
Marjorie Forrester on *The Great Gildersleeve*,
Mrs. Hilliard on *The Adventures of Ozzie and
Harriet*.

**John Brown** (6 series); Key Roles:
Digby O'Dell and Jim Gillis on *The Life of
Riley*, Syd "Thorny" Thornberry on *The Ad-
ventures of Ozzie and Harriet*, Al on *My Friend
Irma*.

**Barbara Eiler** (6 series); Key Roles:
Babs Riley on *The Life of Riley*, Mildred An-
derson on *A Day in the Life of Dennis Day*, Lois
Graves on *Junior Miss*.

**Richard Crenna** (5 series); Key Roles:
Bronco Thompson on *The Great Gildersleeve*,
Walter Denton on *Our Miss Brooks*, Oogie
Pringle on *A Date with Judy*.

**Mary Jane Croft** (5 series); Key Roles:
Alice Henderson on *Beulah*, Daisy Enright
on *Our Miss Brooks*, Janet Archer on *Meet
Corliss Archer*.

Now for some confessions of a moonlight writer which pertain to the text at hand.
Hopefully my comments will let you know
where I'm coming from and help you to realize greater satisfaction from your investment
spent with this book. Writing about comedy
as a species is a new line for me, as anyone familiar with my previous works probably
knows. That's not because I didn't revel in it
when it was aired live—and ever since then by
way of transcriptions. A personal anecdote
will underscore my humble beginnings there.

The very first thing I can remember
about radio (which was to exert a powerful
influence on me for a lifetime) was its comedy. In the 1940s our family traditionally
gathered around the living room set and listened to Senator Claghorn, Titus Moody and
Mrs. Nussbaum put the needle to Fred Allen.
Individually, they supplied snappy ripostes to
his "Question of the Week" during the hu-
morist's recurring visits to Allen's Alley. As a
preschooler and early student, I didn't understand any of it, of course. But I picked up a
pattern that was repeated at our house again
and again. When Allen addressed the
denizens of the Alley, they supplied some
pithy responses to what he had just asked.
With rare exception, no matter what words
fell from the lips of those characters, my parents came quite close to falling out of their
chairs in raucous response. I observed this
happening again and again.

Not until two decades later, in fact,
when I became a passionate collector of vintage radio programs on reel-to-reel tapes, did

I hear some of those shows again and begin to finally realize what had so captivated my folks in the 1940s. I recall that they also introduced me to Edgar Bergen and a wooden dummy at the same time, plus the rib-tickling asides of comic Red Skelton, as well as an inventor of lots of useless stuff—Fibber McGee, along with his wife, Molly. (The latter series was to become one of my all-time radio favorites.) Thus, while I didn't acquire an appreciation for broadcast comedy for the same reasons my folks did back then, through observation I found something comforting in the predictable amusement that it prompted in our home every week.

Incidentally, I have included *Fibber McGee & Molly* and *The Jack Benny Program* within these pages, designating them as "modified situation comedy." Although they maintained some characteristics of variety through vocal and instrumental music each week (a throwback to the vaudeville heritage from which they materialized), the defining elements of pursuing a continuing theme in each installment are there, as much as they may be seen in *Life with Luigi*, *Meet Millie* and *Our Miss Brooks*—sitcoms that did not offer anything beyond humorous plotting. And the fact that people come and go in the *McGee* and *Benny* features doesn't suggest that they don't fit the sitcom mold. Don't visitors methodically come and go in *The Aldrich Family*? Another distinguishing trait to be found in both *Benny* and *McGee* is the integration of the middle commercial in the narrative. None of this, however, in this observer's opinion, prevents it from being a sitcom—at least not a slightly customized one.

So why am I just now getting around to writing about comedy? I simply knew that a surplus of printed works on the genus already exists. Among them is a glut of texts focusing on individual comics, including multiple biographies on vintage icons like Fred Allen, Jack Benny, George Burns, Bob Hope, Groucho Marx and more. There are also volumes that encompass radio comedy as a whole. However, I never found any recent substantial works that dealt exclusively with the aural sit-

uation comedies. As I have channeled my avocation into preserving the broadcasting past for present and future generations, I found a niche that I had been looking for. This book is an attempt to fill an existing void.

An attempt has been made to present as much information about a given series as seems practical, much of it of the sidebar variety. In addition, I've tried to go beyond merely skimming the surface by helping you understand something of the professional and private lives of most of the key performers, especially as it fits within the confines of the aural series on which they worked. While this book was never intended to be a "tell-all" disclosure about the personal lives of the entertainers, there are some revelations that a broad segment of the public may have been unaware of. Providing details will, I hope, not be viewed as a desire on my part to expose an occasional dark secret of a revered luminary, but as an attempt to complete unfinished tales about the characteristics, preferences, choices and lifestyles of the individuals highlighted.

Sometimes those characteristics and behaviors were outwardly manifested in a performer's career; other times, only the individual and possibly those closest to him or her were affected. There should be little cause for alarm when you read that a real-life mom that exuded charm, grace and dignity on her radio and television series relished a dirty joke, smoked as a child and evidently drank liberally with her compatriots early in her professional years. Nor should it surprise you that she—and many, many others to be encountered in these pages—wed more than once, sometimes having divorced multiple times. In many cases, the public knew little about the wives and husbands of the performers, or whether there had been more than one. A prominent father figure in a popular teenage sitcom—prudent in every way for a dozen years as a role model to his radio children and wife—ended his widely acclaimed professional career by appearing *au naturel* in his final movie. It probably wasn't his most venerated contribution to showbiz, but it's a bit of trivia on his vita sheet all the same.

Adultery, substance abuse, illegitimacy, sexual issues, suicide attempts and everyday-life factors had significant effect on a few who enjoyed some degree of notoriety. Admissions of this nature are merely an acknowledgement of the circumstances that prevailed which may have affected resulting behavior in private and sometimes public exhibitions. Rest assured, at no time was the narrative intended to become an exposé, but rather a collection of biographical profiles. The facts seem important in a fuller appreciation of circumstances surrounding these personalities.

Now for some nuts and bolts information you can use.

There were a handful of major national networks during radio's golden age, and they are identified in the text like this:

**NBC**—National Broadcasting Company, which operated two networks until the mid–1940s; the programming in this volume refers to that of the NBC Red network, a chain that went on the air on November 15, 1926, and persisted after the Blue chain was sold.

**NBC Blue**—National Broadcasting Company Blue network, sold in July 1943 and renamed ABC in 1945.

**ABC**—American Broadcasting Company, the new moniker of the NBC Blue web after it was sold.

**CBS**—Columbia Broadcasting System, or the Columbia Phonograph Broadcasting System at its inception on September 27, 1927; then Columbia before the triple call letters came into common usage.

**MBS**—Mutual Broadcasting System, formed September 29, 1934, after four influential stations comprising the Quality Network altered their appellation.

The ratings assigned to the programs featured in this volume are composite averages and should not be considered final measures for complete radio seasons. The figures supplied are instead based upon authentic listening habits of Americans and are documented for a single week in mid-winter each year. The statistics were normally gathered during a January or February week when radio audiences were generally at their listenership peak. The research was conducted by Professor Harrison B. Summers and graduate students in communications at Ohio State University.[9]

There are a couple of appendices at the back of this book which hopefully will add to your enlightenment. In Appendix A you will find a list of 170 sitcoms that appear to qualify for inclusion according to the model outlined above. Consider Appendix B a bonus round. It includes an abbreviated summary of 13 additional compelling sitcoms beyond those 20 featured in separate chapters in the main body of the text. It's an extra I decided to add after my original 20 chapters were completed. I had the help of about a dozen vintage radio hobbyists in determining those shows selected for inclusion, and I'm hoping most readers' favorites will be found either in the main text or in Appendix B.

Finally, as I have admitted in previous works, whatever mistakes you find in this treatise—and I'm certain there will be a few, despite the numerous precautions that have been taken—are mine and mine alone, and I take full responsibility for them. They are, as I've also owned up to before, gaffes of the head and not of the heart. I regret my imperfections.

"Now," as the announcer declared out of a cold vacuum every day at the start of *Lorenzo Jones*, "get ready to smile awhile." As you discover these radio sitcoms for the very first time—or rediscover them again—perhaps you'll find something to smile about, along with the absorbing discoveries you make. Go ahead. Laugh right out loud. It might do you some good. The sitcoms provoked that kind of reaction then, and so much of it is just as funny all these decades later.

# 1

# *The Adventures of Ozzie and Harriet*

## AMERICA'S FAVORITE YOUNG COUPLE

According to the Museum of Television, Ozzie, Harriet, David and Ricky Nelson could be branded "the preeminent icon of the ideal nuclear family." Of course, the designation *nuclear family* wasn't understood by most people—or even in widespread use—during the era in which the Nelsons ruled the airwaves. Still, they were the epitome of families who worked and played together, dined at the same time at the same table and adhered to ideologies that were firmly entrenched in the conscience of most Americans. An inventive Ozzie Nelson was able to "conflate, reduce and transform the professional activities of his family's personal reality into a fictional domestic banality," the museum assured. One pundit suggested that the Nelsons were "radio's most huggable household ... a squeaky-clean nuclear family to gladden the hearts of the Christian Coalition." Relationships were important to them. As they met (often trifling) adversity frequently with an amusing twist, they pulled together to extricate one another. It all began after the parents enjoyed successful careers in the music industry; when they wed and started a family, they went into radio acting, inviting listeners to snoop on their private (albeit scripted) lives. In five years their show reached the coveted Top 10 most popular radio shows. Before it ended they had moved to television, claiming a spot for 14 years as that medium's most enduring sitcom. As an adolescent, Ricky—the youngest—aligned his interests with the professional legacy imparted by his parents, becoming a star in rock 'n' roll madness. His singing career was jump-started by his visibility on *The Adventures of Ozzie and Harriet*, while his story "Boy Makes Good" was a replay of his father's fortune. For a couple of decades, the tribe's numerous achievements offered a pleasant diversion to those who followed their exploits weekly.

❖ ❖ ❖

**Creator-Director:** Ozzie Nelson
**Producers-Directors:** Ozzie Nelson, Glenhall Taylor, David Elton, Ted Bliss, David Nelson
**Writers:** Ozzie Nelson, Harold Swanton, Jack Douglas, John P. Medbury, Sherwood Schwartz, John L. Greene, Ben Gershman, Rupert Pray, Sol Saks, Bill Davenport, Frank Fox, Bill Manhoff, Paul West, Selma Diamond, Hal Kanter, Don Nelson, Dick Bensfield, Perry Grant, Bob Schiller
**Orchestra Leaders:** Billy May, Ozzie Nelson
**Vocalists:** The King Sisters (Donna, Alice, Yvonne, Louise) (ca. 1944–ca. 1946), Ozzie Nelson, Harriet Hilliard Nelson
**Sound Effects Technicians:** Ed Ludes, Monty Fraser, David Light
**Announcers:** Jack Bailey, Verne Smith
**Recurring Cast:** *Ozzie Nelson*, Oswald George (Ozzie) Nelson; *Harriet Hilliard Nelson*, Peggy Lou Snyder Hilliard Nelson; *David Nelson*, Joel Davis (1944–45), Tommy Bernard (1945–49), David Oswald Nelson (1949–54); *Ricky Nelson*, Henry Blair (1944–49), Eric Hilliard (Ricky) Nelson (1949–54); *Syd "Thorny" Thornberry*, John Brown; *Mrs. Hilliard*, Lurene Tuttle; *Emmy Lou*, Janet Waldo, Barbara Eiler; *Gloria*, Bea Benaderet; *Mrs. Waddington*, Bea Benaderet; *Roger Waddington*, Francis (Dink) Trout
**Supporting Cast:** Arthur Q. Bryan, Hans

Conried, Mary Jane Croft, Dix Davis, Bobby Ellis, Verna Felton, William Johnstone, Joseph Kearns, Jack Kirkwood, Elliott Lewis, Johnny McGovern, Marvin Miller, Gerald Mohr, Barbara Nelson, Don Nelson, Alan Reed, Verne Smith, Viola Vonn

**Sponsors:** International Silver Company, for 1847 Rogers Brothers silver patterns (1944–49); H.J. Heinz Company, for Heinz 57 Varieties condiments, sauces and other foodstuffs (1949–52); General Electric Company, for GE phonographs, radios, televisions and home appliances (1952–54); Lambert Pharmacal Company, for Listerine antiseptic mouthwash (1952–54)

**Theme:** "Mary, I'm in Love with You" (Ozzie Nelson and J. Fred Coots)[1]

**Ratings:** High—11.1 (1946–47), Low—2.8 (1953–54), Median—8.7. The show achieved double digits during four seasons: 1946–47, 1947–48, 1950–51, 1951–52.

**On the Air:** October 8, 1944–June 10, 1945, CBS, Sunday, 6:00–6:30 P.M. Eastern Time; August 12, 1945–June 16, 1946, CBS, Sunday, 6:00–6:30 P.M.; September 1, 1946–June 1, 1947, CBS, Sunday, 6:00–6:30 P.M.; August 31, 1947–December 28, 1947, CBS, Sunday, 6:00–6:30 P.M.; January 2–June 11, 1948, CBS, Friday, 9:30–10:00 P.M.; October 3, 1948–March 27, 1949, NBC, Sunday, 6:30–7:00 P.M.; April 3–July 10, 1949, CBS, Sunday, 6:30–7:00 P.M.; October 14, 1949–June 16, 1950, ABC, Friday, 9:00–9:30 P.M.; September 8, 1950–June 22, 1951, ABC, Friday, 9:00–9:30 P.M.; September 28, 1951–June 20, 1952, ABC, Friday, 9:00–9:30 P.M.; October 3, 1952–July 3, 1953, ABC, Friday, 9:00–9:30 P.M.; September 18, 1953–June 18, 1954, ABC, Friday, 9:00–9:30 P.M.

**Extant Archival Material:** Ozzie and Harriet Nelson Papers, 1937–1963: Items about the Nelson clan, with photos; orchestra sheet music; radio–TV series, with scripts (*The Adventures of Ozzie and Harriet, Emmy Lou, The Red Skelton Show* and more); plus radio broadcasts on long-playing recordings and TV show photos archived at the American Heritage Center of the University of Wyoming, 1000 East University Avenue, Laramie, WY, 82071; (307) 766–3756; fax (307) 766–5511; *http://ahc.uwyo.edu/usearchives/default.htm.*

Scripts from 1948–49 season of *The Adventures of Ozzie and Harriet*, with one signed by Ozzie and Harriet and comedian Red Skelton, are archived in the KNX Script Collection, supplied by the Los Angeles CBS affiliate at Thousand Oaks Library, American Radio Archives, 1401 East Janss Road, Thousand Oaks, CA, 91362; (805) 449–2660; fax (805) 449–2675; *www.tol.lib.ca.us.*

Margarite (*sic*) Wallace Scripts, 1945–ca. 1957, includes scripts and some production information for *The Adventures of Ozzie and Harriet*, 1946–52, and some television shows housed at the University of California at Los Angeles (UCLA) Charles E. Young Research Library, Room 22478, Box 951575, Los Angeles, CA, 90095; (310) 825–7253; fax (310) 825–1210; *www.library.ucla.edu/libraries/arts/.*

Forty-eight recordings of *The Adventures of Ozzie and Harriet* shows were in general circulation or held by private collectors as of 2006, sold by vintage radio dealers and traded by old time radio hobbyists.

A log of the series' broadcasts is available from Tom Heathwood, Heritage Radio Classics, Box 16, Chestnut Hill, MA, 02467.

❖ ❖ ❖

Unlike the preponderance of family radio comedies, this one represented the authentic home-grown variety. These characters weren't fictional mirrors of their audio neighbors, with surnames like Aldrich, Anderson (*Father Knows Best*), Andrews, Archer, Brewster, Bumstead, Foster (*A Date with Judy*), Graves (*Junior Miss*), Riley and a host of ancillary nuclear tribes that only *pretended* to be family units. On *The Adventures of Ozzie and Harriet*[2] you got the *real thing.* Partially so, at least. For the most part, the key figures comprised members of the Nelson household. While they were professional actors, they were also genuine living, breathing Nelsons who—placed within the trappings of fantasy scenarios—purportedly lived at home the way audiences heard them on the air. Their fans merely eavesdropped on their personal exchanges and dilemmas by tuning in to new episodes every week.

"One of the reasons for the program's tremendous following was that audiences actually believed that the Nelsons were truly playing themselves, a myth the Nelson family helped perpetuate," conceded one scholar. Ozzie Nelson, for one, opposed giving the writers credit on the air. "We will lose an illusion [if we do so]," he maintained. "They [audiences] think we are really making this up as we go along." Of course, most family conversations aren't scripted and rehearsed. But then "normal" interactions in most clans wouldn't be very interesting to anybody hearing them, either. Fictitious situations were invented, as on every other show. The difference was that the four stars—Ozzie, Harriet, David, Ricky—shared the same family surname and were related. If nothing else, that clearly separated them from most of the other four-member units on the air. Somehow it may have made it all seem more believable, too.

The principals, Ozzie and Harriet—"America's favorite young couple" (after all, an announcer validated it every week for a decade, even as they were approaching their fifties!)—not only starred in but significantly shaped the program named after them. Ozzie's driving influence, in particular, prevented the series from joining a glut of undistinguishable teenage sitcoms in the 1940s. On those latter shows the expressions and crises almost always focused on a younger personality. Think Henry Aldrich, Archie Andrews, Corliss Archer, Joey Brewster, Judy Foster, Judy Graves, et al. *The Adventures of Ozzie and Harriet*, on the other hand, most often began and ended with the parents instead, and predominantly with Ozzie. It didn't even rotate between family members from week to week, as did *Father Knows Best* with its mixture of individuals' personal concerns. *Ozzie and Harriet* simply was what it was. One authority branded it "the Holiday Inn of sitcoms—no surprises."

One chronicler, at least, conjectured that the whiny-voiced Ozzie was the show's foremost figure, citing "his tangents [as] the vehicles to confusion." The historiographer explained: "Once Ozzie had set his mind to something, nothing could dissuade him until disaster had run its inevitable course.... Ozzie would take it to ridiculous lengths, Harriet would gently try to guide him back to reason, David and Ricky would get in a few wisecracks, and Ozzie would be further confused by the ill-timed advice of his next-door neighbor Thorny."[3]

Syd Thornberry's (Thorny's) arrival at the Nelson home was habitually announced by an innocuous "shave-and-a-haircut" rat-tat-a-tat-tat door knock, *sans* the usual "two bits" finish. It became his trademark—in addition

to the rash counsel he dispatched. A couple of other characters were good at giving ill-timed suggestions, too, especially the kind that wasn't helpful or fully appreciated: Mrs. Hilliard, Harriet's mother (her "instructions" were usually meted out by telephone), and the opinionated minor Emmy Lou (who appeared to get along in life without a surname—unless, of course, it was Lou).

Oswald George Nelson, the "preeminent sitcom dad of the 50s," was born of Swedish heritage on March 20, 1906, at Jersey City, New Jersey. He was reared in the affluent suburbs of Ridgefield Park, where, decades later, the street on which his high school stood was renamed Ozzie Nelson. He excelled in sports in his youth and initially thought he was cut out to be a cartoonist. Yet, when he learned to play the ukulele his ambitions changed. He picked up the banjo next. Combining his talent with pianist Frank Leithner, young Nelson performed at local venues. At about 14, he and his chum joined a couple of others their age to form the Syncopation Four. They played garden parties, local clubs and weddings. Ozzie Nelson also vocalized regularly.

Enrolling at Rutgers University in 1923, from which he earned a baccalaureate degree four years later, he demonstrated prowess as an athlete in the boxing ring and on the football field. The athlete-musician worked his way through school coaching football and fronting a band he organized at Rutgers. His entourage played college proms, hotel ballrooms, nightclubs and other tuition-paying venues. His "signature theme" was his alma mater's school song, "Loyal Sons of Rutgers."[4] Nelson systematically worked his way through all the instruments in his musical brigade, allegedly mastering every one except the trumpet. The saxophone was his matchless specialty. Following graduation he remained at Rutgers for three more years, gaining a law degree there in 1930. He was a well-educated impresario in the making.

Although he had prepared himself to become a barrister, by the time he was out of school the Great Depression had plunged the country into economic chaos. Nelson found the money from the dance orchestra simply too promising to let it go. His outfit, in fact, was believed to be one of the nation's best paid at the time. He acquired a permanent spot on a local station that beamed his melodies throughout Gotham.

Young Nelson was a sharp-witted theorist. He set goals and demonstrated early on that he was anything but a laggard. He acquired savvy business acumen as well as an entrepreneurial spirit while coursing along the route to eventual stardom. Those factors helped him reap substantial financial rewards down the road. At the same time, he exhibited a free will that signified he wasn't above priming the pump, resorting to a little manipulation to accomplish his desired ends, particularly during that early epoch.

In 1930, when The New York Daily Mirror printed a poll asking its readers to indicate their favorite radio orchestra, a resourceful Nelson hatched a plan to achieve maximum returns.[5] His manager informed him that the newspaper street vendors received credit for unsold papers they could not disperse by simply returning the front pages of the copies to the publisher. That news—coupled with the fact that the ballots were printed on the back page of the issues—allowed Nelson to stoke the furnace a bit. He surreptitiously dispatched cohorts to retrieve hundreds of leftover back pages as they were discarded. The ballots were filled out with his name and turned in to the paper.

The journal soon announced some startling results: Ozzie Nelson's group surpassed those of the better known national orchestras fronted by conductors like Rudy Vallee (with whom Nelson shared a physical resemblance), the legendary Paul Whiteman and a few more of their eminent stature. Nelson's manager applied the poll as leverage to book the Nelson troupe into the Glen Island Casino, a renowned venue on Long Island Sound that offered radio exposure to dance bands. Nelson, it seemed, was on his way to bigger and better things.

He kept the band going throughout the

1930s and 1940s. In the 1950s, with the demands of weekly radio and television broadcasts, he found the band impractical to manage any longer and dissolved it. In its heyday, however, his musical entourage was composed of a coterie of music-makers that was widely heralded for its impressive impact on the business. Included were Nelson as leader-vocalist; Holly Humphreys, Harry Johnson and Bo Ashford on trumpet; Abe Lincoln and Elmer Smithers on trombone; Charlie Bluebeck and Bill Stone playing clarinet and alto saxophone; Bill Nelson on clarinet and tenor saxophone; Sid Brokaw playing violin and bass violin; Harry Gray and Chauncey Gray on piano; Sandy Wolfe playing guitar; Fred Whiteside on string bass; Joe Bohan on drums; and Harriet Hilliard as feminine vocalist.

Beyond a family movie in which he starred in 1952, Ozzie Nelson's dossier included a half-dozen more theatrical films in which he demonstrated his acting prowess as well as his music: Sweetheart of the Campus (1941), Hi, Good Lookin' (1944), Wave-a-Stick Blues (1944), Take It Big (1944), People Are Funny (1946) and The Impossible Years (1968). In 1939 his was one of 49 bands that NBC Radio carried via remotes over its dual chains. Nelson later turned up in eight one-shot episodes of popular TV fare like The Bob Cummings Show, The Mothers-in-Law, Adam 12, Night Gallery and Love American Style. He wrote, directed and produced the 1965 motion picture Love and Kisses. Furthermore, he directed several assorted series, as well as solo installments, on TV. He toured with his spouse in lighter stage performances like The Marriage-Go-Round. Together they played in an occasional radio anthology drama, such as The Lady Esther Screen Guild Theater in 1946, and Suspense in 1947 (and twice more in 1950). This occurred at the crest of their aural series' popularity.

He was awarded two stars on the Hollywood Walk of Fame, one for television, the other shared with his wife for their radio contributions. In 1973, as he and Harriet were attempting a television comeback, Prentice-Hall

A dual-income family, in more ways than one, Ozzie and Harriet Nelson premiered as showbiz musicians. A lengthy engagement at the Glen Island Casino, plus recordings, films and radio, gave the couple lots of exposure before they chucked it for something else. Engaging in lively jousting before stage audiences prompted a new model for those venues and turned the act into a sensation. That led them to abandon their roots in the industry and concentrate on comedy. Some listeners to their radio sitcom convinced themselves that the family wasn't acting at all—the incidents in their lives weren't rehearsed but transpired at the moment of broadcast. So successful was the duo in their second careers that they persisted in a televised sequel longer than anybody else.

released his memoir, *Ozzie*. In the meantime, that same year Ozzie and Harriet starred in the syndicated sitcom *Ozzie's Girls*, with David Nelson directing. Its premise had the Nelsons renting the boys' rooms to a couple of college coeds. By then the gentler environment of an earlier age had significantly dissipated, however, and viewers had little tolerance for a show like theirs. It didn't survive the season. "It wasn't even up to their radio standards of 25 years before," one authority opined.

Although the couple had been voted "Best Husband-Wife Team in TV" for seven consecutive years by subscribers to the fanzine *TV-Radio Mirror*, the family patriarch was finished. The Internet Movie Data Base (IMDB), a key resource tracking the professional accomplishments of film and television personalities, suggests no new credits for Ozzie Nelson beyond 1973, even on the talk show circuit. By then he was suffering from recurring malignant tumors. He passed away, from liver cancer, in Hollywood on June 3, 1975. For a while prior to his death Harriet slipped into semi-retirement alongside him at their Laguna Beach manor. Until she resumed sporadic TV acting in 1976, she, too, was out of the public spotlight for about three years.

Harriet Nelson was a Midwestern girl. She was born Peggy Lou Snyder in Des Moines, Iowa, on July 18, 1909. Her father, Roy E. Hilliard, 30 at her birth, and mother, Hazel, 22, were "theatrical dramatic artists." Their daughter made her own show business debut at six weeks of age as a "walk-on" in *The Heir to the Hurrah*. The infant was carried onstage in the arms of her singer-actress-dancer mama. At about that time her folks were members of a traveling stock outfit, Morris Brothers Night Company. At age three the child had a speaking role in the Southern opus *Mrs. Wiggs of the Cabbage Patch*. At five she was enrolled in school, and for 11 years she concentrated on her studies—except during school holidays, when she toured with her showbiz elders.

Harriet grew up living in a hotel with her family, so she was unaccustomed to a more traditional home environment.[6] "*Ozzie and Harriet*," noted *The Akron Beacon Journal* in 1994, "did not reflect her life any more than it resembled life in the homes where it was seen." As a young teenager she won a beauty pageant. At 16, three months shy of high school graduation from Kansas City's St. Agnes Academy, she followed her mom— by then separated from her husband, Harriet's dad—to New York City, seeking performing venues. There the young woman joined the Corps de Ballet at the Capitol Theater on Broadway. In 1927, at 17, her career advanced as she became a member of the Gotham-based Radio Keith Orpheum vaudeville circuit, on which entertainers like Gracie Allen and George Burns performed. She worked with Ken Murray for a year as a straight woman—feeding him lines in comedy routines—and later with Bert Lahr in a similar capacity. At about the same time, she danced in the Harry Carroll Revue, the first vaudeville unit on the RKO circuit to play double shows daily.

Writing in 1998, a *New York Times* reporter revealed: "She hung out at the Cotton Club, began smoking at 12, was briefly married to an abusive comedian and lived a high-flying life until she fell in love with Ozzie and handed over her career to him." According to an A&E biography, "She liked a good off-color joke. She enjoyed her cocktails at night. She had the talent to go on and be a big star, but she made that decision to be Ozzie's wife." Such disclosures were a new twist to the veneer that publicists and the public itself ascribed to her. Obviously the image-building eclipsed her earlier life, which, upon reflection, appeared alien to the image concocted for her on radio and on the screen. It was probably a past that she was happy to escape. Eventually her exposure on the stage and vaudeville tours led her to Hollywood, where she appeared in a credited role in the 1932 B-film *The Campus Mystery*.[7]

Several recorders have testified that bandleader Ozzie Nelson—seeking a distaff singer to add to his entourage—saw her in the movie and was impressed enough by her looks and talent to track her down. He found her appearing at a gig in a New York restaurant. Whether he actually saw her in the film before he met her is moot. She clarified this much in 1989 when she met radio interviewer Chuck Schaden: "I went into a very large nightclub called the Hollywood Restaurant in New York City. I was the mistress of ceremonies there.... I met Ozzie at that time."[8] When he offered her a permanent job—he was still performing at the Glen Island Casino—she took it and became no more than the second female in history to vocalize with a big band (Paul Whiteman's Mildred Bailey was the trendsetter). She and Nelson developed a patter-and-tune swap that became an onstage signature. As the band played softly in the background, the duo hurled songs back and forth between them with aplomb. They exchanged jocular repartee, pioneering a technique not seen elsewhere prior to their innovation. "For Ozzie, though he didn't know it then, it was the final stroke of fate that pushed him irrevocably away from the practice of law and cemented him into show business," a historian wrote.

The following year his new lady singer was on network radio, accompanied by Nelson's orchestra, on NBC Blue's *Baker's Broadcast*, aka *The Joe Penner Show*.[9] Harriet Hilliard cut records for four labels—Brunswick, Vocalian, RCA Victor and Blue Bird. During their first summer working together the vocalist and the maestro also fell in love. They wed on October 8, 1935.[10] Her movie career resumed the following year, and over the next 16 years she made another 19 theatrical releases, a few of them with her spouse. Among her film credits are *Follow the Fleet* (1936), *The Life of the Party* (1937), *Cocoanut Grove* (1938), *Sweetheart of the Campus* (1941), *Confessions of Boston Blackie* (1941), *Canal Zone* (1942), *The Falcon Strikes Back* (1943), *Hi, Good Lookin'!* (1944), *Take It Big* (1944) and, of course, *Here Come the Nelsons* (1952).

Harriet performed in lots of stage productions, too, among them *The Impossible Years* and *State Fair*. She was prominent in television. In addition to the two family series in which she co-starred, she appeared in *Once an Eagle*, a 1976 miniseries. Between 1972 and 1989 she made the rounds of TV anthologies, dramas and sitcoms, where she acted in single episodes of *Love American Style*, *The Love Boat*, *Fantasy Island*, *Happy Days* and *Father Dowling Mysteries*. Following Ozzie's death in the mid–1970s, she turned up in a half-dozen made-for-TV flicks, with intriguing titles like *Smash-Up on Interstate 5* (1976), *Death Car on the Freeway* (1979), *The First Time* (1982) and *The Kid with the 200 I.Q.* (1983) among them. An appearance on February 10, 1989, as Sister Agnes on the ABC-TV series of granddaughter Tracy Nelson (Rick's eldest child), *Father Dowling Mysteries*, was allegedly Harriet's final public appearance. She quietly lived out her remaining years at Laguna Beach until October 2, 1994, when she succumbed to congestive heart failure. She was 85.

Five years earlier she replied to the question, "What was the best time for you?" in this manner: "I loved radio best.... You could have a life of your own in radio. It was the best of all worlds. It was big-time. You did it live. Then you had the thrill of working in front of an audience and having one crack at it. You didn't dare make a mistake, so you were absolutely on your best. It only happened once a week, so you could live like a human being the rest of the week. You could go to the movies, you could have people in for dinner. When we went to television, it was 24 hours a day, seven days a week.... I still get such a kick out of those radio shows."[11]

The Nelsons' son David Oswald Nelson was born in New York City on October 24, 1936. By the time he was a teenager the family was in California, where he attended Hollywood High School. While he appeared in 13 theatrical motion pictures in the half-century from 1948 to 1998, the only memorable one (besides the 1952 family epic) was 1957's *Peyton Place*. Others included forgettable titles like *The Remarkable Mr. Pennypacker* (1959), *-30-* (1959), *Up in Smoke* (1978) and *Broken Vessels* (1998).

Much of David's professional career was invested in directing and producing films for the big and small screens, a talent he clearly picked up under the tutelage of his father. The eldest son produced and directed 1973's *Easy to Be Free* and 1983's *Last Plane Out* for the cinemas, while directing a few other films for dual mediums, plus the 1965–66 ABC sitcom *O. K. Crackerby!* He was director of *Ozzie's Girls* in 1973, laboring alongside his parents once again. David also directed a plethora of television commercials. He acted in a quartet of made-for-TV films, including one with his mother, 1976's *Smash-Up on Interstate 5*. Far removed in 1983 from the teen scene, of which he was such a visible part three decades earlier, he turned up that year in the TV movie *High School U.S.A.*, playing, of all people, the janitor. For his TV efforts David Nelson was awarded a star on the Hollywood Walk of Fame.

On May 20, 1961, David Nelson wed June Blair. She joined the television series that year and remained with it until its cancellation five years later. To the pair was born Daniel Blair Nelson on August 20, 1962, and James Eric Nelson on June 8, 1966. The couple divorced in 1975, and David remarried on September 3, 1975, to Yvonne O'Connor Huston. He became the stepfather of Teri Nelson, who married TV game show host Chuck Woolery. David and Yvonne continue sharing their lives together as of this writing.

David's younger brother, Eric Hilliard (Ricky) Nelson, meanwhile, was born at Teaneck, New Jersey, on May 8, 1940. Nobody knew it then, of course, but he was destined to become one of the nation's first teen idols, if not *the* first. Early on he distinguished himself on the family radio and television series, where, according to a critic, "He was the young, cocky boy with his own catchphrase ('I don't mess around, boy') decades before Bart Simpson was born." Life began to turn in a new direction for Ricky, and for the Nelsons themselves, when the juvenile reached his mid-teens.

The commingling of fact and fiction in the family's lives was well illustrated in 1957 when 16-year-old Ricky's impressionable real-life sweetheart developed an overpowering infatuation with rising superstar Elvis Presley. To counter the offender, young Ricky convinced his dad to set up a recording session for him to cut a rock 'n' roll tune. Within a week of its release in April 1957, the youth's single of Fats Domino's hit "I'm Walkin'" sold a million copies and climbed to the second spot on music popularity charts. He was instantly America's newest idol, and the teenyboppers coast-to-coast had a fresh heartthrob. Between then and 1963 Ricky Nelson cut 17 more top-selling single discs that put him high on the record charts and kept him there. They included "Be Bop Baby" (September 1957), "Poor Little Fool" (June 1958), "It's Late" (February 1959), "There'll Never Be Anyone Else but You" (February 1959), "Travelin' Man" (April 1961), "Hello, Mary Lou" (April 1961), "Young World" (February 1962), "Fools Rush In" (September 1963) and "For You" (December 1963). He would have only one more colossal hit after that, a long time coming, "Garden Party" (June 1972). He is assumed to have been second only to Presley in sales of single discs in the late 1950s and early 1960s.

Ricky Nelson's career as a pop singer benefited tremendously from his exposure on a weekly TV series. As the storyline concluded on many episodes, he was surrounded by salivating hordes of yelling, screaming teenyboppers (who were actually paid TV "extras") as he introduced his latest rock 'n' roll number. It wasn't a bad way to launch a promotional campaign. With the support of the music trade papers, his fortune zoomed overnight. All of it exhibited an entrepreneurial spirit that was seemingly passed from father to son. One pundit allowed: "More important than his actual music perhaps was the fact that in giving their blessing to Ricky's career, Ozzie and Harriet demonstrated to millions of timid middle-class Americans that rock and roll was not a satanic threat but a viable musical alternative."

Unlike his sibling David, the younger Nelson remained primarily a performer after the family TV series faded. In addition to recording, he turned up in eight films screened in theaters and in three movies on television. All were less-than-memorable, excepting 1959's *Rio Bravo* and 1960's *The Wackiest Ship in the Army*. He made a few noteworthy guest appearances in a dozen TV episodes of shows like *The General Electric Theater, Hondo, McCloud, The Streets of San Francisco, Owen Marshall—Counselor at Law, The Hardy Boys Mysteries, Tales of the Unexpected, The Love Boat* and *Saturday Night Live*. Rick (he had gotten rid of "Ricky" long before) also hosted the 1967 ABC-TV summer music series *Malibu U*.

On April 20, 1963, he married Kristin Harmon in a ceremony that *Life* magazine touted as the "Wedding of the Year." Like her sister-in-law before her, she too joined the TV series from 1964 until it left the air in 1966. The couple, meanwhile, produced four offspring: Tracy, Matthew, Gunnar and Sam. Tracy Nelson subsequently gained renown as a Hollywood actress, co-starring in *Father Dowling Mysteries* on NBC and ABC from 1989 to 1991.

Despite all the good news, "By the late 70s," according to Wikipedia, "Ricky's life was in shambles. His wife had divorced him [this didn't occur until 1981] and taken their four children. He wasn't making records, and when he played live at all, it was in very small venues."[12] He was still singing and was engaged to wed Helen Blair when they both died in a plane crash on December 31, 1985, at De Kalb, Texas, en route to a New Year's Eve concert in Dallas.

The younger Nelson was admitted posthumously to the Rock and Roll Hall of Fame in 1987. Like others of his family, he also received a star on the Hollywood Walk of Fame. In 2005 *TV Guide* ranked him second on a list of TV's 25 Greatest Teen Idols.

Having "met" the four principals in *The Adventures of Ozzie and Harriet*, we return now to our regularly scheduled feature already in progress.

During their formative professional years, when the parents were musicians,

"Ozzie's deliberate hesitancy and self-deprecating humor were the perfect foil for the sweet and sassy Harriet, who interrupted her songs with sarcastic banter," as one source observed.

In the early 1940s the pair joined the cast of *The Red Skelton Show* on NBC Radio on Tuesday nights, gaining far-reaching notoriety via ongoing performances. On some of those occasions Harriet portrayed the Mean Little Kid's mom, as well as Daisy June and Calamity June. Additionally, the big band routines were replayed, including the husband-and-wife banter Ozzie and Harriet had developed years before. They added some sketches that ostensibly afforded humorous glimpses into their offstage lives. It was all fodder for the creative mind of Ozzie Nelson, who was making notes all the while.

When comic star Skelton was drafted into the Army in 1944, family patriarch Ozzie wasn't sure what their next pursuit should be. But all that changed over dinner one evening at the Brown Derby Restaurant when the couple socialized with old friend Don Quinn, who made his living putting words in the mouths of *Fibber McGee & Molly* every week. He assured Ozzie, "You could write your own show." Ozzie wasn't as confident, but he and Harriet ultimately decided to go for it. He penned a half-hour program, they made an audition tape in a studio with a live audience, and producer John Guedel (*People Are Funny, Art Linkletter's House Party, You Bet Your Life*) flew the trial platters to New York. Within a week the pair signed for a series with International Silver Company. They decided to use child actors to play their sons, feeling their own offspring were not yet old enough to be exposed to entertainment's exploitative nature.

That fall Ozzie and Harriet, plus the boys, shifted their allegiance to CBS on Sunday nights, inaugurating their own domestic sitcom. The 14-year television extension—which superseded the radio version and closely paralleled it in the decades to follow—prompted an astute assessment by Nina Leibman:

From the outset, *The Adventures of Ozzie and Harriet* had a nostalgic feel, resembling Ozzie's 1920s youth in New Jersey more than 1950s Los Angeles. The picket-fenced neighborhoods, the corner drugstore and malt shop featured weekly in this slow-paced half-hour infiltrated American culture at a time of social unease and quiescent distress. In reality, most 1950s fathers were working ten-hour days and commuting long distances to isolated suburbs. For the Nelsons, however, Ozzie was always home, neighbors still chatted over the back fence, and downtown was a brisk walk away. The Nelsons presented an America that never was, but always wished for, and, through their confusion of reality and fantasy, worked to concoct an image of American life that is, to this day, mistakenly claimed not only as ideal, but as authentic.[13]

Another assessor viewed the whole thing similarly:

Ozzie was a guy who never seemed to work: he lounged around his home ... in a sweater and slacks, his whole existence built around his weekly displays of flawed judgment. This even became a running gag for nightclub comics: the question "What does Ozzie Nelson do for a living?" was prime trivia. For the record, he was a bandleader; because most of the action of Ozzie and Harriet was set on weekends when the boys were out of school, his occupation was never a factor. But the notion persisted as the times changed—here was a family from Neverland, far away from Real Life.[14]

At its start the series focused on the foibles of the bandleader and his clan, with numerous references to band rehearsals, road tours and other performing activities. (An aside: did this possibly inspire one of the premises of TV's *I Love Lucy* a decade later? Coincidentally, recall that both shows had a "little" Ricky, also.) Comedy sketches were balanced with full-length songs. The music was dropped completely within two years, and complete storylines filled its 30-minute allotment. Not until April 1949, after Bing Crosby made a guest appearance on the show, accompanied by his son Lindsay, did Nelson become convinced that putting the real David, age 12, and Ricky, age nine, on the air could be a good thing. In a trial run, the boys

first escorted their father on a reciprocal visit to the Crosby show, *Philco Radio Time*. The audience loved it. Replacing the child actors with the authentic adolescents increased the Nelson series' appeal, effectively adding to the verisimilitude of the purely fictional narrative.

Actually, the initial appearance of the Nelson boys on a national radio hookup occurred on the popular CBS matinee feature *Art Linkletter's House Party*. "What do you want to be when you grow up?" the gregarious master of ceremonies asked each of the precocious kids (who say the darndest things!) that day. Eleven-year-old David Nelson, whose hero and mentor was obviously his dad, replied: "Well, I'm going to go to law school and become an attorney and then I'm going on the radio." Like father, like son. And little Ricky, then eight, declared his intent to become one of two things—"a Cub Scout or a Lone Stranger."

At about the same time that was transpiring, Ozzie Nelson bargained for and obtained the very first non-cancellable 10-year contract in broadcasting history when he signed with ABC that year (1949) to air his family sitcom. Pulling that feat off was a coup de grâce that became the talk of the industry and the envy of other entertainers, and set a new standard for future negotiations.[15] Translated, it meant that for a full decade the Nelsons were effectively exempt from any obstructions that the network, their sponsors or advertising agencies might decide to toss into their paths.[16] Even better than that proviso, however, was the fact that they were herewith assured of receiving a basic payment sum for the lifetime of the contract, whether their program aired or not.[17]

Parenthetically, the show maintained ratings that approached or exceeded double-digit figures (considered acceptable, and even good) during the first three years of their 10-year agreement (e.g., 10.0 in 1951–52). However, the numbers plunged to 3.6 in 1952–53 and 2.8 in 1953–54, the last two years they were on radio. By then they were also on ABC-TV, which contributed significantly in reducing the number of radio listeners to a fraction of their former highs, as more and more Americans became mesmerized by the tube.

When Universal Studios released a motion picture, *Here Come the Nelsons*, in 1952, co-starring the tribe with Rock Hudson, it was a smashing success. ABC, meanwhile, took note of the development and believed it had a strong prospect already under contract for an equally award-winning television sitcom. It guessed right, of course, making its infamous 10-year indenture pay off handsomely for the web, as well as its stars.[18] Incidentally, in the two years that both the radio and televersions coexisted, Ozzie Nelson—ever the vigilant overseer, down to the smallest detail—insisted on totally different scripts for the dual formats. The radio show was prerecorded (audio tape had come into vogue then), and the TV series was filmed separately at General Service Studios, a dozen blocks from the Nelson domicile. (Although the Nelsons' program was shot in color in its final two years, an eyewitness noted, "In spirit, and in the popular imagination, they remained black-and-white denizens of the 1950s.")

Nelson's astute business acumen translated into him being actively involved in the 435 chapters of the show aired on television, just as he had been with the radio program. Correctly dubbed a perfectionist, he oversaw the writing, editing, directing and producing of the show, demanding the most rigid criterion be stringently met. When he didn't direct an installment, David Nelson did. Nightlong story idea sessions involving secondary scribes and production personnel were calendared weekly at the Nelson abode in Hollywood Hills. Nothing was left to chance.

"A stickler for quality," affirmed one insider, "Ozzie was adamant that his [TV] program look different from the inferior kinescope products dominating the television schedule." The program was filmed using the highest quality 35 millimeter celluloid available. Once preparatory editing had been completed, Nelson reeled it before an audience situated in a Los Angeles theater he had

rented to determine at what points and how intense the laugh track cues should be. It was a highly professional business; it was much more than merely acting to Ozzie, for he gave it his all—from concept to finished product.

The network publicists dubbed the Nelsons "America's favorite family," and such backslapping persisted for years. While the show's complete title for most of the run was *The Adventures of Ozzie and Harriet*, it was *TV Guide* that pontificated: "There wasn't, in fact, much 'adventure' anyone could discern in the lives of the suburban Nelson clan." Reviewer Gary Brumburgh observed that "Ozzie's dad character came off stammering, hesitant and slightly absent-mined, which meshed perfectly with Harriet's smart, wisecracking appeal."[19]

In their early radio days the Nelsons resided at 1847 Rogers Road, a fact that the critics found "insidious," "despicable" and "shameless." It was no subtle reminder that their long-running sponsor, the International Silver Company, plugged its 1847 Rogers Brothers silver patterns at every commercial break. In television, however—with tableware long a thing of the past—the Nelsons occupied a two-story Colonial in the hamlet of Hillsdale at 822 Sycamore Road, an address that related to nothing. It was hyped as "an exact replica" of their real home in Hollywood, although that hardly seems conceivable. And what would be the point if it was? What percentage of viewers would know or really care? Nevertheless, when the Nelsons transitioned seamlessly onto those small video screens in America's living rooms, "they looked exactly like we thought they would," an observer gushed.

The shows in both mediums chronicled the growing pains of the boys and their parents, and dealt with mundane issues like school, club memberships, girlfriends, hobbies, sports and rivalries. After the boys grew up (on television), they went off to college, returning as storybook attorneys, a profession not so far from their dear old dad's heart. In sweeping generalities the plots frequently could be reduced to a four-part scenario: (a) setup; (b) complication (if one person was responsible for this, it was normally Ozzie); (c) additional complications; and (d) resolution (most often facilitated by Harriet).

In a typical Christmas show aired in the 1940s, the senior Nelsons had just purchased a radio-phonograph combination for their living room. Both mom and dad convinced themselves that this appliance, a rather heavy investment, would satisfy their Christmas needs that year. Each one promised the other not to go behind his/her back and purchase another gift for the partner. Following that setup, the plot thickened as Thorny (played by John Brown), Mrs. Hilliard (Lurene Tuttle) and Emmy Lou (Janet Waldo or Barbara Eiler) contributed separate recommendations for gifts the spouses should consider giving one another—and how disappointed the other would be if he/she didn't receive it. In the end, of course, a covert purchase was made by Ozzie and Harriet and hidden away for a surprise revelation at the family celebration. And they all lived happily until the following week. Once listeners heard a few of these states of affairs they could almost write the predictable outcomes.

Some typical installment titles included the following, some of which prompt intriguing thoughts: "Jury Duty," "The Argument," "Interior Decorator," "The Mustache," "The Circus," "Night School," "The Mystic," "Easter Sunrise Service," "Man and Superman," "Don't Spare the Rod," "Mother's Day," "Boy's Day," "David and Ricky's Punishment," "Father's Day," "Self Confidence," "Fourth of July" and "The Real Estate Deal."

Will the *real* Ozzie and Harriet Nelson please stand up? Unlike his public persona, Ozzie was compulsively attentive to business while Harriet was an alien to the kitchen.

They employed a butler, cook, upstairs maid, chauffeur, gardener and a traveling nursemaid for their journeys from home after they had children. Their dinner guests weren't the Thornberrys of the storyline for the Nelsons routinely entertained the likes of Charles Correll, Art Linkletter, Fred MacMurray and their wives. They also hung out at Don the Beachcomber's and Chasen's, not at the corner drug store soda fountain. What fans heard on the radio or saw on TV didn't resemble how the Nelsons actually lived, even though it was enchanting.[20]

Some biographers have suggested that the Nelsons themselves made the decision to remove their long-running television series from the air in 1966. But David recalled it differently. In an interview 23 years afterward, he admitted, "It was really ABC who made the decision." According to David, "Rick and I were ready, but my father never was."

The Museum of Broadcast Communications observed: "The Nelsons embodied wholesome, 'normal' American existence so conscientiously (if blandly) that their name epitomized upright, happy family life for decades." Conversely, the fact that three of the four members of that kinship divorced a spouse while perpetuating the fantasy of the idyllic domestic environment is an ambiguity. As they portrayed America's ultimate nuclear family, the values that were hypothetically imbued in the national psyche were being lost. In many places, the optimistic idealism which was an underlying theme of those shows no longer prevails. It was Camelot for the common man, a kind of hoped-for impracticality that could never be. Despite that, vast throngs were convinced that it really did exist, if only for the moment.

# The Aldrich Family

## THE PROTOTYPE OF PUBESCENT FARE

Unmistakably casting the mold for future aural equivalents, like Archie Andrews and a glut of significant others, Henry Aldrich was an amusingly bumbling kid, awkwardly racing through adolescence. *The Aldrich Family*—in which he was the pivotal figure—traditionally focused on his misadventures with girls, grades and growing up, and whoever and whatever else he brushed up against. It was analogous to Andy Hardy's exploits, which were all the rage then. A reviewer observed: "Though it now seems among the most dated of its era's entertainment, *The Aldrich Family* in its time was written intelligently, with gentle humor, and was acted wholly appropriately to its primary subject matter." Henry was incessantly flanked by pal Homer Brown, who stuck closer than a brother. Often it was Homer who instigated confusion, mischief and their ensuing troubles. If there was a complicated method of getting through puberty, the chums habitually found it. Storylines often revolved around a shortage of funds. Henry and Homer hailed from emblematic nuclear families—Henry's included a slightly older sister with whom he generally got along, and two parents used to spouting orders and having them executed. Henry's and Homer's attempts to get around the rules of their elders spawned many a plot. Within two years the Aldriches broke the barrier of the top 10 shows measured by the Crossley scale, landing them in the company of *Amos 'n' Andy*,

Jack Benny, Bob Hope and more frontrunners—icons who scratched a long time to get there. The Aldrich clan exhibited a resilience that allowed them to hang on for 13 years—no small feat itself.

❖ ❖ ❖

**Creator:** Clifford Goldsmith
**Directors:** Harry Ackerman, Edwin Duerr, Fran Van Hartesveldt, George McGarrett, Sam Fuller, Bob Welsh, Lester Vail, Joseph Scibetta, Day Tuttle
**Writers:** Clifford Goldsmith, Norman Tokar, Ed Jurist, Ed Joudry, Pat Joudry, Phil Sharp, Sam Taylor, Frank Tarloff
**Orchestra Conductor:** Jack Miller
**Sound Effects Technician:** Bill Brinkmeyer
**Announcers:** Harry Von Zell, Dwight Weist, George Bryan, Dan Seymour, Ralph Paul, Andre Baruch, Dick Dudley, Don Wilson
**Recurring Cast:** *Henry Aldrich:* Ezra Stone (nee Ezra Chaim Feinstone, 1939–42, 1945–51), Norman Tokar (1942–43), Dickie Jones (1943–44), Raymond Ives (1944–November 1945), Bobby Ellis (1952–53); *Homer Brown:* Jackie Kelk (1939–51), Johnny Fiedler (1952), Jack Grimes (1952–ca. 1953), Michael O'Day (1953); *Sam Aldrich:* Clyde Fillmore (1939), House Jameson (1939–ca. 1951), Tom Shirley (1952–53); *Alice Aldrich:* Leah Penman (1939), Katharine Raht (1939–51), Regina Wallace (1952–53); *Mary Aldrich:* Betty Field, Patricia Peardon, Charita Bauer, Ann Lincoln, Jone Allison, Mary Mason, May Rolfe, Mary Shipp, Jean Vander Pyl, others; *Kathleen Anderson:* Mary Shipp, Ethel Blume, Jean Gillespie, Ann Lincoln; *Agnes Lawson:* Judith Abbott; *Will Brown:* Ed Begley, Arthur Vinton, Howard Smith; *Mrs. Will Brown:* Agnes Moorehead, Leona Powers; *Mrs. Anderson:* Alice Yourman; *Dizzy Stevens:* Eddie

Bracken; *Toby Smith:* Dick Van Patten; *Willie Marshall:* Norman Tokar; *George Bigelow:* Charles Powers; *Aunt Harriet:* Ethel Wilson; *Geraldine Love:* Pat Ryan; *Stringbean Kittinger:* Joan Jackson; *Mr. Bradley:* Bernard Lenrow; *Mr. DeHaven:* Ward Wilson

**Supporting Cast:** Ken Christy, Thelma Ritter

**Sponsors:** General Foods Corporation (1939–51), for Jell-O gelatin, pudding and pie fillings, Postum instant hot beverage and Grape Nuts cereals; Sustained (1952–53)

**Themes:** "This Is It" and "All the World's a Wonderland" (aka "Aldrich Theme") (Jack Miller)

**Ratings:** High—31.5 (1942–43), Low—11.9 (1950–51), Median—19.2 (all seasons represented except 1952–53, for which figures aren't available)

**On the Air:** July 2–October 1, 1939, NBC, Sunday, 7:00–7:30 P.M. Eastern Time; October 10, 1939–May 28, 1940, NBC Blue, Tuesday, 8:00–8:30 P.M.; July 4, 1940–July 20, 1944, NBC, Thursday, 8:30–9:00 P.M.; September 1, 1944–August 30, 1946. CBS, Friday, 8:00–8:30 P.M.; September 5, 1946–June 28, 1951, NBC, Thursday, 8:00–8:30 P.M.; September 21, 1952–April 19, 1953, NBC, Sunday, 7:30–8:00 P.M.

**Extant Archival Material:** Scripts from *The Aldrich Family* are included in the Edward Jurist Collection of Radio and Television Scripts housed in the Charles E. Young Research Library at the University of California at Los Angeles (UCLA), Box 951575, Los Angeles, CA, 90095; (310) 825–7253; Fax (310) 825–1210; *www.library.ucla.edu/libraries/arts/*.

Four scripts from *The Aldrich Family* are included in the script collection at The Broadcast ARTS Library, Box 9828, Fort Worth, TX, 76147; (817) 259–0077; *www.broadcastartslibrary.com*.

One hundred and fifty-four recordings of *The Aldrich Family* were in general circulation or held by private collectors as of 2006, sold by vintage radio dealers and traded by old-time radio hobbyists.

❖ ❖ ❖

The preponderance of teenage and twentysomething situation comedies that enveloped radio in the 1940s and the first half of the 1950s exhibited an unambiguous affinity for feminine characters as their key figures. Archetypal examples of the trend were arresting features like *A Date with Judy, Junior Miss, Maisie, Maudie's Diary, Meet Corliss Archer, Meet Millie, My Friend Irma, My Little Margie* and *Our Miss Brooks*. They could be contrasted with but three major programs debuting in the same timeframe that boasted of young men as their protagonists—*The Aldrich Family, Archie Andrews* and *That Brewster Boy*.

It doesn't take rocket science to ascertain that radio was clearly pandering to the single young women among its listening audience. That should be neither alarming nor unnerving. Each of those shows was generally well written, acted and directed, and each developed strong followings. While the gender orientation might have modified the crowd tuning in, it's conceivable that those who were drawn to one of those shows would be receptive to several more, regardless of who the hero or heroine might have been.

*The Aldrich Family* carried the torch for the masculine teenage programs longer, and possibly better, than the others. It became a prototype of the pubescent fare to follow on radio *and* television. For 13 radio seasons it set a lofty benchmark. While its rivals attempted to emulate it, none seriously threatened its position as the leader of the pack. Its perseverance, as well as the sheer numbers who tuned in weekly, allowed it to grow and become the foremost representation the networks could muster to counter the teenyboppers operating on *A Date with Judy, Junior Miss* and *Meet Corliss Archer*.

The Aldrich saga was branded with the entire clan's surname. Nonetheless, listeners knew when they heard Mrs. Aldrich bellowing "*Hen-reeeeeeeee! Henry Al-drich!*" at the top of the show, followed by the youth's inexorable croaking-toned response, "*Coming mother!*," the key figure was Henry, a thrill-seeking 16-year-old Centerville high schooler. Other family members would interact with him and the madcap situations he pushed them into. But it was he who starred, and it was unmistakably the male perspective that was espoused. "Henry Aldrich was an endearingly bumbling kid growing awkwardly into adolescence," observed Wikipedia. "Though it now seems among the most dated of its era's entertainment, *The Aldrich Family* in its time was written intelligently, with gentle humor, and was acted wholly appropriately to its primary subject matter." And all of it provided a boatload of laughs.

While Henry could never be classified as being as nutty as, say, Gracie Allen or (*My Friend*) Irma Peterson, it was nevertheless a forgone conclusion that once he messed with a substance/issue/affair/object/person/theme/dilemma/idea/job/project/place/conveyance or what-have-you (pick any), things would indubitably unravel and ultimately build towards a calamitous finish. There probably wasn't once in 13 years that this wasn't the result. "With Henry, ordinary objects became lethal weapons," proclaimed a media historian. "A telephone was a window to such bizarre convolution that its consequences tested the imagination." (Think of the fun he could have had with a cell phone had he lived today!)

Of course, no man acts alone in creating mayhem, and neither did the underage figures of radio sitcoms. Most had sidekicks who were frequently the inciters of the riots, disturbances, mistakes and misunderstandings that were proffered as weekly fare on such programs. Jughead of *Archie Andrews* fame is a prime example. Another of the leading revolutionaries in deriving absolute pandemonium was Henry's pal Homer Brown, whom a pundit labeled as Henry's "companion in mischief." Incidentally, Homer repeatedly addressed his crony at different times as "Hen," "old man," "old pal" and "old timer." Both were 16, mind you.

While Homer was certainly Henry's co-conspirator, the bedlam frequently *began* and *ended* with Homer, and often persisted *far longer* than it should have *because of* Homer. The opinionated, advice-spouting adolescent seemed to be a few biscuits shy of a full tin. There were times when one could swear that he and Irma and Gracie were cut from the same bolt of cloth (or maybe struck by the same bolt of lightning?). His pronounced "slowness" wasn't intentional, of course. Although he contributed an occasional wacko idea, more often than not his more explicit manifestations arrived when he would unwittingly become a pawn or a culprit.

In one episode, to wit, Mr. Aldrich

(Sam) gleaned some critical business data and wrote it in the margins of a newspaper. Sam Aldrich, by the way, was "no palsy-walsy, sweater-wearing, football-tossing Ozzie Nelson," assured one critic. "He was more in the gruff but understanding Judge Hardy mold." Having written his information in the newspaper margin on the occasion mentioned, Sam left the room, and along came the family behind him—Henry, his slightly older sister Mary, and Mrs. Aldrich (Alice). They divided up the journal for their varied purposes, each taking a portion of it and carrying it to the four winds. Over the course of time, Homer made some added notes on an ad he ripped from the section taken by Henry, and then slipped it into his pocket.

The confusion that abounded as Sam raced all over town trying to retrieve the newspaper in order to make a five o'clock filing deadline at the courthouse (he was an attorney by profession) netted a predictably hilarious romp. After valiant efforts in which everybody in the family joined the desperate patriarch to help him find his missing notes, shortly before five o'clock a dejected Sam admitted defeat, realizing he was losing a windfall. At that juncture Homer—who was with the family every step of the way in their day-long search—reached into his pocket to retrieve the ad he had carried around all day. He called Henry's attention to what *he* had written on the page. There, of course, were also Sam's notes! Despite Henry's chum's total ineptness, Sam filed the brief with 15 seconds to spare. It was all so conventional: Homer, the born loser, ultimately saved the day through no fault of his own. If a denouement like that occurred once on the show, it probably transpired hundreds of times.

Many of the jams that Henry found himself in sooner or later dissolved into situations where he became hard pressed to either confess the truth or cover it up with a measure of fabrication. "Did you know that Homer had borrowed my tuxedo?" his father might inquire of him. Of course Henry was well aware of it: he had loaned it to his buddy without anyone's permission in the first place. Henry could admit what he had done and suffer a consequence, like missing a coveted sporting or social event with his girlfriend, Kathleen Anderson. Or—on the other hand—he could lie about it. But that really wouldn't set a laudable example for America's youth. In a family show, possibly to the credit of the sponsor, ad agency, network censors, writers (or all of them working together in a kind of harmonious integrity), that simply wouldn't do.

The quick-witted logician, therefore, invariably found a third answer. "Father," he might say, "if Homer took your tuxedo, he did so because there was an emergency." Sam Aldrich could ponder aloud: "An emergency? What kind of emergency?" And a resourceful Henry might offer this rejoinder: "Because he knew that if he asked you for it, you would say no; so—needing it in a hurry—he merely borrowed it." Henry was ingenious when it came to rationalizing ways to extricate himself from some very tight spots. When you thought about it for a while, did it actually seem like Homer was the dunderhead here? Or could it possibly have been the adults? (Just a thought for meditative contemplation.)

Another thing that transpired in virtually every show: Henry was perpetually broke. To become flush again he habitually phrased requests to his mother and father for an advance on his allowance, a loan or an outright gift of a specific sum of cash so he could purchase something he just "had to have." It might be fur-lined Army surplus boots (his rationalization: "so I won't catch cold next winter") or some other equally improbable object, or for tickets to a play, a movie, game or concert (whatever was the passion of the moment). If Homer desired the same, he would put the squeeze on *his* folks for similar funding. Sometimes the boys worked opposite sides of the street, Henry attempting to convince Mr. Brown why he should finance an object of desire for Homer, while Homer worked on Mr. Aldrich with a comparable pitch.

Although the boys could be innovative and persistent, their maneuvers usually fell on deaf ears. As a last resort they'd attempt to secure a temporary job (one was as a $6-a-week motorman on a street car trolley, a task for which they were absolutely unsuited—the pair managed to jam the car so it couldn't be easily dislodged). Or they might sell something of little consequence to them (unknowingly a family heirloom, for instance). Or they might hit somebody else up for a loan, or call in some chips for a payback from an earlier transaction. The enterprising duo seldom seemed at a loss for invention.

The real problem was that when they got hold of something—no matter what their pursuit—it almost always backfired. The money might ultimately be forgotten altogether in the process, the least of their troubles, as they sought to extricate themselves from the foul-ups they created. Occasionally they wound up in jail, or, worse, would witness Mr. Aldrich put in the slammer for their grievous mistakes. Sometimes they unintentionally lost or destroyed personal property, stuff of material or sentimental value. Their scheming routinely sowed the seeds of destruction that resulted in colossal and hilarious disasters. While any who were regular listeners could almost routinely predict the outcome, it was still funny.

The show exhibited one of the most distinctive program openings in radio. It also gave listeners one of the medium's most identifiable, powerful marketing messages through the repetitious use of a familiar and catchy jingle sung by the program's dual male leads. At a cue, an announcer went on the air, cold, as the show began.

ANNOUNCER: *And now the Jell-O family presents...*

MRS. ALDRICH: *Hen-reeeeeeeee! Henry Al-drich!*

HENRY: *Coming mother!*

ANNOUNCER: *Yes, it's* The Aldrich Family, *based on characters created by Clifford Goldsmith, and starring Ezra Stone as Henry and Jackie Kelk as Homer. And, yes, it's the Jell-O family.*

HENRY and HOMER (singing): *Oh, the big red letters stand for the Jell-O family!*
*Oh, the big red letters stand for the Jell-O family!*
*That's Jell-O!*
*Yum-yum-yum!*

*Jell-O pudding!*
*Yum-yum-yum!*
*Jell-O tap-i-oca pudding, yes sir-eeeee!*

Few show openings were as unforgettable as that one. Today the jingle is still etched on the brains of millions of that generation who may have heard it hundreds of times. It even outlived the identity of the sponsor that paid for its broadcast.[1]

Henry and company evolved from characters originally appearing in a stage play titled *What a Life!* It was a family-focused narrative by Clifford Goldsmith, an aspiring actor-turned-playwright who until then had largely experienced disappointments in show business. Hailing from East Aurora, New York, he was born March 29, 1899. At Moses Brown High School in Providence, Rhode Island, he was active in that Quaker institute's dramatic society. It helped him affirm a decision to become an actor. Although he tried to pursue his decision on the New York stage multiple times between 1919 and 1922, he later acknowledged that he performed in only a single production. As an understudy for an ailing actor in a play titled *Lightnin'*, he filled in. "After ten days they decided that no matter how sick the original actor might be he would be better than I was," Goldsmith admitted.

He entered Wharton School at the University of Pennsylvania but left before the grades were handed out at the end of his freshman year. Graduating from the American Academy of Dramatic Arts and finding little to encourage him in his preferred vocation, he began taking a paycheck as a publicist for the National Dairy Council. He sustained himself by doing that for the next 16 years. In that capacity one of his primary assignments was to travel on a lecture circuit to high schools. While doing so he consistently made notes on what he saw and heard in that environment, substantial observations that would pay off handsomely for him down the road.

Meanwhile, on the side he tried his hand as a dramatic scriptwriter, a pursuit that almost invariably reached dismal ends. "He had more failures as a playwright than success," observed Irene Heinstein, a modern investigator. "But what a success." In the mid–1930s he penned *What a Life!* So dejected was he by his string of bad luck, however, that he confessed to a journalist some time later that he seriously thought at the time about trading half of his investment in *What a Life!* to a merchant in exchange for a winter garment. Goldsmith's fortunes—indeed his future existence—was substantially altered with the drama, nonetheless. "That play had lots of legs, was produced all over the country and in summer stock, and even revived in 1982 off–Broadway," Heinstein noted.

The powerful domestic presentation bowed at New York's Biltmore Theater on April 13, 1937, and ran for 538 consecutive performances. It starred Ezra Stone as Henry Aldrich, with Leah Penman as his mother. They were the only Aldriches in the production, yet both thespians were tapped for the same roles in the radio incarnation a couple of years later. In the interim, producer George Abbott urged Goldsmith to revamp the show and turn it from a humorless drama into a lighthearted tale of amusement. Goldsmith heeded that advice.

Rudy Vallee attended a performance and requested that the creator develop some sketches for radio based on it. He did that, too, and they were included in 8- to 10-minute snippets on Vallee's 60-minute Thursday night *Royal Gelatin Hour* on NBC. Ezra Stone and others from the stage play were in the cast. That led to 39 weeks on *The Kate Smith Show* on CBS in 1938–39, also on Thursday nights. *Smith* was then underwritten by General Foods Corporation, which was to concurrently sponsor *The Aldrich Family* on NBC on various nights beginning in 1939. Parenthetically, a media scholar speculated: "Henry must have sipped the same magic potion that kept Helen Trent 35 years old for three decades. He had been just 16 in 1937 when he leaped full-blown into Broadway, and he was 16 years old in 1953 when he left the air forever."

In the meantime, the Goldsmith saga was reproduced on the silver screen. *What a Life* was released in 1939, starring Jackie Cooper as Henry and Hedda Hopper—who was destined to become a legendary Hollywood gossip columnist—as Mrs. Aldrich. They were once again the only members of that clan represented. Also appearing in the motion picture was Janet Waldo, soon-to-be star of radio's *Meet Corliss Archer*, and soon-to-be venerated dancer Marge Champion.

Goldsmith wasn't resting on any laurels, however. In addition to turning his original stoic narrative into a comedic radio play, he subsequently capitalized on the same characters by penning three more screenplays: *Life with Henry* (1941), *Henry Aldrich, Editor* (1942) and *Henry and Dizzy* (1942). While Jackie Cooper appeared as Henry in the 1941 production, Jimmy Lydon took over the role in both 1942 screen releases.[2] Although there was no Homer Brown performing in any of the celluloid versions, Henry had a pal on the big screen named Dizzy Stevens. He was introduced in the 1941 film by actor Eddie Bracken (who had lost out to Ezra Stone for the part of Henry on radio), and was replaced by Charles Smith in the latter movies.

Having turned his back on oblivion by then, Goldsmith—earning $3,000 weekly as one of radio's highest paid scriptwriters—penned the screenplay for *Father Was a Fullback*, released in 1949, another family farce featuring Fred MacMurray, Maureen O'Hara, Rudy Vallee, Thelma Ritter and Jim Backus. Eventually the scribe turned his original moneymaking brainchild into a supplementary goldmine: *The Aldrich Family* sitcom ran on NBC-TV from 1949 to 1953. With essentially the same format and premise as the radio adaptation, the video version, like radio, required five separate actors to play the adolescent namesake: Robert Casey (1949–50), Richard Tyler (1950–51), Henry Girard (1951–52), Kenneth Nelson (1952) and Bobby Ellis (1952–53). Of those, only the latter also portrayed the role on radio.[3]

It took just a trio of young thespians to play Homer Brown, however: Jackie Kelk (1949–51), Robert Barry (1951–52) and Jackie Grimes (1952–53). Kelk was the most durable of the Homer Browns in audio. House Jameson, who was Sam Aldrich in the radio run, singularly reprised it on television. One of numerous actresses appearing as the daughter on radio, Charita Bauer (whose crowning achievement was as leading lady Bert Bauer on radio and TV's *The Guiding Light* from 1950 to 1984), introduced the part of Mary Aldrich during the initial season of the TV sequel. Others on TV were newcomers to *The Aldrich Family* cast.[4]

Goldsmith later scripted several episodes of various television series, including *Dennis the Menace*, *The Donna Reed Show*, *The Flying Nun*, *Goodyear Playhouse*, *Leave It to Beaver* and *Petticoat Junction*. He died of undisclosed causes in Tucson, Arizona, on July 11, 1971, at age 71. He left a wife, Cathryn, four sons and a daughter. A self-deprecating man, Goldsmith once said of his children: "Pat, the oldest boy, is the only one who has seen *What a Life*. He wouldn't admit that he liked it—calls the whole thing beginner's luck."

The titles of *The Aldrich Family* episodes—possibly labels ascribed by vintage radio memorabilia collectors—hint at where those situations involving two catastrophe-prone teens were headed. A score of samples: "Crowded Bathroom," "Henry's Engagement," "Henry Loses Gift Watch from Aunt Harriet," "Girl Trouble," "Henry Raises Carrier Pigeons," "Letter from a Loan Company," "Homer's Love Note Goes to Henry's Girl," "Costume Party," "A Quiet Evening," "Henry Wants a School Ring," "Wedding Day Date with a Bride," "Everybody Sleeps Over," "Henry Sends Candy to Two Girls," "French Notes Mix-up," "Blind Date," "Homer Expects a Horse from Agnes," "Henry Takes Gladys to School Play," "Date with a Tall Girl," "Homer Accidentally Engaged," "Henry Alters the School Paper Gossip Column."

Although the part of Henry Aldrich on radio was played by a quintet of actors, it belonged to just one of them—Ezra Stone. His professional career encompassed multiple dimensions of show business. A media cataloguer claims he amassed more than 1,000 credits in radio, television and Broadway, acting, producing and directing across his sweeping professional lifetime.[5] In truth, however, he is remembered for only a solitary thing—Henry. Born under the sobriquet Ezra Chaim Feinstone at New Bedford, Massachusetts, on December 2, 1917, he was the son of a chemist-teacher-philanthropist. At six years of age he appeared with Philadelphia's YMHA players in a production of *Phosphorus and Suppressed Desires*, his initial exposure to the stage. It left an indelible mark on him.

As a younger teen, in 1931–32 he toured with Washington, D.C.'s National Junior Theater. In 1934, at 16 years of age, he graduated from Oak Lane Country Day School of Temple University. He subsequently enrolled at the American Academy of Dramatic Arts (AADA), the same educational institute from which playwright Clifford Goldsmith matriculated about a dozen years earlier. Stone founded and was executive director of a postgraduate professional center of the AADA much later.

He premiered on the New York stage in 1935 in the musical revue *Parade*, portraying seven different roles. A string of comedies followed—*Room Service*, *Three Men on a Horse*, *Brother Rat*—and then the lead in Goldsmith's *What a Life!* Following that triumph, Stone was thrust onto Broadway in *The Boys from Syracuse* and *See My Lawyer*. In the meantime, he was also appearing on Rudy Vallee's and Kate Smith's radio shows. All of it led to the radio role of Henry in *The Aldrich Family* in 1939.

> Although only in his teens, Ezra Stone was both an assistant to [George] Abbott in production and an actor, as well.... But Abbott murmured darkly that he was not right for the part of Henry Aldrich, a high school student who was always in trouble with the superintendent.
>
> In his capacity of production assistant, Stone read the part in try-outs with other actors. For Henry, he used an imitation he did of a one-time schoolmate of his whose voice cracked under the slightest stress. Once before, Stone had used this voice for the part of

a telegraph delivery boy in a nameless sketch performed in the Catskill Mountains. It worked well in the part of Henry Aldrich. Producer Abbott listened attentively to Stone running through the rehearsals, but he seemed to prefer another young actor, Eddie Bracken, for the part.

> Finally, Abbott admitted Stone was being considered along with Bracken for the role. The two young men were told to come back to the office in one hour for the decision from Olympus. When they returned, Mr. Abbott's secretary got up from her chair and handed Stone a single red rose.[6]

With the exception of three years while he was away with the U.S. Army (from 1942 to 1945),[7] the part was his through 1951. Stone's voice earned instant recognition from the bulk of radio listeners who regularly tuned in to the series.

From 1946 to 1958 he taught in the professional training program of the American Theater. Stone penned sketches for *The Aldrich Family* and the shows headlined by comics Danny Thomas, Milton Berle, Fred Allen and Martha Raye. Beyond the major role of his life (Henry Aldrich), however, his acting assignments were sporadic. He turned up in a trio of Bucks County Playhouse stage productions in 1958–59: *Middle of the Night*, *Once More with Feeling* and *The Man Who Came to Dinner*. While he had already appeared in a couple of motion pictures—1940's *Those Were the Days!* and 1943's *This Is the Army*—he played in two made-for-TV flicks, 1972's *A Very Missing Person* and 1981's *The Munsters' Revenge*. Stone performed in a half-dozen dramatic episodes on television series also; *Hawaiian Eye*, *Emergency!* and *Quincy, M.E.* were among the best remembered.

But it was as a director that he remained busiest in his post–Henry days. Stone directed several Broadway productions, including *Me and Molly*, *At War with the Army* and *Wake Up, Darling*. In the quarter-century from 1951 to 1977 he directed a combined 11 television episodes of *The Ezio Pinza Show*, *I Married Joan*, *Bob Hope Presents the Chrysler Theater*, *The Munsters*, *Petticoat Junction* and *Laredo*. In the same period he directed two made-for-TV movies, 1967's *Tammy and the Millionaire* and 1970's *Lassie: Peace Is Our Profession*, plus 11 TV series: *The Hathaways, My Living Doll, Lost in Space, O.K. Crackerby!, Tammy, The Flying Nun, Julia, The Debbie Reynolds Show, Love American Style, The Jimmy Stewart Show* and *Space Academy.*

Even after his induction into the Army in 1942, Stone persisted as Henry for a while. To do so he contributed his then-weekly salary of $1,250 to the U.S. Army. With the opening of the fall season that year, however, his military superiors denied him any further appearances on the air.

Just as Sergeant Stone was interrupting his role as Henry Aldrich for a full-time armed forces commitment, on October 5, 1942, he wed actress-director-teacher Sara Seegar. Eventually they had two children. Ezra and Sara were still married at the time of her death on August 12, 1990. He suffered fatal injuries in a one-car accident on March 3, 1994, at Perth Amboy, New Jersey. Together with Weldon Melick, he had co-authored *Coming Major!* (Lippincott, 1944). His numerous accomplishments were the subject of yet another volume, Kenneth L. Stilson's *Ezra Stone: A Theatrical Biography* (McFarland, 1995).

When Stone left *The Aldrich Family* after Uncle Sam beckoned in 1942, an understudy in the *What a Life!* stage production, Norman Tokar, age 19, succeeded him on radio. But Tokar didn't last long, summoned, as he was, in 1943 to the U.S. Signal Corps. The same thing happened to *his* successor, Dickie Jones, who joined the cast at age 16 (the only one who was Henry's chronological age!). Jones was a true radio veteran, nevertheless; he had debuted on the air at age five and been the voice of Pinocchio in a 1940 Disney cartoon. He was picked from more than 700 young men who tested for the part. When the Army summoned him in 1944, Raymond Ives was tapped as the new radio hero. He lasted until November 1945, when Stone returned to reclaim the part he had inaugurated more than six years earlier. Despite his advancing age, Stone was to remain with the show for another half-dozen years.

When *The Aldrich Family* arrived on radio each week two actors received top billing from the announcer: ... *And starring Ezra Stone as Henry, with Jackie Kelk as Homer!* While three other thespians portrayed the misadventurous Homer during the show's final aural season, the part really belonged (like Stone's) to only *one person*—Jackie Kelk. He, too, possessed a distinctive inflection—in his case, an embedded nasal twang that was symptomatic of the juvenile he was portraying.

Homer wasn't even included in Clifford Goldsmith's original stage play but was added when the show expanded into a weekly audio series. At tryouts for the part, "Every kid in New York was there," Kelk recalled in an interview. "I thought, I'll never get this." Acting on impulse, when it was his time to audition he altered his nuance. "I did that nasal voice—I don't know why, it just popped into my head—and everyone in the booth started cracking up." Over a dozen years he literally grew up in the role. His dark-eyed Jewish co-star, nonetheless, was more than a Stone's throw (pun intended) from the public's perception, looking nothing at all like a gawky all-American boy-next-door. "I looked more the part," Kelk allowed. His build was slight and skinny. "Ezra was this fat little man in a vest who smoked cigars."[8]

Born John Daly Kelk in Brooklyn on August 6, 1921, by age nine the future Homer Brown turned up on Broadway in *Bridal Wise.* Other stage productions followed, including *Goodbye Again,* Cole Porter's *Jubilee* and *Me and Juliet.* At age 10 he was appearing at cinema houses as juvenile Georgie Bassett in seven single-reel Booth Tarkington comedy film shorts based on the famous fictional characters Penrod and Sam. The youngster performed in a trio of movies—1932's *The Run Around,* 1933's *Wrongorilla* and 1934's *Born to Be Bad.*

He concentrated mainly on broadcasting from then on, initially appearing with a company of kids in the 1930s populating *Coast-to-Coast on a Bus,* alongside host Milton J. Cross. Kelk became a hit as an atrocious

*Ezra Stone (right) as Henry Aldrich, and Jackie Kelk (left) as Henry's pal Homer Brown: The two paired up for most of the show's halcyon era (1939–51), except when Kelk was away serving Uncle Sam. Together they routinely landed in hot water, turning simple situations into complex plots that became funnier as they tried to disentangle themselves. Surrounded by parents and pals, the duo formed the template for the adolescent sitcom, turning their characters into memorable figures that were occasionally copied by others.*

brat harassing comics Eddie Cantor, Bert Lahr, Jack Benny, and George Burns and Gracie Allen. The thespian earned further aural credits as a recurring figure in the storylines of *Hello, Peggy* (1935–38), *Dick Tracy* (ca. 1935–ca. 1937, ca. 1938–ca. 1939), *The Gumps* (1936–37), *Hilltop House* (ca. 1937–ca. 1941), *Terry and the Pirates* (1937–39), *Valiant Lady* (ca. 1938–ca. 1942), *Mother o' Mine* (1940–41), *Amanda of Honeymoon Hill* (ca. 1940–ca. 1946) and *Rosemary* (ca. 1944–ca. 1945). For seven years in the 1940s the Professional Children's School alumnus was the voice of cub reporter Jimmy Olsen on *The Adventures of Superman*. By mid-decade he made regular appearances on *The Chesterfield Supper Club* and *Hildegarde's Radio Room*, and put in at least one performance in a *Theater Guild on the Air* drama.

Of course his most memorable role was the part of Homer Brown in *The Aldrich Family*, on radio from 1939 to 1951 and television from 1949 to 1951. He was 30 when he left the role, still featured as the well-known 16-year-old. Age may have caught up with him, but there was a second reason for his absence. For a year he played the lead in the NBC-TV sitcom *Young Mr. Bobbin*. On the small screen, as Alexander Hawthorne Bobbin, he was working his first job while living in the home of a couple of aunts.

Kelk won bit parts in two major motion pictures—*Somebody Up There Likes Me* (1956) and *The Pajama Game* (1957)—and was in a half-dozen guest roles spread across the 1950s in TV episodes of *Those Whiting Girls*, *Leave It to Beaver*, *Bachelor Father* and *The Donna Reed Show*.

An astute businessman, he made numerous profitable investments. Nonetheless, in the 1960s he left the industry proper to earn his livelihood as a casting director at Compton Advertising, a New York City agency. While there, he hired Jane Withers to be "Josephine the Plumber." For a while he also worked for the Louise Shary Literary Agency. Although Kelk didn't return to show business, on a few occasions he put in an appearance at a charity fund-raiser. A longtime alco-

holic, he became a teetotaler in 1981. He never married and succumbed to a lung infection on September 5, 2002, at Rancho Mirage, California. He was 81.

For the bulk of the radio run of *The Aldrich Family*, Sam Aldrich—whom his kids on the show formally addressed as "Father" rather than a softer "Pop," "Dad" or "Daddy"—was played by veteran radio thespian House Jameson. Furthermore, he was the sole actor to play that role in the program's television incarnation (1949–53). Born at Austin, Texas, on December 17, 1902, his given name was copied from the surname of family friend Colonel Edward M. House, an adviser to President Woodrow Wilson. Jameson matriculated in 1924 from New York's Columbia University. Enrolling for private acting lessons in Gotham, he frequently performed on stage locally and with touring stock outfits. In his Broadway debut he toted a spear in a Theater Guild production of *St. Joan*. Such encounters (there were more) thrust him into radio.

In his first sustained broadcast post Jameson won the key role of Inspector Douglas Renfrew of the Royal Canadian Mounted Police in *Renfrew of the Mounted*, initially on CBS (1936–37) and then on NBC Blue (1938–40). Other work followed promptly, including parts as continuing characters in soap operas on NBC's *Young Widder Brown* (1938–42), CBS's and NBC Blue's *This Day Is Ours* (1938–40), NBC's *Hilda Hope, M.D.* (1939–40), CBS's *By Kathleen Norris* (1939–41), NBC's *Brave Tomorrow* (1943–44) and NBC's *Marriage for Two* (1949–50). For a fleeting interlude in 1941 he supplanted Raymond Edward Jones as the host ("Raymond") with the chilling voice who beckoned terrified fans to the *Inner Sanctum Mysteries*. He was in the lead role of ABC's *David Harding, Counterspy* in that thriller's premiering episode in 1942. He was replaced the following week by Don MacLaughlin, who remained with it for a run of 15 years.

Jameson made multiple appearances in narratives aired on *The Columbia Workshop* between 1937 and 1940. He showed up frequently in the cast of CBS's *So This Is Radio*, a 1939 summer entry. During the Second World War he dispatched savings bond appeals and patriotic homilies on NBC's *Cities Service Concert*, and acquired leading roles in *Lands of the Free* and *Words at War*. During the same era he appeared as Jefferson Davis, Thomas Jefferson and James Madison on *The Cavalcade of America*. For a while in the 1940s he carried the namesake role on CBS's *Crime Doctor*. He also performed with companies of on-call actors on *Philip Morris Playhouse* (1941), *This Is War* (1942), *Columbia Presents Corwin* (1944), *American Portrait* (1946), *Philco Radio Playhouse* (1953), *X-Minus One* (1957) and *Suspense* (1960).

When radio faded, House Jameson was just getting his second wind. Television proffered unlimited opportunities, and he took full advantage of them. Between 1956 and 1969 he turned up in 39 episodes of popular video fare, like *Goodyear Television Playhouse*, *Robert Montgomery Presents* (he was on it 14 times!), *Studio One*, *The U.S. Steel Hour*, *Route 66*, *Car 54—Where Are You?*, *Naked City* (eight appearances), *The Defenders*, *Hallmark Hall of Fame* and *N.Y.P.D.* He performed in one made-for-TV flick, 1967's *The Borgia Stick*, and—aside from *The Aldrich Family*—portrayed recurring roles in a quartet of tube features. One was as A. Lawrence Lowell in a 1960 miniseries, *The Sacco-Vanzetti Story*. Jameson was a regular in a trio of daytime serials, playing John H. Phillips in CBS's *The Edge of Night* (1957–58), Dr. Bert Gregory in NBC's *Another World* (1965–66) and Judge Crathorne in ABC-TV's *Dark Shadows* (1967).

Jameson is credited with a dozen Broadway productions, beginning in 1925 and extending all the way to 1968. While most of his gigs before the footlights were short-lived, his last two were enduring: as Dr. James Kimbrough in *Never Too Late* (November 26, 1962, to April 24, 1965) and as Ambassador James F. Magee in *Don't Drink the Water* (November 17, 1966, to April 20, 1968). The busy thespian acted in five features on the silver screen, one of which brought controversial reviews. Beginning his celluloid career with 1948's *The

*Naked City*, he literally posed nude in his final film, 1968's *The Swimmer*, together with a youthful, hard-bodied Burt Lancaster. How far things had progressed since his Sam Aldrich days! Jameson's other movies included *Williamsburg, the Story of a Patriot* (1957), *Parrish* (1961) and *Mirage* (1965).

His first wife, the former Edith Taliaferro, was his senior by a decade. She became the original Rebecca in *Rebecca of Sunnybrook Farm*. Edith Jameson lost her sight in the late 1930s, retired from the stage and died at age 65 on March 2, 1958. Jameson remarried, to the former Elizabeth Mears, who survived him when he passed away in a Danbury, Connecticut, hospital on April 23, 1971. There were no children. He resided at nearby Newtown, Connecticut, from 1939, the year he began the part of Sam Aldrich, until his death.

Katharine Raht portrayed the woman who began every episode of *The Aldrich Family* shouting "Hen-reeeeeeeee! Henry Al-drich!" for the bulk of the show's run. As the matriarch, Alice Aldrich prodded Henry, Sam and Mary, while performing a litany of domestic responsibilities, giving careful attention to every detail in running that household. She was the lady of the house, and it often appeared that she was in charge of it all by herself. Rightly or wrongly she was capable of meddling in everybody else's personal affairs, and often did so without hesitation. It took Sam to balance her at-times-aggressive, overbearing behavior. She seldom stepped back and quietly observed; timid she wasn't, and listeners always knew where she stood in every circumstance.

The thespian playing her most durably, Raht, was a native of Chattanooga, Tennessee. Her own ancestral background is compelling. She hailed from one of the most prominent and affluent clans in east Tennessee. Her grandfather, Julius Raht, of German extraction, arrived in Chattanooga in 1850. His accomplishments are recorded in a Volunteer State history: "In mining [copper] circles and in finance he was one of the most important men of his day."[9] Director of the nearby

Duckwood Copper Mine, Julius Raht discovered a strain that was ultimately named after him, *rahtite*. His son, meanwhile, Katharine's father, enjoyed similar industrial achievements. The published account acknowledges: "He is likewise a large holder of real estate and is altogether one of the foremost business men and progressive citizens of Chattanooga." As a young man he earned an engineering degree from Rensselaer Polytechnic Institute at Troy, New York.

Katharine, his only child, was born in Chattanooga on May 8, 1901. Her mother died when she was but nine years of age, and her dad remarried. She matriculated at Bryn Mawr (Pennsylvania) College and then became a French and history instructor at Foxcroft School, a Middleburg, Virginia, college-prep institute for girls. She also taught at the University of Chattanooga. Nonetheless, harboring a longtime passion for acting, in between school terms in 1937 she worked in summer stock. With a taste for showmanship in her blood, she decided to take a breather from the classroom and enroll for voice training in New York City while seeking employment there.

Following a couple of disappointing stage encounters (plays that opened and closed quickly), Raht was encouraged by a lengthy run of Thornton Wilder's *Our Town*. It premiered on February 4, 1938, and persisted for 336 performances, ending in November 1939. Initially playing a nondescript denizen in crowd scenes, she was eventually elevated to the speaking role of Mrs. Gibbs after actress Evelyn Varden left the show. In subsequent years Raht won stage roles in *The Heiress* (1947–48), *Sabrina Fair* (1953–54), *The Happiest Millionaire* (1956–57) and *Love and Kisses* (1963). When *The Heiress* was revived in New York City in 1950, she was one of a few from the original cast who appeared with it. Coincidentally, Basil Rathbone was among them, too. From 1963 to 1965 Raht was active in regional theater and on the straw hat circuit.

While getting a late start in the profession, the academician-turned-actress jumped into radio with both feet, never looking back. Before long she was playing ongoing roles in a myriad of daytime dramas—*Against the Storm, Aunt Jenny's Real Life Stories, Snow Village Sketches, Young Doctor Malone*—while sporadically appearing in several primetime ventures, including *Crime Doctor, David Harding—Counterspy* and *Stage Door Canteen*. As hostess for the latter she charmed GIs by informing them that she had three sons in the service, all named Henry (Ezra Stone, Norman Tokar and Dickie Jones, who played Henry Aldrich before donning their uniforms). Her claim was always good for a laugh.

Although she didn't make the cut for the televersion of *The Aldrich Family*, in the late 1950s Raht performed in a handful of television episodes of *Ford Star Jubilee, Robert Montgomery Presents* and *Hallmark Hall of Fame*. She also appeared in a made-for-TV movie, 1959's *Children of Strangers*.

While she was approaching middle age by the time she was fully entrenched in show business, Katharine Raht had the stamina and resolve to make it work. As she blazed a trail for herself, she proved that she really could do it all, as she demonstrated weekly in the role of Alice Aldrich. Returning to Chattanooga to retire, the never-married mama of the Aldrich family died there on December 2, 1983, at age 82.

Too many actresses portrayed the role of Mary Aldrich, Henry's sister, to be profiled here. None of a dozen (by some accounts) was enduring. They included at least two names that were to become prolific in radio, however, Jone Allison and Charita Bauer.

Mary Shipp, meanwhile, was the most stable Kathleen Anderson, Henry's sustained love interest—when another girl didn't catch his eye. Shipp's summary is included in the chapter on *My Friend Irma*.

*The Aldrich Family* set the stage for a plethora of teenage comedy dramas to follow. While America's adolescents seemed to think they had complicated lives—as every generation before and after them has—when they heard the troubles of Henry Aldrich and his pal Homer Brown, their own issues may have temporarily paled. On this show, and several more like it, the crowd racing through puberty was—for 30 minutes at least—elevated to princes and princesses of the airwaves. What transpired there not only formed a bond between the fans and some imaginary friends, but also forged a connection between those youth and others of their generation in places sometimes totally different, as well as distant. Ultimately, that may have been this series' most satisfying recompense.

# 3

## The Amos 'n' Andy Show

### THEY SOLD RADIO TO AMERICA

Four score years following its inception, *Amos 'n' Andy* seems more impressive than it did when it originally made it onto the ether. Is there any radio or television sitcom in contemporary times that could so mesmerize a nation for more than three decades? For most, five years would be an incredible achievement in longevity. A decade of new episodes would be categorically unthinkable. Yet *Amos 'n' Andy* grabbed the attention of much of America's populace and appealed to a segment of that audience for an astonishing 32 years! It was a ridiculously improbable run even then. In so doing it persuaded millions to go out and invest in radios of their own so they might bring entertainment directly into their homes, workplaces and vehicles at little expense beyond the initial investment. It was a win-win-win-win scenario for artists, advertisers, audiences and assemblers of radio sets. Turning the show from a nightly serialized comedy into a weekly sitcom after 15 years, the principals augmented their powerful series with familiar voices played by leading black actors and backed by strong writing. The result offered sure-fire laugh-getters. The series remained one of the medium's foremost comedic showcases into the early 1950s, commanding an audience of 40 million in its peak years. At no time did its white creators, dialecticians Charles Correll and Freeman Gosden, try to belittle the Negroes they played. Rather, they magnified a portion of society and its characteristic vernacular,

merely adding hilarious dialogue to the mix. Blacks and whites simply loved it and kept it near the top of the ratings charts for much of its incredible run.

❖ ❖ ❖

**Producers:** Joe Connelly, Freeman Gosden, Bob Mosher

**Directors:** Andrew Love, Glenn Middleton

**Writers:** Freeman Gosden and Charles Correll (1928–43; script supervisors, 1943–55); Robert J. Ross (head writer, 1943–55); Octavus Roy Cohen, Joe Connelly and Bob Mosher, Artie Fisher, Bob Fisher, Paul Franklin, Harvey Helm, Shirley Illo, Hal Kanter, David Schwartz, Arthur Stander (all 1943–46); Robert J. Ross, Joe Connelly, Bob Mosher and two shifting scribes (all 1946–55); Connelly and Mosher (continuing to 1960)

**Organist:** Gaylord Carter (1928–43)

**Orchestra Leaders:** Joseph Gallicchio (1929–32, 1936–37), Lud Gluskin (1943–44, 1945–47, 1954–55), Billy Mills (1944–45), Jeff Alexander (1947–54)

**Vocalists:** The Mystic Knights of the Sea Quartet (1944–45), The Delta Rhythm Boys (Traverse Crawford, Lee Gaines, Carl Jones, Kelsey Pharr, 1945–47), The Jeff Alexander Chorus (1947–49), The Jubilaires (Ted Brooks, J. Caleb Ginyard, John Jennings, George McFadden, 1947–49)

**Sound Effects Technicians:** Ed Lukes and Frank Pittman (1943–48), Gus Bayz and David Light (1948–55)

**Announcers:** Bill Hay (1928–42), Wallace Butterworth (substitute, 1930), Olan Soule (substitute, 1936), Carlton KaDell (substitute, 1936; commercials, 1937; regular announcer, 1945–47), Joe Parker (substitute, 1937–38), Ken Niles (commercials, 1938–43; regular announcer, 1950–51), Ernest Chappell (substitute, 1940), Del Sharbutt (1942–

43), Harlow Wilcox (1943–45, 1951–55), Art Gilmore and John Lake (1947–48), Ken Carpenter (1949–50), Griff Barnett (commercials, 1951–54)

**Recurring Cast:** *Amos Jones:* Freeman Gosden; *Andrew H. Brown:* Charles Correll; *George (Kingfish) Stevens:* Freeman Gosden; *Willie (Lightnin') Jefferson:* Freeman Gosden (1928–51, 1952–55), Horace Stewart, aka Nick O'Demus (1951); *Henry Van Porter:* Charles Correll; *John Augustus (Brother) Crawford:* Freeman Gosden; *Sapphire Stevens:* Elinor Harriot (1937–38), Ernestine Wade (1939–55); *Ramona (Mama) Smith:* Amanda Randolph (1951–54); *Madame Queen:* Freeman Gosden (1928–43), Lillian Randolph (1943–55); *Ruby Taylor Jones:* Elinor Harriot (1935–55); *Arbadella Jones:* Loretta Poynton (1936), Elinor Harriot (1937–39), Barbara Jean Wong (1940–55); *Genevieve Blue:* Madaline Lee (ca. early 1940s–1955); *Dorothy Blue:* Madaline Lee; *Shorty Simpson:* Lou Lubin (1944–50); *LaGuardia Stonewall:* Eddie Green (1947–49); *Algonquin J. Calhoun:* Johnny Lee (1949–54); *Clara Van Porter:* Elinor Harriot (1937–38), Ernestine Wade (1939–44); *Harriet Lily Crawford:* Edith Davis (ca. early 1940s–1943), Ruby Dandridge (1943–55); *Pun'kin:* Terry Howard (1936–37), Elinor Harriot (1937); *Sara (Needlenose) Fletcher:* Ernestine Wade; *Widow Armbruster:* Lillian Randolph

**Supporting Cast:** Elvia Allman, Corny Anderson, Sara Berner, Mel Blanc, Millie Bruce, Ken Christy, Leo Cleary, Dorothy Dandridge, Vivian Dandridge, Roy Glenn, Jester Hairston, Joseph Kearns, Shirley Mitchell, "Wonderful" Smith, Vince Townsend, Jean Vander Pyl, Herbert Rawlinson, Amos Reece, Willard Waterman, Lasses White, Ernest Whitman, Harriette Widmer, Will Wright

**Sponsors:** The Pepsodent Company, for Pepsodent toothpaste (1929–end of 1937); Campbell Soup Company, for Campbell's soups and juices, Franco-American spaghetti and a variety of additional foodstuffs (beginning of 1938–43); Lever Brothers Company, for Rinso detergent, Lifebuoy and Swan hand soaps and other household cleaning and personal care commodities (1943–end of 1950); Rexall Drug Company, for Rexall drug stores and pharmaceutical medications (beginning of 1951–54); Sustained, interspersed with Columbia television sets (1954–55); Brown & Williamson Tobacco Corporation, for Kool cigarettes, and, later, multiple participation (*Amos 'n' Andy Music Hall*, 1954–60)

**Themes:** "The Perfect Song" (1928–41, from *Birth of a Nation*, by Joseph Carl Breil and Clarence Lucas); "Angel's Serenade" (1941–60, by Gaetano Braga)

**Ratings:** High—53.4 (1930–31), Low—2.4 (1955–56), Median—18.8. Figures based on 26 seasons (1930–54 inclusive for *Amos 'n' Andy*, and 1954–56 for *The Amos 'n' Andy Music Hall*). Further documentation unavailable. In the serialized era, numbers fell from a high of 53.4 (1930–31) to a low of 9.4 (1942–43), a decline of 82.4 percent. In the sitcom era (1943–55), figures remained in the double digits for the first 10 of a dozen seasons, a decent level. Overall, *A&A*'s numbers exceeded 20—an exceedingly high ranking—in nine of the 26 seasons reported: 1930–31, 1931–32, 1932–33, 1933–34, 1934–35, 1935–36, 1946–47, 1947–48, 1948–49.

**On the Air:** January 12, 1926–December 18, 1927, *Sam 'n' Henry*, WGN, Thursday–Tuesday, 10:00–10:10 P.M. Central Time; March 19–April 30, 1928, *Amos 'n' Andy*, WMAQ, Thursday–Saturday, Monday–Tuesday, 7:11–7:21 P.M. Central Time; May 1, 1928–August 18, 1929, WMAQ, Thursday–Tuesday, 10:00–10:10 P.M. Central Time; August 19–November 17, 1929, NBC Blue, Wednesday–Monday, 11:00–11:15 P.M. Eastern Time; November 18, 1929–November 8, 1932, NBC Blue, Monday–Saturday, 7:00–7:15 P.M.; November 9, 1932–July 13, 1934, NBC Blue, Monday–Friday, 7:00–7:15 P.M.; September 17, 1934–July 12, 1935, NBC Blue, Monday–Friday, 7:00–7:15 P.M.; July 15, 1935–March 31, 1939, NBC, Monday–Friday, 7:00–7:15 P.M.; April 3, 1939–February 19, 1943, CBS, Monday–Friday, 7:00–7:15 P.M.; October 8, 1943–June 16, 1944, NBC, Friday, 10:00–10:30 P.M.; September 22, 1944–June 1, 1945, NBC, Friday, 10:00–10:30 P.M.; October 2, 1945–May 28, 1946, NBC, Tuesday, 9:00–9:30 P.M.; October 1, 1946–May 27, 1947, NBC, Tuesday, 9:00–9:30 P.M.; September 30, 1947–May 25, 1948, NBC, Tuesday, 9:00–9:30 P.M.; October 10, 1948–May 8, 1949, CBS, Sunday, 7:30–8:00 P.M.; October 9, 1949–May 21, 1950, CBS, Sunday, 7:30–8:00 P.M.; September 24, 1950–June 10, 1951, CBS, Sunday, 7:30–8:00 P.M.; September 30, 1951–May 25, 1952, CBS, Sunday, 7:30–8:00 P.M.; September 28, 1952–May 24, 1953, CBS, Sunday, 7:30–8:00 P.M.; September 27, 1953–May 23, 1954, CBS, Sunday, 7:30–8:00 P.M.; September 13, 1954–March 23, 1956, *The Amos 'n' Andy Music Hall*, CBS, Monday–Friday, 9:30–10:00 P.M.; September 26, 1954–May 22, 1955, *Amos 'n' Andy*, CBS, Sunday, 7:30–8:00 P.M.; March 26, 1956–November 25, 1960, *The Amos 'n' Andy Music Hall*, CBS, Monday–Friday, 7:05–7:30 P.M.

**Extant Archival Material:** More than 160 scripts of *Amos 'n' Andy* broadcasts between 1935 and 1951 are housed in the Broadcasting (loose) and KNX (bound) collections at Thousand Oaks Library, American Radio Archives, 1401 East Janss Road, Thousand Oaks, CA, 91362; (805) 449-2660; fax (805) 449-2675; *www.tol.lib.ca.us.*

An unidentified number of *Amos 'n' Andy* scripts are included on microfilm in Amos 'n' Andy Scripts, 1928–1937, while hard copy scripts from the 1940s appear in the Copyright Deposit Dramas Collection, both archived by the Library of Congress, 101 Independence Avenue Southeast, Washington, DC, 20540, in that body's Manuscript Division at James Madison Memorial Building, Room LM101; (302) 707–5387; Fax (202) 707–6336; *www. loc.gov/rr/mss.*

Three scripts from *The Amos 'n' Andy Show* (1929–54) are maintained in the Script Collection by The Broadcast Arts Library, Box 9828, Fort Worth, TX, 76147; (310) 288–6511; www.broadcastartslibrary.com.

An unidentified number of photographs of *Amos 'n' Andy* are among the Fred Acree Papers, 1920–1947, housed by the University of Texas-Austin's Center for American History, 1 University Station, SRH-2.101, Austin, TX, 78712; (512) 495–4518; Fax (512) 495–4542; *www.cah.utexas.edu.*

An unidentified number of scripts from 1929 of *Amos 'n' Andy* are included in the Scripts and News Transcripts housed by the University of Maryland's Library of American Broadcasting, 3210 Hornbake Library, College Park, MD, 20742; (301) 405–0397; Fax (301) 314–2634; *labcast@umd.edu.*

A total of 222 separate broadcast scripts aired between October 8, 1943, and May 24, 1953, comprise the Amos 'n' Andy Radio Scripts, 1943–1953 collection at the University of California at Los Angeles (UCLA), Charles E. Young Research Library, Room 22478, Box 951575, Los Angeles, CA, 90095; (310) 825–7253; Fax (310) 825–1210; *www.library.ucla.edu/libraries/arts.*

An unidentified number of syndicated rebroadcasts of *Amos 'n' Andy* shows are included in the Archive Research and Study Center Audio Collection of UCLA's Film and Television Archive, Archive Research and Study Center, 46 Powell Library; (310) 206–5388; Fax (310) 206–5392; *arsc@ucla.edu.*

An unidentified number of manuscripts and copies of musical sketches for *Amos 'n' Andy* are housed in the Jeff Alexander Television, Radio, and Motion Picture Music Collection, 1943–1970, at UCLA's Music Library, Special Collections, Room B425, Schoenberg Hall, Box 951490, Los Angeles, CA, 90095; (310) 825–1665; Fax (310) 206–7322; music-spec@library.ucla.edu.

At least 309 transcriptions of *Amos 'n' Andy* broadcasts between 1929 and 1960, plus another eight of *Sam 'n' Henry* (1926–27) are known to be in general circulation or held by private collectors as of 2006, sold by vintage radio dealers and traded by old-time radio hobbyists.

❖ ❖ ❖

"For a significant period of time, life in America came to a virtual standstill when *Amos 'n' Andy* was on the air. Nearly everyone was ... listening to two white guys [Freeman Gosden and Charles Correll] pretending to be two black guys," a series biography proclaimed.[1] Water flow was dramatically interrupted during their quarter-hour on the air, then it resumed in force afterwards, according to public works officials. Shops, restaurants and movie theaters piped in broadcasts of the popular feature as a patronage drawing card—cinema houses suspending their films to air episodes of *Amos 'n' Andy*. Factories altered their shift changes; public transportation ridership was down in that quarter hour. Even a president, Calvin Coolidge, was an inveterate addict. Radio historian John Dunning cited it as "the most popular radio show of all time."[2] He may have been on target. "At its peak," said he, the program "held the hearts and minds of the American people as nothing did before or since."

So compelling were the infamous characters that left an indelible mark on the aural medium that—for many of the nation's denizens—the pair became creatures of listening habit spanning the entire golden age of radio, from 1928–60, more than three decades. Sales of radio sets leaped from $650,550,000 in 1928—the year of their launch—to $842,548,000 the following year when they went national.[3] Who could argue that they were not directly responsible for a sizeable percentage of that increase?

> More than any other program, *Amos 'n' Andy* ... revealed that radio was not just an amusing new form of vaudeville but had unlimited and largely untapped commercial potential.... This ... gave broadcasting the breakthrough megahit it needed to reveal radio as a major medium, a moneymaker, and, mostly, a new art form for the masses....
>
> Listeners during the Depression ... realized they could stay home and be as amused as they could spending money for a vaudeville show, a night-club, a dance, or even a movie. Radio had been readily available, but suddenly it seemed indispensable.[4]

At its peak of popularity, *Amos 'n' Andy* was heard six times weekly by an audience of 40 million listeners, a third of U. S. citizens alive at the time. No other entertainment feature may have ever matched that distinction on a sustained basis. The top-ranking show in 1930, it achieved a rating of 53.4, which is believed to be unsurpassed in the annals of broadcasting.[5] Did anything in the way of amusement generate that kind of enthusiastic response in a Depression-tormented America? Unquestionably, it simply didn't happen. For a while, at least, it soothed the savage beast, if only on the installment plan.

Radio's *Amos 'n' Andy* can be divided conveniently into four distinct eras: (1) 1926–29, the pre-network, pre-halcyon epoch, a trial run in which the innovative masters of aural comedic technique honed their skills to a local audience before carrying them to the nation at large; (2) 1929–43, the serialized show wherein they performed for millions of waiting ears as the country virtually ground to a halt during the initial years to tune in to their nightly quarter-hour; (3) 1943–55, the more sophisticated, glamorized Hollywood epic sitcom that attracted still greater numbers while appealing to a smaller percentage of the population; and (4) 1954–60, an overlapping interval in which the long-esteemed characters stepped down from the lofty perches they once occupied, augmenting their humorous exchanges with radio's predominating format of the period—spinning platters between patter. All of this, in addition to a theatrical film, animated cartoons, comic strip, books, a fleeting and somewhat stormy TV run (1951–53), promotional premiums ad infinitum, public appearances, recordings and merchandising opportunities in myriad forms (including toys, candy bars, apparel and more), kept the duo then and now among the most renowned and best recognized figures in American entertainment.

While the depiction of African Americans in the sitcom version of the show is regarded by some as racially offensive by today's standards, the characterizations on the daily serial version were actually much more sympathetic and rounded than that of other shows of the 1930s, which perpetuated 19th-century minstrel show stereotypes and did not equal the immense success of *Amos 'n' Andy*. Prominent were the blackface act, the *Two Black Crows*, who did two-man comedy routines in vaudeville, short subjects and comedy records, and minstrel headliner Emmett Miller, who recorded a series of popular songs for Okeh Records in the late 1920s.[6]

*Amos 'n' Andy* was a tribute to the two highly versatile men who inspired it: Charles Correll, the short, stocky one with an engaging personality who obviously loved people and let it show; and Freeman Gosden, the tall, thin one who was uncomfortable around strangers but took the lead in micromanaging the team's efforts, with Correll's blessing. Both were Anglo-Saxon whites appearing in the theater of the mind as African-American blacks, or Negroes in the parlance of the day. Their gifts in speaking traditional black dialect—and doing so in scores of different and distinct voices as they "became" multiple characters—made them instant hits with both races. Wikipedia claimed the two men voiced more than 170 different characterizations during the show's initial decade. Meanwhile, their intent was never to belittle or poke fun at Negroes, but rather—using the cultural vernacular—to offer a comedic dialogue in which blacks were the stars and most of the other figures were also black. It had never been done so widely, and Americans of many persuasions were fascinated by the premise. Indeed, by listening to the *Amos 'n' Andy* broadcasts, most of the country was introduced to typical life among an emerging segment of society of whom they were almost totally uninformed.

Charles James Correll was a native of Peoria, Illinois, the very same little burg that was soon to produce Jim and Marian Jordan, the comic actors who gave expression to *Fibber McGee & Molly*. Correll was born to a working-class family on February 2, 1890. His maternal grandmother, Sarah Sabrina Gartman, was a cousin of Jefferson Davis, the president of the Confederacy, a detail worth noting for at least a couple of reasons. (1) The Corrells resided in Illinois at the time of Charles's birth, geographically in Union territory, although the family loyalties during the Civil War likely rested solidly with the South. Like Amos and Andy were destined to do several decades later, the Corrells moved from the deep South, relocating to Illinois during the reconstruction period of the late 1860s and 1870s. A thought to ponder: did this pattern of transferal suggest a scheme to Correll in initiating the radio series? (2) As will be seen shortly, the heritage of Correll's future business partner was presumably vested in the Southern cause, too. Intriguingly, while only speculation on our part, their family histories could have instilled in both men—who would play Southern Negroes seeking work in the North—demonstrably prevailing sympathies for a white-dominated South had they been born only a few years earlier.

During his boyhood, Correll was awestruck by vaudeville shows and eventually landed a part-time job as an usher at the Main Street Theater in Peoria. Moving into adolescence, he acquired an interest in music and dramatics. A piano student at 13, he led the orchestra at Peoria High School, where he also took parts in every narrative stage production he could get. He exhibited tendencies as a prankster and comic, too, while carrying a part-time mailroom job at *The Peoria Journal* during his high school days. It was a preview of the youth's future interests.

Correll also began appearing in amateur minstrel productions staged in and around Peoria, receiving his initial exposure to blackface characterizations. Following high school, he accepted a succession of full-time responsibilities in trades, even working for his dad as a brick-mason for a time. As a sideline, the pianist played during silent movies that were screened nightly at the Columbia Theater in Peoria. Yet he was obviously restless and dissatisfied, preferring a more active role in show business. The path that ultimately took him there began with continuing appearances in amateur and semiprofessional productions in Peoria, and at the nearby Quad Cities.

Correll was eventually hired by a Rock Island vocal ensemble, the Metropolitan Quartet, as the group's accompanist. He continued to develop his performing skills, even filling in as a replacement baritone when needed. Interrupting the continuity for a little while, in 1917 he took a job as a munitions staffer at the Rock Island Arsenal during the height of World War I. The following year—performing at a benefit show—he was "discovered" by the Joe Bren Producing Company of Davenport, Iowa. At the war's conclusion Correll left the Arsenal and hit the road, coaching talent for Bren. One of those routes carried him to Durham, North Carolina. In the late summer of 1919 in Durham he was aligned with another newly-hired Bren agent, Freeman Gosden. The two produced *The Jollies of 1919* at an Elks lodge. It was literally the start of something grand.

Freeman Fisher Gosden was born at Richmond, Virginia, on May 5, 1899, more than nine years after Charles Correll's birth. Gosden's ancestry descended from middle-class Baltimore merchants. Never a part of Virginia aristocracy, his morally upstanding family persisted in a life-long struggle to pay its bills. His grandfather fought in the Civil War on the side of the Confederacy. Given the family's geographical location in the capital of that movement, it may be casually assumed that the clan continued to support the Southern cause.

Young Freeman, in the meantime, was raised near Richmond's theater district and close to Jackson Ward, cited as the commercial and cultural capital of the black Southeast in the years he was growing up. That post exposed him to widely diverse differences in people. All of it "offered young Freeman Gosden a daily window into a complex urban black culture, which most white Americans of the early twentieth century never knew existed," one source postulated.

He was studious while enrolled at Ruffner School near his home. Following grammar school, the boy attended a military institute while residing outside Atlanta with his sister and brother-in-law. Young Gosden returned to Richmond after a year in Georgia and matriculated at John Marshall High School. But when the family's finances grew desperate, at 16 he dropped out of formal education to pursue an income. His work responsibilities included a variety of odd jobs. In the meantime, he suffered unspeakable personal losses. By the year he was 18 (1917), a brother had committed suicide, his father had died after an extended illness, and his mother and only sister were killed in a vehicular crash. All of it left Freeman and two older brothers orphaned, stunned and with deep emotional scars. Despite an ability to make people laugh, young Gosden probably carried his emotional wounds for the rest of his life.

Like his future lifelong business associate, Gosden, too, lost himself in vaudeville. He attended every show that played the nearby Bijou Family Theater. While he had appeared onstage at age 10, under such progressively foreboding circumstances he now lost himself in it completely. Gosden was encouraged in his quest by his closest boyhood friend, Garrett Brown, another orphaned youth—a black boy—whom his family had taken in during childhood. Brown lived with the Gosdens for a decade and had a powerful influence on Freeman's life's work. Among other things, Gosden emulated the idioms that his pal spoke. Brown plainly appeared to teach Gosden everything he knew.

At 18 Gosden gave up minstrelsy to serve in the U.S. Navy during World War I. Because he was prone to seasickness he was assigned to Harvard University to train in wireless communications, establishing a life-long love for the field. In Boston he also entertained sailors at varied venues by strumming on a ukulele. Following his discharge in 1919, he took a succession of non-entertainment jobs. But he was never really happy. As a sideline, he performed at various benefit shows featuring music, dance and comedy in and near Richmond. On one such occasion he was recommended to Joe Bren, then a Chicago theatrical entrepreneur, who offered him a position as a traveling director of benefit productions. On one of his earliest assignments, Gosden was dispatched to Durham, North Carolina, to work with Charles Correll. In retrospect, it seemed to have been providential.

At Durham the two men developed an immediate appreciation for one another. The longer they knew each other, in fact, the greater grew the admiration for the other's abilities. They formed a friendship that was to last for the remainder of their lives, out of which would grow a commercial relationship and personal friendship that would become the envy of many an industry insider. Among their activities with Bren were occasional promotional opportunities on radio, beginning in 1921, where they performed as a harmony act.

In October 1925 they were offered staff positions at Chicago's WGN and left the road to accept, becoming local air celebrities. For an initial $125 weekly the pair worked from 10 A.M. to 2 A.M. announcing, singing, playing piano, swapping jokes, writing and playing in dramatic and humorous skits. Their reach extended well past the Windy City. The powerful station owned by *The Chicago Tribune* had little interference or competition in those days, and was picked up far beyond the confines of Lake Michigan's shores.

They also made musical recordings for the Victor Talking Machine Company. Soon WGN officials urged them to appear in an audio version of a popular newspaper comic strip of the day, *The Gumps*. While the idea of a continuing narrative was to take root with them, they demurred, preferring to develop their own figures, as opposed to some already established. The end result was a couple of black fellows from Birmingham, Alabama, who relocated to Chicago in search of their fortunes—a scenario that mirrored precisely what many of their Southern Negro "brothers" were doing at that time. They chose black characters, Gosden would confess to a journalist in 1981, "because blackface comics could tell funnier stories than whiteface comics." They named their newly minted heroes Sam (Gosden) and Henry (Correll).

*Sam 'n' Henry* became radio's very first comic strip, premiering over WGN on January 12, 1926. It was "the first dramatized feature presenting continuing characters in a continuing story line ever to be heard on American radio."[7] It was to have a considerable effect upon another audio genre which would be appearing shortly, the soap opera, for it exhibited many of the facets of the form. Another of those elements was the casual daily (in their case, nightly) visit with familiar friends. It encouraged the development of an intimate emotional bond between the principals and their audience. "Gosden and Correll became the first entertainers to master the intimacy that radio promised—and in the process, created the basic model for every radio and television program that followed," according to one report.[8] "The program had a profound impact on the evolution of the most basic techniques of dramatic radio itself," insisted another scholar. "Correll and Gosden proved to be the first great radio actors, perfecting a subdued, naturalistic approach to microphone acting that differed sharply from the broad manner that stage actors brought to the air."[9]

In less than a year the program built a strong following throughout the Midwest. It was such an overnight sensation, in fact, that—on the side—Correll and Gosden collected a stunning $2,000 weekly for stage appearances in blackface. It was easy money and absolutely astonishing for 1927. The series' instigators, dreaming still bigger dreams, believed that the radio feature could be successfully reproduced for the benefit of listeners tuning in to stations all over the nation. They were splitting $100 from the radio series itself; a greatly expanded version presumably would boost their bottom line significantly.

At the time, the very first networks (NBC Red and Blue) were just gaining a foothold in broadcasting and didn't reach West beyond the Mississippi Valley. Thus, the radio stars proposed a unique system of recording the show in advance and syndicat-

ing it to outlets far and wide. WGN officials, sensing a threat to "their" innovative programming concept, minced few words in instructing the boys to cease and desist.[10] Faced with no alternative, the pair continued on WGN until their contract expired on December 18, 1927. At that juncture they switched stations, joining a leading Windy City competitor, WMAQ, which was owned by a rival newspaper, *The Chicago Daily News*.[11] After regrouping, to avoid legal action, they proceeded as *Amos 'n' Andy*, debuting on March 19, 1928.[12] Bill Hay, their WGN announcer, was included in a first-year $25,000 contract. He remained with the program to 1942, for all but the final year of the serialized run. His introduction to the characters all those years was a pithy "Here they are."

Although it was essentially the same show as *Sam 'n' Henry* under a new sobriquet, as *Amos 'n' Andy* the boys came from Atlanta instead of Birmingham. Catching a train to the industrial North, they were accompanied by four ham-and-cheese sandwiches and $24 between them. Nevertheless, they had visions of grandeur: ahead of them, they believed, a rainbow awaited at the end of the tracks. With the originating city, their appellations and a softer image being about the only perceptible distinctions between *Sam 'n' Henry* and *Amos 'n' Andy*, the newest Windy City denizens were pretty much like the old ones that Chicago listeners had been hearing the last couple of years. The show's popularity was based on the novelty of overhearing a couple of Negro men "attempting to relate to life in the sophisticated world of telephones and cars, as if they were cave people."[13]

Twelve-inch 78 rpm discs were recorded of every episode far enough in advance of the live WMAQ air dates to be shipped to subscribing stations around the U.S., where they were played locally on the same night that each installment of *Amos 'n' Andy* was performed live in Chicago. At its zenith, according to Wikipedia, some 70 outlets beyond WMAQ were airing the syndicated transcribed series. Simultaneously, *The Chicago Daily News* also offered its readers a comic strip that paralleled the aural feature, and it was widely distributed via syndication, too.

Meanwhile, believing wholeheartedly in the potential of her new acquisition, Judith Waller, WMAQ station manager, went to New York in 1928 to shop the feature, upon which she was spending her whole annual talent budget, to the networks. She began with CBS, as WMAQ had only recently become its Chicago affiliate. Appearing in the office of H.C. Cox, then president of CBS and the Columbia Phonograph Company—this was the period immediately before William S. Paley rescued the floundering chain from almost certain extinction—she later recalled their exchange:

> COX: What is it you're trying to get us to buy, Miss Waller?
>
> WALLER: A daily blackface act.
>
> COX: Well, we have *Moran and Mack* in New York.
>
> WALLER: This isn't a *Moran and Mack*. This is not a song and dance act. This is a continued story.
>
> COX: Miss Waller, do you mean to tell me that you believe an act can go on a network at the same time every day in the week, five days in succession?
>
> WALLER: Yes, I believe that.
>
> COX: I think you'd better go back to Chicago. It's very plain to see that you know nothing about radio.[14]

All of the work in recording those shows became obsolete once NBC responded enthusiastically. Securing an underwriter—the Pepsodent Company—eager to accept *Amos 'n' Andy* as a web series, NBC thus nullified the syndicated version, and with it, the necessity of those cumbersome recordings. The show's setting shifted to New York for its premier on August 18, 1929, where the boys became residents of Harlem after relocating from Chicago. They bought an old flivver which was constantly falling apart—one without a windshield, no less—and thereby operated the Fresh Air Taxi Company as the source of their livelihood. Their show persisted in five-night-a-week serialized install-

ments through February 19, 1943, primarily with Correll and Gosden taking almost all the speaking roles.

The actual origination of those broadcasts, meanwhile, continued from the windowless studios of NBC's Chicago Merchandise Mart until the series transferred to California after Pepsodent bowed out at the end of 1937. Incidentally, the show reportedly moved to the Golden State in response to some health concerns Gosden was experiencing. It situated in Palm Springs for a while but eventually settled in Hollywood for the remainder of its airtime.

In the meantime, the boys who had been mere paupers by signing a $25,000-a-year contract in 1928 were able to renegotiate two years later for a substantially higher fee. This occurred in a period of broadcast history in which firms that measured program popularity had not yet been fully developed; consequently, precise research was still difficult to come by. An enterprising Correll and Gosden didn't let that faze them. Offering listeners a free map in 1930, they were overwhelmed by more than a million requests. As a result, the agency, advertiser and network then had convincing evidence of their stupendous appeal. They agreed that the duo was perceptibly worth more than a mere $25,000 annually—and raised them to $50,000. Within nine years that annual figure approached $400,000 from the radio series alone, not including public appearances, film and recording residuals and merchandising paraphernalia in abundance. To say they found a pot of gold at the end of their rainbow would be an understatement.

In her insightful treatise on the episodic years of *Amos 'n' Andy*, biographer Elizabeth McLeod devotes a chapter to the resonant beauty of the linguistics proffered by the show's familiar figures. She labels the dialect "African American Vernacular English," "Black English Vernacular" or merely "Black English." Zeroing in on the conversational exchanges, McLeod reveals: "The scripts Gosden dictated to Correll for *Amos 'n' Andy* were very specific as to how the characters were to sound. Dialogue was spelled out phonetically, with the lines intended to be read exactly as written."[15]

Among the major events transpiring during the installment-laden era that significantly affected the sitcom epoch was Amos Jones' marriage to Ruby Taylor (actress Elinor Harriot), a college student, medical office receptionist and licensed practical nurse, on December 25, 1935. Subsequently, their little girl, Arbadella (played in order by Loretta Poynton, Elinor Harriot and Barbara Jean Wong) was born October 20, 1936. At Christmas 1940 Amos began reading an inspired account of "The Lord's Prayer" to Arbadella every Yule season, and listeners by the thousands expressed appreciation for it. It was repeated annually through 1954, the final Christmas broadcast in the sitcom format. A 78 rpm record was released with Amos recounting "The Lord's Prayer" on the 'A' side and "Little Bitty Baby" on the 'B' side, featuring Jeff Alexander's Orchestra and Chorus. Parenthetically, there was also a four-record album of previously aired Amos 'n' Andy broadcasts issued during the same period.

Almost from the start, meanwhile, George "Kingfish" Stevens became an integral part of the Amos 'n' Andy plots. While much more will be said at the appropriate time about this schemer who joined the cast in May 1928, by the time the sitcom came along in 1943 he was easily the dominant figure of the story line. Kingfish's official capacity was as head of the fraternity lodge that the two principals joined, the Mystic Knights of the Sea. He was a man who looked for vulnerabilities in his friends, especially Andy Brown, and took full advantage of them for his own purposes, most of which backfired. His familiar catchphrase, "Holy mackerel!" entered the lexicon of millions in his audience. At least one politician, Louisiana's Huey P. Long, was nicknamed "Kingfish" after the flamboyant character.

All About Amos 'n' Andy and Their Creators Correll & Gosden was published in 1930 to satisfy some of the requests NBC and its sponsor were receiving about their heroic duo. That same year RKO Pictures signed the pair to co-star in a theatrical motion picture, Check and Double Check. The title was drawn from one of the show's clichés. With Duke Ellington's orchestra playing in the background, the lead figures appeared in blackface, something that was generally abhorrent to them. Gosden would later allow that the film was "just about the worst movie ever." Offered a contract to star in a sequel, the artisans respectfully declined, although they agreed, possibly reluctantly, to appear in blackface publicity stills. All of it cast aspersions on the ethical interpretation the two were attempting to portray, they maintained. The critics lampooned the celluloid manifestation, but audiences loved it, turning it into a smash hit as Amos 'n' Andy mania hit its stride. While the principals refused a subsequent venture, they did perform in blackface in Paramount's The Big Broadcast of 1936. They also lent their voices to a couple of animated shorts in 1934, The Rasslin' Match and The Lion Tamer. That was about all the screen representation they wanted for a while, however.

The pair did finally make a reappearance of sorts in a visual format nearly three decades later. In 1961 Gosden and Correll once again lent their voices to a cartoon, on that occasion for the ABC-TV juvenile series Calvin and the Colonel. It featured anthropomorphic animals, with situations and inflections strongly resembling Andy and the Kingfish. Although the effort was an attempt to revive the series in a format deemed less racially offensive, it arrived just as major civil rights legislation was being enacted in Congress. That may have in some way influenced its cancellation at the end of its first season. Nevertheless, the show's popularity soared in Australia, and syndicated reruns were repeated there multiple times.

Ratings had begun to erode disturbingly by 1938, and fell to 9.4 in the 1942–43 radio season, dropping the show to 60th place among all entries on the all-important numbers chart. The figures had fallen 82.4 percent from its previous high (53.4 during the show's second season). Drastic measures were inevitable. On top of that, in January 1943 the series' then-current sponsor, Campbell Soup Company, advised that a wartime shortage of tin had forced it to cut domestic soup production by 50 percent. As a result, the firm was unable to maintain the show's $1.8 million annual budget any longer. It offered to underwrite the feature as a weekly half-hour series, but Correll and Gosden politely refused, preferring not to alter the model in the middle of a broadcast season. With little fanfare, therefore, after 4,091 installments the

program simply faded into the woodwork on February 19, 1943.

Temporarily, of course.

That was a watershed experience for the two comedians. When they returned to the air the following October 8, their series had been almost totally overhauled. Premiering as a half-hour sitcom, a model that would persist until the feature was withdrawn a dozen years later, the pair were underwritten by a new sponsor with exceedingly deep pockets. Once again it vaulted into radio's top 10 programs, a spot it held onto for the remainder of the decade.

*Two white guys pretending to be two black guys may have been the principal motivating factor in selling more radio sets to Americans in a brief span during the nation's Great Depression than anything or anybody else. When Charles Correll (at left, who played Andy) and Freeman Gosden (Amos) later turned a 17-year odyssey as black dialecticians into a sitcom in 1943, complete with multiple actors, an orchestra and audience, The Amos 'n' Andy Show bounded back into the upper echelons of the radio ratings, having fallen from first place far down that coveted chart. In sharing the decision-making with others, they saved a novel show from extinction and tickled the nation's funnybone in another of its several formats.*

Pushing Rinso detergent, Lever Brothers relied on *Amos 'n' Andy* to convey to American homemakers just how white their wash could be, in stiff competition with Procter & Gamble's leading Duz brand and Colgate-Palmolive's Super Suds detergent. The significantly padded budget allowed for the addition of a studio audience, an enlarged live orchestra (initially under the baton of Lud Gluskin, and later Billy Mills and Jeff Alexander), a myriad of vocal ensembles and soloists, a significantly expanded comedy cast of talented thespians—with most parts divvied up among several actors for the first time—and the addition of a tested creative writing staff, although Gosden and Correll were still considered the series' "script supervisors." Nevertheless, one can almost hear biographer McLeod audibly sighing as she posits: "As popular as it was, as well remembered as it is, *The Amos 'n' Andy Show* is but a shadow of the series that preceded it."[16]

While Gosden was named executive producer, it seemed clear that in many respects it was no longer "their" show alone; instead, people linked to the advertising agency and the business end of production were calling many of the shots. *Amos 'n' Andy* had, in practical terms, moved from Harlem to Hollywood. In some respects it seemed like—using a modern analogy—a mom and pop store that had sold out to Wal-Mart. The former owners took positions with the conglomerate, but their word in how commerce was conducted was no longer absolute and final.

It wasn't quite that bad, of course. Some of the pervasive decision-making that Gosden and Correll had enjoyed almost exclusively for 15 years was thenceforth shared with the powers that be. In relinquishing some control, however, they had saved a show—and reversed its fortunes (while also insuring their own). The fact that the originators were still actively involved continued to make them a powerful presence that had to be reckoned with when major alterations were contemplated. Hal Kanter, one of the show's writers in the late 1940s sitcom era, differentiated between the namesake principals:

"Freeman was the boss man. He would pace while Correll typed. Freeman was smarter and the voice of authority. Freeman was a rather sophisticated old-school Southern gentleman and a very shrewd businessman, astute and talented and a little bit of a snob, and probably anti–Semitic. Charlie Correll was more down-to-earth and blue-collar—he'd been a bricklayer—and much easier to talk to."

For the first few months as a sitcom the revamped series featured several walk-ons by venerated entertainment figures like Lionel Barrymore, Walter Huston, Peter Lorre, Edward G. Robinson, Ginger Rogers and Ethel Waters. But in February 1944 the insertion of guest stars into the narrative seemed forced to some officials and simply became too much; thus, the practice was abandoned.

There were still other changes in the way things had been done.

> There was an increasing tendency to play to the studio audience—measuring the success of the script by the loudness of the laughs. Where Correll and Gosden had refused to rehearse during the serial era, the sitcom now opened its doors to the public for a live-audience dress rehearsal two days before the actual broadcast.
>
> By 1946, with the arrival of Joe Connelly and Bob Mosher, a writing team with a sharp comic style, the Kingfish had become the central character of the program, and it was he who drove the plots. As a result, the subtle mixture of self-importance, guilelessness and vulnerability that had characterized Andy was gradually replaced by a more generic sort of gullibility—and in order for the Kingfish's increasingly outlandish schemes to work, Andy had to be made not just gullible but more than a little stupid. And Amos receded even further into the background, his presence largely reduced to that of a brief walk-on, in which he would tip Andy off that once again the Kingfish had played him for a fool. [17]

Connelly and Mosher, by the way, would eventually go on to write television's popular *Leave It to Beaver* and *The Munsters*, among a myriad of other TV projects.

Each week, according to McLeod, Andy and the Kingfish "enacted a new variation on the ritual dance of the con man and mark." She added: "The Hollywoodization ... took away ... the sense of a quiet daily visit with close friends." With the "interference" of the studio audience, the protagonists ceased being themselves and dwindled into "simply characters in a show."[18]

Despite all of the changes, however, it was clear that American listeners in the 1940s, and even as late as the early 1950s, were infatuated with the hilarious pursuits of *The Amos 'n' Andy Show*. The season rating of 9.4 in 1942–43 rebounded to 17.1 the following year, the first season of the remodeling into a sitcom. The show became a pawn in the infamous network raids in 1948 when CBS gleefully plucked it from its accustomed spot in NBC's weekly lineup and made it a staple of its all-important Sunday night schedule. In accomplishing the acquisition, CBS paid Correll and Gosden $2.5 million for all rights to the legendary feature.

The domestic sitcom itself often revolved around the Kingfish's attempts to outfox his wife Sapphire, aka "the Old Battle-Ax," after collaborating in some machination that would undermine Andy. The Kingfish was a first-class schemer who was looking out for himself alone, taking advantage of the vulnerable Andy Brown whenever he thought he could get away with it. His sins normally found him out, often attributable to some inadvertent revelation by Amos Jones, and the Kingfish was left with egg on his face. The joy was in getting there.

It probably occurred to many listeners, just as it did to this author, that the show might have been better served after awhile by being re-named *Kingfish 'n' Andy*. Certainly in the sitcom epoch the Kingfish had almost totally replaced Amos as a viable figure who frequently spearheaded moves to trick Andy. A radio historiographer reflected on the trio's ethics as they interacted with each other:

*Amos 'n' Andy* was, in more than one way, a study in black and white. Amos was the most priceless of men, and Andy was the most worthless. Andrew Brown's vanity, ignorance, and laziness contrasted sharply with Amos

Jones's practical intelligence, passion for hard work, and love and respect for family.

The conflict between Amos and Andy was classic. It was the guy who knows all the angles (and how to cut the corners) and to take the square....

Amos's one fault may have been that he was too naïve to be fully believed, while the major drawback to Andy was that he really wasn't crooked enough for sufficient contrast. Clearly something was needed and so the character of George [Kingfish] Stevens was introduced....

The Kingfish was ... an out-and-out crook, but not really clever enough and occasionally too soft-hearted to make a success out of being a confidence man....

Andy Brown was always at the ready with a scheme for sudden wealth, which always somehow involved Amos doing a lot of hard work which Andy could oversee.... Even when Andy ordered Amos about, belittling him, and taking credit for all of Amos's hard work and solid ideas, Amos never seemed to think he was being treated in any way but fairly by his best friend.

Andy was not always as generous toward Amos. If Amos somehow failed to move the piano up the hill all by himself and had a melodically tinkling disaster, Andy would rumble in a slow baritone: "I'se regusted with you, Amos!" [19]

A second scholar contrasted the figures after the Kingfish effectively replaced Amos as one of the dual leads:

George (Kingfish) Stevens ... dominated the show—if not his own harassing wife, Sapphire.... Sapphire was a black Alice Kramden.... [W]hat made his blowhard character even funnier was hearing him cower in Sapphire's presence as she took the wind out of his sails....

Andy was a perpetual naïf, swallowing the Kingfish's outlandish bait-and-switch schemes, but always against his better judgment.... Andy isn't fooled because he's black but because he's too eager to make a fast buck.[20]

One source claimed that *Amos 'n' Andy* "eventually became the longest-running radio program in broadcast history."[21] While its tenure in the aural medium was anything but shabby, a published study concluded that the series qualified as the 28th most durable audio feature, including combining the *Sam* 'n' *Henry* and all *Amos 'n' Andy* years together.[22] The list is topped by the *Grand Ole Opry*, which has broadcast continually without missing a weekly performance since November 25, 1925. It is still airing as this is written. Many more legendary vintage features comprise the list of redoubtable audio epics: *Music and the Spoken Word from the Crossroads of the West* (#2), *The Lutheran Hour* (#3), *The Metropolitan Opera* (#4), *Paul Harvey News and Comments* (#5), *Hawaii Calls* (#6), *National Barn Dance* (#7), *Lowell Thomas and the News* (#8), *Meet the Press* (#9), *The Breakfast Club* (#10), and so forth.

The televised incarnation of *Amos 'n' Andy* appeared on CBS-TV on June 28, 1951. Black actors Alvin Childress (Amos) and Spencer Williams (Andy) were hired. Gosden and Correll, meanwhile, had been apprehensive about the project for a long time and had little to do with it. As it turned out, their fears were well founded. To begin with, they hardly felt that their humorous dialectical exchanges and the interaction of the other characters (most of whom they, themselves, had played during the show's first decade-and-a-half) could be sufficiently transported into a visual medium. There, of course, the dialogue would be significantly diminished. Instead of allowing the audience to form pictures in their minds of what was transpiring, it was to be supplied for them, removing one of the most attractive strengths of the radio feature. But by comparison, that concern was child's play. There was far more to worry about in TV land.

The adventures of *Amos 'n' Andy* presented the antics of Amos Jones, an Uncle Tom–like conservative; Andy Brown, his zany business associate; Kingfish Stevens, a scheming smoothie; Lawyer Calhoun, an underhanded crook that no one trusted; Lightnin', a slow-moving janitor; Sapphire Stevens, a nosey loud-mouth; Mama, a domineering mother-in-law; and the infamous Madame Queen. The basis for these characters was derived largely from the stereotypic caricatures of African-Americans that had been communicated through several decades of popular American culture, most notably, motion pictures.

The program's portrayal of black life and culture was deemed by the black community of the period as an insulting return to the days of blackface and minstrelsy. Eventually, the controversy surrounding the television version of *Amos 'n' Andy* would almost equal that of the popularity of the radio version....

African-Americans were still exuberant over recent important gains in civil rights brought on by World War II. They were determined to realize improved images of themselves in popular culture. To some, the characters in *Amos 'n' Andy*, including rude, aggressive women and weak black men, were offensive. Neither the Kingfish nor Sapphire Stevens could engage in a conversation without peppering their speech with faulty grammar and mispronunciations. Especially abhorred was the portrayal of black professionals. The NAACP, bolstered by its 1951 summer convention, mandated an official protest of the program.[23]

A leading black-owned newspaper, *The Pittsburgh Courier*, spearheaded a drive to remove *Amos 'n' Andy* from television screens. In a hard-fought battle, the journal won some converts while losing many potential supporters. It was an established fact that strong writing and a professional group of thespians turned the show into a rib-tickling riot. That made it a commercial success from its start. Meanwhile, the Negro community's opinion of the series was divided—many laughed at it just as much as their white brethren.

When the controversy began to spill out onto the nation's front pages, however, some powerful advertisers became reluctant to plug their wares in a format that was so well identified with blacks. "Fear of White economic backlash was of special concern to advertisers and television producers," noted one authority. Ultimately, *Amos 'n' Andy* was withdrawn from the tube on June 11, 1953. Media historian Donald Bogel observed: "Neither CBS nor the program's creators were prepared for the change in national temperament after the Second World War.... Within black America, a new political consciousness and a new awareness of the importance of image had emerged." The network seemed blindsided by the furor, although Gosden and Correll were probably thinking to themselves, "We told you so."

Strangely enough, for 13 years after CBS withdrew it, the televersion was repeated in syndicated reruns. Until the modern age the show had only been released on videotape in bootleg versions. As of 2005, however, 71 of its 78 filmed installments turned up in circulation as DVD sets. Its popularity appears to be making a comeback with audiences not even born when it was originally screened.

While Gosden and Correll were prevented from performing in the video version for—of all things—their ethnicity, a handful of the radio actors then appearing on the air reprised their same roles on the small screen. Doing double duty were Ernestine Wade (Sapphire Stevens), Amanda Randolph (Ramona "Mama" Smith), Lillian Randolph (Madame Queen), Johnny Lee (Algonquin J. Calhoun) and Horace Stewart (Willie "Lightnin'" Jefferson). The role of George "Kingfish" Stevens, portrayed on radio by Freeman Gosden, was performed on TV by actor Tim Moore.

Thereafter, TV producers and networks almost universally avoided casting Negroes in shows for the next 15 years, until 1968. "You could count on one hand the number of African-Americans that played significant continuing roles on a TV series during that fifteen year period," allowed one scholar.

CBS had invested a huge amount of money in buying out Correll and Gosden, and needed to do something to recover as much of that investment as they could.

They paid $2.5 million to buy all rights to the property, and had expected that revenue from an A&A TV series would cover that outlay, basing their projections on an anticipated seven-year network run for the TV show. But the series lasted only two seasons, leaving the network desperate not to end up losing money on the deal. Added to that, even though the weekly radio series was still a ratings leader, Rexall Drug Company dropped out as sponsor in 1954, ending the revenue from that source. So the Music Hall was devised as something that could be produced with very little additional expenditure and could be sold on a participating sponsorship basis, maximizing revenue.

Correll and Gosden's ... only role in the production was to come in once or twice a week to tape their inserts. The music and "simulated audience reaction" would then be spliced into the master tape....

The Kingfish acted as master of ceremonies, with Amos 'n' Andy joining him....

One amusing footnote: In 1957 a TV-Radio Mirror reader poll named George "Kingfish" Stevens "the most popular disc jockey in America." Gosden seemed genuinely bemused over the award but accepted it good-naturedly.[24]

The emergence of Correll and Gosden as glorified disc jockeys in 1954 was the *fourth* format the innovative entrepreneurs embraced, following adventure serials, soap operas and situation comedies. Did their talents know no bounds? With the Kingfish leading the way, they jointly performed five nights a week on The Amos 'n' Andy Music Hall. That probably tipped some listeners that it was the beginning of the end. Surprise! In that configuration the "trio" persisted for more than another half-dozen years, until the web at last gave in to the demands of a rebellious cadre of affiliates. The restless local stations had demanded the release of more and more network programming time throughout the 1950s. They felt that they themselves (local stations) could sell the time more profitably to advertisers, rather than receive diminutive trickle-down proceeds from the web.

That finally caused CBS to almost wipe its whole agenda clean on November 25, 1960, the infamous "day radio drama died" and all the decades-long daytime serials breathed their last. Some pundits intimated that—in doing the record show—Gosden and Correll, once highly venerated comedians, fell from grace about as low as they could possibly go while clinging to the fringes of show business.

On the Music Hall there was no money anymore for the large cast of supporting players that augmented the antics of the leads during the dozen-year sitcom era. An occasional guest turned up—stars like Jack Benny and Liberace. Most of the time, however, it was the voices of Amos, Andy and the

Kingfish jawing with one another between pop tunes. A thin comedy plotline typically led off a nightly chapter. The humorous exchanges of a few minutes duration were interspersed among the recorded music of artists like Ray Anthony, Perry Como, Bobby Darin, Ella Fitzgerald, Dean Martin and the Voices of Walter Schumann.

Listenership fell from 12 million *Amos 'n' Andy* sitcom fans to seven million when the humorists began spinning wax. But without the high costs of actors, live orchestra, live vocalists, studio audience and rehearsals, the show became a cash cow for CBS, recouping much of that heavy outlay of a few years earlier.

The personal lives of Charles Correll and Freeman Gosden, in the meantime, appeared to parallel one another in several respects. Both men married within five months of each other, later divorcing those spouses and marrying second wives who were significantly younger than their husbands. In each case the second wife outlived her spouse. Both "second" families resided within a couple of blocks of one another in Beverly Hills, California.

In January 1927 Correll wed Marie James in Chicago. Little is known of her. The childless couple divorced in the same city in May 1937. Before the summer was history, Correll walked the aisle a second time, on September 11, 1937, in Los Angeles, with former dancer Alyce Mercedes McLaughlin, then 29 (he was 47). The couple became parents of five offspring: Dorothy Alyce Correll, born February 1, 1940; Barbara Joan Correll, July 21, 1942; Charles James Carroll, Jr., January 23, 1944 (who died at 60 in 2004); John Joseph Correll, August 3, 1946 (who died at seven of "a mysterious kidney ailment that may have been induced by accidental poisoning," perhaps insecticide or paint); and Richard Thomas Correll, May 14, 1948 (an industrious TV and film thespian, director, writer and producer, starting as a child actor on *Leave It to Beaver* at age 12).

Charles Correll, Sr. succumbed to a fatal heart attack in Chicago at age 82 on September 26, 1972. He and Alyce were visiting the Windy City on the occasion of a WGN veterans' banquet to which Correll had been summoned as an honoree. Survivors included his wife, four children and seven grandchildren.

Gosden, on the other hand, wed Leta Marie Schreiber on June 13, 1927, in Chicago. She was a secretary at *The Chicago Tribune*, WGN's parent owner, the station airing *Sam 'n' Henry* at the time. She was 27 and he was 28. They became parents of two children: Freeman Fisher Gosden, Jr., born November 1, 1928, and Virginia Marie (Ginny) Gosden, who arrived in 1931 (date unconfirmed). Meanwhile, the senior Gosden and his spouse separated in November 1939 and were granted a divorce on December 10, 1940.

She filed legal papers with reference to his radio career and unremitting absences from home, resulting in a dysfunctional lifestyle that both lamented. He expressed regret in a story in *The Los Angeles Times* the month before the divorce became final. During court proceedings Leta Marie Gosden testified that her husband was "sullen and morose," at times refusing to talk to her. He required her to entertain guests on occasions when she was too ill to do so, and sent her home from soirées alone that they attended together if she became too ill to linger. Published reports corroborating her account appeared in papers in Chicago, Washington and other major cities. Syndicated columnist Louella Parsons acknowledged Ms. Gosden's debilitating illness as early as February 19, 1940. Just 15 months following the divorce, Leta Marie Gosden died of a heart ailment on March 25, 1942, at age 42. *The Chicago Tribune* noted that she was in ill health "for the last two years."

Freeman Gosden remarried at Scotia, California, on September 1, 1944, to Jane Elizabeth Stoneham, the daughter of a late owner of the New York Giants baseball team. She was 20; he was 45. The couple resided in Beverly Hills, where Gosden had already been living. Two progeny resulted from their union: Craig Leigh Gosden, born August 31,

1949; and Linda Jane Gosden, January 10, 1953.

A decade after Correll passed, Gosden died, at age 83, of congestive heart failure in Los Angeles on December 10, 1982. He was survived by his wife, four children and five grandchildren. Six years later, *Amos 'n' Andy* was inducted into the Radio Hall of Fame.

Historian Jim Harmon appropriately summarized:

> Amos and Andy had a certain innate innocence, for they were in reality those universal human character types, the back-country provincials who come to the big city and find themselves in conflict with the ways of that city. The dialect was incidental. They might have been immigrant German "Dutch," or Russian "Yids," or Tennessee hillbillies. Because of the minstrel show background of their creators, they were cast as Negroes. In reality, Amos and Andy were all of us, reluctantly leaving the rural unsophistication of the first half of the twentieth century for our inevitable trip into the urban mechanization of the second half.[25]

# 4

# Archie Andrews

## THE BOY WHO WAS EVERYMAN

When the dam burst that had held back the family narratives with adolescent figures at their core—beginning with *The Aldrich Family* in 1939 and continuing through *Meet Millie* in 1954—wave after wave of teen comedies spilled forth. *The Adventures of Archie Andrews* arrived four years after the progenitor of the breed. Although it was unmistakably a copycat of the original, and never surpassed it in audience strength or storyline, it was nonetheless a compelling little farce. In its glory days *Archie Andrews* drew a committed Saturday morning deputation of devoted fans. Its appearance at that point in the weekly schedule instead of primetime was one of its distinctive features, setting it apart from the traditional broadcast pattern of peer sitcoms. It featured a mom and dad raising an "only child," too, a mild departure from most contemporary kid-coms. The key figure in this show consistently surrounded himself with not one but two teenyboppers (and there was a strong indication that he was the object of affection of not just one but both of them). Of course, the protagonist had a lame-brained cohort-in-crime, standard fare for adolescent amusement. Archie's sidekick was awarded an appellation (Jughead) that seemed particularly apropos, a constant reminder of Jug's inability to get even the smallest detail right most of the time. Otherwise, the same fiascoes that teens of the 1940s and 1950s encountered on comparable features occurred here, too. As the program signed

off each week, a gleeful announcer reminded listeners to "be sure and tune in to the merry adventures of Archie Andrews again next week." *Merry* seemed like the operative word there.

❖ ❖ ❖

**Creator:** Bob Montana (comic strip originator), John L. Goldwater

**Producer-Director:** Kenneth W. MacGregor (1945–53)

**Directors:** Herbert M. Moss, Floyd Holm, Anton Leder, Garnet Garrison, Ed King, Frank Papp, Charles Urquhart, Kenneth W. MacGregor

**Writers:** John L. Goldwater, Carl Jampel, Howard Merrill

**Orchestra Leaders:** Leo Kampiniski (1945), Milton Katims (ca. 1945, 1946)

**Organists:** Gene Perazzo, George Wright (ca. 1946–53)

**Sound Effects Technician:** Agnew Horine, Sam Malone

**Announcers:** Kenneth Banghart, Robert L. Shepard, Tex Antoine, Bob Sherry, Dick Dudley

**Recurring Cast:** *Archie Andrews:* Jack Grimes (1943–44), Burt Boyer (1944), Charles H. Mullen (1945–46), Jimmy Dobson (1946), Bob Hastings (1946–53); *Forsythe Pendleton (Jughead) Jones:* Cameron Andrews (1943–44), Harlan Stone (1945–51, 1953), Arnold Stang (1952–53); *Fred Andrews:* Reese Taylor (1943–44), Vinton Hayworth (1945–46), Ian Martin (1946–47), Raymond Edward Johnson (1947), Arthur Kohl (1947–1953), Arthur Q. Bryan (summer run, 1949 only); *Mary Andrews:* Peggy Allenby (1943–44), Alice Yourman (1945–53); *Veronica Lodge:* Vivian Smolen (1943–44), Gloria Mann (1943–51), Jane Webb (1951–53); *Betty Cooper:* Joy Geffen (ca. 1943–44), Doris Grundy (1945–46), Rosemary Rice

(1946–53); *Reggie Mantle:* Paul Gordon (1945–53); *Waldo Weatherbee:* Arthur Maitland; *Hiram Lodge:* Bill Griffis; *Mrs. Hiram Lodge:* Joan Shay; *Agatha:* Pat Hosley; *Uncle Herman Jones:* Art Carney

**Supporting Cast:** Fred Barron, Vivian Block, Maurice Franklin, John Gibson, Ray Hedge, Grace Keddy, Joe Latham

**Sponsors:** Sustained (1943–44, 1945–47, 1948–53); Swift and Company, for Swift's Premium frankfurters and Swift's Brookfield sausage (1947–48); Kraft Foods Company, for Kraft cheese and mayonnaise and macaroni and cheese main dishes, Miracle Whip salad dressing and additional foodstuffs (summer replacement run, 1949)

**Theme:** Sponsor's jingle (1947–48); "Archie Andrews Theme" (all other years)

**Ratings:** Only ratings documented: 4.6 (1947–48, the sponsored season)

**On the Air:** May 31–September 24, 1943, NBC Blue, Monday–Friday (late afternoon, precise time unsubstantiated); October 1, 1943–January 7, 1944, NBC Blue, Friday, 7:05–7:30 P.M. Eastern Time; January 17–June 2, 1944, MBS, Monday–Friday, 5:15–5:30 P.M.; June 2, 1945–August 2, 1947, NBC, Saturday, 10:30–11:00 A.M.; August 9, 1947–October 30, 1948, NBC, Saturday, 10:30–11:00 A.M.; November 6, 1948–September 12, 1953, NBC, Saturday, 10:30–11:00 A.M.; (1948–49); 12:30–1:00 P.M. (1949–50); 11:00–11:30 A.M. (1950–51); 7:30–8:00 P.M. (1951–52); 10:00–10:30 A.M. (1952–53); June 8–September 14, 1949, NBC, Wednesday, 8:30–9:00 P.M. (summer replacement)

**Extant Archival Material:** Fifty-two recordings of *The Adventures of Archie Andrews* shows were in general circulation or held by private collectors as of 2006, sold by vintage radio dealers and traded by old-time radio hobbyists.

❖ ❖ ❖

As noted elsewhere, there was an explosion of copycat series that appeared on radio following the inception of *The Aldrich Family*, the first of the so-called "teen comedies" that swept the medium in the 1940s. Several of them enjoyed concurrent or extended runs during the embryonic era of television, too. *Variety* critically commented that the acting and writing of *Archie Andrews* didn't meet the levels enjoyed by similar teen features like *The Aldrich Family* and *A Date with Judy*. Radio historian John Dunning, whose research is often revered by vintage radio hobbyists and collectors, panned the series ("*Archie* at best was still second-string"), succinctly stating:

"The radio show lost the flavor of the [comic] strip and reflected Archie as just another insane teenager. The plots were virtually copies of *The Aldrich Family*.... Had this show gone on first, it might have been the hit, but it didn't and wasn't." Despite such assessments, *Andrews* still attracted a contingent of chronic devotees. Although the listener numbers were smaller than those engendered by some of its peers, the show corralled a steady following and enjoyed a nine-year air life.

In the subgenre of adolescent features, young women overshadowed their male counterparts as protagonists roughly two to one. By omitting *The Adventures of Ozzie and Harriet*, a program that often involved *all* of the family members (like *Father Knows Best* also did) and wasn't focused exclusively on the offspring, there was but a trio of premier aural features in which pubescent young men were the key players: *The Aldrich Family*, *(The Adventures of) Archie Andrews* and the not-as-memorable *That Brewster Boy*. That triumvirate originated at NBC, incidentally, although all three were heard on the ether at some point beyond the chimes chain.

For a number of reasons it isn't practical to attempt to include every situation comedy in expansive detail in the present volume.[1] *The Aldrich Family* is the subject of a separate chapter, while *That Brewster Boy*—perceived as the weakest of the trio of male-dominated teen entries—has been earmarked for an abridged summation in Appendix B. You will possibly find several of your favorite series outlined in brief detail there, incidentally.

After the precedent set by the prototype series of the genre in 1939 (*The Aldrich Family*) and its first imitator in 1941 (*That Brewster Boy*), *Archie Andrews*, aka *The Adventures of Archie Andrews*, emerged in 1943. With the exception of a full year when it was off the air beginning in the summer of 1944, the program persisted for a decade.

Archie Andrews appeared to be the teenaged equivalent of "everyman." His misadventures seemed plausible enough to have occurred in the best of families. If everyman existed, then in Archie's era that crimson-locked freckled-faced 17-year-old typified the ordinary teenage male as much as anybody.

Like Henry Aldrich and Homer Brown, Archie had a joined-at-the-hip bumbling crony, Forsythe Pendleton Jones, affectionately nicknamed "Jughead." (Harlan Stone, who played "Jug" for most of the run, remembers that, at the initial "cattle call" audition for the role in which he competed with a herd of other young men, before beginning to read some sample lines, he was instructed *not* to sound like Homer on the *Aldrich* show.) Then there was Archie's sweetheart, Veronica Lodge, a well-heeled Southern-sounding debutante who literally drooled over him. There was another girl, too, Betty Cooper, whose precise relationship with Archie forever remained ill-defined. Jughead also attracted a steady girl named Agatha (no surname). Completing the cast of regular characters were Mr. Andrews (Fred) and Mrs. Andrews (Mary), an obnoxious student—Reggie Mantle, plus the high school principal Mr. Weatherbee, Veronica's father and a few occasional figures who appeared when needed.

The origin of *Archie Andrews* is almost as beguiling as the sitcom itself. A goodly number of radio series spawned pulp comics that were patterned after their characters and premises (think *The Shadow*, *The Lone Ranger* and many more). In the situation of *Archie Andrews*, however, the order began with animation—the illustrations of a youthful Bob Montana. Only a short time before he had experienced some of the very trappings of the cartoons he created.

Born October 23, 1920, at Stockton, California, Montana hailed from a family in which the parents consisted of a vaudevillian banjoist (Ray Montana) and an ex–Ziegfeld Follies showgirl (Roberta Pandolfini Montana). By the time he was eight he had visited the 48 states, largely acquiring his education in backstage dressing rooms. In his early teens the Montanas resided in Boston's theater district. After his dad died his mom remarried, and the family moved to Haverhill, Massa-

chusetts. His stepdad operated a theatrical costume emporium at nearby Bradford.

The students and faculty at Haverhill High School, which young Montana attended from 1936 to 1939, influenced the lad far more than anyone realized at the time. It was they who inspired the characters that populated the *Archie* comic books, newspaper strips and broadcast media.[2] During Bob's senior year of high school his family relocated to Manchester, New Hampshire, where he graduated from Central High School in 1940. But his experiences at Haverhill had already set his life's course.

He drew Archie sketches for the December 1941 issue of MLJ's *Pep Comics*.[3] A six-page narrative focused on Archie Andrews and his chums. MLJ was so pleased with the acclaim those illustrations earned that Bob was given a contract to produce *Archie*, a new comic book launched in November 1942. Meanwhile, he spent four years (1942–46) with the U. S. Army Signal Corps and dutifully produced training films for the government.

By the time he returned, the firm had altered its moniker to Archie Publications, in May 1946. Later that year Montana added daily and Sunday *Archie* comic strips that at their zenith appeared in 700 newspapers nationwide. While cross-country skiing at Meredith, New Hampshire, he died of a heart attack on January 4, 1975, age 54. The heritage he left through the widely-acclaimed characters he created continued to live in perpetuity, however. In due course their history will be witnessed in somewhat greater detail.

Meanwhile, in the halcyon days of radio, *Archie Andrews* was a Saturday morning ritual in many of the nation's households, ostensibly influencing millions of adolescents while drawing approximately the same crowd week in and week out. During the Swift-sponsored era the show's opening was distinctively alluring. Actually it was suggestive of both *The Aldrich Family* and *Let's Pretend*, two more popular audio features with juveniles of different age groups: the former because of its shrill exchange between mother and son (*Hen-reeeeeeeee! Henry Aldrich!* and an unremitting-yet-obedient croaked response *Coming mother!*), and the latter show for the Cream of Wheat commercial jingle ("Cream of Wheat is so good to eat, and we have it every day...") led by "Uncle" Bill Adams and a few pretenders (actors).

But whoever the guy was who led the studio audience for *Archie Andrews* in those rousing renditions of the beef-and-pork ditty stood much too close to the microphone—his choice, or by direction—as any casual playback of the vintage shows today verifies. Consistently he was much too vociferous as he stridently bellowed above the adolescents who followed the cue cards and warbled along, just as they had done moments before in the audience warm-up preceding airtime. It was a classic opening, nevertheless, and a memorable one, too.

THEME: A few light bars on the organ

SFX: 4-note signal whistle; repeated

SFX: Scrambling as Jughead throws open his window

JUGHEAD (in the distance): *Hi-ya, Archie. Whadda ya want?*

ARCHIE: *Come on out, Jughead! It's a matter of life or death!*

JUGHEAD (in the distance): *Oh, reeeee-laxxx! Archie ... reeeee-laxxx!*

THEME: A few light bars on the organ as gallery applauds, whistles

ANNOUNCER (theme and noise under): *Yes, here he is again, the youngster millions of readers of Archie Comics magazine know and love so well, brought to you by Swift and Company, makers of Swift Premium franks—Archie Andrews and all his gang....*

GALLERY (sings): *Tender beef...*
*Juicy pork...*
*Known from the West Coast*
*To New York...*
*Swift's Premium franks...*
*Swift's Premium franks....*

ANNOUNCER (reads opening commercial)

Not only was the opening distinctive, so were several other parts of the show—so much so that they became repetitious, and after a while the fans could articulate the words right along with the speakers.

Encounters between Archie, an eternal 17-year-old, and his girlfriend, Veronica Lodge, seldom varied; it didn't matter whether their exchanges were face-to-face or conducted over the telephone. Veronica was a charmingly lithesome, syrupy-voiced Southern lass who Fred Andrews (Archie's dad) thought was a "put-on," but never said as much in Archie's or Veronica's presence. At any rate, their verbal greetings were predictable—and hilarious.

VERONICA: *Hello ... Ah-cheee.*

ARCHIE (laughs rapidly): *Ah-ha-ha-ha-ha-ha-ha-ha-ha.*

VERONICA: *Hi-y'all, Ah-cheekins ... (moaning hum up the scale) Ah-ha-ha-ha-ha-ha-ha-ha-ha. It's awful nice to see y'all, Ah-cheee ... dee-aaaaah! Ah-ha-ha-ha-ha-ha-ha-ha-ha.*

Their customary salutation provoked titters of laughter that rippled through the studio audience. The routine was so familiar to fans that they hung on for the entire episode, intently eavesdropping as Veronica and Archie meted out the anticipated lines and guffaws. Of course, there was never any hint of anything sexual between the pair; in that regard, there was rarely even a smooch. Those lovebirds talked about their feelings, but they never acted upon them. The sponsor and the network censors wouldn't have stood for it!

Real romance got in the way of the storyline infrequently, in fact, usually only when one girl or another displayed a streak of jealousy. Betty Cooper, for instance, was always an enigma in the plots: did she really love and desire Archie or was she just an extraordinarily special friend? As much as she was in his life, turning up at the Andrews' home incessantly, it was difficult to figure. At times she seemed like a third wheel who would have flung herself at him big-time had Veronica found anyone else to make her happy. Maybe she did an incredible job of keeping her true feelings in check. (An Archie movie many years later revealed as much when she literally tried to ravage his body.) There must have been more to it than mere friendship. A contemporary source affirms: "Archie's romantic interests are divided between upper class, refined Veronica Lodge and middle class, athletic Betty Cooper. Betty's girl-next-door demeanor contrasts with Veronica's snobbish behavior, and the two often end up fighting over him." A point to ponder: was he really that much of a prize?

In addition, there was the occasional girl who turned up in a solo installment with whom Archie momentarily became utterly smitten. On one such occasion he fell head-over-heels for a young woman who was about to be married, not realizing that she was the bride-to-be! Most of the time, however, he was content to Ah-ha-ha-ha-ha-ha-ha-ha-ha to Veronica's coy overtures. As mentioned, they talked a lot but did very little on the air; fans were given the impression that they did very little off it, too.

Another predictable staple of every show was the pandemonium that invariably broke loose about three-fourths of the way through the episode. Archie and his friends made such a calamitous racket around Fred Andrews that—in an effort to restore order—the youth's elder screamed repeatedly until there was finally a sudden hush over the crowd: "QUI-ET! ... QUI-ET! ... QUIIII ...— ... EEEET!" (That, too, was followed by rollicking snickers from the audience.) Once there, the radio thespians uttered the same lines every week:

> FRED ANDREWS: *Now listen to me ... all of you. This nonsense has gone far enough ... too far, in fact.*
>
> MARY ANDREWS: *Yes, dear.*
>
> ARCHIE ANDREWS: *Yes, Dad.*
>
> BETTY COOPER: *Yes, Mr. Andrews.*
>
> VERONICA COOPER: *Yes, Mr. Andrews.*
>
> JUGHEAD JONES: *Uh-huh.*

By the time Fred Andrews had reined them all in—and regained some modicum of control in his own domain—he was usually shelling out big bucks from his pocket for damaged garments, ruined hairdos, stolen jackets, broken windows, burst pipes and whatever other destruction had resulted from the melee. Parenthetically, Fred was one of those males who believed he had been bestowed with all the knowledge and ability of a handyman. Therefore, why call a plumber, wallpaper hanger, roofer, electrician, mechanic, bricklayer, carpet installer, appliance repairman, gutter hanger, tree surgeon or the like when he possessed the skills to do it himself "in a jiffy" and save a few bucks? There were three things wrong with that picture: (1) Fred didn't know how to do most of the jobs he tackled, and—with the involvement of Archie and his companions—the project deteriorated rapidly; (2) what could go wrong went wrong and ended up costing Fred far more in capital than he would have spent to have called a professional at the outset; (3) Fred never learned from his mistakes (since nobody enumerated them for him, he made comparable errors in judgment in successive weeks).

Frequently the gang volunteered their services to help him fix, perfect, replace or repair something (hanging wallpaper, changing a flat tire, plugging a roof leak, unstopping a clog in the kitchen sink, etc.). Invariably they collectively did far more damage to themselves and the Andrews property than the problem they set out to resolve. Again, Fred was a slow learner.

Typically, after several colossal mix-ups while trying to change a flat tire on one show, Jughead got himself locked in the trunk of the Andrews automobile. Unfortunately, Archie had the only key and had gone elsewhere. Fred was momentarily absent, too. So while Mary Andrews and Betty Cooper tried to figure some way of getting Jughead out "before he smothers," he repeatedly let out blood-curdling screams that would have halted a panther ready to pounce on a rodent. (The studio audience was in convulsions over this.) To extricate him, Mary at last grabbed a hammer and started bashing in the trunk lid. In the midst of it, everybody else arrived and they were all yelling at one another, although none of them approached the decibel level of those terrifying bellows. Archie, who had the key, was the last to arrive.

In the midst of all the commotion, Jughead was finally released. But it took Fred to shout his "QUI-ET/QUI-ET/QUI-ET" litany to finally get their attention.

Another time Fred brought home a television set as a surprise for Mary and Archie. In those primitive days of TV, Riverdale could attract only a single channel. Fred was determined to sit down and enjoy whatever was on, which turned out to be a travelogue of India. Being unaccustomed to *any* television, they were eager to witness even that. They sat down in front of the set, mesmerized by the small-screen black-and-white account. As luck would have it, while Mary was in the kitchen fixing sandwiches for their supper—which they planned to eat in front of the new one-eyed monster invading their living room—all of Archie's friends showed up one by one.

Jughead was first. He invited himself to supper, requiring more sandwiches, and then he called his mother to tell her where he was. Being unable to hear her above the program, he had them switch off the TV so he could talk on the phone. Subsequently Betty and Veronica arrived individually (the TV had to be turned off to be certain it was the doorbell everybody heard with each new arrival), and in every instance they were so thrilled with the TV that Jughead invited them to stay for supper, requiring still more sandwiches.

As the chapter wound toward its denouement, Fred was missing most of the show he hoped to see. With the lights off so they could view the screen better, in came a tray of sandwiches and glasses of milk. The milk was promptly spilled all over Veronica's new dress, and then Fred sat down in the tray of sandwiches. Listeners knew it was time for yells of "QUI-ET/QUI-ET/QUI-ET" and the standard dialogue to follow. Such fiascoes were commonplace at the Andrews address. On that occasion Fred stood good for one new dress plus having his suit cleaned. It was all so foreseeable, yet still so funny. By then the channel had concluded its broadcast day and signed off—leaving Fred feeling disenfranchised and disgusted because he really

saw nothing on the first day he owned the family's new television set.

In the episode in which the car had a flat tire, they were trying to go to a nearby town to visit Aunt Hattie. After many difficulties in changing the tire—Fred Andrews *never* called in a professional when "I can do the job myself," remember—and once the trunk had been sledge-hammered and Jughead released from it and the tire finally fixed and they were ready to go, who should arrive but none other than Aunt Hattie, who came to visit *them!* A few hours later, as Hattie was ready to return home, *she* had a flat tire! It appeared the tribe's plight might be starting all over again.

Everybody, it seemed, was good at getting Fred Andrews' goat. Here's a typical exchange from a 1947 episode:

FRED: *Oh, Archie, Veronica just called.*

ARCHIE (anxiously): *Gee whiz, she did?*

FRED: *Yes Archie, she did. And she said...*

ARCHIE (interrupting): *Gee, I never heard the phone ring.*

FRED: *Well, it rang and Veronica said...*

ARCHIE (interrupting): *Well, why didn't you tell me?*

FRED (pause): *Archie?*

ARCHIE: *Yes, Dad?*

FRED: *Do you care to hear what Veronica said or not?*

ARCHIE: *Well sure, Dad. Sure.*

FRED: *Then be quiet and I'll tell you!*

ARCHIE: *OK, Dad. OK.*

The endless drivel that went on in that family was enough to drive anybody nuts. Fred got a bellyful of it in every installment.

The repetitions, incidentally, persisted with Mary Aldrich's "for pity's sake" and Archie's unremitting "gee whiz." They were surely the equivalent of stronger idioms in use today. Then there was the surprise element when Jughead put in an unexpected appearance. "Gee whiz! Jughead!" Archie would allow as he took a phone call from his pal or someone greeted him at the door. "Who'd

you expect? Henry Ford? Ah-ha-ha-ha-ha-ha,"
Jughead would giggle. Or he'd throw out
other absurd replies, such as The Cisco Kid?
Bing Crosby? President Truman? Kate Smith?
The Ghost Riders in the Sky? Fred Allen? Jersey Joe Walcott? Groucho Marx? The sheer id-
iocy of it was always good for a robust laugh.

The illuminating episode titles labeling
the vintage radio recordings currently in circulation very well may have been placed there
by hobbyists and traders themselves. Some of
them read: "Trying to Take a Bath," "Veronica's Coming Out Party," "Archie Has the
Hiccups," "Going on a Picnic," "Late for a
Dance," "Archie Borrows a Tire Jack," "Locked
Out of the House," "Relatives Visit Unexpectedly," "Archie Gets a Job at the Drugstore,"
"Careful! Don't Wake Up Father," "Fred's
Sunburn" and "Trying to Hear Ballgame on
the Radio." Most of those offer fans an indication of what to expect, with the understanding that—in the theater of the mind—
all manner of variations are possible.

Charles H. Mullen won the role of
Archie Andrews when the series moved to
NBC in mid–1945. A Brooklynite by birth,
born October 28, 1927, he had already appeared on series like *Coast-to-Coast on a Bus,
Dick Tracy* and *Believe It or Not* when *Archie
Andrews* came his way. Mullen settled in for
what was considered to be a long and happy
run. He was well liked, and the sponsor, network, producer, cast and crew were pleased
with his performance. But Uncle Sam came
calling the following year and he was inducted into the Army. In the interim—until
Bob Hastings arrived, having won the lead
part as Mullen's permanent replacement
(Hastings himself was about to be released by
the Army Air Corps)—for a few weeks Jimmy
Dobson stepped in to cover the role. Hal
Stone, meanwhile, playing the part of
Archie's sidekick Jughead, recalled matters
like this:

> After Mullen spent a few years in the Army,
> following his discharge he came back to NBC
> and asked for his job back.... The deal back
> then was, in recognition of their service to our
> country, returning servicemen were to be

given preference from employers with regards
to being re-hired and getting their old jobs
back. In this instance NBC was very happy
with Hastings playing the role and didn't want
to change horses in midstream. Consequently,
NBC agreed to pay him [Mullen] the same
money it was paying Hastings for a full year,
on top of anything else he might earn.[4]

Following that imbroglio, Mullen had
some brief television exposure, acting on
NBC's *Robert Montgomery Presents* once and
hosting a fleeting CBS children's series. He
left show business altogether when he gained
a post as a Brooklyn sales representative for
the American Tobacco Company. So successful was he in his new venture that he began
receiving promotions that boosted him up
the corporate ladder to district sales manager,
regional sales manager, East Coast sales manager, national sales manager, etc., until he
finally landed as the firm's president and
chief executive officer (1986–92). Mullen returned to acting following retirement, appearing in local theatrical productions and on
Connecticut Public Radio. "I'm proud of
him," Stone—ever the quipster—said not
long ago. "I taught the kid everything I
knew." Mullen died at Darien, Connecticut,
on June 18, 2002.

At the program's peak, Bob Hastings
was the voice of Archie Andrews. The most
enduring of the namesake performers was
born in Brooklyn, New York, on April 18,
1925. He is sometimes confused with a
younger brother, Don Hastings, born April 1,
1934, in Brooklyn, who likewise became a seasoned actor on large and small screens. Don
is best recognized for the role of Dr. Robert
(Bobby/Bob) Hughes on CBS-TV's *As the
World Turns*, a key figure in the daytime serial—he has played the part since 1960 and is
still featured as this volume goes to press.

Bob Hastings, meanwhile, having attended the New York Professional Children's
School, gained a handful of radio credits before becoming a renowned character and
voice actor in visual formats. His preliminary
audio work included regular appearances on
*Coast-to-Coast on a Bus* (late 1920s, early 1930s

on NBC Blue—both Hastings boys were in the cast as their careers began, in fact), plus NBC's *The Lady Next Door,* CBS's *Let's Pretend* and NBC Blue's *Our Barn* all in the 1930s. He was on the latter web's *National Barn Dance* (dubbed "Little Bobby Hastings" while performing as a boy soprano in 1939–40) and the same chain's *The Sea Hound* (as "Bobby Hastings" he played Jerry, young mate of Captain Silver on a 1942–44 ship bound for juvenile adventure). Hastings won recurring roles on NBC's daytime serials *The Right to Happiness* and *This Is Nora Drake* in the 1940s, and joined repertory companies staging that chain's *The Eternal Light* (1955–57) and *X-Minus One* (1955–58). In the interim, a record album he recorded in 1954, *World's Greatest Children's Songs,* with orchestral accompaniment, sold well.

The busy audio thespian segued into television easily. He was Steve Elliot, head of a top-secret planetary defense organization, on NBC's *Atom Squad* (1953–54). He played the leading man, Ed Foyle, in that net's short-lived 1958 daytime serial *Kitty Foyle.* Hastings was Lieutenant Elroy Carpenter in ABC's service sitcom *McHale's Navy* (1962–66). He was Barney on CBS's *The Edge of Night* in 1966. During the 15 years from 1963 to 1978 he contributed voiceovers to a boatload of animated cartoon series on the three major chains: *The New Casper Cartoon Show, The New Adventures of Superman, The Superman-Aquaman Hour of Adventure, The Batman-Superman Hour, Jeannie, The New Scooby-Doo Movies, Devlin, Clue Club, Fred Flintstone and Friends, The C.B. Bears* and *The Challenge of the Super Friends.* Several of those aired for more than one season, incidentally.

In addition, Hastings was prominent in more live-action series. He hosted the pithy syndicated game show *Dealer's Choice* in 1973, appeared in two mini TV series (*Wheels* in 1978, *Studs Lonigan* in 1979) and portrayed the recurring role of police chief Burt Ramsey in ABC's daytime serial *General Hospital* (1979–86). He also provided voiceovers for *Gotham Girls* in 2002.

Hastings wasn't done yet, however—not by a long shot. He turned up in 21 made-for-TV movies as well as 118 single episodes of popular television series, including shows like *Disneyland, The U.S. Steel Hour, The Real Mc-Coys, The Phil Silvers Show, The Untouchables, G.E. Theater, Car 54—Where Are You?, Gunsmoke, Ben Casey, The Twilight Zone, Dr. Kildare, Petticoat Junction, The Munsters, Batman, Hogan's Heroes, The Flying Nun, Here's Lucy, Green Acres, Emergency!, Love American Style, Adam 12, Ironside, The Rockford Files, The Love Boat, Quincy M.E., Alice, Three's Company, The Waltons, The Dukes of Hazzard* and *Trapper John M.D.*

In the four decades from 1961 to 2001 he performed in 23 theatrical motion pictures, although only a handful were memorable flicks: *The Great Impostor* (1961), *McHale's Navy* (1964), *McHale's Navy Joins the Air Force* (1965), *Did You Hear the One About the Traveling Saleslady?* (1968), *Angel in My Pocket* (1969), *The Poseidon Adventure* (1972), *Airport 1975* (1974) and *Harper Valley P.T.A.* (1978).

Hastings married his childhood sweetheart, Joan Rice, in Brooklyn, and they became parents of four children. In modern times he continues to appear sporadically at old-time radio conventions in re-creations of roles in which he participated many years earlier.

The part of Jughead was played for most of the run by the inimitable Harold (Harlan/Hal) Stone, Jr., who, until his death in early 2007, directed and performed re-creations of the shows presented at some of the annual vintage radio conventions around the country (Cincinnati, Los Angeles, Newark, Seattle). A native of Long Island, New York, he was born June 10, 1931. His show business career started young: by age three he was a $10-an-hour child model for commercial photographers engaged by magazines, catalogs, billboards, sales literature and newspapers. (Had the Internet been available then, his chubby cheeks may very well have been plastered about the globe.) He was on stage at eight, performing in *Life with Father.* His vocational horizons seemed set.

Young Stone progressed through a surfeit

of increasingly demanding theatrical assignments before eventually breaking into radio while still a kid. Beginning with the children's fantasy narratives on *Let's Pretend*, in the early 1940s he worked his way through occasional performances on a plethora of daily dramatizations—*My True Story, Portia Faces Life, The Right to Happiness, Road of Life* and more—as well as primetime programs like *Big Town, Death Valley Days* and *Dr. Christian*. He could be heard all over the dial, just like his more mature peers in the industry. At age 13, as *Archie Andrews* moved to NBC, Stone won the part of Jughead amid considerable competition. He maintained it through 1951 and returned to it later. He tells about those days in a self-published memoir:

> From the moment that the entire cast was assembled for our first *Archie* program's rehearsal, it was obvious that it was going to be a very pleasant experience. Being the youngest at 13+, I was definitely made to feel like one of the "grown ups" and treated with respect and warmth by my fellow cast members. That same camaraderie existed between all the regular cast members and the program's writer, Carl Jampel, as well as the many directors we had....
>
> The bottom line: Everyone was a seasoned "Pro." I always approached my job in a very professional manner, thanks to my prior years of training in the theater and numerous other radio programs. That's all anyone ever really cared about. As long as someone was totally professional and held up their end ... they were admired and respected....
>
> In all the years the program was on the air, I don't recall ever having a personality clash or conflict ... with any of the other numerous performers.... And when one of the principals had to leave the show ... the new arrivals instantly became "family" and we didn't lose a beat. That's due to the skill of the directors at finding someone who filled their shoes perfectly.[5]

Following service in the early 1950s in the Air National Guard during the Korean conflict—which carried him far from the part of Jughead—Stone returned to enroll at Hofstra College at Hempstead on New York's Long Island. He also recaptured the part of Jughead. That helped him gain performances

on *The Theater Guild on the Air, The Ethel Merman Show, The Slapsie Maxie Rosenbloom Show* and *The Henry Morgan Show*. By then television had trumped radio, and Stone was acting on the tube on an occasional *Robert Montgomery Presents, Kraft Television Theater* and other anthology productions. Ultimately the thespian left the performing end of the business to become a commercial and television director. When he retired from that, he and his wife Dorothy moved to northern Arizona, where they resided to his death.

Arthur Kohl was cast in the part of Fred Andrews in the halcyon days of *Archie Andrews*. The son of Chicago actor Arthur E. Kohl, the younger Kohl was born there on January 26, 1908. Breaking into Chicago radio in the 1930s, he appeared on a plethora of local series before gaining his first network gigs in 1938: NBC's *Lights Out* and NBC Blue's *Empires of the Moon*. Not long afterward he was on a surfeit of soap operas, some extending through the 1940s: *Bachelor's Children, The Barton Family, Betty and Bob, Girl Alone, The Right to Happiness, The Road of Life* and *The Story of Mary Marlin*. He performed regularly on *The Gary Moore Show* in 1942 and won occasional dramatic roles on *Author's Playhouse* and *The First Nighter*.

By 1944 Kohl left the Windy City to move to Gotham where his broadcasting fortunes were brighter, as many shows were relocating there. That year he co-starred with Elsa Mae Gordon in the fleeting syndicated series *The Callahans* that originated over New York's WMCA. It was a comedy about life in a theatrical boardinghouse. Kohl picked up the part of Fred Andrews in 1947, possibly as a consequence of working on *The Callahans*. His recurring *Archie Andrews* role was the capstone of his netcasting career, and he carried it into the early 1950s. Before the 1940s ended, however, he also made several appearances on ABC's fantasy anthology *Quiet, Please* (1948–49), and—once in 1949—on NBC's *Radio City Playhouse*. His single television exposure occurred on Dumont's *Famous Jury Trials* in 1950. No documentation has surfaced to indicate that Kohl was ever married.

He died at Tampa, Florida, on December 17, 1972, without any survivors.

Kohl's opposite on *Archie Andrews*—appearing for most of the run as Mary Andrews—was Alice Yourman. Born Alice Anderson Thorpe at Oregon, Illinois, on September 17, 1907, she graduated from Lead (South Dakota) High School and later from Columbia School of Expression at Chicago's Northwestern University, where she pursued dramatics. Along the way she produced and acted in a *March of Time* feature at Hammond, Indiana. Subsequently she became active in a Theater Guild fraternity while living at Mount Vernon, Ohio. Alice Thorpe wed Clarence Yourman, a New York City native and industrial engineer, in 1928, and they had two children, Ann and Lee. After Clarence died suddenly in October 1938, Alice left Mount Vernon with her two progeny and relocated to New York, seeking work as an actress.

Yourman found the competition stiff—many aspirants were after the same few roles. She asked herself: "What do I have to offer that these others don't?" Her conclusion was that the only real distinction separating her from them was her Midwestern accent. Yourman capitalized on it and won numerous parts for shows where directors were seeking precisely that. One affirmed, "Her voice has a fresh quality like a prairie breeze."

Like many radio thespians, she enacted ongoing supporting characterizations in soap operas in the 1940s and 1950s. Her litany included *Ethel and Albert, The Guiding Light* (she was Laura Grant in the last three years of the CBS Radio run, 1953–56, and almost from the start of the CBS-TV run, 1953–1962), *Hearts in Harmony, Myrt and Marge, The Right to Happiness, Two on a Clue* (on which she was the announcer, a rarity for her gender, 1944–46) and *Young Widder Brown.* Yourman was part of the anthology contingent staffing Mutual's 1948–49 espionage melodrama *Secret Missions.* And during the *Archie Andrews* years she infiltrated the competition, crossing over to *The Aldrich Family* some weeks to play Mrs. Anderson, mother of Kathleen, Henry's girl-

friend. She joined professional organizations and became active in the American Federation of Television and Radio Artists, the Actors Equity Association and the Screen Actors Guild.

Yourman performed in a 1956 episode of *The Phil Silvers Show* on CBS-TV and appeared as Anita Borkowitz on the same web's daytime thriller serial *The Edge of Night* the following year. In 1976 she turned up in a made-for-TV movie, *Luke Was There.* Her voice was heard on scores of broadcast commercials. She also played in one major theatrical release, 1970's *Dirtymouth.* From 1961 to 1974 she appeared in dozens of theatrical productions on stages across the nation.

She moved to Columbus, Ohio, in 1987 to be near her daughter and several grandchildren. Never remarried, at the time of her death there on October 28, 2000, at age 93, Yourman was survived by two brothers, her son, six grandchildren and 11 great-grandchildren.

Gloria Mann was the most prolific Veronica Lodge in *Archie Andrews,* yet her career and life were all too brief. Born Gloria Mostman on July 7, 1927, in New York City, she entered show business early as part of the *Our Gang* comedy lineup. At eight years of age she appeared on Broadway in Zoe Akins' Pulitzer Prize–winning play *The Old Maid.* She returned to the same venue in 1942 in the short-lived *All in Favor.* In the interim Mann gained momentum in radio. In 1939–40 at age 12 she played one of the twin offspring of the heroine in CBS's daytime serial *The Life and Love of Dr. Susan.* In 1945 she performed in Mutual's *Real Stories from Real Life,* and the next year she was a regular on NBC's *Johnny Morgan Show,* while also launched ongoing acting spots with ABC's *My True Story.*

In the early 1950s Mann turned up on NBC-TV's *Robert Montgomery Presents* and in several other video features. But it was as the stuck-up Dixie chick Veronica Lodge in *Archie Andrews* that she established an unforgettable voice that resonated with legions weekly who found her both predictable and enticing. Hal

Stone contrasted her with the "other" girl in the Andrews plotlines, Betty Cooper, played in 1945–46 by Doris Grundy:

> Gloria was slightly older than Doris (or perhaps she just seemed that way) because she had been in the business for a few years prior to joining our cast and seemed more "sophisticated." And in addition, she wore lots of makeup, so she looked older and more "worldly." Dare I say sexier? Perfect for playing the comic book vamp "Veronica." And Gloria played the part with a put-on Southern Bell [sic] accent that made the voices of the two girls very distinct.... A totally different vocal quality made the characters more readily identifiable to the "ear" of the listener whenever they were in the same scene together.[6]

Retiring from the industry in 1952, Gloria Mann Zipser died of undisclosed causes in Los Angeles on April 21, 1961, at the age of 33. Survivors included her spouse, Stanley Zipser, daughter Lisa Lynn and son Dean Jeffrey, parents, brother and sister.

Better known to radio listeners was Vivian Smolen, an earlier Veronica Lodge, whose daily consternation was exhibited on not one but *two* soap operas, elevating her status to one of the medium's most punishingly beleaguered heroines. For many years in the 1940s and 1950s Smolen played the namesake role on CBS's *Our Gal Sunday*, and was the troubled Laurel "Lolly Baby" Grosvenor, daughter of NBC's *Stella Dallas*. "She played Sunday with a plaintive coolness and a dignity that made you feel that no man ... was really worthy of her," one pundit observed.

Born in February 1916 in New York City, Smolen was the offspring of immigrants—a musician, Max, from Russia, and Pauline, from Austria. Educated at Brooklyn College, Vivian was her family's main breadwinner while she appeared daily on the radio. She was introduced to radio early, appearing on a Sunday afternoon *Children's Hour* series launched on New York's WJZ in 1924. Host Milton Cross dubbed her "the girl with the sympathetic voice." As she grew older, she gained spots in a couple of daytime serials, *Doc Barclay's Daughters* and *Front Page Farrell*.

She was a hostess at the *Stage Door Canteen* (1942–45) and a frequent supporting actress between 1946 and 1955 in the mystery narratives of *Mr. Keen, Tracer of Lost Persons*.

Less than a month before the cancellation of the enduring *Our Gal Sunday* on January 2, 1959, in which she was the heroine for 13 years, Smolen married Harold Klein, vice president of ABC films in New York City. He later joined Plitt Theaters as an executive and transferred to Chicago in 1974, where Vivian performed on *Chicago Radio Theater*. During her time in the Windy City she played the bit part of Mrs. Dunphy in the 1980 motion picture *My Bodyguard*, her solo appearance on the big screen.

In the meantime, after her daytime dramas folded, she provided voiceovers for radio and TV commercials. The couple never had children and retired in the Sunshine State. Harold Klein died in 2001, while Vivian succumbed to death at age 90 in Lake Worth, Florida, on June 11, 2006.

The last of the key continuing characters in *Archie Andrews*, Betty Cooper, was played most durably by Rosemary Rice, a veteran of both radio and television. She was born about 1925 at Montclair, New Jersey. She made her way into radio on the strength of being a pretender in the fairy tale narratives dramatized on CBS's *Let's Pretend* in the 1930s. Her radio repertoire expanded to characterizations in the 1940s and 1950s on a half-dozen popular daytime serials: *Life Can Be Beautiful*, *Ma Perkins*, *The Right to Happiness*, *The Second Mrs. Burton*, *When a Girl Marries* and *Young Doctor Malone*. Rice performed with repertory companies on *The Cavalcade of America*, *Crisis in War Town*, *The FBI in Peace and War*, *Grand Central Station*, *NBC Theater*, *Studio One*, *Suspense* and *The Theater Guild of the Air*. In the 1970s she returned to the microphone for a resurgence of aural drama, appearing on *The CBS Radio Mystery Theater* 22 times and on the syndicated *Radio Playhouse*.

While she was heavily engaged in radio, Rice took time off to appear in a handful of Broadway productions, among them 1941's *Junior Miss*, 1945's *Dear Ruth* and 1947's *Mr.*

*Roberts.* She recorded original and classic children's songs and stories, and won a Grammy for the album *Learning to Tell Time with Grandson Clock.* Unquestionably the most memorable role of her professional life was in the early television family drama *I Remember Mama,* shown live on CBS from 1949 to 1957. As Katrin, Mama's eldest child, Rice's voice opened every episode. While the pages of the family photo album turned, viewers heard her say:

> This old album makes me remember so many things in the past ... San Francisco and the house on Stiner Street where I was born. It brings back memories of my cousins, aunts, and uncles ... all the boys and girls I grew up with. And I remember my family as we were then ... my brother Nels ... my little sister Dagmar ... and, of course, Papa. But most of all ... when I look back to those days so long ago ... most of all ... I REMEMBER MAMA.

The actress went on to other television projects, concurrently and after that impressive venture, playing roles on the *Kraft Television Theater* (1949), *Studio One* (1956) and *The Edge of Night* (1962). She was in demand as a TV spokesperson for a diverse array of commodities, like Campbell's soup, Lady Clairol ("If I have only one life to live, let me live it as a blonde"), Lux toilet soap, Shell oil and a range of automobiles that indicated no partiality—General Motors' Buick, Ford Motors' Ford and Chrysler Corporation's Plymouth. Her marketing efforts were rewarded with a Cleo trophy for outstanding TV commercials.

In the early years of the 21st century Rice attended numerous old-time radio conventions, where she participated in re-creations of some of the vintage aural series in which she performed decades earlier.

The *Archie Andrews* radio adaptation was only one of the spinoffs of Archie Comics. While several decades elapsed before the show was reincarnated in this country into a televised format involving live actors, a glut of animated cartoons came cascading down the tube. All of them championed the high-school high-jinks of Archie and his comrades, just like the illustrated pulps, comic books, comic strips and radio sitcom portrayed earlier. The TV extensions were so omnipresent it seemed as if they would last forever. Here's a litany:

*The Archie Comedy Hour,* CBS, September 14, 1968–September 5, 1970

*Archie's Funhouse,* CBS, September 12, 1970–September 4, 1971

*Archie's TV Funnies,* CBS, September 11, 1971–September 1, 1973

*Everything's Archie,* CBS, September 8, 1973–January 26, 1974

*The U.S. of Archie,* CBS, September 7, 1974–September 5, 1976

*New Archie Sabrina Hour,* NBC, September 10, 1977–November 12, 1977

*The Bang-Shang Lalapalooza Show,* NBC, November 19, 1977–January 28, 1978

*The New Archies,* NBC, September 12, 1987–February 4, 1989

*Archie: To Riverdale and Back Again* (made-for-TV movie), NBC, May 6, 1990

In the storyline of the video flick, all of the familiar adolescent characters were adults and returned to attend a reunion 15 years after graduating from Riverdale High School. Archie was a successful attorney, Forsythe Pendleton (Jughead) Jones was a neurotic psychiatrist with as many (or more) problems as his clients, Veronica Lodge was a socialite and Betty Cooper was an elementary school teacher. Archie was engaged at last, though not to Veronica or Betty, and had to cope with his emotions. To Veronica, he explained, "I have a fiancée." She retorted, "Don't worry, I've had thirteen." When they were alone together, Betty admitted to Archie, "I never forgot how I stood by and watched you chase after Veronica—how I never just went after what I wanted." She turned on the shower, and he inquired, "What are you doing?" A Betty that audiences in the 1940s wouldn't have believed salaciously replied, "Something I always wanted to do with you, Archie. I'm sick of being Miss Goody-Two-Shoes. Treat me like a woman, Archie. Make me wild."

In one of the movie's subplots, the kids'

old hangout, known as Pop Tate's Chocklit Shoppe (a soda dispensary), had been condemned and was about to be demolished.[7] Pop petitioned Archie to save it.

The movie mixed sentimentality with nostalgia. When Archie acknowledged to Jughead, "We had great times in high school before we graduated," Jughead confided, "I wish we never did that." In the final scenes, Archie broke up with his fiancée (Pam), deciding to remain in Riverdale permanently; Jughead planned to return to Riverdale to open a practice; Betty announced that she would come back to teach there; and Veronica, then living in Paris, expected to remain behind for a while before going home. The possibilities seemed, at the least, intriguing.

The film's cast was, of course, populated by people who were born long after Archie became a success in pulp and radio. They included newcomers Christopher Rich as Archie, Sam Whipple as Jughead, Karen Kopins as Veronica and Lauren Holly as Betty. Other unfamiliar names filled out the roster. Although the film was a pilot for a possible television series, it was panned by critics and fans alike and never developed further.

Despite the setback, there have been many other Archie variations over the years that have been successful. Archie has been featured in more than 30 different titles in print; he has appeared in model kits, on cereal boxes, magazines, calendars and numerous additional character collectibles; the comics inspired the creation of the Archies, a pop musical group that scored the hit song *Sugar, Sugar*; and there have been spinoffs like *Josie & the Pussycats* and *Sabrina, the Teenage Witch*.

Archie mania continues to amplify. Archie Comics Entertainment, LLC was formed in 2004 to foster merchandising efforts enveloping the Archie characters. An upscale fashion line was initially introduced for Betty and Veronica. It included dolls, calendars, note cards, bejeweled tops and softcover Archie mad-lib tomes. A large selection of graphic novels was subsequently produced featuring Archie and friends. Global cell phone deals with wallpapers and text messaging backgrounds, video games and a live action movie starring Betty and Veronica were among several concepts being deliberated in 2006 and, apparently, beyond.

"Despite the rampant changes that have occurred in the comic book industry, Archie remains a pleasant and refreshing constant amidst all of the chaos and turmoil," an Archie website affirmed. "It's very good to know that Archie and his gang will be around to entertain young and old alike, well into the new millennium. The times, fads and fashions may change, but the down home values that make Archie great never will."[8] An Archie Publications executive reiterated his firm's commitment to family amusement: "It's what we do best.... We produce a product that parents are comfortable giving to their children...."[9] If that's the case, the Rockwellian paradise of Riverdale will persist indefinitely.

"I have no doubt that the success of the 'Archie' program so many years ago helped us grow," Michael Silberkleit, chairman-publisher of Archie Comic Publications, Inc., said in the present century. There is something intrinsically satisfying in realizing that radio played an integral part in the history that has led to the Archie resurgence. Now, in another century, people around the world are being exposed to Archie and company, including generations that weren't a twinkle in anyone's eye when the tubes of the Motorolas, Philcos, RCA Victors, Crosleys and Atwater-Kents were humming. Network radio may have vanished ages ago, but its inheritance remains. Thanks to Archie Andrews, some of it may persevere for a substantial stretch into the future.

# 5

# *Baby Snooks*

## Imp of the Air

While there never was a sitcom about a truly vile parent or a really gloomy child, *The Baby Snooks Show* was, according to one pundit, "the closest to a family comedy about a bad seed." She was, as another surmised, "the most notorious brat of the air." It seemed ludicrous that a preschool tyke could dominate her parents, and especially her father, with whom she spent so much time, earning little more than a reprimand for it. When he could take no more of her tricks at last, she suffered the consequences. The devilment that she could think up was sure to provoke glee. Her shrill voice made her memorable. She even dressed to impress the studio audience, so closely identifying with the role that it was difficult to separate Snooks from the woman who portrayed her. It was Fanny Brice's second career. Following an illustrious run on stage, including 13 years with the *Ziegfeld Follies*, plus a futile attempt in flicks, she reverted to a younger age, trotting out a figure exhibited to private groups. Now refined and ready for mass consumption, the part rejuvenated her faltering career: the misbehaving imp transformed a falling star into one of entertainment's brightest. Many of the traits Snooks demonstrated reflected on Brice's early beginnings at the turn of the century when she fended for herself in the Big Apple. Out of it grew a little girl who brought giggles to millions for her audacity in standing up to her elders. Her mischievousness was an affront to parental supervision, while it pro-

voked unabashed laughter from her fans. It all ground to a halt when Brice died unexpectedly—there was no attempt to replace her. She was one of a kind, and when she passed her alter-ego did, too.

❖ ❖ ❖

**Creator:** Fanny Brice (nee Fania Borach)

**Producer-Directors:** Mann Holiner (early 1940s), Al Kaye (1944), Ted Bliss, Walter Bunker, Arthur Stander, Roy Rowen

**Writers:** Phil Rapp, Jess Oppenheimer, Devary Freeman, Everett Freeman, Bill Danch, Sid Dorfman, Arthur Stander, Robert Fisher, Jerry Seelen

**Orchestra Leaders:** Meredith Willson (ca. 1937–44), Carmen Dragon

**Vocalist:** Bob Graham (1945)

**Sound Effects Technicians:** Clark Casey, David Light

**Announcers:** John Conte (late 1930s–early 1940s), Tobe Reed (1944–45), Harlow Wilcox (mid-late 1940s), Dick Joy, Don Wilson Ken Roberts

**Recurring Cast:** *Baby Snooks:* Fanny Brice (nee Fania Borach); *Lancelot (Daddy) Higgins:* Frank Morgan, Alan Reed, Hanley Stafford (nee Alfred John Austin); *Vera (Mommy) Higgins:* Lalive Brownell, Lois Corbet (mid–1940s), Arlene Harris (post–1945); *Robespierre Higgins:* Leone Ledoux (1945–51); *Jerry Dingle:* Danny Thomas (1944–45); *Irma Potts:* Fanny Brice (nee Fania Borach); *Uncle Louie:* Charlie Cantor (1945); *Mr. Weemish:* Alan Reed, Ken Christy (ca. 1951)

**Supporting Cast:** Ben Alexander, Elvia Allman, Jack Arthur, Sara Berner, Hans Conried, Georgia Ellis, Stan Farr, Gale Gordon, Earl Lee, Frank Nelson, Lillian Randolph, Celeste Rush, Irene Tedrow, Martha Wentworth

**Sponsors:** General Foods Corporation, for Maxwell House Coffee, Post Toasties cereal, Sanka decaffeinated coffee, LaFrance bleach, Jell-O gelatin, tapioca, puddings and pie fillings and additional foodstuffs and household commodities (1937–48); Lewis Howe Company, for Tums antacid reliever (1949–51)

**Themes:** "Always and Always"; "Thoughts While Strolling" (Meredith Willson); "Good News" (Ray Henderson, Buddy DeSylva and Lew Brown); "You and I" (Meredith Willson); "Rock-a-Bye Baby" (American nursery rhyme); "Little Girl" (Alan M. Rattray)

**Ratings:** High—28.9 (1941–42), Low—12.0 (1950–51), Median—18.1. Ratings based on all 13 complete seasons under multiple appellations.

**On the Air:** November 4, 1937–June 30, 1938, *Maxwell House Presents Good News* (aka *Good News of 1938*), NBC, Thursday, 9:00–10:00 P.M. Eastern Time; September 1, 1938–June 29, 1939, *Maxwell House Presents Good News* (aka *Good News of 1939*), NBC, Thursday, 9:00–10:00 P.M.; September 7, 1939–February 29, 1940, *Maxwell House Presents Good News* (aka *Good News of 1940*), NBC, Thursday, 9:00–10:00 P.M.; March 7–June 27, 1940, *Maxwell House Presents Good News* (aka *Good News of 1940*), NBC, Thursday, 9:00–9:30 P.M.; July 4–25, 1940, *Maxwell House Presents Good News*, NBC, Thursday, 8:00–8:30 P.M.; September 5–October 10, 1940, *Maxwell House Presents Good News*, NBC, Thursday, 8:00–8:30 P.M.; October 17, 1940–July 10, 1941, *Maxwell House Coffee Time*, NBC, Thursday, 8:00–8:30 P.M.; September 4, 1941–July 23, 1942, *Maxwell House Coffee Time*, NBC, Thursday, 8:00–8:30 P.M.; September 3, 1942–June 17, 1943, *Maxwell House Coffee Time*, NBC, Thursday, 8:00–8:30 P.M.; September 2, 1943–June 15, 1944, *Maxwell House Coffee Time*, NBC, Thursday, 8:00–8:30 P.M.; September 17, 1944–June 10, 1945, *Post Toasties Time* (aka *The Baby Snooks Show*), CBS, Sunday, 6:30–7:00 P.M.; September 16, 1945–June 9, 1946, *The Baby Snooks Show*, CBS, Sunday, 6:30–7:00 P.M.; September 6, 1946–May 30, 1947, CBS, Friday, 8:00–8:30 P.M.; September 5, 1947–May 28, 1948, CBS, Friday, 8:00–8:30 P.M.; November 8, 1949–May 5, 1950, NBC, Tuesday, 8:30–9:00 P.M.; October 10, 1950–May 29, 1951, NBC, Tuesday, 8:30–9:00 P.M.

**Extant Archival Material:** Radio scripts for *Baby Snooks*, aired under multiple appellations from 1937 to 1945, are included in two collections—*Baby Snooks Radio Scripts* and the David Freedman Papers, 1930–1940—archived in the Charles E. Young Research Library at the University of California at Los Angeles (UCLA), Box 951575, Los Angeles, CA, 90095; (310) 825-7253; Fax (310) 825-1210; *www.library.ucla.edu/libraries/arts/*, or, for David Freeman Papers, contact: (310) 825-4988; *www.library.ucla.edu/libraries/special/scweb/*.

Some scripts for *Post Toasties Time* (1944–45) featuring *Baby Snooks* are included among the Jerry Seelen Papers, 1912–1965, bulk 1944–1965, housed at the American Heritage Center of the University of Wyoming, 1000 East University Avenue, Laramie, WY, 82071; (307) 766-3756; Fax (307) 766-5511; *http://ahc.uwyo.edu/usearchives/default.htm.*

A single script of *Maxwell House Coffee Time* (1940–44) featuring *Baby Snooks* is archived in the Script Collection of the Broadcast Arts Library, Box 9828, Fort Worth, TX, 76147; (310) 288-6511; *www.broadcastartslibrary.com.*

*The Baby Snooks Scripts*, a volume by Philip Rapp, and edited by Ben Ohmart, contains original scripts from the shows, from BearManor Media, Box 71426, Albany, GA, 31708; (229) 436-4265; Fax (814) 690-1559; http://bearmanormedia.bizland.com/id16.html.

At least 128 *Baby Snooks* broadcasts under the various appellations (including 103 before it was identified as *The Baby Snooks Show*) are known to be in general circulation or held by private collectors as of 2006, sold by vintage radio dealers and traded by old-time radio hobbyists.

Partial logs of series featuring *Baby Snooks* for the periods 1944–48 and 1949–51 are available from Jay Hickerson, 27436 Desert Rose Court, Leesburg, FL, 34748.

Books about Fanny Brice: *Fanny Brice, the Original Funny Girl*, by Herbert G. Goldman (New York: Oxford University Press, 1992); *Funny Woman: The Life and Times of Fanny Brice*, by Barbara W. Grossman (Bloomington, Indiana: Indiana University Press, 1991); *Fabulous Fanny: The Story of Fanny Brice*, by Norman Katkov (New York: Alfred A. Knopf, 1953).

❖ ❖ ❖

Long before Gilda Radner and Lily Tomlin made themselves up for their onstage capers by donning smock frocks and braiding their hair, Fanny Brice, from her late 40s to her late 50s, worked in front of a radio audience garbed in the regalia of a baby-doll dress and bonnet. She was the prototype for other performers coming along behind, a model some would adopt as a pattern for their own acts.

"I love Snooks, and when I play her I do it as seriously as if she were real.... For twenty minutes or so, Fanny Brice ceases to exist," the actress acknowledged. A radio historiographer observed: "A notable change occurred

*Donning a baby-doll dress and bonnet, Fanny Brice—one of the original stars of the Ziegfeld Follies—abandoned her natural voice to schmooze an audience as Baby Snooks. For 14 years the grown-up played a "mean widdle kid" (as Red Skelton might say), a cantankerously rotten brat who was accustomed to wrapping her daddy (played by Hanley Stafford, shown) around her little finger. Snooks was an out-of-control kid who would try anything; it didn't matter that punishment would be waiting. Launched to public acclaim as a skit on The Ziegfeld Follies of the Air in 1936, the figure became a regular the next season on Maxwell House Presents Good News. By 1940 her feature acquired the whole show, and for 11 more years Snooks was an imp that kids of every age adored.*

in Fanny Brice. Her personality slipped into the background as Snooks emerged.... Miss Brice all but abandoned her natural voice in public. Seldom was she out of character; even in interviews she often referred to 'Snooks' almost as a living person."[1]

To avoid ruining the image of the little twerp for the studio audience, she insisted on scripts printed in very large type so she could read them without benefit of eyeglasses. She got into the part by squirming, squinting, mugging and bolting up and down. So meticulous, so fanatical was she about the character that "while she was on the air she *was* Baby Snooks" (as Everett Freeman, one of her scribes, insisted). "And ... for an hour after the show, she was still Baby Snooks. The Snooks voice disappeared, of course, but the Snooks temperament, thinking, actions, were all there."[2]

A writer whose adolescence encompassed Snooks' heyday described the era:

> The brats of Radioland were flabbergasting in their contempt for their elders. Every insult, every bit of snideness was clutched to our hearts. Harassed and put upon as we were by parents, teachers, and any adult who cared to issue us orders, the wine of insolence was heady indeed. And grown-ups didn't seem to mind. Perhaps it was all made acceptable to them by their knowledge that these cheeky and mouthy brats were in reality adults only pretending to be children. No child, in real life, would ever talk to his parents like Red Skelton who played Junior, "the mean widdle kid"; Fanny Brice, ever the classic brat, "Baby Snooks"; and Edgar Bergen, who was both himself and the voice of his ventriloquist's dummy, Charlie McCarthy.[3]

Authors, it seems, had their personal pet "worst" minors among the handful of rotten apples who gave a bad name to all Juveniledom. A few of those scribes put Baby Snooks of Sycamore Lane at the top of their lists. The pranks, incessant queries and badgering she was capable of would have driven any ordinary male to drink. Although a longsuffering Daddy Higgins attempted to take her antics in stride, when he had had enough, he turned his little urchin over his knee and al-

lowed her to experience the wrath of his exasperation. Daddy was initially played by movie thespian Frank Morgan, and then by radio actor Alan Reed. Hanley Stafford, however, created all of the nuances most people associate with that pivotal figure. He was in the part for no less than 13 years (1938–51).

His opposite, Vera (Mommy) Higgins, was portrayed successively by Lalive Brownell, Lois Corbet and Arlene Harris. While she came in for her share of licks from Snooks, it was the incredibly funny exchanges that Lancelot Higgins had with his rebellious offspring that made the show truly entertaining. He utilized many of those experiences as teaching opportunities, although (if they took) Snooks somehow usually understood them in ways that were foreign to her father's intents.

Mommy and Daddy Higgins also fought like cats and dogs, especially over Vera's burned toast and Lancelot's obsession with the charms of other women. On one occasion—when he arrived home with lipstick on his collar and Snooks pointed it out to him—he paid her fifty cents to keep her mouth shut and make sure his shirt got into the wash before "Mummy" saw it. But Snooks, ever a dirty double-crosser, made sure to leave it where her mom would find it anyway! With a kid like Snooks working against him, Pop led a miserable existence. There was also a baby brother in the storyline, Robespierre Higgins, played by child impersonator Lenore Ledoux. With Snooks left to her own devices, that kid hardly had a chance at survival.

As for Snooks, she was a mischievous little monster whose cunning deeds surely made her parents wish at times that she had never been born. With unpleasant punishment a virtual certainty for her craftiness, coupled with whiny-voiced questions and eye-batting innocence, she could tell a lie with a straight face. At the same time, she would be master-minding the downfall of her parents and double-crossing anybody who actually believed she wouldn't. The grandbaby of all comic brats applied every beguiling trick, invariably pushing the right buttons to drive her hassled father to the brink of despair.

The irrepressible tyke could think up more naughtiness than seemed humanly possible, without regard to the consequences. Not only did she hang a beehive where her mom's club was to meet; she slashed her dad's fishing line to shreds; she plucked the fur from her mother's pelt coat, lathered Robespierre with glue, then covered him with fur and sold him for four bits to a neighbor youngster as a pet monkey; and she derailed an important recital by adding marbles to her father's piano. One wag classified her as "a perambulating package of nitroglycerin ... a small rampaging demon." Yet Fanny Brice said of the figure she played for so long, "With all of her deviltry, she is still a good kid, never vicious or mean." And *Variety* affirmed: "Snooks was not nasty or mean, spiteful or sadistic. She was at heart a nice kid." Tell that to her harried dad.

No matter which side one might take, the clever exchanges prevailed. To wit:

DADDY: *If you don't behave I'll have to take my belt off and then you know what'll happen.*

SNOOKS: *Your pants will fall down.*

+ + +

SNOOKS (answering telephone): *Hello....*

MAN (speaking on filter): *Hello. I want to talk to Mr. Higgins.*

SNOOKS: *He ain't here. Who's calling, please?*

MAN (filter): *This is Mr. Mudge from across the street. Who's this?*

SNOOKS: *This is Hortense, the maid.*

MAN (filter): *Well, listen, Hortense. You tell Mr. Higgins to call me as soon as he gets in, see? It's about that brat kid of his.*

SNOOKS: *About Snooks, Mr. Mudge?*

MAN (filter): *Yeah. She went and tied up my little boy with some wire from a radio aerial. I just found him in the coal bin.*

SNOOKS: *Imagine that!*

+ + +

DADDY: *Snooks, I told you to watch your baby brother. Now what have you done with him?*

SNOOKS: *He's playing baseball with the neighborhood kids and they're keeping an eye on him.*

DADDY: *Robespierre's playing baseball?*

SNOOKS: *Yeah. He's home plate.*

Actually, Snooks was simply Brice in another age. "Snooks is just the kid I used to be," Brice allowed. "She's my kind of youngster, the type I like. She has imagination. She's eager. She's alive." Brice was born into a Hungarian Jewish family in New York City's Lower East Side as Fania Borach on October 29, 1891, the third progeny of a couple of moderately-heeled tavern proprietors. John Dunning recalled her early exposure to an array of experiences that shaped her career for the rest of her days:

> Snooks and Borach grew together, playing in the streets near Harlem, running away from school [she dropped out following eighth grade], mooching nickels and dimes at Coney Island. But Snooks lay dormant; Fannie [who altered the spelling of her name in the 1920s] was imp enough for one girl. She entertained whenever she could find an audience with a few pennies. She picked up the earthy accents of European families who had settled into Manhattan a generation before, and learned how to do dialect comedy. By her mid-teens, the pennies had grown to dollars; she was scratching out a slim living playing amateur nights in neighborhood saloons. [On one such occasion, after winning a $10 award at Kenney's Theater in Brooklyn singing "When You Know You're Not Forgotten by the Girl You Can't Forget," she gathered $23 in loose change in addition to her prize—coins the spectators tossed on stage.]
> Her break came in 1910. She met Irving Berlin, then a struggling young songwriter. Berlin had written a piece called "Sadie Salome"; he suggested that she sing it in a dialect at the Columbia Burlesque House, where she was working. Her performance, utilizing the combined tongues of her street people, was seen by Florenz Ziegfeld, who offered her a job in the *Follies*. Money and acclaim began to pour in, and Fannie successfully played a *Follies* girl for the next thirteen years.[4]

That was her first permanent job over a dually-divided entertainment career.

The public got an unmistakable sample of Baby Snooks as early as 1912, nevertheless, a full quarter-century before the figure would become widely known (and Fanny Brice's career would take off in a totally different direction). As the *Titanic* sank, Brice padded her vaudeville act with a pithy routine that spotlighted a preschooler. It was a foretaste of things to come. But at the time, to subsist she didn't need Snooks and focused on supplementary aspects of her showwomanship instead. Combining music with comedy, she drew crowds by vocalizing on standards like "Second Hand Rose." As time progressed, her performances with the *Follies* triumphed. By 1917 she was one of its foremost artists.

When Hollywood beckoned in the late 1920s she was ready and turned up in a handful of celluloid productions, sometimes in uncredited roles: *My Man* (1928), *Night Club* (1929), *Be Yourself!* (1930), *The Man from Blankley's* (1930), *Crime Without Passion* (1934), *The Great Ziegfeld* (1936), *Everybody Sing* (1938), *Hollywood Goes to Town* (1938), *Ziegfeld Follies* (1946) and *The Story of Will Rogers* (1952). In several films Brice sang as well as acted. In her first, *My Man*, titled after her lifelong signature song, she performed the number onscreen, having first recorded it back in 1921. She ultimately waxed about two dozen sides for RCA Victor and several more for Columbia, in fact.

Posthumously, Brice received a Grammy Hall of Fame Award for her recording of "My Man." Other tunes she belted out in the same movie were emblematic of the style that made her popular at stage venues: "I'd Rather Be Blue Over You"; "Second Hand Rose"; "If You Want the Rainbow, You Must Have the Rain"; "I'm an Indian"; and "I Was a Floradora Baby." Even though she earned a star on the Hollywood Walk of Fame for her contributions to the motion picture industry, "Her few starring movies in the early talkie era were unsuccessful," noted one authority.[5] Another delineated, "Brice, a *Ziegfeld Follies* headliner ... had suffered slumps in Hollywood, on Broadway, and in radio appearances as well as failed marriages."[6] Her picks in men proved dismal failures; she wed and divorced a trio of them.

Her career on stage, recordings and film

eventually led Fanny Brice to radio, which, by the 1920s, emerged as the nation's first source of instant, simultaneous amusement and information. Following some scattered guest appearances as early as 1927, in the fall of 1932 she joined bandleader George Olsen and his orchestra as vocalist for a Saturday night half-hour on NBC. It lasted 13 weeks. Yet the feature exposed Brice to a continuing spot before the microphone, while offering America a wider dimension for appreciating her talents. It was followed by a handful of other shows.

In the fall of 1936 she headlined NBC Blue's *Broadway Merry-Go-Round*, which aired under multiple monikers (*Folies Bergere of the Air, Folies de Paree, Revue de Paree*). Brice's spot lasted until the end of 1936 when producers Frank and Anne Hummert replaced her with Beatrice Lillie. In 1939 Brice showed up with Hanley Stafford, Bob Hope and Martha Raye in a play titled *Zazazu* on *The Gulf Screen Guild Theater*. Outside Snooks, however, Brice's most enduring radio performance occurred with Stafford in a Christmas rendition of the beloved fairy tale *Pinocchio*, which was repeated several times on anthologies like *The Camel Screen Guild Players* (1947), *The Lady Esther Screen Guild Theater* (1944, 1945, 1946) and *The Screen Guild Theater* (1948, 1950).

The origin of the character of Baby Snooks is uncertain, as at least two conflicting stories have been cited. One has it that— in preparing for a radio performance—Brice adapted an amusing tale about a man and his nephew, "The Simple Story of George Washington," from Robert J. Burdette's volume of skits *Chimes from a Jester's Bells*. She transposed the nephew to a niece and proceeded to make it a droll bit, introducing a lisping infant to listeners that she labeled "Schnooks." A second plausible tale maintains that the character was a burlesque invention altogether. It extends to her *Follies* days when, as one pundit allowed, Moss Hart became "the least likely man to have fathered Baby Snooks." The famous playwright and director of plays and musical theater purportedly penned a sketch that incorporated the figure

Brice played for the last 15 years of her life. That theory is acknowledged by several scholars, lending some credence to the possibility that Hart really was Snooks' father.

No matter who thought up the concept initially—couldn't it have been Brice herself?—we know *when* it first met audience approval with more certainty. There is a preponderance of evidence suggesting that Snooks' premier on the ether occurred on February 29, 1936, on a CBS broadcast of *The Ziegfeld Follies of the Air*. Her improvisation was so well received that, shortly after the next radio season debuted in the fall of 1937, the Snooks character was integrated into NBC's weekly variety series *Maxwell House Presents Good News* (aka *Good News of 1938*). General Foods Corporation teamed with filmmaker Metro-Goldwyn-Mayer to create an hour-long extravaganza presided over by a string of MGM luminaries (e.g., James Stewart, Robert Taylor, Robert Young, et al.). Part of the feature's billboard allowed: "Your ticket of admission is your loyalty to Maxwell House coffee."

The program not only presented dramatic vignettes from forthcoming MGM motion picture releases, it offered glimpses into the processes that went into the making of movies. It was a sensational hour that included an impressive list of guests from various show business venues, plus the musical backing of one of the most prominent radio impresarios, Meredith Willson, and his orchestra. Monologist Frank Morgan and Fanny Brice (as Snooks) were part of the recurring cast and became its most popular acts.[7] By 1940 the pair took over the whole show, which was reduced to a half-hour in March and renamed *Maxwell House Coffee Time* in October. During half the show Morgan presented comedy routines; Brice's half was devoted to humorous Snooks narratives. Common themes during her portions dealt with hair dyeing, pulling teeth, tonsil removal, playing hooky, fake measles, sneaking out and other childhood maladies and mayhem.

It was re-titled *The Baby Snooks Show* in September 1944 when she acquired all of it and Morgan transferred elsewhere.[8] That same year the producers put up a trial balloon in the form of an alternative sketch focused on Irma Potts (played by Fanny Brice) and Jerry Dingle, a small-town mailman (Danny Thomas). The skits were substituted for Snooks during some of the 1944–45 radio season, but they never were widely accepted by listeners. Baby Snooks rose to the forefront once again, and this time it became Brice's consuming passion for the remainder of her life. "Miss Brice probably emerges as the leading solo female comic of radio," one pundit pontificated.[9]

Thinking back to those days, historian Jim Harmon revealed: "Many listeners began to accept Snooks as a real child. I recall thinking cannily as a small boy that she was probably really a teenager. Fanny Brice's real self was not so much subjugated to Snooks as completely absorbed by the character."[10]

After 11 seasons, General Foods pulled out as sponsor of the long-running Snooks situation comedy, and the show suddenly collapsed, ending with the performance of May 28, 1948. But never say die. Less than 18 months later it found a new underwriter, Lewis Howe (for Tums), and returned to NBC from CBS. It persisted there for another 18 months, minus the usual summer hiatus.

Brice was reportedly so devoted to the show by then that—as the ratings began to slide late in the run (as they did for many durable audio series)—in the final couple of seasons she accepted reduced compensation for her work.[11] Nevertheless, she was still handsomely rewarded for her role as Daddy's infantile nemesis: by 1946 she was earning $6,000 weekly, allowing her to own an 18-room Hollywood mansion. Regarding her wealth, she once told an interviewer that she believed "pearls shouldn't be taken off," that they "needed to be lived in"; therefore she "would sleep in" hers at night.

When the opportunity arose, she carried the character of Snooks to other radio series. In addition to the aforementioned *Pinocchio* performances with Hanley Stafford, Brice trotted out her miscreant on a visit to the daytime game show *Double or Nothing*. When NBC's sensational star-studded radio extravaganza *The Big Show*—headlined by Tallulah Bankhead and backed by Meredith Willson's orchestra, with a vast array of glittering guests every week—premiered at the middle of the 20th century, Brice and Stafford reprised their famous roles on the second night of the impressive big-budget showcase (November 12, 1950). It was their final performance together outside their own series.

In addition to the radio feature, late in her career she cut a string of Capitol record albums for kids that might have been inspirations for monologues by Captain Kangaroo or Mr. Rogers for his Neighborhood years later. Among her benign subjects were "Crossing Streets," "Kindness to Animals," "Table Manners" and "Truthfulness."

During a prolonged illness in 1945 when Brice was off the show, Eddie Cantor, Robert Benchley, Peter Lorre and other stars filled in while "searching for Snooks." She was also absent in 1948 during an extended salary dispute. Although totally absorbed by her character then, there were signs that she was becoming progressively weary of the radio rat race. A source indicated that she intended to retire from show business at the close of the 1950–51 radio season due to being "tired of fighting to stay on top." It was an epoch in which many other radio comedians were transferring their wares to television (e.g., George Burns and Gracie Allen, Jack Benny, Milton Berle, Red Skelton and several more). "That's something a 60-year-old Baby Snooks could not have carried off," the informant acknowledged.

Otherwise she portrayed Snooks until a cerebral hemorrhage took her life in 1951. It occurred on May 24, and she lingered five days, until the day of her scheduled broadcast (May 29), when she passed. That evening NBC aired a musical tribute to the artist during her usual half-hour time period. In a brief eulogy, Hanley Stafford remarked: "We have lost a very real, a very warm, a very wonder-

ful woman." More than 2,000 mourners turned out for her funeral in Hollywood. She had been writing her memoirs for some time, but they remained unfinished.

Although physically gone, Brice was recalled in a myriad of reincarnations. *Rose of Washington Square*, a Hollywood biopic co-starring Alice Faye and Tyrone Power, loosely based on Brice's life through the Snooks introductory period, had been released a dozen years earlier in 1939. A quarter-of-a-century afterward, singer-actress Barbra Streisand took to the Broadway stage in *Funny Girl*, a 1964 musical depicting Brice's life. It was so well received that when Hollywood beckoned she reprised her role in a 1968 film, for which she won an Academy Award for Best Actress. *Funny Girl* in both formats was produced by Ray Stark, Brice's son-in-law (who married Frances Arnstein, Brice's daughter, born in 1919; Brice also had a son, William Arnstein, who grew up to be a successful artist). A sequel, *Funny Lady*, was produced for the silver screen in 1975, also starring Streisand. Streisand recorded both "My Man" and "Second Hand Rose," pop vocals long associated with Brice. Still much later, in 1991 Brice's image was released on one of five U. S. postage stamps celebrating legendary comedians.[12]

In her three marriages Brice was linked with some colorful characters. She seldom referred to her ephemeral span with Frank White, whom she wed at 18 and divorced about three years later (1910–13). More passionate was her encounter with notorious professional gambler Jules (Nicky) Arnstein (nee Jules W. Arndt Stein), her spouse from 1918 to 1927—although separated for much of it while he served time in the slammer. A sentence at Sing Sing, during which Brice visited him weekly, apparently taught him little. Upon his release he became caught up in a conspiracy to carry stolen securities to the District of Columbia. That time he was sent up the creek for a couple of years at Fort Leavenworth. According to Wikipedia, "Nicky shamelessly sponged off her [Brice]. The film [*Funny Girl*] suggests Nicky sold phony bonds;

he was actually part of a gang that stole $5 million of Wall Street securities. Instead of turning himself in, as in the movie, Arnstein went into hiding. When he finally surrendered, he did not plead guilty, as he did in the movie, but fought the charges for 4 years, taking a toll on his wife's finances."[13] Despite their lengthy separations, the couple still managed to produce two kids, Brice's only children. Upon Arnstein's release from prison the last time, a sad but wiser Brice divorced him. Having been single for 16 months, Brice tied the knot a third time in 1929 with composer-stage producer Billy Rose. She also appeared in *Crazy Quilt*, a revue he put together. Brice remained his wife for nine years—equal to the time she was Mrs. Arnstein—before divorcing Rose in 1938. She didn't remarry. Regarding her last two nuptials, she told a reporter: "With Nick Arnstein, I was miserably happy. With Billy Rose, I was happily miserable."

Hanley Stafford was Lancelot Higgins for most of the show's run, and it was he more than any other character that was foiled by Baby Snooks. Born Alfred John Austin on September 22, 1899, at Hanley, Staffordshire, England, he would ultimately derive his stage name from the place of his birth. In 1911 he and his parents relocated to Winnipeg, Canada, where he lived until 1922. Then he moved to his third nation, America, and became a naturalized citizen three years afterward. At 16, meanwhile, he joined a Canadian military platoon and—most likely after his tour of service ended—married an Englishwoman named Doris (her maiden name isn't recorded in U.S. Census Bureau records). Hanley's only child, Graham Stafford, was born in 1921. Oddly enough, Hanley's dad, George Austin, and Hanley both served in World War I, while Graham, Hanley's son and George's grandson, served in World War II. George lost his life in battle, and the other two, both volunteers, were wounded. Consequently, that family paid a hefty price for its military contribution.

Convalescing from his injuries, Hanley passed the time by organizing a theatrical contingent. Upon his discharge in 1919 he gained some bit parts, acting with the Winnipeg Permanent Players. Then he joined a stock company and toured western Canada. When that outfit folded he worked in wheat fields to earn enough dough to return to Winnipeg, exhibiting adaptability to his circumstances and displaying a robust determination to succeed. At home he heaved freight for the Dominion Express and was a stenographer for Grand Trunk Pacific.

In 1922 Hanley and Doris left their adopted homeland and carried Graham, then age one, to Hollywood. Within a year the patriarch found work portraying villains in western films. A couple of years of that landed him back on the stage in a critically acclaimed role in *Six Characters in Search of an Author*. The notoriety from it led to other parts, and by 1928 he was attached to the Los Angeles' Shelley Players as an actor and director of stage productions. There he met Bernice Bonnet, who became his leading lady. Divorcing Doris in the early 1930s, he wed Bernice in 1934.

In the meantime, with the theater reeling from the sharp financial blows of the Depression's fallout, Stafford turned to radio for his livelihood. Believing that more opportunities for aural work existed in New York City, he and his bride took off for Gotham. Within a short while he was playing the lead in NBC's daytime serial *John's Other Wife* (1936–ca. 1938) while simultaneously appearing at least four times a week on CBS's soap opera *Big Sister*. In addition, in 1936–37 on Sunday afternoons he was the namesake hero of NBC's crime drama *Thatcher Colt*. He held the same honor during a portion of the syndicated run of the juvenile serial *Speed Gibson of the International Secret Police* (1937–38). In the mid-1930s he carried a recurring role as Lord Tennington in the youthful syndicated adventure *Tarzan*. In 1937 he was Snapper Snitch the Crocodile in the children's syndicated fantasy series *The Cinnamon Bear*. By 1938 Stafford was Daddy Higgins to Baby Snooks, a part that would last 13 years. A year later he also became J. C. Dithers, the irascible yet compassionate superior to Dagwood Bumstead of CBS's *Blondie* sitcom. He played one of the heroes, Nayland Smith, in the 1939 and 1940 syndicated version of the serialized melodrama *The Shadow of Fu Manchu*. In the summer of 1950 he was Bart Conway in NBC's romantic narrative *Presenting Charles Boyer*.

Stafford discovered more opportunities to ply his craft on the ether as he reached beyond the continuing roles. He turned up in the following dramatic anthologies at irregular intervals: *Calling All Cars* (1934), *The Camel Screen Guild Players* (1947), *The Court of Human Relations* (1934–39), *The Gulf Screen Guild Show* (1939), *Hollywood Hotel* (1938), *The Lady Esther Screen Guild Theater* (1943, 1944, 1945, 1946), *The Screen Guild Theater* (1948, 1950) and *Suspense* (1942).

In a treatise on the difficulty that supporting radio performers encountered in hearing their contributions acknowledged on the ether, critic Leonard Maltin recalled how Stafford overcame the plight of anonymity on *Good News*, where Baby Snooks was introduced as a recurring feature:

> Frustrated because he was given no credit for his work, Stafford seized an opportunity during a lunch break for *Good News* one day. [Radio actor Jerry] Hausner asked if they might get a sandwich, and Stafford replied, "I want to wait until this place clears out; I have something to do."
>
> "So we waited for the theater to empty," said Hausner..."and on the piano was [that week's host] Robert Taylor's script.... So Hanley walks over to the script, takes his pencil out and writes, after 'Fanny Brice as Baby Snooks,' 'with Hanley Stafford as Daddy.' Now when Robert Taylor came back to the studio after lunch, he ... got up to the mike and read the billboard '...with Hanley Stafford as Daddy,' and nobody made anything of it because everybody assumed that it was supposed to be that way...." The billing was repeated the following week and for years to come. Thus, an anonymous actor's name became known to the listening public.[14]

In the years between 1941 and 1956 Stafford returned to the silver screen for 10 more flicks: *Life with Henry* (1941), *Swing It Soldier* (1941), *Three Guys Named Mike* (1951), *Lullaby of Broadway* (1951), *A Girl in Every Port* (1952), *Just This Once* (1952), *Here Come the Marines* (1952), *Francis Covers the Big Town* (1953), *The Affairs of Dobie Gillis* (1953) and *The Go-Getter* (1956). He also did a little television, appearing in 1953 as Lester in the pithy syndicated sitcom *The Hank McCune Show*. From 1959 to 1962 he acted in single episodes on a half-dozen TV series: *Maverick*, *Sugarfoot*, *The Jim Backus Show*, *The Shirley Temple Show*, *Cheyenne* and *77 Sunset Strip*.

Stafford's second marriage, to actress Bernice Bonnet, ended—as did his first—in divorce. But a plucky Bonnet didn't take such circumstances lying down. The couple obtained their divorce decree in April 1939. When Stafford announced his engagement to radio vocalist-actress Viola Vonn (whose first name was sometimes written Veola and Vyola) a short time afterward, Bernice Stafford filed an appeal before a Los Angeles Superior Court judge. In her petition she requested that the divorce decree be overturned, claiming that she and Stafford had reconciled. The judge was sympathetic to her plea. Considerable legal wrangling ensued, including overtures to a higher court in early 1940. Ultimately the appeal was set aside, and Stafford and Vonn wed that year. Vonn and his only child, Graham, survived Stafford upon his passing from a heart attack in Hollywood on September 11, 1968. He was 68.

A personal reflection may suggest the feeling of loss that America experienced on the night Fanny Brice died and *Baby Snooks* vanished forever. This author was an adolescent at the time and a faithful listener to *Snooks*, as were some of my neighborhood pals. I was in the backyard of the home of the children living across the street, playing a game of kick ball with several others, when word reached us of Fanny Brice's death. Somebody plugged in a radio on the screened-in back porch and turned up the volume so we could hear the tribute show while we continued with our game. We ran the bases and attempted to put the opposing team's members "out," but did so in stunned silence, almost disbelieving what we were hearing. It seemed like one of our own had just died. *Baby Snooks* had ceased to be funny.

# 6

# *Beulah*

## THE DEFINITIVE DOMESTIC COMEDY

*Beulah* was peerless in the annals of golden age radio: it dispensed the droll adventures of a black woman, its central character, in a storyline that embraced both black and white characters. During the pre–Civil Rights epoch in America there were limited opportunities for network audiences to find people of dual races in plausible interactive situations which were charmingly amusing. At its peak the "domestic comedy" that gave new meaning to that term kept legions of Americans snickering, however. Its ability to entertain extended for a decade across sundry formats. The novel sitcom reached its zenith as a five-night-a-week quarter-hour serial, progressively introducing a new dilemma every week. Centered on a Caucasian family and their Negro cook-housekeeper-maid, the humorous feature offered lively exchanges as Beulah and her employers found themselves in complicated dilemmas, often provoked by their own ineptness. Beulah's ingenuity usually managed to extricate the rest from their predicaments. In another unusual twist, the namesake character was initially played not by a black woman but by a white man! In fact, *two* such actors portrayed her before a buoyant African American female turned the show into a frothy and compelling romp. Hattie McDaniel, an Oscar-winning movie thespian, imbued Beulah with sparkle and animated energy during the program's halcyon days. Regrettably, the actress was routinely censured by public figures of her own race

for portraying a figure in servitude. She scoffed at their rebuke, however, giving a sterling performance that appealed to fans from both ethnic groups as her series became an enigma to the critics in its time.

❖ ❖ ❖

**Producer-Directors:** Helen Mack (1945–46), Tom McKnight (1947–53), Jack Hurdle (c1953), Steve Hatos (1953–54)

**Writers:** Herb Finn, Bill Freedman, Seaman Jacobs, Arthur Julian, Hal Kanter, Howard Leeds, Phil Leslie, Arthur Phillips, Sol Saks, Sherwood Schwartz, Charles Stewart, Sol Stewart

**Orchestras:** Buzz Adlam, Albert Sack

**Organist:** Gordon Kibbee

**Vocalists:** Penny Piper, Carol Stewart, Eileen Wilson

**Sound Effects Technician:** Vic Livoti

**Announcers:** Hank Weaver (1945); Ken Niles (1945–46), Marvin Miller (1947–53), Johnny Jacobs (1953–54)

**Recurring Cast:** *Beulah:* Marlin Hurt (1945–46), Bob Corley (1947), Hattie McDaniel (1947–51), Lillian Randolph (1951–52), Amanda Randolph (1952–54); *Harry Henderson:* Hugh Studebaker (1947–52), Jess Kirkpatrick (1952–54); *Alice Henderson:* Mary Jane Croft (1947–52), Lois Corbett (1952–54); *Donnie Henderson:* Henry Blair (1947–53), Sammy Ogg (1953–54); *Bill Jackson:* Marlin Hurt (1945–46), Ernie (Bubbles) Whitman (1947–54); *Oriole:* Ruby Dandridge (1947–54)

**Supporting Cast:** Louise Beavers, John Brown (Mr. Jenkins), Kathryn Carnes (Aunt Alice, 1945–46), Dorothy Dandridge, Vivian Dandridge, Roy Glenn, Jester Hairston, Jess Kirkpatrick (Mr. Frink, the egg man), Sam McDaniel, Butterfly McQueen, Marvin Miller, Carol Stewart ("the girl down the street from Beulah's house," 1945–46), Nicodemus

Stewart, Hugh Studebaker (Silly Watson), Lee White

**Sponsors:** Lewis Howe Company, for Tums indigestion distress reliever (1945–46); Procter & Gamble Company, for Dreft dishwashing powder (1947–53); Multiple Participation (1953–54), including General Foods Corporation, for a variety of foodstuffs; General Motors Corporation for Buick automobiles; The Murine Company, Inc., for Murine eye medications

**Themes:** "Got De World in a Jug" (1945–46); "Downhearted Blues" (Alberta Hunter, Lovie Austin); "Lazy Heart" (Alexander Laszlo)

**Ratings:** 30-minute format: 9.3 (1945–46); 15-minute format: High—15.5 (1949–50), Low—3.0 (1953–54), Median—9.7 (1947–54, all seasons except 1952–53)

**On the Air:** July 2–August 20, 1945, *The Marlin Hurt and Beulah Show*, CBS, Monday, 9:00–9:30 P.M. Eastern Time; August 26, 1945–March 17, 1946, CBS, Sunday, 8:00–8:30 P.M.; February 24–March 24, 1947, *The Beulah Show*, ABC, Monday, 9:00–9:30 P.M.; April 2–June 18, 1947, ABC, Wednesday, 9:30–10:00 P.M.; June 25–August 20, 1947, ABC, Wednesday, 9:00–9:30 P.M.; November 24, 1947–July 2, 1948, *Beulah*, CBS, Monday–Friday, 7:00–7:15 P.M.; August 23, 1948–July 1, 1949, CBS, Monday–Friday, 7:00–7:15 P.M.; August 22, 1949–June 30, 1950, CBS, Monday–Friday, 7:00–7:15 P.M.; August 28, 1950–June 29, 1951, CBS, Monday–Friday, 7:00–7:15 P.M.; August 27, 1951–June 27, 1952, CBS, Monday–Friday, 7:00–7:15 P.M.; August 25, 1952–June 19, 1953, CBS, Monday–Friday, 7:00–7:15 P.M.; September 28, 1953–May 21, 1954, *The New Beulah Show*, CBS, Monday–Friday, 7:15–7:30 P.M.

**Extant Archival Material:** More than 400 *Beulah* transcription discs are held in the Hattie McDaniel Collection at the Academy of Motion Picture Arts and Sciences Margaret Herrick Library, 333 South La Cienega Boulevard, Beverly Hills, CA, 90211; (310) 247–3036, extension 218; *www. oscars.org/mhl/sc/index.html.*

Three *Marlin Hurt and Beulah Show* (1945–46) radio scripts are maintained in the private collection of Fuller French, labeled the Broadcast Arts Library, Box 9828, Fort Worth, TX, 76147; (310) 288–6511; www.broadcastartslibrary.com.

Some *Beulah* scripts are included among writer Hal Kanter's Papers in the repository of the Wisconsin Historical Society, 816 State Street, Madison, WI, 53706; (608) 264–6460; *http://arcat.library. wisc.edu.*

No fewer than 36 recordings of *Beulah* shows were in general circulation or held by private collectors as of 2006, sold by vintage radio dealers and traded by old-time radio hobbyists.

❖ ❖ ❖

*Got de world in a jug, Lawd,*
*Got de stopper in my hand.*
—Series inception, 1945–46

From that vocal overture to an irrepressible "Luh-*uhhve* dat man!," *Beulah* was an aural cornucopia of black characterization in postwar America—*with a twist*. An obviously contented Negro domestic servant for an upper middle-class Caucasian family, she was the brains behind the organization. It was often Beulah's pure savvy, in fact, that extracted the Hendersons, her employers, from the complicated situations in which they were mired. Though faced with conventional racial circumstances, an adoring Beulah (who clearly held Harry Henderson, his wife Alice and their son Donnie in near-reverent import), nevertheless, was protective of her "family" at the Henderson residence at 213 Lake Street. At times, it almost seemed as if they were *her* subjects rather than the other way around.

A succinct outline of the brief history of African American broadcasting in the United States will establish a background and foster an understanding of the times in which *Beulah* appeared. While the show became the first network broadcast feature to star a black woman, it achieved that distinction in a rather bizarre manner. More will be said about that presently. For now, a look into the circumstances of non-white aircasting may prove enlightening in regards to *Beulah*'s inception.

The incredible success of *Amos 'n' Andy* is a tale familiar to most vintage radio analysts and hobbyists (see Chapter 3). For the uninitiated, it stems from popular black figures created by a couple of enterprising white men, Freeman Gosden and Charles Correll. Originally introduced as *Sam 'n' Henry*—two boys from the South who made their way to an industrialized North, seeking their fortunes— the feature originated weeknights over Chicago's WGN, dating back to January 12, 1926. It was the first recognized radio series in which black characters were the stars, albeit with Caucasians playing all the roles (but with convincing dialect). An instant hit, the show's fame spread quickly; the upshot was the launch of the similarly-themed *Amos 'n' Andy* on March 19, 1928, over Windy City competing outlet WMAQ, again with Gosden and Correll portraying those figures. That feature expanded to the NBC Blue network on August 19, 1929. The antics of *Amos 'n' Andy* would persist on network radio all the way to November 25, 1960, more than three decades beyond its humble birth.

"*Amos 'n' Andy* ... was all that most whites knew about blacks," a modern critic postulated. "Somehow, Jack Benny's [black] valet, Rochester, and his female counterpart, the wise and loving Beulah, escaped the black wrath that [eventually] tarred Gosden and Correll's show, most likely because Eddie Anderson [Rochester] and Hattie McDaniel [Beulah] were black. *Beulah* beat *Amos 'n' Andy* to TV by eight months, and though she was more of a stereotype, the show remained largely immune from attack."[1] Gosden and Correll's landmark achievement—their feature's audience drew more than 40 million listeners at its peak, as about a third of the nation's citizens tuned in—successfully argued that Americans would accept black characterization in traditional settings. Their early success perpetuated other black-oriented aural series, a few of which thrived while earning striking notoriety.

At about the same time Gosden and Correll were gaining their reputation on the air, WSBC, a rival Chicago station, offered *The All-Negro Hour*, another breakthrough in racial diversity. Debuting November 3, 1929, the variety series combined comedy, music and serial drama. While it persisted about six years, the show's real significance is that it became the first on the ether to proffer an all-black performing staff. Led by ex-vaudevillian Jack C. Cooper, the program not only supplied a venue for black talent, it exposed listeners to diverse contributions of Negro artists.

Like *Amos 'n' Andy*, the feature arrived during a period in which local stations were responsible for much of the entertainment they offered. At that time national and regional networks were just organizing and had not reached their summit in providing amusing fare to the masses, which would occur a short time later. Opportunities thus abounded for local series like *The All-Negro Hour*. Three years after its withdrawal in 1935, innovator Cooper was back on the air with another WSBC black-oriented entry, *Search for Missing Persons*. His purpose there was to reunite black migrants from the South with Yankee relatives and friends with whom they had lost touch. Cooper's success—and that of similar entrepreneurs, plus an eventual trend toward expansion in the radio industry—was to lead to a rise of black-oriented radio stations after the Second World War.

In the meantime, *Amos 'n' Andy*'s phenomenal acceptance paved the way for yet another early network series, *Aunt Jemima* (intermittently aired from 1929 to 1953). CBS signed actress Tess Gardella as the smiling black woman in a minstrel feature with its origins in Gardella's portrayal of the character in a 1920s stage review. As the good-natured mammy of breakfast fame, Aunt Jemima's renowned countenance first appeared on boxes of pancake mix in the early 1890s. Product advertising three decades afterward, in an era before the Quaker Oats Company purchased the brand, propagated a legend: "On the old plantation, Aunt Jemima refused to reveal to a soul the secret of those light fragrant pancakes which she baked for her master and his guests. Only once, long after her master's death, did Aunt Jemima reveal her recipe. It's still a secret."

The first personification of Aunt Jemima was ex-slave Nancy Green, who the pancake mix processors signed in 1893 to make public appearances as the character. Thirty years later, following Green's death in 1923, Gardella—a white thespian wearing blackface (shades of *Amos 'n' Andy* in their nominal public appearances)—was tapped to continue the tradition. After Gardella's stint on the ether ended in 1933, black actress Amanda Randolph (who was also to play *Beulah* two decades later) was engaged to embody the familiar culinary connoisseur in radio and personal appearances. That duty was extended to black singer-actress Edith Wilson in 1948; she perpetuated the figure in television commercials to 1966.

The first news discussion program aimed at African Americans, premiering on a local station from 1946 to 1952, was labeled *Listen Chicago*. It focused on black-oriented religious and social calendars, and topics of discussion of special interest to black listeners.

Although *Beulah* was to make its inaugural appearance on radio in the early 1940s—one of a handful of black-focused audio series—not until late in the decade did a local station hire an all-black announcing staff. That outlet, WDIA of Memphis, was one of a handful of Dixie broadcasters achieving notoriety by focusing on Negro personalities. Atlanta's WERD, for instance, became the nation's first black-owned radio station. John Richbourg, an Anglo-American disc jockey, drew 15 million listeners during his heyday between 1947 and 1973. Appealing to both whites and blacks, he programmed rhythm and blues recordings for his overnight stint on Nashville's powerful 50,000-watt WLAC. DJs in other strategically situated markets offered similar fare, opening the doors to greater acceptance of black music. One source affirmed, "The exposure of white youths to black urban tunes altered American society. Black radio in the 1950s fueled the popularity of rock 'n' roll, blurring cultural barriers between the races."

Into this mix drifted Caucasian entertainer Marlin Hurt, an actor and comedian born at DuQuoin, Illinois, on May 27, 1904. Growing up under circumstances that would not have been unrecognized by the mythical Henderson clan of Beulah's acquaintance, Hurt recalled a black woman named Mary who cooked for his family in his younger years. He depicted her in her thirties, "man-crazy," weighing about 140 pounds, with good teeth, her hair in bangs and a pageboy bob, and attired in short skirts and exceptionally high heels. Her demeanor so stimulated Hurt

that he practiced imitating her voice in order to include it in a hoped-for future show-business career. At the same time, he observed black railroad section hands harmonizing together a cappella as they labored, singing aloud:

> Got de world in a jug, Lawd,
> Got de stopper in my hand.

For 13 years Hurt appeared as part of a stage-and-radio act that included siblings Bud and Gordon Vandover, a trio billed as Tom, Dick and Harry. Hurt (who performed as Dick) was sometimes able to transform his "colorful" vernacular to the airwaves, employing a high-pitched falsetto dialect. He introduced the character of Beulah to network listeners via *Home Town Unincorporated*. NBC beamed the variety series from Chicago to a regional Southern audience between November 26, 1939, and April 28, 1940. Hurt persisted in the recently-contrived feminine impression in the summer of 1940 on NBC Blue's *Show Boat*.

Three years down the road, when Bud Vandover died, Hurt decided to strike out on his own. While appearing in the summer of 1943 on NBC's *That's Life*, aka *The Fred Brady Show*, Hurt's animated portrayal of Beulah was overheard by Don Quinn, the creative genius behind the enormously popular *Fibber McGee & Molly* on NBC. Always looking for fresh ideas, and having lost several recurring voices to wartime service, Quinn envisaged adding Beulah (whose surname was Brown) to the diminishing number of zany characters flowing to and from the McGees' legendary domicile at 79 Wistful Vista. By then Hurt was already 39, far beyond the clutches of the wartime draft, making him even more appealing to Quinn for the *McGee* show.

On January 25, 1944, the McGees (played by Jim and Marian Jordan)—figures who seemingly possessed few of the world's material goods—acquired a black cook named Beulah. She debuted as "a chuckling Aunt Jemima handkerchief-head, not all that far removed from a minstrel show."[2] Marlin Hurt habitually had the studio audience convulsing with laughter at his entrance. Standing with his back to the microphone as McGee hollered for Beulah, Hurt swiftly twirled around to face the microphone and a room full of eyewitnesses and bellowed: "Somebody bawl fo' Beulah?" The effect was uncontrolled hysteria as the studio audience dissolved into bedlam. They were witnessing a white guy performing as a black mammy—from the ridiculous to the sublime.

The introductory question carried over to Beulah's later broadcast years. On occasions it was injected when she witnessed her superiors in deep consternation.[3] She spouted some additional black-oriented colloquialisms, too. One of her best was "On the con-positively-trairy!" When McGee flung one of his convoluted tantrums, she would shake her head and laugh, "Luh-*uhhve* dat man!" It would stay with her for a full decade.

So well received was the Beulah figure by the McGee faithful that in little more than a year a decision was made to spin Beulah off into her own separate series.[4] The transfer wouldn't be without precedent, however. On August 31, 1941, Throckmorton P. Gildersleeve (then played by Harold Peary)—a pompous windbag bachelor who made ladies' girdles (of all things) and sparred endlessly with the homeowner at 79 Wistful Vista—turned up in his own NBC half-hour sitcom, *The Great Gildersleeve.*[5] Suddenly he was flanked by a ready-made family of his own, including a niece and nephew for whom he was the resident guardian, a black housekeeper and cook, a coterie of men friends with whom he regularly sparred and a bevy of stunning girlfriends he enjoyed dating. By then no longer a girdle-maker, he was the water commissioner for the neighboring hamlet of Summerfield.

No one had such drastic changes in mind for Beulah, however. She would continue to be what she already was, a cook-housekeeper-maid combo, pure and simple. Only the host family would change; weekly McGee visitors like Wallace Wimple, Doc Gamble, Mayor LaTrivia, Millicent Carstairs, Abigail Uppington, Mr. Old Timer, Teeny, and announcer

Harlow ("Waxy") Wilcox would remain. Beulah would premier in her new incarnation at CBS as a Monday night half-hour situation comedy under the appellation *The Marlin Hurt and Beulah Show.* The series launched on July 2, 1945, after the McGees left on their usual summer hiatus following the June 26 broadcast. It was scripted for the summer run, in fact, by no less a wordsmith than Phil Leslie, Don Quinn's co-author on *Fibber McGee & Molly.*[6]

In the new incarnation Beulah worked in the household of Marlin Hurt, a business executive who lived with his Aunt Alice, played by Kathryn Carnes. One pundit depicted Beulah in that version as "easily excitable and meddling, and her efforts to resolve domestic crises were the focal point of stories." Her boyfriend, Bill Jackson—a multivoiced Marlin Hurt appeared as himself, as Beulah and as Bill Jackson, too!—was introduced and became a key element in subsequent manifestations of the program. *The Marlin Hurt and Beulah Show* persisted as a seasonal replacement on Monday nights through August 20, 1945, and then shifted to a permanent spot in the CBS lineup on Sunday nights opposite one of NBC's leading comedians, ventriloquist Edgar Bergen and his chief marionette Charlie McCarthy.

*The Marlin Hurt and Beulah Show* held its own, despite the fierce competition at NBC at that hour. Everything was going well until fate stepped in: Hurt dropped over dead on a golf course on Thursday, March 21, 1946, the victim of a heart attack, apparently without warning. The show he spawned immediately left the air. It wouldn't return for 11 months, until budding standup comic Bob Corley, also a Caucasian, was hired to replace Hurt, that time on ABC under *The Beulah Show* moniker.

Born at Macon, Georgia, on May 29, 1924, Corley was just 22. He made a handful of humorous recordings at mid-century and appeared in a couple of 1965 films, *The Legend of Blood Mountain,* a mystery he penned himself, and *Forty Acre Feud,* a cornpone tale loosely interwoven around the singing of multiple *Grand Ole Opry* artists. Otherwise, his career was fairly nondescript. Corley, too, died young, at age 47, on November 18, 1971, in Atlanta, where he finished his career as a local television director. He maintained that "age and hormones" prevented him from continuing as Beulah two dozen years earlier. His portrayal, nonetheless, was soundly rejected by radio listeners, and within six months both the show—and he—were withdrawn.

At that juncture it occurred to someone within the broadcasting hierarchy that perhaps a black woman could play the role of Beulah if the program was to return to the air. What a novel idea! Why hadn't anyone seriously considered that before? Did no African American ladies possess sufficient skills to accomplish it? That couldn't be true. As it turned out, several were well qualified. For most of the radio series' run, all the same, the part was to belong to one of them: well-known film actress Hattie McDaniel, who was inexorably linked to the role for a quadrennial. She infused Beulah with depth and humor, and combined the right amount of sass and dignity to make it an endearing portrayal. Her performance lingered in the public's perception long after she abandoned it, in fact.

The last of 13 children of a Virginia-born freed slave who fought with the Union army, Hattie McDaniel arrived on June 10, 1895, at Denver, Colorado.[7] Fifteen years later she was the only Negro to partake in an event sponsored by the Women's Christian Temperance Movement. On that occasion she recited a poem, "Convict Joe," and won a gold medal for her efforts. That solidified a long-harbored ambition within her to become a professional entertainer. Following her high school sophomore year, Hattie McDaniel left formal training behind to travel with a minstrel entourage fostered by her dad and brothers, Otis and Sam. During that period she also developed as a lyricist for some of the music they performed. It was a proficiency that contributed to her livelihood some years later.

After Otis died in 1916 the group began to lose its impetus. Hattie didn't dawdle over it forever; she caught the next wave of opportunity she encountered, in 1920 latching on to bandleader George Morrison's "Melody Hounds" vaudeville troupe. The unit received excellent reviews of their performances. While with Morrison, in 1923 McDaniel sang over Denver's KOA Radio, becoming the first woman of her race to do so anywhere. That provided the opportunity for her to record several of the songs she had composed. Subsequently, she advanced to a touring circuit under auspices of the black cinema-dominated Theatrical Owners Booking Association. When the stock market collapsed in October 1929, pitching the nation overnight into sustained economic chaos, the 200-pound McDaniel was appearing on stage as Queenie in *Showboat*. Her company abruptly folded, as did thousands of others, and McDaniel was suddenly out of a job. The dispossessed singer-actress related what happened next:

> I had headlined on the Pantages and Orpheum circuits, but vaudeville was dead as last month's hit song. Milwaukee was really my springboard to Hollywood. I landed there broke. Somebody told me of a place as a maid in the ladies' room at Sam Pick's Suburban Inn. I rushed there and took the job. One night, after midnight, when all the entertainers had left, the manager called for volunteer talent from among the help. I asked the boys in the orchestra to strike up "St. Louis Blues." I started to sing "I hate to see the evening sun go down." ... I never had to go back to my maid's job. For two years I starred in the floor show.[8]

Following that stint in Milwaukee, McDaniel landed in Los Angeles in 1931. While seeking work she hired herself out as a domestic, a cook or a washerwoman. She was soon appearing on a local radio show over KNX, *The Optimistic Donuts*, thanks to her brother Sam, who was already on the program. Her developing reputation would soon project her to network radiocasting. In the 1930s and 1940s she randomly appeared on *Amos 'n' Andy*, an institution on the ether. She also performed on *The Eddie Cantor Show*, variously on CBS and NBC. It was the first time an African American had sung on an American nationwide hookup. As a member of American Women's Voluntary Services, she appeared in uniform on Cantor's show in 1942 plugging sales of bonds on behalf of the nation's wartime efforts. Between 1938 and 1947 she sang with a Negro choir on CBS's *Wings Over Jordan* black gospel and preaching series.

In 1932 McDaniel signed to play Hi-hat Hattie in *The Golden West*. It was a nickname given her by announcer Tom Breneman when she turned up for her first *Optimistic Donuts* performance attired in formal evening gown, while the rest of the cast was clad in street clothes. The new handle stuck with her for years. That motion picture, incidentally, was the precursor of no fewer than 80 that followed in the next two decades, mostly of B-movie persuasion.[9] Typical titles included *Impatient Maiden* (1932), *Hypnotized* (1932), *Flirtation* (1934), *Murder by Television* (1935), *Can This Be Dixie?* (1936), *Maryland* (1940), *The Male Animal* (1942), *Thank Your Lucky Stars* (1943), *Hi, Beautiful* (1944), *The Flame* (1947) and *The Big Wheel* (1949). McDaniel was often featured as a domestic in those films.[10] Yet there were some high moments among her celluloid renditions. She sang a duet with Will Rogers in 1934's *Judge Priest*, and with Clark Gable in 1937's *Saratoga*. She performed in movies headlined by some of Hollywood's most notable legends, like Shirley Temple in 1935's *The Little Colonel*. Among her most significant parts were Queenie in *Show Boat* (1936), Fidelia in *Since You Went Away* (1944) and Aunt Tempy in *Song of the South* (1946).

But, incontestably, the role of her lifetime—for which she is still remembered today—was Mammy in 1939's epic *Gone with the Wind*, headlined by Clark Gable, Vivian Leigh, Leslie Howard, Olivia de Havilland, Thomas Mitchell, George Reeves, Butterfly McQueen and a host of lesser-knowns. Producer David O. Selznick tested many aspirants competing for Mammy, among them Louise Beavers, who later succeeded McDaniel as *Beulah* on television; actress Hattie Noel; and

Eleanor Roosevelt's personal maid, Elizabeth McDuffie, a member of the White House servants' amateur theater ensemble. But it was McDaniel who provided the convincing command of the part. She appeared at her audition attired in an authentic maid's uniform ready to work. That choice became the defining moment of her career and overshadowed every professional opportunity she subsequently encountered. Referring to her pivotal contribution there, one source affirmed: "Here she is, in a number of ways, superior to most of the white folk surrounding her."[11]

By then the black actress possessed "enough clout to insist on certain script changes," one scholar pontificated, excising the term "nigger" from the dialogue along with Mammy's own references to "De Lawd."

In a synopsis of that classic film, a critic delineated: "Mammy felt that she owned the O'Haras, body and soul, that their secrets were her secrets.... Mammy emerged from the hall, a huge old woman with the small, shrewd eyes of an elephant. She was shining black, pure African, devoted to her last drop of blood to the O'Haras.... Mammy was black, but her code of conduct and her sense of pride were as high as or higher than that of her owners.... Whom Mammy loved, she chastened. And, as her love for Scarlett and her pride in were enormous, the chastening process was practically continuous."[12]

When the *Gone with the Wind* stars were feted at the film's premier in Atlanta in December 1939, McDaniel sent word to director Victor Fleming beforehand that she would be unable to attend. She knew that her presence would cause a stir in a still-segregated South where emotions ran high over racial differences. When Clark Gable learned of her decision, he announced his intent to shun the grand opening in Atlanta. If McDaniel, with whom he had been friends since *Saratoga* a couple of years earlier, couldn't go, he wouldn't either. Wanting to diffuse racial tensions, however, McDaniel convinced Gable to attend, while she stayed behind.

She wouldn't be shut out forever, however. On February 29, 1940, just two months

*Academy Award–winning actress Hattie McDaniel—who set a standard for excellence among blacks in popular enter-tainment—ushered in nightly visits with namesake Beulah. Portraying a charming domestic, she endeared herself to black and white radio fans of the mid-twentieth century. Shown here with boyfriend Bill Davidson, a shiftless, ami-able character played by Ernie Whitman, McDaniel was very much a part of the Henderson family, her employers. She not only performed her required duties with aplomb, but offered practical wisdom to help the clan navigate complex is-sues. McDaniel was criticized by the NAACP for accepting work showcasing Negroes in servitude. She was a worthy crusader for her race, nevertheless, blazing trails that inspired people of various races.*

after the debut of *Gone with the Wind*, Mc-Daniel became the first Negro to be invited as a guest (not a servant) to the annual Academy Awards presentation dinner at the Coconut Grove at Los Angeles' Ambassador Hotel. On that occasion, in competition with fellow cast member Olivia de Havilland for the coveted prize of Best Supporting Actress, McDaniel was the first of her race to win an Oscar. A reviewer claimed her recognition achieved "the loudest ovation of the evening." After a brief acceptance speech, prepared in advance by the studio, McDaniel broke down in tears before leaving the dais. No African Americans would win an Oscar again until a quarter-of-a-century had elapsed, making her triumph that much more impressive in the annals of filmdom. Parenthetically, upon her death McDaniel willed her Oscar to Howard University. During racial riots on the campus in the 1960s the Oscar was misplaced and has never resurfaced.

Hattie McDaniel unavoidably became a lightning rod in the controversy over racial inequality between the 1930s and her death from breast cancer on October 26, 1952. While she was "the most celebrated black actress of her time," she was constantly perplexed by criticisms and protests ignited by the "mammy" roles she was given to play.[13] There doesn't seem to be much evidence that she intentionally inflamed the masses. Nevertheless, the acting parts that she accepted—particularly those on the silver screen—infuriated her own race as well as the Caucasians, but for different reasons. The dearth of roles available to Negro actresses in that epoch left her little choice but to appear in minstrel settings that depicted humble, predominantly ignorant blacks, or as a housekeeper, cook or maid if she wanted to be in films.[14] Some members of the black community criticized her for her choices, including the NAACP, which railed against those stereotypical images. That body's leader, Walter White, and a few members of the black press were particularly vocal in their protests.

At least one Caucasian scholar took a broad swipe at some of the prevailing practices in that period of racially-slurred broadcasting:

> Although the producers of *Beulah* finally selected a black woman instead of a white man to portray the stereotyped black maid, the appearance in that role of Hattie McDaniel in 1947—and Louise Beavers and Lillian Randolph in the 1950s—did not alter the minstrel model upon which the show was based.
>
> The depiction of America's ethnic minorities as guileful, awkward, or pretentious was a residual of the humor that blossomed in vaudeville and minstrelsy during the time of massive immigration at the turn of the [twentieth] century. Poking ridicule at accents, mannerisms, personality traits, and physical attributes was ultimately the comedy of a race-conscious society that was anything but a melting pot. It was difficult for radio comedians to abandon successful ethnic material.[15]

Nevertheless, at least one contemporary African American activist, Jesse Jackson, professed that shows like *Beulah* and *Amos 'n' Andy* made his racial heritage proud: "Black people had enough sense to appreciate them as funny people playing at their roles.... There was a tradition in our community of funny people. It did not dominate black life to the extent that it has been projected."[16]

"Why should I complain about making $7,000-a-week playing a maid?" McDaniel responded to her detractors on one occasion. "If I didn't, I'd be making $7-a-week being one!" The actress devoted an inordinate amount of her time in later years to defending her professional decisions. At the same time, she angered white Southerners with her impudent, outspoken and opinionated portrayal of Malena, the maid in *Alice Adams*, a 1935 movie. Some simply couldn't abide her perceived insolence.

It was as if she was damned if she did and damned if she didn't! "It's hard to imagine the pain McDaniel endured," wrote a contemporary *PopMatters* editor. "Her life and work surely warrant careful reconsideration." Noting that "Hollywood historians haven't always been kind to the legacy of Hattie McDaniel and black stars of her era," a modern reviewer observed: "Thanks to contemporary scholarship these personas are being revealed with a sharper lens."

Significant alterations in racial acceptance were rapidly approaching during the twilight years of McDaniel's life. It was a far cry from the working environment in which she had begun three decades earlier. The Supreme Court's historic 1954 decision disallowing segregated school systems, and its 1956 ruling against segregation in all public institutions of higher learning and in public transit systems, were watershed occurrences that drastically altered the thinking of the American populace about positions many had held all of their lives.

In broadcasting, by January 1954 the National Negro Network was formed, and a year later premiered *The Story of Ruby Valentine*, a weekday serial starring black vocalist-actress Juanita Hall. (Did *Beulah* prepare the way?) Soon that network was airing a couple of additional short-lived series featuring African Americans: *The Life of Anna Lewis*, with Hilda Simms portraying the title role; and *It's a Mystery, Man*, spotlighting legendary bandleader-showman Cab Calloway. Similarly, Negro Radio Stories was established in the 1950s, and it debuted a quartet of daytime dramas proffering all-black ensembles: *Ada Grant's Neighbors, My Man, Rebeccah Turner's Front Porch Stories* and *The Romance of Julia Davis*. In March 1955 ABC Radio offered its first all-black network series, *Rhythm & Blues on Parade*. African American master of ceremonies Willie Bryant presented all-black talent on that landmark feature.

Rochester, Jack Benny's opinionated manservant, had been laboring for his employer since 1937, of course, and Birdie Lee Coggins—played by Lillian Randolph, who years later would appear as Beulah—had been Throckmorton P. Gildersleeve's beloved but fussy housekeeper and cook since 1941. Yet by the 1950s it was becoming clear that radio was, for the very first time, providing opportunities for black entertainers and audiences that had never been available before. The edicts handed down by the Supreme Court shaped new thought patterns, while radio

officials were surprised in 1954 to find that the national Negro market was worth $15 billion in purchasing power.[17] For a variety of reasons then, it seems logical to assume the nation's collective mind was slowly shifting. Network radio—in its declining years—was progressively bending to accommodate the modification.[18]

Late in life McDaniel organized her Los Angeles neighbors in a protest against segregation, evidence of the new trends occurring across the land. Her lobbying efforts paid off when the U.S. Supreme Court forced white residents to abandon a "restrictive covenant" that had long been in place.

In early 1952, meanwhile, McDaniel succeeded Ethel Waters in the lead role on *The Beulah Show* on ABC-TV, a weekly half-hour sitcom that had premiered in 1950. Only six episodes were filmed featuring McDaniel, however. One source maintains that those installments were never shown, although that isn't confirmed by other scholars. McDaniel was not well, her health rapidly spiraling out of control. Beginning Monday, November 12, 1951, she was succeeded in the radio run by Lillian Randolph (of Birdie Lee Coggins fame on *Gildersleeve*). Randolph remained as Beulah throughout the season, ending June 27, 1952. A heart attack, a stroke and a diagnosis of advanced breast cancer afforded a grim outlook for McDaniel, who was soon bound to a wheelchair. Despite that, CBS Radio publicists remained upbeat, issuing press releases in the latter part of summer 1952 proclaiming that *Beulah* would return to the air after its usual seasonal hiatus on Monday, August 25, 1952. Those dispatches confidently observed that the series' star, McDaniel, would reprise the namesake role again. Trying to put a happy face on the situation, there was no mention of cancer or even illness. CBS was clearly hopeful that the lady who had made the nightly feature a hit would be back.

But it wasn't to be.

McDaniel was dying and would succumb to her illness just two months later. In the meantime, in every Monday edition after the series' resumption, *The New York Times* listed *Beulah* with Hattie McDaniel's name beside the show's title in its daily radio log. Tuesday through Friday each week that post included only the name of the show itself. The pattern persisted until Monday, November 5, when *Beulah*—with no moniker beside it—was printed from then on. McDaniel had died the previous week, on October 26, at age 57. Almost financially destitute after years of abusive men (four marriages, the first ended by a murder, the others by divorce), generous gifts, spendthrift parties and enormous medical bills, her miserable physical plight was only complicated during her latter days. A few months before her death she sold her possessions and moved to the Motion Picture Country Home and Hospital at Woodland Hills, California, a new facility for which she had helped raise capital. Her demise was reported in newspapers a few days afterward. For the most part, an adoring public had been kept in the dark about the nature of her absence as the network re-ran transcriptions of earlier broadcasts. A report indicated that she had prerecorded an additional 12 weeks (60 chapters) of the show that were broadcast as her illness lingered.

McDaniel earned two stars on the Hollywood Walk of Fame—one for her radio work, predominantly as Beulah, the other heralding her film contributions. One of her final requests was to be interred at Hollywood Memorial Park Cemetery. Because it was segregated then, however, her remains were placed at Angelus Rosedale Cemetery in Los Angeles. Forty-seven years later, in 1999, a pink granite monument was unveiled to honor her at Hollywood Forever, the new moniker of Hollywood Memorial Park. And on January 25, 2006, the U.S. Postal Service released a 39-cent commemorative stamp signifying McDaniel's manifold accomplishments in show business.

She is the subject of a 45-minute AMC biography produced and directed by Madison Davis Lacy and hosted by Whoopi Goldberg, *Beyond Tara: The Extraordinary Life of Hattie McDaniel*. There have also been a couple of biographies in print—*Hattie: The Life of Hattie McDaniel*, by Carlton Jackson (Madison, 1990), and *Hattie McDaniel: Black Ambition, White Hollywood*, by Jill Watts (HarperCollins, 2005).

When McDaniel became the first feminine thespian to portray the title role in the radio series, the feature's title was abbreviated from *The Beulah Show* to simply *Beulah*. Not only did the series return to CBS after the six-month fling with Bob Corley at ABC, there were several other alterations in the weekly half-hour sitcom. For one, there was a new sponsor, Procter & Gamble, which purchased time for its Dreft dishwashing detergent. For another, the episodes were shortened to a quarter-hour's duration. Then, the show aired five nights weekly, following the pattern of a handful of serialized daytime dramas (though *Beulah* aired in the evening).[19]

In the new format, "Beulah was like a deferential Lucy Ricardo," said one source, "continually getting her employers [the Henderson family] in—then out—of all kinds of trouble." Usually in every new tale a contrite Beulah confessed, "Yes 'um, it's all my fault." That notwithstanding, she could invariably save the day with her earthy wit and blind persistence.

In addition to the three members of the all-white Henderson tribe, two more characters were on hand who often brought complications to Beulah's life. Both were black.

One was her well-meaning boyfriend of longstanding (about 10 years), Bill Jackson, a mechanic by trade, who could be branded a lazy bum if it wasn't so apparent. Shiftless and clumsy, he found excuses for not working and not keeping appointments, even those with Beulah, which could frustrate even the most forgiving heartthrob. His frequent arrivals at the Henderson home—to the familiar "shave-and-a-haircut" knock on their back door, followed by the anticipated "two bits" sound effect reply—preceded his straight-line greeting to Beulah. It invariably gave her an opening for a crowd-pleasing retort. Their typical exchanges (never with any sexual ramifications in those days) went like this:

BILL: "It's Bill, baby, your home run hitter in the game of love!" *Beulah:* "Well come on in, home run hitter; your grand slam is anxious to score!"

BILL : "It's Bill, baby, your cupid with arrows pointed at your heart!" *Beulah:* "Well, come on in, Bill, you're right on target!"

BILL : "It's Bill, baby, your rowboat in the tunnel of love!" *Beulah:* "Well, come on in, rowboat, and let's paddle along together!"

BILL : "It's Bill, baby, your sumptuous fruit in the orange groves of devotion!" *Beulah:* "Well, come on in, Bill, and give me a squeeze!"

It all sounded pretty inane. But it never failed to provoke a huge studio audience chuckle, its desired end.

Then there was Oriole, the befuddled maid of the family next door to the Hendersons, whose actions invariably led to a cry of: "The sky is falling! The sky is falling!" A pundit suitably labeled her a "birdbrain" after considering her hang-ups and her given name of Oriole. While she dialogued frequently with Beulah, it was the latter who constantly attempted to clear up the poor wretched soul's confusion. If a servile maid spouting malapropisms wasn't precisely a racial slur, one scholar noted, the examples Beulah dealt with on a consistent basis painted black caricatures as ignorant and slow.

Nevertheless, the comedy was a big drawing card, and the interactions between Bill and Beulah, in particular, struck the nation's funnybone. "Who's came knockin' at my door, three hours late?" she inquired once, to which he replied: "It's Bill, baby. No pain, no strain. I rode in here on the crest of a heat wave. Ooooooweeeee, it's hot out dere!" Bill had an answer for every weakness he exhibited.

A radio historiographer posted some observations on Beulah's handling of non-white characters in a predominantly white society:

Beulah ... ran the house, solved domestic dilemmas, and was treated as a member of the family, a concept well ahead of its time....

In those days, many a middle-class home had a maid, and even a maid's room, so it

didn't seem unusual to find the situation duplicated in radio families.... Radio's blacks were listened to and considered "part of the family"—a pleasant myth but, at worst, an unrealized ideal....

Hal Kanter said, "Beulah was really an inoffensive, benign character. Beulah was not stupid. There were stupid characters on the show, but there were a lot of stupid characters on all-white shows, too."[20]

The following outline suggests a typical week during the show's quarter-hour format heyday.

On Monday night a crisis, difficulty or concern was established. This was followed by anticipation or dread as the week went along, reaching a climax midweek or later, with the pivotal issue finally being resolved and dispatched during Friday's dénouement. Thus, boyfriend Bill might announce to Beulah on Monday evening that she would finally get to meet her prospective mother-in-law when the woman arrived in town on Wednesday. That gave Beulah a couple of days to weep and wail loudly in seriocomic fashion as she worked herself into a tizzy. Meanwhile, the well-meaning Hendersons attempted to comfort her while next-door maid Oriole made matters worse by telling Beulah how *she* lost a boyfriend after he brought his mother to town and the two women were at cross purposes. When Bill's mom did arrive, Beulah committed a grievous faux pas and figured her life was over. She received reassurance from every member of the Henderson clan on Thursday, along with Bill. By Friday, just before his mom departed for home, she expressed confidence in Beulah. After the woman left, Bill and Beulah cooed and smooched and signified once more that all was well that ended well.

There were numerous episodes in which one or the other of the Hendersons—father Harry, mother Alice, preteen son Donnie—was at the crux of the impasse to be dealt with. That's where Beulah's compassion for her little family was demonstrated time and time again. "A basic recurring theme," one pundit allowed, "is that they [Harry, Alice and Donnie] were rescued by Beulah's ingenuity and common sense," after having gotten themselves "into dilemmas they were too dumb to resolve on their own." It was shades of the helping-hand characters in daytime radio—like *Just Plain Bill* [Davidson], barber of Hartville; *Ma Perkins*, Rushville Center's beloved lumberyard proprietress; and *David Harum*, the banker of Homeville—who freely extended their advice to people who were incapable of running their own lives. Beulah was similar, and she revealed inordinate depths of insight and benevolence as she meted out good-natured counsel to the little clan. Thus, Donnie's love life and grades improved, attorney Harry's client relationships were advanced and Alice knew how to deal with fussy members of a social circle she belonged to, all thanks to Beulah.

The show persisted in that frame for seven years, almost five with Hattie McDaniel at the helm. Overlapping it was a televised *Beulah*, a half-hour weekly sitcom on ABC-TV that ran from 1950 to 1953. For almost two years Ethel Waters—who achieved greater fame as a gospel singer with evangelist Billy Graham than as an actress—played the namesake role. She was followed for a half-dozen episodes by Hattie McDaniel before McDaniel became too ill to continue.[21] In the final season, actresses Louise Beavers and Amanda Randolph—the latter also featured as the radio Beulah at the time—completed the video run. Both Beavers and Randolph left *The Beulah Show* on TV to play the maid Louise on Danny Thomas's sitcom *Make Room for Daddy*, Beavers in 1953–54 and Randolph from 1955 to 1964.

In the meantime, the aural version of *Beulah* was percolating right along. Preceding McDaniel's death, Lillian Randolph—Birdie Lee Coggins on *The Great Gildersleeve* (1941–54) and Madam Queen on *Amos 'n' Andy*—assumed the lead for the rest of the 1951–52 radio season. The producers signaled a preference for her sibling, Amanda, then playing Saffire's feisty Mama on *Amos 'n' Andy*, but she was temporarily unavailable due to contractual obligations. As soon as she was free,

however, Amanda Randolph took over the lead and maintained it for the rest of the run, from 1952 to 1954, when *Beulah* left the airwaves permanently.[22] During its final season the program was renamed *The New Beulah Show*, its fourth audio-only moniker, and aired a quarter-hour later than its customary seven o'clock. On television, meanwhile, it was always dubbed *The Beulah Show*.

The Randolph sisters were natives of Louisville, Kentucky. Amanda was born September 2, 1896, and Lillian followed on December 14, 1898. Both achieved measures of success on the stage and in films.

Lillian was the more prolific on the screen, appearing in over 50 movies between 1938 and 1979, and more than a dozen television roles, including the 1977 TV miniseries *Roots*, where she was Sister Sara. Her motion picture titles included *Life Goes On* (1938), *West Point Widow* (1941), *Gentleman from Dixie* (1941), *Cooks and Crooks* (1942), *The Great Gildersleeve* (1942), *It's a Wonderful Life* (1946), *Once More, My Darling* (1949), *Hush Hush, Sweet Charlotte* (1964), *How to Seduce a Woman* (1974) and *Once Is Not Enough* (1975). Lillian Randolph died in Los Angeles on September 12, 1980.

Her sibling, Amanda, was a comedienne in black vaudeville. Her first on-screen appearance came in the Vitaphone two-reeler *The Black Network* (1935). Following parts in a few all-black feature films, she became established as a network radio character actress. Of Amanda's 28 screen appearances, half were in celluloid renditions, while the rest were in TV, mostly single outings. Among her films were bit parts in *She's Working Her Way through College* (1952), *Mr. Scoutmaster* (1953), *A Man Called Peter* (1955) and *A Pocketful of Miracles* (1961). In addition to *Beulah* on radio she played the Kingfish's domineering mother in TV's *Amos 'n' Andy* (1951–53) and filled the maid's role on *Make Room for Daddy* for a decade. Amanda Randolph died in Duarte, California, on August 24, 1967.

The recurring radio cast in *Beulah*'s halcyon days, in the meantime—in addition to the principals already mentioned—included seasoned actors Hugh Studebaker and Jess Kirkpatrick as Harry Henderson; veteran Mary Jane Croft and Lois Corbett as Alice Henderson; Henry Blair and Sammy Ogg as their son Donnie Henderson; Ernest Whitman as Bill Jackson; and Ruby Dandridge as Oriole. Most of the successors to the original players were installed following the tumultuous period when Hattie McDaniel hovered between life and death, and transcriptions of previous shows were routinely inserted into the broadcast schedule. As actors depending on work for their livelihood, several moved on to other assignments and were replaced as new episodes resumed. Only Whitman and Dandridge remained from the original cast when the show ended in 1954. Several Negro members of a supporting company were borrowed from a cadre of *Amos 'n' Andy* performers.

The show's mainstay announcers were the ubiquitous Marvin Miller (1947–53) and Johnny Jacobs (1953–54). Miller was instantly recognized by audio listeners of that era. In his lifetime, "the man of a thousand voices" was heard on at least 88 continuing radio network series as announcer, actor, master of ceremonies or commentator. He was also a popular television figure, where he was associated with nearly a score of continuing series and made-for-TV films, and played in 76 big-screen movies. Miller may be best recalled as Michael Anthony, secretary to the benevolent mythical John Beresford Tipton, on CBS-TV's *The Millionaire* weekly from 1955 to 1960. Born Marvin Mueller on July 18, 1913, at St. Louis, Missouri, the legendary performer died February 8, 1985, at Santa Monica, California.

Johnny Jacobs, meanwhile, was born June 22, 1916, at Milwaukee, Wisconsin. He died three years before Miller and on the same day, February 8, at Los Angeles. Over his professional lifetime Jacobs introduced no less than a score of national radio series and half that number on television, proving his mettle as an interlocutor in dual mediums. He was still presenting daytime game shows on multiple networks as late as 1975.

*Beulah* emanated from a rented studio located at 6000 Sunset Boulevard in Hollywood on the southwest corner of Gordon and Sunset. While the structure is still standing in the modern era, its space has been converted into offices. Before *Beulah* became a prerecorded program in its later years, the quarter-hour sitcom originated live at 4 o'clock Pacific Time each weekday afternoon (aired over CBS at 7 P.M. in the East). Stuart Lubin, a vintage radio buff today who was often in *Beulah's* live studio audience when he was a teen, remembers some of those experiences. "In order to get in to see *Beulah*," he recalled, "you had to be in before 'lockdown' at 3:45. I knew many of the guest relations staff, or ushers, and they made many an exception for me. Sometimes I couldn't get there until 3:53 or so. I still got in. [Announcer] Marvin's warm-up was only about six minutes."

Hattie McDaniel and the others playing Beulah had a microphone at stage left. The glass-enclosed operational "fishbowl" was located above stage left, with sound effects at stage right. Two other microphones were situated at center stage for the other actors and the announcer. McDaniel would enter the stage attired in a small apron, obviously for benefit of the studio audience. Among all the regular performers, Lubin remembered that McDaniel cared enough about the fans to linger following each broadcast and to mingle with the studio audience, shaking hands, hugging, engaging in friendly exchanges, answering questions, posing for pictures and signing autographs. "On most days most of the others departed hurriedly when the show ended," Lubin observed. "But not Hattie. She was there maybe 30 minutes afterward, as long as somebody wanted to talk."[23]

McDaniel and her peers brought a smile to the faces of millions who regularly tuned in to her antics every weeknight during postwar America and the Korean epoch—people seeking a little hilarity to cap off what might have been a stressful day. *Beulah* on radio introduced blissful repartee with familiar characters to the nation's living rooms just before television became all-pervasive.

Some authorities have speculated that the individuals who openly disparaged Beulah's portrayal of American blacks quite possibly didn't listen to the radio incarnation habitually, nor watch the televersion. The Caucasian family for whom Beulah was employed consistently found themselves in quandaries they were unprepared for. Again and again they turned to the resolute determination, innate astuteness and unwavering ability of Beulah to pull them out of the fire. McDaniel was a charming comedienne as she delivered her little tribe from the throes of trouble and harm. Beulah clearly maintained affection for the benighted family, and they appreciated her for it. And legions of Americans laughed with her as she applied common sense answers to the Hendersons' anguished calls of distress.

# 7

# *Blondie*

## Don't Touch That Dial

*Blondie* is ostensibly the most widely circulated comic strip in history, its characters having appeared in several other formats. One of the most enduring (and endearing) was radio. Although the show was named for the matriarch of the Bumstead family—as was the comic strip from which it sprang—it was nonetheless unambiguously about the clan's patriarch, Dagwood, and the fumbling foibles in which he found himself (and how the rest of the characters reacted to him). Dagwood Bumstead was a clumsy husband and father who found a way to foul up everything. In terms of ineptness—a quality often ascribed to his gender in radio—he could be certified as Exhibit A. His intents may have been honorable, but he misunderstood the simplest of issues every single time. His idiosyncrasies were never annoying; instead, they came off as witty, resulting in running gags like the mammoth sandwiches he constructed, his physical run-ins with the postman, and exchanges with an irritable-but-lovable superior at work. If a task could be done wrong, slowly or in a complicated fashion, Dagwood filled the bill with clueless abandon. Meanwhile—unlike virtually all of the rival sitcoms that transferred to TV—the *Blondie* radio show simply put its video efforts to shame. The feature never played well on the tube, an ironic development, since it drifted into radio *after* a trio of long-running visual formats—comic strip, movies and comic books. Radio frequently didn't fare well when it competed under such circumstances. In *Blondie*'s case, however, the aural manifestation prevailed for more than a decade, running absolute rings around everything the small screen generated in multiple, flawed attempts.

❖ ❖ ❖

**Creator:** Murat Bernard (Chic) Young
**Producer-Writer:** Ashmead Scott
**Directors:** Eddie Pola, Don Bernard, Glenhall Taylor
**Writers:** Johnny Greene, William Moore
**Orchestra Leaders:** Harry Lubin, Billy Artz
**Sound Effects Technicians:** Ray Erlenborn (1939–48), Parker Cornel (1948–49)
**Announcers:** Bill Goodwin, Howard Petrie, Harlow Wilcox, Ken Niles
**Recurring Cast:** *Dagwood Bumstead:* Arthur Lake (nee Arthur Patrick Silverlake, Jr.); *Blondie Bumstead:* Penny Singleton (1939–46), Alice White (ca. 1946–ca. 1948), Ann Rutherford (1948–50), Patricia Van Cleve (1949); *Alexander (Baby Dumpling) Bumstead:* Leone Ledoux (child impersonator, 1939–43), Tommy Cook (1943–46), Larry Sims (1946–ca. 47), Bobby Ellis (1947), Jeffrey Silver (1949–50); *Cookie Bumstead:* Leone Ledoux (child impersonator, ca. 1942–ca. 1946), Marlene Ames (1946–ca. 1947), Norma Jean Nilsson (1947–ca. 1949), Joan Rae (ca. 1949–50); *Julius C. (J.C.) Dithers:* Hanley Stafford, Arthur Q. Bryan; *Cora Dithers:* Elvia Allman; *Herb Woodley:* Frank Nelson, Harold Peary (ca. 1949–50); *Mr. Fuddle:* Arthur Q. Bryan, Harry Lang; *Alvin Fuddle:* Dix Davis; *Harriet:* Mary Jane Croft; *Dimples Wilson:* Viola Vonn, Lurene Tuttle
**Supporting Cast:** Rosemary DeCamp, Ed MacDonald, Hans Conried
**Sponsor:** R.J. Reynolds Tobacco Company, for Camel cigarettes and Prince Albert pipe tobacco (1939–44); Colgate-Palmolive-Peet, Inc., for Super

Suds detergent, Colgate dental cream, Lustre Crème shampoo, and other household and personal hygiene commodities (1944–49); Sustained (1949–50)

**Themes:** The music used to introduce *Blondie* is believed to be an original and unnamed composition.

**Ratings:** High—17.3 (1946–47), Low—10.4 (1948–49), Median—14.0. Ratings based on 10 complete seasons, 1939–49 inclusive.

**On the Air:** July 3, 1939–June 22, 1942, CBS, Monday, 7:30–8:00 P.M. Eastern Time; September 28, 1942–June 26, 1944, CBS, Monday, 7:30–8:00 P.M.; July 21–September 1, 1944, ABC, Friday, 7:00–7:30 P.M.; August 13, 1944–August 19, 1945, CBS, Sunday, 8:00–8:30 P.M.; August 26, 1945–September 26, 1948, CBS, Sunday, 7:30–8:00 P.M.; October 6, 1948–June 29, 1949, NBC, Wednesday, 8:00–8:30 P.M.; October 6, 1949–May 4, 1950, ABC, Thursday, 8:00–8:30 P.M.; May 11–July 6, 1950, ABC, Thursday, 8:30–9:00 P.M.

**Extant Archival Material:** A single script (unidentified by date) of *Blondie* is maintained in the Script Collection at the Broadcast Arts Library, Box 9828, Fort Worth, TX, 76147; (310) 288–6511; www.broadcastartslibrary.com.

A single script of *Blondie* for the broadcast of April 22, 1940, is included in the Broadcasting Collection of the Thousand Oaks Library, American Radio Archives, 1401 East Janss Road, Thousand Oaks, CA, 91362; (805) 449–2660; fax (805) 449–2675; *www.tol.lib.ca.us.*

Thirty-one recordings of *Blondie* shows were in general circulation or held by private collectors as of 2006, sold by vintage radio dealers and traded by old-time radio hobbyists.

❖ ❖ ❖

This show, which originated in the comics, had so many adaptations it's certainly possible to forget some of them. Beyond the newsprint, there are comic books; a novel; extensive merchandise, including toys, games, clothing and a myriad of additional representations; a sequence of 28 films, one of the most enduring such series in movie history; an 11-year audio run; two pithy televised manifestations; a postage stamp; a Library of Congress exhibition; a signature sandwich now repeatedly mentioned in dictionaries; a chain of restaurants; a website; and at least the possibility—although it hasn't materialized as of this writing—of a stage musical production.

The diverse variations are simply mind-boggling. But who's counting?

*Blondie* was one of the earliest—and longest lasting—sitcoms on the aural ether. Everything you've ever heard about the husband/father/male character being the boob in a show is realized here. Although it was named for the woman playing his wife, the series is, and always was, about the zany individual wearing the pants in the family (only one did in those days, incidentally). Dagwood Bumstead, Blondie's counterpart, was the nitwit who routinely crossed swords with his superior, J.C. Dithers, at the Dithers Construction Company. Bumstead often practiced his tomfoolery there, where he was sometimes employed as an accountant, except when Dithers fired him—more times than a dog has fleas. According to *Radio Life*, "His charm is that he's so splendidly weak, he makes us feel less lonely." Often it was up to his striking, empty-headed better half to plead for the restoration of his job.

Not only that, Bumstead had a knack for creating misunderstandings with his precocious offspring, Alexander and Cookie, as well as his wife. Let's face it: wherever he went, trouble was certain to follow. It was in the *process* of righting his wrongs that the series became endearing to so many who were already exposed to it in print.

"Perfect casting," according to one source, made the difference. Arthur Lake and Penny Singleton fit the Dagwood and Blondie figures so ideally in most of the spin-off adaptations that they could have "easily been Chic Young's inspiration for the comic strip instead of the other way around."[1] Young introduced his characters to American newspaper readers in 1930. They turned up on the silver screen eight years later, and in radio the following year.

Murat Bernard Young, who permanently began calling himself Chic in 1925, although he had been nicknamed Chic as a boy, was born in Chicago on January 9, 1901. His mother, a painter, and father, a shoe store proprietor, encouraged their children in artistic development. The family moved to St.

Louis while Chic was a boy. Chic's older brother, Lyman, grew up to create the comic strip *Tim Tyler's Luck*, which persisted from 1928 to 1996, subsequently produced by his son Bob in its final dozen years following Lyman's death in 1984. That strip also inspired a 12-part movie serial in 1937, a precedent that wasn't lost on his sibling.

When Chic graduated from high school he began seeking work in the field of art. Instead, he found employment with railroads and became a stenographer there. Eventually that took him back to Chicago, where he earned a living in the daytime and studied art at night. After creating the comic strips *The Affairs of Jane* (ca. 1921) and *Beautiful Bab* (1922), in early 1923 Young was hired as a $22-a-week artist with the Cleveland syndicate Newspaper Enterprise Association. Not many months later he was picked up by the venerated King Features syndicate, where he initially filled in for artists who needed a substitute. There he gained valuable tutoring that couldn't have been purchased. By 1924 he sold another comic strip invention, *Dumb Dora*, to King. He would subsequently create *Blondie* (which began running on September 8, 1930, a strip he wisely maintained the rights to), *The Family Foursome* (1931) and *Colonel Potterby and the Duchess* (1935). The latter, his most durable following *Blondie*, was in print 28 years, a bonus strip that appeared in many papers on Sundays running above *Blondie*.

Chic Young married concert harpist Athel Lindorff on October 1, 1927. One of their children, Dean, born in 1937, was destined to succeed his father as the guardian of the *Blondie* comic strip. In the meantime, the family relocated to Hollywood in 1938 as Columbia Pictures was about to start filming the series of *Blondie* motion pictures. The Youngs left California for Florida during Dean's senior year in high school and never departed the Sunshine State, putting down permanent roots at Clearwater. By 1949 *Time* reported that Chic Young was earning $300,000 annually for his creation, turning a personal fortune into an empire and ultimately into a dynasty.[2]

As Chic continued to produce the strip, Dean went to college, graduating to serve on the staff of a Miami advertising agency. After a couple of years Dean resigned to become a sales promotion executive. When his father suggested that he come home to work with him on the comic strip, the younger Young remembers, "I couldn't get packed quickly enough." They labored side by side for a decade, until Chic Young succumbed to a pulmonary embolism on March 14, 1973, at St. Petersburg. He was 72.

As if losing his father—in whom he took great delight—wasn't bad enough, Dean learned that shortly after Chic's passing more than 600 of the 1,600 newspapers carrying the strip in 60 nations were canceling. It was nearly a 40 percent loss in visibility and revenue, a crushing blow to the heir apparent. But in the years since, the departing 600 papers were regained, and 700 new outlets have been added. "I think some of that momentum can be attributed to the characters not becoming anachronisms," said Dean Young, who produces the seven-day-a-week strip in his Clearwater studio with artist Denis Lebrun. The feature currently boasts in excess of 280 million daily readers who follow it in 35 translations in 55 nations around the globe.

At its inception *Blondie* was quite a long way from the suburban environment in which it was to thrive. It actually premiered as a "girlie" strip about Blondie Boopadoop, a flighty, unconventional flapper of the 1920s who was courted by an affluent young heir, Dagwood. His folks disparaged the object of his affections, however, judging her to be beneath their social status. The creative mastermind behind *Blondie*, meanwhile, decided that the Jazz Age figures were becoming immaterial to many readers. In 1933, at the peak of the Great Depression, he wed Blondie and Dagwood and re-focused the strip on their challenges as newlyweds. Dagwood's well-heeled dad cut his son off without a cent, giving the couple a serious trial to confront. Readers embraced the new emphasis on domesticity, and it carried over into the movies, radio and other formats.

Chic Young developed a simple formula for *Blondie*'s plotting from which he seldom strayed. It encompassed a quartet of basic themes: eating, sleeping, raising a family and making a living. The most popular running gags in all of *Blondie*'s various incarnations were Dagwood's confrontations with an irascible but kindhearted Mr. Dithers, battles with itinerant door-to-door salesmen, physical collisions with the postman on the Bumsteads' route, frequent naps, encounters with the dog Daisy and the creation of a Dagwood sandwich containing a monumental amount of leftovers unsteadily stuffed between two pieces of bread. Those indiscriminate culinary innovations, incidentally, became famous in their own right, with the Dagwood included today in some versions of Webster's various dictionaries and labeled "a multilayered sandwich." Despite the updates, the traditional values of life, love, family and work persist.

Dean Young, who speaks of his father almost reverently, calling him "my daddy, the genius, who created this wonderful cast of characters," has gradually updated the Bumsteads. The couple talks on cell phones today, while Blondie operates a catering enterprise and owns a notebook computer. Dagwood has a computer at work, and—instead of hurrying to catch a bus to his job—he carpools now. Young has also launched a restaurant franchise company fostering a chain of Dagwood's Sandwich Shoppes, extending the life of the enveloping brand by giving it still greater visibility.

The Bumsteads remain frozen in their late thirties with two adolescent offspring. Will they grow older? "Not in my lifetime," vows Young. In an age of social upheaval, rocked by divorce and dysfunction, Blondie and Dagwood offer stability. "Here's a family where they actually like each other," Young affirms. "The husband and wife are still in love with each other. He kisses her when he leaves, and kisses her when he comes home. It's fun to look in on a family that actually is going through life in a loving, affectionate way. It's kind of a confidence builder."

Decades after the strip's inception, a newspaper writer provided this assessment of the pulp feature that inspired the radio incarnation:

> Like a lapidary with the gift of magic, Chic Young polished the drab ore of domestic and workaday life into a celebration of the human condition so glowing with warm humor that it attracted and was welcomed by a near-global audience.
>
> Through the Bumstead family ... millions of readers saw the vexations and concerns of life reflected and softened by wit.[3]

Even though *Blondie* celebrated its 75th birthday in 2005, it's still not the most durable of America's comic strips. *Blondie* and five strips ahead of it in longevity were honored with their own U.S. postage stamps in 1995:

1. *Katzenjammer Kids* (since 1897)
2. *Gasoline Alley* (since 1918)
3. *Barney Google and Snuffy Smith* (since 1919)
4. *Thimble Theater/Popeye* (since 1919)
5. *Little Orphan Annie* (since 1924)

*Blondie* premiered on radio via a comedic vignette performed on NBC's *Bob Hope Show* for Pepsodent toothpaste on a Tuesday night in December 1938. From that humble start, plus the momentum of the newly-released *Blondie* movie (which grossed $9 million), the radio embodiment emerged. The first airing of the series occurred six months later. Adopting the thespian principals in the films, it was heard over CBS on Monday, July 3, 1939. It continued for 11 years, even forgoing the traditional warm-weather holiday break normally accorded most season-long entries in seven of those summers (1940, 1941, 1943, 1945, 1946, 1947, 1948). That suggests it was perceived as a hot property, and, in fact, it was: in its first decade on the ether its numbers never fell out of double digits; for half of those years they reached 15.0 or above, a consistently strong showing when compared with some of its competition throughout the 1940s.

On the air, *Blondie* arrived with a unique trumpeting:

Despite idiosyncrasies aplenty and all manner of machinations that may have left audiences wondering which character really was the most aberrant, "Here's a family," said Dean Young, son of Blondie's creator, "where they actually like each other. The husband and wife are still in love with each other. He kisses her when he leaves, and kisses her when he comes home. It's fun to look in on a family that actually is going through life in a loving, affectionate way." Penny Singleton (shown) portrayed the allegedly dizzy blonde namesake role throughout most of the durable radio run, while Arthur Lake was always heard as her lame-brained spouse, Dagwood Bumstead.

ANNOUNCER: *Uh-uh-uh-uh ... Don't touch that dial! Listen to...*

DAGWOOD (bellows): *B-L-O-N-N-N-D-E-E-E!*

Indeed, maybe you *had* to see them. But isn't that why they labeled radio the Theater of the Mind?

The 28 movies in the *Blondie* series and their release dates, which may be the longest running comic strip-inspired series in cinematic history, were:

*Blondie* (1938)
*Blondie Meets the Boss* (1939)
*Blondie Takes a Vacation* (1939)
*Blondie Brings Up Baby* (1939)
*Blondie on a Budget* (1940)
*Blondie Has Servant Trouble* (1940)
*Blondie Plays Cupid* (1940)
*Blondie Goes Latin* (1941)
*Blondie in Society* (1941)
*Blondie Goes to College* (1942)
*Blondie's Blessed Event* (1942)
*Blondie for Victory* (1942)
*It's a Great Life* (1943)
*Footlight Glamour* (1943)
*Leave It to Blondie* (1945)
*Life with Blondie* (1945)
*Blondie's Lucky Day* (1946)
*Blondie Knows Best* (1946)
*Blondie's Big Moment* (1947)
*Blondie's Holiday* (1947)
*Blondie in the Dough* (1947)
*Blondie's Anniversary* (1947)
*Blondie's Reward* (1948)
*Blondie's Secret* (1948)
*Blondie's Big Deal* (1949)
*Blondie Hits the Jackpot* (1949)
*Blondie's Hero* (1950)
*Beware of Blondie* (1950)

There was no shortage of pundits eager to review the motion picture series. The radio installments often seemed like abbreviated editions of the movies, incidentally. Here's a typical appraisal of the movies:

Plotwise, the appealing characteristic of the *Blondie* films is Dagwood's knack for getting himself into trouble. Just when you think he's gotten into enough trouble for one film, and

the rest of it should be spent getting out of it, he gets in still more trouble. And more trouble. And then some more. And still more. Sometimes Blondie pulls him out of it, sometimes blind luck does the job, but regardless, we can't help but laugh and sympathize, laugh and sympathize. Through it all, one thing is certain: the Bumstead family will hang together through thick and thin; their blatant refusal to accept defeat is a quality that can only be admired. Their characters are reflections of ourselves; perhaps another element of the series' appeal rests in how we identify with them and cheer when they pull through in the end. And it helps, of course, that most of the films are outright hilarious.[4]

The televersions, on the other hand, could never be regarded by any gauge as the hit that *Blondie* became on the cartoon pages, in the cinema houses and on radio. Two attempts to transfer the outlandish antics of the bumbling Bumstead and his tribe to the small screen ended in colossal failures. Could it have had anything to do with the casting?

In the first venture on NBC, from January 4 to September 27, 1957 (just 26 episodes aired in that period), only radio's Arthur Lake (Dagwood) and one of the actors who played neighbor Herb Woodley (Hal Peary) crossed the chasm to video. The other thespians taking familiar roles were unfamiliar to the viewers: Pamela Britton, who had never appeared in the movies or on radio, was the new Blondie. Other nondescript names replaced long-running actors who performed as Alexander, Cookie and J.C. Dithers.

A second attempt on the tube was an even bigger fiasco, persisting on CBS from September 26, 1968 to January 9, 1969 only, a mere 13 weeks (minus holiday preemptions). Nobody, including Arthur Lake, who had *always* been Dagwood, transferred from film, radio or the first TV stab to that production. Lake, by then 63, was replaced by Will Hutchins as Dagwood; Patricia Harty was Blondie; and all of the other roles except Dithers (played by Jim Backus) featured total unknowns.

A second contributing factor in the quick demise of both TV incarnations is the fact that too much time passed between the popularity of the radio program and its transfer to television. Audiences had simply moved on. Seven years had elapsed between the demise of the radio series and the launching of the NBC-TV incarnation. People had many more options to which they could devote their time. When the second show arrived on CBS-TV, the radio feature had been history for practically a generation (18 years): many had never even heard of it, while others dismissed it or possibly had even forgotten it. *Ozzie and Harriet* and *Father Knows Best*'s Jim and Margaret Anderson had long since relieved them of a frenetic need to be re-charged by the lame-brained antics of Dagwood and Blondie Bumstead. As audiences lapsed into more lethargic family contentment, the funny business of the 1940s seemed light years behind.

Arthur Patrick Silverlake, Jr., the man who brought Dagwood Bumstead to life in 28 films and a brief TV feature, and enunciated the character for 11 years on radio, said he loved it so much that "how nice it would be if the show could just go on forever." Born April 17, 1905, at Corbin, Kentucky, Silverlake (who eventually simplified his moniker to Arthur Lake) was the product of a couple of performers—acrobatic strongman Arthur Silverlake, Sr. and his legitimate stage actress spouse Edith Goodwin. The nomadic Silverlakes made the rounds of small-time tent shows and lived in a handful of states in Dixieland (South Carolina, Kentucky, Alabama, Tennessee). At the time of Junior's birth, his dad and uncle performed in an aerial act as "the Flying Silverlakes," touring with a road show circus.

Young Arthur's veins flowed with greasepaint quite early: at age one he was carried before the footlights for an ice-jumping scene in a backwater production of *Uncle Tom's Cabin*. He and his sibling, Florence, who also became a thespian of some repute, joined the performing Silverlakes in 1910. After the clan abandoned circus theatrics for vaudeville, they traversed the South and Southwest. In 1917 they settled in southern California

where Arthur Silverlake, Jr. premiered on the silver screen in the silent film *Jack and the Beanstalk*. He subsequently turned up in a plethora of collegiate musicals and westerns, eventually landing a superior role in the 1925 movie *Skinner's Dress Suit*. He signed for a series of *Sweet Sixteen* comedies with Universal Pictures; three years later he played the namesake role in *Harold Teen*, a foretaste of things to come: it was based on a popular comic strip figure of that epoch. A movie veteran by then, within a decade Arthur Jr. was proficient in radio, too.

Lake's celluloid output persevered with the talkies *Dance Hall* (1929), *Cheer Up and Smile* (1930), *Indiscreet* (1931), *Silver Streak* (1934), *Orchids to You* (1935) and *Topper* (1937), among others. He was freelancing when he heard that Columbia Pictures planned a string of low-budget flicks adapted from the *Blondie* comics and was seeking an actor to portray Dagwood Bumstead. Some two dozen leading Hollywood men tested for the part. "But I had a couple of people rooting for me," Lake divulged. It was heavy artillery.

In silent films Lake became known for playing boyish characters, and when he got into talkies his boyish characters were made even funnier by giving them squeaky voices. He met the lady who would become his wife at actress Marion Davies' beach house. Patricia Van Cleve was her niece, and when Lake married Van Cleve, he was Marion Davies' nephew by marriage. Marion Davies ... was courted by the powerful newspaper publisher William Randolph Hearst. [Lake was a pal of Hearst's sons and was thereby a frequent guest at Marion Davies' beach house.] William owned King Features, which published the "Blondie" comic strip. With these two powerful people [Davies and Hearst] in Arthur Lake's corner, he was able to get the much-deserved attention needed to star as Dagwood Bumstead in the Blondie movies....

One evening Lake, his wife and Ms. Davies were at Ciro's night club when Harry Cohn came over to their table. Cohn, who was noted for his rudeness and gaucheries, was the head of Columbia Pictures, which produced the "Blondie" pictures. "Well, Marion," said Cohn, "thanks to me your nephew is now a star. What do you think about that?" Without missing a beat, Marion Davies replied, "You son of a bitch! Thanks to my nephew and the success of those movies, your studio is still in business."[5]

For the first seven years of the radio series, and for all 28 of the movies, actress Penny Singleton appeared as Blondie. After she left the radio show (for a while) to pursue other acting opportunities, one of her temporary replacements was Patricia Van Cleve, Marion Davies' niece, on whom she obviously doted—Patricia was the daughter of Davies' sister Rose. And, of course, Patricia was Arthur Lake's wife.

Some confusion exists among radio historiographers about who succeeded Penny Singleton as Blondie and when. Various sources denote a quartet playing that part (Penny Singleton, Alice White, Patricia Van Cleve, Ann Rutherford), but—even when mentioning all four—they often do so in differing sequences. In 2005 a radio cast member, Jeff Silver, sorted it out again, but without mention of Alice White: "Arthur Lake's wife did not replace Penny Singleton on the radio show. She was replaced by Ann Rutherford for the rest of the run of the show on NBC. When the show moved to ABC his wife did play Blondie on the opening program, but was quickly replaced by Ann Rutherford for the rest of the season, which was the last of the run. By the way, I should know. I was the last boy to play the part of Alexander ... from 1948 through 1950."[6] White appears to have played Blondie after Singleton and before Rutherford. It's certainly possible, though thus far not definitively documented, that Van Cleve also performed in that era, too.

A Wampas Baby star in 1940, Patricia and her husband Arthur Lake maintained a huge home only a few doors from Davies' palatial waterfront estate. The Lakes had two children, Arthur III, who subsequently occupied his parents' house with his own children, and daughter Marion, who moved to Paris in adulthood. In later years Arthur Jr. and Patricia had six grandchildren and 12 dogs, the youngest of which was named "Baby Dumpling." Arthur Jr. died of a heart attack at Indian Wells, California, on January 9, 1987. He was 81.

Penny Singleton, meanwhile, the woman who—more than any other actress—is recalled for bringing *Blondie* to life, was born Mariana Dorothy Agnes Letitia McNulty on September 15, 1908, at Philadelphia. Her Irish journalist dad, Benny McNulty, was kin to Jim Farley, Franklin Roosevelt's campaign manager and eventually the U.S. Postmaster General. In early life Dorothy sang at a silent movie cinema. By the seventh grade she was a member of "the Kiddie Kabaret," a touring vaudeville troupe. She vocalized on Broadway in the following years.

In the 1930s she made her way to Hollywood, accredited as Dorothy McNulty in early films like 1936's *After the Thin Man*. "They threw parts at me that Claire Trevor didn't want," she acknowledged. Trevor was widely recognized for portraying movie bad girls. Still single as her thirties approached, in 1937 Dorothy wed a dentist, Dr. Lawrence Scogga Singleton. Seeking a new professional show business moniker, she selected Penny Singleton (she collected pennies at the time). It stuck with her the rest of her life.

Other movies followed. She acted, sang and danced in 1938's *Swing Your Lady* shortly before being picked to play Blondie Bumstead opposite Arthur Lake. The following year (1939) she and Dr. Lawrence Singleton divorced. By then they were parents of a daughter. Penny Singleton married Robert Sparks in 1941; he produced the first dozen *Blondie* films. He was still her spouse when he died on July 22, 1963. They had a child together, too, and Penny Singleton Sparks never remarried.

*The Penny Singleton Show*, a summer replacement sitcom carried by NBC Radio, appeared from May to September 1950. While Singleton continued to act on stage, her most acclaimed role beyond *Blondie* was Jane Jetson. It was a voiceover portrayal for the animated television series *The Jetsons* that seemed to persist forever. It ran in 1962–64 on ABC, 1964–65 on CBS, 1965–67 on NBC, 1969–71 on CBS, 1971–76 on NBC, 1979–81 on NBC, 1982–83 on NBC, and in syndication in both 1985 and 1987. That was followed by a 1990 silver screen production, *Jetsons: The Movie*.

In the meantime, Singleton, by then again living in New York, took a major role in instigating the Radio City Music Hall Rockettes' first strike ever in 1966, which led to improved working conditions. Three years afterward she was named president of the American Guild of Variety Artists, becoming the first of her gender to head a union affiliated with the powerful AFL-CIO. St. John's University bestowed the honorary Doctor of Fine Arts degree on her in 1974. Two years later, Arthur Lake, then 71, and Penny Single-ton, 67, were reunited for a Milwaukee stage production of *No, No, Nanette*. She died at Sherman Oaks, California, at age 95, on November 12, 2003, from complications of a stroke.

Radio's *Blondie* expired nearly six decades ago. Yet, for those with long memories who were around then, there is still a weekly or daily reminder of its existence in the comic pages of America's newspapers. Few other shows could make a similar claim. It's a pleasant reverie, carrying readers back to an era when one could hear (and see) Dagwood's convoluted contortions via the Theater of the Mind.

# 8

# *Duffy's Tavern*

## THE LITTLE MAN WHO WASN'T THERE

"Archie is just Gardner," said the creator-writer-producer-star of *Duffy's Tavern*, Ed Gardner. Gardner really had no intention of being a performer when he gave birth to the idea of the barkeep Archie in 1938. He desperately sought a thespian who could speak Brooklynese (a native dialect with origins embedded in the real estate between Staten Island and Queens, New York). But repeated auditions didn't turn up the voice he sought. In desperation he demonstrated what he was looking for to the applicants. Not until he glanced through the window into the studio control room did it finally dawn on him that, so far, only *he* had been able to give the character the inflection he was after. He realized it after witnessing the facial expressions and hearing the guffaws of the technical crew looking on. Gardner crafted an exceedingly amusing series that lasted nearly 11 years. The show became the curse of English teachers everywhere as he screwed up modern speech with relish. Flanked by a coterie of wacko sidekicks who were fixtures at the East Side watering hole, Archie—running the joint for an unseen proprietor—possessed an innate ability to disparage anybody who needed it. That included a stream of Hollywood icons, plus some other performing vets from diverse venues that dropped by to feel his needle. It was all in good fun, of course, and the celebrities saw it as an honor. Archie's alter ego, in the meantime, rose to fame and fortune. Gardner

proved a shrewd businessman who kept much of his focus on the bottom line. While some of his methods were dubious, he delivered a show that could be counted on for riotous belly laughs every time out.

❖ ❖ ❖

**Creator-Producer:** Ed Gardner (nee Edward Fredrick Poggenburg)

**Directors:** Rupert Lucas, Jack Roche, Tony Sanford, Mitchell Benson

**Writers:** Abe Burrows, Larry Marks, Larry Gelbart, Ed Reynolds, Norman Paul, Lew Meltzer, Dick Martin, Vincent Bogert, Manny Sachs, Alan Kent, Bill Manhoff, Raymond Ellis, Lou Grant, Bob Schiller, Larry Rhine, Sol Saks, more (dialogue and gags); Ed Gardner (final scripts)

**Orchestra Leaders:** John Kirby (ca. 1941–ca. 1944), Peter Van Steeden (ca. 1944–unsubstantiated date), Joe Venuti, Matty Malneck, Reet Veet Reeves, Walter Gross, Teddy Wilson

**Vocalists:** Johnny Johnston, Benay Venuta, Helen Ward, Bob Graham, Tito Guizar, Clark Dennis

**Sound Effects Technician:** Virgil Reimer (1944–51)

**Announcers:** John Reed King, Jimmy Wallington, Marvin Miller, Jack Bailey, Rod O'Connor, Perry Ward, Dan Seymour, Jay Stewart

**Recurring Cast:** *Archie:* Ed Gardner; *Miss Duffy:* Shirley Booth (March 1941–June 1943), Florence Halop (October 1943–March 1944, ca. late 1947–48), Helen Lynd (April–May 1944), Doris Singleton (May 1944), Sara Berner (May 1944), Connie Manning (May–June 1944), Florence Robinson (September–November 1944), Sandra Gould (November 1944–June 1947), Helen Eley (October-November 1947), Margie Liszt (November 1947–ca.

late 1947), Gloria Erlanger (ca. 1948–February 1949), Hazel Shermet (February 1949–ca. 1951), Pauline Drake (ca. 1951); *Clifton Finnegan:* Charlie Cantor, Sid Raymond; *Eddie:* Eddie Green, Sam Raskin; *Clancy:* Alan Reed (nee Herbert Theodore Bergman); *Colonel Stoopnagle:* F. Chase Taylor; *Wilfred Finnegan:* Dickie Van Patten; *Dolly Snaffle:* Lurene Tuttle

**Supporting Cast:** Bea Benaderet

**Sponsors:** Rainbow, Inc., for Schick dry shavers (1941–January 29, 1942); General Foods Corporation, for Sanka decaffeinated coffee (February 5–June 30, 1942); Bristol-Myers, Inc., for Ipana toothpaste, Sal-Hepatica stomach distress reliever, Trushay hand lotion, Minit-Rub muscle-relaxing liniment, Vitalis men's hair grooming preparation and other personal hygiene and health care commodities (1942–49); Blatz Brewing Co., for Blatz beer (1949–50); Multiple Participation (1950–51)

**Theme:** "When Irish Eyes Are Smiling"

**Ratings:** High—19.6 (1946–47), Low—6.7 (1941–42, 1950–51), Median—13.5. Ratings based on full seasons, 1941–51 inclusive.

**On the Air:** March 1–June 14, 1941, CBS, Saturday, 8:30–9:00 P.M. Eastern Time; September 18, 1941–March 12, 1942, CBS, Thursday, 8:30–9:00 P.M.; March 17–June 30, 1942, CBS, Tuesday, 9:00–9:30 P.M.; October 6, 1942–June 29, 1943, NBC Blue, Tuesday, 8:30–9:00 P.M.; October 5, 1943–June 27, 1944, NBC Blue/ABC, Tuesday, 8:30–9:00 P.M.; September 15, 1944–June 8, 1945, NBC, Friday, 8:30–9:00 P.M.; September 21, 1945–June 14, 1946, NBC, Friday, 8:30–9:00 P.M.; October 2, 1946–June 25, 1947, NBC, Wednesday, 9:00–9:30 P.M.; October 1, 1947–June 23, 1948, NBC, Wednesday, 9:00–9:30 P.M.; October 6, 1948–June 29, 1949, NBC, Wednesday, 9:00–9:30 P.M.; September 29, 1949–September 21, 1950, NBC, Thursday, 9:30–10:00 P.M.; November 10, 1950–April 27, 1951, NBC, Friday, 9:30–10:00 P.M.; October 5–December 28, 1951, NBC, Friday, 9:00–9:30 P.M.; Late 1950s (dates unsubstantiated), NBC, Saturdays and Sundays, between 8:00 a.m. Saturday and 12 midnight Sunday (brief vignettes of a few minutes' duration on *Monitor*, NBC Radio's weekend magazine service)

**Extant Archival Material:**; Bound and unbound scripts of *Duffy's Tavern* aired from 1941 to 1945 are included in the Abe Burrows Papers, 1904–1993, housed at the Billy Rose Theatre Collection of the Performing Arts Library, 40 Lincoln Center Plaza, New York, NY, 10023; (212) 870-1639; fax (212) 870-1868; *www.nypl.org/research/lpa/the/the.html.*

Scripts from *Duffy's Tavern* are included in the Collection of Radio Series Scripts, ca. 1933–1980,

ca. 1940–1959; the Larry Gelbart Papers; the Vincent Bogert Radio and Television Scripts, 1946–1964; and the Jackson Stanley Papers, archived in the Charles E. Young Research Library at the University of California at Los Angeles (UCLA), Box 951575, Los Angeles, CA, 90095; (310) 825-7253; Fax (310) 825-1210; *www.library.ucla.edu/libraries/arts/.*

Scripts, production materials, outlines, synopses, research notes and treatments for various shows, including *Duffy's Tavern*, are among the Hy Freedman Papers, 1945–1978, bulk 1945–1963; the Laurence Marks Papers, 1901–1988, bulk 1940–1988; and the Parke Levy Papers, 1933–1965, archived at the American Heritage Center of the University of Wyoming, 1000 East University Avenue, Laramie, WY, 82071; (307) 766-3756; fax (307) 766-5511; *http://ahc.uwyo.edu/usearchives/default.htm.*

A single script of a *Duffy's Tavern* broadcast is housed among the Script Collection at the Broadcast ARTS Library, Box 9828, Fort Worth, TX, 76147; (310) 288-6511; *www.broadcastartslibrary.com.*

Ninety-six scripts of *Duffy's Tavern* airing between September 13, 1944, and April 6, 1951, are included in the Morris Freedman and Rudy Vallee collections of the Thousand Oaks Library, American Radio Archives, 1401 East Janss Road, Thousand Oaks, CA, 91362; (805) 449-2660; fax (805) 449-2675; *www.tol.lib.ca.us.*

No fewer than 184 recordings of the 30-minute *Duffy's Tavern* shows, plus 53 of the brief segments aired on *Monitor*, are known to be in general circulation or held by private collectors as of 2006, sold by vintage radio dealers and traded by old-time radio hobbyists.

An extensive log and history of *Duffy's Tavern* prepared by Martin Grams, Jr. is available from Bear-Manor Media, Box 71426, Albany, GA, 31708; (229) 436-4265; fax (814) 690-1559.

❖ ❖ ❖

Do you recall the song "The Little Man Who Wasn't There?"[1] Sharing it in the first person, the narrator reveals his encounter with that apparition—not once—but *twice.* Was the little man for real or not?

Duffy was like that. Never seen. Never heard. Only heard *from.* For more than a decade he'd telephone Archie, the manager of the institution bearing his name, as the sitcom that sported a similar sobriquet got rolling every week. While those frequent conversations were all one-sided, Duffy's brusque intervention and ability to be unpleasant rose to the surface. Frankly, with the possible exception of Irish tenors, Duffy was seldom pleased with any idea, person or thing. His minion, meanwhile, weathered his superior's annoyances throughout the episodes as he enumerated names of those he expected to pass through the saloon's doors presently.

The watering hole Duffy owned has been the bane of radio historiographers for years as they derided it with unrestrained abandon. Labeled "the eyesore of the East Side," the establishment which catered to the Irish working crowd—an authentic Irish pub if ever there was one—was physically situated in a seedy slice of downtown Manhattan, New York, ostensibly on Third Avenue at Twenty-Third Street. The joint was little more than "a fly-infested dive," according to one reviewer. "The food was horrible, the service lousy, and the atmosphere dank. The one thing that was kept at a consistently high level at Duffy's was the insanity."[2] True to its ethnic proclivity, some mainstays of its menu were corned beef and cabbage, and pickled pigs' feet. The odors alone could turn some prospective patrons off.

*Duffy's Tavern* sprang from the mind of Ed Gardner, who unintentionally gave voice to the Brooklyn barkeep on an obscure CBS Sunday night series in 1938. Gardner was born Edward Fredrick Poggenburg on June 29, 1901, at Astoria, Long Island.[3] At 14 he briefly played piano in a saloon, a foretaste of things to come, perhaps. The job lasted until his mother caught him there! At 16 he withdrew from Bryant High School and began drifting from one post to another, a diverse "wild ride" that was to persist for a decade. He sustained himself by becoming, among other things, a boxing manager, a stenographer and a salesman extraordinaire. Among the commodities he pushed were pianos, ink, pens, miniature golf courses, typewriters and paint. In 1929 he met and married Shirley Booth. She had also quit school, at 14, to become an actress.

Gardner became a promoter in the publicity department of Crosby Gaige, which led to a post promoting stock companies for Jennie Jacobs. Other opportunities came his way, including summer stock and radio. And that's where everything began to fall into place for him. *Duffy's Tavern* was actually launched when Gardner established the voice of Archie, the Brooklyn barkeep, for an obscure CBS series. He did so in a curious way. He had had considerable exposure in writing, directing, and producing a handful of major network programs in the 1930s, like *Believe It or Not, The Bing Crosby Show, The George Burns and Gracie Allen Show, Good News of 1939, The Al Jolson Show, The Rudy Vallee Show,* et al. That notwithstanding, the critics still assessed him as little more than a third-string actor. "Archie was the making of Gardner," affirmed one.

Parenthetically, in the eight-year period between 1939 and 1947, Gardner made about two dozen radio appearances on series other than his own. Among them: *The Adventures of Ellery Queen, The Columbia Workshop, Texaco Star Theater, Stage Door Canteen, Paul Whiteman Presents, Philco Radio Hall of Fame, Suspense, Command Performance* and *The Alan Young Show.* A number of these featured multiple outings.

Gardner was in Hollywood working on *The Texaco Star Theater* as a director and producer in the radio department at J. Walter Thompson advertising agency when he began to develop *Duffy's Tavern* as a viable project. In late 1938 he created Archie while he was director of the CBS sustaining Sunday night variety hour *This Is New York.* In one portion he intended to feature the voice of a "typical New York mug." But he couldn't find an actor to perform as he thought the part should sound. Less than half an hour before the audition show on July 29, 1940, on the CBS series *Forecast,* he was still hearing potential actors for the part. Deeply frustrated, he took over the microphone, exhibiting how he wanted the dialogue read. Archie surfaced just then. Gardner's obscurity melted into the ether when he donned his apron and battered fedora to welcome the initial guests of *Duffy's Tavern.*

The show was assigned a permanent slot

in the CBS schedule early in 1941, and over the next three-and-a-half months—before a summer break—it began to build an audience. It resurfaced that fall with new listeners acquiring a taste for its madcap brand of comedy. CBS unleashed a flood of press releases to promote the returning series that autumn. The publicists sometimes parodied the craziness of the series they were plugging, as in this epistle issued in September 1941:

### RHYME INSPIRED BY THE OPENING OF A PLACE OF REFINEMENT

I ain't no poet, like the Bard of Avvon
But welcome, folks, to "Duffy's Tavern."
Ladies 'n' gents ... an' kiddies too,
We run our joint for the likes of you.
An' anyone who gets too noisy,
Will wake up in some town in Joisey.
Each Thursday night we take the air.
An' we'll be heard most everywhere.
The network? Only take one guess,
It's coast-to-coast on CBS.
As time goes on, we'll bring you guests,
To entertain with tunes an' jesto.
And Old Man Duffy'll squawk an' moan
About the show, by telephone.
We aim to please an' treat you well,
We have a high-class clientele.
If fun an' music you are havin'
Just tune in on "Duffy's Tavern."
                                        —Archie

The ratings were sufficient to maintain the series for more than a decade, to the end of 1951. In a 10-year span the show's numbers climbed to double digits seven times, an incredibly high percentage. In addition, as was often the case with radio sitcoms, the premise and characters were spun off into a motion picture, released in 1945, and briefly reincarnated as a syndicated television series in 1954—more than two years after it left the aural ether. Furthermore, vignettes of its humorous exchanges appeared on NBC's weekend magazine programming service *Monitor* in the mid-to-late 1950s. While none of the supplementary add-ons reached the level of esteem enjoyed by the radio incarnation, they attested to the triumphs of the fundamental hypothesis.

Wikipedia didn't mince any words when it came to assessing the spin-offs, insisting that "*Duffy's Tavern* didn't translate well to film or TV." Surrounded by more than 30 contract stars at Paramount Studios, the *Duffy* cast seemed rather insignificant, as legends of the silver screen contributed almost nonstop entertainment to the 1945 celluloid production of *Duffy's Tavern*. In the storyline the staff of a war-displaced record manufacturer drowned their sorrows on credit at Duffy's while the firm's proprietor sought means around price controls and war-related attrition that threatened to put them all out of business. In spite of the fact that stars like William Bendix, Joan Caulfield, Bing Crosby, Cass Daley, Betty Hutton, Alan Ladd, Dorothy Lamour and many more turned up to act or put in cameo appearances, the movie was a box-office flop.[4]

While the flick was Ed Gardner's first and last attempt to perform on the big screen, he was perceived by some as dreadful in the televised incarnation which followed. According to radio wordsmith Larry Rhine, the brief video fling was "weighted by Gardner's inability to adapt to camera work." The scribe pontificated: "He couldn't act, and he wouldn't learn camera ... he thought he could do TV, so he left radio, but he was a bad actor and knew it."[5] *TV Guide* opined that the visual format was a "poor adaptation of the popular radio program." For whatever the reason, media scholars Tim Brooks and Earle Marsh omitted any reference to *Duffy's Tavern* or mention of Gardner in the edition we read of their normally reliable and expansive compilation of hundreds of televised series and thousands of entertainers.[6] The tube's syndicated manifestation persisted briefly in 1954. "The radio series had been as much a showcase for guest stars ... as a situation comedy," a television historian clarified. "The TV adaptation was merely the latter."[7]

With the broadcast of October 6, 1942, the radio show was underwritten by its third corporate patron, Bristol-Myers, Inc. It was the start of a business relationship between program, network, advertising agency and sponsor that was to prevail throughout the series' halcyon epoch, concluding with the broadcast of June 29, 1949. A directive filtered down from on high that—to soften the blow to anyone who might be offended by the show's rather potent title—the appellation was to be reduced from *Duffy's Tavern* to a mere *Duffy's* as the firm took over the program's sponsorship.[8] Obviously a well placed individual or individuals within the Bristol-Myers hierarchy was convinced that there could be widespread repercussions in linking their healthful commodity, Ipana toothpaste, with the perceptibly unsavory image of a saloon. As a consequence, Ed Gardner proffered the term *Duffy's Variety*; that alteration was applied for only a few installments before being banished as unwieldy, too.

In noting the name change, a press release advised that "some listeners, the majority being Catholics, had started public protests" over the use of the show's original sobriquet. The publicists acknowledged that *tavern* was a term that glorified drinking, and therefore was offensive to some in the audience, "and should not be used over the radio." Without saying it, of course, the sponsor was afraid that any offensive behavior on its part could turn into outrage on the part of some listeners. It was never a good idea to place a product or its corporate manufacturer in such a potentially compromising position for fear of public rebuke and its resultant loss of sales and possible tarnished image.

The "organized protests" soon fizzled, however. Five months later Bristol-Myers concluded that there weren't very many offended fans after all. There had been a handful of letters opposing the connotations attributed to *tavern*, but little more. The edict preventing its application was reversed. The program reemployed the full designation of *Duffy's Tavern* with the broadcast of March 9, 1944, after a new press release announced: "The sponsor of *Duffy's* apparently has come to the conclusion that the citizenry was not greatly outraged by the alcoholic connotation in the word 'tavern.'" The question was settled for the remainder of the run. Ironically, an alco-

hol beverage maker, Blatz Brewing Company, took over the show following Bristol-Myers' long reign as sole patron.

In reality, taverns have been a source of comedy and drama through the ages. Think of Sir John Falstaff, the fictional comedic character and drinking buddy of Prince Hal, the future King Henry V. Falstaff appears in a quartet of William Shakespeare's famous plays (*Henry IV*, Parts 1 and 2; *Henry V*; and *The Merry Wives of Windsor*). Some of their merry encounters occur at the Boars Head Tavern in Eastcheap, London. More barroom scenes are included in Eugene O'Neill's *The Iceman Cometh* and William Saroyan's *The Time of Your Life*. "But Duffy's ain't that kind of a joint," said one wag. "Archie is part bartender, philosopher, with a touch of reprobate in him."

Through Archie, an eccentric Ed Gardner also turned the malapropism into a national institution, becoming a butcher of speech. Playing the wisecracking, linguistic-deficient barkeep, and communicating in typically nasal Brooklynese, he introduced the weekly performances. He'd interrupt a tinkling piano rendition of the show's theme, "When Irish Eyes Are Smiling," to answer a ringing telephone, invariably discovering Duffy himself on the line, the audience overhearing Archie's side of the conversation: "Duffy's Tavern, where the elite meet to eat—Archie, the manager, speaking—Duffy ain't here ... Oh, hello, Duffy." Over the next half-hour he dispatched one-liners that turned the King's English on its head. A few of the more tantalizing were:

- *Opera is when a guy gets stabbed in the back and instead of bleeding, he sings.*
- *Leave us not jump to seclusion.*
- *Now, don't infirm me that I'm stupid.*
- *Fate has fickled its finger at me.*
- *Get me the lost and foundling division.*
- *Leave me not forget me hospitality.*
- *I tink you've given me da mucous of an idea.*
- *Listen, wit good management, dis place could show a nice overhead.*

*The New York World-Telegram* chided the

show, saying it "drips with grammatical gore." While the inmates at San Quentin prison voted it their favorite program, as a premium offer in 1943 the sponsor shipped thousands of copies of *Duffy's First Reader* to listeners requesting it.

At a salary of 15 dollars weekly, "Archie the manager" wasn't getting rich quick. But an opportunistic, enterprising Archie capitalized on oftentimes questionable and ill-advised machinations that—if they worked out—could significantly augment his income. One historian acknowledged that it was sometimes difficult to understand where the character of Archie and the real-life actor playing him separated: "In a sense it is a mistake to call Gardner a radio actor, because there was very little difference between him and the character named 'Archie' he had been portraying with uniform success."[9]

While the program usually included a weekly billing of well-known guests who entertained the audience, its sustaining power was in some obsession chanced upon by Archie and his pub pals. One week he might scheme for a raise or lavishly prepare for an icon's visit; the following week he might be consumed by making repairs to the establishment, making the books balance or assisting one of the regulars with a specific concern. Foremost among the recurring cast of zany characters was Duffy's air-headed, man-crazy daughter, Miss Duffy (a part originally crafted by Ed Gardner's first wife, Shirley Booth, who carried the role into 1943 and for whom he spent the rest of the series' life searching for a copy). *Radio Life* depicted Miss Duffy as "a gabby, gum-chewing, featherbrained Brooklyn miss who exposes her blissful ignorance every time she opens her mouth," while Archie dubbed her "Mother Nature's revenge on Peeping Toms." Other frequent visitors were Eddie (Eddie Green), a droll waiter and janitor whose sneaky oaths precipitated some of the series' wittiest contributions;[10] Finnegan (Charlie Cantor), a likeable oaf with several screws loose and a demonstrated proclivity for falling for sales scams (Archie branded him "a subnormal chowderhead, a dope, a

low-grade moron"); and Clancy (Alan Reed), a thick-tongued Irish policeman on the beat who freely spouted sage advice.

"The comic grief, consternation and naïve inspirations of the bartender-manager and the cross-play of characters, add up to first-rate diversion, in which the writers and directors do well by the several performers and vice versa," *Variety* expounded. Booth, by the way, must have won partial custody of the Miss Duffy figure: after she left the show she turned up on several other variety series—including those headlined by superstars Fred Allen, Eddie Bracken, George Burns and Gracie Allen—imitating the voice and character precisely, only calling herself Dottie Mahoney for those exhibitions.

In the meantime, Ed Gardner "probably incurred the wrath of many radio performers by advertising that if he wanted a watch at a large discount or a fur coat, he just worked into his program a mention of the manufacturer of those items," said researcher Martin Grams, Jr. "Nor did he endear himself with radio writers when he disparaged their abilities."[11]

The wordsmiths laboring on most radio series worked under contracts, a guarantee that those who wrote for Ed Gardner missed altogether. He had a habit of hiring and firing on a whim. Bob Schiller revealed that he was fired four times as a gag writer for the show's scripts. Gardner's attitude toward the welfare of his scribes was typified by the fact that, as each radio season came to a close, he took off on vacation without having informed the writers if their services would be needed the following September. It was a shameless way to treat fellow professionals, and apparently he had little hesitation about repeating the procedure year after year.

In *Off Mike*, Abe Burrows revealed what writing *Duffy's Tavern* was like for a week in which the show's guest was, for instance, comedian Fred Allen:

> "We call a conference to get a story-line for Fred Allen's appearance.... Somebody remembers that St. Patrick's Day is coming, and ... Duffy ... always holds what he calls his 'Spring

Semi-Annual St. Patrick's Day Musicale and Pig Roast.' ... Why not let Archie try to hire Fred Allen as the M.C. for the Pig Roast? Then Duffy won't want Fred, and Fred will have to audition for him. This will give us a splendid opportunity to louse up Allen and have a lot of fun while Duffy is insulting him....

"We then lay out a three-page synopsis describing what everybody does and when.... We also decide where to place the commercials ... and the musical numbers."

The chore of writing the show was divided among the staff writers, who then gathered with Ed Gardner to go over the material....

[Sol] Saks ... remembers what the weekly grind was like: "We worked all night until airtime to get that script mimeographed, hurried over to the studio where the actors would read it over once, broadcast it, drop the scripts into the wastebasket and go home, and we would go back to work.... It was an eighty-five-hour week, because the last session was twenty-four to twenty-eight hours."[12]

Once in a while reports surfaced that Gardner, who controlled almost every aspect of the show, kept the wages paid the others connected with the show as low as he could get away with. "We were so underpaid in those days," said writer Bob Schiller, "that we'd take the jokes we wrote for *Duffy's Tavern* and send them to *Reader's Digest* and put them in the mouths of our guests and we'd get five dollars." Schiller went on: "He [Gardner] always felt that if we were making a lot of money, which he didn't want to pay, we would get lazy and not write as well."

Despite the evident tightness, however, it still came as a surprise to most insiders when—after Bristol-Myers ended its seven-year ties with the program—Gardner moved the permanent cast, plus a quartet of scripters, to Puerto Rico to take advantage of that nation's favorable tax laws.[13] The rules then in force were particularly profitable to him by substantially reducing the show's bottom line. To persuade business enterprises to relocate their operations there, local officials had passed the Puerto Rican Development Act, proffering a moratorium on income taxes for a dozen years. Thus, the radio series left Hollywood's NBC studios at Sunset and Vine in the summer of 1949 and set up shop in Puerto Rico that fall under the aegis of a new underwriter, Blatz Brewing Company. New shows were transcribed, a broadcasting innovation that had only recently come into widespread use. "He [Gardner] was widely criticized for the move on the grounds that he was ducking the income tax," one authority reported, "and the show's popularity, sadly, would soon fall off to the point where it would be dropped. In order for Hollywood stars to appear on *Duffy's Tavern*, they would have to fly south for rehearsals, and that did not go over very well. Although a few stars did..., the majority of the episodes were supported by the usual *Duffy's* cast."[14]

Long before any of this occurred, the radio guest list was as carefully handled as that on any of the superlative variety features. The specialty of the house was in satirizing whoever arrived; Archie turned the knife with considerable gusto. John Dunning allowed that Gardner "refined the insult and made it an art form."[15] Historian Martin Grams proclaimed: "At *Duffy's* a guest was a person who received a good deal of pushing around—but with hilarity and no pain, as distinguished from the shoddy air of certain audience participation shows, in which the visitor was rendered merely ridiculous. At *Duffy's* the invited dropper-in was prominent and talented folk who could take care of themselves when the insults were flying, and the more rarefied the atmosphere from which they came to spend an evening at the Tavern, the better the time they had."[16]

They had no hesitancy in signing up, either. One source confirmed, "For guest stars it was like going on the Larry King show—if you got on *Duffy's Tavern*, you were validated as a celebrity." The pop idols turning up there were a veritable Who's Who among entertainers of that day, drawn from diverse mediums—most of them major drawing cards that the series relied on heavily in audience-building.

Among the surfeit of show business veterans who called at least once (with many returning for a second or third trip) were legends like these (and there were many more):

Fred Allen
Eddie (Rochester)
    Anderson
Desi Arnaz
Gene Autry
Phil Baker
Lucille Ball
Tallulah Bankhead
Brace Beemer
    (The Lone Ranger)
Ralph Bellamy
Joan Bennett
Milton Berle
Irving Berlin
Humphrey Bogart
Major Edward Bowes
Joe E. Brown
James Cagney
Hoagy Carmichael
Ilka Chase
Charles Coburn
Bing Crosby
Xavier Cugat
Dennis Day
Marlene Dietrich
Morton Downey
Jimmy Durante
Leo Durocher
Clifton Fadiman
Jinx Falkenburg
Gracie Fields
Cary Grant
Sir Cedric Hardwicke
Susan Hayward
(The Incomparable)
    Hildegarde
Hedda Hopper
Betty Hutton
Van Johnson
George Jessel
Boris Karloff
Dorothy Lamour

Gypsy Rose Lee
Peggy Lee
Oscar Levant
Art Linkletter
Ida Lupino
Herbert Marshall
Mary Martin
Tony Martin
Victor Mature
Elsa Maxwell
Lauritz Melchoir
Adolph Menjou
Ethel Merman
Ray Milland
Carmen Miranda
Gary Moore
Henry Morgan
Barry Nelson
Ozzie and Harriet
    Nelson
Louella Parsons
Gregory Peck
Dick Powell
Jane Powell
Basil Rathbone
Martha Raye
Robert L. Ripley
Roy Rogers
Mickey Rooney
Dinah Shore
Kate Smith
Ann Sothern
Risë Stevens
Gloria Swanson
Deems Taylor
Shirley Temple
Rudy Vallee
Willard Waterman
Clifton Webb
Orson Welles
Esther Williams
Ed Wynn

On one occasion the program's guest was Monty Woolley, whose consumption of alcohol was reportedly seldom rivaled. In the two-and-a-half- hour span between the first performance (for the Eastern and Central time zones) and the second (for the West Coast), Woolley and Ed Gardner went to Brittingham's, a fabled bistro adjacent to the CBS studios at Columbia Square. There the pair consumed, according to one estimate, 20 martinis. During the late show performance (which was regularly done without a live studio audience), Woolley fell down on the floor, the script clutched in his hands. "Ed, the ever-thoughtful host, got down on the floor with him and they finished the program lying on their sides, both smashed," observed writer Larry Gelbart.[17]

After forming Edward F. Gardner Productions, the creator of *Duffy's Tavern* produced the 1951 film noir crime thriller *The Man with My Face*. It was his solo credit as a self-employed producer. He penned an episode of the syndicated TV series *Annie Oakley* in 1955, turned up as a guest on a couple of Ed Sullivan's *Toast of the Town* telecasts on CBS in the mid–1950s, and played a couple of roles on NBC's *Alfred Hitchcock Presents* in the early 1960s.

As often happens, marriage partners with dual careers don't achieve the same levels of satisfying success, at least not at the same time. While Gardner was married to Shirley Booth, she became well recognized in theater as he labored in rather obscure anonymity for a few years. "He was a theatrical hustler and promoter," noted one observer, "working for small stock companies in every imaginable capacity, from director to script typist to 'the guy who paints the scenery.'" He was also delivering termination notices for advertising agencies to actors whose services were no longer needed. He confessed that he simply "did not handle his wife's success well."

Following his divorce from Booth in late 1942, Gardner wed New York stage and radio actress Simone Hegeman on March 24, 1943. To that union were born two sons, both in Los Angeles County: Edward Hegeman Gardner, on April 28, 1944, and Stephen Anthony Gardner, on March 25, 1948. During the sojourn of *Duffy's Tavern* in Puerto Rico the Gardners relocated to Spain, where Ed pondered retirement. In a radio interview in

Spain in 1953, to the question "Who is the best actress in America?" Gardner replied: "You will find the best actress among my ex-wives." (He had only one ex.) The family's plans changed and they returned to the United States. He died of a diseased liver in a Los Angeles hospital on August 17, 1963, at the age of 62.

Shirley Booth, meanwhile, went on to bigger and better things, too. Born Thelma Marjorie Ford in New York on August 30, 1898, she attended public schools in Brooklyn, New York, and Hartford, Connecticut, before quitting at 14 to pursue a stage career, in spite of her father's angry opposition. Her first professional performance didn't materialize overnight, however—the year was 1921, in a Hartford production of *The Cat and the Canary*. For more than a year she appeared in stock theater in New Haven, premiering on Broadway in 1925, where she was the leading lady in the play *Hell's Bells*. Another newcomer, Humphrey Bogart, was in the cast of that production, too. For a decade Booth alternated between stock engagements and short-run Broadway shows. In time her repertoire included 600 plays in stock companies and 40 on Broadway. She would later acknowledge, "Acting is a way to overcome your own inhibitions and shyness. The writer creates a strong, confident personality, and that's what you become ... unfortunately, only for the moment."

In the 1950s and 1960s she made a handful of movies. According to *The New York Times*, "She portrayed many quick-witted women with acerbic tongues, but gained her greatest recognition for playing an ingratiating but drab, garrulous housewife clinging to wistful illusions in [1952's] *Come Back, Little Sheba*." For that role, which she had performed in 1950 on Broadway, she captured a Tony and Oscar award. Becoming the first actress to win both a Tony and Oscar for the same role, she was instantly added to stardom's upper echelon. In between those two manifestations, incidentally, in 1951 she appeared on Broadway as the feisty but lovable Aunt Cissy in the hit play *A Tree Grows in Brooklyn*. Booth had already won a Tony for her portrayal of Grace Woods in 1948's *Goodbye, My Fancy*, and earned a third as a romantic tourist in 1952's *The Time of the Cuckoo*. Subsequently she gained a star on the Hollywood Walk of Fame. For several years she was a regular traveler between New York and Hollywood.

Her "greatest recognition" role in *Come Back, Little Sheba* notwithstanding, Booth is quite possibly remembered by more people today as an irrepressible housekeeper, Hazel Burke. She starred on the television sitcom *Hazel*, derived from a comic strip character and seen on NBC from 1961 to 1965, and CBS from 1965 to 1966. "Everybody under forty knows me better from *Hazel*, not from my movies," Booth once told a reporter. She excelled there as a domestic with a penchant for getting into other people's business in humorous ways. In its initial season on the air the video series cracked Nielsen's top 10 list. Her performance as Hazel added two Emmys (in 1962 and 1963) to the trio of Tonys and single Oscar she had previously won, making her only the fourth performer in history to win the Triple Crown of Acting.

For five months in 1973 Booth played Grace Simpson in a second televised sitcom, ABC's *A Touch of Grace*. She was a widow with a gravedigger boyfriend in that now-virtually-forgotten half-hour series. Before retiring from show business in the mid–1970s she appeared in a quartet of made-for-TV movies: *The Glass Menagerie* (1966), *Do Not Go Gentle Into That Good Night* (1967), *The Smugglers* (1968) and—in a voiceover part as Mrs. Santa—*The Year Without a Santa Claus* (1974). She also made a few one-time appearances in the TV dramatic series *Playhouse 90* and *The United States Steel Hour*, plus several guest shots on Ed Sullivan's *Toast of the Town*, *The Perry Como Show*, *What's My Line?*, *The Andy Williams Show* and *The Tonight Show Starring Johnny Carson*.

Following her divorce from Ed Gardner in 1942 (they reportedly remained good friends), she wed an artist and farmer, William H. Baker, Jr., on September 24, 1943.

Booth never had children, and, upon her second husband's death from heart disease in 1951, she never remarried. After a brief illness she succumbed to death at age 94 on October 16, 1992, at her home on Cape Cod in North Chatham, Massachusetts. She was survived by a sister, Jean, 16 years her junior.

*Duffy's Tavern* appeared to have stimulated a myriad of successive televised series with neighborhood taverns as their backdrops. First and foremost was Jackie Gleason's inspired 1950s and 1960s character Joe the Bartender. During sketches on the popular entertainer's Saturday night TV comedy hour, Joe (Gleason) conversed with Mr. Dunahy, an unseen patron, before being joined by Crazy Guggenheim (Frank Fontaine), a Finnegan-like, jovial dolt. Other series employing the neighborhood tavern as a venue included *Archie Bunker's Place*, a spin-off from *All in the Family*, in which the windbag pro-

tagonist ran a blue-collar bar; the daytime serial *Ryan's Hope*, proffering a titular family headed by tavern-owning Irish parents; *The Jeffersons* (final season, 1984–85), wherein actor Danny Wells operated Charlie's Bar on the ground floor of the apartment edifice where George and Louise were tenants; and *Cheers*, a 1980s sitcom co-created by James Burrows, son of *Duffy's Tavern* scribe Abe Burrows, and godson of Ed Gardner.[18]

Whether they were stirred by the radio series or not is anyone's guess, but there is some evidence that innumerable bars are operating across the U.S. right now under the moniker Duffy's Tavern. They extend from Monterey, California, to Wickford, Rhode Island, with the potential for scores of sites in between. The label has weathered well, particularly during times that Americans returned to their roots in a sweeping nostalgia craze. Archie likely would have celebrated it.

# 9

## Father Knows Best

### RADIO'S MOST TYPICAL FAMILY

*TV Guide* called it "the quintessentially comforting '50s sitcom." Make that: in *two* mediums. Like others of its ilk, the tube's *Father Knows Best* was preceded by an audio run—that one of five years' duration. It was a warm-up for performances by an award-winning cast. That troupe hung around for six seasons in original shows, after which the same programs were repeated seven more years on network TV, followed by 13 more in syndication, plus unlimited reruns beyond on multiple cable channels. The warmhearted feature centered on the Andersons in a small hamlet in mid–America whose issues were symptomatic of families everywhere: average dilemmas faced by nuclear clans of the 1950s and usually settled in relatively cool, calm, cooperative ways. Even though the parents often shared differing views, and a trio of kids could be a little testy, their respect for one another was paramount. It was the kind of kinship many people either patterned their own tribes after or profoundly wished for, according to remarks on modern web sites. Nevertheless, the Andersons set lofty ideals that few could attain in a bona fide world, critics said. Central figure-movie star Robert Young was a hero to some: he possessed many of the sterling qualities found in the "good" patriarch, setting a high mark for males in mid-century America. While he could be stubborn, argumentative and persistent, he was kindhearted and devoted to his brood. As time advanced he became a sage to whom

they turned for counsel. By the end of the run he had proved to his family's satisfaction that this dad usually *did* know best, at least most of the time.

❖ ❖ ❖

**Creator-Writer:** Ed James
**Producers:** Eugene B. Rodney and Robert Young
**Directors:** Fran Van Hartesveldt, Murray Bolen, Ken Burton
**Writers:** Paul West, Roz Rogers
**Orchestra Leader:** Roy Bargy
**Announcers:** Marvin Miller, Bill Forman
**Recurring Cast:** *Jim Anderson:* Robert Young; *Margaret Anderson:* June Whitley (audition show), Jean Vander Pyl; *Betty Anderson:* Rhoda Williams; *Bud Anderson:* Ted Donaldson; *Kathy Anderson:* Norma Jean Nilsson (predominant), Helen Strong; *Elizabeth Smith:* Eleanor Audley; *Hector Smith:* Herb Vigran; *Billy Smith:* Sam Edwards
**Sponsor:** General Foods Corporation, for Maxwell House Coffee, Post 40 Percent Bran Flakes, Post Toasties, Instant Postum caffeine-free beverage and other foodstuffs and household products (full run)
**Themes:** "Let's Have Another Cup of Coffee" (Irving Berlin), followed by "Waiting (for Love to Find You)," aka "Father Knows Best Theme" (Don Ferris, Irving Friedman, Leon Pober)
**Ratings:** High—13.4 (1950–51), Low—7.6 (1952–53), Median—10.3. Ratings based on four complete seasons, 1949–53 inclusive.
**On the Air:** August 25, 1949–July 6, 1950, NBC, Thursday, 8:30–9:00 P.M. Eastern Time; September 7, 1950–July 5, 1951, NBC, Thursday, 8:30–9:00 P.M.; September 20, 1951–May 31, 1953, NBC, Thursday, 8:00–8:30 P.M., 9:00–9:30 P.M., 8:30–

9:00 P.M.; September 10, 1953–April 25, 1954, NBC, Thursday, 9:00–9:30 P.M., 8:30–9:00 P.M.

**Extant Archival Material:** Radio scripts for *Father Knows Best*, aired from 1950 to 1954, are included in the Eugene Rodney Collection of Scripts and Production Material, ca. 1950–ca. 1963, archived in the Charles E. Young Research Library at the University of California at Los Angeles (UCLA), Box 951575, Los Angeles, CA, 90095; (310) 825–7253; Fax (310) 825–1210; *www.library.ucla.edu/libraries/arts/*.

A single script of *Father Knows Best* for the broadcast of September 13, 1951, is included in the Marvin Miller Collection of the Thousand Oaks Library, American Radio Archives, 1401 East Janss Road, Thousand Oaks, CA, 91362; (805) 449–2660; fax (805) 449–2675; *www.tol.lib.ca.us.*

The complete run of 197 *Father Knows Best* broadcasts are known to be in general circulation or held by private collectors as of 2006, sold by vintage radio dealers and traded by old-time radio hobbyists

❖ ❖ ❖

*Father Knows Best* was an audio feature about "radio's most typical family," one respected media historiographer proclaimed.[1] Indeed, the Anderson clan that resided in mythical Springfield was about as symbolically expressive of what life was like among nuclear kinships in the United States in the middle of the twentieth century as anybody could hope to emulate. In spite of mild disagreements, they exhibited a unity of purpose that proffered a supportive, caring attitude for one another, one the nation has seldom witnessed to that degree since. There was something profoundly satisfying and rewarding in what listeners—and later, viewers—experienced. Millions recognized wholesome ideals and qualities worth copying. They aspired to lofty goals, sometimes unattainable, practicing them in their own family units as they attempted to replicate the Anderson model. All of it promptly became fair game for critics who disparaged the show's whitebread style for its perceived failures to project reality. Despite that, in a kinder, gentler America, the series resonated with enough people to remain on the air in various incarnations for more than three decades.

*Father Knows Best* was produced by Eugene B. Rodney and Robert Young, the latter also the show's star. They originally met in 1935 and, some years later, formed a business partnership, Rodney-Young Productions, which eventually shifted the feature from audio to video. According to the Museum of Television, the pair "based the series on experiences each had with wives and children; thus, to them, the show represented 'reality.'"[2] Responding to critics who claimed it wasn't genuine and authentic, Young admitted: "No, of course, but that's how we'd *like* it to be." Adding subplots about illness or drugs or serious problems, which media reviewers urged them to do, "would have been like taking a beautiful painting and obliterating it with black paint—and that really would have turned the audience off," Young reasoned. "We never intended the series to be more than a weekly half-hour of fun and entertainment."

Young and Rodney's protestations to the contrary, the placid, benign tone of *Father Knows Best* has been almost singularly credited to writer Paul West, a father of four, depicted as a mellow, mild-mannered man. Hearing an enormous amount of bickering going on between the Andersons in the series' earliest days—when the show's creator, Ed James, was penning the scripts—West "desquabbled" it. Commenting on Young himself, West branded him "easygoing," and affirmed: "He never questioned a word. He'd have read the phone book if we'd have put it in front of him."

The program was characterized by issues of family love, warmth, charity and decency. "Springfield was a make-believe fantasy by today's standards," one pundit assessed, "but back then, it was the majority of real America." Expounding further, he added a personal perspective: "I watched this show every week [on TV] and wished I was a member of the Anderson family. Having belonged to a somewhat volatile family, I had the 30-minute escape every week to be a part of a caring, loving clan." The common-sense values the show upheld may have been a haven for many parents then, and likely would be welcomed by many modern heads-of-households who've followed the erosion of idealism in subsequent decades.

The Anderson family lived at 607 Maple Street in Springfield, and was comprised of five members. The patriarch, Jim, sole breadwinner of the clan (normally affixed at one per household in those days), was an agent of the General Insurance Company. He was played by the veteran movie screen idol Robert Young, "the fresh-faced epitome of decent upstanding American manhood, fatherhood, and husbandhood."[3] It wasn't often that a married male in an ongoing series, especially in radio, rose to become a show's star and central focus of all the other characters—particularly without being portrayed as a fool. If nothing else, such factors distinguished *Father Knows Best* from the bulk of its contemporaries, both dramatic and comedic, including primetime features and daytime serials as well.

For all of the radio run, with the exception of an audition show on December 20, 1948, Jim's wife Margaret was portrayed by voice artist Jean Vander Pyl. She was a woman who spent her professional career saying the lines of dozens of storybook characters, most of them of animated persuasion. In this show she personified a sweet-spirited yet determined matriarch whose feet at times seemed more firmly rooted in terra firma than did those of other members of her tribe. Her domestic servitude was replete with the usual household chores, plus the normal crises in coping with raising three youngsters while attempting to bring out the best in her man, the show's protagonist.

The offspring included eldest daughter Betty (Rhoda Williams), whom Jim nicknamed "Princess"; middle child James Jr., called "Bud" (Ted Donaldson), who rattled off a "Ho-ly cow!" catchphrase incessantly; and precocious younger daughter Kathy (Norma Jean Nilsson), whom Jim nicknamed "Kitten" and "Angel," and Bud dubbed "Shrimp." The first two children were typical adolescents with all the common difficulties and concerns that come with that age, including dates and boyfriends/girlfriends, studies, chores, chums, money woes, part-time jobs, sports and extracurricular activities, driving, etc. The youngest, a preteen, on the other hand, exuded a tomboy spirit while constantly coping with a frustrating adult world. She often required more personal time from the other family members because of her age.

The idyllic setting of Springfield in a presumably Midwestern but otherwise unidentified state (the residents notably possessed no distinctive accents) seemed a million miles from the major concerns of the time period: the Korean Conflict, Civil Rights issues, murders, rapes, robberies, anti–Communist witch hunts and the Cold War, sudden prosperity and the proliferation of gadgetry and materialism in a postwar environment. Everybody was Caucasian. Nor was there any drug addiction, teen pregnancy, quitting school or other "relevant" topics that pass for entertainment now.

Every evening Jim Anderson burst through the door with a cheery "Margaret? I'm home!" It rapidly became an identifying motto. He'd replace his suit jacket with a sweater before interacting with his offspring and spouse, attempting to attack and settle the mundane as well as the complicated issues transpiring in their lives. Unlike some other family comedies of the period, in which one or both parents were floundering idiots, Jim and Margaret were instead helpful, responsible adults. When a family crisis arose, Jim calmed the situation with a caring attitude and thoughtful wisdom.

Early in the radio manifestation father was perceived as a rather awkward bungler. One source suggested that "in the audio version the title of the show ended with a question mark, suggesting that father's role as family leader and arbiter was dubious." Despite the lack of an authentic question mark, father didn't know best 100 percent of the time. Jim Anderson was wrong some of the time, and, on occasion, he lost his temper. He was guilty of mangling even the best of intents.

An example occurred in 1950 after Margaret gave orders that everybody was to honor dear old dad, canceling any personal plans for Father's Day to wait on pop hand and foot. The kids reluctantly agreed, only to discover that pop had planned an all-day fishing expedition for himself with neighbor Hector Smith and was unwilling to give it up to satisfy his family's wishes. To honor the commitments their kin were making to them both, nonetheless, each man agreed to carry his family along on the fishing outing. What started out to be only apprehension resulted in a ruined day after the Andersons showed up late; the women insisted that firewood be gathered and a full breakfast be cooked and consumed before any fishing began, disastrously delaying the men from their appointed rounds; a single mishap resulted in Hector's fishing gear sinking to the bottom of the lake and Kathy falling into the lake, her clothes becoming totally soaked; and finally a government official showed up to inform the men they had been casting their fly rods on the grounds of a protected U.S. fish hatchery. Some days it didn't pay for Jim Anderson to get out of bed!

Despite such pitfalls, by the end of the audio run he had become much more paternal, even exhibiting the traits of a sage counselor when the situation warranted. He presented "an impossible family role model," attested one pundit. It was amazing how far he had come from where he had started. As the television era dawned, it was evident that Jim and his relatives had matured light years from their radio inceptions. In all likelihood they never would have persisted for so many years otherwise. "On TV," affirmed one reporter, "he became an all-knowing fount of wisdom."

Beyond its radio inception, *Father Knows Best* enjoyed greater success in its visual incarnation. Following five years in audio, the last one abbreviated by NBC and with listeners by then in decline (the show was even discontinued altogether by the chain's flagship station in New York a full five months before the network run was withdrawn), it was to sustain far more acclaim in television. There it persisted for six months (1954–55) on CBS before hitting its stride on NBC (1955–58), returning later to CBS (1958–62). Although there was plenty of commendation for it, the show was canceled in March 1955, a result of poor ratings in video, just as in radio. Few children and presumably many parents weren't able to view it at 10 o'clock on Sunday night in the Eastern Time zone. That had a chilling effect on the numbers. NBC picked it up the following fall, however, with a new sponsor and gave it an 8:30 start time in the East. The show caught on, becoming an overnight sensation and winding up in the top 10. Some 203 installments were filmed between 1954 and 1960.

Although the entry reached its peak in popularity during the 1959–60 season on CBS, winning sixth spot in the ratings, after 11 years of playing Jim Anderson, Robert Young announced that he had grown tired of it and wanted out. In a highly unusual move, the network scheduled reruns of the show for two years in primetime (1960–62) beyond the original chapters. Afterward, ABC TV repeated many of those same episodes for its primetime audience during the 1962–63 season while re-screening many more between 1962 and 1967 for its daytime audience. The feature continued in syndication until 1980 and was subsequently repeated again and again on assorted cable networks, clearly telling of its overwhelming acceptance in some quarters.

Fifteen years after it left the weekly airwaves, Rodney and Young collaborated on a TV special that returned the video cast to the cameras once more. The *Father Knows Best Reunion* aired on NBC-TV on May 15, 1977, with moderate success. A second effort, *Father Knows Best: Home for Christmas*, reunited the TV principals again and aired on NBC-TV in December 1977.

Regrettably, as could be expected, not everybody who tuned in to *Father Knows Best* appreciated its elevated intents. A check with various web sites will quickly confirm that at least a handful of evaluators felt quite differently about the series. Philip Rapp, creator-author of *The Bickersons* radio series—whose premise was a virtual nonstop quarrel between marriage partners—named Ozzie and Harriet Nelson and Jim and Betty Anderson as he lamented: "It just made me sick. There was so much sweetness. This was not marriage as I knew it." (His personal battles with Mary, his own spouse, have been well documented, and allegedly inspired *The Bickersons*.) Even one of *Father Knows Best*'s actors, Billy Gray, who portrayed Bud throughout the video run, was a very partial critic of the show, suggesting that the series added to the troubles inherent in domestic life.

> I wish there was some way I could tell kids not to believe it—the dialogue, the situations, the characters—they were all totally false. The show did everybody a disservice. The girls were always trained to use their feminine wiles, to pretend to be helpless to attract men. The show contributed to a lot of the problems between men and women that we see today.... I think we were all well motivated, but what we did was run a hoax. *Father Knows Best* purported to be a reasonable facsimile of life. And the bad thing is that the model is so deceitful. It usually revolved around not wanting to tell the truth, either out of embarrassment, or not wanting to hurt someone.... If I could say anything to make up for all the years I lent myself to that ... it would be: *You* know best.[4]

The family Anderson, however, appears not to have run its course quite yet: a feature-length live-action movie remake of *Father Knows Best*, starring Tim Allen, has been announced by Paramount Pictures and Nickelodeon Movies; it is tentatively scheduled for theatrical release in 2008.

On radio, the show's opening frequently plugged a commodity manufactured by General Foods Corporation. Before any familiar theme or other acknowledgement of the feature transpired, it would begin something like this....

> KATHY: *Mother, are Post 40 Percent Bran Flakes really the best-tasting cereal of them all?*
>
> MARGARET: *Well, your father says so, and Father Knows Best.*

Sly little devils, those!
The fact that General Foods stayed with the series for its five-year radio run indicates that it was convinced that, despite flagging numbers, it had a wholesome, quality program on its hands—the kind a healthful food processor was proud to associate its name and products with.

As was the custom in that epoch, Mom and Dad Anderson occupied separate beds. Of radio's married couples, only Ozzie and Harriet Nelson, in fact, actually got away with sharing a double bed! But Jim and Margaret Anderson were usually united when push came to shove on how to handle their bewildering offspring, a circumstance that actually did matter. Although they faced disagreements, within the span of a half-hour they inevitably harmonized, most often working out their differences in a lot less time. Margaret, while strong-willed, sometimes gave in reluctantly, with at least the implied rationalization "Father knows best."

In spite of whatever handicaps Jim might be burdened with, he was considered among the best TV dads in the land. One source places him among a sterling set of Superdads that encompassed the likes of Andy Taylor (Andy Griffith), Ward Cleaver (Hugh Beaumont), *My Three Sons'* Steve Douglas (Fred MacMurray) and Ozzie Nelson. In a 2004 poll conducted by *TV Guide*, Jim Anderson (Young) was voted the sixth "Greatest TV Dad of All Time."[5] No similar survey focused on radio dads, but he might have performed even better if such an assessment had been made! (There were fewer to choose from.) In addition, on a broadcast shortly before Father's Day in 1950, the National Father's Day Committee (an organization we seldom hear from today) announced that Young had been tapped as recipient of its "Father of the Year" award.

While he won a couple of Emmys for his role as Anderson (and a third a few years later as star of TV's *Marcus Welby, M.D.*), Jane Wyatt—who played his TV wife—earned a trio of Emmys for her role as Margaret Anderson. In video, incidentally, the Anderson offspring were played by Elinor Donahue (Betty), Billy Gray (Bud) and Lauren Chapin

(Kathy). Only Young transferred from radio to the visual medium. Media historians have overlooked explanations for the failure of Young's radio castmates to make the leap to television. In his case, of course, he owned 50 percent of the company producing the show, potentially a contributing factor in his perpetuity with the series.

After Young's father died in an automobile accident caused by a teenage driver, the Inter-Industry Highway Safety Committee approached the actor about spearheading a national campaign to improve teen driving. An outgrowth of their discussions resulted in *Father Knows Best* becoming an active part of the committee's crusade. A Good Driver Club was integrated into the radio scripts, while Young also made direct appeals to listeners. Several million safe-driving agreements between young people and their parents were signed as a result of the coordinated and widespread humanitarian effort.

The situations in *Father Knows Best* frequently could be classified as corny and commonplace, yet the audience found something in their humor to laugh at and possibly even identify with. This exchange before breakfast one morning was emblematic:

KATHY: *Mother, I can't find my skates.*

MARGARET: *Kathy, come in and start your breakfast.*

KATHY: *Ohhhh.... breakfast. Don't you understand, Mother? This is a crisis. How can I go to school without my skates?*

MOTHER: *Eat your breakfast, dear, and we'll look for the skates later.*

KATHY: *Oh, but I have looked for them. I've looked just every place. They simply vanished.*

MARGARET: *Did you look in the hall under the telephone table?*

KATHY: *Mother, that's practically the first place I looked.*

MARGARET: *Well, how about the service porch?*

KATHY: *They aren't there ... they aren't anywhere. Ohhhh, what am I going to do?*

MARGARET: *You're going to eat your breakfast. I'll run out to the garage and see if you left them there ... and don't use too much sugar in your cereal.*

KATHY: *Look way in the back, Mother, near the magazines. Oatmeal ... that's all we get around here is oatmeal.*

SFX: Father yells after hitting skates

FATHER: *Ahhhhhh....*

SFX: Crashing down stairs with a thud at the bottom

KATHY: *Never mind, Mother ... Daddy found them.*

FATHER (barking): *Who left those skates on the stairs?*

KATHY (innocently): *Oh, is that where they were?*

Titles of a handful of typical installments of *Father Knows Best* hint at what the storylines were about: "Betty's Engagement," "Betty's Screen Test," "Time for a New Car," "A New Housekeeper," "Family Car Stolen," "The New Girlfriend," "Father Becomes Ill," "Taking on City Hall," "Jim Inherits a Ranch in Arizona," "Locked Out of the House," "A Diet Discussion," "New Washing Machine," "Should Women Work?," "Bud Quits School," "Selling the House," "The Phantom Prowler," "The Kids Revolt," "Second Family Car," "The Boy Next Door," "Bud Dislikes Girls," "Banged-Up Fender," "The Missing Wedding Ring," "Big Inheritance," "A Date Mix-Up with Leonard and Ralph and Betty," "The Value of Money," "Moving to Chicago" and "False Elopement."

The show's opening theme was a catchy instrumental adaptation of a 1932 composition by the inimitable Irving Berlin, "Let's Have Another Cup of Coffee." The lilting melody was a natural for a sponsor proffering a brand of coffee (Maxwell House). In addition to its sly hint, the lyrics implored the listeners to enjoy a second piece of pie—a favorite method of topping a meal in many households in that epoch. A second piece of music, "Waiting (for Love to Find You)," aka "Father Knows Best Theme," sometimes bridged the gap between the first commercial and the narrative. Don Ferris and Irving Friedman composed the music, and Leon Pober penned the lyrics.

Robert George Young was born February 22, 1907, in Chicago, the son of an Irish immigrant building manufacturer. Raised in Seattle and Los Angeles, the youngster determined early that he wanted to act, and accepted roles in high school drama productions. Following graduation, while covering his overhead via daytime jobs as a bank clerk and a loan collector, he enrolled in night classes at Pasadena Community Playhouse, gaining stage experience in the process. At 21 he premiered in Hollywood films in an uncredited role in 1928's *The Campus Vamp*. It was the first of 98 theatrical motion pictures that would showcase his talents.

The majority of those were of the B variety, with hackneyed monikers like: *New Morals for Old* (1932), *Men Must Fight* (1933), *Hell Below* (1933), *Remember Last Night?* (1935), *Sworn Enemy* (1936), *The Bride Wore Red* (1937), *Married Bachelor* (1941), *Slightly Dangerous* (1943), *Relentless* (1948) and *Bride for Sale* (1949). There were a handful of better-recalled movies, however, including *Northwest Passage* (1940), *Western Union* (1941), *H.M. Pulham, Esq.* (1941), *Claudia* (1943), *Crossfire* (1947) and *That Forsyte Woman* (1949). Young seldom won the girl in the parts in which he was cast. Louis B. Mayer allowed: "He has no sex appeal." Some wags disagreed, citing him as one of the handsomest, most suave lookers among Hollywood's masculinity. Young had his own "take" on his screen experiences: "I was an introvert in an extrovert profession," and, "All those years at MGM I hid a black terror behind a cheerful face."

Slowly he forged a career, not as a leading man but as a dependable thespian that audiences liked. His costars included Joan Crawford, Greta Garbo, Greer Garson, Jean Harlow, Katharine Hepburn, Myrna Loy and Norma Shearer. "My career never had any great peaks," said Young. "But producers and directors knew I was reliable. So when they couldn't really get the big stars, they'd say, 'Let's get Bob.' As a result I always kept working, each time a little higher."

Beyond the silver screen Young appeared in a dozen made-for-TV movies and four TV series—in addition to *Father Knows Best*, there was *Window on Main Street* (a fea-

ture he also created and produced, in 1961–62 on CBS), *Marcus Welby, M.D.* (1969–76, ABC) and *Little Women* (1972, a syndicated miniseries). He also turned up in single episodes and made guest appearances no less than 18 times on a myriad of TV series, among them: *I've Got a Secret, What's My Line?, Toast of the Town, This Is Your Life, The Tonight Show Starring Johnny Carson, The Ford Television Theater, Climax!, The Christophers, Dr. Kildare, The Bell Telephone Hour* and *Bob Hope Presents the Chrysler Theater.*

Parenthetically, while playing the long-running *Marcus Welby*, Young was so convincing as a medical practitioner that—on average—he received an astounding 5,000 letters per week from fans seeking professional medical advice![6] Not only that, his colleague on the show, actor James Brolin, who made house calls on a motorcycle as Dr. Steven Kiley, related: "There was a poll at one time that said the majority of the American people would nominate Robert Young and myself as President and Vice President. People trusted us that much."[7] For Young, of course, the discernment of trustworthiness had a long history extending as far back as two decades when he began appearing as Jim Anderson, the nation's eventual "Father of the Year."

All of his TV performances followed an active history in network radio dating to August 6, 1936, on NBC's *Kraft Music Hall*, with Bing Crosby hosting. Young's first regular series was *Good News of 1938*, with Fanny Brice and Frank Morgan. He often played the leads on a range of dramatic series that included *Cavalcade of America* (numerous times), *The CBS Radio Workshop, Columbia Presents Corwin, Encore Theater, The Fifth Horseman, The Free Company, The Gulf Screen Guild Show/Theater, Hallmark Playhouse, Hollywood Hotel, Hollywood Star Playhouse, Hollywood Star Time, The Lady Esther Screen Guild Theater* (numerous times), *Lux Radio Theater* (numerous times), *Philip Morris Playhouse, The Screen Guild Theater, The Silver Theater, Suspense* (numerous times), *Theater of Romance, This Is Hollywood, This Is My Best, The Victory Theater* and *The Witness.*

For nine weeks in the late summer and early fall of 1943 he was a small-town newspaper editor on CBS's *Passport for Adams*. In the 1944–45 radio season he was emcee and straight man for NBC's *The Frank Morgan Show*. Yet unquestionably Young's most celebrated audio role was as Jim Anderson. He carried it on radio for five years and on television for another six, a total of 400 original half-hour performances in dual mediums (including 197 in radio, 203 in television). It was obvious that he not only mellowed as the years rolled by but that he was in love with the part.

There was another side to Robert Young's existence that was widely reported by the media.

> Despite the characters he played and his public image, Mr. Young was a complex and, in many ways, troubled figure.
> He had a history of alcoholism and depression. In 1991, at 83, he tried to commit suicide by running a hose from his car's exhaust pipe to the interior of the vehicle. The attempt failed because the battery was dead and the car wouldn't start. He later admitted that he had been drinking when he asked his wife to enter into a suicide pact with him and then tried to take his life.[8]

Two decades earlier—in a 1971 interview—he admitted to having been engaged in those battles for much of his professional life. A member of Alcoholics Anonymous for years (even while *Father Knows Best* was airing), Young spoke on behalf of that organization on countless occasions. He initially conquered his addiction in the late 1960s before lapsing into it again some time afterward. Young overcame it a second time following the attempted suicide. Living for another seven years, to July 21, 1998, he succumbed to respiratory failure at his home at Westlake Village, California, in suburban L.A. He was married only once, to his high school sweetheart, Elizabeth Louise Henderson, from 1933 until her death in 1994. Young was 17 and she was 14 when they first met. Together they raised four daughters: Betty Lou Gleason, Carol Proffitt, Barbara Beebe and Kathy Young.

His opposite in *Father Knows Best*, the cool-headed Margaret Anderson, was played for most of the show's run by Jean Vander Pyl. A salesman's daughter who was born on October 11, 1919, at Philadelphia, she gained millions of fans while "few ever knew what she looked like," *All Movie Guide* affirmed. During her childhood her family resided in Memphis, Chicago, Larchmont and New Rochelle, New York, and Long Beach, California, before settling in Los Angeles in 1933.

After graduating from Beverly Hills High School in 1937, Vander Pyl enrolled in dramatics classes at the University of California at Los Angeles. As an undergraduate she gained her first acting role on radio in the CBS West Coast series *Calling All Cars* (ca. 1938–39). She was soon playing damsels in distress on several dramas. Before long she appeared whenever Andy Brown needed a girlfriend on CBS's *Amos 'n' Andy*. At the same time she turned up regularly in supporting roles on the same web's *Lux Radio Theater*. While playing the pivotal character of Margaret Anderson on *Father Knows Best* for the full radio run, she was occasionally heard as an extra in NBC's collegiate-focused narrative *The Halls of Ivy* (1950–52).

The artist reached her zenith in voiceover roles with a brigade of animated television series. Although probably best identified as Wilma Flintstone in the Hanna-Barbera feature *The Flintstones*, shown under multiple monikers from 1960 to 1974 on the three networks, she is recalled as the voice of Rosie the Robot in *The Jetsons*, broadcast between 1962 and 1987 on the three webs and in syndication. But those roles were only the tip of the iceberg. In addition, over a TV career extending from the 1950s to the 1990s, she supplied character voices in all of these cartoons: *The Yogi Bear Show*, *Top Cat*, *Magilla Gorilla*, *The Hillbilly Bears*, *The Atom Ant Show*, *The Secret Squirrel Show*, *The Banana Splits Adventure Hour*, *Dinky Dog*, *Scooby-Doo—Where Are You!*, *Where's Huddles?*, *The Pebbles and Bamm-Bamm Show*, *Inch High—Private Eye*, *Hong Kong Phooey*, *The New Tom & Jerry Show*, *Mister T*, *The All-New Scooby and Scrappy-Doo Show* and *Wake Rattle & Roll*.

In 1995 Vander Pyl told a reporter that she received $250 per episode for her work on *The Flintstones*, and that—when it ended—she happily accepted $15,000 in lieu of residual payments from syndication. As the series has been screened repeatedly in more than 80 countries globally, she realized decades earlier she had made a poor choice. Living in San Clemente at the time, she remarked: "If I got residuals I wouldn't live in San Clemente, I'd *own* San Clemente!" She appeared in only one Hollywood theatrical production, an uncredited role in 1954's *Deep in My Heart*. While devoting the bulk of her professional life to voiceovers, she nevertheless turned up in dramatic roles on a handful of TV series, including *Jane Wyman Presents the Fireside Theater*, *Medic*, *The Donna Reed Show*, *Petticoat Junction*, *Murder She Wrote* and *Leave It to Beaver*. Vander Pyl supplied voices for nearly two dozen animated TV films, in addition to the series on which she worked.

She wed Carroll G. O'Meara, an advertising executive and writer, who became director-producer of *The Jack Benny Program*, *The George Burns and Gracie Allen Show*, *The Kate Smith Show* and others. He won an Emmy for writing *The Halls of Ivy* on television. The couple had three children, Kathleen O'Meara, born October 21, 1940; Carroll Timothy O'Meara, April 22, 1943; and Michael John O'Meara, July 6, 1945. After Carroll O'Meara died at age 53 on February 18, 1962, Jean O'Meara married musician Roger Wells DeWitt. They had a son together, Roger E. DeWitt, on September 15, 1964. R.W. DeWitt died at age 79 on September 11, 1992. When Jean DeWitt died on April 10, 1999, at her home in Dana Point, California, a victim of lung cancer, she was survived by three sons—Timothy, of Northridge, California; Michael, of Dana Point; and Roger, of New York City—and two stepsons, Anthony DeWitt of New York and Peter DeWitt of June Lake, California, and three grandchildren.

Rhoda Elaine Williams, who played Betty Anderson in *Father Knows Best*, was born July 19, 1930, in Denver, Colorado. Her family moved to Galveston, Texas, and then to Hollywood within a brief span. Rhoda grew up with radio, debuting at age nine on NBC's *I Want a Divorce!* She was soon heard on *Dr. Christian*, *One Man's Family*, *The Life of Riley*, *Lux Radio Theater* and other shows. Her most durable and memorable role was as Betty Anderson, a part she played for the full five-year run.

That didn't prevent her from earning a livelihood on both large and small screens, however. For three decades, beginning when she was just 14, she performed in theatrical motion pictures, mostly in uncredited roles and bit parts. Her total of 14 movies include *National Velvet* (1944), *House of Strangers* (1949), *Cinderella* (1950), *The Heart Is a Rebel* (1958), *High School Hellcats* (1958) and *The Sergeant Was a Lady* (1961).

Williams costarred in the fleeting NBC-TV sitcom *Mixed Doubles* in 1949. In addition, she made 21 guest appearances on dramatic and comedy TV series, including *Dragnet*, *Tightrope*, *Zane Grey Theater*, *Twilight Zone*, *Bob Hope Presents the Chrysler Theater*, *The Dick Van Dyke Show*, *Laredo*, *Felony Squad*, *The Big Valley*, *The Jimmy Stewart Show* and *Search*. She appeared in two episodes of Robert Young's *Marcus Welby, M.D.* (1970, 1974), and she wound up her formal acting career in a *Barnaby Jones* installment in 1980.

Having graduated from Hollywood High School, Williams continued her education at the University of California at Los Angeles, earning a bachelor's degree. She followed it with a master's degree in theater in 1972 from California State University, Northridge. The actress subsequently instructed speech and voice classes. She held memberships in the American Federation of Television and Radio Artists, the Screen Actors Guild, and several other professional alliances.

Married to David Van Meter on January 5, 1952, she became the mother of four children. Their names and birthdates: Janis Elaine Van Meter, October 1, 1952; Debra Kathlyn Van Meter, July 28, 1954; Jonathan D. Van Meter, April 24, 1961; and Steven R. Van Meter, October 19, 1963. The Van Meters left Los Angeles in 1992, and Rhoda died of natural causes at Eugene, Oregon, on March 8, 2006. She was survived by her husband; daughters Janis Hayes of Harrisburg, Oregon, and Debra DePew of Eugene, Oregon; sons Jon, of Corvallis, Oregon and Steven, of Tujunga, California; 12 grandchildren; and three great-grandchildren.

Ted Donaldson, Bud in radio's *Father Knows Best*, was born in New York City on August 20, 1933. He possessed a show business heritage, as his parents were venerated musicians. His father, William Donaldson (1891–1954), was a song writer, arranger, vocal coach and performer, penning arrangements with George Gershwin (1916) and Duke Ellington (1927). His mother, Muriel Pollock Donaldson (1895–1971), a Julliard School of Music graduate, was a concert pianist, composer, organist and accompanist, penning rag, jazz, concert and pop music while performing on radio (1925–36), stage and in concert. While Ted Donaldson's own showbiz career was condensed into a pithy interlude, what an impression he made in a brief span!

He premiered on radio as a four-year-old atop the lap of Ireene (sic) Wicker, *The Singing Lady*. Over the next three years his voice resonated from features like *Aunt Jenny's Real Life Stories, Between the Bookends, Life Can Be Beautiful, The March of Time, Our Gal Sunday* and a five-part aural adaptation of Charles Dickens' *A Christmas Carol*.

At seven, in April 1941, young Donaldson went on stage as the youngest son, Harlan Day, in a Broadway production of *Life with Father* that lasted two years. Within weeks after that he was back on the stage in Irwin Shaw's *Sons and Daughters*, starring Gregory Peck, Stella Adler and Karl Malden. A reviewer exclaimed: "The most amusing scene in the play is the work of a small boy named Ted Donaldson. It's impossible to describe just how he is so effective, but the author was wise to give him only a three or four minute bit else he would have walked off with the play amid a gale of laughter. He almost did anyway."

In 1943 Ted narrated a children's record-

ing by the Jack and Jill Singers. He performed on many recordings narrated by Milton Cross, some of those children's musicals and operettas that his mother, under the pen name "Molly Donaldson," composed, with Madge Tucker as arranger.

In the meantime, during the Second World War, weighing 87 pounds by the time he was nine, young Donaldson became a redhaired, pudgy-faced, extremely popular child star on the silver screen. He launched that phase of his career in 1944 in Norman Corwin's *Once Upon a Time*, for which *The Washington Post* critic acknowledged that Donaldson "ran away with the film"—pretty heady stuff since Cary Grant was the movie's star. The adolescent immediately turned up in a second 1944 release, *Mr. Winkle Goes to War*, starring Edward G. Robinson, again earning glowing citations for his work.

Donaldson interrupted his celluloid portrayals to appear with Ireene Wicker in a 1944 Christmas production on television. Thus, at age 11, he became one of only a handful of pre-pubescent thespians to earn the distinction of playing in five entertainment media: radio, stage, recordings, screen and television. The following year (1945), *Parents* magazine dubbed him "one of the finest juvenile stars of the day."

Altogether, Donaldson performed in 19 motion pictures. In a string of *Rusty* movies (*The Adventures of Rusty, The Return of Rusty, For the Love of Rusty, Son of Rusty,* et al.) he portrayed a recurring character, Danny Mitchell, at least eight times. His most celebrated picture was the 1945 Oscar-nominated *A Tree Grows in Brooklyn*. Donaldson carried the title role in 1948's *The Decision of Christopher Blake*.

Following a brink-of-manhood role in 1952's *Phone Call from a Stranger*, he retired from films at age 19. At 21, when *Father Knows Best* left radio, he quit show business altogether as a source of livelihood. Donaldson returned to the stage in 1968 to play the lead in *A Severed Head* in a production by the Ensemble Players of Los Angeles' Loyola University. Rhoda Williams (Betty in *Father Knows Best*) was also in the cast. Most other details of his later life are unrecorded. The Internet Movie Data Base reported that he was employed at a bookshop in the late 1970s, but beyond that no more information has been forthcoming.

Norma Jean Nilsson, *Father Knows Best*'s Kathy Anderson in the radio original, was born in Hollywood on January 1, 1938. At two years of age she was on the silver screen, appearing in 1940's *Emergency Squad*, the first of 17 theatrical motion pictures attributed to her. While most of her roles went uncredited, her major films included *Seventeen* (1940), *Typhoon* (1940), *I Want a Divorce* (1940), *Suspense* (1946), *The Gangster* (1947), *Peter Pan* (1953), *The Actress* (1953) and *The Green-Eyed Blonde* (1957).

Like her "siblings" in the Anderson family, Nilsson, too, got into radio early. By the late 1940s she was performing supporting roles on CBS and NBC's *The Jack Carson Show*, the anthology cast of CBS's *Doorway to Life*, and as Cookie, one of the Bumsteads' bewildering offspring in *Blondie*, a sitcom airing on all three networks. Her most durable role in the audio medium was as Kathy Anderson. After *Father Knows Best* departed, in 1956 Nilsson performed on *The CBS Radio Workshop*. No documented evidence has surfaced confirming that she persisted in broadcasting or movies beyond the release of her 1957 film.

Some footnotes are worthy of note, however. Nilsson registered an IQ of 162 at eight years of age, according to an item in Louella Parsons' column of November 16, 1946. At 11, in 1949, she signed a contract for a weekly salary of $125, which is believed to have made her the highest paid child actress in radio at the time. In December 1949 *The Los Angeles Times* identified Nilsson in a group of 10 students at local Bancroft Junior High School comprising the 500 Club, a contingent of youths who had appeared on at least 500 radio shows.

Finally, in October 2000, Nilsson, Ted Donaldson and Rhoda Williams—the three children on *Father Knows Best*—resurfaced at the annual convention of the Friends of Old Time Radio held at Newark, New Jersey, for a revival of a half-hour episode of their most memorable achievement. It was believed to be the first, and last, time the trio worked together since their radio series left the air.

*Father Knows Best* was at the forefront of a line of domestic situations that emerged on radio in the 1940s. In the minds of many, it outclassed most of the others by demonstrating a compassionate attitude among the members of its nuclear clan, and for its forthrightness in dealing with daily issues affecting average families of its epoch. While most similar sitcoms that began on radio also transitioned to the tube, few prevailed in repeating episodes for two full decades after its original run played out. *Father Knows Best* did. It was a testament to the talent of peerless actor Robert Young and the show's enveloping influence in presenting a microcosmic view of small-town Americana in the midst of the last century.

# 10

# Fibber McGee & Molly

## PAGLIACCIS OF THE AIR

For its edition of October 16, 1972, a scribe at *Newsweek* magazine penned these lines: "He lived in an imaginary house at 79 Wistful Vista, where the closet was filled with more junk than a scrap dealer's front yard. He was incurably lazy and a compulsive liar, but although he was always concocting some scheme to get out of work, he was invariably caught by his wife, who would exclaim: 'Tain't funny, McGee!' And at that precise moment, 48 million Americans sitting around their radios would break into uproarious laughter. McGee was Fibber and his lovable wife was Molly, and together they were one of the hottest regularly scheduled shows on radio." Another pundit delineated: "No twosome was more perfectly attuned to middle-class 1930s sensibilities than *Fibber McGee & Molly*.... The show, which seamlessly blended vaudeville high jinks with radio's cozier atmospherics, came along at the right time— a home remedy for a shaken, insecure, Depression-era America that needed reassuring that its values were still intact, alive and well." Over its lifetime the program made use of dozens of well-worn gags, witty scenarios capitalizing on sound properties that the audience anticipated and embraced every time they were trotted out. Concurrently, it introduced into the American lexicon numerous phrases that were repeated again and again by the public at large. Regularly calling forth an ensemble of eccentric figures that the listeners knew well, the series tickled the nation's sense of humor for two-plus decades. In its prime, no show provoked more laughter for a longer period among the faithful fans in Radioland.

❖ ❖ ❖

**Creator:** Don Quinn
**Producer-Directors:** Cecil Underwood (1930s), Frank Pittman (1940s), Max Hutto (1950s)
**Writers:** Don Quinn (1935–50), Phil Leslie (1943–56), Keith Fowler, Ralph Goodman, Joel Kane, Leonard L. Levinson, Tom Koch (1957–59)
**Orchestra Leaders:** Rico Marcelli (1935–36), Ted Weems (1936–38), Jimmy Grier (1937 on the West Coast), Billy Mills (1938–53)
**Vocalists:** Kathleen Wells, Ronnie and Van, Audrey Call, Gale Page, The Three Kings, the Johnson Merrymen, the Bennett Sisters, Lynn Martin, Joe Bolan, Emery Darcy, Clark Dennis, Bob Hanan, Ronnie Mansfield, Annette King, Kay Donna, the Clef Dwellers (all 1935–36); Perry Como (1936–37); Marvel (Marilyn) Maxwell (1936–37); Donald Novis (1938–39); Jimmy Shields (1939–40); The Four Notes (1939–40); The King's Men (arranger Ken Darby, Jon Dodson, Bud Linn, Rad Robinson, all from 1940–53); Martha Tilton (1941)
**Sound Effects Technicians:** Manny Segal (1935, 1939), Eleanor Weems (1937), Mrs. Ted Williams (1937), Don Mehan (1937), Jack Wormser, (1941), Virgil Reimer (1941), Frank Pittman (1942), Monte Fraser (1944), Warren Allen, Parker Cornel, Cliff Thorsness, Bud Tollefson
**Announcers:** Harlow Wilcox (1935–53), John Wald (1953–56), Don Wilson (1953)
**Recurring Cast:** *Fibber McGee:* Jim Jordan; *Molly McGee:* Marian Jordan; *Teeny:* Marian Jordan; *Mrs. Abigail Uppington:* Isabel Randolph; *Mr. Old-Timer:* Bill Thompson; *Wallace Wimple:* Bill Thomp-

son; *Nick Depopoulouss*: Bill Thompson; *Horatio K. Boomer*: Bill Thompson; *Bessie*: Cliff Arquette; *Wallingford Tuttle Gildersleeve*: Cliff Arquette; *Throckmorton P. Gildersleeve*: Harold Peary; *Mayor Charles LaTrivia*: Gale Gordon; *F. Ogden (Foggy) Williams*: Gale Gordon; *Karl Snarl*: Gale Gordon; *Otis Cadwallader*: Gale Gordon; *George (Doc) Gamble*: Arthur Q. Bryan; *Alice Darling*: Shirley Mitchell; *Beulah*: Marlin Hurt; *Mrs. Millicent Carstairs*: Bea Benaderet; *Silly Watson*: Hugh Studebaker; *Uncle Dennis*: Ransom Sherman; *Lena*: Gene Carroll; *Mrs. Clammer*: Elvia Allman; *Ole Swenson*: Richard LeGrand; *Flossie*: Betty Winkler; *Herbert Appel*: Herb Vigran

**Supporting Cast:** Jim Backus, Parley Baer, Sara Berner, Mel Blanc, Ken Christy, William Conrad, Mary Jane Croft, Bob Easton, Verna Felton, Bernadine Flynn, Lenore Kingston, Jess Kirkpatrick, Peggy Knudsen, Howard McNear, Tyler McVey, Marvin Miller, Frank Nelson, Zasu Pitts, Rolfe Sedan, Bud Stephen, Walter Tetley, Peter Votrian

**Sponsors:** Johnson Wax Company, for an extensive line of floor and vehicle cleaning and polishing agents (1935–50); Pet Milk Company, for Pet evaporated milk (1950–52); Reynolds Aluminum Company, for Reynolds aluminum foil (1952–53); Multiple participation, including Tums, Paper-Mate pens, Richard Hudnut home permanents, RCA appliances, Carters Little Liver pills, Prudential Insurance Company, Dial Laboratories, Armour and Company, Brown and Williamson Tobacco Company, Miles Laboratories, Inc. (1953–56)

**Themes:** "Save Your Sorrow for Tomorrow" (B.G. DeSylva and Al Sherman, 1937, except late 1937, to fall 1940), "Laugh Your Way Through Life" (briefly from October 1937), "Wing to Wing" (Billy Mills, fall 1940–56), "Ridin' Around in the Rain" (secondary refrain applied sporadically)

**Ratings:** High—37.7 (1942–43), Low—2.2 (1955–56), Median—19.8. Ratings based on 21 seasons (1935–56 inclusive).

**On the Air:** April 16–July 2, 1935, NBC, Tuesday, time unsubstantiated; July 8, 1935–March 7, 1938, NBC Blue, Monday, 8:00–8:30 P.M. Eastern Time (transitioned to NBC Red Monday at 8 P.M. in 1936; moved to NBC Red Monday at 9 P.M. in 1937); March 15–June 28, 1938, NBC, Tuesday, 9:30–10:00 P.M.; September 6, 1938–June 27, 1939, NBC, Tuesday, 9:30–10:00 P.M.; September 5, 1939–June 25, 1940, NBC, Tuesday, 9:30–10:00 P.M.; October 1, 1940–June 24, 1941, NBC, Tuesday, 9:30–10:00 P.M.; September 30, 1941–June 23, 1942, NBC, Tuesday, 9:30–10:00 P.M.; September 29, 1942–June 22, 1943, NBC, Tuesday, 9:30–10:00 P.M.; September 28, 1943–June 20, 1944, NBC, Tuesday, 9:30–10:00 P.M.; October 10, 1944–June 26, 1945, NBC, Tuesday, 9:30–10:00 P.M.; October 2, 1945–June 11, 1946, NBC, Tuesday, 9:30–10:00 P.M.; October 1, 1946–June 17, 1947, NBC, Tuesday, 9:30–10:00 P.M.; October 7, 1947–June 1, 1948, NBC, Tuesday, 9:30–10:00 P.M.; October 5, 1948–May 31, 1949, NBC, Tuesday, 9:30–10:00 P.M.; September 13, 1949–May 23, 1950, NBC, Tuesday, 9:30–10:00 P.M.; September 19, 1950–June 12, 1951, NBC, Tuesday, 9:30–10:00 P.M.; October 2, 1951–June 10, 1952, NBC, Tuesday, 9:30–10:00 P.M.; October 7, 1952–June 30, 1953, NBC, Tuesday, 9:30–10:00 P.M.; October 5, 1953–August 27, 1954, NBC, Monday-Friday, 10:00–10:15 P.M.; August 29, 1954–June 23, 1955, NBC, Sunday-Thursday, 10:00–10:15 P.M.; June 27–September 23, 1955, NBC, Monday-Friday, 11:45 A.M.–12:00 noon and June 27–September 22, 1955, NBC, Monday-Thursday, 10:00–10:15 P.M. (repeat broadcasts in evening); September 26, 1955–March 23, 1956, NBC, Monday-Friday, 10:00–10:15 P.M.; June 1, 1957–September 6, 1959, *Monitor*, NBC, Saturdays and Sundays at irregular intervals in three- to five-minute vignettes, with repeat airings in 1960 and 1961

**Extant Archival Material:** A large file on Jim and Marian Jordan, including newspaper and magazine clippings, sound recordings on cassette tape, scripts and books pertaining to *Fibber McGee & Molly*, is maintained in the local history collection by the Peoria Public Library, 107 N.E. Monroe Street, Peoria, IL, 61602–1070; (309) 497–2000.

Sound recordings and scripts of *Fibber McGee & Molly* broadcasts are included in the Archives; and separately in the Tom Price Collection, ca. 1935–ca. 1975, containing thousands of radio program recordings, 1930–60 (although only those transferred to cassettes are available for use), plus extensive research papers pertaining to *Fibber McGee & Molly* and Jim and Marian Jordan; housed at the Pacific Pioneer Broadcasters, Box 4866, North Hollywood, CA, 91617; (323) 461–2121; *www.pacific pioneerbroadcasters.org/archive/html*.

An unidentified number of scripts for *Fibber McGee & Molly* are among the Andy White Papers, 1935–1979, including script summaries for 1935–46, archived by the American Heritage Center of the University of Wyoming, 1000 East University Avenue, Laramie, WY, 82071; (307) 766–3756; Fax (307) 766–5511; *http://ahc.uwyo.edu/usearchives/default.htm*.

Microfilm of S.C. Johnson & Son's corrected copies of scripts, including commercials, are among the Fibber McGee & Molly Scripts, 1935–1950; separately, tape recordings of four 1939 *Fibber McGee & Molly* shows are included with the Hugh Carlson Recordings, 1939–1944; furthermore, there are progressive script drafts and transcripts of an interview with Jim Jordan in the Perry Miller Adato Papers, 1940–1974; all archived at the Wisconsin Historical Society, 816 State Street, Madison, WI, 53706; (608) 264–6460; Fax (608) 264–6486; *http://arcat.library.wisc.edu.*

Three *Fibber McGee & Molly* radio scripts are maintained in the Script Collection by the Broadcast Arts Library, Box 9828, Fort Worth, TX, 76147; (310) 288–6511; www.broadcastartslibrary.com.

Two scripts of *Fibber McGee & Molly*, one for the broadcast of October 14, 1952, the other for May 5, 1954, are preserved in the Monty Masters and Marvin Miller collections at Thousand Oaks Library, American Radio Archives, 1401 East Janss Road, Thousand Oaks, CA, 91362; (805) 449–2660; fax (805) 449–2675; *www.tol.lib.ca.us.*

*Heavenly Days: The Story of Fibber McGee & Molly* by Charles Stumpf and Tom Price, originally published in 1987 by the World of Yesterday, is available from BearManor Media, Box 71426, Albany, GA, 31708; (229) 436–4265; Fax (814) 690–1559; http://bearmanormedia.bizland.com/id16.html.

At least 531 *Fibber McGee & Molly* broadcasts between 1935 and 1956 are known to be in general circulation or held by private collectors as of 2006, sold by vintage radio dealers and traded by old-time radio hobbyists.

A log of *Fibber McGee & Molly* is available from Tom Price at 521 Toyon Drive, Monterey, CA, 93940, and in a catalog available from Terry Salomonson at http://users.aol.com/otrjerry2/terrysol.html.

❖ ❖ ❖

The legitimacy of *Fibber McGee & Molly* (*FM&M*) as a sitcom is somewhat suspect. One reviewer has interpreted it as "really only a series of skits; there were no 'stories' as such, just general themes to be developed by McGee and friends."[1] Another source affirmed: "Actually there was no 'story' to the programs. Usually a situation was established and then various characters would enter the McGee home at 79 Wistful Vista and help or hinder the action."[2]

It was so.

On one broadcast McGee was writing a book, "The Story of the Typewriter." In hunt and peck fashion, he pounded out some ridiculously funny terms and phrases, and applied them to manual typewriters. "Himself"—as Molly frequently dubbed her mate in referencing him to others—was convinced

it would be a work of art, a best seller. Then came the onslaught of Wistful Vista denizens, one at a time. They rang the family's dual chimes and, upon entering, added their personal perspectives on his venture before departing with a door slam.

Whether this was—or was not—a sitcom, *FM&M*'s significance among the annals of aural aircast features is indisputable. One eminent scholar suggests that vintage radio is defined by possibly no more than three programs: *Fibber McGee & Molly, The Lone Ranger* and *The Shadow*, shows that make "everybody's list."[3]

One radio historiographer assessed the series thusly: "Fibber McGee was in the long tradition of American braggarts and bumblers, the ineffectual husband who shouts and sputters while his wife looks on indulgently. He was originally a teller of tall tales in the tradition of frontier humorists Mark Twain, Josh Billings, and Artemus Ward, but by the 1940s McGee had, like Huck Finn, been 'sivilized' by [writer Don] Quinn and was more inept mainstream American male than cracker-barrel yarn spinner. Now he simply exaggerated, dreamed up goofy get-rich-quick schemes, and fumed."[4]

"Not until the success of the *Fibber McGee & Molly Show* by 1940 did the situation comedy become a strong alternative style," assured another. Jim and Marian Jordan "nurtured and refined two characters who comically summarized the conditions of millions of average American families.... The key to success ... was the development of a fallible, recognizable, sympathetic human character with whom listeners could warmly identify. Fibber McGee and Molly were ... familiar people, a blend of rural and urban that was awkward and vulnerable enough to affect the serious emotions as well as the funnybones."[5]

Yet another summarized the Jordans' most important radio venture like this: "*Fibber McGee & Molly* was more than a classic comedy program. It was an institution that upheld national morale during two critical events, the Great Depression and World War II."[6]

And *Radio Guide* depicted the central figures as the "Pagliaccis [Clowns] of the air who were trying their darndest to make America forget its troubles."[7]

Let's go back to the beginning.

James Edward Jordan was born on a farm outside Peoria, Illinois, on November 16, 1896. His future bride, Marian Driscoll, was born a coal miner's daughter in Peoria on April 5, 1898. After the Jordans moved to town, Jim completed eighth grade at St. Marks School, followed by a few more years of formal training while he was enrolled at Peoria's Spalding Institute. Marian was across the street from Spalding studying at the Academy of Our Lady, though she and Jim didn't meet during this time. Both were music lovers: he sang tenor with a trio that entertained locally; she was a contralto, also playing piano and violin. They finally met in December 1915 at a Christmas choral rehearsal at St. John's Catholic Church. After she invited him to a piano recital in January, the pair began dating.

Jordan was continually seeking to improve his financial situation by working short stints for Peoria employers. As a sideline he pursued musical engagements for the Templeton Quartet, which he formed in early 1917. By September he joined a Chicago vaudeville act, "A Night with the Poets," as tenor vocalist. For 39 weeks he toured the western U.S. and Canada, performing about 260 dates before departing for Peoria in April 1918. He was not only homesick but missing Marian Driscoll, who was earning a living as a piano coach. Jordan became a mail carrier. Overcoming the reservations of her family and gaining their blessing, he wed Marian on August 31, 1918. Five days later he was summoned by the Army. World War I was still raging. After six weeks of basic training in Georgia, Jordan was shipped to France, where he promptly contracted dysentery. He was hospitalized long past the Armistice signing. Meanwhile, he organized a camp show, "The Premiere Review," and toured U.S. hospitals throughout France for about six months following the hostilities.

Returning to Peoria, Jordan expanded his livelihood pursuits by gaining experience selling washing machines, vacuum cleaners and life insurance. Ultimately he decided to try show business again—this time with Marian by his side. The couple hired some professional instrumentalists and billed themselves as "The Metropolitan Musical Entertainers." While Jordan performed as a lyric tenor, Marian accompanied him on piano. Traveling by train, they performed in a different locale every day and were a huge success. At the zenith of this enterprise they took in $25,000 in one year. In the same period the Jordans became parents of a couple of progeny: Kathryn, born June 18, 1920, and Jim Jr., born August 3, 1923. For the most part Marian remained with the children in Peoria while Jim continued touring in vaudeville. Occasionally, however, she joined him for some bookings as "Marian and Jim Jordan— Harmony Team."

Jordan vocalized on a Minneapolis radio appearance in 1923, his first broadcast. When the family's outlay overtook their income, Jordan faced reality and temporarily returned to Peoria, where he found work clerking in a dry goods emporium and later sold toys at a department store. In 1925 the couple went on the air as "the Jordans, Marian and Jim" on Chicago's WIBO, their first audio show together, at $10 a week. Jordan later allowed: "That's when a performer learned how because you knew nobody was listening to it anyway, so you caught on how to do it. On that show we didn't speak a word, it was all songs and piano. We didn't talk on the radio until 1927." And yet, between 1925 and 1927 the Jordans routinely performed on a trio of radio stations nightly. While they played numerous features under a myriad of monikers, two stand out: *The Smith Family* and *Smackout*.

The former has been linked to the beginnings of soap opera. In fact, historians of the genre insist that Jim and Marian Jordan might be credited with originating the form itself. Premiering over Chicago's WENR one night weekly, *The Smith Family* was recognized by no less an esteemed authority than Francis

Chase, Jr. as "the great-granddaddy of soap operas." The conversational exchanges of *The Smith Family* were indicative of what would soon be coming down the pike as authentic daytime drivel, making that comic serial—even on a local station—a progenitor of a major genre.

Another of the serials' eminent scholars, Raymond William Stedman, elaborated on the pervasive influence of *The Smith Family*:

> In this open-end drama of family life, Marion [sic] Jordan became the first of the serial mothers, her sources of both delight and anxiety

being two marriageable daughters, one of whom was courted by a jaunty prizefighter (Jordan). The other daughter dated a Jewish boy....

In the brief time it was on the air, *The Smith Family* introduced audiences to continued drama that was more like the first daytime serials than most people realize. The action, though slapstick, concerned home and family. And most of the characters appeared regularly, affording the audience ample opportunity to get to know both them and their habits. In a way, the listener was eavesdropping upon something happening in someone else's home at that very moment—listening to people he

*But will it play in Peoria? These Peorians took a (Doc) Gamble (pun intended) that it would and—like Amos 'n' Andy—came close to embracing the parameters of radio's golden age. Marian and Jim Jordan's audio career took off with a couple of practice runs (The Smith Family, Smackout) in Chicago before the main course. As Fibber McGee & Molly, at their peak they ingratiated themselves to 48 million listeners. Residents of imaginary 39 Wistful Vista, the couple hosted an entourage of eccentric characters who dropped by every Tuesday night from the 1930s to the 1950s, causing America to burst with uncontrollable laughter via running gags and zingers. Although the Jordans became an NBC mainstay, Smackout aired over CBS in 1931, most likely when this photo was snapped.*

could expect to meet again and again.... *The Smith Family* had its place in the soap opera's family tree, if only as a stunted root.[8]

Strangely enough, Marian Jordan denounced any intimation that the pair contributed to soap opera's humble start. While she demonstrated a self-effacing humility throughout her life, there is sufficient evidence that their fledgling efforts may have influenced a genre more than either of them admitted or possibly even realized.

*The Smith Family* prevailed from June 9, 1929, to April 3, 1932. Toward the end of the run WENR raised the Jordans' salary to $60 weekly.

During the same period they became acquainted with an out-of-work commercial cartoonist and gag-writer from Grand Rapids, Michigan, named Don Quinn. Neither realized at the time that this gifted man would become their professional partner for about two decades and be responsible for drawing verbal characterizations for them that would be instantly recognized in homes across the country. The partnership began with Quinn penning *Smackout*, a humorous tale about the proprietors of a small-town grocery that was invariably "smack out" of whatever the patrons requested. Signing a 26-week contract at a guaranteed $250 weekly to start, Marian and Jim Jordan supplied an aggregate of 150-plus character voices during a four-year run. The show aired over Chicago's WMAQ, WENR and KYW (the latter call letters reassigned to Philadelphia late in 1934) from March 2, 1931 (overlapping *The Smith Family* at WENR by more than a year), to August 3, 1935. For at least part of the run, from November 1, 1931, to May 27, 1933, *Smackout* was carried by NBC to a national audience.[9]

The Jordans were growing more affluent in the process. Ironically, Marian received $140 of their weekly $200 salary for a sustaining (unsponsored) show because she played the piano in addition to acting. She was also a member of the musicians union. Out of the remaining $60 that went to Jim Jordan, he shelled out $40 to Don Quinn for his writ-

ing, leaving Jordan with $20 for his own efforts. Needless to say, the National Organization of Women would have loved that turn of events!

While *Smackout* was running, an opportunity emerged that would prove the veracity of an audience of one. Henrietta Johnson Louis, whose spouse, Jack Louis, was a partner in the advertising agency Needham, Louis and Brorby (NLB), prevailed on her husband to tune in *Smackout*, as she was doing daily. She was, not coincidentally, the daughter of H.F. Johnson, an heir to and then running the Johnson Wax Company of Racine, Wisconsin. NLB was Johnson's agency and was then seeking a new radio series on which to plug the firm's commercial wares. The upshot was that, late in 1934, the Jordans were offered a 26-week pact for a new show which NLB would hire Don Quinn to write. It didn't get much better than that. After hammering out a formula for the new feature, *Fibber McGee & Molly* debuted over NBC from New York on April 16, 1935. A published review of the first show read:

> Comedy, orchestra and vocalists. Sponsored by S. C. Johnson Company–NBC network. Fibber McGee, aided by his wife and heckler, Molly, contributes a funny and enjoyable program, one in fact that is likely to send the name of the team into the higher bracketed radio field.... Fibber isn't actually a new wrinkle.... He is sort of an 'Irish Baron Munchausen' ... but the combination of good delivery with good material insures success. First show was well paced and liberally sprinkled with laughs. Storyline involves Fibber's adventures as a tourist and his propensity for murdering the truth. His monolog on the question 'When a Red Light is a Dead Light' was very good. Ditto his story about Ermitrude the camel.... Supporting are Ulderico Marcelli's orchestra, and Ronnie and Van, duet. Kathleen Wells is soloist and handled her two numbers very nicely.... Harlow Wilcox, the announcer, doubled in foiling for Fibber, while the latter also delivered some gag commercials on auto wax.

*Variety*, on the other hand, which would soon alter its opinion, saw the premier in a less favorable light:

More ... a slipshod musical half hour than a refreshing down-to-earth comedy serial. Dialogue weak, with continuity continuously broken up by orchestrations and rural atmospheric sounds. Marian and Jim Jordan play the leading characters, a combo of hen-pecked husband and wise-cracking wife. The nickname explains the kind of humor unrolled. Femme's brogue is definitely Irish, while husband relays in a hinterland twang. No special reason for either of these varied assortment of tongues.... Nary a real out-and-out laugh in the lot, excepting, just once in a while, a carefully planned gag would be timed correctly. Again, the script limitations hampered the duo from ever getting underway.... Auto patter plentiful, with filling stations, mechanics, etc., worked into the story, but it was none too clever. Enamel talk was handled by Harlow Wilcox, who killed a few quips due to his premature laughs. Middle class sound effects never struck an authentic chord. Automobiles chugging, came over like a motor boat pulling into dock.... As it stands, program demands stiffer pacing, punchier lines, and more of Fibber and his frau.

Within 10 months *Variety* changed its tune—either the program was vastly improved or a new scribe was on the staff (or both), as evidenced by this February 12, 1936 citation:

Since first reviewed early in 1935, this program has undergone a change of personnel and a stepping up of tempo.... The program is now delivering a lot of entertainment. Essentially comedy, the pursuit of giggles is along broad and obvious lines. Broad and obvious is always okay for radio, but in this case, a nice timing of gags, and intelligent writing of the dialog has lifted the proceedings above the snappy level that the same material and situations could very easily degenerate into if not given smart treatment. Smartness spreads beyond the entertainment, and includes the commercial speiling, which is reasonable, yet forceful.

Obviously, *FM&M* had turned a corner.

In the early shows the client was most interested in plugging its car wax agents. To supplement that idea the McGees became road warriors, traveling hither and yon over the nation's highways, encountering storyline themes wherever they went. This persisted until the late summer of 1935 when Johnson decided to switch its emphasis from vehicles to floors, highlighting its line of cleansing and polishing agents for home and industry hardwoods, linoleum and other coverings. McGee and Molly came off the road and settled in a mythical place called Wistful Vista. McGee won a raffle, the prize being the little house at 79 Wistful Vista (the street was named after the town), and the couple moved in. It was years later that McGee trimmed a lilac bush that had been blocking their view of the house number and they discovered that they were really living at 81 Wistful Vista. But they had used 79 for so long, they kept it. Quite possibly it became the most universally identifiable address on any radio series.

In their treasure trove of all things McGee, Charles Stumpf and Tom Price paint a word picture of the dual characters. It could be effectively applied to any era of the series' long life:

McGee and his missus remained definite stereotypes. He was "Everyman," in what he did, said, and believed. A childlike showoff, he compulsively acted out his fantasies from week to week—never lacking in a scheme or two for getting rich quick. Exaggeration and overstatement were his trademarks. Without exception, Fibber became the butt of his own schemes. Most of the show's laughs came at his expense. Fibber never held a steady job and lacked responsibility. He was, nonetheless, a dutiful, tough, slightly hen-pecked husband. He loved Molly very much, but had a difficult time telling her so.

For her part, Molly was always a bit smarter than her spouse and much more practical. She shared her hubby's dreams for getting rich overnight, but was wise enough to know that the dreams were foolish and were doomed to failure before they had begun. She never let on though, at least not to the fanciful Fibber. What's more, Molly was a sentimentalist. She was head-over-heels in love with her husband and didn't much care who knew it.[10]

In many respects *Fibber McGee & Molly* compared favorably with another NBC spousal duo from 1937–55, *Lorenzo Jones* and his wife Belle. In that pair's daily serialized yarn, the eccentric Jones was an incorrigible inventor of useless stuff. When he wasn't doing that, he was dreaming up many more haywire plans, including plenty of get-rich-quick schemes. Sound familiar? In one prolonged scenario he fathomed the idea of turning his life story into a motion picture, *Lorenzo Jones, the Man!* Now, who does that remind you of? Such wacky pursuits "made him a character to the town—but not to Belle—who loves him," according to the show's daily epigraph. The similarities between the two men and the women who stood behind them trying to keep them on course were uncanny. For most of the run *Lorenzo Jones* was a humorous soap opera. *Fibber McGee & Molly* could have swapped genres and time periods with them. There they would, no doubt, have been acclaimed by a distaff audience in the midst of matinee mayhem surrounding the Joneses' weekday quarter-hour.[11]

The shows from New York continued for only a few weeks, transferring in the summer of 1935 to Chicago. The era of repeat broadcasts, one for the East Coast and Central region, the other beamed to the West Coast, ended on Monday, March 7, 1938. From then on the program was carried nationwide on Tuesday nights, originating in Chicago at 8:30 P.M.

For more than a few years *FM&M* was a ratings phenomenon. In 16 of its 21 seasons—including 16 of its 18 years as a half-hour show—it posted impressive double-digit numbers. On seven occasions those figures surpassed 30.0, and 10 times they exceeded 20.0, not a shabby accomplishment! In fact, the show's overall median for the 21 years was 19.8, an exceedingly high ranking. By 1937 the Johnson Wax Company was so pleased with its sudden and dramatic increase in distribution of furniture, woodwork, floor and vehicle cleaning and polishing agents—some of its commodities doubled in sales—that it renegotiated the Jordans' contract. Their combined salary was raised to a phenomenal $2,650 per program ($137,800 annually, based on the 52-week season the show was then airing)—not bad in post–Depression America for a couple of rural hoofers and

melody-makers. By early 1941 *FM&M* pushed past Bob Hope, Jack Benny and Edgar Bergen, and the Jordans' income climbed past $3,500 weekly. As the 1941–42 season concluded, the show was first in the nation, with a Crossley rating of 36.5 and a weekly budget of $24,000, less than 50 percent of the outlay other advertisers were spending on comedy series headlined by big names. By 1949 the show was reaching an estimated 40 million listeners weekly, and at its peak it was determined to have been heard by 48 million.

Don Quinn (1900–67) remained with *FM&M* for 15 years, until he decided to branch out into other projects. He subsequently created and oversaw the writing of the NBC series *The Halls of Ivy* (1950–52), starring Ronald and Benita Coleman. Nevertheless, Quinn was with *FM&M* in its heyday. Reporting in *Off Mike*, he offered some insightful perspectives on how the industry should treat an audience.

> The shows which live and build over the years are those for which the listener feels an abiding love and friendship. If you are a star on one of these happy productions, you are, by acclamation, a paid-up life member in good standing of millions of American families.
>
> They will stay home from bridge parties and movies to tune you in. They will agonize over your misfortunes and gloat over your triumphs. And, what is a far more important thing, they will buy your sponsor's product, whether they need it or not. You'd better mind your p's and q's, too, because you're in their homes on sufferance, though you may stay for years and years if you remain nice people.[12]

Quinn normally met with the Jordans every Thursday to give them his written thoughts about the following week's show (aired on Tuesday nights from 1938 to 1953). The Jordans reacted and made suggestions.

Quinn carried their input to his office and began formulating a script. There were further discussions with the Jordans and producers, and additional rewrites. By Sunday afternoon the wordsmith was back at the Jordan residence submitting a completed script. Quinn read the lines of all the actors aloud, except for McGee and Molly; they read their own lines. There was some follow-up discussion and the scribe took notes for improving the finished product. Afterwards, he returned to his office to polish the script into near-final form.

The entire cast assembled at NBC rehearsal studios on Monday mornings for a day-long practice. Some terms and phrases were altered once more, with cast members being urged to speak frankly. Neither Jordan complained if the better lines were spoken by supporting players. The closeness of the group was evident; achieving a quality broadcast was their unified goal. On Tuesday mornings there was a full dress rehearsal that included the 26-piece orchestra, vocal group, announcer and soundman. There were no further rehearsals: the show went on the air live at 8:30 P.M. when it originated in Chicago, and at 6:30 P.M. local time when it was in Hollywood.

Quinn hired Phil Leslie (1909–88) in 1943 to help him with the scripting. Leslie remained with the show until it ended 13 years later, assuming the job of head writer after Quinn departed. In later life Leslie made his living penning episodes of nearly a dozen television series, among them: *Hazel*, *The Farmer's Daughter*, *Petticoat Junction*, *The Addams Family*, *Green Acres*, *Get Smart*, *The Lucy Show*, *Julia* and *The Brady Bunch*.

From the late 1930s to 1953 *FM&M* followed a triple-segmented format, integrating music, commercials and comedy into a 13-point outline.[13] It was all so reminiscent of the vaudeville showcases from which some of its performers emanated.

1. Announcer introduces the show ("The Johnson Wax Program, with Fibber McGee and Molly," for most of the run)
2. Orchestra launches theme song
3. First commercial—announcer
4. Orchestral bridge music
5. Announcer sets the scene for the comedic plot; audience applauds
6. FIRST COMEDY SCENARIO (situation established)
7. First musical number—either by Billy Mills and his orchestra or the Kings Men vocal quartet, backed by the orchestra
8. SECOND COMEDY SCENARIO (situation progresses with second commercial integrated into plot and delivered by announcer)
9. Second musical number—reverse participation from the first musical number
10. THIRD COMEDY SCENARIO (situation resolved)
11. Third commercial—announcer
12. Orchestra launches theme song as McGee and Molly bid farewell ("Goodnight all" was Molly's standard sign-off)
13. Closing comments by announcer[14]

The celebrated closet routine on the *Fibber McGee & Molly* show was doubtlessly the most famous running gag in radio. It became highly identifiable to all of their fans, likely because the listeners' psyches transferred it to a sight gag. Comedian George Burns declared, "No picture could have been funnier than what the listener was seeing."[15] Even people who were born since the radio series was on the air have heard about Fibber McGee's closet. Introduced as a special effect by soundman Manny Segal on March 5, 1940, after McGee yanked open the hall closet door in search of something, the gag had all manner of hell breaking loose. Using a portable staircase for his auditory pop-art, the soundman allowed 10 empty oil cans, a pair of roller skates, a snow shoe, a barrel of broken crockery, a bowling pin, two boxes of kitchenware, a rake, an egg beater, three cowbells and a mandolin to cascade down the stairs following a little shove. A tinkling bell signaled the end of the routine as it rolled around on the floor—much like those in the studio audience seemed to be doing by then.

On rare occasions nothing would happen for a few moments after the door was opened, keeping fans on the edge of their chairs. The gag was repeated on scores of broadcasts in the years that ensued. Now and then somebody other than McGee would yank the door open. When the audience laughter began to die down, McGee invariably muttered: "Gotta clean that thing out one of these days!" Making good on his intents about nearly anything was one of his greatest handicaps, of course.

Wistful Vista hadn't been visited by the latest advanced technology, therefore it was still accustomed to pre-rotary-dial, operator-assisted telephone connections, even when calling locally. McGee often picked up the phone and, in requesting to be linked to his party, invariably heard the familiar voice of Myrt, a switchboard operator at the local telephone company. "Oh, izz-zat you, Myrt?" he'd inquire. The studio audience would break into titters as it eavesdropped on his side of the conversation.

"How's every little thing, Myrt? ... Your brother did what? ... Fell down the stairs and smashed his face and broke off one of his hands? Oh, my gosh...."

At that juncture Molly would cut in with her usual rejoinder: "Heavenly days! The poor lad...."

McGee would complete the routine with Myrt, explaining: "...Dropped his watch again, eh?"

On another occasion his riposte to Myrt was: "Your brother's up the river again, hunh, Myrt?"

"Heavenly days!" Molly replied in despair.

McGee repeated what Myrt had just told him: "...He's convinced the fishing is better up the river than around here, right?"

Another time the set-up line McGee uttered was: "Your kid brother, hunh? Broken back, hunh?"

To which Molly inquired, "Oh, heavenly days—what happened?"

McGee continued, repeating what he'd heard: "...He was hitchhiking to the west coast and got as far as Peoria and ran out of money, and now he's broke 'n back, you say?"

One of the best running gags on the show—which never failed to dissolve the studio audience into raucous laughter—was McGee's penchant for alliteration. Don Quinn worked a mind-blowing tongue-twister

into his scripts almost every week. It was usually inane and irrational, but it brought the house down every time. Here's a sample: "Punch-bowl McGee, I was known as in those days. Pronounced by press and public as the Pugilistic Pixie of the pedigreed paper-weight pugs, pummeling pudgy palookas, pulverizing proboscuses and paralyzing plug-uglies. Pounding a peach of a punch that plunked the punks on their piazzas. The Ping-Pong Poppa of the pineapple punch. A peculiar poke that petrified the pit of the paunch of the pillow-pushers who plopped to the platform too pop-eyed to protest!"

There were plenty of other "Fibberisms," like his frequently exhibited predilection for imagery. "Them springs are tighter than a forty-dollar girdle after a spaghetti dinner," he once observed.

His salutation to Molly could be "Snookie," "Tootsie" or "Kiddo," while she called him "McGee." When McGee was wound up over something, he often muttered "Ah, pshaw!" And legions of Americans picked up Molly's phrase and for years repeated one of the program's most memorable mottoes after it steadily fell from her lips: "T'ain't funny, McGee!" When encountering someone she didn't know, she'd habitually remark: "How do you do, I'm sure."

Marian Jordan was among the show's dialecticians, of which there were several. Her legendary alter ego, Teeny, the precocious neighborhood imp who taunted McGee with incessant whiny-voiced questions when he was focused on something else, was a classic: "Hey mister ... whatcha doin', hunh, mister? ... Hunh? ... Whatcha doin'? ... Hunh? ... Whatcha?" She harassed him until he was completely bumfuzzled, repeatedly working "I betcha" into her pithy ponderings. After McGee ventured to offer some explanation that he hoped would satisfy her curiosity about what he was up to or to solve whatever dilemma she raised—hoping she would run along and leave him alone—she'd sassily retort: "I know it!"

Possibly the most versatile dialectician on the show was the first supporting cast member to be permanently added to the roster, voice actor William H. (Bill) Thompson, Jr. Over a transitory span he acquired a working knowledge of 19 foreign languages while specializing in animal sounds as well, his obituary in *The New York Times* acknowledged. Born to a couple of vaudevillians on July 8, 1913, at Terre Haute, Indiana, he exhibited a talent for mimicry early: at age two he made his first professional appearance on stage, and at five he performed regularly with his parents.

In high school in Chicago he wrote and directed plays and organized theater clubs. He submitted a sketch for an NBC competition that drew 5,000 entrants during the Chicago Century of Progress World's Fair Exhibition in 1933. After performing it like a veteran with its 10 dialects, within a week—at age 20—he was on the ether in a *National Farm and Home Hour* skit. Soon Thompson was singing with a choral group on *The Sinclair Wiener Minstrels* on NBC Blue. By 1934 he was a regular on Don McNeill's daily feature *The Breakfast Club* on the same web. On some occasions, with McNeill, Thompson played a meek, mush-mouthed figure which had a strong bearing on "Mr. Wimple" a few years later. It was the start of something grand. By 1936 he performed on McNeill's Saturday NBC program *Jamboree*. In the meantime, the versatile artist provided the voice of Snifter, the Talking Dog on Morey Amsterdam's fleeting *Night Club* program in 1937, while impersonating a parrot on *The Story of Mary Marlin*, a daytime serial.

On January 27, 1936, in his first appearance on *Fibber McGee & Molly*, Thompson introduced a character with a heavy Greek accent that he had been impersonating on a local program, *The Hoffinghams*, over WENR. When he applied the dialect on *FM&M* the audience went into "hysterics," according to a reporter. Thompson returned the following week as an Irish policeman, hinting at the diversity of his voice abilities. He was quickly hired as an ongoing member of the cast and soon trotted out characters like the Greek Nick DePopolous, a W.C. Fields–sounding

Horatio K. Boomer, Scotsman Angus MacPerson MacKenzie MacTavish, Russian Nikolas Andreviev Alexandrovitch Ivanoffsky Smikelovna and more. In Thompson's vast repertoire, however, there were two that stood head-and-shoulders above all the others, both of which persisted to the end of the half-hour run: Mr. Old-Timer, who was sometimes referred to as the Old-Timer; and a rejuvenated Wallace Wimple.

Mr. Old-Timer, whose real name was Rupert Blasingame, usually saluted the McGees with "Hey there, Johnny!" and "Hello there, daughter!" The feisty codger frequently worked his mama and papa and his gal, Bessie, into his rapid-fire spiel. McGee would make an observation, usually a flat statement in which he expressed an opinion or put a spin on a given issue, only to have the Old-Timer chortle: "Well, that's purty good, Johnny. But that ain't the way I heeee-rrrrd it! The way I heeee-rrrrd it, one feller sez ta t'other feller, sez ... Saaayyy, he sez ..." and then trail off, completing his thought. His expression, "Well, that's purty good, Johnny," and the phrase that followed became one of many slogans to reach beyond the confines of the show. It even surfaced in the Warner Brothers cartoon *Tortoise Wins by a Hare*. Bugs Bunny disguised himself as a bearded old man and reprised portions of the hallmark expression while trying to trick the turtle into revealing how he beat the rabbit. Furthermore, Thompson's Old-Timer has been favorably compared to Parker Fennelly's Titus Moody, a resident of Fred Allen's infamous "Alley."

The other celebrated Thompson characterization, Wallace Wimple, was brought out of mothballs to make his first appearance on *FM&M* on April 15, 1941. It was probably the most memorable of all the voices beyond those of the dual stars. A mild-mannered Wimple addressed the McGees with a down-in-the-mouth "Hello, folks!" The terribly henpecked spouse poked fun at his "big old fat wife, Sweetie Face" (with a given name of Cornelia). He lived in fear of this woman, yet chortled mercilessly over what he'd like to do to her to retaliate for her brow-beating him. None of it did he ever do, of course, except in his dreams.

His hobby was bird-watching, and he often carried his "Bird Book" (emphasizing the B's as he said it) to identify the varieties he witnessed. In dialogue with others—when he liked something he heard—he responded gleefully, "Oh, that's just peachy," as the studio audience erupted into rowdy, foot-stomping convulsions.

Animation film director Tex Avery created a canine figure named Droopy Dog around the Wallace Wimple inflection, which appeared regularly on cinematic cartoon screens. Thompson supplied the voice-overs. It all came to a screeching halt, however, including his appearances on FM&M, when he was summoned to war by Uncle Sam. He served in the Navy from 1943 to 1946, then resumed his radio work while expanding his voice-over career in movies and television. Thompson subsequently turned up on The Edgar Bergen and Charlie McCarthy Show as a guest lecturer, and appeared several times on The CBS Radio Workshop. In the movies he impersonated the Dodo and the White Rabbit in Alice in Wonderland, and the pirate Mr. Smee in Peter Pan, reprising those roles in radio adaptations on Lux Radio Theater.

In 1956 in Lady and the Tramp he delivered five dialects in a single film: Jock the Scottish terrier, Bull the Cockney bulldog, Dachsie the German dachshund, Joe the Italian chef and an Irish policeman in the park. He was Ranger J. Audubon Woodlore in multiple Donald Duck and Humphrey the Bear shorts, and Professor Owl in a couple of musical shorts, including the Academy Award–winning Toot Whistle Plunk and Boom. He recreated both roles in Walt Disney's varied TV series, and in 1967 was the first thespian to voice the comic book namesake character in the movie short Scrooge McDuck and Money. There were many similar ventures.

In 1957 Thompson became an executive in community relations for the Union Oil Corporation in Los Angeles. He continued doing limited work in animation, playing

King Hubert in 1959's Sleeping Beauty and Touché Turtle on TV's Touché Turtle and Dum Dum. His last role was as Uncle Waldo in 1970's The Aristocrats; it was released shortly before he succumbed to a heart attack on July 15, 1971. Thompson was 58, hardly old enough to qualify as Horatio K. Boomer, Mr. Old-Timer, Wallace Wimple and additional voices that made him a joy to hear.

Fibber McGee & Molly distinguished itself by transporting two of its prime comedy artists into their own discrete radio series: Throckmorton P. Gildersleeve, the McGees' neighbor, shifting seamlessly into The Great Gildersleeve in 1941 and prevailing there to 1958; and Beulah, their Negro maid, for whom a series was created under the sobriquet Beulah in 1945, lasting to 1954. There were 1950s television extensions of both spinoff series, incidentally.

Actor Harold Peary joined the McGee cast in Chicago in 1937. Proving a versatile utility player, he turned up in many different roles, and sometimes more than one per episode. A permanent characterization as an overblown, self-important windbag was created for him in 1939 at his request, and he moved in as a resident next door to the McGees. Sparks immediately began to fly between the two men. "You're a haaaarrrrd man, McGee!" was Gildersleeve's anticipated retort to their foolish bickering as audiences ate it up, loving their weekly confrontations. A couple of years later Gildersleeve's popularity mushroomed and he was thrust into his own show. When Harold Peary left the show in 1950, a sound-alike actor, Willard Waterman, won the part and carried on as if there had been no change. Meanwhile, McGee missed his sniping chum and soon found another in Doc Gamble, who would persist through the 30-minute run, ending in the mid–1950s.

Beulah, the McGees' housekeeper-maid-cook-bottlewasher, showed up in the McGee plots on January 25, 1944. The part originated with Marlin Hurt, a male white actor with a range of high-pitched falsetto dialects, perfect for conveying the black mammy. As

Beulah, Hurt ignited roars of unquenchable laughter from the studio audience after standing with his back to the microphone awaiting his cue and—hearing it—whirling around to face the house for the first time, inquiring: "Did somebody bawl for Beulah?" Even though most fans might have realized the part was played by a man, seeing him deliver his lines was still hilarious. The figure grew in popularity, so that, in mid-1945, "she" was dispatched, with the blessings of *FM&M*, to launch *The Marlin Hurt and Beulah Show* on CBS. After Hurt died of a heart attack nine months later, the revised show with other actors was redubbed *Beulah*. In its most unforgettable portrayal, Hattie McDaniel carried the role from 1947 until her own death in 1952.

Many more humorous thespians turned up nearly every week at 79 Wistful Vista. A few of the most widely celebrated are presented here:

- *Mrs. Abigail Uppington* (Isabel Randolph, 1007–1073), a self-aggrandizing socialite McGee addressed as "Uppie." She threw lavish parties for Wistful Vista's "upper-crust" (demarcated by McGee as "a bunch of crumbs held together by dough"). After departing the show in 1943, Uppie was succeeded by a couple of successive elitist snoots who also got under McGee's skin: *Mrs. Millicent Carstairs* (Bea Benaderet, 1906–68) and *Mrs. Clammer* (Elvia Allman, 1904–92).
- *Mayor Charles LaTrivia* (Gale Gordon, 1906–95), a long-winded nerd with a penchant for rambling observations; he constantly tripped himself up over metaphors. He went off on tangents, pontificating about this and that, making missteps along the way. He once mentioned that he had played "possum." When McGee pressed him about it, he responded: "Look, when I said I was playing possum, I merely meant I was lowing lye ... er, lying low ... I never said I was ... You're the one that always mis-con-words my strues ... strue remarks my words! ... Every time I

stake a simple matement ... er, make that a staple mintment ... stinkle statement ... minkel stutmeant ... LOOK ... *You're* the one ... I ... YOU ..." Being utterly defenseless, LaTrivia finally stopped, paused interminably, then calmly said as only the basso-voiced Gale Gordon could bellow: "McGee." (One could hear him meting out in measured syllables "Miss Brooks" or—in later years—"Mrs. Carmichael" after a disaster on other series.) The *FM&M* studio audience had, by then, dissolved into bedlam. "The silence between the climax of his angry tirade and the uttering of 'McGee' was as funny as any piece of dialogue," proclaimed media critic Leonard Maltin. "The actor said he timed those pauses according to the audience sitting in front of him."

"I *listened* to the audience, and it occurred to me one day that when there is silence, what is the audience doing? They are thinking about (a) what you might say, (b) *if* you're going to say it, and *when* you're going to say it.... They're very busy. I used to time those pauses by the audience. I knew just by hearing them when it was time to say 'McGee,' and then it would work.

"Sometimes I'd wait twenty seconds without a breath, sometimes more. I never took a stopwatch and said, 'I'm going to wait twenty seconds.' If I knew they were ... receptive, I'd wait longer.... Jim Jordan used to stand there and start laughing—he couldn't believe that I would wait that long. The people in the booth would say, 'Oh my!' Sometimes they'd wonder whether I'd dropped dead right in front of the mike.... It was the audience; the audience is terribly important to an actor, but so few actors realize it."[16]

For a while after New York City Mayor Fiorello LaGuardia's death in 1947—on whom Mayor LaTrivia was based—His Honor was absent from the *McGee* show, replaced by *F. Ogden Williams*, the Weatherman (also played by Gordon), a visitor whom McGee dubbed "Foggy." Williams didn't try to predict much about the atmosphere; he usually spoke in generalities. He'd depart the McGee domicile with, "Well, good day ... probably."

Gordon also appeared as *Karl Snarl*, manager-with-an-attitude at a local finance firm, and—on rare occasions—as Molly's old swain, *Otis Cadwallader*.

- *Doctor George Gamble* (Arthur Q. Bryan, 1899–1959), supplying a flesh-and-blood nemesis for McGee, a stand-in for Gildersleeve in that pivotal role. For at least a dozen years after his arrival in 1943 Gamble sparred with his adversary, a perfect foil for McGee. McGee's insulting references to the medic ran the gamut of physical alliteration: "tummy thumper," "bone bender" and "serum salesman." In turn, Gamble addressed McGee as "Marble-head," "Neanderthal" and "Gutternose." It was a constant game of one-upmanship in everything the pair did, with the sly old physician usually coming out on top.

And now for some typical gags....

> MCGEE: *As the fat lady said when she took off her corset, that lets me out.* (March 12, 1940)

> MCGEE: *As the ball player said when he told the third baseman "good-bye," I've gotta be heading for home.* (January 7, 1941)

> MCGEE: *I'm a member of the sweater set. I either sweat 'er set.*

> MOLLY: *'Tain't funny, McGee.* (September 30, 1941)

> WALLACE WIMPLE: *My goodness, I haven't seen you for simply weeks. I suppose that's because it's been so rotten out.*

> MOLLY: *No, it's because you've been so written out.* (December 9, 1941)

> MILLICENT CARSTAIRS: *Mr. Carstairs is very interested in antiques.*

> MCGEE: *Now there's a straight line if I ever heard one.* (May 15, 1945)

> MCGEE (after doorbell): *Who's this? Everybody's been here once already.* (April 3, 1951)

> MOLLY: *Sometimes I wish the radio had never been invented. And then when I think how we both like to eat regularly, I'm glad it was.* (date unknown)

> MCGEE: *Ah, there goes a good kid. How she ever puts up with these nasty moods of mine I'll never know ... except she knows that they never last more than half-an-hour ... once a week ... usually Tuesdays.* (date unknown)

The middle commercial in the show took on added emphasis. As it did in *The Jack Benny Program*, the spot was integrated into the storyline as the effervescent Harlow Wilcox dropped by 79 Wistful Vista on Tuesday nights to deliver a spin about a commodity manufactured by the program's underwriter. Although Wilcox referred to McGee as "Pal" almost from the start, and McGee referenced the announcer as "Harpo" during the show's earliest days (possibly because he harped so much about the sponsor's wares) and "Junior" much later, somewhere along the way McGee assigned the appellation "Waxy" to Wilcox. That handle evolved into "Milky" after the Pet Milk Company took over the show's sponsorship in 1950.

Many times when Wilcox showed up on his doorstep McGee would be agitated about something, or be busy with a scheme to prove his worth to the world or make a million dollars for him and Molly. Nonetheless, he'd audibly moan over what he knew was coming: a commercial pitch. It was even worse when Molly was present, for she would innocently inquire something like: "Tell us, Mr. Wilcox, why do you have such a bright shine on your face?" McGee would groan in response. "Oh Molly, now you've gone and done it!" Without missing a beat, Wilcox was off and running: "That bright shine on my face, Molly, is a reflection of the perfect job I get every time I apply Johnson's Self-Polishing Glo-Coat to my hardwood floors!" McGee would interrupt his guest frequently with little rejoinders, qualifying his misery: "Oh, my goodness!" or "Good grief, Waxy!" Few shows attempted to assimilate the advertising into the plot. *FM&M* did so every week. For many fans its droll reverberations became an anticipated moment, a delightful part of the act.

From the very start of each weekly show, Wilcox's familiar audio billboard "The Johnson Wax Program with Fibber McGee & Molly" reinforced the link between the stars and the paste and liquid polishing compound manufacturer. That association grew proportionately as the years rolled by, affording instant subliminal imagery for the company's products. Similar reminders tied Jack Benny's fans to Jell-O and Lucky Strike, *Ma Perkins* to Oxydol, *Jack Armstrong* to Wheaties, *The Great Gildersleeve* to Kraft, and *Amos 'n' Andy* to Pepsodent.

In 1937 the Jordans signed with Paramount Pictures to appear in a FM&M movie, *This Way Please*. On May 3, 1937, the program shifted to the West Coast for 10 weeks. The film starred Charles (Buddy) Rogers, Betty Grable and Ned Sparks. Mary Livingstone made her screen debut in the musical comedy, along with the Jordans, who appeared in multiple brief sketches. The flick premiered on October 7, 1937, at the Paramount Theater in Los Angeles. So pleased with the Jordans' performance were Paramount officials that the duo was signed for three additional films—none of which were made. Marian's health became an issue before work could proceed and that contract was voided.

Nonetheless, there were still three more celluloid productions featuring the Jordans, but filmed at a later date and for RKO Radio Pictures. The next one, *Look Who's Laughing*, a comedy, was released in 1941 and premiered on October 9 at New York's Palace Theater. Receiving top billing were Edgar Bergen and Charlie McCarthy, followed by Jim and Marian Jordan, and Lucille Ball. Several members of the radio troupe appeared with them: Harold Peary (Throckmorton P. Gildersleeve), Bill Thompson (Wallace Wimple), Gale Gordon (Otis Cadwallader) and Isabel Randolph (Abigail Uppington).

In the third film in the series, *Here We Go Again*, a comedy issued in 1942, the stars were again Bergen and McCarthy and the Jordans. Each of the others from the radio series who appeared in the previous movie reprised their roles.

In the last cinematic entry, *Heavenly Days* (1944), another comedy, the Jordans received top billing. The King's Men turned up in that motion picture, but the other cast members did not. Peary was playing in Gildersleeve flicks by then; Gordon was overseas defending the country; and Randolph had left the show.

Getting back to Molly's health, for a while it had been fragile as they made that first picture in 1937. The Hollywood activity on top of a punishing schedule that included the weekly show, personal appearances, interviews and publicity obligations simply proved too much. In September 1937 her physician ordered her to bed for total rest at a sanitarium between weekly broadcasts. She was removed from every other assignment. Her illness progressed, nevertheless, and soon she left the show altogether. The program was introduced as *Fibber McGee & Company* during Marian's prolonged absence.

The Jordans' daughter, Kathryn, age 17 in 1937 when this occurred, spoke on a British Broadcasting Corporation series not long ago about her mother and father's career. She confirmed to the public for perhaps the first time that Marian Jordan had suffered a severe nervous breakdown. Placed in a psychiatric facility for therapy and care, at the peak of her illness she was suicidal. When Marian was able to return home, she continued therapy until she was able to return to the show. It didn't happen overnight. It had been announced that she would rejoin the cast when the show resumed following a summer break in the fall of 1938. But Marian wasn't up to it. Not until the broadcast of April 18, 1939, in fact, did she permanently reappear, her absence lasting about 18 months. There was considerable rejoicing among cast, studio audience and listeners that night!

During her absence from the microphone Marian was protected from public scrutiny and conjecture. Stories surfaced linking her sudden disappearance to fatigue, rheumatic fever, alcoholism and other causes. Discussion continues in the modern era, too: "For 18 months in 1937–38 it [FM&M] aired without Marian, reportedly due to fatigue or a nervous breakdown, but in reality, alcoholism."[17] A contemporary researcher observed: "I'm glad the press didn't pursue the reasons for Marian's departure from the program or she probably would never have been able to return."[18] Can there be much doubt that CNN, FOX, MSNBC and their ilk would have chewed her up and spit her out had they existed then?

The Jordans experienced a taste of California living during the show's 10-week sojourn in the Golden Gate State as their motion picture was being filmed in 1937. Molly's illness was evident a couple of months later. According to series chroniclers Charles Stumpf and Tom Price, Jim Jordan subsequently convinced himself that the balmy temperatures on the West Coast could be incredibly advantageous to Marian's health. He initiated steps to transfer the show's site of origin once more. Jordan persuaded the network, agency and sponsor to go along with him. Processing all the arrangements took awhile. Finally, on January 24, 1939, the *McGee* series signed off for the very last time in the Windy City.

Beginning January 31, 1939, it aired from NBC's Hollywood studios. The new venue became its home for the rest of the run. Accompanying the Jordans on their cross-country trek were Don Quinn, Billy Mills and his orchestra, the Four Notes harmony group (which were replaced a year later by the King's Men, who prevailed for 13 years), announcer Harlow Wilcox and comic-actor regulars Bill Thompson, Harold Peary and Isabel Randolph. Left behind were utility players Hugh Studebaker, Bernadine Flynn and Betty Winkler. The trio had commitments to other Chicago-based shows, including numerous soap operas.

In 1949 Jim Jordan sold the rights to *Fibber McGee & Molly* to NBC. That same year the Jordans made a detour from their usual roles, appearing in CBS's dramatic series *Suspense* in the tense tale "Back Seat Driver." They repeated the narrative there in 1951. Also in 1949 the Johnson Wax Company made it clear that it was ready to transfer the huge investment it had been making in radio to television, where many other firms were focusing the bulk of their advertising budgets. Would there be a televised version of *Fibber McGee & Molly?*

Jim and Marian were not at all sure that the new medium would be well-suited to them. They realized that essentially the success of their

radio program had depended upon the listener's imagination. The key elements being the famous closet door gag and the ... host of outlandish characters played by a mere handful of actors, all of which constituted a program uniquely suited to radio. A show that possibly could not, and most likely would not, lend itself to the revealing eye of the television camera.[19]

Somewhat apathetically, in 1950 the Jordans made a pilot film for a potential TV show. It went nowhere, but Johnson Wax did, taking its money out of the *FM&M* radio show and putting it into NBC-TV's *Robert Montgomery Presents* (1950–57) and *The Saturday Night Revue* (summers of 1953, 1954). The Pet Milk Company (1950–52) stepped into the void left by the departing wax-maker, followed by the Reynolds Aluminum Company (1952–53), after which the show continued with a participating sponsorship arrangement.

There was a *Fibber McGee & Molly* TV series nearly a decade later featuring Bob Sweeny and Cathy Lewis as the celebrated couple. It debuted on NBC-TV on September 15, 1959, and was off the air on January 5, 1960. "While Sweeney and Lewis were outstanding performers in their own right, longtime fans of the radio program simply could not accept them in the all too familiar roles of Fibber and Molly," wrote Stumpf and Price. "The TV series lacked the magic spark that had been provided by the Jordans and their excellent writers and supporting cast."[20] The Jordans' observations of a decade earlier may have haunted the video producers in the failed attempt.

In the meantime, when the show moved to a five-night-a-week quarter-hour format in the autumn of 1953, it was transcribed. It was also heard sans Harlow Wilcox, Billy Mills' orchestra and the King's Men, all victims of drastic budget-cutting. The studio audience was absent, too. The McGees were silent from March 23, 1956 to June 1, 1957, when 10 three- to five-minute sketches began airing on NBC's weekend marathon *Monitor* magazine programming service. These were written mostly by Tom Koch, who penned 1,136 vignettes featuring Marian and Jim. Five were aired throughout the day on Saturdays and another five on Sundays. This continued through September 27, 1959, with about 160 of the features replayed in 1960 and 1961. Thus, with the exception of about 14 months the show didn't air in 1956–57, plus summer vacations, *Fibber McGee & Molly* persisted on radio in one form or another from 1935 to 1961, or about a quarter-of-a-century, a durable run for a couple of kids from Peoria.

Actually, in February 1960 NBC urged the Jordans to sign a new contract for a three-year extension of their *Monitor* feature, with new material. But when Marian consulted a physician she learned she had a malignant ovarian tumor. The Jordans declined NBC's offer. Marian's strength waned for a year. She died at home in Encino on April 6, 1961.

Unaccustomed to being without Marian, Jim Jordan retired from show business and took a vacation to Hawaii. There he met the widow of dialect-comedian Harry Stewart, Gretchen, in the islands under similar circumstances. They returned to their homes but stayed in touch. On January 31, 1962,

they wed in Honolulu and left on an Orient wedding trip. Jordan was 65.

He returned to the microphone a dozen years later for a syndicated audio series, *Fibber McGee and the Good Old Days of Radio*, with seven installments running 55 minutes each. Phil Leslie penned the scripts, vintage radio historian Chuck Schaden hosted, and Hal Peary and Gale Gordon took listeners on a walk down memory lane. Jordan performed several more times on radio before his death on April Fool's Day, April 1, 1988, at 91. His widow and children donated his bound volumes of *Smackout* and *Fibber McGee & Molly* scripts to Chicago's Museum of Broadcast Communications. That organization exhibits a replica of the famous closet in its impressive collection.

"The rise of the *Fibber McGee & Molly Show* led directly to a revival of situation comedy in radio," media historian Fred MacDonald proclaimed. "Eager to duplicate the popularity and profitability of that series, sitcoms proliferated in broadcasting in the 1940s."[21]

In that sense, perhaps, it was a sitcom after all.

# 11

# *The George Burns and Gracie Allen Show*

## The Most Successful Married Couple in Show Business

In retrospect, no radio team may have been better appreciated than Burns and Allen. According to historian Luther Sies, "Their long successful career warrants their recognition as the best comedy team in American Radio's Golden Age." He classified Burns as "a lackluster dancer and former seal trainer" before he met Allen in 1922, "half of a sister dancing act," and they formed a new partnership on and off stage. Burns saw potential in pushing his mate to the forefront. While he was the supreme straight man, she got the laughs from her specious views. "One day, the audience realized I had a terrific talent," Burns habitually insisted throughout his life. "They were right. I did have a terrific talent. And I was married to her for 38 years." Allen was cited by many sources for an impeccable delivery. "Only Jack Benny surpassed her excellent sense of timing," wrote Sies. Burns and Allen were among the few duos who not only successfully transitioned from vaudeville to radio (where they persisted for 18 years), but shifted once again to TV (lasting until Allen retired after eight years). Their radio debut was a replay of their stage routines—pithy sketches and humorous monologues interspersed with tunes proffered by bands, ensembles and soloists. When the ratings went south, Burns smartly overhauled the format, dropping the music and turning the show into a domestic sitcom featuring the married partners. (They had been "singles" onstage until then.) That alteration, in 1941,

turned it around; it gave them another 17 years to wow audiences, with Allen's zany annotations making perfect sense to her but sounding ludicrous to those rolling in the aisles. And nobody ever surpassed her at what she did best.

❖ ❖ ❖

**Directors:** Ed Gardner, Ralph Levy, Al Kaye

**Writers:** George Burns, *head writer*; Willy Burns, Harry Conn, Carroll Carroll, John P. Medbury (all 1930s); Paul Henning, Harvey Helm, Hal Block, Henry Garson, Keith Fowler, Aaron J. Ruben, Harmon J. Alexander, Helen Gould Harvey (all 1940s)

**Orchestra Leaders:** Guy Lombardo (1932–34), Robert Emmett Dolan, Ferde Grofé (1934–35), Jimmy Grier, Jacques Renard (1935–36), Eddy Duchin (July-August 1936), Henry King (September 1936), Ray Noble (1937–March 1938, September 1938–40), Jan Garber (April–June 1938), Glen Gray (July–August 1938), Artie Shaw (1940–41), Paul Whiteman (1941–43), Felix Mills (1943–45), Meredith Willson (1945–48), Harry Lubin (1948–50)

**Vocalists:** Milton Watson (1934–35), Tony Martin (1936–March 1937, July 1937–April 1938, May-August 1938), Dick Foran—"the Singing Cowboy" (April–June 1937), Frank Parker (April 1938, September 1938–40), Jimmy Cash (1941, ca. 1942–45), Richard Haydn (1942), Six Hits and a Miss (1942), The King's Men, Jimmy Newell, The Smoothies, The Les Paul Trio

**Sound Effects Technicians:** David Light (1942–45), Virgil Reimer (1945–49), Al Span (1949–50)

**Announcers:** Ken Niles (1934–37), Ronald Drake (aka Wendell Niles; 1937–ca. 1938), John Conte (ca. 1937–38), Paul Douglas (1938–39), Truman Bradley (1939–40), John Hiestand (1940–ca. 1941), Jimmy Wallington (ca. 1940–41), Bill Goodwin (1941–50), Harry Von Zell, Tobe Reed (1947–49), Ted Husing, Dick Joy

**Recurring Cast:** *George Burns:* George Burns (nee Nathan Birnbaum); *Gracie Allen:* Gracie Allen (nee Grace Ethel Cecile Rosalie Allen); *Tootsie Sagwell:* Elvia Allman; *"The Happy Postman":* Mel Blanc; *Mrs. Billingsley:* Margaret Brayton; *Muriel:* Sara Berner; *Herman* (the duck): Charles Nash; *Waldo:* Richard Crenna; *Blanche Morton:* Bea Benaderet; *Harry Morton:* Hal March

**Supporting Cast:** Jim Backus, Dawn Bender, Tommy Bernard, Henry Blair, Hans Conried, Lois Corbett, Barbara Eiler, Verna Felton, Gale Gordon, Tommy Gordon, Sandra Gould, Bob Jellison, Joseph Kearns, Walter Woolf King, Sheldon Leonard, Cathy Lewis, Elliott Lewis, Wally Maher, Lou Merrill, Marvin Miller, Gerald Mohr, Frank Nelson, Isabel Randolph, Mary Lee Robb, Richard Ryan, Sarah Shelby, Doris Singleton, Eric Snowden, Irene Tedrow, Lurene Tuttle, Viola Vonn, Anne Whitfield, Ernest Whitman, Paula Winslowe

**Sponsors:** General Cigar Company, for Robert Burns Panatella cigars (1932–33); General Cigar Company, for White Owl cigars (1933–35); Campbell Soup Company, for Campbell's tomato juice (1935–37); General Foods Corporation, for Grape-Nuts cereal and other foodstuffs (1937–38); Liggett & Myers Tobacco Company, for Chesterfield cigarettes (1938–39); Lehn & Fink Products Company, for Hinds' Honey and Almond Cream personal care goods (1939–40); George A. Hormel and Company, for Hormel ham, sausage, bacon and other pork products, Dinty Moore beef stew and chili, Spam luncheon meat and other foodstuffs (1940–41); Lever Brothers Company, for Swan soap and other personal care and household commodities (1941–45); General Foods Corporation, for Maxwell House coffee and other foodstuffs (1945–49); Block Drug Company, Inc., for Amm-i-dent toothpaste (1949–50)

**Themes:** "Comin' Through the Rye" (1932–34), "Crazy People" (1934–35), "The Campbells Are Coming" (1935–37), "The Very Thought of You" (1937–39), "Love Nest" (1941–50)

**Ratings:** High—30.2 (1933–34), Low—13.2 (1949–50), Median—19.3. Ratings based on 18 seasons (1932–50 inclusive).

**On the Air:** February 22–May 18, 1932, *The Robert Burns Panatella Program*, CBS, Monday, 10:00–10:30 P.M. Eastern Time; May 25–December 28, 1932, CBS, Wednesday, 9:00–9:30 P.M.; January 4–May 17, 1933, CBS, Wednesday, 9:30–10:00 P.M.; May 24, 1933–June 13, 1934, *The White Owl Program*, CBS, Wednesday, 9:30–10:00 P.M.; September 19, 1934–May 22, 1935, *The Adventures of Gracie*, CBS, Wednesday, 9:30–10:00 P.M.; May 29–September 25, 1935, CBS, Wednesday, 10:00–10:30 P.M.; October 2, 1935–September 16, 1936, *The Campbell's Tomato Juice Program*, CBS, Wednesday, 8:30–9:00 P.M.; September 23, 1936–March 24, 1937, *The George Burns and Gracie Allen Show*, aka *Burns and Allen*, CBS, Wednesday, 8:30–9:00 P.M.; April 12, 1937–August 1, 1938, NBC, Monday, 8:00–8:30 P.M.; September 30, 1938–June 23, 1939, CBS, Friday, 8:30–9:00 P.M.; October 4, 1939–April 24, 1940, CBS, Wednesday, 7:30–8:00 P.M.; May 1–June 26, 1940, CBS, Wednesday, 6:30–7:00 P.M.; July 1, 1940–March 24, 1941, NBC, Monday, 7:30–8:00 P.M.; October 7, 1941–June 30, 1942, CBS, Tuesday, 7:30–8:00 P.M.; October 6, 1942–June 29, 1943, CBS, Tuesday, 9:00–9:30 P.M.; August 31, 1943–June 13, 1944, CBS, Tuesday, 9:00–9:30 P.M.; August 15–December 26, 1944, CBS, Tuesday, 9:00–9:30 P.M.; January 1–June 25, 1945, CBS, Monday, 8:30–9:00 P.M.; September 20, 1945–May 30, 1946, NBC, Thursday, 8:00–8:30 P.M.; September 5, 1946–May 29, 1947, NBC, Thursday, 8:30–9:00 P.M.; September 4, 1947–June 10, 1948, NBC, Thursday, 8:30–9:00 P.M.; September 30, 1948–June 23, 1949, NBC, Thursday, 8:30–9:00 P.M.; September 21, 1949–May 17, 1950, CBS, Wednesday, 10:00–10:30 P.M.; November 18–December 29, 1959, CBS, randomly scheduled, five minutes

**Extant Archival Material:** An unidentified number of scripts of *The George Burns and Gracie Allen Show* are included in the Script File of Duke University's John W. Hartman Center for Sales, Advertising and Marketing History, Box 90185, Durham, NC, 27708; (919) 660–5827; Fax (919) 660–5934; *http://scriptorium.lib.duke.edu/harman/*.

The Burns and Allen Collection is comprised of 82 volumes of radio scripts, 1932–1950, television scripts, scrapbooks, clippings, 600 disc recordings and films of the television series *The George Burns and Gracie Allen Show*, archived in the Cinema-Television Library of the University of Southern California, Doheny Memorial Library, 3550 Trousdale Parkway, Los Angeles, CA, 90089; (213) 740–8906; Fax (213) 821–3093; *www.usc.edu/isd/archives/arc*.

Transcriptions of Andy Devine's appearances on *The Jack Benny Program* and scrapbooks citing his radio performances are among the Andy Devine Papers, while the James Stewart Papers include transcriptions of Stewart's appearances on radio shows from 1939 to 1953, both collections archived at Brigham Young University's Harold B. Lee Library, Provo, UT, 84602; (801) 422–3175; Fax (801) 422–0461; *specialcollections@byu.edu*.

An unidentified number of scripts of *The Jack*

*Benny Program* are among over 5,000 drawn from multiple radio and TV series housed by the University of Maryland's Library of American Broadcasting, 3210 Hornbake Library, College Park, MD, 20742; (301) 405–0397; Fax (301) 314–2634; *labcast@umd.edu.*

An unidentified number of scripts of *The George Burns and Gracie Allen Show* are in the Collection of Radio Series Scripts, ca. 1933–1980, ca. 1940–1959, in the Arts Library, Special Collections, of the University of California at Los Angeles (UCLA), Charles E. Young Research Library, Room 22478, Box 951575, Los Angeles, CA, 90095; (310) 825–7253; Fax (310) 825–1210; *www.library.ucla.edu/libraries/arts.*

An unidentified number of scripts of *The George Burns and Gracie Allen Show* are among the Ben Blue Papers, plus the Collection of Miscellaneous Phonograph Records, ca. 1940–1971, includes some recordings of the same radio series, both compilations housed at the Department of Special Collections of the Charles E. Young Research Library, Box 951575, Los Angeles, CA, 90095; (310) 825–4988; *www.library.ucla.edu/libraries/special/scweb/.*

At least 122 broadcasts between 1934 and 1950 (and likely scores more) of *The George Burns and Gracie Allen Show* are known to be in general circulation or held by private collectors as of 2006, sold by vintage radio dealers and traded by old-time radio hobbyists.

A log of *The George Burns and Gracie Allen Show,* with some gaps, is available from Jay Hickerson (*jayhick@aol.com*).

The volume *George Burns and Gracie Allen, a Bio-Bibliography* (Greenwood Publishing), by Cynthia Clements and Sandra Weber, includes a complete radio and television log.

❖ ❖ ❖

BURNS: *Gracie, those are beautiful flowers. Where did they come from?*

ALLEN: *Don't you remember, George? You said that if I went to visit Clara Bagley in the hospital I should be sure to take her flowers. So, when she wasn't looking, I did.*

For more than a quarter-century in multiple expressions George Burns was the quintessential straight man for his giddy, seemingly scatterbrained spouse. Nowhere in the pages of history can one find a greater champion of empty-headed reasoning than Gracie Allen. She claimed the title as she created an entertainment subgenre centering on ingénues who portrayed ditzy dames—to the delight of listeners (and TV watchers) everywhere. Think Jane Ace of *Easy Aces,* Allen's contemporary, and Marie Wilson, *My Friend Irma* (Peterson), who followed in her wake. Yet, despite her seeming lack of brainpower, "Gracie was different from the usual female flake.... She came across not as a flighty dope or blond nitwit but as a lovable eccentric," according to one assessor. Her partner-husband allowed that she was merely "off-center," claiming: "Women understood her. Men thought they were married to her. And everybody knew somebody just like her." Applying oblique reasoning, she nevertheless figured out the truth—though most times in complicated, circumvented style.

Burns and Allen played themselves in a hugely exaggerated fabrication of their lives as a couple of radio (and, eventually, television) performers. By the time they first employed the sitcom model on October 7, 1941, they had already been on the air for nearly a decade. After the pair graduated from vaudeville to radio in the early 1930s, their program was spun from what they termed their "flirtation act." It was borrowed from the couple's vaudeville and short film routines. Mixed with comedic monologues and skits was a strong emphasis on music, performed on radio by a live orchestra, soloists, and vocal and instrumental ensembles. That combination perpetuated the variety-like atmosphere that was prevalent in their pre-radio performances.

But by the fall of 1941, with their ratings having fallen by half from their program's inception, Burns realized the "flirtation act" was no longer holding audiences, and it had to be fixed in a hurry—or the Burns family would be unemployed very soon. In the meantime, his best friend, Jack Benny, had been plugging along on radio with a modified situation comedy format that usually allowed him to occupy the top spot of the ratings heap. Benny's interpretation was to develop a series of skits around a common theme for each week's installment, leaving the music intact. Burns came to the conclusion that he and his bride should follow a similar pattern.

The music continued for a while but was progressively downplayed and eventually abandoned altogether, turning the show into a pure half-hour domestic sitcom. "The new format's success made it one of the few classic radio comedies to completely re-invent itself and regain major fame," one source proclaimed.[1]

Burns had long ago proven that he could learn new tricks: in the vaudeville era he and Allen made the shocking discovery that audiences were amused by her delivery of straight lines that were never meant to be all that funny. "If Burns had returned Gracie's loony remarks with wise-guy zingers of his own, it wouldn't have worked; it would have upset the delicate comic balance and put too much of a strain on the jokes," one scholar averred. Learning that, Burns had the good sense to reverse their roles. *He* became the straight man, allowing *her* to get the laughs by offering comebacks that absolutely cracked up the crowds in front of them. He cited it as one of the smartest decisions he ever made.

In their new radio adaptation, for the

*Nobody played a wacko better or longer than Gracie Allen. She checks over the scripts for an upcoming broadcast with her partner-husband George Burns. The George Burns and Gracie Allen Show, which persisted on radio, and later television, had its origins in vaudeville, where the two played for many years. When Burns realized then that Allen was getting bigger laughs with purely straight lines, he reversed their roles, tossing the intended funny stuff to her. Affirming what others had said, he allowed, "They were right. I did have a terrific talent. And I was married to her for 38 years." On radio, a contingent of ongoing characters interacted with the pair, playing off Allen's bizarre method of looking at life. She thought they were out of touch, and so turned a ditzy dame into a widely adored figure.*

first time they played themselves as a married couple. Until that point they performed as younger singles. For a while Allen was the object of affection for both Burns and announcer Bill Goodwin. In time, the latter pursued other women (his prowess as a "ladies' man" was repeatedly emphasized), while Burns and Allen remained just friends but not wedded partners. All that changed when Burns directed his writers to revamp the show into a sitcom, focusing on the couple's married life. It included situations involving friends, neighbors and acquaintances who visited the Burns domicile. And like *The Jack Benny Program*, the revised *George Burns and Gracie Allen Show* portrayed the stars as entertainers with their own weekly radio series. (After the radio show disbanded, they became "television stars" in a continuation of their embellished existence in video.) Meanwhile, the shift from single friends to wedded bliss was, of course, a pretty dramatic switch for a couple of comedians. Audiences quickly adapted, nevertheless; they had known all along that Burns and Allen were husband and wife in real life, of course.

Gracie Allen also shared a common trait with another famous performing wife. She and Jack Benny's actress wife Mary Livingstone dreaded the ordeal of appearing before the microphone every week. For that reason, George and Gracie performed sans audience in their first season. Paper was taped over glass doors to prevent any staring passersby from looking in. The show was subsequently moved to the Willard Hotel where footlights before the mics shielded Gracie from a thousand onlookers. Gracie was even given an enlarged mic to prevent eye contact with audience members. Spectators were asked not to laugh at or applaud the jokes, a rather sterile environment for a comedy show.[2]

From 1941 to the end of their radio and television runs the pair was a working show business duo trying to negotiate ordinary issues. The writers projected circumstances and accompanying dialogue that were consistent with the characters' personalities and ages. The themes of each installment purposely avoided topical humor, implausible characterizations and absurd contrivances—in their place focusing on more conventional aspects of daily living. All of it was, of course, strongly influenced by Allen's character's "illogical logic." Cultivated from their vaudeville routines, it was often referred to as a "Dumb Dora" characterization.

Branded by an early film of the same appellation featuring a pivotal, addlepated distaff figure, her nonsensical reactions were much more progressive than the Dumb Dora stereotype, just as was Burns' understated straight man. A critic labeled her "a brilliant comedian" whose exchanges with others in the plots "left her verbal opponents dazed and confused, and her audiences in stitches." Often her thinking was aided and abetted by their mythical neighbors, Harry and Blanche Morton (Hal March and Bea Benaderet), who were introduced into the plotting during the sitcom epoch; by the show's announcer, Bill Goodwin; and by Mr. Beasley, the happy mailman (Mel Blanc on radio; Rolfe Sedan on TV). There were also the unidentified members of Allen's ladies' club, the Beverly Hills Uplift Society.[3] It was a set-up simply waiting for the laughs to begin. With Gracie Allen nearby, that didn't take long.

The real guffaws resulted from Allen's skewed perspective of the world and the confusion that resulted from her misguided impressions. The preponderance of the show's dialogue and speaking parts were written specifically for Allen. She was credited with having the genius to deliver lengthy diatribes in a fashion that made it sound as though she was making her arguments up right on the spot.

Allen is forever remembered as the one who was mixed up, although—to her—it appeared that everybody else couldn't get it right.

BURNS: *Gracie, why should I give your mother a bushel of nuts? What'd she ever give me?*

ALLEN: *Why, George, she gave you me. And I'm as good as nuts.*

"Gracie Allen took little interest in the radio show and could have done it in her sleep," noted one scholar. "She made few creative contributions beyond her own enchanting personality, and usually didn't attend rehearsals." Instead, Mary Kelly, Jack Benny's original "true love"—their wedding plans fell shy of the altar because Benny was a reform Jew and she was a devout Catholic—often substituted for Allen preceding the actual radio performances.

Burns and Allen first made it to radio as comedy relief for bandleader Guy Lombardo, whose *Robert Burns Panatella Program* had been running on CBS since the network was organized in 1927. The droll duo joined the show in early 1932. Parenthetically, not long afterward Burns and Allen went to the West Coast to shoot a movie. Their radio contract required them to bear the sizeable cost of maintaining telephone lines carrying their voices across the nation, allowing them to continue to perform "live" on the show. "We lost $200 a week every week we were on the radio," said Burns. "The phone call was that much more than what we were getting."

On the other hand, at least a segment of listeners who were addicted to "the sweetest music this side of heaven" balked, finding the interruption for a few laughs not to their tastes. Burns reported in his memoir, *The Third Time Around*, that a college fraternity basing weekly dance parties around Lombardo's audio program expressed strong disapproval with the sudden adjustment in format. No matter, the show's ratings more than doubled in a single year after Burns and Allen came aboard, to the extent that the sponsor retained them but—in 1933—dumped Lombardo, his brothers and the remainder of his entourage. Burns and Allen were the new headliners; the greatly reduced music that persisted from then on played only second fiddle to the comic sketches that had been a mainstay of the couple's earlier vaudeville careers. Decades afterward, Burns remembered:

> Gracie and I were perfect for radio. Both of us could stand still in front of a microphone and read out loud. Gracie had a terrific voice, and I had Gracie. And that's all it took. We were on the air for almost twenty years. I think I loved being in radio more than any other part of my career. Radio meant show business, and I wanted to be in show business. Radio was that place where performers who couldn't do anything except talk, could talk. [4]

There were lots of running gags on their show, just as on other radio sitcoms. One pertained to Allen's displaced brother. It became such an issue that eventually she began turning up on other network programs in cameo roles on a nationwide pursuit of her lost sibling. The whole thing grew to such epic proportions that her real-life brother, George Allen, a San Francisco accountant, became openly resentful. According to one source, he vamoosed and went into hiding. He asked the entertainers to suspend the mythical hunt. While they did so, he was continually a hot topic of discussion in the couple's closing vignettes on their weekly television series two decades later.

In 1940 Allen ran for President of the United States, representing the imaginary Surprise Party. During a year-long campaign she made many speeches on her own show, as well as those hosted by countless other NBC comedians. The sponsor even released a book, *Gracie Allen for President*, including photographs of the "candidate" and her family. In the end, in November of that year Allen gained a number of write-in votes in the national election. It was certainly a unique means of plugging one's own venue.

Burns' questionable ability to vocalize in harmony was a constant thorn in most people's sides, although never his wife's. Instead, she praised his singing, dubbing him "Sugar Throat." In the meantime, there was a running gag about her idolization of actor Charles Boyer, with whom she was not only thrilled but infatuated. Burns never seemed to let it get the best of him, however.

In one long-running gag, which carried over from radio to television, Burns fired the show's announcer every couple of episodes. He also was involved with the scribes far more than the public probably realized. Hollywood critic Leonard Maltin discussed the writing of the *Burns and Allen* show in one of his texts:

The audience never knew—or suspected, most likely—that George was "the brains of the outfit," that he was more than simply a great straight man. (When Paul Henning wrote to his mother and said he was going to write for George Burns, she replied, "Congratulations, that's wonderful, but who writes for Gracie? *She's* the one who says the funny things.")

"I used to be in the [writers'] room all the time," George explained. "I never took billing as a writer, but I know what made Gracie and myself a really good team was that I had a talent off the stage, and Gracie had it on the stage. I was able to think of it and Gracie was able to do it. And that's what made us a good team."

One of Burns' staff writers was his brother, who bore the brunt of George's occasional bursts of temper. Longtime associate Paul Henning recalls, "If he had to let off steam, he'd let off steam to Willy; he'd just give him hell, blame him for anything. One day Willy said, 'Listen, George, I don't have to take this from you. I can go back to Brooklyn and do what I was doing before I came out here.' And George—brought up short—said, 'What was that?' And Willy said, 'I was sitting at home and you were sending me $50 a week.'"

Willy was in fact a valued member of the team. And George was a respected boss. Years of experience in vaudeville had given him tremendous comedy know-how.[5]

In 1948 William S. Paley, the head honcho at CBS, came courting NBC stars, making several of them attractive tax incentive offers they simply couldn't refuse. After Jack Benny, the chimes chains' top entertainer, defected, he became a general in Paley's army, persuading some of the others to follow suit. It didn't take much for him to convince his pals George Burns and Gracie Allen that they could do better; that the CBS brass would appreciate them far more than they were being cherished (not just in dollars but in genuine pride and joy) by the NBC brass. Once the dust settled from the talent raiding, Red Skelton, Edgar Bergen and Charlie McCarthy, Harold Peary (*The Great Gildersleeve's* key player) and Ozzie and Harriet Nelson joined the parade from NBC, along with Bing Crosby and Groucho Marx from ABC. The outcome positioned CBS to be the primetime leader in both radio and television, which was just around the corner.

On October 12, 1950, *The George Burns and Gracie Allen Show* transitioned to television, becoming one of the first sitcoms to make the leap. The characters that audiences had become familiar with in radio shifted seamlessly to the tube, affording most fans a first glimpse of what those individuals actually looked like. (Several members of the radio troupe continued on TV in their accustomed roles.) The show was also scripted by a cadre of wordsmiths who had penned it for audio, some of them even going back to preparing gags for the couple's vaudeville performances. The early shows were "simply a copy of the radio format," affirmed one pundit.

The first half-dozen episodes of the TV series originated in New York City; after that the whole company relocated to Hollywood. In its first couple of seasons the video performances were live but aired every other week, alternating with other series, to provide what Burns deemed as "necessary time" for rehearsals. Thereafter the show was filmed in a studio without benefit of spectators, followed by a screening for an audience before showing it on television. The reactions of those witnesses were recorded, and then they, as Burns explained, "sweetened the laughter when a joke went flat and there was no way of eliminating it from the film." The show persisted on CBS-TV through September 22, 1958, when Allen's health necessitated her retirement.[6]

An innovative Burns was the first TV entertainer to apply the theatrical convention of "breaking the fourth wall" between the audience and the performer. On several occasions during each show he stepped out of a scene and out of character to address the audience, commenting on the action in progress. Following a puff on his cigar, he'd step back into the scene, and the storyline resumed. Burns applied the device again in some successive TV ventures. Although a few others tried to imitate the pattern, it was never effectively applied until standup comedian Garry

Shandling reprised it from 1986 to 1990 on his own Showtime and Fox sitcom, *It's Garry Shandling's Show*. In the plotting there he appeared as himself, portraying—are you ready for this?—the star of a TV situation comedy. Where did that idea originate? (With Benny or Burns, so it would seem.)

In yet another departure from the norm, weekly installments were followed by a pithy (and witty) dialogue between the two stars, attired in formals, a throwback to their vaudeville days of yore. In those exchanges the pair often conversed about members of Allen's family, her eccentric brother being a favored subject.

> ALLEN: *George, did you know my brother eats concrete?*
>
> BURNS: *Your brother eats concrete?*
>
> ALLEN: *Of course! Mother asked him to stay for dinner but he told her he was going to eat up the street.*

Invariably the lunacy ended with Burns petitioning, "Say goodnight, Gracie." She obligingly countered, "Goodnight." Never once, as some historians have incorrectly surmised, did she say, "Goodnight, Gracie." That erroneous attribution may have been perpetuated after viewers repeatedly heard Dan Rowan's sign-off on NBC-TV's *Laugh-In* (1968–73) wherein he beseeched his partner, Dick Martin, to "Say goodnight, Dick." His opposite invariably shot back: "Goodnight, Dick!"

Burns was just getting warmed up for television when Allen retired. He immediately attempted a solo effort, which netted a disappointing outcome. *The George Burns Show*, another sitcom, ran on NBC-TV for an abbreviated 1958–59 season, lasting less than five months. Without Allen to play off the marvelous straight lines he customarily delivered in the past, the spark was missing and the show fell flat. Burns attempted to replicate what he had going with Allen in a subsequent ABC-TV sitcom, *Wendy and Me*, in which Connie Stevens appeared as a daft dame. But that, too, failed and was pulled after one season (1964–65). A quarter-century

later, in the fall of 1989, he again tried to make a go of it in television as the medium's oldest host (he was then 89). In his own TV series swan song he presided over CBS-TV's *George Burns Comedy Week*. The humorous anthology lasted just three months. Burns insisted throughout his life, obviously correctly so, that Gracie Allen really *was* the best thing that happened to his professional career. Both entertainers, in fact, attributed their success to the other spouse.

Although the couple never had children in the natural way, in the 1930s they adopted a girl, Sandra Jean Burns, and a boy, Ronald John Burns. Both performed on the *Burns and Allen* TV show. Sandra's visits to the show were fleeting, although Ronnie became a permanent presence in 1955 and stayed with it until the show ended in 1958. Appearing as himself, he portrayed a serious college dramatics student who was generally appalled by his parents' comedic efforts.

Following Allen's death in 1964, the senior Burns threw himself into his work, becoming more involved than ever before. "George Burns was better known in the last two decades of his life than at any other time in his life and career," Wikipedia maintained.[7] He toured the nation in nightclub and theater engagements, playing opposite such disparate entertainers as Carol Channing, Betty Davis, Connie Haines, Dorothy Provine and Jane Russell. He also played a sequence of solo concerts on university campuses and in prestigious New York venues like Carnegie and Philharmonic halls. Often he performed before capacity crowds with his show-stopping patter, humorous asides, singing and dancing.

His career was rejuvenated in 1974 when—upon the death of his dear friend Jack Benny—he was assigned to replace him in a film version of Neil Simon's *The Sunshine Boys*. Despite crushing grief over losing his pal of so many decades, he won an award as Best Supporting Actor for his work. He also assumed a number of nightclub dates that Benny had been too ill to fulfill. Burns later put whatever "no talent" argument existed permanently to rest when he starred in the title role of what ultimately became a trilogy of theatrical motion pictures: 1977's *Oh, God!*, 1980's *Oh, God! Book II* and 1984's *Oh, God! You Devil*.

While continuing to perform, Burns also took an active role in the business affairs of the television industry, demonstrating considerable savvy in more than one facet of showbiz. Taking a cue from Lucille Ball and Desi Arnaz's Desilu Productions, Burns established McCadden Productions (named for the street his brother lived on). The outfit not only created commercials but turned out sitcoms, including *Mr. Ed*, *The Bob Cummings Show*, *No Time for Sergeants*, *The People's Choice*, *Mona McCluskey* and *The Marie Wilson Show*. Marie Wilson, you will recall, played the Gracie Allen–type character in *My Friend Irma* on both radio and television, a characterization that Burns seemed naturally drawn to.

George Burns was born Nathan Birnbaum in New York City on January 20, 1896. His father was a surrogate cantor at the local synagogue but didn't work all that much. When a flu epidemic killed the elder Birnbaum in 1903, he left a wife and 12 children. Thus, at age seven, Nattie—as Burns was affectionately nicknamed by his clan, and was privately addressed by Gracie Allen years later—began earning a few pennies here and there by doing whatever he could: he sold newspapers, shined shoes, ran errands and made syrup in the basement of a nearby candy emporium. Down in that cellar his show business career started to bud.

Four neighborhood kids about the same age started harmonizing together. When they drew a small crowd they saw visions of something better. Naming themselves the Peewee Quartet, they sang on street corners, ferryboats and in taverns, passing their hats among the spectators for small change. While in the fourth grade, Nattie Birnbaum dropped out of school altogether to pursue a life in entertainment. Trick roller skating, instructing in dance routines, vocalizing and adagio dancing in small-time vaudeville formed the foundation of his early career.

During that period he adopted "George Burns" as a stage moniker.

In the meantime, Grace Ethel Cecil Rosalie Allen had been born into an Irish Catholic show business family in San Francisco on July 26, 1895. She lost her father early, too; after he abandoned her when she was five, leaving her mother with four daughters and a son, Gracie Allen purportedly never spoke of her dad again. Thus, both future famous entertainers had in common the loss of their fathers at an early age.

Allen was educated at Star of the Sea Convent School before joining her sisters Bessie, Hazel and Pearl in a vaudeville act in 1909. That was later trimmed to Bessie and Gracie. Gracie Allen met George Burns in 1922 while she was enrolled in a secretarial school. Her roommate invited her to accompany her to Union Hill, New Jersey, to meet George Burns and Billy Lorraine, a vaudeville act that was breaking up. The roomie saw it as a chance for Allen to go back on the road by selecting one of the partners and creating a new act. Allen and Burns hit it off from the start. They premiered at Newark's Hill Street Theater at $5 daily. The audience quickly fell in love with her, but it took Burns more than three years to negotiate a more personal arrangement. Actually, she had to get out of an engagement to wed somebody else, according to one story, in order to marry Burns.

Their wedding in Cleveland on January 7, 1926, was somewhat daring for the period in which it transpired. Burns was Jewish; Allen was Catholic. Before their nuptials the dual faiths hadn't been combined into unions all that much, and certainly not among public figures. At about the same time, a Jewish Jack Benny and his first serious sweetheart (of several years' duration), Mary Kelly, a staunch Catholic, were unable to reconcile their differences over religion in order to wed. Their case was not atypical of popular traditions in that era. Interestingly, Burns and Allen and Benny and the girl he finally did marry, Mary Livingstone, also Jewish, became lifelong friends. Benny and Burns considered one another their "best friend."

Burns, incidentally, strayed at least once during his 38-year marriage to Allen. While the account has been retold by numerous media historians in several variations, here's Burns' own recollection of the incident:

> I had my affair in the early 1950s. It was with a beautiful starlet. I don't remember her name, but she was very pretty and very sexy....
>
> Gracie and I were having a little fight at the time. She wanted to buy a silver centerpiece that cost $750. I didn't want to buy a silver centerpiece...."What do we need another one for?" I asked Gracie. "We already have two. You can only use one at a time." But Gracie wanted this centerpiece.
>
> Then I cheated with this girl. I had my one-night affair. I don't know why I did it ... but it had nothing to do with the centerpiece. I wasn't very good at cheating, maybe because I hadn't done it before. Somehow Gracie found out, and I found out that Gracie had found out. So she knew, and I knew she knew, but I didn't know if she knew that I knew that she knew....
>
> Gracie never said a word. That was even tougher than if we had gotten into a big fight. The longer she went without saying anything, the more guilty I felt. Finally, after a few days I couldn't take it anymore. I went out and bought her the $750 silver centerpiece and a $10,000 diamond ring and gave them to her. I never told her why I'd bought them for her and she never asked, and she never said a single word about my affair. At least she didn't say a word for seven years.
>
> Seven years later she was out shopping with Mary [Livingstone] Benny and they were in the silver department at Saks. Gracie found a centerpiece she really liked and she said to Mary, "You know, I wish George would cheat again. I really need a new centerpiece."
>
> Look, I was very lucky that Gracie handled it the way she did. My mistake could have ruined both of our lives. But she was so smart, she just never mentioned it. If she had decided to make a big deal about it, we might not have had another decade together. And, in her own way, she forgave me.[8]

In regard to the affair, Wikipedia proclaimed: "To the day he died he considered it the biggest regret of his life—and considered himself fortunate to have his wife's forgiveness."[9]

Getting a start in theatrical films with a sequence of comic shorts, Burns & Allen's celluloid credits in the 1930s included *The Big Broadcast of 1932*, *International House* (1933), *Six of a Kind* (1934), *The Big Broadcast of 1936*, *The Big Broadcast of 1937*, *A Damsel in Distress* (1937) and *College Swing* (1938).

Gracie Allen suffered a series of heart "episodes" (her term for those ongoing palpitations, in reality a form of heart disease) during the final half-dozen years of her life. A nitroglycerine pill placed under her tongue usually brought relief. At 58, however, she was overcome by a fatal attack on August 27, 1964, succumbing at Hollywood's Cedars of Lebanon Hospital.

In his later years, long after Allen's death, Burns penned a passel of volumes in lighthearted style, some of which became best sellers. Among his titles were *I Love Her, That's Why*; *Living It Up: Or, They Still Love Me in Altoona!*; *The Third Time Around*; *How to Live to Be 100—or More: The Ultimate Diet, Sex and Exercise Book*; *Dr. Burns' Prescription for Happiness*; *Dear George: Advice and Answers from America's Leading Expert on Everything from A to B*; *Gracie, a Love Story*; *All My Best Friends*; *Wisdom of the '90s*; and *George Burns: In His Own Words*.

Burns never remarried. He maintained for many years that he planned to live to be 100, and reached his goal on January 20, 1996. Up until a short time before that he continued to appear in public and occasionally entertained. Burns died of natural causes in Beverly Hills on March 9, 1996.

A historian labeled Burns and Allen "perhaps the most successful husband-and-wife team in show business history."[10] Burns appeared as if he was a bystander who meandered over to befriend a befuddled but beguiling broad and discovered—to his astonishment—he couldn't walk away. "It was a deceptively simple but seductive format that remains fresh, effortless, and inspired to this day," an observer summarized.[11]

And the jokes are as funny now as they were then. While the actress was noted as a judicious professional in timing, her husband chose the words for her that remain timeless.

# The Great Gildersleeve

## THE MOST POMPOUS WINDBAG ON THE AIR

*The Great Gildersleeve* has been branded as the first non-nuclear family sitcom. At its core was a kindhearted, blustery bachelor–Romeo who was the custodian of his late sister's teenage daughter, Marjorie, and adolescent son, Leroy. At the same time, the lothario pursued—and was regularly shadowed by—a bevy of beauties, usually (though not always) one at a time. On several occasions they nearly got him to tie the knot, "nearly" being the operative word. "Gildy," as his cronies dubbed him, was born on another long-running radio comedy, *Fibber McGee & Molly*. When he attracted widespread acclaim, the character was spun off into a new entry in which the heretofore supporting actor became the featured star. In addition to his niece and nephew and a live-in Negro maid, Gildy was surrounded by a host of local denizens—much as were the McGees in his former environment—who put in appearances weekly. In contrast to the mother (and father) series, the plotlines of *The Great Gildersleeve* were more broadly developed. Instead of the others merely dropping by his residence, as the McGees' friends did almost every week, the water commissioner (Gildy's post for most of the run) encountered his pals at home, at their places of livelihood, at social and civic events and especially at gatherings of the oft-crossed Jolly Boys, a lodge. While it was lighthearted fare, Gildy had the ability to cause a stir: sometimes he reacted vociferously to actions with which he dis-agreed, for he was an opinionated and outspoken fellow. His ability to spar so nobly, tenaciously and relentlessly was honed at the master's feet—those of Fibber McGee.

❖ ❖ ❖

**Creators:** Don Quinn and Harold Peary (nee Harrold José Pereira de Faria)

**Producer-Directors:** Cecil Underwood, Frank Pittman, Francis D. Van Hartesveldt, Virgil Reimer, Karl Gruener

**Writers:** Leonard L. Levinson (1941–42), John Whedon and Sam Moore, Jack Robinson and Gene Stone, John Elliotte and Andy White, Paul West, Virginia Safford Lynne, Francis D. Van Hartesveldt

**Orchestra Leaders:** William Randolph (1941), Billy Mills (1941–42), Claude Sweeten (1942–mid 1940s), Jack Meakin (mid-to-late 1940s), Robert Armbruster (1950s)

**Sound Effects Technicians:** Floyd Caton, Virgil Reimer, Monty Fraser

**Announcers:** Jim Bannon (1941–42), Ken Carpenter (1942–45), John Laing (1945–47), John Wald (1947–49), Jay Stewart and Jim Doyle (1949–50), John Hiestand (ca. 1950–ca. 1957)

**Recurring Cast:** *Throckmorton P. Gildersleeve:* Harold Peary (nee Harrold José Pereira de Faria) (1941–50), Willard Waterman (1950–57); *Leroy Forrester:* Walter Tetley; *Marjorie Forrester:* Lurene Tuttle (1941–44), Louise Erickson (mid–1940s), Mary Lee Robb (late 1940s–1957); *Judge Horace Hooker:* Earle Ross; *Birdie Lee Coggins:* Lillian Randolph; *J.W. Peavey:* Richard LeGrand (1941–ca. mid 1950s), Forrest Lewis (ca. mid 1950s–1957); *Floyd Munson:* Arthur Q. Bryan; *Police Chief Gates:* Ken Christy; *Leila Ransom:* Shirley Mitchell; *Adeline Fairchild:* Una Merkel; *Eve Goodwin:* Bea Benaderet (1944); *Kathryn Milford:* Cathy Lewis (1950s); *Bashful Ben:* Ben

Alexander (mid 1940s); *Bronco Thompson*: Richard Crenna; *Rumson Bullard*: Gale Gordon (1940s, early 1950s), Jim Backus (1952); *Craig Bullard*: Tommy Bernard; *Bessie*: Pauline Drake, Gloria Holliday; *Brenda Kickerbocker*: Barbara Whiting; *Babs Winthrop*: Barbara Whiting; *Ellen Bullard Knickerbocker*: Martha Scott; *Paula Bullard Winthrop*: Jean Bates; Kathie Lee (as herself); *Oliver Honeywell*: Hans Conried

**Supporting Cast:** Ben Alexander, Elvia Allman, Jack Arthur, Sara Berner, Georgia Ellis, Stan Farr, Earl Lee, Frank Nelson, Celeste Rush, Irene Tedrow, Martha Wentworth

**Sponsors:** Kraft Foods Company, for Parkay margarine, Kraft cheese in countless varieties, Miracle Whip salad dressing, Philadelphia cream cheese and a wide line of additional foodstuffs (1941–54); Multiple participation (1954–58)

**Themes:** "Big Boy" (Jack Meakin and Forest Carling)

**Ratings:** High—19.7 (1945–46), Low—3.2 (1955–56), Median—12.3. Ratings based on 15 seasons (1941–56 inclusive).

**On the Air:** August 31, 1941–July 5, 1942, NBC, Sunday, 6:30–7:00 P.M. Eastern Time; August 30, 1942–June 27, 1943, NBC, Sunday, 6:30–7:00 P.M.; August 29, 1943–June 25, 1944, NBC, Sunday, 6:30–7:00 P.M.; September 3, 1944–July 1, 1945, NBC, Sunday, 6:30–7:00 P.M.; September 2, 1945–June 9, 1946, NBC, Sunday, 6:30–7:00 P.M.; September 11, 1946–June 4, 1947, NBC, Wednesday, 8:30–9:00 P.M.; September 10, 1947–June 2, 1948, NBC, Wednesday, 8:30–9:00 P.M.; September 8, 1948–June 1, 1949, NBC, Wednesday, 8:30–9:00 P.M.; September 21, 1949–June 14, 1950, NBC, Wednesday, 8:30–9:00 P.M.; September 6, 1950–May 30, 1951, NBC, Wednesday, 8:30–9:00 P.M.; September 5, 1951–June 2, 1954, NBC, Wednesday, 8:30–9:00 P.M.; September 27, 1954–June 30, 1955, NBC, Sunday-Thursday, 10:15–10:30 P.M.; October 20, 1955–April 5, 1956, NBC, Thursday, 8:00–8:25 P.M.; October 11, 1956–March 21, 1957, NBC, Thursday, 8:00–8:25 P.M.; 1957–March 27, 1958, NBC, Thursday, 8:00–8:30 P.M.

**Extant Archival Material:** The Walter Tetley Papers, including materials of the actor who appeared as Leroy Forrester on *The Great Gildersleeve*, are a collection privately held by Charles K. Stumpf, 803 Hazelwood Apartments, Hazelton, PA, 18205; (570) 454–4261.

An unidentified number of scripts for *The Great Gildersleeve* are among two collections, the Gene Stone Papers, 1947–1989, and the Jackson Stanley Papers (outlines only), archived in the Charles E. Young Research Library at the University of California at Los Angeles (UCLA), Box 951575, Los Angeles, CA, 90095; (310) 825–7253; Fax (310) 825–1210; *www.library.ucla.edu/libraries/arts/*.

An unidentified number of scripts for *The Great Gildersleeve* are among three collections: the Andy White Papers, 1935–1979, including scripts between 1935 (initially on the progenitor series, *Fibber McGee & Molly*) to 1947; the Francis D. Van Hartesveldt Papers, 1941–1963, also containing story ideas, outlines, correspondence, contracts and other memorabilia; and the John Whedon Papers, 1928–1973, also embracing outlines and other materials, all housed at the American Heritage Center of the University of Wyoming, 1000 East University Avenue, Laramie, WY, 82071; (307) 766–3756; Fax (307) 766–5511; *http://ahc.uwyo.edu/usearchives/default.htm*.

Microfilm of the Kraft Foods Company's corrected copies of scripts, including commercials, are among the Great Gildersleeve Scripts, 1942–1954, archived by the Wisconsin Historical Society, 816 State Street, Madison, WI, 53706; (608) 264–6460; Fax (608) 264–6486; http://arcat.library.wisc.edu.

A single script of *The Great Gildersleeve* for the broadcast of September 10, 1952, is preserved in the Marvin Miller Collection at Thousand Oaks Library, American Radio Archives, 1401 East Janss Road, Thousand Oaks, CA, 91362; (805) 449–2660; fax (805) 449 2675; www.rtohlibrary.org.

*The Great Gildersleeve*, by Charles Stumpf and Ben Ohmart, is available from BearManor Media, Box 71426, Albany, GA, 31708; (229) 436–4265; Fax (814) 690–1559; http://bearmanormedia.bizland.com/id16.html.

At least 499 *The Great Gildersleeve* broadcasts are known to be in general circulation or held by private collectors as of 2006, sold by vintage radio dealers and traded by old-time radio hobbyists.

A log of *The Great Gildersleeve* is available from Terry Salomonson at http://users.aol.com/otrjerry2/terrysol.html.

❖ ❖ ❖

Some modern radio historians and hobbyists have mistakenly given the honor of "radio's first true spin-off program" to *The Great Gildersleeve* while obviously overlooking the grandame of soap opera, Irna Phillips. It's not our intent to reduce the worthy contributions of *The Great Gildersleeve*, which, in this writer's opinion, is genuinely deserving of—and will receive—sufficient acclaim. Nevertheless, setting the record straight, Phillips is more likely to have been the first to bring forth one show from the womb of another. It's an error that many media historians continue to make, incidentally.

In 1939, a couple of years before *Gildersleeve* emerged from the long-running *Fibber McGee & Molly*, Phillips plucked one of her most popular threads from what has become, when the televersion is added to it, the most enduring narrative on the air: *The Guiding Light* (1937–present). She flung it out over the ether as *The Right to Happiness*. So durable was that offspring drama that it—along with a trio of its peers—survived until the radio serials collectively reached their final broadcasting gasps on November 25, 1960. That quartet outlived some 300 soap opera contemporaries over a triple-decade timeframe.

To offer additional credit where it may be due, Phillips applied at least a modified form of the spinoff as early as 1933. That year she reprised her original series, *Painted Dreams*, by launching a tale on the air with similar themes and characters under the moniker *Today's Children*.[1] And if we're splitting hairs, *Bright Horizon*, a daytime serial that Phillips *did not* create, was spun off from yet another long-running narrative, *Big Sister*, on Monday, August 25, 1941. *The Great Gildersleeve* didn't arrive until the following Sunday, August 31. That puts it no less than third in line among true spinoff series, and possibly even further down the line (depending on how *Today's Children* is designated), negating one of the venerated claims often repeated about its heritage.

All that notwithstanding, *Gildersleeve* may have been the first evening situation comedy spun off from an earlier show (although scholars claiming its first-place spinoff status invariably leave out the "evening" part). Its origins, in *Fibber McGee & Molly*, date to September 26, 1939, when Throckmorton P. Gildersleeve moved in as the McGees' next door neighbor. There, "the most pompous windbag on the air" became, according to radio historian Jim Harmon, "undoubtedly the most important supporting character ever on the show."[2] (Even the name of the character sounded haughty.) The role originated

with Harold (Hal) Peary (nee Harrold José Pereira de Faria). He joined the McGee cast in 1937 as a utility player, performing as different people for a couple of years—sometimes two or more figures per installment. Often he applied ethnic and foreign dialects, a feat he readily accomplished with recurring ease. On occasion he played a figure by the name of Gildersleeve, although the part wasn't consistent.

After a while Peary—a scholar whose ability to speak fluently in five languages belied his often blustery stage presence—asked McGee creator-writer Don Quinn to develop a fuller role for him, turning Gildersleeve into an every-week member of the company. He suggested that Gildersleeve reside next door to 79 Wistful Vista and exhibit an ostentatious personality that McGee could play off. Anybody who's familiar with McGee knows he was never happier than when sparring with someone he could sink his teeth into. He made no exception for Gildersleeve, a portly fellow weighing 230 pounds with an infectious giggle that became an on-air brand. His hallmark chuckle, incidentally, is often ascribed by media chroniclers as a "dirty laugh." Quinn loved it and put him at 83 Wistful Vista, then turned the two reprobates loose on one another. The result was predictable anarchy every week. They glared at each other across the fence while playing their little-boy tricks, even engaging in an outrageous water fight on one occasion. Quinn gave McGee's nemesis a catchphrase, which Gildy uttered in exasperation on nearly every show, a line that became a newly-minted American idiom: "You're a haaaarrrrd man, McGee!"

"Quinn knew at once the value of sarcasm in comedy," an observer wrote. "Never again would McGee fail to have a rival in the long battle of words." He was constantly at cross purposes with Gildersleeve, and often jousted with the haughty socialite Mrs. Abigail Uppington (whom he dubbed "Uppie"), as well as several others. His most pointed and persistent wrangling, however, was reserved for Doctor Gamble. Gamble possessed a cool, calculating, abrasive demeanor that was prominently exhibited for McGee's benefit. He saved his best nicknames for McGee, too, like "bird brain," "mental lightweight" and "mindless midget."

Wordsmith Leonard L. Levinson, who drew the assignment of penning the first year's scripts for *The Great Gildersleeve*, recognized the value of infighting characters, too. On the very first outing, Levinson engaged Throckmorton P. Gildersleeve and crusty, cantankerous, nasal-sounding Judge Horace Hooker (Earle Ross) in a battle royal, setting the pace for subsequent weekly meetings for the next 17 years. With a billy-goat laugh, Hooker was for sure the Billy Goat Gruff. Gildy even called him "you old goat." While their harangues were never unexpected, they made for some pretty funny exchanges between two grouches who cared a great deal about one another. Under the cover of crotchety façades, they tried very hard to hide their innermost feelings.

Gildy's mounting popularity with listeners on the McGee show won the spinoff and his very own half-hour sitcom. The new entry was a genuine situation comedy, as opposed to a series of comic sketches like those comprising the McGee program. At the time, Gildy operated a girdle factory in Wistful Vista somewhere in mid–America. (Jim and Marian Jordan, McGee & Molly's alter egos, hailed from Peoria, Illinois, and their show maintained a distinctively Midwestern flavor even after it was produced in Hollywood.) Gildersleeve Girdle Works' motto was a classic: "If you want the best of corsets, of course it's Gildersleeve."

As the first show kicked off, Gildersleeve was at the Wistful Vista depot leaving for Summerfield, where he was on a mission of personal business involving a niece and nephew, his sister's children, who had become orphans. He hoped to be named their legal guardians. Surrounding him as he boarded his train were his employees, who referred to him as "T.P." As a parting jest he admonished them to "uphold Gildersleeve girdles to the best of your ability while I'm away." Listeners never really knew what became of the undergarments concern beyond that. Wistful Vista was literally in Gildy's wistful past and was seldom mentioned again, his future assured with new "foundations" (pun confessed).

The bachelor did become the guardian of wiseguy Leroy Forrester (Walter Tetley), age 12 (to whom "Unc" would frequently growl "Lee-eee-roy!"), and his sister Marjorie (Lurene Tuttle, Louise Erickson, Mary Lee Robb), an incredibly sophisticated teenager. Gildersleeve demonstrated an enveloping compassion for his wards that added warmth to the character. Surprisingly, however, there was little attempt to reference the children's late parents or to assuage the kids' devastating loss. While bringing that to the forefront from time to time would not have been humorous, it would have been human and humane. But Gildy appeared to all but ignore the passing of his late sister. While it's possible to envision empathetic conversations on a variety of sobering topics conducted by *Father Knows Best's* Jim Anderson with his progeny, particularly in the TV era, radio comedy didn't handle reality very well. Consequently, if Marjorie and Leroy missed their mom and dad (and why wouldn't they?), they said little about it. Listeners were left to contemplate that matter by themselves, just as Marjorie and Leroy did. Though we don't know how far back in their past the children's parents died (it might have been a while or possibly just before their uncle joined them), Gildersleeve—on his arrival in Summerfield—didn't dwell on sympathy, then or later. Given the perspective of time, to ignore a matter of that import now would be absolutely unthinkable. Almost universally, radio comedy writers either didn't sense its significance or perhaps weren't adept at handling it.

At the Forrester home in Summerfield Gildersleeve also inherited Birdie Lee Coggins (Lillian Randolph), the family's Negro live-in cook and housekeeper. She was a hilarious woman who didn't mind speaking her own mind to her superior when it seemed

*Don't let the looks fool you! Walter Tetley, left, was already 26 when The Great Gildersleeve went on radio in 1941. By the time it left the air in 1958 he was about 43, a child impersonator still playing Leroy Forrester. Leroy was the 12-year-old nephew of Summerfield water commissioner Throckmorton P. Gildersleeve, a figure introduced on the Fibber McGee & Molly series by Harold Peary (shown). In this photo, "Unc" or "Uncle Throckmorton" is comforted by Leroy and his sibling Marjorie (actress Lurene Tuttle). Tuttle was 35 when she began playing the teen—about 16 then— and 38 when she left the role three years later. One of the magical attributes of radio was that actors could be almost any age or physical type, and the Theater of the Mind conveniently convinced the audience otherwise.*

prudent, even though she also nearly smothered him and the children as the substitute mother figure. "Lillian Randolph's Birdie was a much more sympathetic and realistic character than Beulah on the McGee show," one reviewer asserted.[3]

Hal Peary acquired another catchphrase early in his newest radio series: "You're a briiii-iight boy, Leroy!" Leroy reluctantly practiced piano lessons, brought home disappointing report cards and never learned not to slam the door. While admiring his Uncle Mort, he was quick to deflate his kin's ego

with reactions of "Ha!" or "What a character!" One of his recurring epithets was "Aw gee, Unc, for corn's sake!" automatically followed by his custodian's "Lee-eee-roy!" By the spring of 1949, while in junior high school, Leroy began to notice girls, particularly Rumson Bullard's daughter across the street. By 1951 he was infatuated with Brenda Kickerbocker and then Babs Winthrop, both portrayed by Barbara Whiting.

During the 1949–50 radio season Marjorie met, fell in love with and—on May 10, 1950—wed Walter (Bronco) Thompson

(Richard Crenna), football star at the local college. The event created such a stir that *Look* magazine took note of it, assigning an incredible five pages to the nuptials in its May 23, 1950, issue. After living under the Gildersleeve roof for a while, the Thompsons—including twins subsequently born to them, Linda and Ronnie—purchased the house next door to Gildersleeve, Leroy and Birdie.

In a striking forerunner to later television hits *Bachelor Father* (1957–62) and *Family Affair* (1966–71), shows that proffered affluent uncles taking in offspring of deceased siblings, Gildersleeve was a bachelor raising two children as a middle income wage earner, initially in private business but in the public arena by his second year. On October 18, 1942, Gildy was appointed water commissioner of Summerfield. As one wag clarified, it was "an illustrious career that might be described as doing nothing at all." Between time with the ladies and nights with the boys, it could hardly be thought of as a difficult lifestyle. "*The Great Gildersleeve* may have been the first broadcast show to be centered on a single parent balancing between child-rearing, work, and social life, done with taste and genuine wit, often at the expense of Gildersleeve's now slightly understated pomposity," according to one authority.

Throckmorton P. Gildersleeve interacted with a number of the town's longstanding citizens. It wasn't unusual for him to visit their places of business or to encounter them elsewhere on weekly episodes. All of that was reminiscent of the cast of characters who dropped by the McGee dwelling every week on the progenitor series. Gildy developed strong bonds with the town druggist, a meek little man named Peavey (Richard LeGrand, Forrest Lewis) whose down-in-the-mouth apologetic motto found its way into the nation's lexicon, too: "Well now, I wouldn't say that, Mr. Gildersleeve." The water commissioner maintained ties with Floyd Munson (Arthur Q. Bryan), the Summerfield barber, as well as police chief Gates (Ken Christy), who wasn't known to have a first name beyond "Chief." With the addition of Judge

Hooker, the quintet formed the Jolly Boys Club, a contingent of oddballs whose regular meetings were characterized by disputes as often as the harmony they gathered together to sing. "Fel-las! Fel-las! Let's all be Jolly Boys!" the peacemaker-chief would plead incessantly.

Gildy had a roving eye, too, and simply adored the ladies. While he never got hitched, he had little trouble keeping a gorgeous dame hanging on his arm. His was purportedly the only radio sitcom that forthrightly faced a single middle-aged person's romantic side. *Our Miss Brooks*, on the other hand—in theory and in practice—spent almost no time actually courting, although she talked about it a lot. Gildy possessed a healthy masculine libido, considering himself a ladies' man, even as he quivered in the very presence of a strikingly beautiful, unattached female.[4]

Over the show's long run he had multiple semi-permanent girlfriends, the most enduring being Leila Ransom (played by Shirley Mitchell), a nearby neighbor, widow and Georgia native with a pronounced Dixieland drawl. Gildy came close to marrying her on June 27, 1943, but halted just shy of the altar. The following year, in a similar situation, on June 25, 1944, he barely escaped getting hitched to school principal Eve Goodwin (Bea Benaderet). After nearly saying, "I do!" to Leila's cousin Adeline Fairchild (Una Merkel) during the 1948–49 season, he dated nurse Katherine Milford (Cathy Lewis) in the 1950s. A couple of siblings of Gildersleeve's surly neighbor Rumson Bullard (Gale Gordon, Jim Backus) maintained on-again/off-again affairs with Gildy: Ellen Bullard Knickerbocker (Martha Scott) and Paula Bullard Winthrop (Jean Bates). At one point Gildy also turned his attention to free-spirited folk singer Kathie Lee, who appeared as herself.

Historian Elizabeth B. Thomsen, who has made a study of *The Great Gildersleeve*, recording much of what is currently available about the series, speculated in some detail about the origin of the character's moniker:

The name "Gildersleeve" was said to be selected because it was the most pompous name the writers could think of. And it does have a certain ring to it. Perhaps there are subtle, unconscious connections with the idea of "gilding" or making something appear to be golden, and the haberdashery sound of "sleeve" that make you think of a vain and slightly ridiculous man. Or perhaps the Gildersleeve writers were unconsciously remembering the name of Basil Lanneau Gildersleeve, the noted classical scholar of whom Professor Paul Shorey of the University of Chicago said that, during fifty years of American classical scholarship, "the figure of Gildersleeve had dominated throughout." Basil Lanneau Gildersleeve was the author of standard Greek and Latin textbooks, so writers may have been familiar with it from their school days....

The "Throckmorton P." part of the name is easier to trace—Peary lived on Throckmorton Place![5]

It may be further noted that, on the *Fibber McGee & Molly* broadcast of October 22, 1940, Gildersleeve explained that the "P" in his name represented "Philharmonic." It may have been the only time in which the middle name was delineated. Before leaving the topic of the unusual appellation, in an early episode of *The Great Gildersleeve* the water commissioner was presented a key to the city by the officials of Gildersleeve, a small hamlet within the boundaries of Portland, Connecticut.

"The show holds up better than many other radio sitcoms, feels closer to us in time, is less gimmicky, and seems a little more honest than most," one critic maintained. Names for individual *Gildersleeve* episodes have been assigned by hobbyists and collectors over the years. Here are some representative appellations which suggest various themes the series pursued: "Pranks at School," "Birdie Quits," "Leroy Smokes a Cigar," "Matchmaker," "Leroy Runs Away," "Ten Best Dressed," "Gildy's New Neighbors," "Dinner for Judge Hooker," "Gildy Produces a Play," "Quiet Evening at Home," "Toothache," "Fibber & Molly Visit," "Auto Accident with Judge Hooker," "Low Water Pressure," "Gildy Runs

for Mayor," "Leroy Suspended from School," "Teaching Marjorie Domestic Arts," "Falling Out of the Jolly Boys," "Gildy Contemplates Early Retirement," "Birdie Takes a Vacation," "Marjorie's Hot Rod Boyfriend," "Stuck with Water Department Money Overnight," "Gildy Tries to Give Up Smoking" and "School Board Election—Gildy vs. Hooker."

Harold Peary was at the forefront of everything that was emblematic of Gildersleeve, of course. "The key to the show was Peary," Wikipedia insisted, "one of the most gifted voice actors of his generation ... whose booming voice and facility with moans, groans, laughs, shudders, and inflection was as close to body language and facial suggestion as a voice got. Peary was so effective, and Gildersleeve became so familiar a character, that he was referenced and satirized [sic] periodically in other comedies and in a few cartoons."[6]

You will recall that Peary had asked *Fibber McGee & Molly* scribe Don Quinn for an expanded role in that series as early as 1939. The creation of the ongoing character of Throckmorton P. Gildersleeve was the upshot. As time progressed, nevertheless, is it possible that he grew weary of the repetitious nature of that figure? A few historiographers have hinted as much. After consistently playing the role for more than a decade on dual programs, and also starring in a string of motion pictures as the inimitable character that Quinn established specifically for him, in 1950 Peary left *The Great Gildersleeve*. Apparently the decision was at his own volition after the star clashed with either the network or sponsor—or both. Multiple sources affirm that he attempted to carry the show to CBS and keep the rights to the Gildersleeve moniker and character for himself, none of which happened. One pundit summarized, "He outsmarted himself and lost the role of a lifetime."

The controversy erupted during an epoch of fallout that extended from the infamous broadcasting talent raids of the late 1940s. On that occasion CBS wooed several long-playing members of NBC's invincible troupe of comedians—*Amos 'n' Andy*, Jack Benny, Edgar Bergen and Charlie McCarthy, George Burns and Gracie Allen, and Red Skelton—as well as ABC's stellar crooner Bing Crosby and comic-quizmaster Groucho Marx. For its own undisclosed reasons, in the meantime, the Kraft Foods Company—*The Great Gildersleeve*'s solo sponsor in its first 13 seasons as a separate entry—plainly wasn't interested in shifting the program to CBS. Peary lost in his quest to retain rights to the program, too; they had never been his, even though the figure was fashioned specifically for him.

Upon his departure from NBC, therefore, he launched a new sitcom for CBS titled *Honest Harold*—one he owned and produced.[7] But he got the short end of the stick that time, too. The show petered out after a 39-week season (September 17, 1950, to June 13, 1951), vanishing from the ether altogether. It never attracted a sufficient audience. After just two broadcasts, in fact, in its issue of September 29, 1950, *Radio Life* panned it as "just another show," castigating it for plagiarism and lackluster attributes. Certainly it offered more than enough echoes of Peary's former series.

> Its failure was ... attributed to several factors.... Peary seemed to be hanging on to too many *Gildersleeve* elements. Peary had professed boredom with the role but had emerged on the rival network with a strong sound-alike, complete with the famous "dirty laugh."
>
> As Honest Harold Hemp, he lived with his mother and nephew.... Among his friends was Doc "Yak-Yak" Yancy, a strange cross between the crustiness of Judge Hooker and the nasal whine of Mr. Peavey, both notable *Gildersleeve* characters.... The show opened with the dirty laugh and closed with Peary giving background dialogue over credits, all *Gildersleeve* throwbacks.... *Harold* was the near-equal of *Gildersleeve* in several respects. Shows on tape reveal funny writing and well-drawn characters, and the supporting cast and production crew were first-rate.[8]

There was a strong suggestion, made by more than one scholar, that Peary operated under the assumption that—without him in the lead—*The Great Gildersleeve* would simply fold. Whether that was so or mere hyperbole, for the fans of the durable NBC series the chain was fortunate to have in its arsenal an actor who sounded enough like Peary to fool many listeners. One of the program's wordsmiths, Paul West, remembered: "Hal wanted a piece of the show, and his agent, MCA, was so sure they wouldn't continue the show without him that they sold him on the idea he was irreplaceable. Even though he'd worked with him before, Hal forgot that Willard Waterman was waiting in the wings."[9]

When Waterman stepped before the microphone as the program returned from its summer break in the fall of 1950, some members of the listening audience didn't even realize that another actor was in the part of the Summerfield water commissioner, paying little attention to the list of cast credits. "Waterman did an amazing job in nearly perfectly capturing the tone and subtleties of Peary's voice on a consistent basis," wrote reviewer Bob Beckett. "It was a great imitation. But there was really only ONE Throckmorton P. Gildersleeve, and that, of course, was Mr. Harold Peary. Waterman just imitated him and did a wonderful job in keeping the integrity and spirit of the originator."[10] Fortunately for Kraft, however, the protagonist had earned even greater acclaim with a fawning public than the show's star had. That aided and abetted the series' seamless transition from Peary to Waterman.

Waterman worked with Peary on several previous occasions on local and national broadcast series beamed from Chicago in the mid–1930s. His voice was considered a "near-perfect match" to Peary's. But he felt that Peary possessed a signature laugh that he shouldn't attempt to copy, and stood by that as long as he played Gildersleeve. Otherwise, there was little noticeable difference in the two men's inflections.

There were some other alterations in the program during the 1950s that were much more apparent to everybody who tuned in regularly. In 1952 some of the mainstays among the cast began reporting for duty less and less. For months at a time Judge Hooker, Floyd Munson, Bronco and Marjorie Thompson, and others were frequently missing in action. In their stead the storyline introduced a hypochondriac, Mrs. Potter, and a door-to-door egg farmer-salesman, Mr. Cooley, who made recurring appearances. Meanwhile, Gildy's romantic entanglements sometimes ended abruptly, his girlfriends often replaced by new ones for short flings—and without explanation. It must have seemed choppy to the continuing listener.

With radio in decline as the 1950s marched along, by 1954 the ratings were spiraling downward at a hefty clip. The Kraft Foods Company decided to shift the bulk of its advertising dollars to television to get the most bang for the buck, as so many other major radio sponsors were doing. In an attempt to hold its audience, NBC decided to try something new for two of its premier comedies that had been paired in the past: from Sunday through Thursday nights beginning in the fall of 1954 the web offered listeners quarter-hour back-to-back episodes of *Fibber McGee & Molly* and *The Great Gildersleeve* in the 10 o'clock Eastern Time half-hour.[11] (Friday nights at 10 o'clock were reserved for Gillette's *Friday Night Fights* boxing matches, a tradition then in its sixteenth season on varying networks.)

The weeknight strip was abandoned in the fall of 1955, however, when *The Great Gildersleeve* was reduced to a 25-minute Thursday night entry. That was further confirmation that the show was in a descent, a trend not limited to it alone but encompassing most of the remaining aural primetime fare by the mid–1950s. *Gildersleeve* was off the air for more than six months in 1956 before it returned for its sixteenth season, a "season" that lasted just five months. And previous shows were repeated during a portion of its final year, 1957–58, still occupying its customary Thursday night timeslot.

By then most long-playing nighttime radio features had either died or jumped to television. Gildersleeve (the continuing char-

acter) had been around since 1939, airing almost 19 years and surpassing the track records of almost every other mythical radio figure. While the show clearly suffered poor writing quality as the 1950s wore on, it still offered listening satisfaction and enjoyment to a diminishing group of fans, many of whom had been with it for years. And in its halcyon days there was hardly a more consistently entertaining family sitcom on the ether.

As with so many of its contemporaries, *The Great Gildersleeve* spawned movie and television incarnations. The big screen productions were generally well received, in contrast to the TV attempt which regrettably failed miserably.

Prior to a quartet of *Gildersleeve* films featuring Hal Peary in the namesake role (along with all the other Summerfield characters), the actor had appeared as Gildy in a quintet of celluloid productions: *Comin' Round the Mountain* (1940), *County Fair* (1941), *Look Who's Laughing* (1941), *Here We Go Again* (1942) and *Seven Days' Leave* (1942). Shortly after the radio series grew out of *Fibber McGee & Molly*, Peary starred in *The Great Gildersleeve* (1942), *Gildersleeve on Broadway* (1943), *Gildersleeve's Bad Day* (1943) and *Gildersleeve's Ghost* (1944). All of the radio cast then appearing, with the exception of Walter Tetley (Leroy), performed in those flicks. Tetley was a "child impersonator" by profession. Born in 1915, he was between 27 and 29 years of age when the quartet of films was released and thus unable to play a 12-year-old lad. Actor Freddie Mercer filled the bill in the big screen productions, although Tetley had a bit part as a bellboy in *Gildersleeve on Broadway*.

Unlike most of its peer radio sitcoms that gained additional mileage on network television in the early 1950s, *The Great Gildersleeve*'s producers labored under no fewer than two handicaps—and maybe three—when they took their show to the tube. In the first place, it was one of the few without the guaranteed audience and promotional savvy of a network, as it was produced for syndication. That probably had a limiting effect on the number of markets in which it was seen. Secondly, it didn't arrive until 1955, later than several other family sitcoms which had gained a foothold with television audiences. Viewing patterns for some watchers were already set. In addition, since *The Great Gildersleeve* had been around since the late 1930s, quite possibly its stabilized environment simply wasn't attractive to viewers by the mid–1950s, who had so many fresher options to select from.

Willard Waterman played Gildy in the televersion, which lasted one 39-week season. Lillian Randolph (Birdie), Forrest Lewis (Peavey) and Shirley Mitchell (Leila Ransom) reprised their radio roles on the small screen, while more actors were imported for the other characters. The radio show was taped on days when the TV production was inactive.

One source deduced: "The television program ignored all of the development that had happened on radio, and reverted to a broader style. On television, Gildersleeve was portrayed almost as a caricature of the radio character the petty bureaucrat [sic], the pompous fool, the womanizer."[12] In summarizing the pithy video effort, Wikipedia concluded: "The TV version is considered now to be somewhat of an insult to the *Great Gildersleeve* legacy. Gildersleeve himself was sketched as less loveable, more pompous, and a more overt womanizer, an insult amplified when Waterman himself said the key to the television version's failure was its director not having known a thing about the radio classic."[13] Directors of the TV show were Charles Barton and Robert S. Finkel. IMDb offered this enlightenment: "Waterman's talent can't save the tedious scripts, but the show does give a lot of incidental if unintended info about life in the 50s—not only the material furnishings and styles, but also production values. For example, one can readily see the early stages of evolution of sitcoms and how light and harmless (un-controversial) the issues are. [It was] strictly check your brain in at the door type of comedy. "[14]

There were further spinoffs from the original radio series.

At the zenith of the show's popularity, Harold Peary, as Gildersleeve, recorded a collection of children's fairy tales for Capitol Records. The stories were issued in heavy book-style albums containing four 78 rpm discs with full orchestral accompaniment. In 1945 the first of these, *Stories for Children, Told in His Own Way by the Great Gildersleeve*, included "Jack and the Beanstalk," "Puss in Boots" and "Rumplestiltskin." In 1946 a second album, *Children's Stories as Told by the Great Gildersleeve*, included "The Brave Little Tailor" and "Hansel and Gretel." A third and final release, in 1947, employed the title of the first in the series and embraced "Cinderella" and "Snow White and Rose Red."

Gildersleeve was also satirized in an animated cartoon, *Hare Conditioned*, featuring Bugs Bunny and shown in cinema palaces.

While *The Great Gildersleeve* was on summer hiatus in 1947, NBC—and Kraft—aired a one-time comedy and musical variety series, *Summerfield Bandstand*, between June 11 and September 3 in Gildy's time period. It featured a staff orchestra, vocalist Ken Carson, guest stars and comedic vignettes with Throckmorton, Leroy, Marjorie and other members of the regular series on a rotating basis. Few characters had their cake and ate it too, but Gildersleeve obviously did.

Harrold José Pereira de Faria, who legally altered his stage name late in his career to Harold (Hal) Peary in April 1958, was born July 25, 1908, at San Leandro, California, the son of Portuguese immigrants. He developed an interest in music early in life and performed as a boy soprano at weddings, parties, banquets and other festive occasions by age 11. At 13, about 1921, he was featured on the air as *The Oakland Tribune's Boy Caruso*. A baritone at 17, he routinely toured with companies staging musical comedy shows. Peary became firmly entrenched in Bay Area radio in subsequent years, moving across the bay to San Francisco by 1928, where he was billed as *The Spanish Serenader* on a live NBC West Coast feature. He was poised to accept many more opportunities in radio; some of the doors that opened for him went well beyond mere singing. Peary became a comic and an actor, too, occasionally combining the three strains. Before relocating to Chicago in 1935, where he gained a significant foothold in the audio medium, he turned up in occasional support roles on *One Man's Family*, aired from San Francisco.

Early in his career in the Windy City he appeared as an Italian student's father on NBC's madcap comedy-variety series *Kaltenmeyer's Kindergarten*. At the same time, he was heard as Dr. Haines in *Welcome Valley*. Peary and Willard Waterman, and a host of other Chicago-based thespians, performed as leads and in supporting roles on the horror drama *Lights Out* during the same epoch. In 1935–36 Peary portrayed both Tony the Wop and Major Fellowes on NBC's juvenile aviation adventure serial *Flying Time*.

Returning to the West Coast in 1937, in Hollywood he became a dependable utility player on *Fibber McGee & Molly*, which led, of course, to *The Great Gildersleeve* and subsequently to *Summerfield Bandstand* and *Honest Harold*. From 1937 to 1939 he raised his voice in harmony with a dozen-member choral troupe that regularly performed on *The NBC Minstrels*. In 1941 Peary appeared as Smagooznok on the NBC West Coast comedy *The Signal Carnival*. For a brief while in the 1940s he was Herb Woodley, the Bumsteads' neighbor on *Blondie*. Peary also made single-shot guest appearances on a host of dramatic anthology series: *Lux Radio Theater* (1943), *The Lady Esther Screen Guild Theater* (1945, in which he reprised his role from the film *Gildersleeve's Bad Day*), *Hollywood Star Time* (1947), *The Sealtest Variety Theater* (1948–49 season) and *The Philip Morris Playhouse* (1949).

In addition to the previously named nine motion pictures in which he played Throckmorton P. Gildersleeve—four as the star—Peary made another seven low-budget movies (sometimes in uncredited roles) between 1954 and 1973. None are memorable. He didn't fade into oblivion following *Honest Harold*'s transitory tenure, however. In fact, some of his best performances were ahead of him as he turned his attention pri-

marily to the tube, which was rapidly siphoning off radio's homegrown audience.

Peary turned up in guest slots at least two dozen times on TV series, usually but not always in dramatic parts. Among them were: *Toast of the Town, Disneyland, Stars Over Hollywood, Schlitz Playhouse of Stars, Public Defender, The Spike Jones Show, The Bob Cummings Show, Circus Boy, Tombstone Territory, Surfside 6, The Dick Van Dyke Show, Perry Mason, My Mother the Car, The Addams Family, My Three Sons, Petticoat Junction* and *The Brady Bunch*. He also won recurring roles in a couple of TV series: as Perry Bannister in 1955 on CBS's *Willy,* and—having obviously come full circle—returning to where his notoriety began in a not-so-ironic twist as Mayor LaTrivia on NBC's short-lived *Fibber McGee & Molly* in the fall and early winter of 1959. At the end of his career Peary provided voiceovers for a couple of animated Christmas movies in 1976 and 1979.

While radio listeners perceived Harold Peary as an arrogant yet adorable windbag in the defining role of his professional life, in private he maintained a very complicated existence that occasionally spilled out onto the pages of the print media. On June 20, 1946, he and his first wife, the former Wanda (Betty) Farquhar, were granted an interlocutory decree—pronounced during the progress of a legal action and having only provisional force, according to Webster—pending a formal divorce decree that took effect on June 21, 1947. The couple had no children. Subsequently, Peary and radio–TV actress Gloria Holliday tied the knot in Tijuana, Mexico, on August 8, 1946, seven weeks after the interlocutory decree was issued. They were prevented from marrying in the United States until his divorce was final, although they did re-marry in June 1947. Gloria was two months pregnant on her first wedding day and gave birth to a son, Page Peary, on March 9, 1947, a few months before his dad was legally available to wed in America.

In the meantime, at the home of an acquaintance, on July 2, 1946, Betty Peary, Hal's first wife, accused a woman of taking his side in the divorce action. Their dispute erupted into a physical altercation. Betty was charged with "batting" the woman on her head with a water tumbler. Two days afterward she was charged yet again, that time with drunkenness during a film colony nightclub brawl.[15]

Before her hearing in a Los Angeles courtroom on the battery charge, Betty Peary fainted three times in the hallway outside. A judge found her guilty, fined her $100, placed her on probation and meted out a 30-day suspended jail sentence.[16] At some point Gloria Holliday (Peary) assumed the role of Bessie, Gildersleeve's secretary at the Summerfield Water Department, a role initiated by Pauline Drake. Holliday also appeared as PBX operator Gloria in Honest Harold on CBS.

A longtime resident of Manhattan Beach, California, in 1956 Peary was named honorary mayor of the city. He succumbed to a heart attack at Torrance, California, on March 30, 1985, at the age of 76. He was survived by his wife and son.

Peary's successor in his defining role, Willard Lewis Waterman, was born at Madison, Wisconsin, on August 29, 1914, the son of a building materials manufacturer. Educated at his hometown University of Wisconsin, where he enrolled in electrical engineering to scratch an itch (possibly an outgrowth of the family's livelihood?), he gave it up when he discovered his passion for theater was even greater. Waterman was skipping the classes he was enrolled in to sit in on drama courses when the dean of the engineering school advised him to think about acting if he was going to keep missing scheduled subjects. He needed no further prompting, switched his major and won parts in collegiate dramatics productions while working in local radio.

He left school to pursue an acting career, winding up in Chicago in 1935 at the hub of national radio activity at that time. Actually, Waterman and Hal Peary—whose destiny would overlap and become intricately intertwined—both got to the Windy City within a few months of each other. Fate, and a single role, eventually would make both of them stars. The pair appeared together on several of the same shows, concurrently and separately, standing in for one another, as the two men's voices were noticeably analogous. Peary's departure from Chicago a couple of years later, when he frequently was heard by the name of Gildersleeve, opened up a whole new vista for Waterman.

The latter's aural credits included dramatic roles in a company of Chicago thespians playing on Lights Out between about 1935 and 1939. For a couple of those early years Hal Peary also found work on the show. The two actors were linked when they showed up in the cast of The Tom Mix Ralston Straight Shooters, a weekday juvenile western-adventure serial that ran on all the chains except CBS. Waterman was heard sporadically in supporting roles on that series for nearly a decade.

A newspaper reporter, writing in 1937, allowed:

> It is there then [Chicago] that we discover the man of many deaths. Willard Waterman is his name. His life in the radio theater has been a dying one ever since he started on the ether waves two years ago. Although he has been given up dead many times and is killed continually, he still remains very much alive on the Girl Alone program in which you hear him as "Leo Warner."
>
> Waterman has been dying on the air ever since his first production, in which he was killed off in the first chapter of a radio serial.... Most of his dying has taken place in Arch Oboler's midnight thrillers, Lights Out. But out of these deaths Waterman has been able to make a very good living.[17]

During the same period he turned up in the casts of a couple of other venerable daytime serials, The Romance of Helen Trent and Ma Perkins. He was a frequent contributor to The Chicago Theater of the Air in the 1940s, too, joining a contingent of Windy City artists for another dramatic anthology. For a spell early in the decade to mid–1942 he was the masculine lead, John Fairchild, in the CBS soap opera Kay Fairchild, Stepmother. He took a similar position in the CBS and MBS sitcom Those Websters from 1945 to 1948. Between

1947 and 1949 he impersonated Roger Barton during a two-year span in which *The Guiding Light* emanated from Los Angeles. By 1949 he performed in narratives aired on *The Damon Runyon Theater*. That summer (1949) Waterman was featured in supporting roles on *Four-Star Playhouse*, as well as in the fleeting NBC sitcom *Me and Janie*. During the 1949–50 radio season he and Shirley Mitchell (Leila Ransom of the *Gildersleeve* cast) were teamed for the CBS sitcom *Leave It to Joan*, starring Joan Davis. During the same year he made multiple appearances on the NBC dramatic anthology *Screen Director's Playhouse*.

Occasionally he showed up in supporting roles on *The Amos 'n' Andy Show* and *My Friend Irma*. In January 1950 he performed on *Lux Radio Theater*, and from 1950 to 1952 he was board member John Merriweather on *The Halls of Ivy*. In 1950, of course, he signed to replace Hal Peary as the namesake lead on *The Great Gildersleeve*. Waterman remained with it until new episodes played out in the mid–1950s. By then he was already giving attention to the same part in the video version, a show that lasted one season.

Like most of his peers, Waterman did not concentrate on radio to the exclusion of other entertainment media. In addition to the short-lived TV entry of his most famous effort, he was seen many times on large and small screens. Between 1949 and 1973 he made 35 motion pictures of the B variety, with such incredibly uninspiring titles as *So You're Having In-Law Trouble* (1949), *No Man of Her Own* (1950), *So You Think You're Not Guilty* (1950), *Darling, How Could You!* (1951), *It Happens Every Thursday* (1953) and *How to Be Very, Very Popular* (1955). Waterman was uncredited in many of his film roles.

Meanwhile, he performed in one made-for-TV movie, an uncredited role in 1959's *Moochie of the Little League*. He was Carl Foster, a recurring character in CBS's *The Eve Arden Show*, lasting five months in the 1957–58 television season. Furthermore, Waterman made 38 guest-shot appearances in the dramatic and comedic casts of TV series, appearing in some multiple times. Among his repertoire were *The Adventures of Jim Bowie, The Real McCoys, Circus Boy, December Bride, Casey Jones, The Adventures of Rin Tin Tin, 77 Sunset Strip, How to Marry a Millionaire, Lawman, Bat Masterson, General Electric Theater, Bonanza, Laramie, Wagon Train, Dennis the Menace, Cheyenne, The Joey Bishop Show, Maverick, Mr. Ed, My Favorite Martian* and *Vacation Playhouse.*

Beginning in 1966 the versatile actor appeared in the smash Broadway musical *Mame,* which continued for 1508 performances in New York and another 443 in London. After finishing all of his broadcast, stage and screen assignments, in 1980 he was cast in a Sony radio commercial. Even it was a winner, garnering a CLIO trophy after being voted the best commercial of that year in its sphere.

In 1937 Waterman was a founding member of the American Federation of Radio Artists (AFRA), now the American Federation of Television and Radio Artists (AFTRA). He is believed to have been the only member of the union's board of directors in four different locales: Chicago, Los Angeles, San Francisco and New York. He served on the union's board until 1990. That group ultimately cited him for his "distinguished career," as well as his "dedication to the welfare of performers everywhere."

Waterman died on February 2, 1995, at Burlingame, California, a victim of bone marrow disease. He was 80. His wife of 57 years, Mary Anna, and two daughters, Lynne Ansara of Burlingame and Susan Waterman of Canoga Park, plus three granddaughters and a great-granddaughter, survived him.

Other gifted performers among *The Great Gildersleeve* players had equally impressive careers. In an atypical turn, several—but not all—were born during the 19th century.

Lurene Tuttle (1906–86), who originated the part of Marjorie, Gildersleeve's niece, left radio early to perform on screen; over a lengthy career she appeared in 44 theatrical motion pictures, plus 12 more on television. She won running parts in five TV series, and turned up in guest shots on a myriad of video features another 114 times.

Walter Tetley (1915–75), already 26 when the show began, played Gildersleeve's genial 12-year-old nephew, Leroy, for the full run of the radio show.

Lillian Randolph (1898–1980), who was Birdie in the four Gildersleeve movies, also remained the one and only portrayer of her part on the radio series. She transitioned to the television embodiment as well, becoming the only individual to appear in all three media versions of *Gildersleeve*.

Judge Hooker's alter ego, Earle Ross (1888–1961), and Mr. Peavey's, Richard LeGrand (1882–1963) were radio veterans who acted on numerous aural series before they arrived in Gildy's neighborhood.

Arthur Q. Bryan (1899–1959), the barber of Summerfield, carried still greater weight when he retraced Harold Peary's pathway to join *Fibber McGee & Molly* as the irascible resident nemesis Doc Gamble.

And Shirley Mitchell (1919–), Gildy's girlfriend Leila Ransom for a while on radio and TV, concentrated her career on scads of dramatic and comedic video roles after her radio days passed.

In the decade prior to the middle of the twentieth century and for a few years thereafter, *The Great Gildersleeve* was a reliable source of amusement for many radio listeners. Fans knew the characters well and loved the contortions that the water commissioner went through as he faced issues linked with running a home, making a living, conflicting with chums and being a persistent ladies' man. In the end, the show proved at least a couple of things: (1) that an enormously well-liked character in one series could harvest still more acclaim in a separate vehicle that was created just for him; and (2) few would notice when an actor with a similar-sounding inflection was brought in to replace the original.

Actually, not until there were significant slip-ups in the scriptwriting as the 1950s advanced was the flow interrupted in what listeners had come to expect and accept. An experiment with a daily quarter-hour model seemed to drive more of the audience away. With radio's fortunes fading fast by then, the once-amusing little sitcom was finally reduced to repeat (and familiar) transcriptions. Nonetheless, during the feature's heyday, the rivals of *The Great Gildersleeve* were few in number, at least those with an ability to consistently deliver the obligingly lighthearted fare that this show did for a comparably enduring interlude. Unquestionably that made it one of the most universally beloved sitcoms of radio's golden age.

# 13

## The Jack Benny Program

### RADIO'S PREMIER ENTERTAINER

Jack Benny could well be voted the most beloved comedian of the golden age of radio. The aura surrounding him persists unabated; an energized following casts the venerated entertainer as an incomparable figure worthy of unbridled adulation, the level of passion at times almost defying belief. Surprisingly, many of his most rabid fans weren't even born by the time of their idol's death in 1974. Yet a new generation is laughing tumultuously at Benny's side-splitting antics, hearing aural transcriptions in a myriad of formats while watching DVDs and videotapes of the master of his profession. His ascendancy began with Ed Sullivan, the journalist-turned-showman who interviewed him on the ether. That pushed Benny onto the airwaves permanently, and with him came a cast of characters that Americans found enormously satisfying. They had the country eating from their hands from the 1930s into the mid–1960s with their radio and television incarnations. The situations were modestly simple and familiar. Perhaps that's what drew listeners initially. But they were also uproariously funny. A half-dozen gags were replayed nearly every week: incidents pertaining to Benny's alleged stinginess, his "permanent" age of 39, his Maxwell automobile, his professing to be a concert virtuoso while insufferably sawing a fiddle. Although the gags were routine, the jokes were not. Studio audiences fell into the aisles, doubled over in laughter. During the radio season it was a tradition

every Sunday night. It was clean fun, too. America had an itch, and Benny knew where to scratch. Most people would likely say his show was one of the best things radio did for them. The hero worship attests to it.

❖ ❖ ❖

**Producers:** Irving Fein, Hilliard Marks
**Directors:** Robert Ballin, Hilliard Marks
**Writers:** Henry Conn (1932–36); Al Boasberg, Howard Snyder and Hugh Wedlock, Jr. (1936); Ed Beloin and Bill Morrow (ca. 1936–43); George Balzer, Milt Josefsberg, Sam Perrin, John Tackaberry (1943–55)
**Orchestra Leaders:** George Olsen (1932), Ted Weems (1932), Frank Black (1933–34), Don Bestor (1934), Jimmy Grier (1934), Johnny Green (1934–36), Phil Harris (1936–52), Mahlon Merrick (ca. 1946–ca. 1948), Bob Crosby (1952–55)
**Vocalists:** Ethel Shutta (1932–33), James Melton (1933), Frank Parker (1933–34), Michael Bartlett (1934–35), Kenny Baker (1935–39), Dennis Day (1939–44, 1946–58), Larry Stevens (1944–46), the Sportsmen Quartet (including, at different times: Gurney Bell, Bill Days, Jay Mayer, John Rarig, Thurl Ravenscroft, Max Smith, Marty Sperzel)
**Sound Effects Technicians:** Jimmy Murphy, Virgil Reimer, Gene Twombly
**Announcers:** George Hicks (1932–33), Howard Claney (1933), Alois Havrilla (1933–34), Don Wilson (1934–58)
**Recurring Cast:** *Jack Benny:* Jack Benny (nee Benjamin Kubelsky); *Mary Livingstone:* Mary Livingstone (nee Sadie Marks); *Ethel Shutta:* Ethel Shutta (1932–33); *Kenny Baker:* Kenny Baker (1935–42); *Phil Harris:* Phil Harris (1936–52); *Rochester Van Jones:* Eddie Anderson (1937–58); *Dennis Day:* Dennis Day

(1939–44, 1946–58); *Schlepperman*: Sam Hearn (1935–?); *Maxwell* (Benny's car): Mel Blanc (ca. 1935–58); *Train Depot PA Announcer*: Mel Blanc (1945–58); *Professor LeBlanc*: Mel Blanc (1945–58); *Polly* (Benny's parrot): Mel Blanc (1945–58); *Sy*: Mel Blanc; *Mr. Kitzel*: Artie Auerbach; *Gladys Zybysko*: Sara Berner; *Mabel Flapsaddle*: Sara Berner; *Gertrude Gearshift*: Bea Benaderet; *Martha*: Jane Morgan; *Emily*: Gloria Gordon; *Ed*: Joseph Kearns

**Supporting Cast:** Joe Besser, Mel Blanc, Dix Davis, Joel Davis, Andy Devine, Verna Felton, Frank Fontaine, Sandra Gould, Sheldon Leonard, Eddie Maher, Frank Nelson, Minerva Pious, Benny Rubin, Ethel Shutta, Blanche Stewart

**Sponsors:** Canada Dry Bottling Company, for Canada Dry Ginger Ale (1932–33); General Motors Corporation, for Chevrolet automobiles, trucks, parts and service (1933–34); General Tire Corporation, for General tires (1934); General Foods Corporation, for Jell-O gelatin, puddings, tapioca and pie fillings, Grape-Nuts cereal and a wide line of additional foodstuffs (1934–44); American Tobacco Company, for Lucky Strike cigarettes and other brands (1944–55); Multiple participation (1956–57); Home Insurance Corporation, for varied insurance coverages (1957–58)

**Themes:** "Beyond the Blue Horizon" (1932–33), "Yankee Doodle Boy," segueing into "Love in Bloom" (opening theme); "Hooray for Hollywood" (closing theme)

**Ratings:** High—36.4 (1934–35), Low—5.8 (1954–55), Median—25.5. Ratings based on 22 seasons (1933–55 inclusive)

**On the Air:** May 2–October 26, 1932, *The Canada Dry Ginger Ale Program*, NBC Blue, Monday and Wednesday, 9:30–9:45 P.M. Eastern Time; October 30–December 29, 1932, CBS, Sunday, 10:00–10:15 P.M. and Thursday, 8:15–8:30 P.M.; January 1–January 26, 1933, CBS, Sunday, 10:00–10:15 P.M. and Thursday, 8:00–8:15 P.M.; March 17–June 23, 1933, *The Chevrolet Program*, NBC, Friday, 10:00–10:30 P.M.; October 1, 1933–April 1, 1934, NBC, Sunday, 10:00–10:30 P.M.; April 6–September 28, 1934, *The General Tire Show*, NBC, Friday, 10:00–10:30 P.M.; October 14, 1934–July 14, 1935, *The Jell-O Program*, NBC Blue, Sunday, 7:00–7:30 P.M.; September 29, 1935–June 21, 1936, NBC Blue, Sunday, 7:00–7:30 P.M.; October 4, 1936–June 27, 1937, NBC, Sunday, 7:00–7:30 P.M.; October 3, 1937–June 26, 1938, NBC, Sunday, 7:00–7:30 P.M.; October 2, 1938–June 25, 1939, NBC, Sunday, 7:00–7:30 P.M.; October 8, 1939–June 16, 1940, NBC, Sunday, 7:00–7:30 P.M.; October 6, 1940–June 1, 1941, NBC, Sunday, 7:00–7:30 P.M.; October 5, 1941–May 31, 1942, NBC, Sunday, 7:00–7:30 P.M.; October 4, 1942–May 30, 1943, *The Grape-Nuts Program*, NBC,

Sunday, 7:00–7:30 P.M.; October 10, 1943–June 4, 1944, NBC, Sunday, 7:00–7:30 P.M.; October 1, 1944–May 27, 1945, *The Lucky Strike Program*, NBC, Sunday, 7:00–7:30 P.M.; September 30, 1945–May 26, 1946, NBC, Sunday, 7:00–7:30 P.M.; September 29, 1946–May 25, 1947, NBC, Sunday, 7:00–7:30 P.M.; October 5, 1947–June 27, 1948, NBC, Sunday, 7:00–7:30 P.M.; October 3–December 26, 1948, NBC, Sunday, 7:00–7:30 P.M.; January 2–May 29, 1949, CBS, Sunday, 7:00–7:30 P.M.; September 11, 1949–May 28, 1950, CBS, Sunday, 7:00–7:30 P.M.; September 10, 1950–June 3, 1951, CBS, Sunday, 7:00–7:30 P.M.; September 16, 1951–June 1, 1952, CBS, Sunday, 7:00–7:30 P.M.; September 14, 1952–June 7, 1953, CBS, Sunday, 7:00–7:30 P.M.; September 13, 1953–June 6, 1954, CBS, Sunday, 7:00–7:30 P.M.; September 26, 1954–May 22, 1955, CBS, Sunday, 7:00–7:30 P.M.; October 28, 1956–July 7, 1957, *The Best of Benny*, CBS, Sunday, 7:00–7:30 P.M. (repeats); September 29, 1957–June 22, 1958, CBS, Sunday, 7:00–7:30 P.M. (repeats)

**Extant Archival Material:** Transcriptions of Andy Devine's appearances on *The Jack Benny Program*, and scrapbooks citing his radio performances, are among the Andy Devine Papers, while the James Stewart Papers include transcriptions of Stewart's appearances on radio shows from 1939 to 1953, both collections archived at Brigham Young University's Harold B. Lee Library, Provo, UT, 84602; (801) 422–3175; Fax (801) 422–0461; *specialcollections@byu.edu*.

An unidentified number of scripts of *The Jack Benny Program* are among over 5,000 drawn from multiple radio and TV series archived by the University of Maryland's Library of American Broadcasting, 3210 Hornbake Library, College Park, MD, 20742; (301) 405–0397; Fax (301) 314–2634; *labcast@umd.edu*.

An unidentified number of scripts of *The Jack Benny Program* are found in the Ben Blue Papers and the Jack Benny Papers, 1930–1974, the latter collection including photographs, personal and business records from 1935 to 1955, tapes, magazine articles, memorabilia and awards, housed by the University of California at Los Angeles (UCLA) Charles E. Young Research Library Department of Special Collections, Box 951575, Los Angeles, CA, 90095; (310) 825–4988; *www.library.ucla.edu/libraries/arts/*.

A corrected script of *The Jack Benny Program* for December 6, 1953, is maintained by Stanford University's Special Collections and University Archives, 557 Escondido Mall, Stanford, CA, 94305; (650) 725–1026; *speccollref@stanford.edu*.

Musical scores and arrangements for the Sportsmen Quartet's performances on *The Jack Benny Program* and other radio and TV shows (1943–70) are housed by the Pacific Pioneer Broadcasters, Box 4866, North Hollywood, CA, 91617; (323) 461–2121; www.pacificpioneerbroadcasters.org/archive/html.

An unidentified number of scripts for *The Jack Benny Program* are among the Milt Josefsberg Radio Scripts, 1938–1946, archived by the American Heritage Center of the University of Wyoming, 1000 East University Avenue, Laramie, WY, 82071; (307) 766–3756; Fax (307) 766–5511; *http://ahc.uwyo.edu/usearchives/default.htm.*

A total of 96 scripts from *The Jack Benny Program* (1932–58) are maintained in the Script Collection by the Broadcast Arts Library, Box 9828, Fort Worth, TX, 76147; (310) 288–6511; www.broadcastartslibrary.com.

About 120 scripts, with brief show synopses, of *The Jack Benny Program* (1945–57) comprise the Bob Crosby, Milton Josefsberg, Fletcher Markle and Hilliard Marks collections at Thousand Oaks Library, American Radio Archives, 1401 East Janss Road, Thousand Oaks, CA, 91362; (805) 449–2660; fax (805) 449–2675; *www.tol.lib.ca.us.*

The International Jack Benny Fan Club is accessed at *www.jackbenny.org.*

At least 795 *Jack Benny Program* broadcasts between 1932 and 1955 are known to be in general circulation or held by private collectors as of 2006, sold by vintage radio dealers and traded by old-time radio hobbyists.

Logs of *The Jack Benny Program* are available from Jay Hickerson (*jayhick@aol.com*), and Larry and John Gassman (*lgsinger@sbcglobal.net*).

❖ ❖ ❖

What can be said about Jack Benny that hasn't been stated hundreds, even thousands of times in legions of books and magazines and newspapers and on websites and in databases and libraries and museum collections large and small? He was the classic archetypical performer, the consummate comedian: beloved by an adoring public, respected by colleagues, idolized by fans. A gifted artist whose talent far outweighed mere metaphors, he exhibited an unbridled generosity that belied his stage persona. If vintage radio was to be defined by a single entertainer, Jack Benny would be at the top of many people's lists. At least one radio historian (and plenty more, quite likely) accorded him status as "the most popular and best loved comedian of radio's Golden Age."[1]

Born Benjamin Kubelsky in Chicago of Polish heritage and Jewish descent on February 14, 1894, he took his first bow on Valentine's Day. Growing up in nearby Waukegan, where his father ran a haberdashery, at his parents' insistence young Kubelsky took up violin, which he detested. They projected for him the life of an accomplished concert artist, though he hated lessons, practice— everything about it. He was also a poor student in school, routinely failing his courses of study, frequently being a truant and successively getting kicked out of Central High School and Waukegan Business College. He went to work for his poppa but was dismissed there, too, after several screw-ups. The only thing to that point that he had really been good at was cracking people up with his jokes.

He learned to play piano, and he could play the fiddle. At eight he performed for Saturday children's matinees at the Phoenix Opera House. At 17, for $7.50 weekly, he was in the pit orchestra of Waukegan's Barrison Theater, a vaudeville palace. In 1911 the Marx brothers came to town with their stage manager-director mother. She was so impressed by Kubelsky's skills as an accompanist and sight reader that she offered him $15 weekly plus room, board and travel expenses to join their act. His parents saw it differently, however, and gave an unqualified "no." The young showman reflected, "If I had gone on the road then, I might have become so successful as a pit musician that I never would have become a comedian." While not projecting himself as a comic, "I did think how nice it would be to be a straight man in a comedy team because the straight man wore good clothes and carried a cane and a straw hat."

Over his parents' initial protests, young Kubelsky succeeded in going on the road at 18, nevertheless. In September 1912 he left town in the company of Cora Salisbury, a recently widowed ex-vaudevillian who returned to work with a piano-violin act. During that epoch he experienced a succession of name changes. When concert violinist Jan Kubelik threatened to sue him unless he altered his appellation, he adopted Ben K. Benny; the act was known as Salisbury and Benny. In a few years, when he was performing solo, Ben Bernie had long been doing a similar act and sent word that Ben Benny had best find a new name. Sailors traditionally greeted one another as "Jack" then. His new stage name was derived from that: Jack Benny. Except for a stint in the Navy in the waning days of the First World War, when he was once more known as Benny Kubelsky, he was forever after Jack Benny.

When Ms. Salisbury left the road after a couple of years, Benny teamed with Lyman Woods, a young Chicago pianist. For five years they played the better theater circuits, earning $350 weekly together. Their gigs were interrupted by Benny's service at the Great Lakes Naval Training Station near Waukegan. As a sailor he appeared in a show where—for the very first time—he was required to speak on stage. It was a watershed experience; he set his sights on comedy thereafter, with music merely as something to fall back on, his fiddle becoming not much more than a stage prop to hold in his hand.

*Jack Benny—Aristocrat of Humor* was his solo act billing following the war. In his travels he met Gracie Allen and George Burns (the latter would become his best friend for life). All of them were single then. In 1921 he met Sadie Marks, an Orthodox Jew like himself and a distant relative of the infamous Marx brothers (the comedians changed the spelling of their birth surname from Marks). At the time she was 14; he was 27. Romance didn't blossom just then, but it followed with love in full bloom. He labeled her "the love of my life." They wed in Waukegan on January 14, 1927; she was 19, he was 32. It was the only marriage for both, a fact he took great pride in.

The following year his stage partner, who was playing a "dumb girl," went to the hospital. While she was away, with Sadie resisting all the way (she experienced stage fright throughout her life, a circumstance to be revisited shortly), Benny temporarily replaced his associate with his wife. The act was an overnight hit, and Sadie permanently replaced the girl—over Sadie's strong protests.

She was given the stage name of Mary Livingstone. Sometime afterward she had her moniker legally altered. She was known as Mary Livingstone for the rest of her days. Even Benny said he often forgot to call her "Sadie" when they were at home.

Benny's acquaintance, newspaper columnist Ed Sullivan, was launching a weekly quarter-hour interview series on CBS on January 12, 1932. Sullivan had been favorable to Benny in his column. The standup comic reasoned: how could I ignore Sullivan's request when he asked me to appear on his first show gratis? Benny couldn't. Sullivan told him to wing it, but Benny came prepared anyway. His initial radio spiel began: "This is Jack Benny talking. There will be a slight pause while you say, 'Who cares?'" The head of the ad agency representing Canada Dry Ginger Ale was listening and liked what he heard. That translated into hiring Benny to headline his own variety half-hour over NBC Blue less than four months later, debuting May 2, 1932. The original *Ed Sullivan Show*, then on radio, had brought Benny before the nation.

A couple of years following his series' inception, in July 1934 the Bennys adopted a two-week-old daughter, Joan Naomi. She became the apple of her daddy's eye. In 1990 she released his long-planned, still-unpublished memoir, augmented by her own editorial comments. The result was a captivating volume of personal perspectives—his, hers and those of his industry friends: *Sunday Nights at Seven*, named for his enduring timeslot on a trio of national audio hookups.

Returning to Mary Livingstone, over her constant protestations, she too became a permanent part of the radio cast. Her daughter remembered a well-publicized dynamic surrounding those occasions at a time when Joan was a high school senior:

> Mother had become increasingly nervous and apprehensive about appearing in front of an audience. She had long since passed stage fright. Panic-stricken was more like it! ... In 1950, after eighteen years on the show, she had reached a point of near hysteria. By noon on Sunday her hands looked as though they

would burst into flame. She told Daddy she simply couldn't face it any longer.

I think he knew this would happen.... He still needed Mary Livingstone because she was such an integral part of the radio show.... So he made a deal with her—she would continue to do the radio shows for the next year, but he would work out a way for her not to have to go to the studio or perform in front of an audience....

By that time the technology had reached a point so this plan was feasible. On Saturdays, recording equipment was brought to our house and Mother could read her lines, Daddy feeding her the cues. On Sundays I went to the studio in her place, read at the rehearsal and did the show. After Daddy explained to the studio audience how and why this was happening, I played Mother's part live—trying to imitate her voice, her timing.... Of course when the show was aired, her voice had been spliced into the tape, so the listening audience heard the real Mary Livingstone and not me.[2]

Parenthetically, in the subsequent televised exhibition of *The Jack Benny Program*, viewers learned to live without Mary Livingstone altogether. Wikipedia reported that "Livingstone appeared rarely if at all" on the TV series due to "a striking case of stage fright." In 1958 she permanently retired from entertainment and almost never went back.

*The Jack Benny Program* developed from a variety show unifying sketch comedy and musical interludes into a situation comedy model. One source explained: "Although each week's episode usually had a theme or starting premise, the actual playing out of that premise often evolved into a loose collection of skits."[3] NBC's *Fibber McGee & Molly* successfully adapted the formula to its weekly half-hour after launching three years after *Benny*'s inception. For his part, Benny played an illusory version of himself. Fictionalizing Benny the radio star provided the backdrop for plotting the installments. Numerous possibilities could be translated into the germ of an idea for a single episode: hosting a celebration, a golfing excursion, a shopping trip, transporting the cast by rail to Chicago or New York for appearances away from L.A., impressing a sponsor, preparing for the following Sunday's show, celebrating a birthday or borrowing something from the neighbors. Other characters played off that theme, reacting and contributing in their own unique ways.

For most of the run they included Mary Livingstone, a wisecracking comrade who wasn't a girlfriend in the true sense of that term but who liked Benny (yet could also unabashedly dish out light insults, too); the inimitable Rochester, Benny's valet, a Negro with an acerbic tongue who didn't mind putting his "boss" in his place—he was "the closest thing the Benny character had to either a spouse or a best friend" one authority surmised; Don Wilson, a portly announcer with an identifyingly hearty chuckle; Phil Harris, a loudmouth jive-talking impresario who exhibited a proclivity for wine, women and risqué repartee; and Dennis Day, an Irish tenor who was portrayed as a naïve youth leading an incredibly sheltered existence who overcame all of it to upstage his superior. When it was time for a musical number, Day and Harris (or their stand-ins) vocalized solos, or the band provided an instrumental. With the exception of Rochester, incidentally, who was impersonated by Eddie Anderson, all of these individuals performed under their own monikers.

They were the main players, and yet there were many others in supporting roles, some of whom appeared almost every week. They included Mel Blanc, the man of a thousand voices; Frank Nelson, who also played dozens of character roles, some again and again; Sheldon Leonard; bandleader Bob Crosby, who succeeded Phil Harris; Verna Felton, Dennis Day's "mom"; and several others whose dialects were familiar to the fans.

There were also lots of guest appearances by celebs like Fred Allen, Edgar Bergen, George Burns and Gracie Allen, Ronald and Benita Colman, Bing Crosby, Bob Hope, Red Skelton, Frank Sinatra, Barbara Stanwyck, James Stewart, Orson Welles and many more. Some of those had their own radio series, and Benny turned up as "their" guests, too. In 1937 he and Fred Allen launched a running

*A typical broadcast of* The Jack Benny Program *featured—from left to right—Benny and wife, actress Mary Living-stone, impresario-comic Phil Harris, singer-comic Dennis Day, Eddie Anderson (who played Benny's valet Rochester) and announcer Don Wilson. The orchestra is in the background, while the foreground includes a portion of the studio audience. During a radio run that spanned a quarter-century the Benny series aired separately on three networks at the same time on the same day of the week for 23 seasons. It consistently occupied one of radio ratings' top spots, often capturing first place. Among all the comics on the air, his peers considered Benny as the master of timing. Long before his audio run ended the showman added a video version that persisted for 15 years.*

quarrel on the ether, and the audience-building ploy became an institution, popularizing a device that spilled over into other shows.

It began when Allen cited a juvenile fiddler who had performed on his show as something to undercut "a certain alleged violinist" on NBC Sunday nights. Benny replied in kind, and the pair (fast chums outside the studio) fought like cats and dogs on the air for a decade. Every now and then they appeared on each other's show, perpetuating the feud myth. Crosby and Hope, W.C. Fields and Charlie McCarthy, and several

more radio duos applied the same blueprint with varying degrees of success, but perhaps none as well as Allen and Benny did.

By the way, a humorous incident in regard to the violin is worth repeating, particularly in light of the high-alert emphasis on security in the modern age. Benny was a personal friend of Harry S Truman, and was picked by him to be master of ceremonies at the President's inaugural ball on January 20, 1949. On the comic's arrival at the White House, a security guard pointed to his violin case. "Mr. Benny, what do you have in there?" The visitor jokingly whispered, "It's a Thompson submachine gun." Replied the guard: "Oh, that's a relief. I was afraid it was your violin."

During the show's heyday the direction for each of the Sunday night programs didn't crystallize until the prior Tuesday evening. That night, by telephone, the quartet of wordsmiths who worked on it for a dozen years exchanged ideas with each other and with Benny. A draft was completed on Wednesday and Thursday, with the writing double-teamed: Milt Josefsberg and John Tackaberry formed one scripting unit, while George Balzer and Sam Perrin comprised another. Each squad penned about half the show. They consulted with each other again on Thursday evening. The finished work was typed and reproduced for a meeting at Benny's house on Friday morning—or in a hotel room if the show was on the road. After a thorough cleansing, the script went to the studio for mimeographing.

The entire cast and the writers met Saturday morning at 10 o'clock for an initial reading and timing of the show. Following that, the cast was dismissed, and Benny and the writers conferred again, sometimes for three hours or more. They cut, revised and improved the final script. The cast reassembled at 10 o'clock on Sunday morning for a second reading. Afterward they ran through it before the microphone. There wouldn't be much further practice—Benny was cool to it, afraid of losing spontaneity by over-rehearsing. At four o'clock Pacific Coast Time they were on the air.

One of the show's scribes, George Balzer, recalled those years of working alongside Benny: "He was unbelievable in this business for his attitude toward the show and his writers, for the performers. There was no one like him—he had complete respect for everybody. I never heard him say anything to anybody that might be overheard that could be embarrassing—never. He was easy to work with, always ready to listen and never insisted on doing anything if there was someone who didn't feel it was right."[4]

All of which belied the image of self-importance, of regal splendor, that he exhibited onstage. And, of course, there was that matter of miserliness.

In what was arguably the most memorable gag pulled during the series' lengthy run, one night Benny was walking from neighboring Ronald and Benita Colman's home back to his own: the radio audience could hear the sounds of Benny's footsteps, then those of a second figure gaining on him. The unannounced individual purportedly thrust a gun into Benny's ribs.

"Your money or your life," snarled a holdup man (actor Eddie Maher). There was an incredibly pronounced interval.

Benny had instructed Maher to stand there with a straight face, oblivious to the studio audience's reaction, without saying a word until he—Benny—touched his left ear lobe. That was quite a long time. The audience, of course, was howling with laughter. After an exceedingly lengthy pause, when Benny finally touched his ear ...

"Come on, hurry up," the thief directed, impatiently.

"I'm thinking it over," Benny replied, the audience dissolving into further convulsions of unbridled hilarity. By the clock, the laughter on that single occasion exceeded two full minutes, considered by some vintage radio hobbyists to be "the longest response to any provoked laughter in radio history." Whether or not that was indeed the case, the occasion was definitely an upper, and Benny referred to it years later as his "masterpiece of stingy jokes."

There were legions more, of course. Here are a few of Benny's favorites:

❖ ❖ ❖

The Bennys were dining with Gloria and Jimmy Stewart. The waiter brought the check. "I'll take it," Benny allowed rather tenuously.

"Oh, no," Stewart retorted. "I'll take it."

"I couldn't let you do that, Jimmy."

"I'd feel better if I paid the check."

"Oh, well, Jimmy, if your health is involved...."

❖ ❖ ❖

Benny's French violin teacher (played by Mel Blanc) remarked: "Monsieur Benny, you 'aven't pay me for your violin lesson today."

"Ah, yes, how thoughtless of me, professor. Have a chair."

"I had a chair last time. Today I want the money."

❖ ❖ ❖

Returning home from a country club—his chauffeur and manservant Rochester at the Maxwell's wheel—Benny called out: "Rochester?"

"Yes, boss."

"Maybe we ought to go back to that golf course and look for my ball some more."

"We ain't never gonna find it. Why don't you give up?"

"Give up? Give up? Rochester, suppose Columbus gave up! He never would have discovered America. Then what would have happened?"

"We'd be looking for that ball in Spain, boss."

❦ ❦ ❦

Benny testified long afterward, "I wasn't really a cheapskate. Once, many years ago in the Moulin Rouge, a Hollywood nightclub where the standard tip was a quarter, I tipped the hatcheck girl a dollar. She returned it.

"'Please, Mr. Benny,' she said, 'leave me with some illusions.'"

❖ ❖ ❖

Then there was the infamous vault in the subbasement of the Benny home at 1002 North Roxbury Drive. There Benny purportedly stashed his valuables. He remembered it like this: "One of the miracles of radio was its power to suggest anything by ingeniously using sound effects. With a few noises, your imagination would paint the whole picture. When I had to go down to the vault, you heard my descent, step by step. You heard steps, steps, steps, steps. Then the steps ceased and the audience knew I was resting. Then the steps, steps, steps, steps continued downward. You heard chains clanking, whistles screaming, bells ringing, tumblers turn-

ing, iron doors groaning...." A guard remained in the depths who never surfaced, but held many funny conversations with his employer. It was an act that transferred well to television in subsequent years.

❖ ❖ ❖

Benny talked about the running gags his writers constantly employed, particularly the attention to his depiction as a penny-pinching cheapskate:

No other phase of my image has the longevity and the laugh-arousing power of the stinginess.... I'd sometimes complain to the writers that they were getting into a rut. I'd say, "Let's cut out these tired jokes about the Maxwell, being thirty-nine, wearing a toupee, the lousy violin playing and for heaven's sake, guys, enough with the stingy jokes."

I found we could get away with leaving out Phil Harris, Rochester, the fiddle, the Maxwell, Mary Livingstone—but the listeners wanted stingy jokes. So I tried rationing them. I wouldn't allow more than one stingy joke a program.[5]

In real life, nevertheless, Benny was anything but a penurious miser. "I can't imagine a man more generous and thoughtful than my father," his daughter Joan insisted. One example of his generosity will have to suffice. He hosted an anniversary party for friends at Chasen's restaurant. The husband of the couple being feted observed that, when the waiter arrived with the check, Benny handed it back to him with: "Put whatever you want on it." Benny's guest remarked, "Aren't you concerned about that?" Replied Benny, "Not at all. Whatever they put on is less than they would expect me to give. If I sign the bill, no matter what I do, it's not enough. If they sign the bill, whatever they put on is fine with me and we both go away happy."

Then there was the memorable exchange repeated every now and then between Benny and Mel Blanc, the latter posing as a Little Mexican figure. Benny often encountered him at the depot; the Hispanic man was given to "small talk," and the gag went like this:

BENNY: *Are you waiting for the train?*

LITTLE MEXICAN: *Sí.*

BENNY: *Are you meeting someone?*

LITTLE MEXICAN: *Sí.*

BENNY: *A relative?*

LITTLE MEXICAN: *Sí.*

BENNY: *What's your name?*

LITTLE MEXICAN: *Sy.*

BENNY: *Sy?*

LITTLE MEXICAN: *Sí.*

BENNY: *This relative you're waiting for ... is it a woman?*

LITTLE MEXICAN: *Sí.*

BENNY: *What's her name?*

LITTLE MEXICAN: *Sue.*

BENNY: *Does she work?*

LITTLE MEXICAN: *Sí.*

BENNY: *What does she do?*

LITTLE MEXICAN: *Sew.*

BENNY: *Sew?*

LITTLE MEXICAN: *Sí.*

BENNY (exasperatedly): *Now ... cut that out!*

There were lots of other catchphrases on the show. Here are a few more:

SHELDON LEONARD (to Benny): *Psst! Hey, buddy.*

PHIL HARRIS (to Benny): *How ya doin', Jackson?*

ANDY DEVINE (to Benny): *Hi-ya, buck!*

TRAIN ANNOUNCER: *Train now leaving on track five for Anaheim, Azusa and ... Cuc—amonga!*

FRANK NELSON (after Benny calls to floor-walker, "Oh mister! ... Mister!"): *Y-e-e-e-s-s-s-s-s?*

FRANK NELSON (after Benny says to floor-walker, "You really *do* hate me, don't you?"): *Oooooooooh, do I?*

MR. KITZEL (sings in Jewish accent):
*Pee-kle in the mee-dle and the mustard on top!
Just the way you like them and they're always hot!*

In regard to his faith and heritage, "Benny had shed his Jewish identity along with his Jewish name on his way from vaude-ville to radio. The character he and his writers sustained on the airwaves for four decades had no ethnicity or religion."[6]

The sponsors, meanwhile, were sold—literally—on *The Jack Benny Program*. In Benny's own words, "Jell-O was the talk of the country. It became so famous that from being only a trademark for a type of gelatin powder, it became the generic name for all gelatin desserts. The mountains of unsold Jell-O disappeared. Even the warehouses ran out of supplies. People liked it. They kept buying it. The more we kidded it, the more they bought. The Jell-O campaign was the greatest success story for radio as a selling medium."[7]

*The Jack Benny Program*, incidentally, was one of two prominent NBC sitcoms to integrate the middle commercial into the plot-line. Benny didn't vehemently protest the arrival of Don Wilson to plug Jell-O, Grape Nuts or another commodity in mid-story. But his counterpart, the patriarch of *Fibber McGee & Molly*, sure did when Harlow Wilcox turned up at 79 Wistful Vista with the gleam in his eye twinkling off a can of Johnson's Self-Polishing Glo-Coat wax. Obviously, those two sponsors sold more merchandise than they would have if their shows paused for a commercial break (as other programs did), interrupting the flow of the humorous narrative.

While Benny was top of the proverbial heap on NBC, CBS czar William S. Paley cast a hungry eye upon the comedian. Paley apparently had good reason to believe Benny could be had: he learned that NBC refused to deal with Benny in terms of buying Benny's holding company package (a tax break major entertainers usually enjoyed in those years).... Paley reached out to Benny and offered him a deal that would allow that package-buy—a tremendous capital gains tax break for Benny at a time when World War II had meant taxes as high as 90 percent at certain high income levels.

But Paley, according to CBS historiographer Robert Metz, also learned that Benny chafed under what he came to see as NBC's almost indifferent attitude toward the talent that brought the listeners. NBC, under the leadership of David Sarnoff, seemed at the time to think that listeners were listening to NBC because of NBC itself. To Paley, according to Metz, that was foolish thinking at best: Paley believed listeners were listening because of the talent, not because of which platform hosted them. When Paley said as much to Benny, the comedian agreed. Because Paley also took a personal interest in the Benny negotiations, as opposed to Sarnoff (who had actually never met his top-rated star), Benny was convinced at last to make the jump—and, in turn, he convinced a number of his fellow NBC performers (notably Burns & Allen and Kate Smith) to join him.[8]

After 16 years as an NBC luminary, with the program of December 26, 1948, Benny left the chimes chain.[9] The following week, on January 2, 1949, he resurfaced at CBS at the same hour on the same day of the week, where he remained entrenched for the rest of his radio run and for 14 of his 15 years on television (1950–64). Benny returned to NBC for a final year, 1964–65, after he was canceled by CBS. NBC was only too happy to have him back, but by then there wasn't a lot of demand for an aging standup comedian with his acting skills. The sitcom faded into oblivion at the end of the season, having completed 32 years on the air, including 25 on radio (1932–55, 1956–58) and 15 on TV, giving him four decades of exposure in dual mediums. With his long television tenure, only Bob Hope exceeded Benny among radio comics in broadcast longevity. Benny surpassed most of his remaining contemporaries, legends that included Fred Allen, Edgar Bergen, Milton Berle and George Burns, each with credentials in audio and video.

Benny's accomplishments ratings-wise were also unparalleled. While Bob Hope achieved an almost unbelievable 40.9 rating in 1942–43, a few seasons previously Benny reached an almost unthinkable plateau with a combined audience on two nights of 44.8. (Only *Amos 'n' Andy* was known to have surpassed him.) For 20 seasons Benny destroyed his competition with double-digit figures.[10] But despite such heady success, by the early 1950s many sound lovers began bailing out, leaving audio icons to fend for themselves, and some fading radio stars feeling like guests of honor at a wake. Benny hung on, refusing to abandon a ship that was taking on more water all the time—until May 22, 1955. But

he wasn't finished quite yet with the medium that had made him an exalted superstar in entertainment's universe.

Seventeen months later, again at his customary seven o'clock hour on Sunday nights, CBS returned him to the air. According to wordsmith Milt Josefsberg, the hour and the day was "one of the few constants we could rely on in a rapidly changing world." In an unusual move, the web repeated *The Best of Benny* programs for eight months in the 1956–57 season, and again for nine more months in the 1957–58 season, until CBS pulled the plug forever on June 22, 1958. It had been a marvelous run. Benny was still airing every week on CBS-TV. The show, with many of its familiar characters still in place, would go on for another seven seasons.

There had been indications that Benny never really wanted to do TV. He admitted, on one occasion, that in 1959—while waiting for his own series to air—he switched channels a half-hour before it was time for his program. He began watching the hour-long western adventure *Bonanza*. So absorbed was he in it that he forgot about his own show. "If I won't even watch me, what chance do I have?" he pondered.

It was quite evident that Benny appeared far more relaxed in radio, his "first love." In 1946, four years before he went on the tube with his own show, while getting a taste of it in a 45-minute special, he informed a reporter: "Hold off television! Science be damned! Long live radio!"[11] For years he was guarded about the visual medium; some critics thought he was seldom comfortable in it and frequently cited references to his fondness for radio. He clearly understood the one-eyed fiend for what it was:

> By my second year in television I saw the camera was a man-eating monster. It gave a performer a close-up exposure that week after week threatened his existence as an interesting entertainer. I don't care who you are. Finally, you'll get on people's nerves if they get too much of you. I don't care how wonderful or handsome or brilliant or charming you are—if the public gets too much of you, they'll be bored. Given that kind of magnification combined with intimacy that's characteristic of television, the essence of

a comedian's art becomes inevitably stale. The audience gets to know you inside and outside. Your tone of voice, your gestures, your little tricks, the rhythm of your delivery, your way of reacting to another performers' moves, your facial mannerisms—all of these things, so exciting to an audience when you are a novelty, soon become tedious and flat.[12]

With a quarter-century to his credit in radio, Benny believed people loved him in a different way. "I came at them gently—quietly, through their ears. I suggested images to them, picture jokes. I was like a friendly uncle, a slightly eccentric, mad uncle—now [with 15 years in TV] I became something too much. The television camera is like a magnifying glass and you can't enjoy looking at anything blown up for too long."[13]

Media critics claimed Benny offered little visual appeal. A biographer concluded, "It contrasted with the magic of radio listening when Benny could create an imaginative show of an inestimable appeal."[14]

Beyond his radio and television work, Benny also acted in 27 theatrical films plus a trio that were made for television. He was in dozens of additional movies where he appeared as himself. His acting career in celluloid began with *Chasing Rainbows* in 1930. Among his notable features were *Broadway Melody of 1936* (1935), *The Big Broadcast of 1937* (1936), *Buck Benny Rides Again* (1940), *Love Thy Neighbor* (1940), *Charley's Aunt* (1941), *To Be or Not to Be* (1942), *The Horn Blows at Midnight* (1945), *It's a Mad, Mad, Mad, Mad World* (1963) and *A Guide for the Married Man* (1967). The public's less-than-favorable reaction to *The Horn Blows at Midnight* became a running gag on his radio series. Benny was caricatured in several Warner Brothers cartoons, too: *Daffy Duck and the Dinosaur* (1939, as Caspar the Caveman), *Slap-Happy Pappy* (1940, as Jack Bunny), *Malibu Beach Party* (1940, as himself) and *The Mouse That Jack Built* (1959, as himself). For the latter animation, Benny, Mary Livingstone, Eddie Anderson, Don Wilson and Mel Blanc were engaged to reprise their familiar inflections in voiceover roles.

Furthermore, there were scores of television guest appearances, and Benny acted 22 times in serious or comedic parts on a handful of TV series: *The Jackie Gleason Show, General Electric Theater, Shower of Stars, The George Burns Show, Make Room for Daddy, Checkmate, The Lucy Show* and *The London Palladium Show*.

Following his broadcasting career, Benny again performed as a standup comedian. With his health failing in October 1974, he canceled an appearance in Dallas after suffering a dizzy spell and resulting numbness in his arms. In December inoperable pancreatic cancer was discovered. He passed away at age 80 in Los Angeles on December 26, 1974. Mary Livingstone survived him (she died at age 78 of heart disease on June 30, 1983), along with Joan Benny Baker and four grandchildren: Michael, Maria, Robert and Joanna Baker. During Benny's funeral George Burns was unable to complete the eulogy he had prepared. Bob Hope took over: "For a man who was the undisputed master of comedy timing, you'd have to say that this was the only time when Jack Benny's timing was all wrong. He left us much too soon."

A cultural arts facility, designated The Jack Benny Center, was established in his memory at Waukegan, Illinois. No fewer than four biographies have surfaced on the celebrated performer thus far. Benny was inducted into the Radio Hall of Fame in 1989. In August 1991 he joined several other comics on commemorative stamps issued by the U.S. Postal Service.[15] In recent years a veteran actor from stage and television, Eddie Carroll, a dead ringer for Benny in stage appearance, mannerisms and inflection, has been showcasing his talent across America. His one-man performance is close enough to the original to leave audiences convinced they've spent an evening with Benny.

The president of the International Jack Benny Fan Club, Laura Leff of Piedmont, California, believes that the simplest, yet most complete depiction of the comedian is probably the one that garnishes his grave: "A Gentle Man." He was that. And so much more.

# 14

# *The Life of Riley*

## WHAT A REVOLTIN' DEVELOPMENT THIS IS!

Chester A. Riley was a hardhat with a soft heart—and a genius at turning order into chaos. Although he worked for Stevenson Aircraft in Los Angeles in assembly-line production, it was mostly at home that he disrupted the lives of those about him. He possessed an uncanny ability for offering ill-timed interventions into mild situations, turning them into unexpected complexities that extended well beyond their original deficiency. Sometimes he applied words out of context that sounded somewhat like those he intended. The awkwardly-lumbering daddy and spouse consistently had high aims but failed to connect with reality before running off on tangents that usually left him looking foolish. He was staunchly supported by a caring clan that tried to recognize, comprehend and accept the hair-brained notions which led him—and sometimes, *them*—into absurd quagmires. *The Life of Riley* suffered false starts in both its radio and television incarnations. Few remember its fleeting inception on the aural airwaves, occurring before a memorable seven-year run that starred William Bendix as the lovable lout. When Bendix wasn't available for a TV sequel, a youthful, bug-eyed Jackie Gleason substituted. Though Gleason would achieve great acclaim elsewhere, he failed to persuade audiences in his initial national exposure, and the series rapidly left Videoland. It didn't return until Bendix was free. The revised show satisfied a large segment of early viewers and

persisted for five years. The dual mediums gave the series a combined airlife of 14 years, plus exposure on the silver screen. Looking back, it could hardly be classed as a poor run for a daddy with a big heart and a slow brain.

❖ ❖ ❖

**Creator-Producer-Writer:** Irving Brecher
**Directors:** Leonard Bercovici (1941), Marx Loeb (1941) Al Kaye (1944–?), Don Bernard (?–1951)
**Writers:** Leonard Bercovici (1941), Sidney Harmon (1941), Reuben Ship, Ashmead Scott, Alan Lipscott, Robert Sloane, Dick Powell (not the actor)
**Orchestra Leader:** Lou Kosloff (1944–51)
**Sound Effects Technician:** Monty Fraser
**Announcers:** Jackson Wheeler (1941), George Bryan (1941), Ken Niles (1944–45), Ken Carpenter (1945–49), Jimmy Wallington (1949–51), Harry Von Zell
**Recurring Cast:** *J. Riley Farnsworth:* Lionel Stander (1941); *Maude:* Grace Coppin (1941); *Dave:* Jack Grimes (1941); *Peggy:* Peggy Conklin (1941); *Chester Arthur Riley:* William Bendix (1944–51); *Margaret (Peg) Riley:* Paula Winslowe (1944–51); *Junior Riley:* Conrad Binyon, Scotty Beckett, Jack Grimes, Bobby Ellis, Tommy Cook; *Babs Riley:* Sharon Douglas (1944–46), Barbara Eiler (1947–51); *Jim Gillis:* John Brown (1944–51); *Olive (Honeybee) Gillis:* Shirley Mitchell (1944–51); *Digby (Digger) O'Dell:* John Brown (1944–51); *Waldo Binney:* Francis (Dink) Trout (1944–51); *Carl Stevenson:* Alan Reed, Ken Christy; *Uncle Buckley:* Charlie Cantor (1944–51); *Uncle Baxter:* Hans Conried (1944–51)
**Supporting Cast:** Elvira Allan, Shirley Mitchell, others
**Sponsors:** Sustained (1941); American Meat Institute (1944–45); Procter & Gamble Company, for Teel mouthwash, Draft detergent, Prell shampoo,

Ivory Flakes detergent, Drene shampoo, Lava soap and more household and personal care commodities (1945–49); Pabst Blue Ribbon Company, for Pabst Blue Ribbon beer (1949–51)

**Theme:** "What'll You Have?" (Pabst Blue Ribbon beer jingle, 1949–51)

**Ratings:** High—18.4 (1947–48), Low—7.2 (1944–45), Median—13.4. Ratings based on consecutive run, from 1944–51. The show achieved double digits during five of those seven seasons, 1945–50 inclusive, an extremely remarkable return.

**On the Air:** April 26–June 28, 1941, CBS, Saturday, 10:00–10:30 A.M. Eastern Time; July 5–September 13, 1941, CBS, Saturday, 11:00–11:30 A.M.; January 16–July 2, 1944, ABC, Sunday, 3:00–3:30 P.M.; July 9, 1944–July 8, 1945, ABC, Sunday, 10:00–10:30 P.M.; September 8, 1945–July 6, 1946, NBC, Saturday, 8:00–8:30 P.M.; September 7, 1946–July 5, 1947, NBC, Saturday, 8:00–8:30 P.M.; September 6, 1947–June 26, 1948, NBC, Saturday, 8:00–8:30 P.M.; August 27, 1948–May 27, 1949, NBC, Friday, 10:00–10:30 P.M.; October 7–December 30, 1949, NBC, Friday, 9:00–9:30 P.M.; January 6–June 30, 1950, NBC, Friday, 10:00–10:30 P.M.; October 6, 1950–June 29, 1951, NBC, Friday, 10:00–10:30 P.M.

**Extant Archival Material:** Three hundred twenty-five audiotapes of *The Life of Riley* (1944–51) are included in the Irving Brecher Collection, archived at the University of Southern California's Doheny Memorial Library, 3550 Trousdale Parkway, Los Angeles, CA, 90089; (213) 740-8906; fax (213) 821-3093; www.usc.edu/isd/archives/arc/.

Two hundred fifty-six recordings of *The Life of Riley* shows were in general circulation or held by private collectors as of 2006, sold by vintage radio dealers and traded by old-time radio hobbyists.

❖ ❖ ❖

*The Life of Riley* was a good example of something that occurred in radio more times than is now remembered: one show appearing under a single moniker that was broadcast in two or more dissimilar forms that might seem to have very little in common with one another. Actually, it happened quite frequently on the ether during the golden age. There were altered manifestations, for instance, of *Amos 'n' Andy, Burns and Allen, Cities Service Concerts, Front Page Farrell, Lorenzo Jones, Mr. Keen—Tracer of Lost Persons* and quite a few more.

In the case of *The Life of Riley*, as one pundit succinctly put it, the earliest incarnation (as a Saturday morning feature lasting five months in 1941) "bore scant resemblance to the far better known William Bendix series that followed" (from 1944 to 1951, mostly on a variable weekend night). Another scribe maintained that there was "no real connection" between the two series beyond the title they shared.

It was the later incarnation, of course, that provided radio listeners with a litany of memorable one-liner catchphrases that were repeated ubiquitously and rapidly incorporated into the national idiom. The namesake character, for example, was immortalized for his recurring expression "What a revoltin' development this is!" He delivered it at least once every installment, most often when it was revealed that he, himself, had become the victim of his own shenanigans. Mortician Digby (Digger) O'Dell, on the other hand, wowed the audience with a morbidly sepulchral sense of humor, dispatching metaphors like, "You are looking well ... very natural," and, "Business is a little dead right now," and his classic farewell, "Cherrio ... I'd better be ... shoveling off." Digger delighted in informing potential patrons that he was in "real estate." In one unforgettable rejoinder he quipped, "You may not like flowers at first, but eventually they'll grow on you."

The key to making the whole show work was Chester Arthur Riley, portrayed by William Bendix. His character was a run-of-the-mill blue-collar factory employee, a riveter for an aircraft manufacturer. As head of his household, Riley stereotypically was the breadwinner for an average Irish-American nuclear clan residing in close proximity to Los Angeles. If the show did nothing else, it demonstrated that people like him could be humorous subjects—and lead funny lives. It also gave the protagonist ample chances to toss occasional barbs at the pretensions of elitists who sometimes looked down their long noses at the lower rungs of the socioeconomic ladder.

*The Life of Riley* was one of a handful of quasi-ethnic shows witnessed through non-ethnic eyes. Like much of American popular culture of the period, *The Life of Riley* and *Life with Luigi* and their counterparts took a distinctly White Anglo-Saxon Protestant (WASP) stance.

"Bendix played Riley in a manner that resembled many of his supporting roles in Hollywood films of the 1940s," an observer affirmed, "as a heavy-handed, obstinate, yet ultimately sensitive lummox. Each week, Riley first became flustered, then overwhelmed by seemingly minor problems concerning his job, his family, or his neighbors. These small matters—once Riley became involved—escalated to the verge of disaster.... Catastrophe was ultimately averted by a simple solution, usually the clarification of a fact."[1]

Another source characterized Riley as an unpretentious "dese-dems-dose mug." He wasn't stupid, but he wasn't intensely sharp. He could be unfazed by circumstances. His intentions may have been honorable most of the time, yet he got mixed up in endless amusing complexities. This clown with a heart might never have come off as well had there not been a William Bendix to play him. Predictable plotting was hammered out in assembly-line fashion. But it didn't hold Bendix back; he gave all he had, reflecting America's working-class transferal from urbanized living to suburban neighborhoods. [2]

Riley was flanked by a cast of characters who contributed to turning that premise into reality every week. Aside from O'Dell, played by the busy radio comedian John Brown (who also performed double duty in the same show as Riley's pal Jim Gillis), there were three Riley kinfolk adding to the levity: his wife Peg (Paula Winslowe) and two kids, Junior (Conrad Binyon, Scotty Beckett, Jack Grimes, Bobby Ellis and Tommy Cook) and Babs (Sharon Douglas and Barbara Eiler). Several other recurring figures added mirth to the plots.

Mirroring fads that came into vogue in the postwar economic boom, the Rileys lived comfortably but not extravagantly, and were not only helped but occasionally frustrated by the invention of time-saving devices that were supposed to improve everybody's lives. Media historiographers have dubbed Riley "an American everyman," a guy that possessed a heart of gold. Yet he was unmistakably gullible, invariably bumbling and normally well-intentioned. Such attributes allowed him to turn mere trials into earthshattering tribulations as he went about inadvertently undoing the doings of his family and friends. In that regard he could level a superstructure as readily as he could level a playing field.

The individual who stood squarely behind *The Life of Riley*—its creator, inspirer and longtime trustee—was show business creator-writer-director-producer Irving S. Brecher. Born of Czechoslovakian parentage in New York City on January 17, 1914, Brecher's early history in the industry included gag-writing for comic Milton Berle. When the wordsmith scribbled his first screenplay, *New Faces of 1937*, it proffered a line of work that was to become far more important to him over the next quarter-of-a-century than a mere fleeting diversion. He penned the screenplay, contributed some of the dialogue, or adapted existing works to the motion picture screen 17 times. Among his big-screen credits are such notable flicks as *The Wizard of Oz* (1939), *Meet Me in St. Louis* (1944), *Ziegfeld Follies* (1946), *Summer Holiday* (1948), *The Life of Riley* (1949), *Somebody Loves Me* (1952) and *Bye Bye Birdie* (1963). Brecher wrote the teleplay for a 1959 TV adaptation of *Meet Me in St. Louis*, too. Aside from directing *The Life of Riley*, he also performed those duties for *Somebody Loves Me* and *Sail a Crooked Ship* (1961).

Between 1982 and 1996 he appeared as himself on television on multiple occasions, frequently on specials honoring the amusing Marx brothers.[3] Groucho Marx had figured prominently in the inspiration and development of *The Life of Riley* decades earlier.[4] The idea that resulted in *Riley* actually originated as a basis for a potential radio series to be named *The Flotsam Family*. It was projected as a domestic comedy that was to feature a miscast Marx in the key role as the head-of-household. It never got past its pilot outing, however; a prospective sponsor recoiled from it, expressing a preference for some other model for the potential star.

Subsequently, producer Brecher witnessed William Bendix portraying inept taxi firm proprietor Tim McGuerin (a role Bendix eventually parlayed into a trio of movies) in the 1942 film *The McGuerins from Brooklyn*. Brecher instantly recognized in Bendix the answer to his quest for Riley. As a result, *The Flotsam Family* was modified, and *The Life of Riley* was reborn (recall that it was on the air with a disparate theme in 1941). Bendix became the clumsy average Joe. So successful was the radio program that—five years later—it inspired a 1949 motion picture featuring Bendix in the lead. There followed a couple of NBC televersions, one with Jackie Gleason (1949–50), the other with Bendix (1953–58).

Brecher penned and directed *The Life of Riley* motion picture, although Groucho Marx was credited with the original storyline. The celluloid version co-starred Rosemary DeCamp ("Doctor Christian's office") as Peg Bendix. James Gleason (no known relation to Jackie) appeared as Riley's pal Gillis, Meg Randall was Babs Riley, Lanny Rees was Junior Riley and John Brown returned in his radio role as Digger O'Dell. Other notables in the flick were Bill Goodwin, Beulah Bondi and Ted de Corsia. Bendix, DeCamp, Randall and Brown appeared before the CBS *Lux Radio Theater* microphones on May 8, 1950, for an hour-long audio adaptation of the feature film.

In the silver screen tale, Burt Stevenson the son of Riley's business owner, Carl Stevenson, was in financial arrears, yet Burt was privy to a trust fund that could erase his indebtedness altogether. There was just one catch: he had to be married in order to claim the trust. As Riley's line supervisor at the plant, Burt arranged to give Riley a promotion, along with a hefty raise. On the sly Burt informed Riley's daughter Babs that the only way he was able to persuade his father to accept Riley's advancement was to convince him that he (Burt) intended to wed Babs. Although she had the hots for Jeff Taylor, she wrestled with the delicate position Burt had placed her in: her dad wanted, needed and had earned the pending promotion. Was she willing to sacrifice her own happiness for his? The crisis was set in motion.

Jackie Gleason appeared in the title role in the initial television expression that followed. (William Bendix was hung up with a film commitment at the time.) Brecher remembered Gleason from a visit he made in the late 1940s to the Hollywood nightclub Slapsie Maxie's. Then a thin and hungry comic, Gleason was reportedly unreliable and owed everybody money. Brecher hired him and welcomed him to TV by giving him a set of golf clubs, only to learn a short time later that the enterprising Gleason promptly sold the gift to a prop man. When Gleason's bad teeth screwed up the soundtrack by whistling uncontrollably, Brecher paid half his star's dental bills. Brecher, the producer-director, recalled later, "Jackie got tears in his eyes. He picked me up and said, 'You're the nicest Jew I ever met!'"

Alongside Gleason in that early television endeavor, Rosemary DeCamp (Peg), Lanny Rees (Junior) and John Brown (Digger) reprised their celluloid roles for the small screen. Gloria Winters joined their number, performing as Babs. For their collective efforts, the company received video's first Emmy for "Best Film Made for and Shown on Television." It was the earliest sitcom to be filmed (presumably by kinescope recording) for later presentation.

Despite everything the series seemed to have going for it, by any assessment Riley's malapropisms and oafish behavior were poorly suited to Gleason's wisecracking nightclub style. "Gleason may have been too brash, too like his Ralph Kramden bully of a decade later on *The Honeymooners*," allowed an eyewitness, "not the blustering softie created by, and personified by, Bendix on radio." Gleason's Ralph Kramden was painted as "more complex, rowdier, meaner, fatter, and funnier" than the Riley audiences had come to love in theaters and on their radios. Wikipedia decreed:

In several ways, Riley was a prototype for such later blue-collar sitcom protagonists as blustery get-rich-quick schemer Ralph Kramden and his animated Stone Age counterpart Fred Flintstone, blustery bigot Archie Bunker, benign but bighearted Dan Connor, and *King of Queens* Doug Heffernan. Bendix's Riley especially was perhaps too guileless to be their true prototype, but for making blue-collar characters as operable on television as on radio or in film, Chester Riley earned his place in broadcasting history.[5]

Television historian Alex McNeil concurred: "More than any other comedy of the 1950s, it [*The Life of Riley*] resembled *All in the Family*, as both shows centered around a blue-collar husband and father who frequently found life a bit too perplexing."[6] *TV Guide*, meanwhile, depicted Chester A. Riley as "an Archie Bunker without the attitude."[7]

In the meantime, although the show was expected to resume after a 26-week run—with Gleason replaced by Bendix in the lead—when the network refused to guarantee its continuation beyond six installments, Brecher balked and turned thumbs down altogether. One missive indicates that in 1950 he thought of TV as a fad, while another attributes some similar skepticism to Bendix himself.

Nevertheless, three years later Brecher was persuaded to renew the idea, with Bendix playing Riley. On that occasion the creator licensed his series to NBC for five years at $120,000 annually. Brecher would not direct the new TV feature, however.

Brecher wasn't particularly crazy about either of the men who played Riley. Bendix's manager once went to Brecher and asked that the program's title be revised to The William Bendix Show. "That's fine," Brecher retorted. "And when he quits or dies we'll just locate another actor named William Bendix, hire him and continue as if nothing happened." In a way, Brecher observed, "Bendix was a schmuck."

Brecher remembered that manufacturers often sent him a sample after a product's name was cited in the show's dialogue. On one occasion, Longines-Wittnauer timepieces

were mentioned, and a couple of watches soon showed up on his desk. Brecher passed one along to Bendix. On another occasion, Chevrolets were referred to in a script and Brecher was given the keys to one. On receiving that gift, he promptly heard from Bendix's manager. "When is Bill getting his Chevrolet?" he inquired. Relating the tale some years afterward, Brecher noted that he was quick on his feet, replying: "I'm running out of Chevrolets but tell him I'll send over a couple of fenders." As a postscript to this recollection, Brecher added: "He was a real schmuck!"[8]

Reading between the lines, the question arises: was it Bendix or perhaps his spokesman, the unidentified manager, who was the schmuck? Just a thought. (Will the *real* schmuck please stand up?)

In the Bendix televersion, by the way, Marjorie Reynolds played Peg, Wesley Morgan was Junior, and Lugene Sanders was Babs. Furthermore, in the series' first four seasons on television its rating ranged between 29.9 and 37.4, more than respectable enough to maintain it within the top 25 shows on the air. With a score of 35.0 the show ranked 13th among all shows from October 1953 to April 1954.

The origins of the program's title have provided ongoing and enticing debate among trivia buffs. More than one theory surrounds the line that inspired it.[9]

"Living the life of Riley" suggests an ideal life of prosperity and contentment, possibly living on someone else's money, time or work. Rather than a negative freeloading or golddigging aspect, it instead implies that someone is kept or advantaged. The expression was popular in the 1880s, a time when James Whitcomb Riley's poems depicted the comforts of a prosperous home life ... but it could have an Irish origin: After the Riley clan consolidated its hold on County Cavan, they minted their own money, accepted as legal tender even in England. These coins, called "O'Reillys" and "Reilly's," became synonymous with a monied person, and a gentleman freely spending was "living on his Reillys." Thus, the radio–TV title has an ironic edge.[10]

The notion of a carefree, bountiful, yet humble lifestyle was the inspiration for a comic song penned by Pat Rooney that illustrated someone who had struck it rich. Becoming infamous in the decade of the 1880s, one of its lyrics suggested, "A hundred a day would be small pay," while another verse of "Is That Mr. Reilly?" asked:

Is that Mister Reilly, can anyone tell?
Is that Mister Reilly that owns the hotel?
Well, if that's Mister Reilly they speak
 of so highly,
Upon my soul Reilly, you're doing
 quite well.[11]

The titles of some of the *Riley* radio episodes (possibly labeled by hobby collectors or dealers) are indicative of Riley's diverse calamities: "Riley Gets Junior Two Dates for a Dance," "Riley Lies to Peg about Going to a Wrestling Match," "Riley and Gillis Buy a Car Together," "Riley's Night Job," "Riley's Tonsillectomy," "Riley's Jilted Sister Visits," "Riley Invites Himself to His Boss's New Year's Eve Party," "Riley Coaches Junior's Basketball Team," "Riley's Old Flame, Bertha," "Riley Talks in His Sleep about Gertrude," "Riley Is Held Up," "Thanksgiving Dinner with the Boss," "Riley Drives a Cab for Babs' Boyfriend," "Riley's Southern Female Neighbor," "Riley's Rent Controversy with His Landlord," "Peg in a Beauty Contest," "A Love Letter from Boopsie," "Riley's First Car and Traffic Court," "Riley's Troubles with a New Foreman," "Peg's Father Comes to Visit," "Charleston Dance Lessons with Louella," "Louella Stays with the Rileys," "Riley and Louella—a Kiss in the Dark," "Babs Wants Privacy and Moves Out," "Riley, the Boxer," "Riley and the Free Press" and "Riley, the Forger."

In an emblematic installment in 1945, a five-dollar bill goes missing from the cream jar that Riley said he placed the money in earlier. He verbalizes all of the possibilities he can think of in an attempt to account for the missing bill. "A thief wouldn't take it because it would put him in a higher tax bracket," he concludes as he finally convinces himself that his own son Junior snitched it when nobody was looking. After severely scolding, then punishing, the boy for the missing cash, even though Junior denies any involvement, Riley suffers humiliation when Peg discovers the missing bill in her spouse's pocket: he only *thought* he had added it to the cream jar savings! "What a revoltin' development this is!" Riley experiences an emotional roller coaster as he punishes himself for his insensitivity before he catches up with Junior and confesses his misdeed. He apologizes profusely in an attempt to right his wrong, telling Junior he would buy him a new lawn mower! The episode was a classic example of the breadwinner's foolhardy action coming home to roost after his longsuffering wife made yet another crucial revelation. This pattern was repeated scores of times across the show's lengthy tenure.

An examination of William Bendix, the lead actor, provides a fascinating look into a brief life of a celebrated thespian. His first glimpse of the light of day occurred on January 14, 1906, in a midtown flat in New York City's Manhattan borough. The Bendixes resided near the tracks of the Third Avenue Elevated Railway ("the El," as locals were fond of saying), tracks that were demolished five decades later. A descendant of composer Felix Mendelssohn-Bartholdy, and the son of occasional musical performer Oscar Bendix,[12] young William gained his first public exposure to entertainment at age five. At that time his pop was securing his principal livelihood by performing odd jobs at Vitagraph Studios. Oscar Bendix was lucky enough to obtain a bit part for his progeny in a Lillian Walker motion picture filmed at Vitagraph.[13]

It would be 1942—some 31 years later—before Bendix returned to celluloid. In the meantime, he selected a myriad of colorful pursuits. Quitting high school before finishing, he joined the New York Yankees as a bat boy.[14] As fortune had it, he boasted of witnessing the legendary George Herman "Babe" Ruth hitting in excess of 100 home runs. The story goes that at age 15 young Bendix was delegated by the celebrated player to run his personal errands. That assignment was to take on additional import more than a quarter-of-a-century afterward when he—Bendix—played the Babe himself in the 1948 movie *The Babe Ruth Story*. Parenthetically, on October 21, 1948, Bendix was joined by Charles Bickford and Lurene Tuttle at the NBC microphones, reprising their roles on *The Screen Guild Theater*'s adaptation of the movie.

Bendix had, in the meantime, acquired an acute interest in dramatics as early as the 1920s. He joined a neighborhood settlement house company on New York's Lower East Side, the Henry Street Players. To augment his income he took a job as a singing waiter at a local restaurant. On October 22, 1927, he wed Theresa Stefanotti, and the couple remained together until his death some 37 years later. To their union was born two daughters.

Some time following their marriage, Theresa's dad helped Bendix secure a position managing a New Jersey grocery store. At night the new groom entertained in nightclubs and played small parts in what a critic characterized as "a series of Broadway flops." The erstwhile grocery business soon folded, meanwhile, as the economic debacle of the Great Depression engulfed America. Bendix moved on, identifying himself with the U.S. Works Progress Administration's Federal Theater Project (1935–39). It was the largest and most ambitious effort to offer employment for idle theatrical professionals during the Franklin D. Roosevelt presidency. That led him into the New York Theater Guild, where in 1939 he was cast as police officer Krupp in William Saroyan's Pulitzer Prize–winning play *The Time of Your Life*. Seen there by Hollywood producer Hal Roach, Bendix was offered a film contract, which he accepted.

His third outing on the silver screen, 1942's *Wake Island*—in which he played private Aloysius K. "Smacksie" Randall—brought him an Academy Award nomination and confirmed his skills as a supporting player in motion pictures. Bendix would star

in only a few of the 64 theatrical films in which he performed from 1942 to 1965. Among his better known flicks, which inadvertently overlapped his *Riley* radio run, were *Lifeboat* (1944), *A Bell for Adano* (1945), *Sentimental Journey* (1946), *The Blue Dahlia* (1946), *The Time of Your Life* (1948), *The Babe Ruth Story* (1948), *A Connecticut Yankee in King Arthur's Court* (1949), *The Life of Riley* (1949), *Kill the Umpire* (1950) and *Detective Story* (1951).

Bendix frequently "looked the part," exhibiting body traits that netted him many unique roles. His burly physique and an ability to speak Brooklynese stood him in good stead for playing both genial lugs and vicious thugs. He was frequently cast as a soldier, gangster or detective in movies. Jut-jawed and broken-nosed, he perfectly fit the image of the various figures he portrayed on both large and small screens. He often appeared as the time-weathered evildoer with a kindhearted spirit, and was sometimes typecast as dumb and brutish characters that were similar to his familiar Chester A. Riley interpretation.

Simultaneously, Bendix was adding more radio triumphs to his permanent dossier. He appeared in a glut of anthologies in the 1940s and 1950s, including *The Cavalcade of America* (on multiple occasions), *The Columbia Workshop*, *The Fifth Horseman*, *Hollywood Star Playhouse*, *The Hour of Mystery*, *The Lady Esther Screen Guild Theater* (multiple times), *Lux Radio Theater* (multiple times), *The Railroad Hour*, *The Screen Guild Theater*, *Suspense* (multiple times), *This Is Hollywood* and *This Is My Best*.

In an abbreviated career, he played in two made-for-TV films; was the lead in NBC-TV's hour-long western series *Overland Trail*, which aired for seven months in 1960; and 42 times appeared in single TV episodes, often anthologies, among them: *Fireside Theater*, *Lux Video Theater*, *Philco Television Playhouse*, *Goodyear Television Playhouse*, *Ford Television Theater*, *Screen Directors Playhouse*, *Robert Montgomery Presents*, *The Twentieth Century Fox Hour*, *Wagon Train*, *Westinghouse Desilu Playhouse*, *Playhouse 90*, *Schlitz Playhouse of Stars*,

The Untouchables, Mister Ed, General Electric Theater, The Dick Powell Show and Burke's Law.

Following a stomach ailment, Bendix died in Los Angeles on December 14, 1964, of lobar pneumonia, having also suffered malnutrition. He was just 58, perceptibly at the peak of his professional show business achievements. Had he lived longer he surely could have added many more credits to an already impressive list. Survived by his wife and daughters, Bendix is remembered with a star on the Hollywood Walk of Fame.

Playing his opposite on The Life of Riley radio series as his spouse Margaret (Peg) Riley was Paula Winslowe. Born March 23, 1910, she appeared in a couple of theatrical films near the start of her professional career, both in uncredited roles: 1937's Saratoga and 1942's Bambi. They were to be her only motion pictures, as she primarily concentrated her efforts on broadcasting. She was, in fact, a prolific radio actress between the late 1930s and the late 1950s. From 1937–39 Winslowe was Miss Foster, secretary to newspaper managing editor Steve Wilson on CBS's Big Town. She played the star's love interest, Jill, on The Joe E. Brown Show on the same chain in 1938–39.

But it was as part of a company of seasoned West Coast actors that Winslowe put a lasting stamp on the ether. Often appearing in anthologies as well as an occasional comedy, she was regularly heard on Arch Oboler's Plays, Broadway Is My Beat, The Cavalcade of America, The CBS Radio Workshop, Crime Classics (on multiple occasions), Escape (multiple times), Forecast, The George Burns and Gracie Allen Show (multiple times), Gunsmoke, The Halls of Ivy, The Lady Esther Screen Guild Theater, Lux Radio Theater (multiple times), On Stage, Romance, The Screen Guild Theater, The Silver Theater (multiple times), Suspense (multiple times) and Treasury Star Parade. She carried the role of Peg Riley for the duration of the second aural run of The Life of Riley (1944–51).

As radio began to fade Winslowe turned her focus to television. From 1953 to 1958 she was cast in the recurring part of Martha Conklin, the principal's spouse in CBS-TV's rendition of its popular radio favorite Our Miss Brooks. Between 1953 and 1966 she also turned up in 22 single episodes of various video series. They included The Adventures of Ozzie and Harriet, Climax!, I Love Lucy, The Gale Storm Show, You Are There, The George Burns and Gracie Allen Show, Rawhide, Michael Shayne, The Life and Legend of Wyatt Earp, The General Electric Theater, Perry Mason and My Mother the Car. In the early 1960s Winslowe provided voiceovers for multiple episodes of ABC-TV's The Flintstones, an animated cartoon. She died on March 7, 1996.

Irving Brecher reportedly bragged that The Life of Riley was radio's first family sitcom. He was likely mistaken because The Aldrich Family clearly preceded it on the air by no less than 21 months. Yet Riley was the first family sitcom to successfully project a lower middle-class tribe as subjects of a humorous narrative in primetime every week. It did so successfully for nearly a decade, with popular film and video derivatives added. In that regard, The Life of Riley was foremost among all radio series, blazing a trail that other producers attempted to emulate. Its longevity is likely attributable to its star, Bendix, who thoroughly imbued the part with his personal traits and habits, so much so that it could be difficult to recognize where he stopped and his character began. Perhaps no higher compliment could be paid an artist.

# 15

# *Life with Luigi*

## THE LITTLE IMMIGRANT

*Life with Luigi* broke all the current conventional rules set out to protect everybody of every stripe from anything that might be considered distasteful. When the show aired, however, what now might be termed racial slurs and insults were perfectly acceptable. Fat-girl jokes were abundant. Slaps at minorities of every type were commonplace. Although all of it could be branded as far too offensive for modern ears, in the first half of the 20th century Americans were conditioned by stage shows, films, nightclub comics and vaudeville acts to roar appreciatively at the expense of some population segments. The laugh-crafters of broadcast mediums enjoyed a field day cranking out jokes that put down minorities. In that mindset, a show like *Life with Luigi*, about a quiet little immigrant come to America, flourished, a harbinger for stereotypical chortles directed at people of foreign extract. Not until the pendulum swung in the opposite direction in the 1950s did *Luigi* and its contemporaries find themselves in jeopardy. As Congress passed sweeping anti-discriminatory legislation, sponsors fled and audiences questioned if some of the audio fare they were hearing matched the widespread acceptance and inclusion of diversity gradually coming into vogue. The transitory phase was speeded up by the networks, which killed off most of their remaining features that could offend certain groups. Yet, while it prevailed, *Life with Luigi* was a simple tale of heroes and patriotism that focused on one man attempting to do right in the midst of adversity. The show was caught in a time warp, its fate sealed with the shifting mores, its put-downs no longer funny to the majority that were underwriting the broadcast's bills.

❖ ❖ ❖

**Creator-Producer:** Cy Howard
**Producer:** Pat Burton
**Directors:** William N. Robson (1948), Mac Benoff (1949–53)
**Writers:** Hy Kraft and Arthur Stander (1948), Mac Benoff and Lou Derman (1949–53)
**Orchestra Leaders:** Wilbur Hatch, Lyn Murray, Lud Gluskin
**Sound Effects Technicians:** Jack Dick, Ray Kemper, James Murphy, others
**Announcers:** Charles Lyon, Bob Lemond, Bob Stevenson
**Recurring Cast:** *Luigi Basco:* J. Carrol Naish (nee Joseph Patrick Carrol Naish); *Pasquale:* Alan Reed (nee Herbert Theodore Bergman); *Rosa:* Jody Gilbert (nee Josephine Gilbert Swartzburg); *Jimmy O'Connor:* Gil Stratton, Jr., Alan Reed, Jr. (on rare occasions); *Miss Spaulding:* Mary Shipp; *Schultz:* Hans Conried; *Horowitz:* Joe Forte; *Olsen:* Ken Peters
**Supporting Cast:** Gale Gordon, Ed Max, Gerald Mohr
**Sponsors:** Sustained (1948–50, 1954); William J. Wrigley Company, for Wrigley's Spearmint chewing gum (January 10, 1950–March 3, 1953)
**Theme:** "Chicago" (full orchestra), segueing into accordion rendition of "Oh, Marie"
**Ratings:** High—16.4 (1949–50), Low—8.8 (1952–53), Median—11.8. Ratings based on sponsored years only (1950–53), others unavailable.

While the numbers began with a high-water mark, they plunged appreciably each season thereafter.

**On the Air:** September 21, 1948–January 4, 1949, CBS, Tuesday, 9:00–9:30 P.M. Eastern Time; January 9–July 3, 1949, CBS, Sunday, 10:00–10:30 P.M.; July 10–September 25, 1949, CBS, Sunday, 8:30–9:00 P.M.; September 27, 1949–January 3, 1950, CBS, Tuesday, 9:30–10:00 P.M.; January 10–June 13, 1950, CBS, Tuesday, 9:00–9:30 P.M.; August 15, 1950–July 3, 1951, CBS, Tuesday, 9:00–9:30 P.M.; August 28, 1951–May 27, 1952, CBS, Tuesday, 9:00–9:30 P.M.; August 12, 1952–March 3, 1953, CBS, Tuesday, 9:00–9:30 P.M.; 1954 (specific dates undocumented), quarter-hour weekday series

**Extant Archival Material:** Lou Derman Papers, 1944–1975, includes *Life with Luigi* scripts from 1948 to 1953 at the University of California at Los Angeles (UCLA) Charles E. Young Research Library, Room 22478, Box 951575, Los Angeles, CA, 90095; (310) 825–7253; fax (310) 825–1210; *www.library.ucla.edu/libraries/arts/*.

A single script of the *Life with Luigi* broadcast of February 7, 1950, appears in the Broadcasting Collection of the Thousand Oaks Library, American Radio Archives, 1401 East Janss Road, Thousand Oaks, CA, 91362; (805) 449–2660; fax (805) 449–2675; *www.tol.lib.ca.us*.

No fewer than 63 recordings of *Life with Luigi* shows are known to be in general circulation or held by private collectors as of 2006, and many more are believed to be available (although unconfirmed), sold by vintage radio dealers and traded by old-time radio hobbyists.

❖ ❖ ❖

Media historian Fred MacDonald observed, "One of the most controversial areas in which radio found rich comedic material was in its caricature of ethnic minorities. A staple of stage comedy of the nineteenth and early twentieth centuries, racial comedy abounded in radio and was warmly received. Some of the most important series in radio history, in fact, exploited ethnic humor."[1]

A spate of ethnic comedies during radio's golden age may have embarked upon the most difficult subspecies of all to carry off satisfactorily: dialect humor. At least a half-dozen series excelled at it—*Abie's Irish Rose, Amos 'n' Andy, Duffy's Tavern, The Goldbergs, Lum and Abner* and Cy Howard's second fabrication (less than 18 months after his

*My Friend Irma* was firmly entrenched at CBS), *Life with Luigi*. The latter entry was categorically in a class by itself: fashioned by a Jewish innovator and starring an Irish (Catholic) thespian, it was an American sitcom with Italian immigrants as its core subjects.

Ironically, the Irishman who portrayed the central figure, dialectician J. Carrol Naish, never impersonated a party from his own heritage. Instead, he built a reputation by performing in many other vernaculars. Over a lengthy professional life the skilled artisan voiced personalities of African American, East Asian, Eastern European, Hispanic, Mediterranean, Middle Eastern-North African, Native American, Polynesian and South Asian descent. Not many of his contemporaries could match Naish's ability to convincingly portray such a diverse range of characters so well. "Being funny in a strange tongue magnifies the difficulty beyond the scope of all but a few talented actors. One such actor was J. Carrol Naish," a radio scholar affirmed.[2] Two other equally gifted dialecticians were cast here—Alan Reed, who played Pasquale, radio's "man of a thousand voices," and the incomparable Hans Conried, who could also carry off many a foreign parlance.

The series for which Naish is best remembered, *Life with Luigi*—cited as "radio's last hit ethnic sitcom,"[3] opened and closed with the namesake protagonist, Luigi Basco, reading aloud a letter he penned to his dear mother back in his native Italy in which he updates his present circumstances. What he said there was often funny, for the adopted Chicagoan pensively attempted to make sense of nuances concerning customs and language that he—with a limited history in this country—could only have little comprehension of and appreciation for. Thus, to him, when he promised his mama he would write to her often, he was merely following an American tradition by penning a *promissory note*. Basco, who operated an antique shop at 21 North Halstead Street in Chicago's Little Italy sector, assured his mom: "Everybody here is crazy for old things ... old furniture ... old lamps ... old chairs.... Also is lotsa people crazy about Old Grand Dad. He must be a fine man." A live studio audience responded heartily to such malapropisms.

In the very first episode of *The Little Immigrant* (the title of the audition show aired June 15, 1948, and a signature that Basco added as he finished his weekly letters to his Mama Mia), the mild-mannered antique connoisseur discovered why his family's old friend Pasquale—who some years earlier had arrived from Italy with his wife and daughter, Rosa (Jody Gilbert)—was anxious to be his chum's American sponsor and benefactor, paying Luigi's boat passage to the U.S.A.: Pasquale fully intended to cajole, coerce or dupe Basco into marrying his by-then massively obese and unappealing offspring (so— among the myriad of explanations he offered—"I can be your father-in-law!"). Pasquale operated the Spaghetti Palace, an Italian bistro, in the building immediately adjacent to Luigi's small rented emporium.

"Pasquale was a lying, conniving plotter, a heartless saboteur of Luigi's love life," claimed one historian. Another averred: "Pasquale ... was essentially an Italian version of *Amos 'n' Andy*'s George 'Kingfish' Stevens. But while the Kingfish's modus operandi was to make a quick buck, Pasquale's one-track-mind was focused only on marrying off ... Rosa." The con artist aspect was an underlying theme of virtually every chapter. Pasquale persisted in a merciless, often deceitful crusade that never ended. A high-pitched 300-pound Rosa giggled a lot and possessed an unmistakable and uncontrollable belly laugh (which would be summoned by any mild provocation).

At crucial moments in the plot, the Italian chef, who often had more trouble with the King's English than the newcomer, advised: "Just so happen I'm-a bring-a my little baby with-a me. I'm-a gonna call-er over ... Oh, Roooossa! ... Rooooossa! ... ROSA!" His progeny screeched buoyantly: "You call me, Papa?" Pasquale cooed: "Say allo to Luigi." Rosa convulsed with a quivering, raucous fat-girl belly laugh, followed by a shrill "Hello,

Luigi." It became a running gag, a feature of the show that audiences came to anticipate. After a while it wouldn't have been right without it.

That element notwithstanding, Luigi exhibited a burning desire to discover all he could about America, about its history, its people and its government. Jimmy O'Connor (Gil Stratton, Jr.), a 12-year-old whiz kid whom he hired to clerk at the antiques shop, helped the immigrant sort out many things with which he was unfamiliar. The Italian native's misconceptions of countless American practices were consistently good for a few snickers every time out. Beyond them, however, the show also became a weekly lesson in civics.

Luigi was prepared to swear his allegiance to the United States Constitution and to the flag that symbolized it. He so wanted to become a contributing citizen of his new homeland that he enrolled in a class designed to inform immigrants about America's past, precepts and opportunities. Taught by the buxom Miss Spalding (Mary Shipp), with whom Luigi developed a mild infatuation, the class included other ethnics and plenty of opportunity for mirthful adventures into patriotic concepts. Among his peers in the classroom were Schultz (Hans Conried), a crusty German who constantly complained, "My rheumatism is killing me!"; a Russian Jew, Horowitz (Joe Forte); and a Scandinavian, Olsen (Ken Peters). Celebrating nationalism and the immigrant experience as related by a grateful European, the show delivered a message that Americans were eager to hear.

The students' exchanges with one another and their instructor were carefully crafted to generate laughs. This bit of dialogue, from a broadcast near the end of 1949, is typical of the jovial interaction. Notice the emphasis on dialects.

> LUIGI: Excuse-a me, Miss Spaulding, but ... soon-a is gonna be New Year's Eve and ... I'm-a no have enough-a money to call my Mamma on the telephone....
>
> MISS SPAULDING: Aw....
>
> OLSEN: Oh, poor Luigi ... he is homesick....

SCHULTZ: Schtop, Olsen ... Luigi iss here mit us ... how can he be home *zick?* Schmile, Luigi ... I'm just trying to sheer you up....

HOROWITZ: Luigi ... Luigi ... how much would it cost to make a telephone call from Chicago to Italy?

LUIGI: Well, uh ... how much is-a cost to make-a the call?

HOROWITZ: Yes, how much?

LUIGI: I was-a ask long distance operator. She's-a tell me she's-a cost with-a government tax, fifteen dollars-a first three minutes ... five dollars each-a next minute....

SCHULTZ: Ach! If you give a hiccup by mis-chtake you lost *three dollars!*

MISS SPAULDING: Yes, it is quite expensive. If you should speak to your mother for only ten minutes it would cost about fifty dollars.

OLSEN: Gee, that's a lot of money for a phone call.

HOROWITZ: True ... true. But when you wanta talk to your mother, a t'ousand dollars ain't too much. Wait, Luigi ... I got an idea for you—why don't you lend the fifty dollars from your friend Pasquale?

MISS SPAULDING: Mr. Horowitz, it is not *lend* ... it is *borrow* fifty dollars from Pasquale.

SCHULTZ: What's the difference? Either vay *he ain't gonna get it....* Luigi, I got an even *better* idea: go into Pasquale's schtore ven he's not dere and make the call on his telephone....

LUIGI: No. No thanks-a, Schultz. But-a now I know what I'm-a do.... It's-a hard to get-a money from-a Pasquale ... but maybe he's-a gonna let me use-a his telephone and when-a the bill has-a come, I'm-a gonna pay off-a little by little....

HOROWITZ: That's a good idea!

SCHULTZ: Oh, Luigi, are *you* a schmartkopf! Schmile. And vat if you don't pay him back zo quick? Vat can Pasquale do to you? Can he zue you in court? Can he take avay your schtore? Can he make you marry his daughter Roza?

LUIGI: (*timidly*) Schultz-a, can he?

SCHULTZ: About the zuing and the houze, I don't know. But about Roza ... on dat I can giff you my *guarantee!*

Luigi Basco did not always comprehend the meaning of everything he encountered in his adopted homeland. He frequently took matters far too literally as a result of his mis-understanding. At the same time, he exhibited a gentle, sweet spirit that won over the hearts of most of the people about him. While he loved his new country, he also took solace in his new countrymen, optimistically looking for the best in them and discovering it wherever he could. He was a model citizen, especially not to already be one. He gratefully acknowledged the good things he witnessed, fostering a kind of inspired nationalistic pride among the listeners. Some of them could have been led to acknowledge their blessings and attempt to imitate his exem-plary model.

The last immigrant to arrive on radio's showboat, Basco routinely encountered ob-stacles of many descriptions. A few are ascer-tained in the episode titles that vintage radio collectors have assigned to the various *Luigi* aircasts, among them: "Luigi Discovers Amer-ica," "Medical Insurance," "Luigi Needs to Get Married to Keep Jimmy," "First Date with an American Girl," "Character Refer-ences," "Income Tax Problems," "Luigi's First Car," "The Electric Bill," "Luigi's Toothache," "Pasquale's Birthday Party," "Life Insurance Policy," "Fire Code Violation," "Homesick," "Hit and Run Witness," "Stock Investments," "The City Zoning Commission," "The Post Office Breaks Luigi's Christmas Present to Mama," "Luigi's First Citizenship Papers," "Flunking the Final Exam," "Luigi Finds a Wallet," "Fire in the Store," "Not Counted by the Census Bureau," "A Visit from the Immi-gration Service," "Miss Spaulding Resigns," "Rosa's Makeover for Antique Dealers' Dance," "Mama Thinks Luigi Is a Million-aire," "Luigi, Square Dance Caller," "Luigi Takes Rosa to the Movies," "Rosa Attends Luigi's Night School Class," "Luigi May Lose His Home" and "No Girl for the Dance."

Like many of its counterparts in the same era, the radio series was successful enough to be spun off into a video derivative. Yet it could never be declared as much a hit there as it had been in its aural environment. Specifically, it appeared that audiences didn't take kindly to the notion (perceived or otherwise) of poking fun at ethnics of any type. And potential sponsors were absolutely scared stiff. Parenthetically, *Amos 'n' Andy*, possibly radio's most popular single series at any one time, lasted just two seasons on TV, largely being banned in a stereotypical witch hunt. If *Amos 'n' Andy*—which was incredibly admired as an audio property—couldn't make it on the tube, *Life with Luigi* had virtually no chance at all.

The transition from aural to visual conception occurred on CBS-TV on September 22, 1952, with most of the radio cast making the leap across the chasm (J. Carrol Naish, Alan Reed, Jody Gilbert, Mary Shipp, Joe Forte, Ken Peters and more—with the noticeable exception of Hans Conried, whose Schultz character was portrayed on TV by Sig Ruman). The same themes that prevailed on radio turned up on the small screens in America's living rooms. But viewers who had been so receptive to funny lines about minorities on the ether were not pleased when they saw those same people delivering those lines before their very eyes. So poor was their reception, in fact, that in three months they were history, canceled on December 29, 1952.

But Cy Howard and CBS were prepared to give it the old college try. They revived the show three months later, substituting a new cast for the familiar voices and, by then, faces. Vito Scotti was Luigi, Thomas Gomez was Pasquale, Muriel Landers was Rosa. It was to no avail. If the audience hadn't liked it when the people they fell in love with on radio performed their roles on television, why would they like it any more with a cluster of neophytes? The second edition languished just nine weeks—from April 9 to June 4, 1953—when the network mercifully pulled the plug and banished it forever. The weekly primetime outing on radio had already been yanked, on March 3, 1953, only a couple of months after the original televersion departed. Keeping sponsors satisfied—or just keeping sponsors—had much to do with it. Highlighting the differences between people was becoming a cruel joke on the air.

Unlike many of *Life with Luigi*'s contemporary radio features (think *The Life of Riley*, *My Friend Irma*, *Our Miss Brooks*, *Ozzie and Harriet*, et al.), *Luigi* never inspired a Hollywood production. Although the program was popular with many, the truth is that it never reached the proportion of the mass audience that would have been required to encourage promising box office returns. While it couldn't be declared a failure, it simply never was the hit series that several of its rivals became.

A number of authorities have attempted to soothe the troubled beast by stating that—during much of its run—this show faced stiff competition in its customary timeslot in the form of comedian Bob Hope on NBC. That factor, they explained, negated any real chance for *Luigi* to pull ahead in the ratings. Some have speculated that if the show had aired at a different time, or if it had arrived on the ether a few years earlier, it would have made a more lasting impression. At this distant vantage point such an idea leads to still more conjecture and little substantiation, although the theory may have some merit. Nevertheless, it appears that the significantly diminishing—or, in some cases, the complete departure of—ethnic-oriented network series in the early 1950s, like *Amos 'n' Andy*, *Beulah*, *The Goldbergs* and comparable fare (including their radio and television adaptations), could have been prompted by multiple issues. It's probably reasonable to hypothesize that the same concerns could have finally sealed the fate of *Life with Luigi* in dual mediums, too.

Suggesting that everything old is new again, a key thesis of *Life with Luigi* was reprised during the 1986–87 television season when eight immigrants representing various nations enrolled in a night class preparing them for U.S. citizenship. The syndicated sitcom *What a Country!* had its origins in the British comedy *Mind Your Language*, which was telecast from 1977 to 1979 and again in 1986. American viewers who had heard or seen *Luigi* more than three decades earlier must have thought it was déjà vu.

The celebrated actor who played Luigi was born Joseph Patrick Carrol Naish in New

York City on January 21, 1897. But he wasn't descended from stage stock, as were so many of his peers. To the contrary, some of Naish's ancestors were well-connected Irish politicians and civil servants. Educated at St. Cecilia Academy in Gotham, Naish enlisted in the Navy at 16 and was dispatched to the European theater in World War I. Deserting to join an Army buddy while there, he flew missions with the Aviation Section and received his discharge in France. Naish traversed the Continent, picking up work wherever he could find it. Altogether he spent a decade seeing the world, absorbing the languages, dialects and customs of far-flung nations.

At the same time, he gained experience on the Parisian and New York stages, and in stock companies. His training and experience prepared him for what was to be his most important life's work. At 29 Naish performed in his first film, 1926's *The Open Switch*. In all he appeared in 195 theatrical celluloid productions. While most of his motion pictures were of the "B" variety—1931's *Ladies of the Big House,* 1933's *Notorious but Nice,* 1936's *Two in the Dark* and 1939's *Persons in Hiding* being prime examples—there was an occasional flick that gained prominence: 1950's *Annie Get Your Gun,* 1951's *Across the Wide Missouri,* 1953's *Beneath the 12-Mile Reef* and 1954's *Sitting Bull* (in which Naish starred as the namesake Native American).

In many of these he was robed in foreign garb and spoke a foreign tongue. He flourished during the early days of talking pictures, drawing upon his almost matchless ability to communicate in an incredible number of dialects. It seemed to make little difference what a part required; he adroitly turned up playing Chinese, French, Italian, German, Japanese, Native American, Portuguese and South Seas Islander subjects. Although many of his roles were evildoers (often appearing as a crime czar, for example, in the late 1930s), he earned a couple of Oscar nominations for some sensitive parts: as a wretched prisoner of war in 1943's *Sahara,* and as the destitute dad of a deceased Mexican war hero in 1954's *A Medal for Benny.*

During this same timeframe Naish was performing regularly on multiple radio anthologies. His resume included appearances on *The Camel Screen Guild Players, The Fifth Horseman, Hollywood Hotel, Lux Radio Theater* (on numerous occasions), *The Screen Guild Theater, Suspense* (many times) and *The Witness.*

In addition to *Life with Luigi,* in 1957 the veteran actor portrayed the hero in a syndicated televersion of *The New Adventures of Charlie Chan.* Beyond those series he turned up on the tube in a couple of made-for-TV films and visited various shows a combined total of 29 times, mostly acting in anthologies. Among them: *The Cavalcade of Stars, Toast of the Town, Lux Video Theater, Climax!, Schlitz Playhouse of Stars, The Alcoa Hour, Whirlybirds, The Texan, Westinghouse Desilu Playhouse, Wanted—Dead or Alive, Cimarron City, The Untouchables, Wagon Train, The Christophers, Route 66, Burke's Law, I Dream of Jeannie, The Man from U.N.C.L.E., Green Acres, Bonanza* and *Get Smart.*

After illness forced his retirement in 1969 he was enticed to return for one more film the following year. Sporting false teeth, Coke-bottle glasses and a wheelchair, he turned up in the ultra-cheap flick *Dracula vs. Frankenstein* (he was the latter), released in 1971. It was the capstone of his career, and, according to one reviewer, "Naish managed to act the rest of the cast right off the screen."

He married actress Gladys Heaney (1907–87) in 1928. They met when they were castmates in the stage play *The Shanghai Gesture* (1926–28). The couple had one daughter, Carrol Elaine Naish (1931–87), who wed businessman-contractor-investor-philanthropist Jack Sheridan and bore him five children. Sadly, Elaine died about a half-year after her mom's passing. Both had survived J. Carrol Naish, who succumbed to emphysema at La Jolla, California, on January 24, 1973. That was Elaine's forty-second birthday, ironically. Her dad had just turned 76. A single star on the Hollywood Walk of Fame commemorates his many television triumphs. Yet, incongruously, he performed far more times in motion

*Once again—with effect. J. Carrol Naish at left (Luigi) and Alan Reed (Pasquale) underscore their points with gusto on a broadcast of* Life with Luigi. *It was an ethnic sitcom in the vein of* Amos 'n' Andy, Duffy's Tavern, The Goldbergs *and* Lum and Abner *about an Italian immigrant who tried to be a model citizen. His encounters with language, customs, laws and people generated the laughs. Never intended to ridicule any sect, the show was pure fun. It aired in an epoch that saw its barbs putting down minorities, however, something that was going out of vogue as the 1950s wore on. Naish and Reed were gifted dialecticians. Naish spoke eight languages fluently and was comfortable delivering many foreign tongues on the dial, TV and in film, playing in a near-record 195 movies.*

pictures, and confirmed his broadcasting viability with the most memorable and widely accepted role of his life in *radio*—not television.

Theodore Alan Reed (nee Herbert Theodore "Teddy" Bergman) played Pasquale (without surname) in *Life with Luigi*. Like J. Carrol Naish, he was a fellow native New Yorker but born a decade after Naish, on August 20, 1907. His parents were real immigrants, his attorney-father arriving from Austria, his mother from Russia. Following high school the youngster joined his cousin Harry Green in vaudeville stock companies. When he got into broadcasting, he altered his moniker in 1940 from Teddy Bergman to Alan Reed "to break the trap of his Jewish identity." Too often, he discovered, his birth name limited him to roles where he replicated ethnic brogue, an experience that he later turned to his advantage.

His earliest aural performances were on *The Eveready Hour, The Collier Hour* and *True Detective Mysteries*. He was present when network radio began in 1926 and performed throughout the golden age on at least 49 series. A few of his many audio mainstays: *Abie's Irish Rose, The Adventures of Ellery Queen, The Adventures of Philip Marlowe, The Adventures of Sam Spade—Detective, Al Pearce and His Gang, Big Sister, December Bride, Duffy's Tavern, The Eddie Cantor Show, Escape, Flash Gordon, Ford Theater, The Fred Allen Show, The Halls of Ivy, The Life of Riley, My Friend Irma, Myrt and Marge, Philip Morris Playhouse, The Rudy Vallee Show, The Shadow, The Six Shooter, True Detective Mysteries* and *Valiant Lady*.

While he performed on Broadway with legendary stage veterans Alfred Lunt and Lynn Fontanne, Reed's impact was even greater on the West Coast, where he transitioned into a busy film actor. Between 1944 and 1978 he appeared in 34 celluloid productions, among them: *Days of Glory* (1944), *The Postman Always Rings Twice* (1946), *Perfect Strangers* (1950), *The Redhead and the Cowboy* (1951), *Here Comes the Groom* (1951), *I, the Jury* (1953), *The Far Horizons* (1955), *Lady and the Tramp* (1955), *The Desperate Hours* (1955), *The*

*Revolt of Mamie Stover* (1956), *Peyton Place* (1957), *Marjorie Morningstar* (1958), *1001 Arabian Nights* (1959), *Breakfast at Tiffany's* (1961), *Alice in Wonderland or What's a Nice Kid Like You Doing in a Place Like This?* (1966), *The Man Called Flintstone* (1966), *In Name Only* (1969) and *The Seniors* (1978).

Reed was eventually active as a television actor and voiceover specialist, too. In addition to the fleeting *Life with Luigi* in 1952, he reprised his radio role in the 1954 syndicated *Duffy's Tavern*. He performed recurrently in CBS's *Mr. Adams and Eve* (1957–58), NBC's *Peter Loves Mary* (1960–61) and ABC's *Mickey* (1964–65). From 1951 to 1955 he was the insufferable guest poet Algernon Archibald Percival Shortfellow on NBC's madcap kiddy tease *Smilin' Ed McConnell and His Buster Brown Gang*. Reed provided the voice for Fred Flintstone in *The Flintstones* on ABC (1960–66) and NBC (1967–70), and on CBS's *The Flintstones Comedy Hour* (1972–74). He also gave voice to Mad Dog Maloney on CBS's *Where's Huddles?* (1970).

On April 5, 1932, Bergman (Reed) wed Finette Walker, age 22, a stage and radio vocalist. The pair met while appearing at CBS. She survived him 45 years later when he died at age 69 on June 14, 1977, in Los Angeles following a long illness. To their union were born three sons: Alan Jr., Steve and Christopher. There were also 10 grandchildren at the time of his passing.

The actress who played his daughter on *Luigi*, the giggly, pleasingly plump Rosa, was Jody Gilbert. Born Josephine Gilbert Swartzburg at Fort Worth, Texas, on March 18, 1916, at 18 she studied acting at the Pasadena Playhouse. At 19 she studied voice and acting at New York's Columbia University, and performed in a vocal recital at Carnegie Hall. At 20 she signed for a motion picture, an uncredited part in *Confession*, released in 1937. It was the first of some 88 theatrical features in which she was to appear over the following four decades.

Many times Gilbert turned up in uncredited bit parts, her roles often identified on cast lists only by physical traits of the full-figured girl: "fat woman" (no fewer than six films), "stout woman who can't swim," "plump hostess," "burly woman cab driver," "buxom woman," "big woman," "fat lady" (no fewer than three films), "fat girl," "large woman," et al. Those cavalier sketches depicted an ingénue who was a natural for the 300-pound Rosa when *Life with Luigi* jumped from radio to television in 1952. While B-films dominated her on-screen inventory, a few stood out: *Everything Happens at Night* (1939), *Seventeen* (1940), *Star Dust* (1940), *Grand Ole Opry* (1940), *Never Give a Sucker an Even Break* (1941), *Hellzapoppin'* (1941), *Life with Blondie* (1945), *My Friend Irma Goes West* (1950), *Butch Cassidy and the Sundance Kid* (1969) and *Lifeguard* (1976).

In radio, on the other hand, Gilbert acquired few noteworthy credits beyond *Luigi*. She appeared in two television films and played in single episodes on a handful of TV series: *The Dick Van Dyke Show*, *The Lucy Show*, *Dragnet 1967*, *Batman*, *Night Gallery*, *Here's Lucy*, *Mannix*, *Policewoman*, *Switch*, *Love American Style*, *Sanford and Son* and *Starsky & Hutch*. At 62 she died of injuries sustained in a motor vehicle accident. The never-married Gilbert passed away on February 3, 1979, in Los Angeles, survived by her mother and two siblings, all of Los Angeles.

Gil Stratton, Jr., who played Jimmy O'-Connor, Luigi Basco's young helper at his antiques enterprise, was born in Brooklyn, New York, on June 2, 1922. Near the end of his career three-quarters of a century later, Stratton confirmed that he had been a Brooklyn Dodgers fan all his life and loved sportscasting from the age of eight. Bill Stern was, in fact, his childhood idol. All of this was to have a pronounced effect on the direction he later took. "Acting was a means of getting there," he confessed.

At 19 Stratton debuted as Bud Hooper in *Best Foot Forward*, a Broadway musical production at the Ethel Barrymore Theater in which he sang and danced for a run of 326 performances. The show was produced and directed by George Abbott, choreographed by Gene Kelly, and featured Nancy Walker

and June Allyson in its original cast. When the play was released as a motion picture in 1943, Stratton acquired a small uncredited part. That same year he earned his first speaking role in a film starring Mickey Rooney and Judy Garland, *Girl Crazy*. His show business career soon expanded into radio, principally in the cast of *One Man's Family*, in addition to *Life with Luigi*.

Critics observed that Stratton had a "young, wholesome juvenile look" which gave him a "slight, apple-cheeked" appearance. Obviously his looks were in his favor: he worked in 21 theatrical motion pictures, two made-for-television films, one TV series (CBS's *That's My Boy* in 1954–55) and single episodes of multiple TV series, among them: *Dragnet*, *Shower of Stars*, *The Damon Runyan Theater*, *Wonder Woman*, *Archie Bunker's Place*, *Disneyland*, *Cagney and Lacey*, *Remington Steele*, *Boy Meets World* and *Malcolm & Eddie*. His silver screen features, meanwhile, included *Mr. Belvedere Goes to College* (1949) and *Stalag 17* (1953), in addition to a plethora of B films.

Stratton's performances as Junior Jackson in the sitcom *That's My Boy* turned heads at KNXT, the Los Angeles CBS affiliate, and in 1954 he was offered the permanent post of weekday sportscaster. He accepted and remained on the job more than two decades, gaining a reputation as one of the nation's premier sportscasters. One of his assignments included being the television voice of the Los Angeles Rams professional football team. He also aired sports reports over local KNX Radio. Moving to Hawaii in 1984, he purchased and managed radio stations KKON and KOAS-FM at Kealakekua on the western shore of the Big Island near Kailua-Kona. The veteran broadcaster returned to L.A. in 1987 and rejoined KNX Radio and KCBS-TV (formerly KNXT) as a reporter and sportscaster, persisting for more than a decade in his second sojourn, to early 1998 at age 75. As of this writing he lives in North Hollywood. He was elected to the board of the Thousand Oaks Library Foundation in 2002.

Stratton was married three times: to Audrey Botkin, who appeared alongside him in

Broadway's *Best Foot Forward*, on May 8, 1942; to Camille Sellars, on November 24, 1945, in Chicago (they had two children born in California, Gilda Woolsey Stratton, on March 26, 1950, and Gilbert "Gibby" Montague Stratton, on December 26, 1951—Camille and Gil separated on November 1, 1958); and television actress D'Arline Marie Norvas (Dee Arlen) in March 1961.

Mary Shipp, the night class teacher Miss Spaulding in *Life with Luigi*, and Hans Conried, the frequently inciting and obnoxious German student Schultz, are profiled in the chapter on *My Friend Irma*, on which show both also appeared in supporting roles.

*Life with Luigi* arrived on the airwaves shortly before the door slammed on the kind of entertainment it represented. In its earliest days people laughed uproariously at the antics of the mild little man who wanted nothing more than to support his adopted country. Unfortunately, his country didn't reciprocate, and he fell victim to a nation's social customs in drastic upheaval. Had *Luigi* arrived on the air just a decade before, the show might have been far more appreciated, and the fans might have gone on laughing for a few additional years. By its end, however, many Americans were beginning to turn a corner: the program's demise was a clear sign that even the hint of alleged ridicule of minorities wasn't going to be tolerated—or even be considered all that funny—any more.

# 16

## Meet Millie

### DIZZY DAMES AND ASSORTED NUTS

By the time CBS presented *Meet Millie* to radio's ears, the chain was on a roll. Having already introduced a spate of sex-and-the-single-girl comedies—sans the sex but squarely fixed on unattached broads—the web was enjoying a semblance of comeback successes. The web decided to stay with a winner. In this latest entry a gal Friday was at the apex of a troupe of wacko figures drawn from personal and professional quarters who turned the show into one of audio's late-season bloomers. Given her circumstances, Millie Bronson was incapable of distancing herself from cohorts who demonstrated less than "normal" behavior. A couple of those nuts lived in the same boardinghouse as she. One was a fruitcake who thought he was a poet. Far out. Millie's own mother could be similarly branded. She was a one-theme-only MOM: Marry Off Millie. As so much of her own existence was derived from her single daughter and the eccentricities that swirled about her, what would poor mama do, the thinking fan must have ruminated, if the unimaginable occurred? But that matter was left unscripted. Millie's habitual complications with her boss and his son—the latter whom she fancied more than a passing acquaintance, to poppa's chagrin—kept the plots boiling. Side-splitting outcomes were the order of the day via the screw-ups, poor judgment, misinformation and misunderstandings, typical of lighthearted fare that radio sitcoms dispensed while the medium

ebbed its way toward a final conclusion. Although *Meet Millie* never commandeered a liberal segment of the rapidly dwindling aural audience, for the fans who tuned in it made the downward spiral a much more pleasant ride.

❖ ❖ ❖

**Creator-Producer:** Frank Galen
**Director-Producer:** Bill Manhoff
**Writers:** Bill Manhoff, Joel Kane
**Orchestra Conductor:** Irving Miller
**Announcer:** Bob Lemond
**Recurring Cast:** *Millie Bronson:* Audrey Totter (1951–ca. 1953), Elena Verdugo (ca. 1953–54); *Bertha (Mama) Bronson:* Bea Benaderet, Florence Halop; *Alfred E. Printzmetal:* Marvin Kaplan; *J.R. Boone, Sr.:* Earle Ross; *Johnny Boone, Jr.:* Rye Billsbury; *Morton:* Bill Tracy
**Sponsors:** Sustained (1951–52); Multiple participation (1952–54), including County Chemicals (for Brylcreem men's hair dressing), Nestle Company (for Nescafé instant coffee), Procter & Gamble Company (for Lava soap)
**Theme:** "Meet Millie"
**Ratings:** 6.0 (1952–53, only season for which documentation is substantiated)
**On the Air:** July 2–August 20, 1951, CBS, Monday (time unsubstantiated); September 4–11, 1951, CBS, Tuesday (time unsubstantiated); October 9, 1951–January 1, 1952, CBS, Tuesday, 10:00–10:30 P.M. Eastern Time; January 6–May 18, 1952, CBS, Sunday, 9:30–10:00 P.M.; May 25–June 29, 1952, CBS, Sunday, 6:00–6:30 P.M.; July 6–August 31, 1952, CBS, Sunday, 9:00–9:30 P.M.; October 23, 1952–September 23, 1954, CBS, Thursday, 8:00–8:30 P.M.

**Extant Archival Material:** *Two Meet Millie*

radio scripts are maintained in the private collection of Fuller French by the Broadcast Arts Library, Box 9828, Fort Worth, TX, 76147; (310) 288–6511; www.broadcastartslibrary.com.

Scripts, production notes and related memos from long runs of *Meet Millie* are archived in the KNX Script Collection supplied by the Los Angeles CBS affiliate at Thousand Oaks Library, American Radio Archives, 1401 East Janss Road, Thousand Oaks, CA, 91362; (805) 449–2660; fax (805) 449–2675; *www.tol.lib.ca.us.*

Eleven recordings of *Meet Millie* shows were in general circulation or held by private collectors as of 2006, sold by vintage radio dealers and traded by old-time radio hobbyists.

❖ ❖ ❖

*Meet Millie* was one of a handful of primetime domestic comedies featuring unattached young women that arrived on CBS Radio just as audio's fortunes began to wane. As the 1950s progressed, that factor became even more pronounced as more and more listeners chose to become viewers. In fact, such series as *Meet Millie*, *My Friend Irma*, *My Little Margie* and *Our Miss Brooks*—all amusing tales of single, working-class gals—plugged holes in the CBS schedule that departing shows left vacant. In some cases, the predecessors went over to TV; in others, they vanished entirely when they simply couldn't compete with the newer medium any longer.

Nevertheless, those humorous narratives continued to wow unwavering audiences that weren't quite ready yet to abandon their longstanding aural traditions. For a few more years *Meet Millie* and her kind kept the faithful laughing at their hilarious hijinks one night a week. And with the exception of *My Little Margie*, which premiered on video and subsequently added an audio version, the other late-in-the-golden-age comedies listed above all inspired reincarnations on the small screen. Radio listeners of that era were therefore on the cutting edge of some of television's incubatory conceptions. It was a day in which moderately successful radio features turned up on the home screen frequently, often with most of the original cast intact.

All of those humorous entries proffered varying tweaks and twists to set them apart

from their contemporaries: Millie lived with her mom, Margie lived with her dad, Irma had a roommate of the same gender and Connie Brooks lived alone but dialogued intermittently with her aging landlady. A couple of these namesake leading ladies were inordinately bright, while the remainder, at times, appeared to have checked their marbles at the door. Millie Bronson, a personal secretary, belonged to the latter category. She and a few more of the show's recurring characters were usually responsible for mix-ups occurring in the plotline. If *My Friend Irma* Peterson was the quintessential airhead of the airwaves—certainly so among the unattached gals—there isn't much doubt that Millie Bronson was one of her more flighty rivals.

*Meet Millie* debuted on July 2, 1951, just as radio's slide was starting to become noticeable. By the time the show left the aural ether with its final broadcast on September 23, 1954, radio executives were in full-fledged panic mode. Even though the televersion of *Meet Millie* outlived the original—it began on October 25, 1952, and persisted on CBS-TV through February 28, 1956—the departure of the real McCoy was one of many signals that network radio's entertaining programming days were numbered.

The series was set in Jackson Heights, New York, where Millie and her widowed mother, Bertha, shared a brownstone apartment. Mama's overriding passion was to marry Millie off. She wanted a grandchild "to bounce on my knee while I still have a little bounce in me." Bertha took every opportunity she could manufacture to push her obsession with Millie's future to respectable limits. Millie was a young, attractive, middle-class secretary who indulged a fantasy of her own, albeit somewhat clandestinely at times. She hoped one day to become the bride of Johnny Boone, the offspring of her investment counselor employer, J.R. Boone, Sr. While Millie's mom encouraged her daughter's dream, the senior Boone was cool to the idea.

A major impetus in the storyline was Millie's neighboring pal Alfred E. Printzmetal, an employee at Schercases Delicatessen. He, too, nurtured a longstanding fantasy—to become a noteworthy poet, author and composer. Women perceived Printzmetal as physically striking "in an eerie sort of way." An outspoken J.R. Boone, Sr., on the other hand, classified him as "peculiar" and a harbinger of bad luck. He lobbied for returning the misguided "artist" to Mars! An unperturbed Printzmetal loved to recite his original stanzas to others, which tended to confirm Boone's skeptical assessment.

"Ode to a Wristwatch," one of numerous illustrations of the aspiring poet's verse, went like this:

> Hail to you, old faithful 17-jewel,
> Automatic-winding, shockproof time piece
>     with the pigskin band;
> You're so hard for me to understand....
> Tick tock, tick tock, do you feel hurt?
> Do you think life is shoddy
> Because you have a face and hands...
> But you ain't got no body?

Then there was this one, which he introduced as "My Heart Is Alone, by Alfred":

> My heart is alone since you have left
> Of your sweet presence I am bereft;
> I feel locked out, like a man who's lost
>     his house keys...
> If you don't come back, dear, gloriosky!

The stanzas didn't have to resemble intelligent sagacity, of course. For instance, there was "Apology to a Housefly":

> You little housefly, I'm saluting
> Flitting hither, flitting yon,
> I hate to tell you, you're polluting
> All the food you're sitting on ...
> Don't look at me with pleading eyes,
> You're too small for me to wash you...
> Would you like to go to Paradise?
> You would? Sit still. I'll squash you.

Finally, another example—"Song for a Statue in the Park":

> Hail to thee, brave statue, noble monument
> Braving summer's heat and winter's cold...
> Bronze general on your bronze horse

> Sitting silent in the night...
> What stories, oh metal equestrian, could
>     you tell if you could talk?
> Of park bench, whispered love words
> And things written on your horse's flank
>     and jaw;
> Keeping your secrets, telling not a smidgen
> As you brave the indignities of man, and
>     boy, and pigeon?

Robert Frost, Henry Wadsworth Longfellow and Walt Whitman needn't have worried about being upstaged by Alfred E. Printzmetal. No prizewinning rhyme poured from his lips. But radio listeners found his tangential digressions hilarious even when—because?—they often didn't make any sense.

These were the principals involved in *Meet Millie*'s farcical escapades every week. Installments offered titles, perhaps subsequently assigned by radio hobbyists, like "Take in a Roomer," "Painting the Town Red," "Aunt Emily Visits" and "Mama's Home Cooked Meal."

In the first of those, to meet some expenses Mama rented her room to an ex-con without knowing anything about him. When she figured it out she and Millie connived to rid themselves of him. He had been hauled into jail on a traffic violation, the audience learned, but of course Millie and Mama—who didn't hear that—imagined far worse. When he accidentally pulled the phone out of the wall, thereby disconnecting it, and told them he was going to the kitchen for a knife, their worst fears seemed about to materialize. He told them he had something in his trunk he wished to share with them, once he had it cut up. While the boarder was doing that, Alfred showed up and they rapidly dispatched him to fetch the police as they awaited their fate. The upshot of it was that the man brought the ladies some fudge he had made while in prison. He revealed to them that he only got a traffic ticket but he couldn't pay the fine so he went to jail for 30 days. They told him they had sent Alfred for the police, but he never did anything he was supposed to. Just then there was banging on the door, shrill whistles and Alfred shouting: "Don't touch those women, you brute! The joint is surrounded!" It was typical *Meet Millie* fare.

The video version of the same show was one of the early series to emanate from CBS's Television City in Hollywood. It also underscored the difficulty that the major filmmakers had with the encroachment of TV on their turf. In no uncertain terms they laid down the law to series lead Audrey Totter: she wouldn't be permitted to have her cake and eat it too. While she would be allowed to persist as the key figure in the aural manifestation of *Meet Millie*, the studio simply would not consent to letting the movie actress play the same part on television. It was one of many retaliatory swipes the studios took in those days toward the rapid encroachment of TV on its perceived turf. TV was presumably costing the studios tons of money by keeping many of their regular patrons away from the theaters—they stayed home to check out the powerfully influential new medium. As a result, in this instance actress Elena Verdugo was brought in to play Millie Bronson in the TV adaptation of the popular radio feature. Before long Totter became so disenchanted with the studio's treatment of her over it that she threw in the towel altogether, left the show and paved the way for Verdugo to inherit the aural role as well. It was an unfortunate outcome for Totter, although Verdugo had demonstrated on TV that she was capable of reaching the worthy performance levels of her predecessor.

Totter was the progeny of European émigrés, a Viennese dad and a Swedish mom, and made her debut in the world at Joliet, Illinois, on December 20, 1918. Stagestruck at an early age, she eagerly accepted roles in high school shows. Her pop had imbued her with a love for acting, having carried her to the theater in Chicago many times, where she was exposed to plays, the ballet and opera. Her mother, meanwhile, loved movies and took her young daughter to cinema palaces. The aspiring young thespian broke into radio in the Windy City. In the part of Violet, she circulated throughout the country with a performing ensemble in *My Sister Eileen*. By the time they reached New York City she was 21 and started actively appearing in network radio dramas. Not long afterward she won a recurring role in the CBS daytime soap opera *Bright Horizon* (1941–45). She played before the footlights in several stage productions, too.

While Totter would surface in numerous television shows in succeeding years, it was on the silver screen that her career flourished in the pre–TV age and for which she became well identified. Signing her first celluloid contract in 1945 with MGM (and in the early 1950s with Columbia, and eventually with 20th Century–Fox), in motion pictures she was often featured as a fragile, nononsense leading lady and femme fatale. Her theatrical appearances included roles in *Main Street After Dark* (1945), *The Postman Always Rings Twice* (1946), *Lady in the Lake* (1947) and *Any Number Can Play* (1949). Her most striking characters were in "film noir," a powerful breed that dominated celluloid in the United States in the late 1940s. Totter was frequently a murderess or a crime victim there. "One is certainly hard-pressed to think of another true 'bad girl' representative so closely identifiable with film noir than hard-looking blonde actress Audrey Totter," a source confirmed.[1] Ultimately she performed in 43 movies screened in theaters and another half-dozen made-for-TV films shown on home screens, the last one, as of this writing, in 2004.

Although denied the opportunity to portray Millie Bronson in *Meet Millie* on television in the early 1950s, Totter eventually landed continuing roles in a trio of other video series. For one season, 1958–59, she was boardinghouse proprietress Beth Purcell in NBC-TV's hour-long western *Cimarron City*, starring George Montgomery. Another year, 1962–63, she was the feminine lead in the ABC-TV half-hour sitcom *Our Man Higgins*, featuring Stanley Holloway and Frank Maxwell. From 1972 to 1976 Totter was simply known as Nurse Wilcox in the hour-long

CBS-TV drama *Medical Center*, with James Daly and Chad Everett as leading men.

Notwithstanding all of these, her most prolific professional journey beyond *Meet Millie* was in single episodes of televised narratives. In all, the actress turned up no fewer than 50 times in dramatic TV installments. Some of her best work included performances in *Four Star Playhouse*, *Science Fiction Theater*, *The Ford Television Theatre*, *Lux Video Theatre*, *Zane Grey Theater*, *The Californians*, *Climax!*, *Cheyenne*, *Hawaiian Eye*, *General Electric Theater*, *Alfred Hitchcock Presents*, *Route 66*, *Rawhide*, *Perry Mason*, *Dr. Kildare*, *Bonanza*, *Ironside*, *The Virginian*, *Hawaii Five-O*, *Disneyland* and *Murder, She Wrote*. She officially retired after the latter show in 1987, although she has appeared on television a couple of times since.

In her personal life the gossip columnists enjoyed a field day pairing Totter with actors Clark Gable, John Payne and Ross Hunter. But at 34, in 1953 she wed the love of her life, Dr. Leo Fred, assistant dean of medicine at the University of California at Los Angeles. They were together 42 years when he died. A daughter was born to them. By June 2004, Totter, 85, was living at the Motion Picture and Television Country House and Hospital at Woodland Hills, California.

Elena Angela Verdugo was tapped to portray Millie Bronson in the televersion of *Meet Millie* and, as recounted already, acquired the same role in the radio series when Audrey Totter resigned. Verdugo was born April 20, 1925, in Paso Robles, California, a descendant of a Spanish clan that had settled in the Golden State in 1776 when it was designated a territory. She took Terpsichore lessons in Latin dancing at three years of age. By age six she made her film debut in *Cavalier of the West*, a western starring Harry Carey, Sr. Not until her teen years, however, did she become widely noticed. Most of those years were devoted to playing Mexican peasants, gypsy girls, harem handmaidens and exotic South Sea islanders.

But the years of early training in Latin American artistry ultimately paid off when she briefly appeared in 1940's *Down Argentine Way*, a movie that launched Betty Grable to stardom. Verdugo's subsequent performance in 1942's *The Moon and Sixpence* brought her renewed critical acclaim. At about the same time, she recorded "Tico-Tico" with an instrumental troupe, headlined by Latin bandleader Xavier Cugat, with whom she vocalized for a short while.

Of 30 feature-length films she appeared in over a lengthy career, among the most prominent were *Belle Starr* (1941), *House of Frankenstein* (1944), *Cyrano de Bergerac* (1950), *Gene Autry and the Mounties* (1951) and *Angel in My Pocket* (1969). Verdugo also turned up in a quartet of made-for-TV movies. Beginning in 1959, and for a few years thereafter, she recalled her early rhythmic training, performing on the straw-hat circuit around the country in musicals like *Oklahoma!* and *South Pacific*. Before and after this period she showed up in one-shot guest spots on television series 25 times, including *Dangerous Assignment*, *Cavalcade of America*, *The Bob Cummings Show*, *The Gale Storm Show*, *Rawhide*, *Route 66*, *77 Sunset Strip*, *Petticoat Junction*, *Mannix*, *Ironside*, *Daniel Boone*, *Love American Style* and *Scarecrow and Mrs. King*.

In addition to *Meet Millie*, Verdugo won recurring roles in a trio of pithy TV sitcoms: CBS's *The New Phil Silvers Show* (1964), in which she appeared as Silvers' sibling Audrey; CBS's *Many Happy Returns* (1964–65), where she was mercantile store clerk Lynn Hall; and NBC's *Mona McCluskey* (1965–66), as Alice Henderson, the romantic obsession of a U.S. airman. None of those possessed the staying power that allowed *Meet Millie* to persist into its fourth season. However, Verdugo won widespread respect and is fondly recalled by viewers as Consuelo Lopez, the pragmatic but warmhearted nurse-receptionist in a fifth TV series, ABC's *Marcus Welby, M.D.* (1969–76).

Verdugo married radio and screenplay wordsmith Charles R. Marion, scriptwriter for *The Abbott and Costello Show*, in 1946. The couple had a son, Richard, who became an actor and director. Richard was the victim of a fatal heart attack at age 50. His parents, meanwhile, had divorced in 1955. Seventeen years later his mother remarried, to Charles R. Rockwell, and they are still together as this is prepared in 2006. In 2005 she appeared at a western film fair in Charlotte, North Carolina, alongside several legendary Hollywood thespians.

The part of Bertha Bronson, "mama" to the key figure in Meet Millie, was introduced by Beatrice (Bea) Benaderet, who appeared extensively in radio and television comedy. While her nasal-sounding banter was easily distinguished, more often than not it was her inimitable giggle that instantly confirmed her identity to audiences tuning in. Born in New York City on April 4, 1906, she descended from a charming heritage: her dad, Samuel Benaderet (1880–1954), was of Sephardic Jewish lineage and in 1900 migrated to the U.S. from Turkey, where his birth family spoke Spanish (you read that right) as its native tongue.[2] On the other hand, Bea's mom Margaret—born in New York City—was the offspring of Catholic parents who migrated from Northern Ireland to America.

The Benaderets relocated to San Francisco shortly after Bea's birth. Despite her half–Jewish ancestry she was raised Catholic and graduated from St. Rose's Academy, a private church institute in the City by the Bay. She gravitated toward entertainment early and in her twenties broke into radio over local stations. By the mid–1930s she was an actress at San Francisco's KFRC, an outlet that affiliated about then with the Don Lee–Columbia (CBS) West Coast chain. Sylvester L. (Pat) Weaver, a future NBC president, was then station manager. Benaderet moved to Los Angeles permanently about 1936 and made her debut on network radio in a weekly hour-long CBS anthology produced by Orson Welles, The Campbell Playhouse (1938–41). From 1943 to 1962 she performed in 47 Hollywood flicks, a preponderance in voiceover roles for Warner Brothers animated cartoons. But it was on the air that her voice—and eventually her face—became so widely recognized in the common American household.

Her broadcasting dossier reads like an encyclopedia of dual mediums. Benaderet appeared in all of the following California-based radio sitcoms: The Adventures of Ozzie and Harriet (as Gloria and as Mrs. Waddington), The Amos 'n' Andy Show (in non-recurring roles), Duffy's Tavern (non-recurring), Fibber McGee & Molly (Millicent Carstairs), The George Burns and Gracie Allen Show (Blanche Morton), Granby's Green Acres (Martha Granby), The Great Gildersleeve (Eve Goodwin), The Jack Benny Program (Gertrude Gearshift), Maisie (non-recurring), Meet Millie (Bertha Bronson), My Favorite Husband (Leticia Cooper and Iris Atterbury), Our Miss Brooks (non-recurring) and countless others. In serious narrative parts she played on The Adventures of Sam Spade, This Is Your FBI and a myriad of other West Coast detective-crime dramas.

On television she performed on single-shot episodes for numerous series, frequently cast in different parts in multiple installments of the same show. Included were (with some considerable voiceover work) I Love Lucy, Screen Directors Playhouse, The Bob Cummings Show, The Flintstones, The George Burns Show, The Restless Gun, General Electric Theater, 77 Sunset Strip, The Bugs Bunny Show, Peter Loves Mary, The Chevy Show, Top Cat, Vacation Playhouse, The Danny Kaye Show, The Famous Adventures of Mr. Magoo, The Road Runner Show, The Bugs Bunny-Road Runner Hour and Merrie Melodies Starring Bugs Bunny and Friends.

In the 1950s Benaderet reprised her role as Blanche Morton on The George Burns and Gracie Allen Show on CBS-TV while doing the same as Gertrude Gearshift on The Jack Benny Program on the same network. She was denied the part of Ethel Mertz in I Love Lucy because she was contracted to Burns and Allen. Subsequently, she was Cousin Pearl Bodine in at least 24 episodes of CBS-TV's The Beverly Hillbillies in the 1960s. The capstone of her career was the part of Kate Bradley, a role she played scores of times in the 1960s on two CBS-TV sitcoms: Green Acres and the sister feature in which she finally starred, Petticoat Junction. She remained with those series until she finally became too ill to continue.

Benaderet died of pneumonia and a relapse of lung cancer in Los Angeles on October 13, 1968, at age 62. She was divorced from Jim Bannon after a dozen years of marriage (1938–50), with whom she had two children— John James (Jack) Bannon, born June 14, 1940, and Margaret Bannon, born March 4, 1947. Jack Bannon grew up to follow in his mom's footsteps: he won continuing acting roles in a couple of hour-long TV dramas, CBS's *Lou Grant* (1977–82) and ABC's short-lived *Trauma Center* (1983). Long before that, however, Bea Benaderet had wed a second time, to Jack Benny's sound effects tech, Gene Twombley, in 1957. Twombley suffered a fatal heart attack just four days after Bea's demise.

Bea Benaderet was succeeded in the part of Bertha Bronson by Florence Halop, who filled the role in radio and television manifestations, the latter for the full run. Born in Jamaica Estates, New York, in the Queens borough on January 23, 1923, Florence was already on the air by 1927! A year later she was among the gang featured on Milton Cross's *Coast-to-Coast on a Bus*. As she grew older she worked other ongoing radio stints on *Duffy's Tavern*, *The Falcon*, *The Jimmy Durante Show* and *The Jack Paar Show*. While she was in minor roles in a trio of theatrical movies—1939's *Nancy Drew, Reporter*, 1940's *Junior G-Men* and 1966's *The Glass Bottom Boat*—she eventually concentrated on the small screen, which emerged at about the time her career was at full throttle.

Halop was cast in a trio of made-for-TV movies and a trilogy of continuing series beyond *Meet Millie*. She was a regular performer on ABC-TV's *Holiday Hotel*, aka *Don Ameche's Musical Playhouse*, in 1950–51. Then she turned up in a couple of recurring roles—as the chronically pesky Mrs. Hufnagel, a patient in the NBC-TV medical drama *St. Elsewhere* (1984–85), and as feisty bailiff Florence Kleiner on the same web's sitcom *Night Court* (1985–86). The latter part might have persisted longer had Halop not died of lung cancer in Los Angeles on July 15, 1986. Ironically, she had replaced Selma Diamond as the

unmistakably raspy-voiced, short-statured court officer who also succumbed to lung cancer after one season with the same show. Both actresses were heavy smokers.

The bulk of Halop's video efforts were nevertheless focused on single-shot guest appearances in both serious and comedic shows. Among 39 such outings, she performed on *Goodyear Television Playhouse*, *I Love Lucy*, *Playhouse 90*, *The Untouchables*, *The Dick Van Dyke Show*, *I Spy*, *That Girl*, *The Mod Squad*, *Love American Style*, *Here's Lucy*, *Police Woman*, *All in the Family*, *The Love Boat*, *CHiPs*, *The Betty White Show*, *Soap*, *Archie Bunker's Place*, *Barney Miller*, *Alice*, *Hill Street Blues* and *Diff'rent Strokes*.

Marvin Kaplan portrayed the poet wannabe Alfred E. Printzmetal in *Meet Millie*'s dual incarnations. He was born in New York's Brooklyn borough on January 24, 1924. The stocky-bodied, round-faced, bespectacled comic actor with the distinctive Brooklynese inflections was available at the right places at the right times. As a result, he earned numerous career broadcasting credits. Now semi-retired, except for an occasional commercial spot or guest appearance, as of 2005 he had performed in 36 single TV episodes, eight continuing TV series, four made-for-TV movies and 23 full-length motion pictures. Kaplan wasn't prolific in radio, however, *Meet Millie* being his most prominent exposure in the aural medium.

Trained as a teacher at New York University and Brooklyn College, he left that profession after a brief foray to concentrate on acting and playwriting in the late 1940s at the University of Southern California. Legendary Hollywood actress Katharine Hepburn saw him in a campus production there and recommended him for a bit part in her 1949 film *Adam's Rib*. The rest is history. Among his silver screen celluloid features were *Francis the Talking Mule* (1950); *I Can Get It for You Wholesale*, *The Fat Man* and *Angels in the Outfield* (all 1951); *Wake Me When It's Over* (1960); *The Nutty Professor* and *It's a Mad Mad Mad Mad World* (both 1963); *The Great Race* (1965); and *Freaky Friday* (1976).

But it was in television that Kaplan became widely noticed by the average American. Often it was his voice that was instantly recognized, in cartoon series like ABC's *Top Cat* (1961–62), NBC's *The C.B. Bears* (1977–78), NBC's *The Smurfs* (1982–90), CBS's *Saturday Supercade* (1983–85) and the syndicated *Wake, Rattle & Roll* (1990–91). He turned up in live-action series, too, as Marvin the accountant in CBS's sitcom *The Chicago Teddy Bears* in 1971; as TV producer Dwight McGonigle on ABC's short-lived sitcom *On the Air* in 1992; and—much more memorably—as telephone lineman Henry Beesmyer, a regular delicatessen patron on CBS's sitcom *Alice* from 1978 to 1985.

The shows on which Kaplan appeared only once or twice were profuse: *The Ford Television Theatre, General Electric Theater, Shower of Stars, Make Room for Daddy, Alcoa Theatre, M Squad, Gomer Pyle U.S.M.C., My Three Sons, Petticoat Junction, The Mod Squad, I Dream of Jeannie, Love American Style, Charlie's Angels, CHiPs, Disneyland, MacGyver, Cagney & Lacy, My Two Dads* and *E.R.*

Playing the part of Johnny Boone, Jr., Millie Bronson's boyfriend in the radio version, was Rye Billsbury, nee J. Riordan Billsbury, who sometimes professionally appeared under the moniker Michael Rye. (He was supplanted by Ross Ford in the TV series.) Billsbury was born in 1918 in Chicago, the son of a theatrical booking agent. Entertainment was a way of life for his family for generations, reaching back to England, where ancestors were stage show producers and actors. By the early 1940s the younger Billsbury's voice was beamed from the Windy City to everywhere. In addition to *Meet Millie*, his radio work extended into the mid–1950s, including long-running identities with *The Cisco Kid; The First Nighter; The Guiding Light; Heartbeat Theater; Jack Armstrong, the All-American Boy; Ma Perkins;* and *Tales of the Texas Rangers.* He definitely possessed one of the richer masculine voices on the airwaves.

The performer subsequently made a mint out of supplying voiceovers for animated TV series for the small fry: *The Lone Ranger* (1966–69, CBS, in which he played the lead); *Hot Wheels* (1969–71, ABC); *Sky Hawks* (1969–71, ABC, again the lead); *Super Friends* and similar monikers (1977–83, 1984ff, ABC); *Scooby and Scrappy-Doo* and similar monikers (1979–81, 1983ff, 1985–86, ABC); *The Super Globetrotters* (announcer, 1979–80, NBC); *The Smurfs* (1981ff, NBC); *Spider-Man* (1981–82, NBC); *The Incredible Hulk/Amazing Spider-Man Hour* (1982ff, NBC); *Super Friends* (1984–85, ABC); *The 13 Ghosts of Scooby-Doo* (1985–86, ABC); *The Gummi Bears* (1985–89, NBC; 1989–90, ABC); *The Super Powers Team—Galactic Guardians* (1986, ABC); *The Flintstone Kids 'Just Say No' Special* (1988, ABC); *Tale Spin* (1990–94, syndication); *The Pirates of Dark Water* (1991–92, ABC); plus several more.

Rye appeared in no fewer than 14 single episodes of ongoing television dramas, including hits like *The Adventures of Rin Tin Tin, Wagon Train, M Squad, Perry Mason, The Lone Ranger, Mission Impossible* and *The Incredible Hulk.* He turned up in a quartet of full-length motion pictures: *Two Lost Worlds* (1951); *Hands of a Stranger* (1962); *Cougar Country* (1970, as the narrator); and *The Nativity* (1986, in multiple voiceover roles). He also performed in a 1983 made-for-TV flick, *The Secret World of Og.* Rye and his spouse, the former Patricia Foster (born 1939), daughter of character actor Donald Foster (1899–1969), still resided on Los Angeles' South Irving Boulevard as of mid–2006.

*Meet Millie*'s boss, J.R. Boone, Sr., was portrayed by actor Earle Ross in both radio and video versions (the latter for one season only, replaced in June 1953 by Roland Winters).[3] Born in Illinois on March 29, 1888, Ross's comparatively limited dossier includes appearances in five B-movies between 1936 and 1941, none memorable; the continuing role of the irascible Judge Hooker in a brief syndicated screening of *The Great Gildersleeve* in 1955; and single guest appearances in two other 1955 TV shows, CBS's *Our Miss Brooks* and the syndicated *Wild Bill Hickok.* Ross's death, attributed to cancer, occurred in North Hollywood, California, on May 21, 1961.

For detailed information on the life of Robert W. (Bob) Lemond, *Meet Millie*'s interlocutor, see the chapter on *Our Miss Brooks* in this volume. Lemond presented a handful of audience participation sitcoms in that era, including *Honest Harold, Life with Luigi, My Favorite Husband, My Friend Irma* and a few more.

*Meet Millie*, with its zany characters and situations, was a delightful reverie in an epoch in which dial-twisters were still searching for something amusing. It was kept alive by a charitable network that was obviously smitten by the series' potential, enough to sustain it for a full season until willing underwriters were signed. Such perseverance rewarded listeners with some entertaining, lighthearted fluff.

# 17

# My Favorite Husband

## A Dress Rehearsal for the Main Event

*My Favorite Husband* was a sort of *I Love Lizzy*, according to one scholar. Indeed, it was the warm-up act for bigger things to come in broadcasting—specifically, Lucille Ball's *I Love Lucy*, which cast a country into a frenzy that bordered on rabid hysteria before it subsided. *My Favorite Husband* took the social-climbing and show-business ambitions of ordinary homemaker Liz Cooper (who debuted as Liz Cugat) and blew them far out of proportion. As an only slightly toned-down Lucy Ricardo, Liz offered enough zaniness that the resemblance was unmistakable. Living on a quiet residential street in a Midwestern village, Liz had wed, a decade before, a nondescript banker, George Cugat/Cooper, who obviously rated fairly low on his industry's totem pole. But she had visions of grandeur and would stop at little to realize them. Over his strong protests she engaged in all sorts of connivance to improve her/their lot in an effort to not just be accepted by her peers but elevated somewhere above them. It was a prelude to the more memorable and exaggerated *Lucy* that was coming soon to a TV nearby. Lucille Ball was at mid-career, temporarily starring in radio as she made the transition from B-movie actress to Emmy-winning video legend. Her opposite, Richard Denning, was another prolific B-flick thespian who probably is better recalled for his TV contributions, too. Broadcasting veterans Gale Gordon and Bea Benaderet, cast in supporting roles, augmented their situations as early

blueprints of Fred and Ethel Mertz. It was a charming comedy that set the stage for better appreciated efforts by Ball. And while it lasted, audiences had a ball with it, too.

❖ ❖ ❖

**Producers:** Gordon T. Hughes, Jess Oppenheimer

**Directors:** Harry Ackerman, Gordon T. Hughes, Jess Oppenheimer

**Writers:** Bob Carroll, Jr., Phil Cole, Jack Crutcher, Bill Davenport (summer 1948), Frank Fox (summer 1948), John Michael Hayes, Jess Oppenheimer, Madelyn Pugh, Martin Weinter

**Orchestra Leaders:** Lud Gluskin, Wilbur Hatch, Marlin Skiles

**Sound Effects Technician:** Clark Casey (1948), Bill Gould

**Announcer:** Bob Lemond

**Recurring Cast:** *Liz Cooper:* Lucille Désirée Ball; *George Cooper:* Lee Bowman (premier episode), Richard Denning (nee Louis Albert Heindrich Denninger); *Rudolph Atterbury:* Gale Gordon; *Iris Atterbury:* Bea Benaderet; *Katie:* Ruth Perrott; *Leticia Cooper:* Bea Benaderet (initially), Eleanor Audley

**Supporting Cast:** Frankie Albertson, Harry Bartell, Tommy Bernard, Gloria Blondell, Jack Carroll, Hans Conried, Richard Crenna, Barbara Eiler, Laurette Fillbrandt, Sandra Gould, Ira Grossel (aka Jeff Chandler), Florence Halop, John Hiestand, William Johnstone, Joseph Kearns, Erwin Lee, Hal March, Ed Max, Gerald Mohr, Frank Nelson, Jay Novello, Isabel Randolph, Ruth Rickaby, Janet Scott, Mary Shipp, Doris Singleton, Gil Stratton, Jean Vander Pyl, Viola Vonn

**Sponsor:** Sustained (1948); General Foods Corporation, for Jell-O gelatin, puddings, pie fillings and tapioca desserts, Sanka instant coffee, LaFrance bleach and other foodstuffs and household agents (1949–51)

**Ratings:** High—10.8 (1949–50), Low—8.8 (1950–51), Median—9.5.

**On the Air:** July 5–September 24, 1948, CBS, Friday, 9:00–9:30 P.M. Eastern Time; October 2–December 25, 1948, CBS, Saturday, 7:00–7:30 P.M.; December 26, 1948, CBS, Sunday, 7:00–7:30 P.M.; January 14–July 1, 1949, CBS, Friday, 8:30–9:00 P.M.; September 2, 1949–March 31, 1950, CBS, Friday, 8:30–9:00 P.M.; April 2–June 25, 1950, CBS, Sunday, 6:00–6:30 P.M.; September 2, 1950–March 31, 1951, CBS, Saturday, 9:30–10:00 P.M.

**Extant Archival Material:** About 125 scripts of My Favorite Husband broadcasts (possibly all those aired) are housed in the KNX Collection at Thousand Oaks Library, American Radio Archives, 1401 East Janss Road, Thousand Oaks, CA, 91362; (805) 449-2660; fax (805) 449-2675; www.tol.lib.ca.us.

At least 96 transcriptions of My Favorite Husband are known to be in general circulation or held by private collectors as of 2006, sold by vintage radio dealers and traded by old-time radio hobbyists.

❖ ❖ ❖

My Favorite Husband grew to have a powerful influence on entertainment's future. The radio adaptation was inspired by characters created by novelist Isabel Scott Rorick for her 1941 best-seller Mr. and Mrs. Cugat: The Record of a Happy Marriage, which resulted in the 1942 comedy flick Are Husbands Necessary? starring Ray Milland and Betty Field. The CBS Radio manifestation, however (while a highly amusing sitcom in its own right from 1948 to 1951), was merely the warm-up act for the principal attraction, which followed immediately over most of these same CBS stations, albeit on television—I Love Lucy (1951–57) and a myriad of successor laugh riots: The Lucy-Desi Comedy Hour (1957–60), The Lucy Show (1962–68), Here's Lucy (1968–74) and Life with Lucy (1986). While there was a video sequel of My Favorite Husband from 1953 to 1955, in which Barry Nelson and Joan Caulfield starred, the series itself is probably best remembered for its audio interpretation. That provided Lucille Ball's prime exposure to an aural-only audience, flanked by Richard Denning, whose celebrity was also on the upswing.

The radio series' weekly epigram introduced it as the story of "two people who live together and like it." It proffered the tale of George (Denning) and Liz Cooper (Ball), a somewhat seemingly mismatched couple who wed a decade earlier. While blissfully in love and childless—rather unusual by radio's family sitcom standards—the pair offered distinct contrasts between the leading characters.

George Cooper was a conservative, level-headed, don't-ruffle-any-feathers, no-nonsense businessman. His position as fifth executive vice-president at Sheridan Falls National Bank would have been totally boring had it not been for the frequent interference of his society-minded spouse, Liz. She was his opposite in more ways than one, cited as "scatter-brained and determined to help other people solve their problems." That was, of course, something that characters of serious and humorous radio narratives had been doing for a couple of decades by the time the Coopers arrived. The various scenarios focused on the catastrophes occurring after Liz's well-meaning interventions foundered. Her indisposed spouse invariably was drawn into the middle of her shenanigans, although he would have preferred to have been anywhere else. Think Lucy and Desi. The Coopers lived at 321 Bundy Drive in the relatively quiet Midwestern hamlet of Sheridan Falls, by the way.

Lucy ... er ... Liz saw herself as a society woman, an ambitious "climber," one unafraid to try anything to advance her own social standing, her husband's career, or to meet a passing celebrity. (Did we say "think Lucy"?) Her best friend was Iris Atterbury (Bea Benaderet), with whom she often coordinated her schemes at getting ahead. Iris was the wife of George's boss, Rudolph Atterbury (Gale Gordon). It was he who delivered the show's most memorable catchphrase: "Ah, Liz girl, George boy." The two couples' activities were intermingled on many shows.

When Liz's grandiose plans went awry, it was often because of her relationship with Iris that George's job was ultimately saved: Liz gave "Mr. Atterbury" (the respectful appellation by which they invariably addressed the boss, even though they were on friendly terms with him and his wife) plenty of reason to let George go. The Coopers also had a maid, Katie, who sometimes aided and abetted the lady of the house's elaborate conspiracies. And then there was George's mother, Leticia Cooper, an aristocrat who looked down her long nose at Liz, giving her daughter-in-law plenty of incentive to aspire to a higher rung on the social ladder.

If the parallels between *My Favorite Husband* and *I Love Lucy* seem outrageously uncanny, there was a pretty strong reason for their similarity. In two words, it was: Jess Oppenheimer. His hand unequivocally guided the series more than any other, including the writing, casting, directing and producing. And the qualities he brought to the show was but a foretaste of greater things to come.

Born at San Francisco on November 11, 1913, young Jessurun James Oppenheimer (in truth!) was attracted early to the footlights and decided to spend his life in show business. "From the moment I first set foot inside a radio studio, I was hooked," he recalled years later. The station was the City by the Bay's KFRC, an outlet that affiliated with the Don Lee–Columbia (CBS) West Coast chain while he was there. The de facto manager in those days was Sylvester L. (Pat) Weaver, Jr. This was the very same Weaver who would be running NBC as president a few decades later while creating sterling television programming like *Today*, *Tonight* and *Home*, and infamous radio features like *Monitor* and *Weekday*. Among a contingent of talented actors participating in various KFRC programming in those days was Bea Benaderet. For the year that young Oppenheimer was at the station he was in stimulating company, and all of it was to have a profound effect on him later.

Leaving San Francisco in October 1936, he committed himself to pursuing the greater opportunities in entertainment that Los Angeles appeared to afford. With considerable luck, the 22-year-old Oppenheimer landed a job almost immediately with the influential Young & Rubicam advertising agency. Y&R

had only a small presence in Los Angeles at the time, but gargantuan expansion was on its horizon. As it turned out, Jess Oppenheimer was to become a pivotal cog in the wheel of that power-driven machine. Initially he was hired for the writing staff of *The Packard Hour*, an NBC Tuesday night half-hour musical variety series hosted by silver screen dancer Fred Astaire. At $125-a-week, Oppenheimer realized he had caught the brass ring, making the big time in his very first try.

Subsequently he wrote for more than a few additional Y&R-produced series, as well as a handful of other programs that carried some very big names as their stars. His impressive repertoire included, in chronological sequence, *The Jack Benny Program* ("without a doubt the easiest writing job I ever had," declared the wordsmith); *Hollywood Mardi Gras*, hosted by vocalist Lanny Ross; *The Chase and Sanborn Hour*, featuring Edgar Bergen and Charlie McCarthy; a few installments of *The Texaco Star Theater*, starring actor Adolphe Menjou; *The Lifebuoy Program*, with vocalist Al Jolson; *The Gulf Screen Guild Show*, which attracted celluloid legends like Fred Astaire, Jack Benny, Joan Crawford, Bette Davis, Judy Garland, Robert Montgomery, George Murphy, Basil Rathbone, Loretta Young and many more; *The Rudy Vallee Show*; and *Baby Snooks*, starring Fanny Brice, beginning in 1943. By the time he joined Vallee in the spring of 1941, Oppenheimer's salary had risen to $500 weekly—$26,000 a year—not all that bad for a 27-year-old more than six-and-a-half decades ago.

After war broke out in late 1941, Oppenheimer joined the U.S. Coast Guard the following year. Rising to the rank of chief petty officer, he was stationed at the Wilmington Patrol Base in Los Angeles. During his tenure he was assigned to interview men returning from overseas, dramatizing their exploits for a radio narrative, *Together We Serve*. The series was co-hosted by Mary Astor and Rudy Vallee. Meanwhile, the scribe also penned Coast Guard recruitment shows featuring enlisted musicians from some of the venerable big bands, like Jimmy and Tommy Dorsey,

Woody Herman, Ted Lewis, Freddy Martin, Raymond Scott, Fred Waring and more.

About 1944 the Coast Guard's chief commandant discovered that Oppenheimer had been moonlighting as a scriptwriter for *Baby Snooks* over the previous year. The younger man was informed, in no uncertain terms, that if he persisted in that activity he would forfeit his weekly Coast Guard salary of $75. Oppenheimer never slowed down. By then his paycheck from penning *Snooks* every week exceeded $750. He continued turning out scripts for the show following his discharge from the service in 1946, right until Fanny Brice flung a fit in May 1948 and stormed off the air after being asked to accept a salary cut of $2,500 weekly from the $5,500 she was getting. The advent of TV had prompted severe reductions in the compensation paid several major radio stars. For a while, at least, Brice didn't intend to be one of them. When she wouldn't play ball, for the first time in a dozen years Oppenheimer found himself without a steady income.

Only a short time earlier, on August 5, 1947, he had married Estelle Weiss, the manager of the pop record department at a Los Angeles record emporium, Music City. When he lost his job in May 1948, Estelle (whom he affectionately called "Es") was five months pregnant. Three months later—after near-panic had set in—Oppenheimer was contacted by Harry Ackerman, CBS Radio's West Coast programming guru. Ackerman invited him to submit a script for *My Favorite Husband*, starring Lucille Ball. The show was an unsponsored sitcom that had been running since early July. Bill Davenport and Frank Fox, then "on loan" from *The Adventures of Ozzie and Harriet*, were scripting it, although they would soon return to their regular digs for a new radio season. Wordsmiths Bob Carroll, Jr. and Madelyn Pugh had been enlisted to pick up the slack.

> The idea that I came up with for a segment of *My Favorite Husband* was something of a departure from the scripts that Harry [Ackerman] had sent me. I decided to make Liz Cugat [Ball's surname through 1948] a little bit less

sophisticated, a little bit more childlike and impulsive, than the character who had appeared in the first few shows—in short, more like Baby Snooks. She would be a stage-struck schemer with an overactive imagination that got her into embarrassing situations. This would give me an excuse to engage Lucy in some broad slapstick comedy.[1]

Can you see the hand of fate at work here? If you have ever watched even one installment of *I Love Lucy*, do you not begin to catch a glimmer of where it all came from? Stay tuned; there's more to come.

After the episode that Oppenheimer had written aired in early October 1948, he received a follow-up call from Ackerman.

> "Jess," he [Ackerman] said excitedly. "This was a terrific show. How would you like to be head writer of *My Favorite Husband*? I'd like to sign you for a five-year exclusive contract with CBS, whether or not the show stays on the air."
>
> I told him I'd have to think it over. In the weeks since that first call from Harry, all of my friends had advised me not to take a job writing for Lucille Ball. When I attended a rehearsal I had noticed that the producer-director [Gordon T. Hughes], sitting in the control room, had eight or nine prescription bottles ... before him. I remember making a mental note ... that somewhere in this group there must be, shall we say, a "strong personality." ... The "strong personality" had turned out to be Miss Ball.
>
> On the other hand, something had "clicked" when she performed the broad comedy that I had written for her.... There was definitely something special about Lucille Ball, and I decided to take a chance.[2]

On his first day at CBS, Oppenheimer met the two young people who had been penning most of the scripts for *My Favorite Husband* over the previous couple of months, Bob Carroll, Jr. and Madelyn Pugh. He characterized them as red-eyed, trembling and worn-out. The pair had been turning out up to five scripts weekly, doing lots of rewrites in their attempts to satisfy a contentious star, producer-director and network. Oppenheimer assured the duo that it was his experience that—with few exceptions—radio scripts could be completed during normal office hours. His statement met disbelieving stares that seemed to scream "Convince me." Oppenheimer set about doing that, soon winning a couple of converts as he patiently exhibited techniques to accomplish heretofore impossible feats. To the trio's utter delight, they also found that their personalities meshed well. It was definitely the start of something grand!

A week afterward, Harry Ackerman told Oppenheimer that Gordon Hughes was out as producer-director, and he would like Oppenheimer to add those duties to his assignment as head writer for an additional $100 weekly. That time the scribe accepted on the spot. He recalled what happened next: "I had three, maybe four, idyllic weeks in my new position as producer-director-head writer, and then the proverbial fan suffered a direct hit."[3]

In his book he recounted in extensive detail how the show's writing staff had prepared a script that simply didn't work. Midway through a rehearsal, Oppenheimer dismissed the players, telling them the wordsmiths could improve it by morning. Working through the night, they came up with a hilarious dialogue that was a sure-fire laugh-getter, but with one problem: they were never satisfied with the last line. At daybreak Lucy arrived with her agent, Don Sharpe. She sat down to read through the freshly written script, holding her sides as she roared at the funny lines—until she got to the last one. Disagreeing with it completely, she flew into an out-and-out rage. Using profanity and gutter language galore, she stomped, screamed, tossed the script across the room, picked it up and tore the pages into shreds and let them fall to the floor. When her tirade subsided, Oppenheimer said he walked over to her and remonstrated:

"Lucy, I thought we had a team effort going here. We're happy to stay up all night or all week, and break our butts to make the script right for you. But not if you're going to ignore a major rewrite, which you loved, and crucify us over one little line, which can easily be fixed. We need quite a bit more respect than that." I took her hand and shook it and said,

"I can't say that it's been a pleasant experience working with you, but at least it's over."[4]

At that Oppenheimer left the building. By the time he had walked a half-block away, Don Sharpe caught up with him. "She's crying and hysterical," he reported. "She knows she's wrong and agrees with you and wants to apologize." The upshot was that Oppenheimer returned, Lucy apologized, and he told her she must do so to Bob Carroll and Madelyn Pugh, too, or he wouldn't come back. She did. "Once I established that kind of relationship there were just no problems," Oppenheimer affirmed.

From that experience he learned an important lesson about Lucille Ball that was to have a powerful effect not just on their working relationship in the future but in determining the direction of the fabled characterizations he would write for her in radio and television. "I had discovered that Lucy, despite her tough demeanor, was actually quite insecure and required somebody to lean on; she really needed to be dominated." Thus, when he penned a scenario in which George Cooper, Liz's usually passive spouse, played by Richard Denning, became fiery angry over something she had done and didn't mince any words in putting her in her place for it, after the first run-through Lucy said to Oppenheimer, eyes beaming: "Write more scenes like this! That's great. Let him really tell me off." Oppenheimer assured her he would, while thinking to himself: "And I see how I have to act with you in the future, too."

Gregg Oppenheimer, "Es" and Jess Oppenheimer's second child, born March 6, 1951, turned an 85-page autobiographical manuscript that his father left unfinished into a published book after he died at age 75 on December 27, 1988. In the modern epoch the younger Oppenheimer has developed a compelling audio and visual narrative that he has delivered multiple times before vintage radio, television and nostalgia audiences. There he highlights his dad's sweeping professional career. Those who have witnessed his presentation, including this author, marvel at how he picks up the threads that stress certain consistencies in the senior Oppenheimer's work and masterfully weaves them together through his gentle storytelling.

At some point a revelation suddenly dawns on his listeners: there is unmistakable evidence that three popular broadcast shows on which Jess Oppenheimer labored are inextricably related, joined at the hip so to speak. The *Baby Snooks* character, a squalling brat when she doesn't get her own way, who is repeatedly reprimanded by a strong male presence (in *her* case, Daddy Higgins), is simply transposed over an analogous character in *My Favorite Husband*, who similarly requires (yea, *welcomes*) an occasional sharp rebuke delivered by another strong male presence, her spouse George Cooper. And finally, in the ultimate manifestation, the unbridled Lucy Ricardo must be constantly reined in by her beloved Ricky in *I Love Lucy*, a series created by (need we say more?) Jess Oppenheimer. Do you begin to see a pattern emerging here? It's one that's quite difficult to miss once you place the three side-by-side, as Gregg Oppenheimer does while taking his audience by the proverbial hand and leading it along his media history pilgrimage. Snooks Higgins ... Liz Cooper ... Lucy Ricardo. There's simply no way to dismiss the consistent and enveloping parallels.

Several modifications, some of a purely cosmetic variety, were made in *My Favorite Husband* once General Foods Corporation agreed to underwrite the show beginning in January 1949. (It had been sustained by the network until then.) Also, possibly only coincidentally, to that point the lead characters were known as George and Liz Cugat, adopting the surname from Isabel Scott Rorick's fictional account upon which those figures were based—*Mr. and Mrs. Cugat*. Did it sound too much like a famous Latin bandleader with that moniker? Possibly. And it was definitely so to impresario Xavier Cugat and his vocalizing spouse Abbe Lane. The pair was obviously unimpressed by the resemblance; they sued the radio series. The Cugats of *My Favorite Husband* suddenly became the

Coopers of the same series—without further adieu or explanation. One can't help wondering what the offended real-life Cugats thought of the book upon which it was all based in 1941 and the subsequent movie in 1942. Why didn't it cause a stir then?

Whereas the fictional *Cugats* had belonged to a rather upscale, elitist fragment of the populace—their names on the social register by virtue of George's post as a bank vice president and Liz's background as an ex-debutante—his post was now downplayed and the newly-identified *Coopers* were clearly middle-class citizens who only *aspired* (she, in particular) to greater acceptance. This gave the series more opportunity to concentrate on the foibles she presented instead of the somewhat mundane life of a banker.

As a counterpoint to the Coopers, the Atterburys were inserted into many chapters. Although Rudolph was George's superior at the bank, thereby keeping that angle in play as needed, his spouse Iris and Liz Cooper were best friends, gossiping, conniving and generally screwing things up together. At last Liz had someone to help her carry out her sometimes bizarre machinations, often involving wives vs. husbands. Now where have we seen this in reruns since? Think Fred and Ethel Mertz. Suffice it to say that—by the time the show began plugging Jell-O—the typecast figure that Lucille Ball was to become in multiple sitcoms that followed was firmly entrenched. She was already "in character" long before *Lucy* appeared, refining the role every week on *My Favorite Husband*.

Titles of a handful of those weekly installments (probably designated by hobbyists and vintage radio program collectors) offer hints about the typical dilemmas the principals faced: "George's Old Flame," "The Kissing Booth," "Matrimony on the Rocks," "Liz Has Her Fortune Told," "The Boys Think Liz Is Pregnant," "George Attends a Teen-age Dance," "Is There a Baby in the House?," "Be Your Husband's Best Friend," "Piano and Violin Lessons," "Absolute Truth," "Absent-mindedness," "Mother-in-Law," "Give Away Program," "Time Budgeting," "Over Weight,"

"Getting Old," "Liz in the Hospital," "Hair Dyed" and "Liz Changes Her Mind."

Despite the strong writing that Oppenheimer, Pugh and Carroll gave to *My Favorite Husband*, CBS repeatedly carped that the trio weren't providing material to be found running on several other shows at the time. On *Fibber McGee & Molly*, for instance, a sequence of repeating characters showed up in every installment, netting humorous dialogue with the show's chief protagonist (McGee) before slipping off into the sunset for another week. (A modified form of that model occurred on *The Jack Benny Program* some weeks, too.) "We did *whole* stories—*situation* comedy," Oppenheimer explained. When CBS told him it wouldn't work, he persisted, and fun-loving audiences regularly returned for more of the same.

By 1950 Lucille Ball—who had been married to native Cuban bandleader Desi Arnaz for a decade—decided to figure out a way for them to work together. He was constantly on the road performing here and there, while she was stuck in Hollywood making pictures and concurrently appearing in the weekly radio series. The final solution, of course, turned out to be CBS-TV's *I Love Lucy*, created by the senior Oppenheimer, which premiered on October 15, 1951. It became an overnight ratings sensation, the kind of smash hit that provided impetus for a glut of television receiver manufacturing and sales as it mesmerized a nation every Monday night for nearly all of the 1950s. Getting there, however, was a complicated situation.

CBS was eager to have Ms. Ball starring in a video sitcom but initially refused to take her spouse, Arnaz, as she insisted. The web maintained that "nobody will believe the two of you are married." Lucy's response: "But we *are* married!" The couple went on the road together during *My Favorite Husband*'s summer hiatus in 1950, putting on a musical and comedy stage extravaganza designed to showcase their combined talents and convince the public and CBS that they could provide an enthusiastic draw. The itinerant performers were well received everywhere, but at the end of the trip CBS still wasn't buying. Taking the advice of Young & Rubicam, the couple dug into their own pockets to finance a kinescope (film) recording of a pilot show, which they intended to shop to the highest bidder. NBC expressed more than passing interest in acquiring the services of Ms. Ball. That possibility pushed CBS over the cliff, and a deal was struck at last.

Oppenheimer was named head writer, and Carroll and Pugh were kept on. Oppenheimer determined to remain close to the mock-up provided by *My Favorite Husband* because it "worked so well" for Ball. The new series' premise could be summarized by a pithy description: "A show about a middle-class working stiff who labors hard at his job as a bandleader and likes nothing more than to come home to his wife, who doesn't like staying home and is dying to get into show business herself." Of course, Lucy's means of accomplishing that were often unscrupulous, manipulative and deceptive. Sometimes her efforts netted disastrous results, but they were uproariously funny nevertheless. She had 44 million Americans eating out of her hand at one time. A modern media historian nonchalantly observed, "Casting Desi as a Cuban bandleader fending off his wife's showbiz ambitions went back to the original book about the Cugats. Somehow the concept had been overlooked by bandleader Ozzie Nelson and Harriet Hilliard, his real-life band-singing wife, who was revamped on radio as an obedient hausfrau."[5]

Few listeners have reason to recall that—in a unique reversal of normally progressive chronology—*I Love Lucy* enjoyed a fleeting run on CBS Radio in 1952. According to one source, "*Lucy* was hedging its bets in the scary new world of video; six of the *My Favorite Husband* scripts later turned up as *Lucy* TV episodes."

Parenthetically, a little remembered fact is that Jess Oppenheimer acquired a patent for his invention of the Teleprompter, a device using a half-silvered mirror in front of the TV lens that projected words from a rolling script set in large type. It was a boon

A hunky Richard Denning and a gushing Lucille Ball perform a warm-up act for greater things ahead, when Ball and real-life husband Desi Arnaz would co-star in TV's I Love Lucy. In My Favorite Husband (1948–51), characters were introduced that were later refined on the video series (1951–57). Denning and Ball were veteran B-film actors who were merely stopping by radio briefly while en-route to greater opportunities on the small screen. As George and Liz Cooper, they were middle-class denizens, but one of them had far greater ambitions. Liz was also stagestruck, constantly seeking methods of latching on to notoriety in order to attach her name to fame—much to George's chagrin. It was the draft of an outline that would become very familiar to TV watchers in time.

to actors and news anchors, permitting them to seemingly look directly into TV cameras without glancing at a typed manuscript in front of them or at cue cards held by a stage-hand. Oppenheimer originally devised the Teleprompter especially for Ball to read commercials from, but it quickly became an industry standard, adapted by newsmen and drama and comedy thespians.

Lucille Désirée Ball was born in Jamestown, New York, on August 6, 1911. Her lifelong interest in show business carried her to New York City, where she modeled and was a chorus girl. In 1932 a Metro-Goldwyn-Mayer rep pointed her to Hollywood, where—from the 1930s to the 1970s—she played in 92 mostly B-films, all but a dozen of which were released in the 1930s and 1940s. Ball's early features included forgettable inane monikers like *Broadway Through a Keyhole* (1933), *Hold That Girl* (1934), *Men of the Night* (1934), *Three Little Pigskins* (1934), *His Old Flame* (1935), *I Dream Too Much* (1935), *Mess 'Em Up* (1936), *So and Sew* (1936), *Don't Tell the Wife* (1937), *Go Chase Yourself* (1938), *Room Service* (1938), *Next Time I Marry* (1938), *You Can't Fool Your Wife* (1940), *Without Love* (1945), *Two Smart People* (1946) and *Easy Living* (1949). After gaining notoriety, Ball performed in a somewhat improved grade of flick, including *Fancy Pants* (1950), *The Fuller Brush Girl* (1950), *The Long, Long Trailer* (1954), *A Guide for the Married Man* (1967) and *Mame* (1974).

Though television was to dominate her professional career, her radio work was extensive. In 1938–39 she was a recurring cast member on *The Wonder Show*, a Friday night musical variety series starring Jack Haley on CBS. In 1941–42 Ball appeared with Herbert Marshall and others on the NBC Blue variety series *The New Old Gold Program*, initially on Mondays and later on Friday nights. She was also a semi-regular on MBS's panel discussion *Leave It to the Girls* on Saturday nights between 1945 and 1947, and Friday nights between 1947 and 1949. She frequently turned up on other radio panels, comedies and dramatic series, among them *Screen Guild The-* *ater*, *Suspense* and *Twenty Questions*.

In her personal life, Ball wed Desi Arnaz, whose affairs with other women were widely reported and never ceased, on November 30, 1940. To their union were born two children: Lucy Désirée Arnaz, July 17, 1951; and Desiderio Alberto Arnaz IV, aka Desi Arnaz, Jr., January 19, 1953. The couple formed Desilu Studios in 1950 and were pioneer producers of American TV fare during the medium's infancy. They divorced May 4, 1960, but remained friends throughout their lives. Ball married stand-up comic Gary Morton—a dozen years her junior—on November 19, 1961. She went on to become a three-time Emmy Award winner and charter member of the Television Hall of Fame, and made dozens of guest appearances on TV shows, in addition to the series in which she starred: *I Love Lucy* (1951–57), *The Lucy-Desi Comedy Hour* (1957–60), *The Lucy Show* (1962–68), *Here's Lucy* (1968–74) and *Life with Lucy* (1986).

Following a heart attack, while recovering from open heart surgery lasting seven hours at Cedars Sinai Medical Center in Los Angeles, Ball died after her aorta ruptured. Death came on April 26, 1989; she was 77, survived by her husband and two children from her marriage to Desi. Her television features continue to be screened daily, almost nonstop throughout the world.

Louis Albert Heindrich Denninger, aka Richard Denning, was born at Poughkeepsie, New York, on March 27, 1914. Growing up in Los Angeles, he studied accounting at the city's Woodbury Business College before joining his father in the garment industry, working his way from office boy up to vice president. The young man was more attracted to the Little Theater groups he participated in than commerce, however, and made the break when Paramount Studios offered a contract. The studio insisted that he alter his surname from Denninger because it resembled Chicago gangster John Dillinger's moniker too closely.

The tall, blond, square-jawed Denning with a hunky physique appealed to directors and audiences alike. He appeared in 91 theatrical productions over his lifetime, mostly of the B persuasion, with 48 of them coming in a five-year period (1937–42). They included *The Big Broadcast of 1938*, *Some Like It Hot* (1939), *The Gracie Allen Murder Case* (1939), *The Farmer's Daughter* (1940), *Seventeen* (1940), *Beyond the Blue Horizon* (1942) and *Ice-Capades Review* (1942). After sailing in the South Pacific with the U.S. Navy during the war, Denning returned to perform in *Black Beauty* (1946), *Creature from the Black Lagoon* (1954), *An Affair to Remember* (1957), *No Greater Love* (1960) and a final film, *I Sailed to Tahiti with an All Girl Crew* (1968).

When the crime series *Mr. and Mrs. North* added a television adaptation to its long radio run, Denning was tapped as book publisher Jerry North, the male half of the amateur sleuthing duo. The drama ran for a year on CBS-TV (1952–53) and for six months on NBC-TV (1954). At that juncture Joseph Curtin relinquished his dozen-year portrayal of North on radio, and Denning won the role in its final season on CBS. Subsequently he appeared as Greg Graham, *The Flying Doctor*, in a fleeting 1959 syndicated TV series. He was the namesake private eye *Michael Shayne* in an NBC-TV incarnation in 1960–61. In the 1964–65 television season Denning played Steve Scott on the NBC sitcom *Karen*. He capped his professional career with a part for which he is probably best remembered, in a series in which he wasn't the star or the star's sidekick: for a dozen years, from 1968 to 1980, he appeared sporadically as Governor Philip Grey of the Aloha State on CBS-TV's popular hour-long crime drama *Hawaii Five-O*. Furthermore, between 1952 and 1974 Denning turned up in about two dozen single episodes of acclaimed TV dramatic fare, like *The Cavalcade of America*, *Celebrity Playhouse*, *Cheyenne*, *Crossroads*, *Ford Television Theater*, *General Electric Theater*, *I Spy*, *Lux Video Theater*, *McCloud*, *Schlitz Playhouse of Stars*, *Studio One* and *TV Reader's Digest*.

When production ended on *Hawaii Five-O*, which was filmed in Honolulu, Denning remained in Hawaii. He became active in community affairs, serving as an executive director of the Boy Scouts of America. He was also designated honorary president of the Maui Chamber of Commerce. "I'm very grateful for a career that wasn't spectacular but always made a good living," he allowed in retirement. "I have wonderful memories of it, but I don't really miss it."

In real life Denning wed 1940s horror movie queen Evelyn Ankers on September 6, 1942. To do it she broke her engagement with film actor Glenn Ford, then on location. Ankers, 24 at the time and of British descent, was born at Valparaiso, Chile. Her family returned to its own native homeland in the 1920s, where she was exposed to the theater and grew up with aspirations as an actress. She gained roles in British movies. When war clouds swept over Europe in the 1930s, Ankers immigrated to America, arriving in New Jersey in September 1939. Within a decade—until officially retiring from the silver screen at 32 in 1950—she had turned up in 52 celluloid productions.

She was known as the "Queen of the Screamers" for her blood-curdling outbursts in numerous B suspense thrillers. Her portfolio included *Murder in the Family* (1938), *The Claydon Treasure Mystery* (1938), *Hold That Ghost* (1941), *The Wolf Man* (1941), *The Ghost of Frankenstein* (1942), *Sherlock Holmes and the Voice of Terror* (1942), *Son of Dracula* (1943), *The Mad Ghoul* (1943), *The Invisible Man's Revenge* (1944), *The Frozen Ghost* (1945), *The Fatal Witness* (1945) and *The Lone Wolf in London* (1947). Later Ankers appeared in an episode of television's *Mr. and Mrs. North*, in which her husband co-starred, along with several 1950s TV dramatic anthologies. In 1960 she returned to cinema a final time to appear with Denning in *No Greater Love*. She died at their home in Maui, Hawaii, of ovarian cancer on August 29, 1985, at age 67. She was survived by her spouse and their only child, Diana Dee Denning Dwyer (Mrs. Robert M. Dwyer), born in September 1944, and two granddaughters.

On April 26, 1986, Denning, then 72,

married Patricia Leffingwell, who survived him, along with his daughter and granddaughters, following his death on October 11, 1998. According to wire reports he was visiting relatives in southern California when he died at Palomar Medical Center in Escondido after a long bout with emphysema. At the time of his passing Denning maintained homes at Kihei, Maui, Hawaii, and Rancho Bernardo, California.

*My Favorite Husband* was like a pilot for a television series that has never ceased. While the final production was better than its forerunner, every sitcom requires a rehearsal.

In that regard its originators and refiners took comfort in the fact that their inspired little interpretation of humorous married life prompted a "spinoff" that is "Now Playing" somewhere on the globe virtually every day—and has been for many decades. Out of that, billions of people from several generations have been exposed to the kind of madcap plots that listeners were introduced to on *My Favorite Husband*. What went around then, so it seems, keeps coming around now.

Gregg Oppenheimer has cause to be proud of his daddy!

# 18

# My Friend Irma

## IS IT TRUE BLONDES HAVE MORE FUN?

Have you ever dealt with a perennially confused mind? The characters in this show were accustomed to doing that on a routine basis. Nearly every facet of any state of affairs drifted from common sense viewpoints when Irma Peterson was involved. To the urban clerical staffer, life and circumstances seemed perfectly ordinary, even normal. Perhaps because there wasn't a malicious bone in the body of this airhead, her absolute purity and innocence allowed her to witness only the positive traits in those with whom she interacted. But her concept of logic was skewed far differently from that of nearly everybody else she met. Irma believed that flypaper was an airline's stationery. She argued against the draft or compulsory conscription, advocating instead that "A girl shouldn't have to go out with a sailor unless she wants to." The frequency of small-minded (literally!) misunderstandings that prevailed on this show kept it afloat. The sitcom focused on the inept- yet well-meaning central figure, gleaning laughs from how she screwed everything up and how her friends, neighbors and associates handled the amusing fallout. So impeccably charming was she—and so improbable was the environment in which she operated—that the radio entry became an audio citadel. Added to the network schedule shortly before the aural medium began its long slow slide toward oblivion, the series drew ample applause (and attendant ratings). Its theme was perpetuated in reproductions in a couple of other media-

ums. The original audio format which spawned the offshoots persisted for seven years. If that made it the seven-year itch, plenty of Americans seemed willing to scratch.

❖ ❖ ❖

**Creator-Writer-Producer-Director:** Cy Howard
**Director:** Parke Levy
**Writers:** Parke Levy, Stanley Adams, Roland MacLane, Jack Denton
**Orchestra Conductor:** Lud Gluskin
**Choral Ensemble:** The Sportsmen Quartet
**Sound Effects Technician:** James Murphy
**Announcers:** Carl Caruso, Bob Lemond, Frank Bingman, Wendell Niles, Johnny Jacobs
**Recurring Cast:** *Irma Peterson:* Marie Wilson; *Jane Stacy:* Cathy Lewis (1947–53), Joan Banks (briefly in early 1949); *Kay Foster:* Mary Shipp (1953–54); *Kathleen O'Reilly:* Jane Morgan (1947), Gloria Gordon (ca. 1947–54); *Al:* John H. Brown; *Professor Kropotkin:* Hans Conried; *Richard Rhinelander III:* Leif Erickson; *Milton J. Clyde:* Alan Reed; *Mrs. Rhinelander:* Myra Marsh
**Sponsors:** Sustained (summer 1947); Lever Brothers Company, for Swan soap (1947–51); Pearson Pharmacal Company, for Ennds chlorophyll breath mints and Eye Gene eye solution (1951–52); R.J. Reynolds Tobacco Company, for Camel and Cavalier cigarettes (1952–53); Multiple participation, for commodities including Arrid deodorant, Bobbi Pin Curl home permanent, Carter's Little Liver pills, White Rain shampoo (1953–54)
**Theme:** Main—"Friendship" (Cole Porter), Secondary—"Street Scene" (Alfred Newman)
**Ratings:** High—21.5 (1948–49), Low—5.0 (1953–54), Median—12.4 (all seasons represented

except 1951–52, for which figures are unsubstantiated)

**On the Air:** April 11–June 20, 1947, CBS, Friday, 10:30–11:00 P.M. Eastern Time; June 30–July 28, 1947, CBS, Monday, 8:30–9:00 P.M.; August 4, 1947–June 27, 1949, CBS, Monday, 10:00–10:30 P.M.; August 29, 1949–June 26, 1950, CBS, Monday, 10:00–10:30 P.M.; September 4, 1950–June 25, 1951, CBS, Monday, 10:00–10:30 P.M.; October 14, 1951–May 11, 1952, CBS, Sunday, 6:00–6:30 P.M.; May 18–June 15, 1952, CBS, Sunday, 9:30–10:00 P.M.; October 7, 1952–June 30, 1953, CBS, Tuesday, 9:30–10:00 P.M.; December 1, 1953–August 24, 1954, CBS, Tuesday, 9:30–10:00 P.M.

**Extant Archival Material:** Scripts, production notes and related memos from long runs of *My Friend Irma* are archived in the KNX Script Collection supplied by the Los Angeles CBS affiliate at Thousand Oaks Library, American Radio Archives, 1401 East Janss Road, Thousand Oaks, CA, 91362; (805) 449-2660; fax (805) 449-2675; *www.tol.lib.ca.us.*

Scripts for radio and television programs written by Parke Levy, including *My Friend Irma*, are among the Parke Levy Papers (1933–1965) archived at the American Heritage Center of the University of Wyoming, 1000 East University Avenue, Laramie, WY, 82071; (307) 766-3756; fax (307) 766-5511; *http://ahc.uwyo.edu/usearchives/default.htm.*

Sixty-seven recordings of *My Friend Irma* shows were in general circulation or held by private collectors as of 2006, sold by vintage radio dealers and traded by old-time radio hobbyists.

❖ ❖ ❖

As radio matured, a subtle emphasis emerged in some programming sectors that linked audiences to favorite series by ostensibly fostering a kind of superficial ownership of some of the shows they heard. One of the more discernible methods of accomplishing that objective was to cultivate monikers that sought to make a program a natural part of a listener's experience. The application of the adjectives *my*, *our* and *your*, for instance, gently hinted at one's personal involvement in a continuing feature. To wit:

*My Best Girls*
*My Favorite Husband*
*My Friend Irma*
*My Good Wife*
*My Little Margie*
*My Son and I*
*My Son Jeep*
*My True Story*
*Our Barn*
*Our Gal Sunday*
*Our House*
*Our Miss Brooks*
*Our Secret Weapon*
*Your America*
*Your Blind Date*
*Your Dream Has Come True*
*Your Family and Mine*
*Your Hit Parade*
*Your Invitation to Music*
*Your Radio Theater*
*Your Song and Mine*
*Your Unseen Friend*

One resourceful historiographer tallied 23 aural series beginning with the word *my*, 24 beginning with *our* and a whopping 52 beginning with *your*![1] That's 99 altogether that start with one of those three little words. All of them denote a deeper, more personal connection with a given series than, say, dispassionate titles like *Beat the Clock*, *Comedy Playhouse*, *House of Mystery* and *Invitation to Learning*.

Several of the series covered in this text apply this principle, including *My Favorite Husband*, *My Friend Irma*, *My Little Margie* and *Our Miss Brooks*—all sitcoms that premiered in the late 1940s and early 1950s. Many of the *my-our-your* features debuted in that chronological period, signaling an explicit fascination in the industry with highlighting the correlation between listeners and programming. While not all of their broadcast dates have been preserved, no fewer than 35 of the 99 *my-our-your* shows (more than a third) can be certified as beginning in that epoch. There may be several more. *My Friend Irma*, which arrived early in 1947, was clearly on the cutting edge of that trend.

In the meantime, when the Foote, Cone & Belding ad agency took America by storm with an ingenious query for Clairol—*Is it true blondes have more fun?*—the number of women who made up their minds to become flaxen-haired dolls rose by more than 400 percent.

The curious question, proffered by FCB creative copywriter Shirley Polykoff, arrived on the heels of Polykoff's already successful motivational pitch for the same client: *If I have only one life ... let me live it as a blonde.* It was, in reality, an era in which distaff blondes stood out in this country. The musical *Gentlemen Prefer Blondes*, based on a 1925 novel by Anita Loos, became a colossal hit on the Broadway stage in 1949. Four years later Jane Russell and Marilyn Monroe starred in a celluloid production of smashing proportions that repeated the well-worn theme. A 1926 Broadway play and a silent movie in 1928 had preceded those renditions, adding to the national mania over blonde beauties.

All of this obsession coincided with the appearance—initially in radio, then on the big screen, and finally on television—of *My Friend Irma*, a half-hour feature played for laughs with a ravishingly sexy blonde at its core. Mired in mirthful plotting, in its original manifestation the feature captivated audiences for more than seven years. To spice it up and thereby make it stimulating to fans, Irma Peterson became the most scatterbrained single girl ever to cross the airwaves. She was, with little doubt, the dimmest bulb on the Christmas tree. "Irma was possibly the kookiest secretary in the entire world," said one source. "She was friendly, enthusiastic ... just had no sense of logic." As the quintessential giggly girl, she was the embodiment of the classic dumb blonde. And although we may not have branded the phenomenon as unkind, immoral or stereotypical in those days, in the years afterward we have not only recognized but been collectively shamed by our politically incorrect callousness.

It was a model that Gracie Allen had conceived and perfected many years earlier. As a mature comedienne, Gracie might have been forgiven the eccentricities that she displayed as she aged. Irma Peterson, on the other hand—portrayed by the well-seasoned starlet of a plethora of Hollywood B-movies, Marie Wilson—was young, hip, modern, and, as evidenced by screen appearances, a knockout. Exhibiting high cheek bones, she owned

a wide slash for a mouth and a figure that simply wouldn't quit. In 1952—the zenith of her career—her measurements were 39D-23-38. "Wilson, in real life a curvy blond sexpot, spoke in a voice that sounded as if she had a permanent head cold, portraying a sweet, vacant dame—a characterization so terminally sexist that the show is almost unthinkable now," penned one modern journalist. As Irma, Wilson was simply too dimwitted to be believed; she carried the legendary role of her professional career to extreme proportions. She was usually good for one outburst of tears per episode—often the result of her own ineptness—and the weeping and the stupidity sounded awfully convincing.

The show was created by writer-director-producer Cy Howard, "a reformed introvert," according to a critic. Born in Milwaukee on September 27, 1915, he studied at the universities of Wisconsin and Minnesota, earning a degree in economics from the latter. He apprenticed in radio at Houston's KTRH and Chicago's WBBM. By 1943 he was contributing to comic Jack Benny's radio scripts. Between 1944 and 1948 Howard acted on Broadway, and scripted and edited the dialogue for several stage productions. In 1946 he landed at CBS "with *Irma* on his mind." While he wrote for comedians Milton Berle and Danny Thomas in that era, both in the CBS fold, he was clearly gearing up to launch what would become his most noteworthy endeavor, *My Friend Irma*. Eighteen months later (in late 1948) he followed with a second potent entry, *Life with Luigi*, for the same web. Both features went to television in 1952. Things were definitely looking up.

Once Howard penned the librettos for two *Irma* films, new doors opened. He wrote the screenplay for 1951's *That's My Boy*, which the Writers Guild of America nominated a year later as the "Best Written American Comedy." He was its associate producer and served in the same capacity for both *Irma* movies, incidentally. Following a few solo televentures, in the late 1950s he signed with Desilu Studios. For five years he produced and developed scripts for one of the West Coast's most influential production houses. Later he scripted another trio of motion pictures, albeit some being less than memorable: *Marriage on the Rocks* (1965), *Every Little Crook and Nanny* (1972) and *Won Ton, the Dog Who Saved Hollywood* (1976). He directed a couple of theatrical films in that era, *Lovers and Other Strangers* (1970) and *Every Little Crook and Nanny*, plus a made-for-TV flick, *It Couldn't Happen to a Nicer Guy* (1974).

With a cadre of wordsmiths, Howard won an Emmy in 1969 for "Outstanding Writing Achievement in Comedy, Variety or Music." They had collaborated on CBS-TV's *The Smothers Brothers Comedy Hour*. Married three times, Howard and his first wife, radio and Broadway vocalist Nan Wynn (1915–1971), divorced in 1948. He wed actress Gloria Grahame (1923–1981) in 1954, and they split three years later.[2] He remained with his third spouse, Barbara Warner, daughter of Warner Brothers' Jack Warner, from their nuptials in 1964 until his death from heart failure on April 29, 1993, in Los Angeles. He was also survived by a daughter, Paulette Howard, whose mother was Gloria Grahame.

As he branched out into new territory, Howard leaned heavily on one of his key writers for *Irma*. Edward Parke Levy, born in Philadelphia on April 19, 1908, and an alumnus of Temple University, contributed to the storylines of eight mainly B-grade motion pictures before *Irma*'s launch. They included such forgettable monikers as *Happy Heels* (1936), *Ready to Serve* (1937), *Hurray for Hooligan* (1937), *Dates and Nuts* (1937) and *Having Wonderful Crime* (1945). In the meantime he was also a scribe for radio entertainers Joe Penner, Ed Wynn, Ed Gardner, Jack Pearl and Ben Bernie. With that experience under his belt, Levy was a natural wordsmith for *Irma*. When Cy Howard needed still more help, Levy not only became the show's head writer, but directed some of its installments. He contributed significantly to the *Irma* movie scripts, too.

The years as an understudy prepared him to create his own winning broadcast entry. Using his mother-in-law as a model (who lived in his house in 1942), Levy developed the character of Lily Ruskin on CBS Radio (1952–53) and Television (1954–59) for *December Bride*. If the show did nothing else, it partially dispelled the black eye mothers-in-law had been saddled with for a lifetime. Actress Spring Byington imbued the figure of the widowed elder with love rather than formulaic conflict while she resided in her daughter's home.

Levy died March 8, 1993, only about seven weeks before Cy Howard's demise. He left behind his wife, the former Beatrice Spritzler of Philadelphia, a grown daughter, son and two grandchildren.

*My Friend Irma* was narrated by Jane Stacy in George Burns style—acknowledging the audience's presence by addressing it directly. Played by Cathy Lewis, Jane was Irma's roommate and best friend during the show's first half-dozen years.[3] She referred to Irma as "Cookie." Jane's categorical fondness for Irma and concern for her well-being was demonstrated time after time. She particularly took offense at Irma's overwhelming fascination with a man she (Jane) considered little more than a street hustler. For that's what he was. "Al has no job, no money, no clothes, no car, no prospects and no future," she contended. Irma replied wryly: "I know, but I have to stick with him in case things get tough." Al also had a number of shady characters in his life. One, whom he telephoned on each show ("Hello, Joe!") advised him on how to get ahead or solve a specific problem, often by circumventing the law.

It certainly couldn't have been easy for Jane to cope with the lame-brained rationalizations that Irma relayed, nor the complex dilemmas her roommate found herself in. Frequently Jane and others among their sphere of friendships were drawn into those crises, too. The resulting frustration often required all of the patience Jane could muster, even though she was demonstrably tender-hearted, dispatching gentle rebukes when they were absolutely necessary.

After Jane departed from the storyline

Men were drawn to this lighthearted piece of fluff, affirmed one radio historian, by "Wilson's sexy nasal voice and the sparky-sounding Lewis." My Friend Irma (actress Marie Wilson, right) was narrated by Jane Stacy (played by Cathy Lewis) in George Burns style—acknowledging the audience's presence by addressing it directly. For most of the run Jane and Irma (Peterson) were roommates and chums. Jane dubbed Irma "Cookie." A level-headed Jane's attitude toward the dimwitted ditzy dame was manifest in a concern for her emotional and mental health, expressed in sundry ways. Jane exhibited her feelings strongly when it came to Irma's selection of a boyfriend. Al, whom Irma chose, was regrettably shiftless, unemployed and carelessly content to mooch as well as smooch.

in 1953—her absence explained by a sudden move to Panama—Irma was linked with newspaper journalist Kay Foster as her new roommate. The character was brought to life by actress Mary Shipp.

There were others who fleshed out the plotting, contributing to a profusion of absurdities which each new chapter introduced. Among them was Irma's boyfriend, Al (actor John Brown), who apparently never offered a decipherable surname. Worse, for several years he had no job, although it didn't seem to faze him one bit. The impoverished, ambitionless con artist–suitor also had his own pet name for his sweetie pie: "Chicken." Al was so shiftless that at times it appeared Irma was the brains behind the organization. Scary! If that was the case, heaven help them. The fans knew how desperately in trouble that pair really was!

Another prominent member of the show's roster was the affluent investment counselor Richard Rhinelander III, Jane Stacy's bachelor employer, played by Leif Erickson. Jane was smitten with him, and—while she was level-headed—she desperately hoped he would ask her to marry him.[4] On one occasion, Jane mused pensively to Irma: "Wouldn't it be great if I wound up being Mrs. Richard Rhinelander the third?" "What good would that do if he's got two other wives?" Irma asked (seriously) in retort.

Others in the continuing cast included Irma's and Stacy's boardinghouse landlady, an aging Irish lass, Mrs. Kathleen O'Reilly (initially played by Jane Morgan, then by Gloria Gordon). The address of their rather ramshackle, rundown abode was 8224 West 73rd Street in New York City.

There was an upstairs tenant in the building, Professor Kropotkin (Hans Conried), a violinist whom the pair of roommates labeled "Maestro." He fiddled his time away at the Paradise Burlesque. The prof labeled the lower boarders "musical masterpieces," dubbing Jane a "Strauss Waltz" and Irma a "Nutcracker Suite." Furthermore, he kept the widowed Mrs. O'Reilly at arms' length, for she chased him perpetually. The musician

cared neither for her nor the falling down facility she managed. While she threw bouquets, he threw barbs.

Also appearing in the storyline was Alan Reed (nee Teddy Bergman) as frustrated attorney Milton J. Clyde, Irma's boss, and Myra Marsh as Mrs. Rhinelander, Richard's mom. While the latter was a wealthy socialite, she always seemed to sympathize with Irma and Jane and their plights. It was an uplifting touch and added a pleasant reverie to the calamity-prone plots. Finally, for a period in early 1949, as Cathy Lewis (Jane) recuperated from a brief illness, actress Joan Banks supplanted her.

The action in *My Friend Irma* ranged from the ridiculous to the sublime, but was clearly enough to keep audiences coming back. With the exception of *Our Miss Brooks*, launched in mid–1948, which persisted for nine years on radio, no other comedy narrative that debuted in that era (late 1940s, early 1950s) maintained its hold on audiences as effectively and durably as *My Friend Irma*. And none—including *Brooks*—premiering in that period earned the astonishing ratings that *Irma* consistently touted.[5] For three seasons (1947–50), in fact, it single-handedly approached, and even twice surpassed, the highly venerated level of 20.0 in the Hooper numbers. That was an almost unthinkable plateau for a fresh sitcom arriving that late in network radio's history.

In one late 1950 performance, Jane and Irma discussed their families. Jane hailed from nearby Connecticut; thus, she got to see her folks on at least an infrequent basis. It was evident that Irma was quite lonely in New York City, however, with all of her clan residing more than 1,500 miles away at the familial homestead in Minneapolis.

"They're just an average family just like me, perfectly normal people," she explained, punctuated by studio audience guffaws. Then she enumerated her tribe.

"There's Bertha Peterson, my younger sister—she's not as old as I am." (More laughter.)

"There's my brother, Ernie Peterson.

He's engaged—to be married, of course."
(Snickering.)

Jane inquired: "What about your parents?"

"I miss them the most," Irma replied. "They were just like a mother and father to me." (Further chortling.)

It was that kind of cornball dialogue that distinguished the show from most of its contemporaries. Beginning in 1950, after *George Burns and Gracie Allen* discontinued their radio series and moved to television exclusively, only *My Friend Irma* tendered such a prominent dame imbued with that much featherbrained fervor.

Irma once told Mr. Clyde, her employer, she was preoccupied with something.

"What do you mean?" he inquired.

"I mean, when I'm here, I'm not all there," she explained.

"You can say that again!" he shot back.

In another episode—in an exchange with Jane—the two women were looking at a global illustration. "What's this dotted line on the map of the world?" Irma pondered.

"Dotted line?" began Jane's reply. "Oh, that's the International Date Line."

Irma enthused: "Isn't that wonderful? Getting the boys and girls from different countries to go out with each other!"

Senseless to a fault it was.

The premises of the plots were as simple as the dialogue. One week Irma was writing a column for the local shopper newspaper. Jane told her if she wasn't careful about what she said she could be held for libel. "Liable for what?" was Irma's not totally unanticipated reply.

Another week, Richard was traveling to England for business on the Queen Mary. The girls threw him a bon voyage party shortly before his departure. Through the inevitable mix-ups, one could be certain that somebody who wasn't in the traveling party would still be aboard, mistakenly of course, once the ship was at sea. Surprise! It wasn't Irma. She was on the shore waving to Jane, Professor Kropotkin, Mrs. O'Reilly and Al, who didn't get the word to disembark!

Another time the girls and the professor were certain the boardinghouse was haunted, all of them claiming they saw a ghost in the hallway. The upshot of it was that one of the tenants left his clothes behind and slipped into the night wearing a sheet so as not to tip his wife off about the poker party he was routinely attending. (Sometimes the plots were as thin as the air Irma seemed to be breathing.)

Still another time the girls staged a costume party. That way, one of Al's cronies—wanted by the police for assorted offenses—was able to appear in disguise and never be recognized by the cops, who had been called to the address, even though the culprit was right under their noses. You had to have been listening for it to make any sense at all.

Nevertheless, the radio series created such a hullabaloo that not one but two films were produced, capitalizing on the theme of the ditzy blonde. The first, simply titled *My Friend Irma*, was released in 1949 and is primarily recalled for introducing moviegoers to Dean Martin and Jerry Lewis. The music-comedy duo's exposure led to even more screen time for the pair in the sequel *My Friend Irma Goes West*, released in 1950.

In the preliminary flick Martin and Lewis were showbiz wannabes who earned their livelihoods as juice bar operators. They were "discovered" after self-proclaimed talent scout Al, Irma's unemployed swain, heard Martin's golden-throated warbling. Jane, meanwhile, who originally wanted to marry her affluent boss, was ultimately attracted to Martin, while Irma meddled in her roommate's romance, inescapably confusing several issues. In addition to Martin (Steve Laird) and Lewis (Seymour, sans surname), Marie Wilson played Irma, Diana Lynn was Jane, John Lund was Al, Don DeFore was Richard Rhinelander III, Hans Conried was Professor Kropotkin, Kathryn Givney was Mrs. Rhinelander and Gloria Gordon was Mrs. O'Reilly. Thus, three of the radio cast won their same roles in the initial flick.

In the second flick Steve (Dean Martin), Seymour (Jerry Lewis) and Irma (Marie Wilson) were mistaken when they convinced themselves that Steve had secured a Hollywood movie deal. The trio boarded a train for California only to be thwarted by a screwball kidnapping plot involving a Tinseltown celebrity, her pet monkey and some menacing mobsters. "This is easily the funniest and most deep-down-hardy chuckle-inducing film that the fabulous comedy duo of Dean Martin and Jerry Lewis have ever starred in," attested a critic. "In between Martin's dulcet tones as he sings some original songs ... Jerry is at his peak, complete with his legendary, goofy humor, delayed-reaction one-liners, and pratfalls." Beyond the principals, the cast included Diana Lynn and John Lund reprising their earlier roles. New characters were portrayed by Corinne Calvet and Lloyd Corrigan.

All of this eventually prompted a *My Friend Irma* television series, which appeared on CBS from January 8, 1952, through June 25, 1954. It was the very first continuing program to be telecast from CBS's brand new Television City in Hollywood, and it originated live. The video cast included these from the radio series in their usual roles: Marie Wilson, Cathy Lewis, Mary Shipp and Gloria Gordon. Playing Al on TV was Sid Tomack; Brooks West appeared as Richard Rhinelander III; Margaret DuMont was Mrs. Rhinelander; Sig Arno was Professor Kropotkin; and Donald McBride was Milton J. Clyde. Other notable actors in the small screen adaptation included Hal March (as Joe Vance) and John Carradine (as Mr. Corday, an eccentric actor who turned up in 1953 after the professor departed from the storyline).

Katherine Elizabeth (Marie) Wilson was born very near Hollywood at Anaheim, California, on August 19, 1916. Although she demonstrated talent on the East Coast early in her entertainment pursuits—originally as a Broadway dancer—at 18 she migrated back to her roots to win parts in 51 mostly B-level motion pictures between 1934 and 1962. They included less-than-memorable monikers like *Ladies Crave Excitement* (1935), *The Big Noise* (1936), *Public Wedding* (1937), *Boy Meets Girl* (1938), *Should Husbands Work?* (1939), *Harvard, Here I Come!* (1941), *You Can't Ration Love* (1944), *No Leave, No Love* (1946), *The Fabulous Joe* (1947), *Linda Be Good* (1947) and *Marry Me Again* (1953).

As time wore on Wilson became stuck in lighthearted plots as a proverbial featherbrained figure, the kind that made her such a famous hit on *My Friend Irma*. Nevertheless, she must have harbored at least some resentment of the depiction, for she once told a reporter: "Show business has been very good to me and I'm not complaining, but some day I just wish someone would offer me a different kind of role. My closest friends admit that whenever they tell someone they know me they have to convince them that I'm really not dumb. To tell you the truth, I think people are disappointed that I'm not." The tinge of sadness in her revelation was unmistakable. While the show made Marie Wilson widely known, it pigeonholed her beyond redemption.

*Radio Life* noted: "She has that same touching sincerity, the same steady wide-eyed gaze. She can keep an admirable poker face through the most idiotic conversations.... She loves everything and everybody, and there isn't a person in the world that she doesn't call 'honey' with sincerest regard." *My Friend Irma* creator and wordsmith Cy Howard concurred. "She's so much like Irma that I have to rewrite the things she says to make them believable," said he.

Wilson appeared in a couple of made-for-TV films, in addition to the large body of theatrical productions. She vocalized in one TV special, turned up in 11 single guest shots on the tube (*The Tennessee Ernie Ford Show*, *Toast of the Town*, *Burke's Law*, *Love American Style* and a few more) and played in one added feature besides *My Friend Irma*: she provided voiceovers for CBS-TV's pithy *Where's Huddles?* summertime animated cartoon series (originated in 1970, rerun in 1971).

Beyond all of that she starred in summer stock and dinner-theater productions like *Born Yesterday* while appearing in commercials and pursuing a nightclub act after her celluloid career began to fade. Married three times, Wilson was divorced twice. She was the wife of Robert Fallon from December 15, 1951, until her death from cancer at age 56 on November 23, 1972, in Hollywood. A biography, *Not So Dumb: The Life and Career of Marie Wilson*, by Charles Tranberg, was released by BearManor Media in 2006.

Cathy Lewis (Jane Stacy) was born December 27, 1916—just four months after Marie Wilson—in Spokane, Washington. Lewis (her real name) arrived in Hollywood in 1936 with the intent of becoming a vocalist, something she made good on as she sang early in her career with bandleader Kay Kyser's venerated outfit. Following an apprenticeship in acting at the Pasadena Playhouse, she signed a contract with Metro-Goldwyn-Mayer. Between 1940 and 1962 she appeared in 15 cinematic productions, also of the B-flick persuasion. They included long since forgotten titles like *Soak the Old* (1940), *Model Wife* (1941), *Double Trouble* (1941), *Slightly Dangerous* (1943) and *The Party Crashers* (1958). Following *My Friend Irma*, Lewis performed as the longsuffering spouse in a short-lived NBC-TV rendition of *Fibber McGee and Molly*. She acted opposite Bob Sweeney there in 1959–60.

Like Marie Wilson, Lewis, too, made 11 single-shot television appearances on such popular series as *Route 66*, *Death Valley Days*, *Hazel*, *Wagon Train* and *F Troop*. But unlike Wilson, Lewis devoted a whole lot of her early career to radio, where her name was quickly recognized by legions of listeners in the 1940s and 1950s. Introduced to prolific radio impresario Elliott Lewis[6] by a mutual acquaintance who reveled in the coincidence of their last names, Elliott Lewis and Cathy Lewis became man and wife on April 30, 1943. Before their divorce some 15 years later,[7] the couple worked together in radio frequently, including playing supporting roles in *The Adventures of Sam Spade, Detective* (1946–51), *The Clock* (1948), *I Love a Mystery* (1940s–1952), *Plays for Americans* (1942), *Suspense* (1953) and *The Whistler* (1940s, 1950s).

Without any doubt, however, their most memorable professional collaboration was on CBS Radio's *On Stage* dramatic anthology, often listed as *Cathy and Elliott Lewis On Stage*. It ran weekly between January 1, 1953, and September 30, 1954. Radio scholar John Dunning offered his readers an insightful perspective on the series:

> The time was right in 1952, when they [the Lewises] had reached the top in radio; known in the industry as "Mr. and Mrs. Radio," they were the busiest people on the air. In addition to producing and directing *Suspense*, Elliott was running *Broadway Is My Beat*.... He was also playing his greatest comedy role, the hard-drinking guitar player ... Elliott Lewis ... on *The Phil Harris/Alice Faye Show*. Cathy was busy as Jane Stacy on *My Friend Irma*, on radio and TV. The TV show was the time-killer, she said: it took many times the commitment of the radio series, and she was to drop it in 1953.
>
> In late 1952, the Lewises ... began forming their own production company. This was called Haven Radio Productions, named for the home they occupied in Beverly Hills. Through this entity they would produce and transcribe their show. The stories would be rooted in powerful male-female situations, with two characters of equal strength.... Many transcriptions were saved, and the present is enriched by *On Stage* on tape, a vivid example of how good radio could be.

Director George Allen, who presided over radio's *The Whistler* crime melodrama from 1944 to 1955, observed that Cathy and Elliott Lewis were both "full-range players." Allen added: "Elliott can sound like the average guy under pressure, and he builds emotion fast and holds it at a peak. Cathy has the same qualities as Elliott, the female counterpart of the average guy in her ability to sound absolutely genuine."

In addition to the preceding credits, Cathy Lewis was also in the recurring casts of radio's *The Amazing Mrs. Danberry* (1946), *The Eddie Bracken Show* (1945, 1946–47), *The Great Gildersleeve* (1950s), *Michael Shayne* (1945–47) and *Whispering Streets* (1950s). She turned up in the repertory companies fleshing out *The Adventures of Bill Lance* (1944–45), *The Dreft Star Playhouse* (1943–45), *The Theater of Famous*

*Radio Players* (1945–46) and *Twelve Players* (1945, 1948).

Cathy Lewis died of lung cancer at age 50 in Hollywood on November 20, 1968. Succumbing to cancer in her fifties in Hollywood were yet three more uncanny parallels the actress shared with her old "roomie" Marie Wilson.

Mary Shipp was Lewis's replacement on *My Friend Irma*, in the character of Kay Foster. Her vita sheet is sparse at first glance when compared with those of the other leads. She was born at Los Angeles on September 17, 1915, studied ballet and performed on stage at age eight. Subsequently she majored in dramatics at Los Angeles City College. Her only film was 1953's *Jennifer*; her only TV series beyond *My Friend Irma* (1953–54, concurrent with the last year on radio) was CBS's *Life with Luigi*. (*Luigi* and *Irma* were both fashioned by an imaginative Cy Howard, you will recall.) In 1952–53 she reprised her radio role there as Miss Spaulding. Shipp appeared on nine single installments of other video series, however, among them *You Are There*, *Dragnet*, *Zane Grey Theater*, *Perry Mason* and *The Donna Reed Show*.

After debuting on NBC's *The Packard Show* in 1937, Shipp became a busy radio thespian, turning up in recurring roles in a quintet of aural sitcoms: *The Aldrich Family* (1939–1940s, where she appeared in two parts at various times, as Henry's sister Mary, and as his girlfriend Kathleen Anderson), *The Great Gildersleeve* (ca. late 1940s, early 1950s, as one of Throckmorton P.'s bevy of beauties), *Life with Luigi* (1948–53, as Miss Spaulding, Luigi's night school teacher who taught him U.S. civics), *My Best Girls* (1944–45, as Linda Bartlett, one of three daughters and *Rocky Jordan* (1951).

Beyond those steady assignments Shipp was active on several radio series, sporadically performing on *Broadway Is My Beat* (1949–54), *Make-Believe Town, Hollywood* (1949–50), *The Milton Berle Show* (1947–48), *The Saint* (ca. 1947–51) and *The Whistler* (ca. 1942–1955). In 1939 she wed radio producer Harry S. Ackerman (1912–91),[8] and the couple

adopted a son. They divorced shortly before he wed Elinor Donahue, 25 years his junior, of *Father Knows Best* fame, in 1961.[9]

Mrs. O'Reilly, the Irish landlady who ran the rooming house Irma and her friends lived in, was briefly portrayed by Jane Morgan, but for most of the run by Gloria Gordon. Morgan's biography appears in the chapter on *Our Miss Brooks* in this text, a sitcom with which she is much better identified.

Gloria Gordon, the mother of Gale Gordon (Osgood Conklin in *Our Miss Brooks*, Rudolph Atterbury in *My Favorite Husband*, Mayor LaTrivia and the Weatherman on *Fibber McGee & Molly*, and Lucille Ball's incessant foil on multiple TV sitcoms), was born in England on May 7, 1884. She became a stage actress and married a vaudevillian, Charles Aldrich.[10] Later, in this country, Gordon earned a handful of radio credits, among them a recurring characterization on NBC's *The Jack Benny Program* in the mid-to-late 1940s, supporting roles in a syndicated *Favorite Story* (1946–49), a continuing part in NBC's *The Halls of Ivy* (1950–52) and an ongoing role in that web's daytime soapy saga *Doctor Paul* (1951–53).

Before that, beginning with 1926's *Dancing Days*, Gordon appeared in a quartet of B-movie theatrical releases. In addition, she performed in 1949's *My Friend Irma*, reprising her radio role as Mrs. O'Reilly on the big screen. She did the same in the TV incarnation (1952–54), and also made one other appearance on *The Jack Benny Program* on CBS-TV in 1954. Gordon died in Hollywood on November 21, 1962. She was 78.

The part of Al was played by John H. Brown, another native English actor, born at Hull, Great Britain, on April 4, 1904. Later, in America, while attempting to break into radio, he derived his principal livelihood as a mortician's clerk in New York City. It seems ironic, since one of the most unforgettable roles he would later play—in dual mediums— was as an undertaker. As a sideline, Brown turned up in a handful of pithy New York stage productions, including *Peace on Earth* (1933–34 and a reprise in the following spring), *The Milky Way* (1934) and *The Pirate* (1942–43). Meanwhile, when the call finally arrived for a radio audition, it didn't take him long to reach the big time.

Brown's dossier could have given rise to the hackneyed expression "Well I'll be John Brown!" The industrious thespian packed a normal lifetime for most audio entertainers into an all-too-brief 52 years, ending with his demise on May 16, 1957, at West Hollywood, California. Brown might not have been stretching the truth when he guessed that he was part of 15,000 radio programs, including 10,000 airing live and half as many via transcriptions. He was active on more than two dozen network gigs.

He won continuing roles in all of the following: *The Adventures of Ozzie and Harriet* (1944–54, where he was neighbor "Thorny" Thornberry), *The Amazing Mr. Smith* (1941), *The Bickersons* (1946–48, 1951), *The Busy Mr. Bingle* (1943, in the namesake role), *The Charlotte Greenwood Show* (1944–46), *The Damon Runyon Theater* (1948–49, as "Broadway," the narrator), *The Danny Kaye Show* (1945–46, as "Mr. Average Radio Listener"), *A Date with Judy* (1944–50, as Melvin Foster, Judy's dad), *A Day in the Life of Dennis Day* (1946–51, as Mr. Willoughby, Day's employer), *December Bride* (1952–53), *The Fred Allen Show* (1939–44, as "John Doe"), *The Gay Mrs. Featherstone* (1945), *The Life of Riley* (1944–51, in dual roles, as Gillis, Riley's chum and colleague, and Digby "Digger" O'Dell, "the friendly undertaker"), *Lorenzo Jones* (ca. 1937–ca. 1939, as Jim Barker, Jones' employer), *Maisie* (1945–47, 1949–51, 1952), *The Mel Torme Show* (1948, as Torme's college dean), *The Saint* (1940s, as Inspector Fernak) and *Tillie the Toiler* (1942, as Simpkins, Tillie's employer).

In addition, Brown played in repertory companies that supplied actors for multiple series: *Beulah* (1947–54), *Columbia Presents Corwin* (1941), *The Eddie Cantor Show* (1935–39, 1940–49), *The Edgar Bergen and Charlie McCarthy Show* (1940s, ca. early 1950s), *Lincoln Highway* (1940–42), *The Mercury Theater on the Air* (1946), *Mystery in the Air* (1945), *The Shadow* (1940s), *Twelve Players* (1948) and *The Whistler* (1942–55).

Furthermore, he reprised one of his most memorable radio roles on television. Brown was mortician Digby "Digger" O'Dell on NBC-TV's *The Life of Riley* in 1949–50 but did not return to the show when it was renewed from 1953 to 1958. In the meantime, in 1951 he resurfaced for a few weeks as Harry Morton, next door neighbor of CBS-TV's *George Burns and Gracie Allen*. He didn't last long, however, discarded after being blacklisted during the "red scare" of the early 1950s for being perceived as a communist sympathizer.[11]

For most of the run, the part of Professor Kropotkin—the fiddler on the roof (er, ah, second floor) at the rooming house where Irma Peterson and her roommates resided—was played by a fantastic dialectician, Hans Conried. Few voice actors equaled his versatility in portraying eastern European figures. "His inimitable growl and impeccable diction were perfectly suited for portraying comic villains and other mock-sinister or cranky types," one reviewer assessed. His wide range of inflections had a profound effect on the myriad of roles he won over an intensely demanding professional career. Born of Jewish parents at Baltimore, Maryland, on April 15, 1917, Hans Georg Conried Jr. grew up there and in New York City, studying dramatics at the latter's Columbia University.

He played many classical Shakespearean characterizations onstage before radio, where he worked profusely in a score of network series. There were recurring portrayals in *Blondie* (1939–1940s), *December Bride* (1952–53, as the cheerless, pessimistic neighbor Pete Porter), *The Gallant Heart* (1944), *It's a Great Life* (1948), *Joan Davis Time* (1947–48), *The Judy Canova Show* (1943–44, 1945–ca. 1953, as the cantankerous houseguest Mr. Hemingway), *The Life of Riley* (1944–51, as Uncle Baxter, an eternal parasite who unremittingly reminded Riley that he once loaned him a pint of blood), *Life with Luigi* (1948–53, as Schultz, a surly German pupil at Luigi's night school), *Maisie* (1945–47) and *The Mel Blanc Show* (1946–47, as Mr. Cushing, president of "The Loyal Order of Benevolent Zebras," Mel's lodge).

Conried was also regularly tapped for appearances in the radio casts of *The George Burns and Gracie Allen Show* (1942–50), *The Damon Runyon Theater* (1948–49), *Escape* (1947–54), *Favorite Story* (1946–49), *Orson Welles Theater* (1941–42, 1944), *Plays for Americans* (1942), *Romance* (1954–57), *The Sears Radio Theater,* aka *The Mutual Radio Theater* (1979–81) and *The Whistler* (1942–55). Director George Allen of the latter series branded the thespian "a marvelous straight lead with tangents, a lead with two faces, a split personality."

In the late 1940s and early 1950s the versatile Conried occasionally directed an episode of CBS Radio's *Stars Over Hollywood* dramatic anthology. In 1953–54 he performed in the original cast of Cole Porter's Broadway hit *Can-Can.* His sharp wit and intellect made him a natural for television and theatrical films, too. The seemingly inexhaustible entertainer appeared in 90 movies in cinema palaces and in 22 more screened on television. He was cast 91 times in solo TV performances and turned up in 19 video series, including eight animated cartoons, where he provided voiceovers for continuing figures.

While the majority of Conried's earlier full-length motion pictures were quickly forgotten B-flicks—*Unexpected Uncle* (1941), *The Big Street* (1942), *His Butler's Sister* (1943), *The Beach Nut* (1944), *Chew-Chew Baby* (1945) and *Well Oiled* (1947)—as time progressed, he won roles in a few memorable films. In addition to 1949's *My Friend Irma,* where he exhibited one of his most famous radio roles, there was *I'll See You in My Dreams* (1951), *You're Never Too Young* (1955), *Bus Stop* (1956), *The Big Beat* (1958), *1001 Arabian Nights* (1959), *The Patsy* (1964) and *The Shaggy D.A.* (1976).

From 1956 to 1964 Conried portrayed Uncle Tonoose on *The Danny Thomas Show,* aka *Make Room for Daddy,* at different times on the ABC and CBS television networks. In a sequel, *Make Room for Granddaddy,* on ABC-TV in 1970–71, Conried again played Uncle Tonoose. He was Wyatt Franklin on CBS-TV's *The Tony Randall Show* (1977–78).

Among the myriad shows Conried stopped by for solitary visits were *To Tell the Truth, The Jack Paar Tonight Show, Pantomime Quiz, The Tonight Show Starring Johnny Carson, This Is Your Life, Match Game 77, Disneyland, Mr. and Mrs. North, I Love Lucy, Four Star Playhouse, The Alcoa Hour, Playhouse 90, Schlitz Playhouse of Stars, The Real McCoys, Dragnet, The Californians, The Donna Reed Show, The U.S. Steel Hour, Have Gun—Will Travel, Mister Ed, The Lucy Show, Dr. Kildare, Burke's Law, Ben Casey, Gilligan's Island, Hogan's Heroes, Lost in Space, The Beverly Hillbillies, Daniel Boone, The Brady Bunch, Here's Lucy, Love American Style, Laverne & Shirley, The Love Boat, Alice* and *Fantasy Island.*

Conried married Margaret Grant on January 29, 1942. She bore him four children. He was still married to her when he died of cardiovascular disease in Burbank, California, on January 5, 1982. It was three weeks shy of the couple's 40th anniversary. His body was donated to medical science.

Not to be confused with an Icelandic explorer named Leif Erickson (980–1025 A.D., with multiple spellings of the moniker)—whose voyages to Norway, Greenland and Newfoundland are recorded in the history books—the actor Leif Erickson (who was actually born under the appellation William Anderson) portrayed Richard Rhinelander III in *My Friend Irma* on radio. He was Jane Stacy's employer and, for a while, at least, her all-consuming passion.

Born October 27, 1911, at Alameda, California, the entertainer was a vocalist and instrumentalist before turning up in the first of his 77 motion pictures, playing a singer backed by Ted Fio Rito's band in 1933's *Sweetheart of Sigma Chi.* Some other B-movies in his repertoire: *Girl of the Ozarks* (1936), *One Third of a Nation* (1939), *Are Husbands Necessary?* (1942), *Pardon My Sarong* (1942), *The Snake Pit* (1948), *Johnny Stool Pigeon* (1949), *Love That Brute* (1950), *Three Secrets* (1950) and *The Tall Target* (1951). Erickson also appeared in his share of better known, better received flicks, including: *Sorry, Wrong Number* (1948), *Show Boat* (1951), *With a Song in My Heart* (1952),

*Carbine Williams* (1952), *On the Waterfront* (1954), *Tea and Sympathy* (1956), *A Gathering of Eagles* (1963) and *I Saw What You Did* (1965).

In addition, Erickson performed in nine made-for-television films, one series (as the hero of NBC-TV's hour-long western *The High Chaparral*, 1967–71), and 71 one-time-only video outings (among them: *Schlitz Playhouse of Stars, Climax!, Alfred Hitchcock Presents, General Electric Theater, The Millionaire, The Rifleman, Zane Grey Theater, Playhouse 90, Rawhide, Wagon Train, Hazel, Burke's Law, Bonanza, The Virginian, Daniel Boone, Gunsmoke, The Mod Squad, Marcus Welby, M.D., The Streets of San Francisco, Cannon, The Rockford Files* and *Fantasy Island*).

Twice wed, both times to movie actresses, Erickson divorced Frances Farmer on June 12, 1942, after six years of marriage. He walked the aisle with Margaret Hayes on June 12, 1942, and their union ended in divorce a month later.[12] His death, by cancer, occurred at Pensacola, Florida, on January 29, 1986. He had no children.

In the aural incarnation, Alan Reed (nee Theodore Alan Bergman) was Milton J. Clyde, *My Friend Irma*'s superior in the storyline. A native New Yorker, he was born in that city on August 20, 1907, ultimately emerging as a talented and busy thespian on both the small and big screens. Reed is particularly recalled for his robust, matchless voice. His versatility encompassed 22 dialects. "He gave vocal life to the prehistoric cartoon character Fred Flintstone on the prime-time TV series *The Flintstones* in the 60s," one pundit assessed. He derived the catchphrase "Yabba dabba doo!" that contributed to making the animated figure so unforgettable. "It is this direct association that has kept his name alive long after his passing," the critic surmised.

For several years after high school, Teddy Bergman and his cousin, Harry Green, worked for stock companies touring vaudeville circuits. Majoring in journalism at Columbia University, Bergman acted at Provincetown Playhouse, too. Eventually he landed on Broadway. In the meantime, radio had debuted, offering all sorts of opportunities for serious and comedic acting. Bergman altered his moniker to Alan Reed, reportedly "to break the trap of his Jewish identity." In radio he discovered that his birth sobriquet often limited him to parts with ethnic brogues.

His arrival on the ether coincided with the launching of the national chains, his introduction being by way of *The Eveready Hour* variety show on NBC (1926–30). Over a radio career that persisted to the latter days of the medium's golden age, Reed performed regularly on more than four dozen network series, among them: *The Adventures of Philip Marlowe* (1947, 1948–50, 1951), *The Adventures of Sam Spade, Detective* (1946–51), *Baby Snooks* (1936, 1937–ca. mid–1940s), *Big Sister* (ca. late 1930s–mid–1940s), *The Collier Hour* (ca. 1927–32), *December Bride* (1952–53), *Duffy's Tavern* (1940, 1941–ca. 1944), *Escape* (1947–54), *The Fred Allen Show* (1939–44), *The Halls of Ivy* (1950–52), *The Life of Riley* (ca. 1941, ca. 1944–ca. 1951), *Life with Luigi* (1948–53), *Myrt and Marge* (ca. 1930s, early 1940s), *The Rudy Vallee Show* (mid–1930s–ca. early 1940s), *The Shadow* (ca. 1930s) and *Valiant Lady* (1938–ca. 1944). Most of the time Reed was on radio as a thespian; a few times he was the designated announcer, introducing, narrating, delivering commercial pitches and signing off shows.

After his comic part as Falstaff Openshaw folded in 1944 on *The Fred Allen Show*—Reed was one of the original residents of Allen's Alley—he left New York to relocate in the Los Angeles area. That same year he developed into a B-movie thespian. By the time of his demise more than three decades later he had turned up in 34 celluloid productions screened in cinema palaces, several of which took him beyond the usual unmemorable B-flicks like *Actors and Sin* (1952), *Teachers Are People* (1952), *Two Weeks Vacation* (1952), *Woman's World* (1954) and *He Laughed Last* (1956) to some pretty stunning fare: *The Postman Always Rings Twice* (1946), *The Redhead and the Cowboy* (1951), *Lady and the Tramp* (1955), *The Revolt of Mamie Stover* (1956), *Peyton*

*Place* (1957), *Marjorie Morningstar* (1958), *1001 Arabian Nights* (1959) and *Breakfast at Tiffany's* (1961).

Reed performed in ongoing roles in nine television series, two-thirds of which were voiceovers for animated cartoons. The rest were as Pasquale in CBS's *Life with Luigi* (1952–53), Charlie Finnegan in the syndicated *Duffy's Tavern* (1954) and Happy Richman in NBC's *Peter Loves Mary* (1960–61). He was tapped for a quartet of made-for-TV movies and appeared in another 36 one-time-only episodes of TV series, such as *TV Reader's Digest*, *Goodyear Television Playhouse*, *Damon Runyon Theater*, *Alfred Hitchcock Presents*, *The Gale Storm Show*, *The Bob Cummings Show*, *The Donna Reed Show*, *Have Gun—Will Travel*, *Richard Diamond—Private Detective*, *Michael Shayne*, *The Lucy Show*, *The Dick Van Dyke Show*, *My Favorite Martian*, *The Addams Family*, *Dr. Kildare*, *Batman*, *The Mothers-in-Law*, *The Beverly Hillbillies* and *Petticoat Junction*.

Alan Reed was married only once, to actress Finnette Walker (1909–2005), from 1932 until his death. She was in the chorus line of the original 1934 Broadway production of *Anything Goes*, starring Ethel Merman. The Reeds produced a trio of sons; one, Alan Reed, Jr., followed in his dad's footsteps, becoming a renowned actor. Following a lengthy illness, the elder Reed died of a heart attack on June 14, 1977, in Los Angeles.

Finally, playing Mrs. Rhinelander, Richard's mom, in radio's *My Friend Irma* was Myra Marsh. Born in Maine on July 6, 1894, between 1935's *Paddy O'Day* and 1955's *The Cobweb*, she was showcased in 37 (mostly B) motion pictures. They included *Your Uncle Dudley* (1935), *Anthony Adverse* (1936), *More Than a Secretary* (1936), *Rascals* (1938), *Boy Friend* (1939), *The Dog in the Orchard* (1941), *The Moonlighter* (1953), *Down Three Dark Streets* (1954) and more. She was also a visitor to a half-dozen television series for single outings, including *Hopalong Cassidy*, *I Love Lucy*, *Dragnet* and *Letter to Loretta*. Marsh died October 29, 1964, in Los Angeles.

In contemporary America it seems almost unthinkable that a broadcast series about a deficient legal stenographer whose elevator plainly didn't go all the way to the penthouse could have created much of a stir—pulling in millions of followers. And it did so not merely as a solitary summer replacement but by persisting for more than *seven* radio seasons! Even more startling is the fact that such fare spawned a couple of full-length motion pictures that packed the Bijous, Rialtos and Orpheums all over the land. And that there was a television run that proffered the same premise for two full seasons, concurrent with the radio articulation's later run. It happened, nonetheless. *My Friend Irma* wowed 'em. Much of America laughed out loud at her dimwitted antics at mid–20th century. While the program was unabashedly stereotypical, for that epoch it was all in jest. Legions got a large charge out of it every time out.

## 19

# *Our Miss Brooks*

## THE TEACHER YOU ALWAYS WISHED YOU HAD

She was the favorite schoolmarm of her pupils "and of all America," one pundit conjectured. Miss Constance Brooks (Eve Arden in real life), English teacher at the fictional Madison High School—with a penchant for witty comebacks and acerbic reproofs—was celebrated by more than one generation of her countrymen at the middle of the last century. Real students and parents viewed her clever put-downs of sophomoric study approaches by—who else?—sophomores as one of acceptance rather than rebuke, the latter left for "legitimate" teachers. Not only that, Miss Brooks turned out to be the perfect challenger to the blustery buffoon who was principal Osgood Conklin (played by Gale Gordon). He barked orders to the minions of his little domain—and became a man that she and the students enjoyed pulling a good-natured prank on. Who couldn't love a teacher like that? Too bad for her that those cataclysms she activated often backfired, and her involvement was inexorably exposed to Mr. Conklin. In a real world she would have been fired after so many infractions, but this was radio and she was insulated against anything that ghastly. In the meantime, on the sidelines Miss Brooks pursued a one-sided courtship with a bashful biology instructor that was simply going nowhere; it, too, could be funny in (not) getting there. She linked herself with ingenious and dimwitted scholars whose attempts to carry out the simplest instructions were somehow inescapably beset by ill fortune, often prompting colossal mix-ups that netted hysterical consequences. Their sitcom arrived shortly before radio's heyday began to wane. For nine years the feature was a mainstay in the nation's homes, as the antics of this cool, calculating academician inspired laughs galore and made every high school student in America wish for a "genuine" instructor like *Our Miss Brooks*.

❖ ❖ ❖

**Producer:** Larry Berns

**Director-Chief Writer:** Al Lewis

**Co-writers:** Arthur Alsberg, Lou Derman, John Quillan

**Musical Director-Orchestra Conductor:** Wilbur Hatch

**Sound Effects Technician:** Bill Gould

**Announcers:** Bob Lemond, Jimmy Mathews, Roy Rowan

**Commercial Spokesman:** Verne Smith (1948–54)

**Recurring Cast:** *Connie Brooks:* Eve Arden (nee Eunice Quedens); *Osgood Conklin:* Gale Gordon (nee Charles T. Aldrich, Jr.); *Philip Boynton:* Jeff Chandler (1948–53), Robert Rockwell (1953–57); *Walter Denton:* Richard Crenna; *Margaret (Maggie) Davis:* Jane Morgan; *Fabian (Stretch) Snodgrass:* Leonard Smith; *Harriet Conklin:* Gloria McMillan; *Edgar T. Stone:* Joseph Kearns; *Daisy Enright:* Mary Jane Croft; *Mr. LeBlanc:* Maurice Marsac; *Jacques Monet:* Gerald Mohr; *Martha Conklin:* Virginia Gordon

**Sponsors:** Sustained (July–September 1948); Colgate-Palmolive-Peet, Inc., for Colgate Dental Cream and tooth powder, Lustre Crème shampoo, Palmolive soap and brushless shaving cream, Vel dishwashing liquid and other personal care and household goods (October 3, 1948–June 27, 1954);

American Home Products, for Anacin pain reliever, Kolynos toothpaste, Bi-So-Dol analgesic, Kriptin antihistamine, Freezone corn remover, Dristan and Primatene cold remedies and other health care commodities (1954–56); The Toni Company, for Toni home permanent, Toni Crème shampoo and rinse, White Rain shampoo, Deep Magic beauty cream and other hair care and cosmetics preparations (1954–56); Multiple Participation (1957)

**Theme:** "Brooks Theme," aka "Our Miss Brooks Theme" (Wilbur J. Hatch)[1]

**Ratings:** High—14.6 (1949–50), Low—4.3 (1955–56), Median—9.1 (1948–56 only)

**On the Air:** July 19–September 13, 1948, CBS, Monday (time unsubstantiated); September 19, 1948–August 28, 1949, CBS, Sunday, 9:30–10:00 P.M. Eastern Time; September 11, 1949–May 28, 1950, CBS, Sunday, 6:30–7:00 P.M.; September 3, 1950–July 1, 1951, CBS, Sunday, 6:30–7:00 P.M.; October 7, 1951–June 29, 1952, CBS, Sunday, 6:30–7:00 P.M.; October 5, 1952–June 28, 1953, CBS, Sunday, 6:30–7:00 P.M.; October 4, 1953–June 27, 1954, CBS, Sunday, 6:30–7:00 P.M.; September 26, 1954–June 17, 1956, CBS, Sunday, 8:00–8:30 P.M. (1954–55), 8:05–8:30 P.M. (1955–56).; January 6–June 30, 1957, CBS, Sunday, 7:30–8:00 P.M.

**Extant Archival Material:** Six *Our Miss Brooks* radio scripts are maintained in the private collection of Fuller French by the Broadcast Arts Library, Box 9828, Fort Worth, TX, 76147; (310) 288–6511; *www.broadcastartslibrary.com.*

Scripts, production notes and related memos from long runs of *Our Miss Brooks* are archived in the KNX Script Collection supplied by the Los Angeles CBS affiliate at Thousand Oaks Library, American Radio Archives, 1401 East Janss Road, Thousand Oaks, CA, 91362; (805) 449–2660; fax (805) 449–2675; *www.tol.lib.ca.us.*

Al Lewis Radio and Television Scripts, 1943–1954, including *Our Miss Brooks* scripts that the head writer-director penned between 1948 and 1954, are archived at the University of California at Los Angeles (UCLA) Charles E. Young Research Library, Room 22478, Box 951575, Los Angeles, CA, 90095; (310) 825–7253; fax (310) 825–1210; *www.library.ucla.edu/libraries/arts/.*

The Lou Derman Papers, 1944–1975, includes *Our Miss Brooks* scripts from December 1953 to June 1954 at UCLA's Charles E. Young Research Library (see above).

*Our Miss Brooks* Scripts, 1950–1956, a collection of the radio scripts for April 1950 to April 1956, with some gaps (episodes 82–336), and television scripts for February 1952 to April 1955 (episodes 1–100), are housed at UCLA's Charles E. Young Research Library (see above).

No fewer than 185 recordings of *Our Miss Brooks* shows were in general circulation or held by private collectors as of 2006, sold by vintage radio dealers and traded by old-time radio hobbyists.

❖ ❖ ❖

When CBS added a half-hour situation comedy to its Sunday night lineup in the summer of 1948 that glorified the public school classroom, professional educators nationwide took notice. Large numbers rose up en masse to give the feature their unqualified endorsement—and their undivided attention. With few exceptions, most found the new series to their liking: it seemed to recognize—and even ordain—the rather thankless and unheralded tasks they had been performing all along. "At last, a teacher was seen as something other than a boring, sexless, freak of nature," declared a reviewer, recalling the stereotypically rigid instructors that the airwaves had heretofore traditionally fostered on listeners.

Now, for the first time ever, the ether was presenting a comely, wisecracking, down-to-earth woman who possessed a colossal amount of charm and the ability to cope with the daily grind required of teachers. Simultaneously, she exhibited resolute strength that allowed her to withstand and not take too seriously the sometimes incredible pressures meted out by an overbearing administrator's demands. "*Our Miss Brooks* ... dared to depict a woman, funny, attractive, wise, competent and working—outside the home, marriage, and children," a radio scholar astutely perceived. This teacher was, another observer allowed, among broadcasting's "noblest working women: the center of a highly successful show, toiling in a realistically portrayed, and unglamorized career." It proffered a novel premise at an auspicious moment.

*Our Miss Brooks* turned into a boisterous siege of unbridled glee. It became one of CBS's most universally beloved comedies. For nine years, in fact—as their weekends drew to a conclusion—legions of radio listeners across America routinely dissolved into side-splitting laughter via the aural antics of mythical Madison High School English teacher

Constance (Connie) Brooks. She was flanked by a cadre of recurring and decidedly eccentric characters, giving rise to her misbehavior.

So popular was this audio celebration of American education that its star, actress Eve Arden, was offered several authentic teaching jobs. (This, despite the fact that she only completed high school. "I wasn't as smart as Connie Brooks," said she. "I played Connie as I remembered my third grade teacher, Miss Waterman.")

Thousands of communications arrived for her annually, nonetheless. In addition to letters from a broad-based spectrum of admiring fans, Arden received scads of appreciative and heartfelt correspondence from educators who poured out their frustrating plights in dealing with school-related responsibilities. They absolutely adored her when she reminded everybody how poorly—as a teacher—she was paid! At the same time, Arden was invited to address PTA meetings all over the country, while being elected to honorary membership in the National Education Association and, in 1952, awarded a citation by the Teachers College of Connecticut alumni for "humanizing the American Teacher." The academicians indeed rose up to call her blessed!

A radio historiographer surmised: "*Our Miss Brooks* was several notches above most radio comedies of the period, but what really raised it above the competition was Arden's softly muttered put-downs of the clowns, loudmouths, and fatheads—mostly male— who surrounded her on campus. She stood out amid the banal Betty Andersons and Harriet Nelsons."[2]

At the peak of the radio feature's popularity, before the inception of a TV embodiment, author Christopher Sergel penned a new volume that gained widespread appeal: *Our Miss Brooks: A Comedy in Three Acts* (Dramatic Publishing, 1950).

The show itself habitually followed a pattern of involving Miss Brooks in some convoluted issue that normally required her expertise beyond sheer classroom instruction. She would help the announcer by assisting with the narration, speaking directly to the audience tuning in (a paradigm George Burns perfected in the television era), saying something like this after the announcer's introduction: "That predicament began last Thursday morning as I was making my way toward Madison High as Walter Denton's heap jerked and hissed all over the road. Suddenly, we found ourselves on an expanse of open road when the motor finally gave up the ghost. As steam billowed from the front of the car, I turned to Walter and remarked ..."

No matter how a situation began, it would almost always in due course involve the high school's pompous principal, Osgood Conklin. Conklin was played by versatile character actor Gale Gordon, who enjoyed a lifelong career performing as blustery windbag figures in scads of radio and television series. His ability to deliver the "slow burn" response was a legendary trademark, and he made frequent use of it here. While he and Miss Brooks pursued the welfare of Madison High's students as their utmost priority, they usually approached it from opposing extremes. That often temporarily put the pair at cross purposes.

The storyline was frequently shrouded in minor misunderstandings, mistaken identities, or a nefarious or duplicitous undertaking either sanctioned or instigated by Miss Brooks. As the tale wound toward its conclusion, a showdown finally occurred with Conklin. Although the audience couldn't guess how the denouement would play out, anticipation emerging from past experiences pointed toward the inevitable climactic eruption. Fans could be virtually certain that Conklin would be left with egg on his face—and at the hands of a withering Connie Brooks, whose mischief was uncovered at last. At that juncture Conklin could slay a dragon after his well-intentioned mission was torpedoed.

An absolute master of timing, actor Gale Gordon never failed to bring the house down in those situations as he applied the slow burn. Prolonging a pause unremittingly, he initiated raucous studio laughter by merely calling the name of his nemesis, applying his deepest basal-toned timbre in slowly doing so: "Miss Brooks?" Following her acknowledgment of his summons (a soft-spoken, shaky, high-pitched "Yes, Mr. Conklin?" by a subject who knew she'd been had), there was yet another extraordinarily lengthy pause before he went for the jugular. Speaking deliberately, calmly, almost reassuringly, his remarks were measurably doled out, slowly building to a crescendo. When he got there, he lost his temper completely and chastened her foolhardiness, raising his level of modulation to its highest crest. Without fail, the onlookers were in total convulsions by then, while his cornered prey could hardly utter a peep. It was one of the funniest—and most predictable—moments in radio, and it occurred virtually every week. The scripting was positively brilliant, incidentally, giving those thespians some inspired material to work with.

There were others in the sitcom that aided and abetted Miss Brooks' conspiracies, of course. One was her eternal heartthrob, a man who seemingly didn't realize that *she*—and romance—coexisted on the planet. The bashful yet deliriously handsome unattached biology instructor, Mr. Philip Boynton—initially played by actor Jeff Chandler and later by Robert Rockwell—wasn't aware of much beyond his beloved frog McDougall. Boynton was almost totally preoccupied with studies about amphibious organisms that couldn't do much more than croak. McDougall gave new meaning to the term "teacher's pet." (In one installment the frog got drunk and spent his airtime hiccupping in class!) For that Miss Brooks was head over heels? Only when pressed into service in one of her schemes was Boynton able to shake loose from his toad in order to think outside the glass box.

Then there was Walter Denton—Richard Crenna in real life—a nerdy perpetual pupil with an incessant pubescent whine in his voice. He was available to drive Miss Brooks to school on those days her own vehicle was in the shop, which was most of the time. When he didn't exhibit enough of a

warped imagination of his own—which was seldom—he did her bidding, completing the complicated designs upon which the weekly tales hung. The squeaky-voiced Denton was the Henry Aldrich of this show, a smart kid who often fouled everything up. Romantically he had eyes for Harriet Conklin (actress Gloria McMillan), the principal's daughter, whose very involvement in their machinations was troubling to her doting father. Mr. Conklin had little patience with Denton, relegating him to a pawn in Miss Brooks' hands, an observation that wasn't far off the mark. Did anyone ever wonder: If Denton was a mediocre or better student, which he apparently was, why some nine years after entering high school (while the show was still airing) he hadn't graduated yet?

Young Denton, as Conklin was apt to refer to him, possessed a poetic bent, incidentally. On the first day back following the extended Christmas break one year, for example, he rhapsodized to Miss Brooks: "This is the morning when the glorious gates of learning fling open anew. When the tantalizing aroma of chalk and pencil shavings beckons to us all, teachers and pupils alike, to join hands and amidst the clanging of bells, come gaily skipping back to the black hole of Calcutta." Maybe that's why Miss Brooks apparently found in him her perfect soul-mate.

In addition to the characters already named, there was also Fabian (nicknamed Stretch) Snodgrass, the school idiot, played by actor Leonard Smith. Miss Brooks once branded him "Madison's athletic giant and mental midget." On another occasion, when Mr. Conklin disparaged young Denton as his daughter's "lame-brain boyfriend," Miss Brooks shot back: "Oh, Walter isn't so bad ... compared to his pal, Stretch Snodgrass, his mentality is positively Einsteinian!" If anyone could bamboozle an issue it was this simple-minded basketball star, whose inability to spell anything correctly was a foregone conclusion. He was little more than a "D" student, and Miss Brooks often tutored the inept repeater in order to help him maintain his eligibility for Madison High's team.

Only there did he excel. He was experienced in lousing up the best of intents and confusing almost every issue, and thus was an important contributor to many of the plotlines.

Finally, there was Mrs. Maggie Davis, Connie's widowed, batty landlady, whose mind wondered; she often forgot what she was saying in mid-sentence. "Mrs. Davis was always naïve and sometimes seemed slightly senile, making remarks in a patter of logical lunacy taken from the Gracie Allen-Marie Wilson cloth," affirmed one reviewer. She was frequently accompanied by a ubiquitous cat named Minerva. (This show was filled with oddball characters, more than one of which was of the non-human variety.) Parenthetically, Minerva exhibited a vocabulary of unremitting meows precisely timed to accentuate the specific comments of Connie Brooks. The chief function of Mrs. Davis, incidentally (played by actress Jane Morgan), was to awaken Miss Brooks every morning (this teacher had a lousy automobile, and obviously her wages were such a pittance that she couldn't afford an alarm clock!). Mrs. Davis routinely called her boarder to breakfast. Their lively exchanges provided a setting for the academic to project a premise for the week's episode while awaiting Denton's jalopy that was to ferry her to school that day.

There were a few more recurring figures in the show that were called upon when the comedy required their presence. Among them was Mrs. Martha Conklin, played by Virginia Gordon (an actress who was the real-life spouse of Gale Gordon), and Mr. Stone, played by Joseph Kearns, the superintendent of schools and Conklin's superior. Also, there were several other teachers: Miss Daisy Enright (Mary Jane Croft), who also taught English and was Miss Brooks' chief rival for the affections of Mr. Boynton (he didn't seem to get it that they sparred over him); Mr. LeBlanc (Maurice Marsac), a French teacher whom Miss Brooks used as a decoy to make Boynton jealous (he didn't get that, either); Mr. Jacques Monet (Gerald Mohr), still another French teacher with whom she tried the same tactics, again without success; and

occasionally a few others (plus sundry students who made rare appearances in the dialogue).

These, then, were the contributors to the zany plots that were spearheaded by Al Lewis, chief writer and series director, who led a team of inventive minds that collaborated with him on the scripting. While one week's situation sounded much like that of another, the ingenious details in arriving at those uproarious finishes brought listeners back week after week and year after year.

In one installment, for example, after some obvious arm-twisting, Connie was to be accompanied to a faculty dance by Boynton. In preparation for her big evening, Walter Denton carried her to Antoine's Beauty Parlor. Who should be there but Daisy Enright, who—knowing already that Connie had won the evening's prize she sought for herself—managed to sabotage her rival's hairdo and makeup.

Connie invariably got off some good lines when she sparred with her opponent. Once, Enright assured her: "When I was in my teens, there weren't very many stars on television." Hearing this, Brooks shot back: "When you were in your teens, there weren't many stars on the flag!"

In another episode, Connie's colleagues were mistakenly convinced that she had found a hundred dollar bill, although she had only 45 cents to her name. She hoped Mr. LeBlanc would buy her dinner. However, because they were observing French Sadie Hawkins Day, he felt it only proper that a woman of such perceived wealth should instead purchase his meal as well as her own. Connie misunderstood his French, thereby inviting Walter Denton and Mr. Boynton to accompany them. Mr. Conklin joined in the festivities. When Connie realized the truth, she stalled at the restaurant until the holiday officially passed so she wouldn't get stuck with the bill.

Another time, when Connie babysat for a couple, she believed she contracted measles and was quarantined. Not realizing she was quarantined, several of her buddies showed up, and in so doing became confined, too, including Mr. Conklin, a most unhappy fellow. All of them learned too late that Connie didn't have measles after all but only an allergic reaction after eating strawberries. Before they could depart after making their newfound discovery (having been incarcerated together for some prolonged and rather miserable hours), a visitor with real measles showed up, exposing them all to the disease!

Let's examine in greater detail a couple of typical 1950 plots.

In the first, the superintendent of schools, Mr. Stone, was to make his annual ceremonial visit to Madison High. Principal Conklin planned a special ritual for the occasion, complete with flag-bearers and the entire student body lined up outdoors to acknowledge the school chief's presence. Even young Denton was asked by Mr. Conklin to pen an editorial for *The Madison Monitor* on the theme "What the Board of Education Means to Me." Miss Brooks was to proofread it, but when she learned Denton had vented his spleen on various issues—taking Stone and the board to task for their perceived shortcomings—she wisely urged Mr. Conklin to write such an editorial himself. It was to be read aloud to the whole school and to Mr. Stone. As one might anticipate, the notion evolved into a series of colossal mistakes.

Copies of both Conklin's and Denton's editorials were literally torn apart, as well as a biology essay by Snodgrass. Unknown to Miss Brooks, it was left to Stretch to paste the various pages together in a usable form for the public presentation. Denton, meanwhile, was cooking up a batch of powder in a chemistry lab to mark the occasion explosively, using an outdated war cannon on the school grounds to carry out his ploy: "When Mr. Stone gets here, we'll give him a salute that he'll hear till he's 90," Denton exclaimed to his pal Stretch.

When the cannon went off, it was Mr. Conklin who reacted instead—by going totally deaf, the result of standing too near the cannon. Not wanting Stone to know of his condition, he asked Miss Brooks to read his editorial aloud, with himself (Conklin) making appropriate gestures of approval as if he was hearing every word. At Conklin's signal, she proceeded—with uproarious results. Conklin—pleased with himself—informed Miss Brooks that he would like to read the final page aloud. He proceeded: "Having observed Mr. Stone's educational methods, I'm convinced that his outstanding talent is his ability to eat bananas while hanging by his tail." Stone left in a huff and promised an investigation. For that fiasco Conklin assigned Brooks to write a new editorial. Having to miss a date with Mr. Boynton to do so, she later decided to tell Mr. Conklin what she thought of him—since he couldn't hear her anyway. Meanwhile, the audience learned that he could indeed hear, having regained his full range of audio capabilities a short time before Miss Brooks entered his office.

"I've got some things to tell you that I've been saving up for years," she began. "It's going to be a great pleasure to coo them into your dainty plugged-up ear." Calling him an "inconsiderate, maladjusted, sub-human tyrant," she continued: "Of all the puffed-up, overstuffed pompous windbags I've ever met, you take the marble cake, marble head. Rather than try to talk some sense into that addlepated, mule-brained little head of yours, I'll do the work this afternoon. Does that make you happy, you beady-eyed, beetle-browed old buzzard?" Mr. Conklin replied: "Yes, Miss Brooks. That makes me very happy." When she fully comprehended that he hadn't missed a word she uttered, he proceeded, meting out his words in measured delivery: "You realize, of course, Miss Brooks, that any chastisement you have suffered in the past is mere child's play when compared with what's in store for you now?" By then, of course, the studio audience—and presumably the listeners at home—were convulsively rollicking and rolling on the floor. It was the kind of stuff which made *Our Miss Brooks* so compelling and so deliriously amusing.

In another example from 1950, Mr. Conklin admonished his minions to participate in an annual National Clean-Up, Paint-Up,

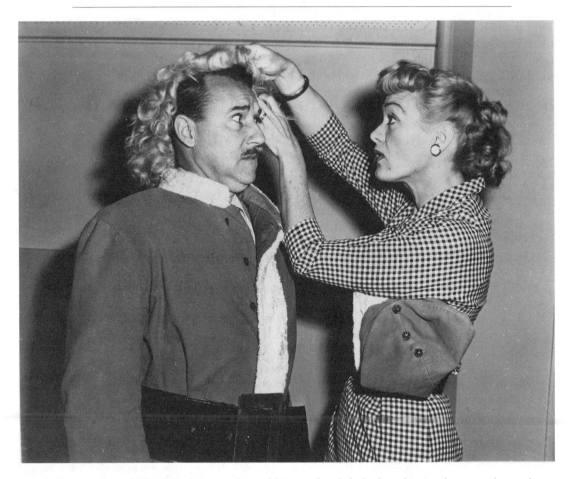

*There wasn't a more likable curmudgeon on radio—and TV, too—than Gale Gordon, who reacted in expected ways when Eve Arden as Our Miss Brooks put a needle to him. Gordon played the stern-hearted taskmaster-principal of Madison High where Arden was an English instructor, her nemesis on the popular Sunday night feature. Invariably the two were at cross purposes: they had the students' best interests at heart, but went about their tasks in opposite ways that resulted in predictable hilarity in every installment. They were flanked by a handful of humorous academicians, and various bright and not-so-bright pupils who were often caught up in Miss Brooks' schemes. In the photo, she helps her superior place a Santa Claus wig on his head, quite likely part of a scheme to pull more wool over his eyes.*

Fix-Up Campaign. It began when he asked Walter Denton to remove all the old files stored in Conklin's office closet and burn them. Furthermore, he instructed Miss Brooks to open a batch of mail he had just received: "Digest its contents, and if it is not of sufficient importance to demand my personal attention, tear it up!"

Later, Stretch Snodgrass—at Miss Brooks' direction—joined Denton to assist in destroying the files. The pair of student culprits encountered a six-year-old letter from Edgar T. Stone, chairman of the school board, written to Conklin's predecessor. It

warned that ex-principal that if he did not reverse his frequently observed "tyrannical methods" towards the faculty and student body, he would be relieved of his position. It was addressed only to "Principal's Office" rather than to an individual. Denton decided to have some fun with it. He typed in Conklin's name above the address lines, informing Stretch that it would cause the principal to shudder that "he's gonna get the old heave-ho" unless he begins "acting like a human being around here."

After Conklin read the letter, he had a virtual heart transplant. "It has always been my warmest desire to take the burden off my teachers, make them as light as possible," he told Miss Brooks. "If you have any suggestions which might help me achieve this desire, you have but to mention them and I am your willing slave. Your wish is my command." She replied: "I don't know who you are, but what are you doing with Mr. Conklin's head on?" During the lunch period that day, Conklin asked Miss Brooks, Mr. Boynton, Denton and Snodgrass to prepare a list of his faults in order to help him remain humble.

Before they could present their list to him, however, Harriet found the old letter to her dad's predecessor and asked him about it, calling attention to the 1944 postmark, then six years old. Conklin realized he had once again been had. He subsequently welcomed the foursome to his office with their list of grievances, playing along with the ruse. Enumerating Conklin's faults, Miss Brooks read aloud from their prepared text: "I readily admit that on many occasions I have acted like a pompous, puffed-up, ill-tempered blowhard." Conklin interjected: "Forgive me, but it seems to me you've omitted maladjusted." The quartet proceeded, with each of the four contributing to the dialogue: "On other occasions I have bellowed like a bull," "screamed like an elephant," "hissed like a viper," "snorted like a buffalo," "and otherwise exhibited the behavior of a maladjusted nincompoop." At that juncture, Conklin could no longer maintain his calm demeanor. He turned his full venom on them, revealing that he knew about the 1944 postmark before they entered his office. He branded them "perfidious malcontents." For her participation in the ploy, Miss Brooks was required to remain after school and write on the blackboard hundreds of times: "Our principal is the best principal that any school ever had." While the punishment may seem silly given current anti-discriminatory stipulations, audiences considered it a riot at the middle of the 20th century.

In its halcyon epoch through the early 1950s *Our Miss Brooks* originated live from CBS's Columbia Square in Hollywood at Sunset Boulevard and Gower Street on Sunday afternoons at 3:30 P.M. Pacific Time. That broadcast was beamed to the nation's middle section and to the Eastern seaboard. The cast returned to the same microphones for a second live performance before a new studio audience at 8 P.M. Pacific Time that evening. CBS transmitted that rendition to stations west of the Rockies.

*Our Miss Brooks* was among a handful of radio series of that epoch to transition into a televised incarnation while continuing its radio presentation. For four years, from 1952 to 1956, it appeared one night weekly (never on Sunday night, the night of the radio broadcasts) as a popular half-hour sitcom over CBS-TV. The principals in the radio cast followed the show to video, where they reprised their roles in separate comical tales. To juice up the ratings, in 1955 the TV environment was altered, with the cast leaving Madison High to join a private elementary institute. In a total turnabout, minus the services of Mr. Boynton for a while, a muscle-bound physical education coach, Gene Talbot (played by actor Gene Barry), pursued Miss Brooks (rather than the other way around).

There was yet one more manifestation of the radio series. In 1956 Warner Brothers released a feature-length theatrical motion picture titled *Our Miss Brooks* that featured the same popular radio–TV cast. In the silver screen storyline Miss Brooks continued to carry a torch for handsome, clueless Mr. Boynton. She was at last able to arouse his attention by being courted by the single dad of a student she tutored. A diversionary subplot involved some petty crimes. And Mr. Conklin continued to blow his stack at the slightest provocation. The "feel good" movie reached its climax with the nuptials of Brooks and Boynton (something never accomplished on the ether), and presumably they lived happily ever after. Although the celluloid form wasn't considered by critics to be as successful as the broadcast versions—possibly begging the question: why purchase something you can get at home every week for free?—it nevertheless captured the spirit of the radio theme.

A look at the individuals who appeared week after week and year after year in those recurring roles will provide insight into the enormous success enjoyed by *Our Miss Brooks*. Perhaps it will also indicate why the series persisted with but one change among the principal cast over its nine-year run, something almost unheard of in any broadcast series with as many players.

Eve Arden was born Eunice Quedens on April 30, 1908, at Mill Valley, California, just north of San Francisco.[3] Wanting to be on the stage from the time she was a young girl, she quit school at 16 to join the Henry Duffy Players, a San Francisco stock company, and went on the road.[4] She transitioned to a band box repertoire company with just four members. Then Arden performed in a revue at the Pasadena Playhouse, which projected her onto Hollywood. Her debut in film came at age 25 when she performed under her birth moniker in 1929's *Song of Love*. In 1934 she interrupted what appeared to be a budding career in celluloid to go to New York City as a Ziegfeld Follies girl. By 1936 she was the understudy there for comedienne Fannie Brice, whose name was about to loom large in radio as *Baby Snooks*.

Arden stayed with the Gotham stage for three years before returning to Hollywood to pursue filmdom once more. She shifted back and forth between Hollywood films and the New York venues for awhile but eventually settled on the West Coast, ultimately appearing in 65 motion pictures. Most of those were of the B-movie variety with less-than-thrilling titles like *Oh Doctor* (1937), *Big Town Czar* (1939), *Obliging Young Lady* (1942), *My Dream Is Yours* (1949) and *Paid in Full* (1950). But she also gained a few noteworthy credits on her movie dossier, too.

Cast in a minor role for 1937's *Stage Door*, by the time the movie was completed her part had been noticeably enlarged. She molded her screen persona as a cynical would-be actress in that film. Arden, who had adopted her new name by then,[5] was a confidante of the movie's lead and characterized as a charming, wisecracking, fast-talking gal. For her efforts she was singled out by critics and audiences alike as they took note of her ability to deliver sharp, wry lines that never concealed her essential warmth as an entertainer. Although Arden didn't realize it then, she had introduced a type of character that was destined to be hers for the rest of her professional life. While her witty asides might actually have prevented her from becoming a film lead, she found plenty of work in the years ahead. She also moved well beyond the traditional girlfriend and secretary roles that were customarily dispensed to many screen actresses.

Her career "lay squarely on the border between leading lady and character actor," Wikipedia affirmed.[6] She was an acrobat, for instance, in a 1939 Marx brothers madcap, *At the Circus*, possibly becoming the only female to ever get the best of venerable comic Groucho Marx. Arden played a Russian sharpshooter in 1944's *The Doughgirls* comedy. She was nominated for an Academy Award as Best Supporting Actress following a dazzling performance as the wisecracking Ida Corwin in 1945's *Mildred Pierce*, starring Joan Crawford.

"If this tall, attractive blonde didn't exactly invent the character of the leading lady's sardonic, wisecracking—and usually dateless—best friend," observed film critic Leonard Maltin, "she certainly set the standard for all the others."[7] Her snappy ripostes brought her growing recognition and put her in line for a new radio series that CBS anticipated launching in 1948. Arden had already gained some aural exposure before that, having premiered three years earlier on a couple of variety series: NBC's *The Sealtest Village Store*, in which she shared the hosting spotlight with Jack Haley (1945–47) and Jack Carson (1947–48); and CBS's *The Danny Kaye Show*, aka *Pabst Blue Ribbon Town* (1945–46), for which she turned up now and again.

In an unusual departure from the norm, in early 1948 CBS owner-chairman William S. Paley approached her at an Ambassador Hotel discotheque and asked her to dance

("He was a wonderful dancer," she remembered). Two weeks later he asked her to consider the title role of a nine-week CBS Radio sitcom debuting that summer that was to focus on a public school educator. Arden wasn't impressed by the original script she received. But a subsequent draft penned by a couple of newly-appointed wordsmiths, Al Lewis and Joe Quillan, led her to think differently. She planned to leave the coast for the summer to vacation with her children and told Paley she would agree only if the show could be transcribed in advance of its seasonal run. By then Bing Crosby and Groucho Marx had already broken longstanding network barriers that were previously inscribed in stone against recording shows for later airing. Now the new practice was becoming commonplace throughout the industry. Paley granted her request.

For the first time, she would be the sole star. It was what she had worked for—and for what fate had prepared her—for all of her years in show business. She was 40 then, having pursued entertainment as her livelihood for 24 years. She was ready. Arden played the lead in *Our Miss Brooks* on its opening night of July 19, 1948, and on its closing night of July 7, 1957—and in every performance in between. Vacationing at a friend's farm in the summer of 1948, she took a telephone call from CBS president Frank Stanton. "Congratulations," he enthused. "*Miss Brooks* is the number one show on the air." The summer diversion developed into such an overnight ratings hit that Arden knew "there was no going back." The show persisted—resumed— before a live audience that fall. With the exception of temporary recesses, it never left the airwaves for the next nine years.

In addition to the radio manifestation there were 154 performances on television (not replays of radio performances, or even vice versa)[8] over a quadrennial (1952–56).[9] Arden also starred in the feature-length film of the same title. In some ways she made a career of the part. She would be recognized decades later by ordinary citizens who addressed her by her character's name—they

figured out who she was not by her looks but by her unforgettable voice. Miss Brooks was the most memorable acting part of Arden's professional life.[10] And for it she won an Emmy.

She didn't quit performing after *Our Miss Brooks* faded, of course. The movie roles kept coming, and some of them were better than she had been accustomed to before her broadcast days. She appeared as defense attorney Jimmy Stewart's wistful secretary in 1959's explicit mystery drama *Anatomy of a Murder*. In the same film, Arden's real-life spouse, Brooks West, portrayed the prosecutor who opposed Stewart's character.[11] She also appeared in a few more well-known theatrical releases following her "career" as Miss Brooks: *The Dark at the Top of the Stairs* (1960), *Sergeant Deadhead* (1965), *Grease* (1978), *Under the Rainbow* (1981) and *Grease 2* (1982). As Principal McGee in the two *Grease* films, "She still had the wisecracks and screen presence to bring back the fond memories of Miss Connie Brooks," a reviewer posted.

She subsequently starred in the unsuccessful CBS-TV sitcom *The Eve Arden Show*, which aired from September 17, 1957, to March 25, 1958. In it she played Liza Hammond, a widow who earned her livelihood as a travel lecturer. The show boasted several supporting characters, none of them holdovers from *Our Miss Brooks*. Included was a housekeeper played by Frances Bavier, who would soon be sequestered with a zany assemblage on *The Andy Griffith Show* (1960–68) and *Mayberry, R.F.D.* (1968–70), where she appeared as the beloved Aunt Bee. Arden, meanwhile, wouldn't headline any more TV shows until she was paired with Kaye Ballard as co-star of the NBC-TV sitcom *The Mothers-in-Law*. It ran from September 10, 1967, to September 7, 1969. Arden portrayed Eve Hubbard, a lawyer's wife. The show's executive producer was Desi Arnaz, who occasionally appeared in the plots as bullfighter Raphael del Gado. Conversely, Miss Brooks' old nemesis, Mr. Conklin, played by Gale Gordon, was simultaneously employed by Arnaz's ex-wife, Lucille Ball. Between the 1940s and 1980s, in fact, he appeared as Lucy's foil on four different CBS sitcoms. (Details appear under his entry, to follow.)

Earlier in the 1960s Arden assumed the stage roles of Dolly Levi and Mame, respectively, in productions of *Hello, Dolly!* and *Auntie Mame*. Her appearances in Chicago theater won for her the Sarah Siddons Award in 1967. Lamentably, in the early 1980s she starred in several preview performances of one of Broadway's most notorious flops, *Moose Murders*.[12] Signed for the role of Hedda Holloway there, Arden was hastily replaced when it became apparent that she was no longer able to memorize her lines. (She was approaching her 75th birthday.) That likely would have been the end of her career had she not had a myriad of television guest shots to fill (*Ellery Queen, Disneyland, Maude, Alice, The Love Boat, Hart to Hart, Masquerade, Falcon Crest*, et al.). In addition to the trio of TV shows in which she starred, Arden appeared as a guest or actress in single episodes of 44 video features, including a spate of made-for-TV movies (1972's *All My Darling Daughters* was among them). She was inducted into the Radio Hall of Fame in 1995 for her tenure as Madison High's favorite English teacher. For her multidimensional contributions to the entertainment industry, she received a star on the Hollywood Walk of Fame.

While her death in Los Angeles on November 12, 1990, was officially listed as heart failure, she was suffering from advanced colorectal cancer. "Hers was a unique comic talent," Leonard Maltin observed, "and the screen is much poorer for her absence."[13] Her autobiography, *Three Phases of Eve* (St. Martin's Press, 1985), was cited by pundits "for its discretion in regard to Arden's many co-stars and her loyalty to the Hollywood studio system that nurtured her career."

Her opposite and adversary on *Our Miss Brooks*, Mr. Conklin, was played by Gale Gordon, one of broadcasting's most versatile veterans, and who made a career out of performing as overstuffed shirts. Born Charles T. Aldrich, Jr. in New York City on February 20, 1906, the popular character actor came by his talent naturally. His mom was a British stage actress, Gloria Gordon (who became an Irish housekeeper on CBS Radio's *My Friend Irma* in the late 1940s); his dad, Charles Aldrich, was a vaudevillian. His parents imbued him with a love of the footlights.

From age one to nine, young Gordon lived with his family in England, where his parents found work on the stage. He returned to New York until he was 17, then went back to England to graduate from Woodbridge School in Suffolk. He had been bitten by the performing bug just like his parents. His initial exposure came in a small part as an extra in a 1923 Canadian stage play, *The Dancers*, which starred Richard Bennett, father of Constance, Joan and Barbara. Bennett taught him what he knew about makeup, acting and voice training, all of which prepared the youth for what was to follow. Gordon moved to Hollywood in 1925, and the following year premiered on the air strumming a ukulele and singing "It Ain't Gonna Rain No More, No More." He wasn't paid for it and said later, "I nearly killed radio that day." He never played an instrument on the ether again.

While he would appear in theatrical motion pictures (there were 16 on his resume, starting with an uncredited part at age 27 in 1933's *Elmer, the Great*, then several movies in which he was cast as stuffy military officers, ending with a minor role at age 83 in 1989's *The 'burbs*), it was overwhelmingly his appearances on radio, then television, for which Gale Gordon would be remembered by legions of doting fans. He ultimately won continuing portrayals on about three dozen broadcast series in a professional career that spanned six decades, from the 1930s into the 1990s. Gordon acquired multiple radio parts that kept him occupied when he wasn't focused on a handful of major roles that turned him into a legend. His peripheral assignments, which kept him busy while significantly improving his bottom line[14] (though not necessarily well-remembered by audiences) were:

*Tarzan* (1932–34), as Cecil Clayton, in a series fed to local stations thrice weekly by disc transcriptions.

*Parties at Pickfair* (1934–36), where in various dramas he played the male lead with star Mary Pickford, for which he was compensated $100 weekly, "a fantastic salary" in the depths of the Great Depression, he attested.

*Irene Rich Dramas* (1935–44), frequently as the male lead in a plethora of narratives.

*Flash Gordon* (1935), in the namesake role.

*Stories of the Black Chamber* (1935), as the master spy Paradine.

*The Cinnamon Bear* (1937), in an occasional supporting role.

*Big Town* (1937–42), as an arrogant District Attorney Miller, possibly the first time he portrayed a killjoy character, a defining trait that would become his trademark.

*The Joe E. Brown Show* (1938–39), as a usually enraged Mr. Bullhammer, Brown's superior at a talent agency.

*The Wonder Show* (1938–39), as a recurring thespian in a company that included Lucille Ball—their first working association, one destined to prevail for half a century.

*The Amazing Interplanetary Adventures of Flash Gordon* (1939), a syndicated feature in which he was again featured in the namesake role.

*The Shadow of Fu Manchu* (1939, 1940), as Dr. James Petrie, one of two heroes who opposed the menacing Fu Manchu.

*Orson Welles Theater* (1941–42), a member of the dramatic thespian company.

*Treasury Star Parade* (1942–44), a member of the recurring acting company.

*The Whistler* (1942), as the titled narrator who knows "many secrets hidden in the hearts of men and women who have stepped into the shadows."

*The George Burns and Gracie Allen Show* (1942 and a few years thereafter), as Harry Morton, the Burns' next door neighbor.

*The Judy Canova Show* (1943–44), as neighbor Mr. Simpson, and (1945–50) as publicity agent Gordon Mansfield.

*The Fabulous Dr. Tweedy* (1946), as Alexander Potts, an educator—did this lead to Mr. Conklin perhaps?

*Jonathan Trimble, Esquire* (1946), playing the title role of the turn-of-the-century journalist who was dubbed "a pompous gentleman, a tyrant in his own household"—more validation for the Conklin selection?

*The Casebook of Gregory Hood* (1946–47), in the title role of the amateur detective whose livelihood was derived from importing.

*Johnny Modero, Pier 23* (1947), as a San Francisco waterfront priest, Father Leahy.

*Junior Miss* (1948–50, 1952–54), as Harry Graves, father of Judy Graves, the namesake protagonist.

*The Phil Harris–Alice Faye Show* (1948–54), delivering commercial pitches for the Rexall Drug Company as a rather stressed Mr. Scott, the firm's representative, whose part was integrated into the show's scripts.[15]

*Granby's Green Acres* (1950), in the title role as John Granby, who traded in his city banking job for the chance to run a ramshackle farm in the country.

*The Penny Singleton Show* (1950), as Judge Beshomer Grundell, who schemed to win the affections of a newly-widowed Penny Williamson, the lead figure.

*Mr. and Mrs. Blandings* (1951), as Bill Cole, attorney for the Blandings—two central figures who also turned their backs on city life to move to the country, a seemingly "catching" ploy that reached its zenith in the CBS-TV sitcom *Green Acres* (1965–71).

Because he was born well before radio was entrenched as a viable amusement alternative in American homes, Gale Gordon was already 35 when his first truly defining opportunity on the ether arose. He was introduced in the continuing part of Mayor Homer La Trivia on NBC's popular sitcom *Fibber McGee & Molly* on October 14, 1941. At a later date he began appearing there as F. Ogden "Foggy" Williams, the weatherman. In both personifications his voice carried a slight edge as he habitually sparred with the irascible homeowner at 79 Wistful Vista. It established a dimension in characterization for him that was to lead to a lifelong occupational stereotype.

During that same interval Gordon also picked up the role of Rumson Bullard on *The Great Gildersleeve*, a spinoff sitcom with origins in the *McGee* show. Bullard was an affluent but abrasive neighbor who resided across the street from Summerfield's water commissioner, Throckmorton P. Gildersleeve. Gildersleeve, like McGee, could enjoy a good jest, but could also be provoked by some denizens he encountered, including Bullard. It was a situation tailor-made for his neighbor, and it contributed to the typecasting that was developing around Gordon. The actor was already showing signs that he would demonstrate in the future characters he was to portray. Each new personality pointed toward the cantankerous curmudgeon for which Gordon would become best known. He once told a reporter, "I am never nasty, unless I get paid for it."[16]

In the late 1940s he was fortunate to obtain two roles that honed his evolving character even more, making him memorable to audiences of millions. One prize was that of Osgood Conklin. The other came only four days after the arrival of *Our Miss Brooks*, on July 23, 1948, when Gordon turned up as a short-tempered banker named Rudolph Atterbury. As such, he was the boss of George Cooper on CBS Radio's *My Favorite Husband* sitcom. The show starred Lucille Ball and Richard Denning as Liz and George Cooper. It was Ball's first broadcast shot at the type of character that was to make her famous around the globe. On occasions Gordon appeared in Lucy and Desi Arnaz's epic comedy *I Love Lucy* on CBS-TV (1951–57) as Alvin Littlefield, owner of the Tropicana Club where Ricky Ricardo's band performed.[17] Gordon also showed up now and then on *The Lucy-Desi Comedy Hour* (1957–60), which followed.

The droll actor developed a rapport with Ball that persisted on a trio of additional TV sitcoms in which she starred while he performed as *her* nemesis (and possibly vice versa): CBS's *The Lucy Show* (Gordon joined the cast in 1963 after the show had been running for a year, and remained with it to the end of the run in 1968), again as a banker, Theodore J. Mooney, with Lucy Carmichael (Ball) as his secretary; CBS's *Here's Lucy* (1968–74), where he portrayed Harrison Carter, brother-in-law of Lucille Carter (Ball) (she was his secretary at the employment agency he operated); and ABC's *Life with Lucy*, lasting only eight episodes in the fall of 1986 before being yanked, in which Gordon played Curtis McGibbon, business partner of Lucy Barker (Ball) (McGibbon's son and Barker's daughter were also wed to one another).[18] With that show, Gale Gordon turned out to be the only actor to co-star or guest-star in every weekly series—on radio and television—that Lucille Ball had been in, dating back to the 1930s.

Gordon's other TV credits include *The Brothers* (1956–57), a half-hour CBS sitcom co-starring Bob Sweeney (the pair of siblings operated a San Francisco photography studio, and the show absolutely bombed), NBC's *Sally* (1958), in which Gordon played Bascomb Bleacher Sr., manager of the Banford and Bleacher Department Store employing Sally Truesdale (Joan Caulfield) as a sales clerk; CBS's *Pete and Gladys* (1961–62), a spinoff from *December Bride*, where Gordon was Uncle Paul to Pete Porter (Harry Morgan), whose ditzy wife Gladys was played by Cara Williams; and CBS's *Dennis the Menace* (1962–63), in which Gordon played a neighbor following the death of actor Joseph Kearns. Gordon seldom lacked for anything to do.

That wasn't all, by any stretch. He appeared in numerous single episodes of a myriad of television series (*Climax!*, *The Real McCoys*, *Playhouse 90*, *Studio One*, *Westinghouse Desilu Playhouse*, *The Danny Thomas Hour*, et al.), and in a few made-for-television films, including 1977's *Lucy Calls the President*. He was given a star on the Hollywood Walk of Fame and posthumously named to the Radio Hall of Fame in 1999. He was married for 58 years to actress Virginia Curley, who played Mrs.

Conklin in *Our Miss Brooks* on radio and television.[19] The pair died within a month of each other; both were residents of the same nursing facility. His passing, from lung cancer on June 30, 1995, in Escondido, California, followed hers. They had no children.

The only role in *Our Miss Brooks* that had to be re-cast across a nine-year run, overlapping the four-year television manifestation of the show, was that of Mr. Boynton. It occurred when the originating actor, Jeff Chandler, decided to concentrate on films rather than broadcasting for the bulk of his professional career. After five seasons on radio and one on TV he left the program in 1953. He was succeeded in both versions and in the 1956 film by movie actor Robert Rockwell.

Born Ira Grossel to a Jewish family in Brooklyn, New York, on December 15, 1918, Chandler attended Erasmus Hall High School, the alma mater of numerous stage, broadcast and film entertainers. He enrolled in a drama course after graduation and had been appearing with stock companies for two years before Uncle Sam summoned him during World War II. Following the war, Chandler returned to take roles in *Escape* and many other radio dramas, and debuted in celluloid in an uncredited role in 1947's *Johnny O'Clock*. It was the first of 46 theatrical motion pictures in which he would appear over the next 15 years. While the bulk of those would be forgotten by an admiring public, he would also shake the image of Mr. Boynton.

Whereas he had played the timid, hesitant-sounding biology instructor on *Our Miss Brooks* (who seemed to possess few concerns beyond his pet frog), Chandler turned out to be a rugged, virile leading man. His co-stars included June Allyson, Joan Crawford, Rhonda Fleming, Susan Hayward, Maureen O'Hara, Jane Russell and Esther Williams. In the 1950s he played in westerns, action dramas and an occasional soap opera. He was readily identified by his silvery hair, dimpled chin, muscular physique and unique voice. Old-time radio historian John Dunning affirmed: "Chandler became a major film star in the 1950s, promoting such a he-man image

that few would remember his notable comedy role."[20] The actor told gossip columnist Sheila Graham, upon the release of the film *Jeanne Eagles* in 1957: "I thought that for once I could keep my shirt on and not have to shave my chest. But today, for a man to be a hit on the screen, he has to take his shirt off."

His filmography included *Because of You* (1952), *The Great Sioux Uprising* (1953), *Foxfire* (1955), *Female on the Beach* (1955), *Away All Boats* (1956), *The Tattered Dress* (1957), *Drango* (1957), *A Stranger in My Arms* (1959), *Thunder in the Sun* (1959), *Ten Seconds to Hell* (1959), *Return to Peyton Place* (1961) and *Merrill's Marauders* (1962). He also starred in a single made-for-TV flick, 1960's *A Story of David*. In addition, he produced one film, composed the music for two more and was lyricist for the title songs of three others. He played the violin and owned Chandler Music, a publishing outfit. At the pinnacle of his fame in movies he vocalized on several Liberty Records albums.

Chandler was standing on the threshold of still greater accomplishments when he went under the knife to repair a herniated spinal disc on May 13, 1961. An artery was damaged during the operation; he hemorrhaged, requiring more than seven hours of added surgery, during which he was given 55 pints of blood. In a third operation he received 20 more pints. By then the 14 to 18 pints in a normal adult had been replaced as much as five times, and he died from blood poisoning on June 17, 1961. A malpractice lawsuit rewarded his two daughters, born in 1947 and 1948, handsomely. He had divorced their mother, Marjorie Hoshelle, in 1954 after seven years of marriage.

In a revealing 1999 autobiography, *The Million Dollar Mermaid* (Simon & Schuster), screen star Esther Williams divulged that Chandler—with whom she had an affair— was a cross-dresser (dressing up as a woman for sexual gratification).[21] When entertainer Sammy Davis, Jr. lost an eye in an accident and was in danger of losing the other, Chandler offered to give him one of his own eyes. Parenthetically, both of Chandler's daughters,

Jamie and Dana, died of cancer, as did his mother, maternal aunt, uncle and grandfather. He is recalled in a couple of published works: *Jeff Chandler*, by Marilyn Kirk (lst Books Library, 2003), and *Jeff Chandler: Film, Record, Radio, Television and Theater Performances*, by Jeff Wells (McFarland, 2005).

Robert Rockwell—the *other* Mr. Boynton—was born in Chicago on October 15, 1920. He earned a master's degree from the Pasadena Playhouse and launched a career as a contract player for Republic Studios. Over his lifetime, between 1948's *You Gotta Stay Happy* and 1995's *Perfect Alibi*, he won parts in 26 theatrical films. Included were *The Red Menace* (1949), *Task Force* (1949), *Call Me Mister* (1951), *The Prince Who Was a Thief* (1951), *War of the Worlds* (1953) and *Our Miss Brooks* (1956).

Although he sustained no other major network radio roles beyond that of Mr. Boynton in *Our Miss Brooks*, Rockwell made over 350 TV appearances across half a century, acting in episodes of many popular series: *Stars Over Hollywood, Racket Squad, The Lone Ranger, Adventures of Superman, Sky King, Cavalcade of America, Toast of the Town, Tales of Wells Fargo, The Millionaire, Westinghouse Desilu Playhouse, Gunsmoke, Surfside 6, Checkmate, Death Valley Days, Maverick, The Lucy Show, Perry Mason, Lassie, Green Acres, Petticoat Junction, Here's Lucy, Eight Is Enough, Benson, Charlie's Angels, Knots Landing, Mama's Family, Diff'rent Strokes, E/R, Hunter, Dynasty, Dallas, Falcon Crest, Newhart, Growing Pains, Beverly Hills 90210* and a host of others. There were also a handful of made-for-TV flicks, and recurring roles in a trio of video series beyond *Our Miss Brooks*: ABC's *The Man from Blackhawk* (1959–60), in which he starred as insurance investigator Sam Logan; NBC's *The Bill Cosby Show* (1969–71), with a minor role as Tom Bennett; and CBS's *Search for Tomorrow* daytime serial (1951), in an obscure bit part but returning to the cast later (1977–78) in the continuing role of Dr. Greg Hartford.

Rockwell performed in more than 200 commercials and voiceovers. His most memorable may have been in a Werthers candy spot as the grandfather treating his grandson to a confection. Highlighting a lengthy stage career were Rockwell's 1946 appearances on Broadway in *Cyrano de Bergerac* opposite Jose Ferrer, and a 1960s San Diego production of *A More Perfect Union* opposite Ginger Rogers. A founding member of the California Artists Radio Theatre, Rockwell was married to Elizabeth Weiss from 1942 until his death by cancer on January 25, 2003, at Malibu, California. Together they raised five children.

One of entertainment's sterling talents, Richard Crenna was launched on his career path by playing Walter Denton in *Our Miss Brooks*, even though he had already acted on previous series. *Brooks* was to become the watershed moment for him, leading to a glut of teenage character roles that prepared him for more diverse things to come. Then still a teen, Crenna's fortuitous opportunity carried him far beyond what anyone might have dreamed. Shortly before his death more than a half-century later he was still appearing nearly every week in a widely acclaimed television series. He simply never quit working, constantly applying the gifts he was imbued with that he had first demonstrated in the 1940s.

Born Richard Donald Crenna on November 30, 1927, at Los Angeles, as a youngster he got into acting nearly by accident. The son of a local pharmacist, he attended L.A.'s Virgil Junior High School and signed up for a dramatics class. "I'd already taken wood shop," he said years later. "I noticed that the prettiest girls were in dramatics and also the goof-offs. That was for me."

One day while on the school playground a teacher arrived to inform the students that local station KFI's *Boy Scout Jamboree* radio series was looking for young talent to become "the Beaver Patrol." He and eight classmates were ultimately tapped for simple roles, with compensation of 25 cents weekly. Crenna was a kid on the show who did everything wrong. It was a humble beginning that eventually saw him playing the high-pitched, squeaky-voiced Denton, America's perennial high school pupil, just after he graduated from high school himself. (At the show's inception

Crenna was also enrolled at the University of Southern California at Los Angeles.)

Other radio roles flowed his way. He turned up in occasional parts on CBS's *Dear John* (1942–44), starring Irene Rich; NBC's *One Man's Family* (1940s, 1950s); *I Love a Mystery* (1940s, 1950s) on NBC Blue, CBS and MBS; MBS's *Red Ryder* (1948–49); CBS's *My Favorite Husband* (1948–51), starring Lucille Ball; CBS's *Gunsmoke* (1952–61); CBS's *Romance* (1954–57); and MBS's *The Zero Hour* (1973, 1974). In the meantime, during the 1940s Crenna was Waldo on *The George Burns and Gracie Allen Show*, alternating between CBS and NBC. From 1946 to 1950 he portrayed Oogie Pringle, Judy Foster's boyfriend on ABC's *A Date with Judy* sitcom, starring Louise Erickson as the "lovable teenage girl who's close to all our hearts." Crenna turned up in the 1950s on NBC as Bronco Thompson, who wed Marjorie Gildersleeve, niece of *The Great Gildersleeve*. From 1952 to 1953 he was Andy Hardy's best friend Beasey in MBS's *The Hardy Family* sitcom, yet another tale of typical teenage misadventures in a nuclear family.

Of course, he was engaged as Walter Denton from 1948 to 1957 on radio, 1952 to 1956 on television and for the 1956 movie based on the broadcast series. "I was really too old to continue playing Walter," Crenna confessed years later. "And at first I refused. But Eve [Arden] had great loyalty to her fellow workers and she liked to keep us around." When the series departed the airwaves at last, "teenaged" Denton (Crenna) was 29. He had made a career of playing similar characters, and might have fleetingly wondered if he was all washed up. He didn't have long to ponder such fears, however.

In 1957, as *Brooks* was ending on radio, Crenna was signed to play a thirtysomething married Luke McCoy on television. He became the grandson of Amos McCoy, played by veteran actor Walter Brennan, and the patriarch of *The Real McCoys* (1957–62, ABC; 1962–63, CBS). The role affirmed Crenna's ability to portray characters other than teenaged rabble-rousers. Furthermore, while

in that part he moved into directing—initially commercials only, then whole episodes of the series.

He expanded his talents further, shedding his image as a comic actor by winning the lead in CBS-TV's *Slattery's People* (1964–65). The hour-long drama focused on an idealistic leader of the minority party in the legislature of an unnamed state. By then Hollywood was convinced that Crenna would be a hit in motion pictures. He appeared as the comic, courageous Captain Collins in the 1966 epic drama *The Sand Pebbles*, playing opposite Steve McQueen. Roles as a criminal (Mike Talman) terrorizing Audrey Hepburn in *Wait Until Dark* (1967), and as astronaut Jim Pruett in *Marooned* (1969), followed. From the 1950 movie *Let's Dance*, in which he had an uncredited bit part, to 1998's *Wrongfully Accused*, where he portrayed Lieutenant Fergus Falls, Crenna performed in 35 theatrical releases. Among the most notable: *The Pride of St. Louis* (1952), *Doctors' Wives* (1971), *Red Sky at Morning* (1971), *Jonathan Livingston Seagull* (1973), *Body Heat* (1981), *First Blood* (1982), *The Flamingo Kid* (1984), *Rambo: First Blood Part II* (1985), *Rambo III* (1988), *Jade* (1995) and *Sabrina* (1995).

Crenna appeared in about 100 television series and films, mostly in single episodes but occasionally in guest shots as himself. Among their number: *I Love Lucy*, *The Millionaire*, *Medic*, *Cheyenne*, *Rowan & Martin's Laugh-In*, *Dinah!*, *The John Davidson Show*, *Saturday Night Live*, *JAG*, *Cold Case*, *Chicago Hope* and *Murder, She Wrote*. He was the subject of a *This Is Your Life* spotlight in 1972, for which several of his former associates on *Our Miss Brooks* returned to pay him homage. Among his TV movies: *Double Indemnity* (1973), *Breakheart Pass* (1975), *First You Cry* (1978), *Mayflower: The Pilgrims' Adventure* (1979), *The Rape of Richard Beck* (1985—he won an Emmy playing the namesake role), *A Case of Deadly Force* (1986), *On Wings of Eagles* (1986 mini-series, with Crenna as H. Ross Perot), *The Case of the Hillside Stranglers* (1989), *Murder in Black and White* (1990), *Last Flight Out* (1990), *Terror on Track 9* (1992), *A Place to Be Loved* (1993),

Jonathan Stone: Threat to Innocence (1994), Janek: The Silent Betrayal (1994), Race Against Time: The Search for Sarah (1996), 20,000 Leagues Under the Sea (1997), The Day Reagan Was Shot (2001) and Out of the Ashes (2003).

Crenna was an ongoing figure in another quartet of television series after Our Miss Brooks, The Real McCoys and Slattery's People. They included a 1981 syndicated magazine show he hosted, Look at Us; the role as surgeon Sam Quinn in the ABC drama It Takes Two (1982–83), opposite Patty Duke Astin; as private detective Mitch O'Hannon, with actor James Earl Jones (Gabriel Bird), in the ABC light crime drama Pros & Cons (1991–92); and as the wealthy globe-trotting entrepreneur Jared Duff in CBS's family courtroom drama Judging Amy. The latter may have been the most successful of the four, and certainly was a crowning achievement in such a prolific career. Crenna won the role at age 72 in 2000. He played the intended husband of Amy's mom, Maxine Gray (Tyne Daly), and was still at it when he passed away, a victim of pancreatic cancer, on January 17, 2003, in Los Angeles. Later, he was eulogized on that series in a single episode.

In addition to his performing duties, Crenna directed one or more episodes for 10 television series and films, including notables like The Real McCoys, The Andy Griffith Show, The Rockford Files and Lou Grant. He also produced a couple of TV movies—1966's Baby Makes Three and 1972's Captain Newman, M.D. A longtime member of the Screen Actors Guild, in the 1950s Crenna worked tirelessly to ensure that actors received residuals for their TV work. He was a member of the SAG board of directors at the time of his death. He wed Penni Sweeney in 1959; she and their three children survived him.

Jane Morgan was Connie Brooks' landlady, Maggie Davis, in Our Miss Brooks' multiple incarnations. Born in England on December 6, 1880, following a lengthy illness (she was bedridden the last five years of her life), she died of a heart attack on January 1, 1972 at Burbank, California, and was buried at sea. Raised in the United States, Morgan was in show business for more than six decades, initially as a classical violinist and afterwards as a character thespian. She appeared at renowned venues such as the Ziegfeld Theatre. Soon after her marriage to Leo Cullen Bryant, a symphony orchestra conductor, she left musical recitals to play in serials in the early days of radio.

Throughout much of the 1940s she appeared as Evelyn Hanover, the romantic interest of the storekeep-philosopher-mayor Ben Willet (Cliff Arquette) of mythical Point Sublime. The show shifted frequently, from the NBC West Coast chain to the MBS-Don Lee hookup and at last to ABC. From 1942 to 1951 Morgan was the heroine in the daytime serial Aunt Mary carried by the NBC West Coast web, which MBS beamed to the nation during 1946–47. As Mary Lane, she was cast as "a wise old lady philosopher who displayed great character in the Ma Perkins mold," according to one pundit. At about the same time she and Gloria Gordon (Gale Gordon's mom) turned up on The Jack Benny Program as Martha and Emily, a couple of aging broads that Benny found irresistible.

Seemingly discovering a niche, Morgan played Mrs. O'Reilly, owner of the rooming house where Irma Peterson (Marie Wilson) and Jane Stacy (Cathy Lewis) were roommates on CBS's debuting My Friend Irma in 1947. (Morgan was soon succeeded in the part by Gloria Gordon after Our Miss Brooks required Morgan's services as its landlady.)

Morgan acted in a surfeit of dramatic series aired from the coast, including NBC's Mystery in the Air (1947), that net's Presenting Charles Boyer (1950), CBS's The Adventures of Philip Marlowe and ABC's Richard Diamond, Private Detective. The thespian played Mother Hemp to CBS's Honest Harold (Harold Peary) in 1951. She turned up in scores of CBS's Lux Radio Theater dramatizations, and was a regular visitor to that network's Suspense and The Sweeney and March Program, as well as to NBC's Cavalcade of America, The Great Gildersleeve, and The Bob Hope Show. Morgan also played in numerous mysteries and other narrative fare on all four webs. All the while, of course, she still cared for Minerva, her pet cat, at the house she owned where Connie Brooks boarded.

Morgan showed up in a couple of movies, too—in an uncredited role in 1951's *Three Guys Named Mike*, and, of course, in 1956's *Our Miss Brooks* as Maggie Davis. The actress is often confused (particularly on the Internet) with Jane Currier Morgan, a popular vocalist who was born in Boston on December 25, 1920. The singer performed on numerous major television variety series from the 1950s to the 1970s.

Leonard Smith's history in the annals of entertainment is brief. He acquired the role of Stretch Snodgrass, the village idiot of Madison High, at age 14 following a brief stint as Tooth Johnson in the MBS comedy *Vic and Sade* in 1946. He was only 10 when he appeared in the first of his five theatrical films: *A Canterbury Tale* (1944) as Leslie, *Our Miss Brooks* (1956) as Snodgrass, *Take a Hard Ride* (1974) as Cangey, *Shining Star* (1975) as an unnamed bouncer and *High Risk* (1981) as Mike. In all of his movies Smith's name appears far down the list of performers, indicating that his on-camera time was limited. No further details of his professional or personal life have surfaced.

Gloria McMillan, who played Principal Osgood Conklin's daughter Harriet and the love interest of Walter Denton, is the last of the key personalities in the cast of *Our Miss Brooks*. Her vita sheet, too, is sparse. She won one more radio role as a teenager's girlfriend, however. In *Mayor of the Town*, a comedy drama running at varied times between 1942 and 1949 on NBC, CBS, ABC and MBS, she played Sharlee Bronson, the girl that Roscoe "Butch" Turner (actor Conrad Binyon) was sweet on. He was the ward of the town's mayor (actor Lionel Barrymore).

Aside from two theatrical films—1956's *Our Miss Brooks*, where McMillan reprised her role as Harriet Conklin, and 1975's *Smile*, in which she played an unnamed lady judge— the remainder of her public exposure is relegated to a handful of largely uncredited TV appearances in addition to *Our Miss Brooks*

(1952–56): NBC's *Dr. Kildare* (two visits in 1966), *Most Wanted* (a made-for-TV movie in 1976), a performance as Clara Brumbaugh in the 1978 NBC-TV mini series *Centennial*, and the role of Mrs. O'Neil in an episode of ABC's *Perfect Strangers* (1990).

While specific data on McMillan's birth remains elusive, a *Los Angeles Times* article published in late 1954 revealed that she planned to wed a University of Southern California student, Gil Allen, age 20, on November 24, 1954, in Westwood, California. "Miss McMillan," the story announced, "who joined the *Our Miss Brooks* cast seven years ago when she was 13, considers the cast her 'second family,' and they will participate in the wedding." Eve Arden was to stand with McMillan's mother (a widowed Hollywood agent, Hazel McMillan) at the ceremony, reported the newspaper account. Gale Gordon would give the bride away; Richard Crenna would usher; Jane Morgan would serve at a reception; and producer Larry Berns' son, Larry, would light the altar tapers. When the cast of *Our Miss Brooks* got involved in something, they made a substantial splash! Parenthetically, Gil Allen, McMillan's husband, became a Presbyterian minister and served several southern California parishes.

The director and lead writer for the radio version of *Our Miss Brooks*, who also penned a handful of installments for the television incarnation, was Al Lewis. Even though he had helpers in the writing department, Lewis was singularly credited every week at the show's opening by announcer Bob Lemond: "It's time once again for another comedy episode of *Our Miss Brooks*, written by Al Lewis." Lemond furthermore announced Al Lewis's name at the end of each installment, that time as its director. Who was this multitalented fellow? Born October 25, 1912, he contributed to the writing of a trio of motion pictures—1946's *Ziegfeld Follies*, 1949's *Ma and Pa Kettle* and 1956's *Our Miss Brooks* (the latter he also directed). He penned an episode of TV's *Vacation Playhouse* and one of *Valentine's Day*, both in 1964, plus he was the scriptwriter for the TV series *Julia* in 1968. Lewis died of congestive heart failure on February 3, 2002, at Huntington Beach, California.

Announcer Robert W. (Bob) Lemond—who introduced *Our Miss Brooks* for Colgate-Palmolive-Peet during the show's heyday—was a native Texan, born in April 1911.[22] He was affiliated with Los Angeles' KEHE before leaving it for a brief rendezvous with San Francisco's KYA. He returned to KEHE in 1938. The following year he departed from the station once again, relocating at nearby KNX. Lemond was just getting his feet wet in network radio when—in 1942—he was summoned to the U.S. Army Air Corps. As a special services officer, he was linked with Armed Forces Radio. Shortly after his return he became an established presence on multiple comedy and dramatic radio features, with no fewer than 20 series to his credit. In addition to *Our Miss Brooks*, they included *The Bob Hawk Show*, *The Hoagy Carmichael Show*, *Honest Harold*, *Life with Luigi*, *Meet Millie*, *My Favorite Husband* and *My Friend Irma*.

During the 1950s and 1960s Lemond presented a quintet of sitcoms airing on a trio of national video chains: *Life with Father* (1953–1955, CBS); *The Ann Sothern Show* (1958–1961, CBS); *Fibber McGee & Molly* (1959–1960, NBC); *Westinghouse Playhouse*, aka *The Nanette Fabray Show* (1961, NBC); and *The Farmer's Daughter* (1963–1966, ABC). In the summer of 1955 he announced the NBC-TV comedy variety feature *And Here's the Show*.

Finally, there was Verne Smith, who delivered the commercials during *Our Miss Brooks*' halcyon era: pitches extolling "soft, glamorous, caressable hair" (Lustre Crème shampoo) and urging listeners to "clean your breath while you clean your teeth and help stop tooth decay" (Colgate Dental Cream). Born November 25, 1909, in New York City, he, too, interrupted a promising career in radio in 1943 to report for duty with Uncle Sam's Army. Returning to the air, he introduced a plethora of network series, among them: *The Adventures of Ozzie and Harriet*, *A Day in the Life of Dennis Day*, *The Great Gildersleeve* (as the show's commercial spokesman),

*The Judy Canova Show*, *The Louella Parsons Show*, *The Roy Rogers Show*, *Truth or Consequences*, and more than a dozen others. Smith died in Seattle, Washington, on March 4, 1978.

In examining the lives of the principal actors of *Our Miss Brooks*, a small detail leaped off the pages of documented records. Of the most prominent quartet of characters in the show—Connie Brooks, Osgood Conklin, Philip Boynton and Walter Denton—four of the five actors playing those parts (Mr. Boynton was re-cast once, you recall) suffered advanced cancer at the time of their deaths. In fact, the malady was the cause of death in three cases for sure, and may have contributed to the fourth. The only person who wasn't so diagnosed (Jeff Chandler) was the first to die, cut short in his prime at age 42, apparently the victim of malpractice during a routine surgical procedure. Astoundingly, both of Chandler's children, his mother, grandpa, aunt and uncle fell victim to cancer's fatal scourge. As the disease is often prevalent in families, would Chandler have met the same fate had he lived longer? Nevertheless, the fact that so many from one small group of thespians shared the same debilitating illness is bewildering, especially if one considers the mirthful madcap mayhem their fun-loving characters produced. The coincidence seems both uncanny and appalling.

On a more pleasant note, *Our Miss Brooks* earned for itself many accolades while winning the hearts of a host of faithful followers during its interval as one of radio's final tour de force situation comedies. Radio comedy is often stilted and badly dated, but this show remains convivial as well as comical even today. One assessment hit the nail on the head: "Miss Brooks' surrogate family, her pupils and colleagues ... loved and respected her while she looked on with mild disdain, too dignified and polite to say anything truly mean—except out of the corner of her mouth to us, her sympathetic listening audience.... It was we who were her secret allies. This most capable and charming of quasi-moms truly was *our* Miss Brooks."[23]

# 20

## The Phil Harris–Alice Faye Show

### RADIO'S NEW LEADER IN SARCASTIC COMEDY

According to one pundit, *The Phil Harris–Alice Faye Show*—preceded by a two-year stint featuring the pair during the flagging days of *The Fitch Bandwagon*—was "radio's new leader in sarcastic comedy." The reviewer added: "The lines were punchy, riotously funny, and expanded the basic format created by Jack Benny. Harris had learned his comedy well during his long years as Benny's stooge."[1] For a decade the bandleader-turned-humorist honed his craft with Benny before acquiring a show of his own with his legendary Hollywood star bride. The format persisted in the Benny tradition, with many scenarios focused on the duo in rehearsal or on behind-the-scenes rows with an unimpressed, unshakable sponsor. Usually there were separate musical numbers by Harris and Faye, a throwback to *Fitch's* longstanding musical heritage. Of course, Benny, *Fibber McGee & Molly* and other comedy series still integrated melodies into their shows. Harris was the true star, although he was aided and abetted by actor Elliott Lewis appearing as Frankie Remley, a boozing buddy who played in Harris's band—although no one ever heard him play. There were a couple of other eccentrics, plus thespians appearing as the couple's daughters (the real progeny weren't old enough). Harris's loudmouth reputation on the Benny series was toned down now that he was a "family man." Offstage he seemed more like the husband-father rather than the womanizer out for good times. Harris and Faye,

who had both been married before, turned out to make a durable team. Their vows lasted to his death 54 years later. By Hollywood standards, it seemed like eternity.

❖ ❖ ❖

**Producer-Director:** Ward Byron (1946–48), Paul Phillips (1948–54)

**Writers:** Ray Singer and Dick Chevillat (1946–50), Ed James, Ray Brenner, Al Schwartz, Frank Gold

**Orchestra Leader:** Walter Scharf

**Vocalists:** The Sportsmen Quartet

**Announcer:** Bill Forman

**Recurring Cast:** *Phil Harris*: Phil Harris (nee Wonga Philip Harris); *Alice Faye*: Alice Faye (nee Alice Jeanne Leppert); *Frankie Remley*: Elliott Lewis; *Julius Abbruzio*: Walter Tetley; *Alice Harris Jr.*: Jeanine Roose; *Phyllis Harris*: Anne Whitfield; *Willie Faye*: Robert North (1946–53), John Hubbard (1953–54); *Mr. Scott*: Gale Gordon

**Supporting Cast:** Arthur Q. Bryan, June Foray, Sheldon Leonard, Jane Morgan, Frank Nelson

**Sponsors:** F.W. Fitch Company, for Fitch shampoo (1946–48); Rexall Drug Company, for Rexall drug stores and pharmaceutical medications (1948–50); Sustained (1950–January 28, 1951); Radio Corporation of America, for RCA appliances and entertainment devices (February 4, 1951–1954)

**Themes:** "That's What I Like About the South" (1946–48), "Sunday" (main theme, 1948–ca. 1954), "Rose Room" (secondary theme), "It's a Big Wide Wonderful World" (ca. 1954)

**Ratings:** High—22.2 (1947–48), Low—3.0 (1953–54), Median—12.5. Ratings based on seven of eight seasons, excluding 1950–51.

**On the Air:** September 29, 1946–May 25, 1947,

*The Fitch Bandwagon*, NBC, Sunday, 7:30–8:00 P.M. Eastern Time; October 5, 1947–May 23, 1948, NBC, Sunday, 7:30–8:00 P.M.; October 3, 1948–June 26, 1949, *The Phil Harris–Alice Faye Show*, NBC, Sunday, 7:30–8:00 P.M.; September 18, 1949–June 4, 1950, NBC, Sunday, 7:30–8:00 P.M.; October 1, 1950–January 28, 1951, NBC, Sunday, 7:30–8:00 P.M.; February 4–May 27, 1951, NBC, Sunday, 8:00–8:30 P.M.; September 30, 1951–May 25, 1952, NBC, Sunday, 8:00–8:30 P.M.; October 5, 1952–June 28, 1953, NBC, Sunday, 8:00–8:30 P.M.; September 18, 1953–June 18, 1954, NBC, Friday, 9:00–9:30 P.M.

**Extant Archival Material:** Memorabilia, scripts, sound recordings and photographs comprise a volunteer-maintained collection of *The Phil Harris–Alice Faye Show*, plus limited representations of other shows on which they performed, in a bank cellar designated as The Phil Harris–Alice Faye Museum, Regions Bank, Box 560, Linton, IN, 47441; (812) 847–4635.

The Walter Tetley Papers, including materials of the actor who appeared as Julius Abbruzio on *The Phil Harris–Alice Faye Show*, are a collection privately held by Charles K. Stumpf, 803 Hazelwood Apartments, Hazelton, PA, 18205; (570) 454–4261.

An unidentified number of scripts for *The Phil Harris–Alice Faye Show* are among the Ray Singer Papers, 1944–1969, archived by the American Heritage Center of the University of Wyoming, 1000 East University Avenue, Laramie, WY, 82071; (307) 766–3756; Fax (307) 766–5511; *http://ahc.uwyo.edu/usearchives/default.htm*.

185 scripts of *The Phil Harris–Alice Faye Show* are maintained in the Script Collection by the Broadcast Arts Library, Box 9828, Fort Worth, TX, 76147; (310) 288–6511; www.broadcastartslibrary.com.

An unidentified number of sound recordings of *The Phil Harris–Alice Faye Show* are among the 26,000-program audio collection privately held as Roger Rittner's "Minds Eye Theatre," 2148 Lambert Drive, Pasadena, CA, 91107; (626) 792–5449.

All of *The Fitch Bandwagon* and *The Phil Harris–Alice Faye Show* broadcasts from 1946 to 1954 are known to be in general circulation or held by private collectors as of 2006, sold by vintage radio dealers and traded by old-time radio hobbyists.

❖ ❖ ❖

Phil Harris was brash and boisterous—a boozing, babe-chasing braggadocio that benefited bountifully from big breaks in binary businesses: bandleading and broadcasting. Besides, he could bury the best of basic communications as he blathered blithely, brutalizing and butchering the King's English bit by bit.

Despite his reputation as a wisecracking, jive-talking hipster, Harris's real-life persona was perceptibly softer and somewhat subdued. Writing in the mid–1970s, one critic affirmed: "Offstage, Harris has a reputation as a polite, almost shy man—a complete reversal of his radio image." Fronting a top novelty band on a national hookup at Los Angeles' Coconut Grove brought him to Jack Benny's attention. In 1936 the comedian snapped him up as the musical director of his show. That good fortune set Harris up for life. His name became familiar overnight in legions of households nationwide. When Benny discovered that his impresario could also dish out clever ripostes to offstage banter, he threw his curly-headed maestro some lines on the show. Before long Harris was a regular contributor to the plots, filling the role of an insult comic. "Hi-ya, Jackson!" he'd quip offhandedly to his boss.

Harris was depicted as a trendy, hotheaded, hard-drinking lad from Dixie whose good nature barely overcame a ferocious ego. Ironically, the Hoosier native's signature song was a rowdy rendition of "That's What I Like about the South." "Like Benny, Harris played a character who in real life would be intolerable. That both men projected themselves through this charade and made their characters treasures of the air was a notable feat."[2]

A decade later Harris and his wife—by then he was the spouse of ex–Hollywood glamour girl Alice Faye—co-starred in the waning vestiges of *The Fitch Bandwagon*. The brassy Sunday night broadcasts had aired since 1938, presenting some noteworthy instrumental ensembles, including Harris's. The series took on the personality of a variety show when comedienne Cass Daley headlined it for a season (1945–46). Because *Fitch* immediately followed Benny's show on NBC, Harris slipped from one studio to another at the station break. Sometimes a plot introduced on Benny's program would be resumed and finished on *Fitch*.

Parenthetically, a study released following the 1946–47 radio season showed that *The Jack Benny Program* ranked first among all

*In addition to the Ozzie Nelsons, the Phil Harrises were musicians who parlayed their artistry into a family sitcom of their own. Phil was well positioned as Jack Benny's impresario and insult comic by the time they inherited* The Fitch Bandwagon *in 1946, turning it into* The Phil Harris–Alice Faye Show *in two years. Faye was a popular vocalist in movies and recordings. In the early 1940s they formed a private and professional alliance that defied the odds. Skeptics gave them little chance at longevity, but the pair fooled them: 54 years later they were still together at the time of Phil's death—by Hollywood standards, a near-record. Their Sunday night series, while not often occupying a spot among the top 10 shows, generated a faithful following and persisted for eight years during network radio's waning days.*

comedy series in November 1946, while *The Fitch Bandwagon*, with Phil Harris and Alice Faye, was mired in 12th place.[3] A whole lot of the audience simply wasn't following Harris as he made the turns from Benny's studio into his own.

Kindly allow further digression for some historical perspective.

> Even though many people thought that *The Fitch Bandwagon* was lucky to be sandwiched in between Jack Benny at 7:00 P.M. and Edgar Bergen at 8:00 on NBC, the *Bandwagon* program actually occupied its Sunday-night-at-7:30 time-slot long before the other two programs

were added to the Sunday line-up. *The Bandwagon*, in fact, pioneered in Sunday evening entertainment programming because prior to its appearance most broadcasters felt that Sunday programming should be of a more religious or serious nature ... even in the evening.[4]

Newspaper media critic John Crosby disparaged Harris and Faye's Sunday night features as "the crudest and least inhibited comedy show in the first fifteen of the Hooper ratings, and my only explanation for its persistently large audience is the fact that it reposes comfortably between Jack Benny and

Edgar Bergen."[5] Wasn't it radio's new leader in sarcastic comedy?

All of this transition from one venue to another worked rather well, nevertheless, until Benny shifted to CBS on January 2, 1949, a product of the network talent raids. At that point he was airing from a facility two blocks from NBC, where Harris's show originated. The Benny writers solved Harris's dilemma of being on two back-to-back series on different chains by including him in the first quarter-hour of their show. By cutting through parking lots, in a couple of minutes Harris could zip at a quick pace from CBS to NBC. That gave him time to warm up his own audience and be on the air as Benny signed off every week.

A humorous portrayal of domesticity, leisure life and the music business pervaded the sitcom about Harris and Faye and their two daughters in that half-hour. Their own offspring were not far beyond the infant stage, so they were impersonated by actresses: Jeanine Roose as Alice Jr. and Anne Whitfield as Phyllis.

Aside from Harris himself (Alice Faye notwithstanding), the most obvious and persistent second banana in the bunch was Harris's pal, left-handed guitar-playing Frankie Remley portrayed by actor Elliott Lewis. As it turned out, Remley was a real musician in Harris's band. The real Remley auditioned for the speaking role of himself but failed to win it. He remained in oblivion, though his name became well-known as the moniker of his superior's hard-drinking buddy. Somehow it always seemed like the series should be titled The Phil Harris–Frankie Remley Show, for obvious reasons. He had far more speaking lines in most installments than Alice Faye, although she was usually good for a ballad in the midst of the action. Late in the run, when Harris was no longer officially affiliated with the Benny troupe, Elliott Lewis performed under his own name.

Born in New York City on November 28, 1917, the son of a printer and journalist, Lewis considered a career in civil engineering. But he was attracted by stage lights and relocated to the West Coast, studying acting at Los Angeles City College. He landed an acting job at KHJ, a CBS affiliate, on a series labeled The Life of Simon Bolivar. Lewis initially made his mark in radio in the late 1930s as an actor, writer, director and producer. Although he expanded into television and fleetingly into recordings and film, radio was always his "first love." He became not only one of the medium's most talented professionals but also one of its most prolific and thereby most influential. Across an extraordinary career, a diversified Lewis earned credits for his connection with more than three dozen audio series:

Adventures by Morse (1944–45, actor)
The Adventures of Nero Wolfe (1946, actor)
The Adventures of Sam Spade, Detective (1946–51, supporting cast)
Arch Oboler's Plays (1945, supporting cast)
Broadway Is My Beat (1949–54, producer-director)
The Casebook of Gregory Hood (1948–49, actor)
Cathy and Elliott Lewis on Stage, aka On Stage (1953–54, actor-producer-director)
The CBS Radio Workshop (ca. 1957, director)
The Cinnamon Bear (1937, actor)
The Clock (1948, acting company)
Columbia Presents Corwin (1948, acting company)
Crime Classics (1953–54, creator-producer-director)
Escape (1947–54, acting company)
The Fitch Bandwagon, aka The Phil Harris–Alice Faye Show (1946–54, actor)
The George Burns and Gracie Allen Show (late 1940s, supporting cast)
Hawk Larabee (1946, actor)
The Hermit's Cave (1940–44, acting company)
I Love a Mystery (1939–42, 1943–44, supporting cast)
The Jack Benny Program (1940s, 1950s, supporting cast)
Jungle Jim (1942, actor)
Junior Miss (ca. late 1940s, actor)
Knickerbocker Playhouse (1939, actor)
The Lineup (1950–53, producer-director)
Maisie (1945–47, 1949–52, actor)

*Meet Me at Parky's* (1945–48, supporting cast)

*Mr. Aladdin* (1951, director)

*One Man's Family* (1940s, 1950s, supporting cast)

*Orson Welles Theater* (1941–42, acting company)

*Plays for Americans* (1942, supporting cast)

*Pursuit* (1949–50, producer-director)

*The Sears Radio Theater*, aka *The Mutual Radio Theater* (1979, ca. 1980–ca. 1981, producer-director)

*Speed Gibson of the International Secret Police* (1937–38, supporting cast)

*Suspense* (1950–54, producer-director)

*This Is Judy Jones* (1941, actor)

*The Voyage of the Scarlet Queen* (actor, 1947–48)

*The Whistler* (1940s, 1950s, acting company)

*The Zero Hour* (1973, director)

Lewis's film work, nevertheless, was pithy. He performed in four movies: *The Winner's Circle* (1948), *The Story of Molly X* (1949), *Ma and Pa Kettle Go to Town* (1950) and *Saturday's Hero* (1951). He directed a trio of television series—*Petticoat Junction*, *The Mothers-in-Law* and *Mayberry R.F.D.*—and produced a quartet of TV series—*This Man Dawson*, *The Lucy Show*, *O.K. Crackerby!* and *The Mothers-in-Law*. He also produced a handful of single episodes of other TV shows. In 1985–86 he was executive script consultant for 34 episodes of TV's *Remington Steele*. His voice is heard on Gordon Jenkins' classic Decca recording of *Manhattan Tower* in 1945. In retirement he penned mystery novels. Beginning in 1980 with *Two Heads Are Better*, which a *Los Angeles Times* critic cited as "a striking novelistic debut," Lewis wrote a succession of eight books about Fred Bennett, a bitter, alienated ex-cop-turned-private detective.

The multitalented artist spent his married life with two well-known actresses. He wed Cathy Lewis on April 30, 1943, and appeared with her in tandem on numerous radio broadcasts. They separated on their 14th anniversary (in 1957) and were divorced on April 16, 1958. He wed Mary Jane Croft in 1960 and was her spouse at his death on May 20, 1990, at home in Gleneden Beach, Oregon, the result of cardiac arrest. He was 72. Lewis was never a father but was survived by Croft and a sibling, Raymond Lewis, of Larkspur, California.

Wordsmith Ray Singer, who was fired from *The Phil Harris–Alice Faye Show* for scripting that was considered too borderline risqué, recalled that Remley in essence became Phil Harris there. Singer depicted Remley as a crude, hard-drinking character, one that Harris used to be before he wed Faye and had a couple of daughters.[6]

Remley was prone to inviting trouble into his chum's life with regularity. The guitarist became the point man for all of the band's palpable traits: dense, lethargic and intoxicated. That perception, while fictitious, was a far cry from the outfit Ozzie Nelson was conducting on another sitcom at the same time. Remley had a way of stranding his bragging, boozing, schmoozing buddy. "I know a guy..." was his preface to putting Harris in touch with a pro in whatever type of trouble arose during an episode. Invariably, the specialist worsened the situation dramatically.

One week Remley convinced Harris he could save a fortune by buying steaks "on the hoof" at a fraction of supermarket prices. Going along with the deal, much too late Harris learned his crony had bought—and brought to his home—a live steer. By the time the animal was transported, slaughtered and the non-usable portions trimmed away, the meat cut, packaged and stored in a rented locker, Harris realized he was spending a small fortune. It was costing far more than any grocer would have charged for the same beef. It was Remley's way of helping out; time after time Harris fell for it lock, stock and steer. The maestro's misplaced trust hinted at just how dense he really was!

Let's face it: he was portrayed as a bumbling buffoon, short of brain power, and became the butt of almost every joke, provoking genuine guffaws from the audience that sounded like canned laughter today. The sound was helped along by microphones strategically placed above the audience to enhance their audible reaction. The jokes became predictable after a while. Listening to them today on recordings, it's difficult to force even a faint grin for many of those gags. For instance, in virtually every show there was at least one misconstrued issue.

On one occasion, Harris—flanked by his family and the ever-present Remley—was in his garage polishing a new English roadster he had just purchased on a European vacation. It was obvious that he was infatuated with it. "You know, Alice," he said, "I'm the luckiest man on earth. Here I am a successful bandleader with my own show, two wonderful children and you—you gorgeous, beautiful, lovable thing." A thinking listener would, of course, realize he meant the car, and not find it all that funny. But the studio audience didn't seem to get it. Or maybe they had been instructed to laugh wildly at everything. When Alice responded, "Why, Phil, that's the nicest thing you've said to me in a long time," he protested at once: "I wasn't talking about *you*, Alice. I meant this dreamboat of a car!" The studio onlookers broke into convulsions, as if it was the most incredibly side-splitting line they'd heard in a while. But after a similar scenario was revisited week after week, some of its luster became tarnished and the joke fell flat, at least with some of those tuning in.

> Remley ... was someone Harris could ridicule and humiliate, but the guzzling and womanizing macho twosome wore a little thin; the one-joke concept fit more amusingly into a quick three-minute segment on the Benny show....
>
> The type finally seems to have exhausted its comic welcome, and become politically incorrect, but Harris was acceptably funny because on the Benny show he only *talked* about his drinking; he never appeared drunk on either his own or Benny's show. He stood in stark contrast to the uptight, probably teetotaling Benny, ... provoking Benny's disdain toward a man he plainly despised as a lush and a letch, a vulgarian even lower down on the social ladder than himself.[7]

There were a handful of additional figures that came across as foils for Harris, too.

One became a fixture, nearly as much as Remley—an excruciatingly confrontational delivery boy from the local market, Julius Abbruzio. It was never very clear to fans why neither of the Harrises, or their surrogates, were prevented from going to the grocery store (fear of recognition, perhaps?). Instead, they always had their purchases delivered, and, apparently, there was only one boy who could do it. (Did he never go to school—or aspire to anything greater?) He got in on whatever was making life miserable for Harris every week and turned the screw a little tighter. Ostensibly he left Harris with egg on his face, and the audience, once again, in stitches.

Julius was played by Walter Tetley, who spoke in high-pitched Brooklynese. There was something familiar about that inflection, by the way. And there should have been! One night a week he was the precocious 12-year-old nephew of Throckmorton P. Gildersleeve on NBC's *The Great Gildersleeve*. Tetley, a child impersonator, played that role for 17 years, beginning in 1941, so his voice was easily distinguished by listeners here. In the *Harris-Faye Show*, nonetheless, he was far more assertive and abrasive than he ever was before his dear old "Unc." Uncle Mort wouldn't have stood for it. His best lines, oft repeated, were: "Are you kiddin'?" and "Get outta here!"

Then there was Willie, Alice Faye's shiftless, lazy, good-for-nothing bum of a brother who lived under their roof. He was played by Robert North for most of the run, and by John Hubbard in the show's final year. The problems of this deadbeat were obvious; having little else to do, he merely exacerbated the troubles that Harris already found himself in. He also found a spot he liked among the unemployed and rested comfortably there, despite Harris's attempts to rectify that situation.

The last of the major recurring figures was Mr. Scott during the Rexall-sponsored years. Played by the marvelous character actor Gale Gordon, a stern Scott was a mythical Rexall official who was constantly in conflict with Harris. He held the bandleader's feet to the fire by subjecting him to constant interrogation, innuendo and reprimand. It was a part that came naturally for Gordon, who appeared in similar commanding roles on *Fibber McGee & Molly*, *My Favorite Husband*, *Our Miss Brooks* and a myriad of other radio series, as well as several *Lucy* TV incarnations.

The show's star—Wonga Philip Harris— was born June 24, 1904, at Linton, Indiana. Most of his adolescent years were spent in Nashville, Tennessee, however, during a pre–*Grand Ole Opry* epoch. One wonders what direction the flashy showman-musician might have taken had he arrived, say, a decade or two later. Might he have been one of the nation's earliest and most universally beloved country music stars? We'll never know, although music was never far from any of his pursuits.

After relocating to San Francisco, where he launched a professional career as a drummer, in the late 1920s Harris and Carol Lofner jointly organized an orchestra. Prosperity smiled on them when they were signed for a protracted commitment at the St. Francis Hotel. After the partnership dissolved in 1932, Harris formed his own outfit, which he headlined both as director and vocalist. He shifted his entourage to Los Angeles not long afterward and married an Australian woman, Marcia Ralston. In time the duo adopted a son, Phil Harris Jr., born in 1935. Four years later the couple divorced.

Harris's life as an entertainer had been on the upswing as the 1930s progressed. He appeared on Rudy Vallee's *Fleischmann Hour* on radio, during which he met Alice Faye, though nothing came of it then. His impressive stint at the Ambassador Hotel's Coconut Grove in Los Angeles wasn't far behind. NBC Blue beamed *Let's Listen to Harris*, featuring the showman and his band, on Friday nights for 18 months (June 23, 1933–December 14, 1934). By then he was also performing in pictures, starting with *Melody Cruise* in 1933. His career encompassed 37 theatrical films by the time he provided a voiceover for 1991's *Rock-a-Doodle* before he retired. Among his movies were *The High and the Mighty* (1954), *Anything*

*Goes* (1956), *The Patsy* (1964), several features in which he appeared as himself, and a fairly large number with voiceover assignments.

Reviving his music career after his radio series faded, Harris made 45 guest appearances on various television series, mostly as himself. They included *The Colgate Comedy Hour*, *The Dinah Shore Chevy Show*, *This Is Your Life*, *The Jack Benny Program*, *The George Gobel Show*, *The Ed Sullivan Show*, *The Andy Williams Show*, *The Pat Boone Show*, *The Dean Martin Show*, *Hollywood Palace*, *Rowan & Martin's Laugh-In*, *The Eddie Fisher Show*, *Shower of Stars*, *This Is Tom Jones*, *Here's Lucy*, *Ben Casey*, *Burke's Law*, *F Troop*, *The Lucy Show*, *Fantasy Island* and *Love Boat*. He also performed on a couple of television specials—*Everything You Always Wanted to Know about Jack Benny but Were Afraid to Ask* in 1971; *NBC Salutes the 25th Anniversary of the Wonderful World of Disney* in 1978—and a made-for-TV movie, 1968's *Mitzi*.

He turned out scads of recordings, his best seller being *The Thing* in 1950. It was a novelty tune about a hapless finder of a box with a mysterious secret and his inability to rid himself of it. Furthermore, Harris summoned his talents as a maestro from mothballs late in his career, conducting a band that frequently performed in Las Vegas in the 1970s and early 1980s. Nevertheless, he still tipped his hat to radio for its powerful influence on his life. "If it hadn't been for radio," he told a reporter, "I would still be a traveling orchestra leader. For 17 years I played one-night stands, sleeping on buses. I never even voted, because I didn't have any residence."

Much later, ex–Harris-Faye wordsmith Ray Singer recalled:

> The six years on *The Phil Harris–Alice Faye Show* were six of the happiest years of my life. They're wonderful people, and it was a writer's paradise, because Phil was the kind of a guy who loved living, and didn't want to be bothered with work or anything else. And he left us alone. We never had to report to him. Dick [Chevillat, his writing partner] and I would work out the premise and write the script. Phil

and Alice lived in Palm Springs; they'd come in on Friday. And we rehearsed, we'd do a rewriting on Saturday, and do the show Sunday and they'd go back to Palm Springs. He never knew what was gonna happen. And it was left in our hands, which is a wonderful thing to do; and it spoiled us for everybody else.[8]

And what of Alice Faye?

She was born Alice Jeanne Leppert, to a father of German descent and an Irish-American mother, in New York City on May 5, 1915. "She rose from the mean streets of New York's Hell's Kitchen to become the most famous singing actress in the world," A&E's *Biography* touted. Getting into entertainment at age 13 as a vaudeville chorus girl with Chester Hale's company, Alice made it to Broadway the following year (1929) in George White's *Scandals*. She appeared on Rudy Vallee's *Fleischmann Hour* on NBC between 1932 and 1934. That's when she was introduced to bandleader Phil Harris, who was performing on the same bill.

Alice received her first big film break in 1934 when Lillian Harvey quit the lead role in a movie adaptation of *Scandals*, in which Vallee was also performing. Originally engaged to sing with Vallee, Alice was thrust into the show's feminine lead. Eight days following her father's death in late 1935 she changed her name, adopting Alice Faye as her stage moniker. Celluloid audiences of the 1930s loved her, and 20th Century–Fox producer Darryl F. Zanuck accepted her as his special charge. "He softened Faye from a wisecracking show girl to the youthful but somewhat motherly figure she played in a few of Shirley Temple's hit films," Wikipedia observed. "Faye also received a physical makeover, from being something of a singing version of Jean Harlow to sporting a softer look with a more natural tone to her blonde hair and more mature makeup."[9] *Newsweek* scribe Jack Kroll called her "a luscious marshmallow sundae of a girl," and her ripe figure fit the movies in which she played.

Primarily cast in musicals, she introduced many popular hit parade songs, such as "You'll Never Know" in the 1943 release *Hello, Frisco, Hello*. Irving Berlin acknowledged that he would choose Faye over any other singer to introduce his songs, while George Gershwin and Cole Porter dubbed her "the best female singer in Hollywood" in 1937. "Color film flattered Faye enormously," Wikipedia disclosed, "and she shone in the splashy musical features that were a Fox trademark in the 1940s."[10] In situations ranging from poignant to comic, she often portrayed a performer who was on the way up, displaying a husky singing voice. "I made six films with Don Ameche, and in every one of them my voice was deeper than the plot," she quipped. Included among her cinematic appearances of the era were *Poor Little Rich Girl* (1936), *In Old Chicago* (1937), *Alexander's Ragtime Band* (1938), *Rose of Washington Square* (1939), *That Night in Rio* (1941) and *Weekend in Havana* (1941). In all, she made 35 films through 1945's *Fallen Angel*, which became a turning point in her career.

The title of that movie could have been written for her. It was supposed to be "her" film. But Zanuck had a new lady-in-waiting, starlet Linda Darnell, whom he had recently taken under his wing. He significantly reduced the scenes with Faye after they had been shot to increase the exposure for Darnell. His former movie queen decided not to take it lying down. She left the Fox studios in a huff, vowing never to return. Zanuck struck back by having her blackballed for breach of contract, effectively ending her motion picture career. For a time it was the talk of the industry. Even though Faye returned to make eight more films later—most of them *much* later (late 1970s to mid–1990s)—her only substantive achievement was 1962's remake of *State Fair*, and even that brought mild notoriety. She played Pat Boone's mother. "I don't know what happened to the picture business," she declared. "I'm sorry I went back to find out. Such a shame."[11]

Nevertheless, for her contributions to motion pictures Faye gained a star on the Hollywood Walk of Fame. Today many of her films are hits at revival theaters across the country. Ironically, she is more popular in Great Britain now than in the United States, according to the IMDb. Toward the close of her career she was hired to promote the virtues of an active senior lifestyle as a spokeswoman for Pfizer Pharmaceuticals.

On September 4, 1937, she wed singer Tony Martin. They were granted a divorce on March 23, 1940, with a final decree of March 27, 1941. They had no children. She and Phil Harris were attracted to one another and soon became an item. Gossip columnist Louella Parsons reported on April 30, 1941: "The only thing that stands in the way is Phil's decree which will not be final for several months.... Phil is telling anybody interested that he'll marry her the minute he can." Although Harris wasn't free to marry in this country until September 20, 1941, the pair went to Mexico and wed on May 12, 1941. On the day his decree became final, the couple remarried in Galveston, Texas. By then they were expecting their first child. Daughter Alice Jr. was born May 19, 1942, and daughter Phyllis Wanda followed on April 26, 1944.

After her conflict with Fox, Faye retired to devote herself to her growing family. The advent of the radio series (*The Fitch Bandwagon*, 1946–48, and *The Phil Harris–Alice Faye Show*, 1948–54) let her keep her hand in show business while allowing her to develop the domestic side. "Her life after Hollywood was charmingly simple," one source reported.

Reminiscing much later about her years at Fox and her transition to motherhood, Faye described the studio as a kind of penitentiary: "So I decided to make a new life for myself. A home life. I had been chauffeured to work, made up, dressed, given my meals and chauffeured back home. I thought, wouldn't it be wonderful to be independent? I equated independence with seeing daylight during the week and learning how to drive a car."[12]

In 1987, she told an interviewer: "When I stopped making pictures, it didn't bother me because there were so many things I hadn't done. I had never learned to run a house. I didn't know how to cook. I didn't

know how to shop. So all these things filled all those gaps."[13]

On the radio shows Faye's honey contralto was a good fit for the ballads and swing numbers she performed. In addition, she was given some tart one-liners to keep up with Harris and Remley. Running gags included portraying her as an heiress ("I'm only trying to protect the wife of the money I love," Harris would remind her). Hanging onto the recent past, on several occasions she tossed barbs at Zanuck with references to *Fallen Angel*.

In a four-decade span starting in 1957 Faye, appearing as herself, turned up in more than a dozen episodes of *This Is Your Life, Hollywood Palace, The Dean Martin Show, The Tonight Show Starring Johnny Carson* and other TV features of that ilk. She also appeared in a quartet of television specials: *Night of 100 Stars* (1982), *Happy 100th Birthday Hollywood* (1987), *61st Annual Academy Awards* (1989) and, paradoxically, *20th Century–Fox: The First 50 Years* (1997). The latter was her final performance.

Late in their careers Harris and Faye donated a large amount of their entertainment memorabilia to the public library in Harris's hometown of Linton, Indiana. Today a museum named for them is operated in Linton and staffed by volunteers. Phil Harris also established some scholarships for promising high school students in Linton while returning to his birthplace to perform at the high school. He hosted an annual celebrity golf tournament there. In 1993 he was inducted into the Indiana Hall of Fame.

The Harrises settled in Rancho Mirage near Palm Springs, where they lived until their deaths. Harris died of a heart attack in Palm Springs, California, on August 11, 1995. Faye died there on May 9, 1998, of stomach cancer. Their daughters, Alice Harris Regan and Phyllis Harris, survived their parents, along with four grandchildren and four great-grandchildren.

The commercials on their programs were something else. The representative of the Rexall Drug Company, who spoke in a monotone during that firm's sponsorship, must have reminded listeners of an unfriendly mortician. While he did his job, his delivery was staid, deficient and uninspiring. If anything, fans hardly were persuaded to run out and buy something from a druggist bearing an orange-and-blue sticker in the window. The guy was dry, his style among the least flattering hawkers in the business. (To clear up any confusion, the actor portraying the Rexall announcer was *not* Gale Gordon. The latter appeared as a Rexall store official in a handful of episodes in which he encountered Phil Harris. On those occasions Gordon exhibited his characteristically cheerless, straightforward, unbending persona—the kind of figure that invariably made him such fun to listen to.)

On the other hand, under the Fitch aegis, the show bounced on the ether with a rousing chorus—and probably millions of listeners—singing, whistling, even jigging to a memorably happy refrain sung to the tune of "Smile for Me":

> *Laugh a-while,*
> *Let a song be your style,*
> *Use Fitch Sham-poo!*
> *Don't despair,*

*Use your head, save your hair,*
*Use Fitch Sham-poo!*

There was little in common between the commercials of the Fitch and the Rexall years. When Rexall pulled out, *Harris-Faye* was left dangling for a few months until RCA, NBC's parent owner, stepped in to rescue it from impending doom. The electronics and appliance manufacturer remained with the series for more than three years, even as the show's ratings plummeted to the single-digit basement, the halcyon days having long passed.

The branding of *The Phil Harris–Alice Faye Show* as "radio's new leader in sarcastic comedy" might be challenged by some, although there is probably enough evidence to justify it. Some listeners who liked the rambunctious, loudmouthed style that often characterized *The Jack Benny Program* were further gratified by a weekly dose of *Harris-Faye*. While domesticity was emphasized on the latter series, in many respects—even after the two features were broadcast on different webs—they often appeared as parts of a whole. And fans of both shows doubled their pleasure as a result of radio comedy's unique experiment.

# Appendix A: A Directory of Network Radio Sitcoms

This compendium covers 170 sitcoms broadcast as recurring American radio features. It includes the years they aired, the chains on which they were heard and the actors most often linked with each show's leading roles. TV incarnations, if any, are noted by their years and webs or syndication.

## Abie's Irish Rose

1942–44; NBC
Sydney Smith, Richard Coogan, Richard Bond, Clayton "Bud" Collyer (Abie Levy); Betty Winkler, Mercedes McCambridge, Julie Stevens, Marion Shockley (Rosemary Levy)

## The Adventures of Maisie

(*See* Maisie)

## The Adventures of Ozzie and Harriet

(*See* Chapter 1)
1944–54; CBS/NBC/CBS/ABC
Ozzie and Harriet Nelson (themselves); Tommy Bernard, David Nelson (David Nelson); Henry Blair, Ricky Nelson (Ricky Nelson); John Brown (Syd "Thorny" Thornberry); Lurene Tuttle (Mrs. Hilliard)
TV: 1952–66, ABC

## The Adventures of Topper

(aka *Topper*)
1945; NBC
Roland Young (Cosmo Topper); Hope Emerson (Henrietta Topper); Paul Mann, Tony Barrett (George Kerby); Frances Chaney (Marion Kerby)
TV: 1953–55, CBS

## The Alan Young Show

1944–47, 1949; NBC/ABC/NBC
Alan Young (himself); Jean Gillespie, Doris Singleton, Louise Erickson (Betty Dittenfeffer); Ed Begley (Papa Dittenfeffer)
TV: 1953, CBS (Young starred in other formats/shows under the same banner)

## The Aldrich Family

(*See* Chapter 2)
1939–51, 1952–53; NBC/NBC Blue/NBC/CBS/NBC
Ezra Stone, Norman Tokar, Dickie Jones, Raymond Ives, Bobby Ellis (Henry Aldrich); Jackie Kelk, Johnny Fiedler, Jack Grimes, Michael O'Day (Homer Brown); House Jameson, Clyde Fillmore, Tom Shirley (Sam Aldrich); Katharine Raht, Lea Penman, Regina Wallace (Alice Aldrich); Betty Field, Patricia Peardon, Charita Bauer, Ann Lincoln, Jone Allison, Mary Mason, Mary Rolfe (Mary Aldrich)
TV: 1949–53, NBC

## The Amazing Mrs. Danbury

1946; CBS
Agnes Moorehead (Mrs. Jonathan Danbury)

## The Amos 'n' Andy Show (aka *Amos 'n' Andy, The Amos 'n' Andy Music Hall*)

(*See* Chapter 3)
1929–60 (sitcom years 1943–55); NBC Blue/NBC/CBS/NBC/CBS
Freeman Gosden (Amos Jones, George "Kingfish" Stevens); Charles Correll (Andrew H. Brown); Ernestine Wade (Sapphire Stevens); Amanda Randolph (Mama); Harriette Widmer (Madame Queen); Elinor Harriot (Ruby Taylor Jones)
TV: 1951–53, CBS

## Archie Andrews

(*See Chapter 4*)
1943–44, 1945–53); NBC Blue/MBS/NBC
Charles Mullen, Jack Grimes, Burt Boyar, Bob Hastings (Archie Andrews); Harlan Stone, Cameron Andrews (Forsythe Pendleton "Jughead" Jones); Vinton Hayworth, Reese Taylor, Arthur Kohl (Fred Andrews); Alice Yourman, Peggy Allenby (Mary Andrews); Joy Geffen, Doris Grundy, Rosemary Rice (Betty Cooper); Vivian Smolen, Gloria Mann (Veronica Lodge)
TV: 1968–76, 1977–78, 1987–89 (animated cartoons), CBS/NBC; 1990 (made-for-TV movie), NBC

## Arthur's Place

1947; CBS
Arthur Moore (himself)

## Baby Snooks (aka *Maxwell House Presents Good News, Maxwell House Coffee Time, Post Toasties Time, The Baby Snooks Show*)

(*See Chapter 5*)
1937–48, 1949–51; NBC/CBS/NBC
Fanny Brice (Snooks Higgins); Alan Reed, Hanley Stafford (Lancelot "Daddy" Higgins); Lalive Brownell, Lois Corbett, Arlene Harris (Vera "Mommy" Higgins); Leone Ledoux (Robespierre Higgins)

## Beulah

(*See Chapter 6*)
1945–46, 1947–54; CBS/ABC/CBS
Marlin Hurt, Bob Corley, Hattie McDaniel, Lillian Randolph, Amanda Randolph (Beulah); Hugh Studebaker, Jess Kirkpatrick (Harry Henderson); Mary Jane Croft, Lois Corbett (Alice Henderson); Henry Blair, Sammy Ogg (Donnie Henderson); Bill Jackson (Marlin Hurt, Ernie "Bubbles" Whitman); Oriole (Ruby Dandridge)
TV: 1950–53, ABC

## The Bickersons (aka *Drene Time, The Old Gold Hour, The Don Ameche Show*)

(*See Appendix B*)
1946–48, 1951; NBC/CBS
Don Ameche, Lew Parker (John Bickerson); Frances Langford, Marsha Hunt (Blanche Bickerson); Danny Thomas, Frank Morgan (Amos Jacobs)

## The Billie Burke Show (aka *Fashions in Rations*)

1943–44; CBS
Billie Burke (herself), Earle Ross (Julius Burke),

Lillian Randolph (Daisy), Marvin Miller (Banker Guthrie, Colonel Fitts)
(*See also* The Gay Mrs. Featherstone)

## Blondie

(*See Chapter 7*)
1939–50; CBS/NBC Blue/CBS/NBC/ABC
Arthur Lake (Dagwood Bumstead); Penny Singleton, Alice White, Ann Rutherford, Patricia Van Cleve (Blondie Bumstead); Leone Ledoux, Tommy Cook, Larry Sims, Bobby Ellis, Jeffrey Silver (Alexander "Baby Dumpling" Bumstead); Leone Ledoux, Marlene Ames, Norma Jean Nilsson, Joan Rae (Cookie Bumstead); Hanley Stafford, Arthur Q. Bryan (J. C. Dithers)
TV: 1957, NBC

## Bright Star

1952–53; Syndication
Irene Dunne (Susan Armstrong); Fred MacMurray (George Harvey)

## Bringing Up Father

1941; NBC Blue
Mark Smith, Neil O'Malley (Jiggs); Agnes Moorehead (Maggie); Helen Shields, Joan Banks (Nora); Craig McDonnell (Dinty Moore)

## Burns and Allen

(*See* The George Burns and Gracie Allen Show)

## The Busy Mr. Bingle

1943; MBS
John Brown (J.B. Bingle); Ethel Owen (Miss Pepper); Jackson Beck (Whizzer, Tommy); Elizabeth Moran (Mrs. Bingle)

## Captain Flagg and Sergeant Quirt

1941–42; NBC Blue/NBC
Victor McLaglen, William Gargan (Captain Flagg); Edmund Lowe (Sergeant Quirt); Fred Shields (Sergeant Bliss); John Smith (Major General)

## The Cass Daley Show

1950; NBC
Cass Daley (herself); Fred Howard (Mr. Daley); Lurene Tuttle (Mrs. Daley)

## Charlie and Jessie

1940–41; CBS
Donald Cook (Charlie); Diane Bourbon, Florence Lake (Jessie)

## The Charlotte Greenwood Show

1944–46; NBC/ABC
Charlotte Greenwood (herself); John Brown (Mr. Anderson); Harry Bartell (Tommy Brooks); Ed MacDonald (Roger); Janet Waldo (Barbara Barton); Cliff Carpenter (Jack Barton); Dix Davis (Robert Barton)

## Chicken Every Sunday

1949; NBC
Harry Von Zell (Jim Hefferen); Billie Burke (Emily Hefferen)

## The Cobbs

1954; CBS
William Demarest (Jim Cobb); Katie Cobb (Hope Emerson)

## The Couple Next Door

1937, 1957–60; MBS/CBS
Peg Lynch (Mother); Alan Bunce (Father); Margaret Hamilton (Aunt Effie); Madeleine Pierce (Betsy)
TV: A sketch reprised on the daytime variety series The Frances Langford-Don Ameche Show, with Jack Lemmon and Cynthia Stone as young marrieds, 1951–52, ABC

## Cousin Willie

1953; NBC
Bill Idelson (Willard O. Knotts); Marvin Miller (Marvin Sample); Patricia Dunlap (Fran Sample); Dawn Bender, Bridget DeCarl (Susan Sample); Stuffy Singer, Tony Kaye (Sandy Sample)

## The Creightons

1942–43; NBC
John Griggs (Christopher Creighton); Ethel Owen (Serena Creighton); Norman Tokar (Victor Creighton); Sammie Hill (Crottie Creighton)

## A Date with Judy

(See Appendix B)
1941, 1942, 1943, 1944–50; NBC/ABC
Ann Gillis, Dellie Ellis, Louise Erickson (Judy Foster); Paul McGrath, Stanley Farrar, Joseph Kearns, John Brown (Melvin Foster); Margaret Brayton, Bea Benaderet, Georgia Backus, Lois Corbett, Myra Marsh (Dora Foster); Tommy Bond, Tommy Cook, Johnny McGovern, Dix Davis (Randolph Foster); Harry Harvey, Richard Crenna (Oogie Pringle); Lurene Tuttle, Ann Gillis, Sandra Gould (Gloria); Mercedes McCambridge, Louise Erickson, Georgia Backus, Sandra Gould (Mitzi Hoffman)
TV: 1951–52, 1953, ABC

## A Day in the Life of Dennis Day

(aka The Dennis Day Show)

(See Appendix B)
1946–51, 1954–55; NBC
Dennis Day (himself); Sharon Douglas, Barbara Eiler, Betty Miles (Mildred Anderson); Francis "Dink" Trout (Herbert Anderson); Bea Benaderet (Clara Anderson); John Brown (Homer Willoughby)

## Dear Mom

1941; CBS
John Walsh (Private Homer Stubbs); Dolph Nelson (Corporal Red Foster); Marvin Miller (Sergeant Mike Monihan); Herb Butterfield (Colonel Willoughby); Lou Krugman (Ulysses Hink)

## December Bride

1952–53; CBS
Spring Byington (Lily Ruskin); Doris Singleton (Ruth Henshaw); Hal March (Matt Singleton); Hans Conried (Pete Porter); Verna Felton (Hilda Crocker)
TV: 1954–59, CBS

## Doc, Duke and the Colonel

1945; NBC
Jess Pugh (Doc); Clarence Hartzell (Duke); Cliff Soubier (Colonel)

## Duffy's Tavern (aka Duffy's Variety)

(See Chapter 8)
1941–51, segments in late 1950s on Monitor; CBS/NBC Blue/NBC
Ed Gardner (Archie); Shirley Booth, Florence Halop, Helen Lynd, Doris Singleton, Sara Berner, Connie Manning, Florence Robinson, Sandra Gould, Helen Eley, Margie Liszt, Gloria Erlanger, Hazel Shermet, Pauline Drake (Miss Duffy); Charlie Cantor, Sid Raymond (Clifton Finnegan); Eddie Green, Sam Raskin (Eddie); Alan Reed (Clancy)
TV: 1954, Syndication

## Easy Aces (aka Mr. Ace and Jane)

(See Appendix B)
1931, 1932–34, 1935–46 (daytime serial most of the run); CBS/NBC/NBC Blue/CBS/Syndication
Goodman and Jane Ace (themselves); Mary Hunter (Marge Hall); Paul Stewart (Johnny Sherwood); Peggy Allenby (Mrs. Benton); Ethel Blume (Betty); Alfred Ryder (Carl); Martin Gabel (Neil Williams); Helene Dumas (Laura); Ann Thomas (Miss Thomas)
TV: 1949–50, Dumont

## The Eddie Bracken Show

1945, 1946–47; NBC/CBS
Eddie Bracken (himself); Ann Rutherford (Connie Pringle); William Demarest (Sheriff Pringle)

## Ethel and Albert (aka The Private Lives of Ethel and Albert)

(See Appendix B)
1944–50; NBC Blue/ABC
Peg Lynch (Ethel Arbuckle); Alan Bunce, Richard Widmark (Albert Arbuckle); Madeleine Pierce (Baby Suzy)
TV: 1953–54, 1955–56, NBC/CBS/ABC (debuted as a segment on NBC's The Kate Smith Hour in 1952–53)

## The Ethel Merman Show

1949; NBC
Ethel Merman (herself); Allen Drake, Arthur Q. Bryan (Homer Tubbs); Leon Janney (Eddie McCoy)

## The Fabulous Dr. Tweedy (aka The Frank Morgan Show)

1946–47; NBC
Frank Morgan (Thaddeus Q. Tweedy); Nana Bryant (Miss Tilsey); Harlan Stone (Sidney Potts); Janet Waldo (Mary Potts); Gale Gordon (Alexander Potts); Harry Von Zell (Timothy Welby); Will Wright (Beauregard Jackson); Sara Berner (Kitty Bell Jackson)

## Fashions in Rations

(See The Billie Burke Show)

## Father Knows Best

(See Chapter 9)
1949–54; NBC
Robert Young (Jim Anderson); Jean Vander Pyl (Margaret Anderson); Rhoda Williams (Betty Anderson); Ted Donaldson (Bud Anderson); Norma Jean Nilsson, Helen Strong (Kathy Anderson)
TV: 1954–62, CBS/NBC/CBS

## Fibber McGee & Molly

(See Chapter 10)
1935–56, brief segments aired on Monitor from 1957 to 1959; NBC Blue/NBC
Jim Jordan (Fibber McGee); Marian Jordan (Molly McGee, Teeny); Bill Thompson (Wallace Wimple, Mr. Old-Timer, Nick Depopoulouss, Horatio K. Boomer); Gale Gordon (Foggy Williams, Charles La-Trivia, Otis Cadwallader, Karl Snarl); Arthur Q. Bryan (Doc Gamble); Bea Benaderet (Millicent Carstairs); Isabel Randolph (Abigail Uppington); Richard LeGrand

(Ole Swenson); Hal Peary (Throckmorton P. Gildersleeve); Marlin Hurt (Beulah)
TV: 1959–60, NBC

## The First Hundred Years

1949; ABC
Sam Edwards (Chris Thayer); Barbara Eiler (Connie Martin Thayer)
TV: 1950–52, CBS (daytime serial)

## Forever Ernest

1946; CBS
Jackie Coogan (Ernest Botch); Lurene Tuttle (Candy Lane); Arthur Q. Bryan (Duke)

## Four Corners, USA

1938–39; CBS
Arthur Allen (Jonah Crowell); Parker Fennelly (Eben Crowell); Jean McCoy (Mary Crowell)

## Frank Wantabe and the Honorable Archie (aka Honorable Archie and Frank Wantabe)

1930–33, 1934; NBC West Coast/NBC Blue
Eddie Holden (Frank Wantabe); Reginald Oldfield (Archibald Chiselberry)

## The Fresh-Up Show

1945–46; MBS
Bert Wheeler (himself); Walter Kinsella (Doc Fickett); Annette Warren (Viola Fickett); Lee Brady (Melville Fickett); Arthur Elmer (Mr. Fuddle). Note: There was a replacement cast for this series at the end of 1945 that included Bert Lahr, Alan Bunce, John Gibson, Leon Janney and Pert Kelton

## The Gay Mrs. Featherstone

1945; NBC
Billie Burke (Dora Featherstone); John Brown (son-in-law); Florence Lake (daughter)
(See also The Billie Burke Show)

## The George Burns and Gracie Allen Show (aka The Robert Burns Panatella Program, The White Owl Program, The Adventures of Gracie, The Campbell's Tomato Juice Program, Burns and Allen)

(See Chapter 11)
1932–50, 1959 (sitcom years 1941–50); CBS/NBC/CBS/NBC/CBS/NBC/CBS

George Burns and Gracie Allen (themselves); Hal March (Harry Morton); Bea Benaderet (Blanche Morton); Mel Blanc ("the Happy Postman"); Elvia Allman (Tootsie Sagwell)

TV: 1950–58, CBS

## The George O'Hanlon Show

1948–49; MBS

Principals portrayed by George O'Hanlon, Lurene Tuttle, Cliff Young, Alan Reed

## Gibbs and Finney, General Delivery

1942; NBC Blue

Parker Fennelly (Gideon Gibbs); Arthur Allen (Asa Finney)

## The Gibson Family (aka Uncle Charlie's Tent Show)

1934–35; NBC

Loretta Clemens (Dot Gibson); Jack Clemens, Al Dary (Bob Gibson); Adele Ronson (Sally Gibson); Bill Adams (Father Gibson); Anne Elstner (Mother Gibson)

## The Goldbergs (aka The Rise of the Goldbergs)

1929–34, 1936, 1937–45, 1949–50 (daytime serial most of the run); NBC Blue/NBC/MBS/NBC/CBS/NBC/MBS/CBS

Gertrude Berg (Molly Goldberg); James R. Waters, Philip Loeb (Jake Goldberg); Alfred Ryder, Larry Robinson (Sammy Goldberg); Roslyn Silber, Arlene McQuade (Rosalie Goldberg)

TV: 1949–51, 1952, 1953, 1954–55, CBS/NBC/Dumont/Syndication

## Gramps

1947; NBC

Edgar Stehli (Gramps); other principals portrayed by Craig McDonnell, Anne Seymour, Joan Lazer, Edwin Bruce, Arthur Q. Bryan, Edwin Bruce, Bartlett Robinson

## Granby's Green Acres

1950; CBS

Gale Gordon (John Granby); Bea Benaderet (Martha Granby); Louise Erickson (Janice Granby); Parley Baer (Eb)

## The Great Gildersleeve

(*See Chapter 12*)

1941–57 (recurring character introduced on *Fibber McGee & Molly* in 1939–41); NBC

Harold Peary, Willard Waterman (Throckmorton P. Gildersleeve, 1950–57); Walter Tetley (Leroy Forrester); Lurene Tuttle, Louise Erickson, Mary Lee Robb (Marjorie Forrester); Lillian Randolph (Birdie Lee Coggins); Earle Ross (Horace Hooker); Richard LeGrand, Forrest Lewis (J.W. Peavey); Arthur Q. Bryan (Floyd Munson); Shirley Mitchell (Leila Ransom); Bea Benaderet (Eve Goodwin); Richard Crenna (Bronco Thompson); Gale Gordon, Jim Backus (Rumson Bullard)

TV: 1955, Syndication

## Great Gunns

1941; MBS

Bret Morrison (Chris Gunn); Barbara Luddy (Veronica Gunn); Bob Jellison (Buster Gunn); Phillip Lord (Pop Gunn); Marvin Miller (Lorson Snells)

## The Grummits

1934–35, 1936–37; NBC/MBS

Ed Ford (Pop Grummit); Eunice Howard (Mom Grummit)

## The Gumps

1934–35, 1936–37; CBS

Wilmer Walter (Andy Gump); Agnes Moorehead (Min Gump); Lester Jay, Jackie Kelk (Chester Gump)

## The Halls of Ivy

(*See Appendix B*)

1950–52; NBC

Ronald Colman (William Todhunter Hall); Benita Hume (Victoria Cromwell "Vicky" Hall); Herb Butterfield (Clarence Wellman); Willard Waterman (John Meriweather); Elizabeth Patterson, Gloria Gordon (Penny)

TV: 1954–55, CBS

## Hap Hazard

1941; NBC

Ransom Sherman (Hap Hazard); Cliff Soubier (Mr. Pittaway); Ray Grant (Cyclone)

## The Hardy Family

1952–53; MBS

Mickey Rooney (Andy Hardy); Lewis Stone (Judge James Hardy); Fay Holden (Emily Hardy); Richard Crenna (Beasey); Eleanor Tanner (Polly Benedict)

## The Harold Peary Show

(*See Honest Harold*)

## Harold Teen

1941–42; MBS
Charles Flynn, Willard Farnum, Eddie Firestone, Jr. (Harold Teen); Bob Jellison (Shadow Smart); Loretta Poynton, Eunice Yankee (Lillums Lovewell); Rosemary Garbell (Josie); Marvin Miller (Beezie Jenks)

## Harv and Esther

1935–36; CBS
Teddy Bergman (Harv); Audrey March (Esther)

## Here Comes Elmer

1944–45; CBS
Al Pearce (Elmer Blurt); Arlene Harris (Arlene)

## His Honor, the Barber

1945–46; NBC
Barry Fitzgerald (Judge Bernard Fitz); Bill Green (Sheriff McGrath); Dawn Bender (Susan Fitz); Leo Cleary (Joel Pearson)

## Hogan's Daughter

1949; NBC
Shirley Booth (Phyllis Hogan); Howard Smith (Tom Hogan); Betty Garde (Kate Hogan); Everett Sloane (Marvin Gaffney); Betty Garde (LaVerne); Johnny Roventini (Johnny)

## Holiday and Company

1946; CBS
Ray Mayer (Tom Holiday); Edith Evans (Shirl Holiday); Frances Heflin (Nora Holiday)

## Honest Harold (aka The Harold Peary Show)

1950–51; CBS
Harold Peary (Harold Hemp); Kathryn Card, Jane Morgan (Mother Hemp); Sammy Ogg (Marvin); Gloria Holliday (Gloria); Parley Baer (Pete); Joseph Kearns (Doctor Yak Yak)

## Honorable Archie and Frank Wantabe

(See Frank Wantabe and the Honorable Archie)

## The Hoofinghams

1935; NBC
Murray Forbes (Mr. Hoofingham); Helene Page (Mrs. Hoofingham)

## House of Glass

1935–36, 1953–54; NBC
Gertrude Berg (Bessie Glass); Joseph Greenwald, Joseph Buloff (Barney Glass); Ann Thomas (Sophie)

## It's Always Albert

1948; CBS
Arnold Stang (Albert); other principals portrayed by Jan Murray, Pert Kelton

## It's Higgins, Sir

1951; NBC
Harry McNaughton (Higgins); Vinton Hayworth, Arthur Cole (Philip Roberts); Peggy Allenby, Vera Allen (Elizabeth Roberts); Denise Alexander (Debbie Roberts); Pat Hosley (Nancy Roberts)

## It's the Barrys

1953; NBC
Jack Barry (himself); Marcia Van Dyke (Marcia Barry); Jeff Barry (himself)

## The Jack Benny Program (aka The Canada Dry Ginger Ale Program, The Chevrolet Program, The General Tire Show, The Jell-O Program, The Grape-Nuts Program, The Lucky Strike Program, The Best of Benny)

(See Chapter 13)
1932–55, 1956–58; NBC Blue/CBS/NBC/CBS
Jack Benny (himself); Mary Livingstone (herself); Phil Harris (himself); Eddie Anderson (Rochester Van Jones); Dennis Day (himself)
TV: 1950–65, CBS/NBC

## The Jack Carson Show

1943–47; CBS
Jack Carson (himself); Dave Willock (Tugwell); Arthur Treacher (Tristan); Elizabeth Patterson (Aunt Sally); Mel Blanc (Hubert Peabody); Jane Morgan (Mrs. Foster)

## The Jack Paar Show

1947; NBC
Jack Paar (himself); others portrayed by Elvia Allman, Hans Conried, Florence Halop, Lionel Stander
TV: Multiple series unrelated to the radio feature but similarly titled—1953–54 and 1955–56, CBS; 1962–65, NBC; 1973, ABC; plus host of The Jack Paar Tonight Show, 1957–62, NBC

## The Jack Pearl Show (aka Baron Munchausen, Jack and Cliff)

1932–34, 1936–37, 1948, 1951; CBS/NBC/CBS/NBC

Jack Pearl (Baron von Munchausen); Cliff Hall (Sharlie)

Note: See Peter Pfeiffer also

## Jimmy Gleason's Diner

1946; ABC

Jimmy Gleason (himself); Lucille Gleason (herself)

## Joan Davis Time (aka The Joan Davis Show, Joanie's Tea Room, Leave It to Joan)

1945–50 (embracing a trio of sitcom situations); CBS

Joan Davis (herself); Andy Russell (Andy, Seranis); Harry Von Zell (Josh Weatherbee, Simon Hackaday); Shirley Mitchell (Barbara Weatherbee, Penny Prentiss); Verna Felton (Rosella Hipperton III); Sharon Douglas (Mabel); Lionel Stander (Lionel); Andy Russell (Tom Hinkle); Joseph Kearns (Pops Davis)

TV: 1952–55 (I Married Joan), NBC

## Joe and Ethel Turp

1941, 1943 (daytime serial); Syndication/CBS

Jackson Beck (Joe Turp); Patsy Campbell (Ethel Turp); Art Carney (Billy Oldham); Jean Ellyn (Dolly Dunkle); Jack Smart (Uncle Ben)

## Joe and Mabel

1941, 1942; NBC

Ted de Corsia (Joe Spartan); Ann Thomas (Mabel Stooler); Betty Garde (Adele Stooler); Jack Grimes (Sherman Stooler); Walter Kinsella (Mike)

## The Johnson Family

1937–50; MBS

Jimmy Scribner (all voices)

## Jones and I

1941–42, 1945–46; CBS/ABC

Sammie Hill (Sally Jones); Scott Farnsworth (Jack Scott); Mason Adams (Ned Scott)

## The Judy Canova Show

1943–44, 1945–53; CBS/NBC

Judy Canova (herself); Ruth Perrott, Verna Felton (Aunt Aggie); George Dietz (Benchley Botsford);

Ruby Dandridge (Geranium), Mel Blanc (Pedro); Gale Gordon, Joseph Kearns (Mr. Simpson); Gale Gordon (Gordon Mansfield); Verna Felton (Patsy Pierce); Jim Backus (Hubert Updyke)

## Junior Miss

(See Appendix B)

1942, 1948–50, 1952–54; CBS

Shirley Temple, Barbara Whiting (Judy Graves); Elliott Lewis, Gale Gordon (Harry Graves); Mary Lansing, Sarah Selby (Grace Graves); K.T. Stevens, Barbara Eiler, Peggy Knudson (Lois Graves); Myra Marsh (Hilda); Priscilla Lyon, Beverly Wills (Fuffy [sic]Adams)

## Keeping Up with Wigglesworth

1945, 1946; Syndication/MBS

Jack Ayres (Snuffy Wigglesworth); other principals portrayed by Bill Adams, Floyd Buckley, Marilyn Erskine, Eunice Howard, Charles Miller, Anthony Rivers

## Lawyer Tucker

1947; CBS

Parker Fennelly (Dan Tucker); Maurice Wells (Warren Biggers); Mae Shults (Sarah Tucker); Arthur Anderson (Mark Davis)

## Leave It to Joan

(See Joan Davis Time)

## Leave It to Mike (aka Paging Mike McNally)

1945–46; MBS

Walter Kinsella (Mike McNally); Joan Alexander (Dinny); Jerry Macy (Mr. Berkeley); Hope Emerson (Mrs. Berkeley)

## Lefty

1946; CBS

Jack Albertson (Lefty); Joan Alexander (society reporter); Maxine Stewart (secretary)

## The Life of Riley

(See Chapter 14)

1941, 1944–51; CBS/ABC/NBC

William Bendix (Chester A. Riley); Paula Winslowe (Margaret "Peg" Riley); Conrad Binyon, Scotty Beckett, Jack Grimes, Bobby Ellis, Tommy Cook (Junior Riley); Sharon Douglas, Barbara Eiler (Babs Riley); John Brown (Digby "Digger" O'Dell); Jim Gillis); Francis "Dink" Trout (Waldo Binney)

TV: 1949–50, 1953–58, NBC

## Life with Luigi

(*See Chapter 15*)
1948–53, 1954; CBS
J. Carrol Naish (Luigi Basco); Alan Reed (Pasquale); Jody Gilbert (Rosa); Mary Shipp (Miss Spaulding); Hans Conried (Schultz); Gil Stratton, Jr., Alan Reed (Jimmy O'Connor)
TV: 1952, 1953, CBS

## Li'l Abner

1939–40; NBC
John Hodiak (Li'l Abner Yokum); Laurette Fillbrandt (Daisy Mae Scruggs); Clarence Hartzell (Pappy Lucifer Ornamental Yokum); Hazel Dopheide (Mammy Pansy Yokum)

## Lorenzo Jones

1937–55 (daytime serial—emphasis shifted from sitcom to melodrama in 1952); NBC
Karl Swenson (Lorenzo Jones); Betty Garde, Lucille Wall (Belle Jones)

## Lum and Abner

(*See Appendix B*)
1931, 1932–40, 1941–50, 1953–54; NBC/MBS/NBC Blue/CBS/NBC Blue/ABC/CBS/ABC
Chester Lauck (Lum Edwards and numerous other voices); Norris Goff (Abner Peabody and numerous other voices); Jerry Hausner (numerous voices); Frank Graham (numerous voices); Lurene Tuttle (numerous voices)

## Ma and Pa

1936–37; CBS
Parker Fennelly (Pa); Margaret Dee, Effie Palmer (Ma)

## Maggie and Jiggs

(*See Bringing Up Father*)

## The Magnificent Montague

1950–51; NBC
Monty Woolley (Edwin Montague); Anne Seymour (Lily Boheme Montague); Pert Kelton (Agnes)

## Maisie (aka *The Adventures of Maisie*)

(*See Appendix B*)
1945–47, 1949–51, 1952; CBS/Syndication/MBS
Ann Sothern (Maisie Revere)

## Major Hoople

1942–43; NBC Blue
Arthur Q. Bryan (Major Amos Hoople); Patsy Moran (Martha Hoople); Mel Blanc (Tiffany Twiggs); Franklin Bresee (Alvin Hoople)

## The Marriage

1953–54; NBC
Hume Cronyn (Ben Marriot); Jessica Tandy (Liz Marriot); Denise Alexander (Emily Marriot); David Pfeffer (Peter Marriot)
TV: 1954, NBC

## Maude and Cousin Bill

1932–33; NBC Blue
Maude Ricketts (Maude); Bill Ricketts (Uncle Bill)

## Maudie's Diary

1941–42; CBS
Mary Mason, Charita Bauer, Carol Smith (Maudie Mason); William Johnstone (Mr. Mason); Betty Garde (Mrs. Mason); Marjorie Davis (Sylvia Mason); Robert Walker (Davey Dillon); Carol Smith (Pauley)

## Mayor of the Town

1942, 1943, 1944–48, 1949; NBC/CBS/ABC/MBS
Lionel Barrymore (Mayor Russell); Agnes Moorehead (Marilly); Conrad Binyon (Roscoe "Butch" Gardner)
TV: 1954, Syndication

## Me and Janie

1949; NBC
George O'Hanlon (himself); Lurene Tuttle (Janie O'Hanlon); Jeffrey Silver (Tommy O'Hanlon); Willard Waterman (Mr. Lamb)

## Meet Corliss Archer

(*See Appendix B*)
1943, 1944–45, 1946, 1947–48, 1949–53, 1954, 1956; CBS/NBC/CBS/ABC/CBS
Priscilla Lyon, Janet Waldo, Lugene Sanders (Corliss Archer); Bill Christy, Burt Boyar, Sam Edwards, David Hughes, Irving Lee (Dexter Franklin); Frank Martin, Fred Shields, Bob Bailey (Harry Archer); Gloria Holden, Irene Tedrow, Mary Jane Croft, Helen Mack (Janet Archer)
TV: 1951, 1952, 1954, CBS/Syndication

## Meet Me at Parky's

1945–48 (recurring character introduced earlier on the Eddie Cantor and Al Jolson radio features); NBC/MBS

Harry Einstein (Nick Parkyarkarkas); Betty Jane Rhodes (Betty); Opie Cates (Opie); Sheldon Leonard (Orville Sharp); Joan Barton (Joan); Ruth Perrott (Prudence Rockbottom)

## Meet Me in St. Louis

1950; NBC
Peggy Ann Garner (Esther Smith); Vinton Hayworth (Alonzo Smith); Brook Byron (Tootie Smith); Agnes Young (Anne Smith); Jack Edwards (Glenn Smith); Billy Redfield (John Truitt); Ethel Wilson (Katie)

## Meet Millie

(*See Chapter 16*)
1951–54; CBS
Audrey Totter, Elena Verdugo (Millie Bronson); Bea Benaderet, Florence Halop (Bertha "Mama" Bronson); Marvin Kaplan (Alfred E. Printzmetal); Earle Ross (J.R. Boone Sr.); Rye Billsbury (Johnny Boone, Jr.)
TV: 1952–56, CBS

## Meet Mr. McNutley (aka *The Ray Milland Show*)

1953–54; CBS
Ray Milland (Ray McNutley); Phyllis Avery (Peggy McNutley); Gordon Jones (Pete "Petey" Thompson); Jacqueline DeWitt (Ruth Thompson)
TV: 1953–55, CBS

## Meet Mr. Meek (aka *The Adventures of Mr. Meek; Meet the Meeks*)

1940–42, 1947–49; CBS/NBC
Wilbur "Budd" Hulick, Frank Readick, Forrest Lewis (Mortimer Meek); Adelaide Klein, Fran Allison (Agatha Meek); Doris Dudley (Peggy Meek); Jack Smart, Cliff Soubier (Uncle Louie); Charles Cantor (Walter Barker); Jeanette Nolan (Birdie Barker)

## The Mel Blanc Show (aka *Mr. Blanc's Fix-It Shop*)

1946–47; CBS
Mel Blanc (himself, Zookie); Mary Jane Croft (Betty Colby); Joseph Kearns (Mr. Colby); Jill Walker, Bea Benaderet (Mrs. Colby); Hans Conried (Mr. Cushing)

## Mennen Shave Time

1946–47; MBS
Principals portrayed by Lou Parker, Ann Thomas

## The Merry Life of Mary Christmas

1945; CBS
Mary Astor (Mary Christmas); Paul Marlon (Mr. Christmas)

## Meyer the Buyer

Mid–1930s; Syndication
Harry Hershfield (Meyer); Teddy Bergman (Mayor Mizznick); Paul Douglas (Lawyer Feldman)

## Mr. and Mrs.

1929–31, 1946; CBS/NBC
Jack Smart (Joe); Jane Houston (Vi); Eddie Albert (Jimmy); Georgia Field (Jane)

## Mr. and Mrs. Blandings

1951; NBC
Cary Grant (Jim Blandings); Betsy Drake (Muriel Blandings); Gale Gordon (Bill Cole); Anne Whitfield (Susan Blandings); Patricia Ianola (Joan Blandings)

## Mr. Feathers

1949–50; MBS
Parker Fennelly (Mr. Feathers); Elinor Phelps (Bunny Feathers); Mert Coplin (Norbert Corbett); Lee True Hill (Emma Klause); Wendell Holmes (Doc Bellows)

## Mortimer Gooch

1936–37; CBS
Bob Bailey (Mortimer Gooch); Louise Fitch (Betty Lou)

## Mother and Dad

1942–44 (daytime serial during its initial year); CBS
Parker Fennelly (Dad); Charme Allen, Effie Palmer (Mother)

## Much Ado About Doolittle

1950; CBS
Jack Kirkwood (Doolittle)

## The Munros

1941; NBC Blue
Neal Keehan (Gordon Munro); Margaret Heckle (Margaret Munro)

## My Best Girls

1944–45; ABC
Roland Winters, John Griggs (Russell Bartlett);

Mary Shipp (Linda Bartlett); Mary Mason (Penny Bartlett); Lorna Lynn (Jill Bartlett)

## My Favorite Husband

(*See Chapter 17*)
1948–51; CBS
Lucille Ball (Liz Cugat/Cooper); Richard Denning (George Cugat/Cooper); Gale Gordon (Rudolph Atterbury); Bea Benaderet (Iris Atterbury); Ruth Perrott (Katie)

## My Friend Irma

(*See Chapter 18*)
1947–54; CBS
Marie Wilson (Irma Peterson); Cathy Lewis, Joan Banks (Jane Stacy); Jane Morgan, Gloria Gordon (Kathleen O'Reilly); John Brown (Al); Hans Conried (Professor Kropotkin); Leif Erickson (Richard Rhinelander III)
TV: 1952–54, CBS

## My Good Wife

1949; NBC
Principals portrayed by John Conte, Arlene Francis

## My Little Margie

(*See Appendix B*)
1952–55; CBS
Gale Storm (Margie Albright); Charles Farrell (Verne Albright); Clarissa Odetts (Verna Felton); Gil Stratton, Jr. (Freddie Wilson); Will Wright (George Honeywell); Shirley Mitchell (Connie); Doris Singleton (Roberta Townsend)
TV: 1952–55, CBS/NBC (TV run began six months before radio run)

## My Mother's Husband

1950; NBC
William Powell (Harvey Jefferson Brickel); Sarah Selby (Dorothy Brickel); Sharon Douglas (Virginia Brickel); Lillian Randolph (Ella Mae); Tom Tully (Uncle Willie)

## My Silent Partner

1949; NBC
Principals portrayed by Faye Emerson, Lyle Sudrow, Harold (Hal) Stone, Ruth Gilbert, Cameron Andrews

## My Son Jeep

1953, 1955–56; NBC/CBS
Donald Cook, Paul McGrath (Dr. Robert Alli-

son); Martin Huston, Bobby Alford (Jeep Allison); Joan Lazer (Peggy Allison); Lynn Allen, Joyce Gordon (Barbara Miller); Leona Powers (Mrs. Bixby)
TV: 1953, NBC

## The Nebbs

1945–46; MBS
Gene Lockhart (Rudy Nebb); Kathleen Lockhart (Fanny Nebb); Conrad Binyon (Junior Nebb); Francis "Dink" Trout (Obie Slider); Ruth Perrott (Sylvia Appleby); Dick Ryan (Buck); Patricia Dunlap (Donna); Billy Roy (Herb)

## Niles and Prindle

1945; ABC
Wendell Niles (himself); Don Prindle (himself)

## The Opie Cates Show

1947–48; ABC
Opie Cates (himself); Noreen Gommill (Cathy); Fred Howard (Pa Bushkirk); Barbara Fuller (Ma Bushkirk)

## Our Miss Brooks

(*See Chapter 19*)
1948–57; CBS
Eve Arden (Connie Brooks); Gale Gordon (Osgood Conklin); Jane Morgan (Maggie Davis); Richard Crenna (Walter Denton); Jeff Chandler, Robert Rockwell (Philip Boynton); Leonard Smith (Fabian "Stretch" Snodgrass); Gloria McMillan (Harriet Conklin); Joseph Kearns (Edgar T. Stone); Mary Jane Croft (Daisy Enright)
TV: 1952–56, CBS

## Ozzie and Harriet

(*See* The Adventures of Ozzie and Harriet)

## Paging Mike McNally

(*See* Leave It to Mike)

## The Parker Family

1939–44; CBS/NBC Blue/ABC
Leon Janney, Michael O'Day (Richard Parker); Jay Jostyn (Walter Parker); Linda Carlon-Reid, Marjorie Anderson (Helen Parker); Patricia Ryan (Elly Parker); Mitzi Gould (Nancy Parker); Roy Fant (Grandfather Parker)

## The Peabodys

1946–47; Syndication
Norman Gottschalk (Harvey Peabody); Fran Allison (Helen Peabody); Joan Alt (Harriet Peabody)

## Peewee and Windy

1930s; NBC
Jack MacBryde (Peewee); Walter Kinsella (Windy)

## The Penny Singleton Show

1950; NBC
Penny Singleton (Penny Williamson); Sheilah James (Sue Williamson); Mary Lee Robb (Dorothy Williamson); Bea Benaderet (Margaret); Jim Backus (Horace Wiggins); Gale Gordon (Judge Beshomer Grundell); Sara Selby (Ida)

## Peter Pfeiffer

1935; CBS
Jack Pearl (Peter Pfeiffer); straight man portrayed by Cliff Hall
Note: See The Jack Pearl Show also

## The Phil Harris–Alice Faye Show
(aka The Fitch Bandwagon)

(See Chapter 20)
1946–54; NBC
Phil Harris (himself); Alice Faye (herself); Elliott Lewis (Frankie Remley); Walter Tetley (Julius Abbruzio); Jeanine Roose (Alice Harris, Jr.); Anne Whitfield (Phyllis Harris)

## Phone Again, Finnegan
(aka That's Finnegan)

1946–47; NBC/CBS
Stu Erwin, Frank McHugh (Fairchild Finnegan); Florence Lake (Miss Smith); Harry Stewart (Longfellow Larsen)

## Point Sublime

1940–44, 1947–48; NBC (West Coast)/MBS (West Coast)/ABC
Cliff Arquette (Ben Willet); Jane Morgan, Verna Felton (Evelyn "Evie" Hanover); Earle Ross (Howie MacBrayer); Mel Blanc (August Moon)

## The Redhead

1952; ABC
Principals portrayed by Mary McCarty, Dick Van Patten, Vinton Hayworth

## The Rookies

1941; MBS
Principals portrayed by Jay C. Flippen, Joey Faye, Loulie Jean

## The Sad Sack

1946; CBS
Herb Vigran (Sad Sack); Jim Backus (Chester Fenwick); Sandra Gould (Lucy Twitchell)

## The Sealtest Village Store

1943–48 (introduced earlier on The Rudy Vallee Show); NBC
Principals featured: Joan Davis, Jack Haley, Eve Arden, Jack Carson; others portrayed by Penny Cartwright, Verna Felton, Gil Lamb, Shirley Mitchell

## Shorty Bell

1948; CBS
Mickey Rooney (Shorty Bell); Jeanne Bates (Joan); Parley Baer (Packrat)

## The Simpson Boys of Sprucehead Bay

1935–36 (daytime serial); NBC Blue
Principals portrayed by Arthur Allen, Parker Fennelly

## The Slapsie Maxie Rosenbloom Show

1948; NBC
Slapsie Maxie Rosenbloom (himself); others portrayed by Patricia Bright, Betty Harris, Phil Kramer, Florence MacMichael, Bernie West

## Smackout (aka The Smackouts)

1931–35; CBS/NBC
Jim and Marian Jordan

## The Smiths of Hollywood

1946, 1947, 1948–49; Syndication/MBS
Harry Von Zell (Bill Smith); Brenda Marshall (Nancy Smith); Arthur Treacher (Sir Cecil Smythe)

## Snow Village Sketches
(aka Soconyland Sketches)

1928–35, 1936–37, 1942–43, 1946 (daytime serial in 1942–43); NBC/MBS
Arthur Allen (Dan'l Dickey); Agnes Young, Kate McComb (Hattie Dickey); Parker Fennelly (Hiram Neville)

## The Stebbins Boys

1931–32; NBC/NBC Blue
Parker Fennelly (Elsy Stebbins); Arthur Allen (John Stebbins)

## Sweeney and March

1946–48, 1951; CBS/ABC
Bob Sweeney (himself); Hal March (himself)

## Tales of Willie Piper (aka *Willie Piper*)

1946–48; ABC
Dick Nelson, William Redfield (Willie Piper);
Elaine Rost, Jean Gillespie (Martha Piper); Charles
Irving (Mr. Gillespie); Stewart McIntosh (Mr. Bissell)

## Tena and Tim

1944–46 (daytime serial); CBS
Peggy Beckmark (Tena); George Cisar, James
Gardner, Frank Dane (Tim); John Goldsworthy (Mr.
Hutchinson); Gladys Heen (Mrs. Hutchinson)

## That Brewster Boy

(*See Appendix B*)
1941–45; NBC/CBS
Eddie Firestone, Jr., Arnold Stang, Dick York
(Joey Brewster); Louise Fitch, Patricia Dunlap (Nancy
Brewster); Hugh Studebaker (Jim Brewster); Con-
stance Crowder (Jane Brewster); Billy Idelson (Chuck);
Bob Bailey (Phil Hayworth)

## That's Finnegan

(*See* Phone Again, Finnegan)

## That's My Pop

1945; CBS
Hugh Herbert (Pop); Mary Wickes (Mom); Peggy
Conklin (Daughter); Ronald Liss (Son)

## That's Rich

1954; CBS
Stan Freberg (Richard "Rich" E. Wilk); Alan
Reed (Jonathan Wilk); Patte Chapman (Susie El-
wood/Freckles); Myra Marsh (Mrs. Elwood); Daws Butler (Hugh McHugh); Jeanne Bates (Mrs. Carlson)

## This Is Judy Jones

1941; NBC Blue
Mercedes McCambridge (Judy Jones); Wally
Maher (Creighton Leighton); Ben Alexander (Junior
Sheldon); Marvel McInnes (Betz Bowman); Elliott
Lewis (Mr. Peterson); Betty Wilbur (Mrs. Jones)

## Those Websters

1945–48; CBS/MBS
Willard Waterman (George Webster); Constance
Crowder (Jane Webster); Gil Stratton, Jr. (Billy Web-

ster); Joan Alt (Liz Webster); Jerry Spellman, Bill Idelson (Emil Stooler); Jane Webb (Belinda Boyd)

## Tillie the Toiler

1942; CBS
Caryl Smith (Tillie Jones); Billy Lynn (Mac Mac-
Dougal); John Brown (Mr. Simpkins); Margaret Burlen
(Mrs. Jones)

## The Timid Soul

1941–42; MBS
Billy Lynn (Casper Milquetoast); Cecil Roy
(Madge Milquetoast)

## Today at the Duncans

1942–43; CBS
Frank Nelson (John Duncan); Mary Lansing
(Mary Duncan); Dix Davis (Dinky Duncan)

## Tommy Riggs and Betty Lou

1938–40, 1942–43, 1946, 1950–52 (daytime serial
in latter incarnation); NBC/CBS/NBC/CBS
Tommy Riggs (himself, Betty Lou); Bea Benaderet
(Mrs. Wingate); Verna Felton (Mrs. MacIntyre); Wally
Maher (Wilbur Hutch); Ken Christy (Mr. Hutch)

## Tony and Gus

1935; NBC Blue
Mario Chamlee (Tony); George Frame Brown
(Gus); Elsie Mae Gordon (Mrs. Grainger); Charles Slat-
tery (George); Arthur Anderson (Buddy)

## Too Many Cooks

1950; CBS
Hal March (Father); Mary Jane Croft (Mother)

## Topper

(*See* The Adventures of Topper)

## The Truitts (aka *The Trouble*
*with the Truitts*)

1950, 1951; NBC
John Dehner (Elmer Truitt); Constance Crowder
(Gert Truitt); Barbara DuPar, Jane Webb (Gladys Tru-
itt); Dawn Bender (Maggie Truitt); Eddie Firestone,
Jr., Gil Stratton, Jr. (Clarence Truitt); Parley Baer,
Ralph Moody (Gramps); Billy Idelson (Hugo); Charles
Woolf (Roscoe)

## Two on a Shoestring

1938 (daytime serial); MBS

Principals portrayed by Eleanor Phelps, Peggy Zinke

## Uncle Abe and David

1930–31; NBC
Parker Fennelly (Uncle Abe); Arthur Allen (David)

## Uncle Walter's Doghouse

1939–42 (variety with domestic skits initially; sitcom focus from early 1942); NBC
Tom Wallace (Walter Wiggins); Charles Penman (Mr. Wiggins); Kathryn Card (Mrs. Wiggins); Beryl Vaughn (Margie Wiggins); Betty Arnold (Mrs. Dramp)

## Vic and Sade

(*See* Appendix B)
1946 (earlier versions emphasized stand-alone sketches); MBS
Art Van Harvey (Victor Gook); Bernardine Flynn (Sade Gook); Bill Idelson, Johnny Coons, Sid Koss (Rush Gook); Clarence Hartzell, Merrill Mael (Uncle Fletcher); Carl Kroenke (Chuck Brainfeeble); Ruth Perrott (Dottie Brainfeeble); David Whitehouse, Johnny Coons (Russell Miller); Hugh Studebaker (Mayor Geetcham, Rishigan Fishigan)

## Willie Piper

(*See* Tales of Willie Piper)

## You Can't Take It with You

1944, 1951; MBS/NBC
Everett Sloane, Walter Brennan (Grandpa Vanderhof); Lois Corbett (Penny Sycamore); Charles Lung (Paul Sycamore); Barbara Eiler (Alice Sycamore)
TV: 1987, Syndication

## Young Love

1949–50; CBS
Jimmy Lydon (Jimmy); Janet Waldo (Janet); Herb Butterfield (Dean Ferguson); Shirley Mitchell (Molly Belle); John Heistand (Professor Mitchell)

# Appendix B:
# Additional Radio Sitcoms

It simply wasn't feasible to feature more situation comedies in this text in full chapters while maintaining a manageable size. Consequently—as you will observe by perusing Appendix A—there are plenty of radio comedy serials that were denied the full treatment out of necessity. Believing that a handful beyond the 20 highlighted in the volume merit further accentuation beyond a directory listing, a baker's dozen (13) of the better recognized, widely acclaimed sitcoms were targeted for extra coverage here. About a dozen vintage program collectors assisted in helping the author determine the final picks for this section. Hopefully, you will discover one or more personal favorites among them. Sitcoms selected for representation in this omnibus collection are:

| | |
|---|---|
| *The Bickersons* | *Junior Miss* |
| *A Date with Judy* | *Lum and Abner* |
| *A Day in the Life* | *Maisie* |
| *of Dennis Day* | *Meet Corliss Archer* |
| *Easy Aces* | *My Little Margie* |
| *Ethel and Albert* | *That Brewster Boy* |
| *The Halls of Ivy* | *Vic and Sade* |

## The Bickersons

Can a show with multiple monikers also be so unique it can't be mistaken? Auditioned a few times from 1939 in sketches on *The Chase and Sanborn Hour*, headlined by Edgar Bergen and Charlie McCarthy, and reprised there in the final quarter of 1948, the King and Queen of Confrontation proffered a quartet of appellations over a pithy span as a separate sitcom: *Drene Time* (1946–47), followed by *The Old Gold Show* and *The Don Ameche Show*

(1947–48), and concluding with a 13-week stint as *The Bickersons* (1951). The final sobriquet characterized it all, as the wedded duo that fought like cats and dogs became the ether's unhappiest campers. Rather than being a mere doormat, like poor Albert Arbuckle to *his* intimidating bride Ethel, John Bickerson gave as much as he got. His and Blanche's matrimony was tainted by verbal abuse the likes of which radio audiences had never heard. One critic noted that John was "in a permanent state of seething exasperation," while Blanche "alternated between victim and viper." The two took delight in inflicting flagrant, unrelenting torment. Eavesdropping on their non-stop parade of insults prompted some fans to ponder why the pair weren't divorced. That would obliterate the show, of course, something the producers couldn't sanction. Yet the slightest provocation escalated into full-scale battle. The effect was raucous hilarity and gargantuan repercussions for spar-zones still to come: think *The Honeymooners*, *The Jeffersons*, *All in the Family*, *Married ... with Children* and *The Simpsons*, all populated by quarrelsome twosomes. There's not much doubt that the bickering Bickersons were the architects of the blueprint used by all.

❖ ❖ ❖

**Announcers:** Marvin Miller, Tobe Reed, John Holbrook

**Recurring Cast:** *John Bickerson:* Don Ameche (1946–48), Lew Parker (1951); *Blanche Bickerson:* Frances Langford; *Amos Bickerson:* Danny Thomas (1946–47)

**Supporting Cast:** Marsha Hunt (1948), Pinky Lee (1946–47), Frank Morgan (1947–48)

**Sponsors:** Procter & Gamble Company, for Drene shampoo and other personal care and household cleaning agents (1946–47); P. Lorillard, Inc., for Old Gold cigarettes (1947–48); Philip Morris Company, for Philip Morris cigarettes (1951)

**On the Air:** September 8, 1946–June 1, 1947, *Drene Time*, NBC, Sunday, 10:00–10:30 P.M. Eastern Time; September 24–December 24, 1947, *The Old Gold Show*, aka

*The Don Ameche Show*, CBS, Wednesday, 8:00–8:30 P.M.; January 2–June 25, 1948, CBS, Friday, 9:00–9:30 P.M.; June 5–August 28, 1951, *The Bickersons*, CBS, Tuesday, 9:30–10:00 P.M.

## A Date with Judy

NBC's *A Date with Judy* and CBS's *Meet Corliss Archer* could be considered the feminine counterparts of *The Aldrich Family* and *Archie Andrews*, both NBC staples in the 1940s. The quartet established the underpinnings of a sub-segment of radio programming that embraced teenagers ("bewildering offspring," in Carlton E. Morse parlance) in a funny sort of way. Growing up was tough in that epoch in nuclear families. For support, most teens could normally rely only upon a mother, father, one or more siblings, possibly grandparents, an occasional doting aunt or uncle, a sympathetic teacher, and peers of the same and opposite gender, with maybe a boyfriend or girlfriend among the latter. Judy Foster fit neatly into that mix, emblematic of the classic adolescent girl facing a myriad of challenges that swirled around boys, studies, parents, peers and wish lists—the usual hang-ups that complicate and sometimes threaten an active young person's life. One critic compared her series with its competitors for the same audience: "The plots were almost interchangeable with others involving teenagers of either sex: less zany, certainly, than *The Aldrich Family*, about on a par with *Corliss Archer*, and perhaps more palatable than *Archie Andrews*." Judy had a younger sibling, Randolph, who had little use for girls. She also had a steady beau, Oogie Pringle, a model of Radioland youth. Like her aircast equivalents, she ran with a crowd of kids with similar interests drawn from both sexes. While the predicaments from which she had to extricate herself seem silly when juxtaposed with "real" concerns, to a teenage queen, losing out to a rival in some mindless quest could feel like "the end of the world."

❖ ❖ ❖

**Announcers:** Frank Barton, Bill Goodwin, Doug Gourlay, Larry Keating, Ralph Langley, Ken Niles, Marvin Miller (1949–50)

**Recurring Cast:** *Judy Foster:* Ann Gillis (1941), Dellie Ellis (1942), Louise Erickson (1943–50); *Melvin Foster:* Paul McGrath (1941), Stanley Farrar (1942), Joseph Kearns (1943), John Brown (1944–50); *Dora Foster:* Margaret Brayton (1941, 1942), Bea Benaderet (1943), Georgia Backus (1944), Lois Corbett (1944), Myra Marsh (1945–50); *Randolph Foster:* Tommy Bond (1941), Tommy Cook, Johnny McGovern (ca. 1942), Dix Davis (1943–50); *Oogie Pringle:* Harry Harvey (1943–46), Richard Crenna (1946–50); *Gloria:* Lurene Tuttle (1941), Ann Gillis, Sandra Gould; *Mitzi Hoffman:* Mercedes McCambridge, Louise Erickson (1942), Georgia Backus, Sandra Gould; *Mr. Pringle:* Fred Howard; *Edgar:* Barry Minch; *Barbara:* Jan Ford

**Sponsors:** The Pepsodent Company, for Pepsodent

toothpaste and tooth powder (1941–42); Bristol-Myers, Inc., for Sal-Hepatica acid analgesic and other pharmaceutical and personal care goods (1943); Lewis Howe Company, for Tums acid analgesic (1944–49); Revere Camera Company, for Revere cameras (1949–50); Ford Motor Company, for Ford vehicles, parts and service (1950)

**On the Air:** June 24–September 16, 1941, NBC, Tuesday, 10:00–10:30 P.M. Eastern Time; June 23–September 15, 1942, NBC, Tuesday, 10:00–10:30 P.M.; June 30–September 22, 1943, NBC, Wednesday, 9:00–9:30 P.M.; January 18, 1944–June 22, 1948, NBC, Tuesday, 8:30–9:00 P.M.; September 28, 1948–January 4, 1949, NBC, Tuesday, 8:30–9:00 P.M.; October 13, 1949–May 4, 1950, ABC, Thursday, 8:30–9:00 P.M.

## A Day in the Life of Dennis Day

No matter what the venue—and there were multiple—the entertainer born Eugene Denis McNulty (Dennis Day) maintained his innocence, earmarked by clever ripostes delivered in the same style that he advanced on *The Jack Benny Program*. Day was first widely noticed there in 1939 and remained with that show while headlining a separate series. Initially he played a soda jerk at Willoughby's Drug Store in mythical Weaverville, working for proprietor Homer Willoughby. Millie Anderson was the love of his life there, but her parents, Herbert and Clara—who ran the Anderson Boarding House where he resided—were none too impressed with the luckless suitor. Their preference for their daughter's hand was Victor Miller, a contemptible fellow who nonetheless seemed to possess cash, status and a plan—things that Day usually found in short supply. An effervescent personality didn't count a great deal with them. The plots focused on Day's efforts to improve his lot in order to impress a henpecked Herbert—in particular, to add standing by significantly increasing his income. When his attempts fell short, which was almost a given, he dealt with the aftermath of disappointment in himself and the reactions of the Andersons. A musical number by Day normally opened and closed every installment, his singing a carryover from his appearances with Benny. By mid-century the show evolved into a variety series, with Day presiding, thereby effectively ending the earlier situation comedy. Although his series never made it to Videoland, Day turned up on the tube just the same, as a continuing figure in Benny's entourage. He was also acclaimed as a popular recording artist.

❖ ❖ ❖

**Announcers:** Verne Smith, Jimmy Wallington, Frank Barton

**Recurring Cast:** *Dennis Day:* Dennis Day; *Mildred Anderson:* Sharon Douglas, Barbara Eiler, Betty Miles; *Herbert Anderson:* Francis (Dink) Trout; *Clara Anderson:* Bea Benaderet; *Homer Willoughby:* John Brown; *Miss Baker:* Isabel Randolph

**Sponsors:** Colgate-Palmolive-Peet Company, for Cashmere Bouquet beauty soap, Colgate dental cream, Lustre Crème shampoo, Palmolive shaving cream and other personal care commodities (1946–51); NutraLite Company, for NutraLite health products (1954–55)

**On the Air:** October 3–December 19, 1946, NBC, Thursday, 7:30–8:00 P.M. Eastern Time; December 25, 1946–June 25, 1947, NBC, Wednesday, 8:00–8:30 P.M.; August 27, 1947–June 30, 1948, NBC, Wednesday, 8:00–8:30 P.M.; August 28, 1948–June 25, 1949, NBC, Saturday, 10:00–10:30 P.M.; August 27, 1949–July 1, 1950, NBC, Saturday, 9:30–10:00 P.M.; October 7, 1950–June 30, 1951, NBC, Saturday, 9:30–10:00 P.M.; September 19, 1954–March 20, 1955, *The Dennis Day Show*, NBC, Sunday, 5:30–6:00 P.M.

## Easy Aces

Following a two-year rest in which they netted $150,000 by allowing a syndicator to peddle disks of 13 years of their dialogue, Goodman and Jane Ace returned to the studio in 1948. For 10 months "radio's laugh novelty" was a sitcom under the banner *Mr. Ace and Jane.* They played a long-suffering, cynical husband and dim-witted wife, supported by a troupe of thespians and backed by an orchestra and live audience. Jane's deadbeat brother Paul was in their midst often. Launched in 1929 by accident, *Easy Aces* was born when *Kansas City Post* reporter Ace reviewed films over KMBC. An act to follow one day failed to materialize, and he was told to "keep talking." Ace summoned his wife waiting at the studio, and the duo fell into a witty exchange concerning a bridge game. Listener reaction was swift and positive. The couple soon talked their way to Chicago's WBBM and on to CBS and New York. Arriving about the same time as Gracie Allen, it was apparent Jane Ace was cut from the same cloth. In *her* case she never met a malaprop she didn't apply: "Time wounds all heels" she'd allow, and "You have to take the bitter with the batter." Ace was equally amiss in his verbalizations: "Mother, you're so pessimistic," he'd say, "why can't you be more of an optician?" Or, "Make it short and sappy." Or, "There's a fly in the oatmeal somewhere." The pair kept fans in stitches. The laugh-getters were created on Ace's own typewriter, and he later proved a prolific wordsmith for popular radio–TV artists (Bankhead, Berle, Como, Kaye, Newhart). Media scholar Luther Sies maintained: "The Aces produced some of the finest comedy ever broadcast."

❖ ❖ ❖

**Announcers:** Ford Bond (1930–47), Ken Roberts (1948)

**Recurring Cast:** *Goodman Ace:* Goodman Ace (nee Asa Goodman); *Jane Ace:* Jane Sherwood Ace; *Marge Hall:* Mary Hunter; *Johnny Sherwood:* Paul Stewart; *Mrs. Benton:* Peggy Allenby; *Betty:* Ethel Blume; *Carl:* Alfred Ryder; *Neil*

*Williams:* Martin Gabel; *Laura:* Helene Dumas; *Miss Thomas:* Ann Thomas; *Paul Sherwood:* Leon Janney; *J.K. Norris:* Eric Dressler; *Miss Anderson:* Florence Robinson; *Cokey:* Ken Roberts

**Supporting Cast:** Frank Butler, John Griggs, Cliff Hall, Pert Kelton, Everett Sloane, James Van Dyk, Evelyn Varden

**Sponsors:** Lavoris mouthwash (1932–33); Jad salts (1933–35); American Home Products Corporation, for Anacin pain reliever, Old English floor polish and other pharmaceutical and household commodities (1935–45); U.S. Army and Air Force Recruiting Service, for enlistment purposes (winter, spring, summer 1948); General Foods Corporation, for a wide line of foodstuffs and household goods (autumn 1948)

**On the Air:** October 5, 1931–January 2, 1932, CBS, trial series airing from Chicago (undocumented schedule); March 1–March 12, 1932, CBS, Tuesday/Thursday/Saturday, 10:15–10:30 P.M. Eastern Time; March 14–July 1, 1932, CBS, Monday/Wednesday/Friday, 10:15–10:30 P.M.; September 26, 1932–January 25, 1933, CBS, Monday/Wednesday/Friday, 10:15–10:30 P.M.; January 26–May 30, 1933, CBS, Tuesday/Thursday/Saturday, 10:15–10:30 P.M.; October 10, 1933–April 27, 1934, CBS, Tuesday–Friday, 1:30–1:45 P.M.; May 2–December 14, 1934, CBS, Monday/Wednesday/Friday, 3:45–4:00 P.M.; January 7–January 31, 1935, CBS, Monday–Thursday, 3:45–4:00 P.M.; February 4–May 29, 1935, NBC, Monday–Wednesday, 7:30–7:45 P.M.; June 4–September 26, 1935, NBC Blue, Tuesday–Thursday, 4:15–4:30 P.M.; October 1, 1935–October 22, 1942, NBC Blue, Tuesday–Thursday, 7:00–7:15 P.M.; October 28, 1942–November 26, 1943, CBS, Wednesday–Friday, 7:30–7:45 P.M.; December 1, 1943–January 17, 1945, CBS, Wednesday, 7:30–8:00 P.M.; 1945–47, Syndicated by Frederick Ziv Company (previous shows reprised), five quarter-hour installments weekly; February 14–May 29, 1948, *Mr. Ace and Jane*, CBS, Saturday, 7:00–7:30 P.M.; June 4–unsubstantiated date, 1948, CBS, Friday, 8:00–8:30 P.M.; Unsubstantiated date–December 31, 1948, CBS, Friday, 8:30–9:00 P.M.

## Ethel and Albert

There was a handful of "conversational" sitcoms that frequently depended heavily upon verbal exchanges between two or more leading figures during much of their airtime. While some were supported by added characters, it often seemed that a large percentage of those shows' weight fell on their principals. Prime examples include *Doc, Duke and the Colonel; Easy Aces; Jimmy Gleason's Diner; Lum and Abner; Ma and Pa; Maude and Cousin Bill; Mother and Dad; Niles and Prindle; Peewee and Windy; Vic and Sade* and a few more. There was also *Ethel and Albert* and the series that preceded and succeeded it, *The Couple Next Door* (1937, 1957–60). The latter ultimately became an extension of *Ethel and Albert*, transferring the same actors and author to the subsequent serial. The similarities were so pronounced that it seemed only the names had been changed to protect the networks, sponsors or advertising agencies owning the rights to them. Here was the story of a married couple, Ethel and Albert Arbuckle (with Baby Suzy in the wings), who appeared to love one another but seemed to have difficulty expressing it. While they weren't at all like *The Bickersons*, who argued incessantly and piercingly, the Arbuckles consisted of a mild-mannered milquetoast man who was accustomed to hearing his spouse air her opinions on everything ad infinitum. She constantly nudged him in whatever direction she preferred and was seldom satisfied with the status quo. They spent a half-dozen years in radio, complemented by three more on TV, followed by another three on radio again as the nameless *Couple Next Door*. Could it be they were speaking not only *to*— but also *for*—millions of American households?

❖ ❖ ❖

**Announcers:** George Ansbro, Glenn Riggs, Fred Cole, Cy Harrice, Don Lowe, Herb Sheldon
**Recurring Roles:** *Ethel Arbuckle:* Peg Lynch; *Albert Arbuckle:* Richard Widmark (1944), Alan Bunce (1944–50); *Baby Suzy:* Madeleine Pierce
**Sponsor:** Sustained
**On the Air:** May 29–August 11, 1944, *The Private Lives of Ethel and Albert*, NBC Blue, Monday–Friday, 4:00–4:15 P.M. Eastern Time; August 14, 1944–June 24, 1949, NBC Blue/ABC, Monday–Friday, 6:15–6:30 P.M.; January 16, 1949–August 28, 1950, ABC, Monday, 8:00–8:30 P.M.

## The Halls of Ivy

A small liberal arts college provided the backdrop for this sitcom. The school's president, Dr. William Todhunter Hall (Ronald Colman), and his wife Vicki (Benita Hume—Mrs. Colman in real life) appeared each week in a lighthearted narrative. Colman was a distinguished actor of notable repute, while his spouse had appeared in musical productions. Both occasionally turned up as "neighbors" on *The Jack Benny Program*. The new show was a departure for talented scribe Don Quinn, who conspired for nearly two decades with Jim and Marian Jordan to pen their *Fibber McGee & Molly* sitcom. While he didn't write most of *Halls'* episodes, Quinn created it and inspired the situations from which they were drawn. In the plotline, President Hall of Ivy College wrestled with contentious board of governors members, as well as interacting with faculty, staff, students, parents, alumni, vendors, contributors and other publics of the institute. Stories were generally warmhearted, allowing the administrator and his wife to share their experiences and perspectives with individuals whose issues had usually evolved into conflict. Hall applied corollaries to supply helpful answers for those dilemmas. Humor and witty banter were sprinkled liberally in the dialogue. The show opened and closed to a male glee club harmonizing in an echo chamber about the mythical institution: "*Oh we love the halls of Ivy ... That surround us here today ... And we shall not forget ... Though we be far, far away.*" It was, as one source attested, "a warm, literate comedy" that still "holds its charm" several decades after it appeared. The aural series subsequently inspired a television adaptation that ran for a year on CBS (1954–55).

❖ ❖ ❖

**Announcer:** Ken Carpenter
**Recurring Cast:** *William Todhunter Hall:* Ronald Colman; *Victoria Cromwell (Vicky) Hall:* Benita (Colman) Hume; *Clarence Wellman:* Herb Butterfield; *John Merriweather:* Willard Waterman; *Penny:* Elizabeth Patterson, Gloria Gordon; *Professor Jeremiah Warren:* Arthur Q. Bryan; *Professor Heathcliff:* Alan Reed
**Supporting Cast:** Ken Christy, Sam Edwards, Virginia Gregg, Stacy Harris, Jerry Hausner, Sam Hearn, Raymond Lawrence, Sheldon Leonard, Johnny McGovern, Rolfe Sedan, Charles Seel, Sarah Selby, Jeffrey Silver, Bob Sweeney, Jean Vander Pyl, Herb Vigran, Paula Winslowe
**Sponsor:** Joseph Schlitz Brewing Company, for Schlitz beer (1950–52)
**On the Air:** January 6–May 5, 1950, NBC, Friday, 8:00–8:30 P.M. Eastern Time; May 10, 1950–June 27, 1951, NBC, Wednesday, 8:00–8:30 P.M.; September 26, 1951–June 25, 1952, NBC, Wednesday, 8:00–8:30 P.M.

## Junior Miss

After a six-month tryout in 1942, which came about just as the teen sitcoms were flooding the airwaves, this one wasn't heard from again for a half-dozen years. Though the format featured the same family both times, and projected the same adolescent in comparable growing-up imbroglios, in the intervening years the cast was replaced and a sponsor added. Furthermore, upon its resumption, for a while at least the program shifted from primetime to a Saturday morning slot, a time zone popularized already by one of its youthful counterparts, *Archie Andrews*. Judy Graves was the so-called average teen with problems revolving around home and school. Her misadventures were analogous to those encountered by Corliss Archer, Judy Foster (*A Date with Judy*), Kathleen Anderson (Henry's girlfriend on *The Aldrich Family*), Betty Cooper and Veronica Lodge (*Archie Andrews*), Betty Anderson (*Father Knows Best*) and a bevy of young ladies whose concerns—to them—seemed overwhelming. Each series had a small twist to distinguish it from its peers: in this one, Judy Graves had a sister, Lois, a year older, who was totally boy-crazy. At 15, meanwhile, Judy hadn't yet discovered the opposite sex, at least not to the point that it occupied every waking thought. In that regard, too, her series departed from the model exhibited by most radio comedies of the subgenre. She also lived in an apartment building in New York's Manhattan borough, a far cry from Smalltown, U.S.A., where most of her Radioland competition resided, complete with two-story home surrounded by a white picket fence on a residential street in a mythical burg. While the locale may have been different, the contortions were much the same.

❖ ❖ ❖

**Announcers:** Durwood Kirby, Ben Gage, Johnny Jacobs, Jimmy Wallington

**Recurring Roles:** *Judy Graves:* Shirley Temple (1942), Barbara Whiting (1948–50, 1952–54); *Harry Graves:* Elliott Lewis (1942), Gale Gordon (1948–50, 1952–54); *Grace Graves:* Mary Lansing (1942), Sarah Selby (1948–50, 1952–54); *Lois Graves:* K.T. Stevens, Barbara Eiler (1942), Peggy Knudson (1948–50, 1952–54); *Hilda:* Myra Marsh (1948–50, 1952–54); *Fuffy* [sic] *Adams:* Priscilla Lyon (1942), Beverly Wills (1948–50, 1952–54)

**Sponsors:** Procter & Gamble Company, for a wide line of household and personal care goods (1942); Lever Brothers Company, for a wide line of household and personal care goods (1948–50); Multiple participation (1952–54), including Raymond Laboratories, for Rayve shampoo, rinse, home permanents and other hair care products

**On the Air:** March 4–August 26, 1942, CBS, Wednesday, 9:00–9:30 P.M. Eastern Time; May 8, 1948–December 30, 1950, CBS, Saturday, 11:30 A.M.–12 noon; October 2–December 25, 1952, CBS, Thursday, 8:30–9:00 P.M.; December 29, 1952–June 5, 1953, CBS, Monday–Friday, 7:15–7:30 P.M.; June 7–September 20, 1953, CBS, Sunday, 8:00–8:30 P.M.; September 28–November 7, 1953, CBS, Monday/Wednesday/Friday, 7:30–7:45 P.M.; November 12, 1953–July 1, 1954, CBS, Thursday, 8:30–9:00 P.M.

## Lum and Abner

In 1936 the hamlet of Waters, Arkansas, near the Oklahoma border, legally altered its name to gain visibility as the site of the mythical *Lum and Abner* radio comedy. The village became Pine Ridge, where a Jot 'Em Down Store—a general mercantile emporium like those two geezers ostensibly ran—is still in business today, commemorating its namesake. The locals persist in gathering to swap stories and learn what's happening in people's lives that makes it worth living. Arkansawyers Chester Lauck (a levelheaded Lum Edwards) and Norris Goff (a hotheaded Abner Peabody) initiated their series over Hot Spring's KTHS in early 1931. Lauck was convinced "the simple philosophy of the Arkansas hills, genuine and unadorned, is interesting." Taking a page from the *Amos 'n' Andy* playbook, the pair devised numerous voices representing dialects of mostly country folks hailing from the foothills of the nearby Ozark Mountains. Like their mentors, for several years the duo performed all the speaking parts—until "progress" intervened and advertising agencies and networks added bigger budgets and casts. Although most of the show's quarter-century history was meted out in serialized seg-

ments, from 1948 to 1950 it appeared as a 30-minute sitcom in primetime with all the usual trimmings, including a live audience. Country had dressed up and gone to town. In spite of this, the same backwater figures mouthing earthy colloquialisms that populated the 15-minute version continued to generate laughs. Lum and Abner's charm lay in their rustic, folksy wit and idioms ("By dogies, Lum!"). Their homespun homilies represented a kinder, gentler America that hordes of listeners were hesitant to abandon.

❖ ❖ ❖

**Announcers:** Charles Lyon, Del Sharbutt, Gene Hamilton, Carlton Brickert (chronologically 1931–38); Lou Crosby (1938–44); Gene Baker (1944–45); Forrest Owen (1945–48); Wendell Niles (1948–50); Bill Ewing (1953–54)

**Recurring Cast:** *Lum Edwards:* Chester Lauck; *Norris Goff:* Abner Peabody; *Cedric Weehunt:* Chester Lauck; *Snake Hogan:* Chester Lauck; *Grandpappy Spears:* Chester Lauck; *Dick Huddleston:* Norris Goff; *Mousy Gray:* Norris Goff; *Doc Miller:* Norris Goff; *Squire Skimp:* Norris Goff; *Diognes Smith:* Frank Graham; *B.J. Webster:* Frank Graham; *Ellie Conners:* Lurene Tuttle; *Dr. Benjamin Franklin Withers:* Clarence Hartzel; *Phinus Peabody:* Elmore Vincent

**Supporting Cast:** Cliff Arquette, Francis X. Bushman (numerous roles), Opie Cates, Andy Devine, Jerry Hausner (numerous roles), Zasu Pitts, Francis (Dink) Trout

**Sponsors:** The Quaker Oats Company, for Quaker cereals (1931), Oustailled (1932, fall 1949, 1953); Ford Motor Company, for Ford vehicles, parts and services (1933–34); J & W Horlicks Company, for Horlicks malted milk beverage (1934–38); General Foods Corporation, for Postum instant beverage (1938–40); Miles Laboratories, Inc., for Alka-Seltzer acid distress reliever, One-a-Day multiple vitamins, Miles Nervine calmative and other pharmaceutical commodities (1941–48); Frigidaire Corporation, for Frigidaire refrigerators and other kitchen appliances (1948–49); Ford Motor Company, for Ford vehicles, parts and services (1950); Local commercials delivered by transcription by Abner Peabody (1953–54)

**On the Air:** July 27–August 8, 1931, NBC, Monday–Saturday, 8:00–8:15 A.M. Eastern Time; August 24–December 26, 1931, NBC, Monday–Saturday, 8:00–8:15 A.M.; January 11–April 1, 1932, NBC, Monday–Friday, 8:00–8:15 A.M.; April 4–April 29, 1932, NBC, Monday/Wednesday/Friday, 8:00–8:15 A.M.; May 2–June 27, 1932, NBC, Monday–Friday, 8:00–8:15 A.M.; August 1–October 7, 1932, NBC, Monday–Friday, 8:00–8:15 A.M.; November 14, 1932–May 19, 1933, NBC, Monday–Friday, 8:00–8:15 A.M.; May 22, 1933–March 29, 1934, NBC, Monday–Thursday, 7:30–7:45 P.M.; May 26, 1933–March 30, 1934 NBC, Friday, 10:45–11:00 P.M.; April 2–June 14, 1934, MBS, Monday–Thursday, 6:15–6:30 P.M.; June 18–December 15, 1934, MBS, Monday–Saturday, 6:15–6:30 P.M.; December 17, 1934–August 30, 1935, MBS, Monday–Friday, 6:15–6:30 P.M.; September 2, 1935–November 26, 1937, NBC Blue, Monday–Friday, 7:30–7:45 P.M.; November 29, 1937–February 25, 1938, NBC Blue, Monday/Wednesday/Friday, 7:30–7:45 P.M.; February 28–July 1, 1938, CBS, Monday/Wednesday/Friday, 6:45–7:00 P.M.; September 5–September 23, 1938, CBS, Monday/Wednesday/Friday, 6:45–7:00

P.M.; September 26, 1938–June 30, 1939, CBS, Monday/
Wednesday/Friday, 7:15–7:30 P.M.; August 28, 1939–March
29, 1940, CBS, Monday/Wednesday/Friday, 7:15–7:30 P.M.;
May 26, 1941–July 3, 1942, NBC Blue,; Monday/Tuesday/
Thursday/Friday, 6:30–6:45 P.M.; July 6, 1942–June 28,
1945, NBC Blue/ABC, Monday–Thursday, 8:15–8:30 P.M.;
July 2–July 19, 1945, ABC, Monday–Thursday, 8:00–8:15
P.M.; September 3, 1945–October 2, 1947, ABC, Monday–
Thursday, 8:00–8:15 P.M.; October 6, 1947–September 24,
1948, CBS, Monday–Friday, 5:45–6:00 P.M.; September 26,
1948–January 16, 1949, CBS, Sunday, 10:00–10:30 P.M.; January 23–June 26, 1949, CBS, Sunday, 8:30–9:00 P.M.; November 2, 1949–April 26, 1950, CBS, Wednesday, 10:30–
11:00 P.M.; February 16–May 15, 1953, ABC, Monday–
Friday, quarter-hour installments, time unsubstantiated;
November 9, 1953–May 7, 1954, Syndicated, Monday–Friday, quarter-hour installments

## Maisie

"I'm in show business," a dazzlingly stunning
Maisie Revere told listeners in a brief epigram at the
start of her weekly sitcom (also known as *The Adventures of Maisie*). "It seems I'm either walking to a
job that is ready to fold or walking back from one
that has." The down-on-her-luck entertainer appeared to get the shaft in every circumstance, usually a result of poor choices on her part. The thrust
of most installments during the show's CBS days
was her incongruent aim to get rich quick while simultaneously helping every one of life's downtrod-
den she encountered—and there were plenty. Existing from one paycheck to the next was a constant
hazard; she'd find ways to "improve" her lot—like
sneaking out of hotel rooms on fire escapes without
paying. Maisie also bore a habit of peppering her
language with "Likewise, I'm sure," which became
a fixture in the lexicon of some denizens tuning in.
The aural sitcom evolved from 10 *Maisie* motion
pictures (1939–47) that a critic labeled "B-fare," who
opined: "The radio series was more of the same."
Nevertheless, in the first two seasons (1945–47) of
its audio incarnation the program earned a median
10.8 rating, a respectable figure for the time. When
it went into syndication, the theme was adjusted
slightly: by then Maisie had settled at a Brooklyn
boardinghouse where one of the residents was loser-
in-life Eddie Jordan, a man who couldn't hold a job
and obviously didn't care for one, yet was a dreamboat in Maisie's eyes. He was invariably behind on
his rent; still, she found work for him at tasks he
was never thrilled about. From its original premise
to that one, the sitcom remained focused on losers.
Only, in the latter version there were two of them
instead of just one.

❖ ❖ ❖

**Announcers:** John Easton, Jack McCoy
**Recurring Cast:** *Maisie Revere*: Ann Sothern; *Bill*:
Elliott Lewis

**Supporting Cast:** Elvia Allman, Hy Averback, Joan
Banks, Edgar Barrier, Harry Bartell, Bea Benaderet, Griff
Bernard, Tommy Bernard, John Brown, Arthur Q. Bryan,
Herb Butterfield, Bob Cole, William Conrad, Hans Con-
ried, Norman Field, Hal Gerard, Roy Glenn, Sandra
Gould, Virginia Gregg, Jerry Hausner, Sammy Hill, Byron
Kane, Earl Lee, Peter Leeds, Sheldon Leonard, Ed Macks,
Wally Maher, Pat McGeehan, John McGovern, Howard
McNear, Marvin Miller, Stanley Miller, Gerald Mohr,
Frank Nelson, GeGe Pearson, Barney Phillips, Isabel Ran-
dolph, Jeffrey Silver, Lurene Tuttle, Stanley Waxman,
Ernest Whitman, Ben Wright, Donald Woods, Will
Wright
**Sponsors:** Eversharp Company, for Eversharp writing
instruments (1945–47); Sustained or local underwriters
(1949–51, 1952)
**On the Air:** July 5–August 16, 1945, CBS, Thursday,
8:30–9:00 P.M. Eastern Time; August 22–September 5,
1945, CBS, Wednesday, 10:30–11:00 P.M.; September 12,
1945–February 27, 1946, CBS, Wednesday, 9:30–10:00
P.M.; March 8–June 28, 1946, CBS, Friday, 10:30–11:00
P.M.; August 16, 1946–March 28, 1947, CBS, Friday, 10:30–
11:00 P.M.; November 24, 1949–1953 (date unsubstantiated), syndicated by MGM; January 11–December 26,
1952, MBS, Friday, 8:00–8:30 P.M. (simultaneous with
transcriptions)

## Meet Corliss Archer

In the aggregate of 94 months it was on the
air, *Meet Corliss Archer* occupied 17 timeslots on
three chains, pausing at CBS on a trio of occasions.
On average the show moved every five or six
months. Ratings for similar teen sitcoms (*The
Aldrich Family*, *A Date with Judy*) in a single season
were about 115 percent higher than *Archer*. Did the
difficulty in *finding* the latter show cause some fans
to give up, partly explaining why it wasn't as well received? Still a good show, on a level playing field it
could have competed well with others of its ilk.
Corliss was a normal teen; her abject boyfriend,
Dexter Franklin, was—as one observer depicted—
"one of the biggest bumblers ever to walk through
Radio Row." Dexter's incessant expression "Holy
cow!" was applied ad nauseam, but that seemed
mild compared to his blood-curdling scream every
time he approached the Archer residence:
"COOOORRRRRR ... LAISSS!" Corliss was given
parents like most of the other teeny-boppers in Radioland: a sensible mom, Janet, who attempted to
keep everything and everybody on track, straighten-
ing them out when they derailed; and a biting, acid-
tongued father, Harry, an attorney, whose penchant
for conniving seemed compatible with his calling.
Dexter was the older man's nemesis, yet the youth
could be useful when Harry got himself into a jam.
Corliss, meanwhile, was constantly in makeover
mode—improving Dexter's looks, actions, disposi-
tion, talent, aims, studies—when he would much
rather have been left to his own devices. A few pals

of both genders contributed to the complex situations of growing up. It was, for certain, emblematic adolescent fare. And in scheduling, it probably deserved better.

❖ ❖ ❖

**Announcers:** Ken Carpenter, Jack Hartz, John Hiestand, Del Sharbutt

**Recurring Cast:** *Corliss Archer:* Priscilla Lyon (1943), Janet Waldo (1944–54), Lugene Sanders (1956); *Dexter Franklin:* Bill Christy (1943), Burt Boyar (1943), Sam Edwards (1944–56), David Hughes, Irving Lee; *Harry Archer:* Frank Martin (1943), Fred Shields (1943–56), Bob Bailey; *Janet Archer:* Gloria Holden (1943), Irene Tedrow (1943–56), Mary Jane Croft, Helen Mack; *Uncle George:* Norman Field (1943); *Louise:* Mary Wickes (1943); *Raymond Ames:* Tommy Bernard, Kenny Godkin; *Mildred:* Bebe Young, Barbara Whiting; *Betty Cameron:* Dolores Crane

**Supporting Cast:** Arlene Becker, Frank Driscoll

**Sponsors:** Sustained (1943, 1956); Anchor Hocking Glass Company, for Anchor Hocking glass products (1944–45); Campbell Soup Company, for Campbell soups and juices, Franco-American spaghetti and other main dishes and other foodstuffs (1946–48); The Pepsodent Company, for Pepsodent toothpaste (1948); Electric Company Cooperatives, for local electric suppliers (1949–53); Carter-Wallace, Inc., for Carter's Little Liver pills (1954, partial sponsorship); Nelson Harris Company, for Toni home permanents and other hair-care commodities (1954, partial sponsorship)

**On the Air:** January 7–February 25, 1943, CBS, Thursday, 8:00–8:30 P M. Eastern Time; March 10–April 7, 1943, CBS, Wednesday, 10:30–11:00 P.M.; April 11–June 6, 1943, CBS, Sunday, 8:00–8:30 P.M.; June 11–September 24, 1943, CBS, Friday, 8:00–8:30 P.M.; January 8–July 1, 1944, CBS, Saturday, 5:00–5:30 P.M.; July 6, 1944–August 23, 1945, CBS, Thursday, 9:30–10:00 P.M.; April 28–September 29, 1946, CBS, Sunday, 9:00–9:30 P.M.; April 6, 1947–May 2, 1948, CBS, Sunday, 9:00–9:30 P.M.; June 15–September 7, 1948, NBC, Tuesday, 10:00–10:30 P.M.; July 31, 1949–June 25, 1950, CBS, Sunday, 9:00–9:30 P.M.; August 27, 1950–July 1, 1951, CBS, Sunday, 9:00–9:30 P.M.; September 9, 1951–April 6, 1952, CBS, Sunday, 9:00–9:30 P.M.; April 13–June 29, 1952, CBS, Sunday, 9:15–9:45 P.M.; October 3, 1952–June 26, 1953, ABC, Friday, 9:30–10:00 P.M.; December 25, 1953, ABC, Friday, 9:30–10:00 P.M.; August 30–November 29, 1954, CBS, Monday, 8:00–8:30 P.M.; June 24–September 30, 1956, CBS, Sunday, 8:00–8:30 P.M.

## My Little Margie

In an unusual turn of events, *My Little Margie* was one of a handful of shows launched during TV's embryonic era that afterward added a radio adaptation. (Among them were: *Howdy Doody*; *Have Gun, Will Travel*; *Hopalong Cassidy*; *Tom Corbett, Space Cadet*; and *What's My Line?*) The engaging sitcom appeared on CBS-TV June 16, 1952, switched to NBC-TV September 2, 1953, and ended its video run August 24, 1955. For much of that time there was also a transcribed radio feature airing. The protagonist

was a twentysomething daughter who shared a high-rise Manhattan apartment with her widowed and quite eligible 50-year-old pappy. Verne Albright was an investment counselor at Honeywell Industries and could be dubbed striking and debonair. That brought him to the attention of a barrage of women, most of whom his offspring fended off. While Margie had a permanent love interest, Freddie Wilson, she encountered more than the normal difficulties with men. Wilson was floundering, unemployed and lacking in ambition, the typical weakened male such shows usually projected. Margie, meanwhile, plotted incessantly. She took neighborly Mrs. Odetts into her confidence, and the pair routinely conspired to outfox the men. The essential ingredient in virtually every chapter, according to one reviewer, was simply: "When Margie does something and Vern finds out, he decides to teach her a lesson. However, as Vern tries to teach Margie a lesson, she finds out and turns the tables by trying to teach him a lesson for trying to teach her a lesson." Oh, what a tangled web we weave.

❖ ❖ ❖

**Announcers:** Johnny Jacobs, Roy Rowan

**Recurring Cast:** *Margie Albright:* Gale Storm; *Verne Albright:* Charles Farrell; *Freddie Wilson:* Gil Stratton, Jr.; *Clarissa Odetts:* Verna Felton; *George Honeywell:* Will Wright; *Roberta Townsend:* Doris Singleton; *Connie:* Shirley Mitchell

**Sponsor:** Philip Morris Company, for Philip Morris and Parliament cigarettes (1952–55)

**On the Air:** December 7, 1952–June 26, 1955, CBS, Sunday, 8:30–9:00 P.M. Eastern Time

## That Brewster Boy

*That Brewster Boy* aired one night a week for three-and-a-half years (1941–45), almost coinciding with the start and close of the Second World War. "The usual adolescent problems of Joey Brewster made the program somewhat reminiscent of the earlier Henry Aldrich show," one historiographer observed. Added another: "It [*Brewster*] centered around a typical American teenage boy and the loving endurance of his parents as he became involved in various problems with girls, at school, and with his friends." A third revealed: "Joey's 'cohort in crime' is his best friend Chuck, an all-talk, no-action kid who always gets Joey into more trouble than he is already in—and who always manages to disappear when things get hot, leaving Joey to face the music alone." Chuck was another instigator of the misfortunes that plagued the heroes of these shows, yet Henry Aldrich's and Archie Andrews' buddies usually stuck around for the consequences. There was another distinguishing characteristic on display here: Joey and Phil (sibling Nancy's love interest) resented one another mightily, which was unusual for these shows. Joey considered the collegiate Phil an opportunist, one of life's losers; Phil thought no better of Joey, addressing him as "Small Fry" and "Sprout." Aside from these few differences, the themes that listeners heard about growing up in the Brewster household were pretty much what they encountered elsewhere in adolescent fare.

❖ ❖ ❖

**Announcer:** Marvin Miller

**Recurring Cast:** *Joey Brewster:* Eddie Firestone, Jr., Arnold Stang, Dick York; *Jim Brewster:* Hugh Studebaker; *Jane Brewster:* Constance Crowder; *Nancy Brewster:* Louise Fitch, Patricia Dunlap; *Chuck:* Billy Idelson; *Phil Hayworth:* Bob Bailey

**Sponsor:** Quaker Oats Company, for Quaker Oats cereals (full run)

**On the Air:** September 8, 1941–March 2, 1942, NBC, Monday, 9:30–10:00 P.M. Eastern Time; March 4–June 3, 1942, CBS, Wednesday, 7:30–8:00 P.M.; June 5, 1942–March 2, 1945, CBS, Friday, 9:30–10:00 P.M.

## Vic and Sade

They were branded "radio's home folks." They truly were "down-home" folks of the earthy variety. They included characters like Chuck and Dottie Brainfeeble, Mayor Geetcham, Rishigan Fishigan (from Sishigan, Michigan, no less!), Blue-Tooth Johnson, Sweet Corn McBlock, Smelly Clark and Cracky Otto. Yet the enduring, compelling narrative that brought them to life gathered a whole lot of listeners and held them close to their radios for about 14 years. *Vic and Sade* occupied soap opera slots for much of its run and was presented in quarter-hour segments, belying the fact it wasn't a serial at all. Its pithy skits could be easily separated from what preceded or followed every sequence: "Each was a little slice of life, an American original, in a category of its own making, as inimitable as its author's fingerprint," observed a critic. Wordsmith Paul Rhymer located the Victor Gook home

"halfway up the next block" on Virginia Avenue in mythical Crooper, Illinois. The couple who lived there adopted a son, Rush, to add flexibility to the plots. Said historiographer Luther Sies: "Rhymer's whimsically warm-hearted look at the Gook family, their friends and acquaintances and the slightly off-center world they inhabited was a genuine contribution to American humor." Those bits of folksy wit so impressed poet Edgar Lee Masters that he labeled them "the best American humor of its day." Fans included Ray Bradbury, Stan Freberg, Franklin Roosevelt and James Thurber, perhaps a cut above your average Blue-Tooth, Sweet Corn, Smelly and Cracky.

❖ ❖ ❖

**Announcers:** Bob Brown (1932–40), Vincent Pelletier, Ed Roberts, Ralph Edwards, Ed Herlihy, Glenn Riggs, Jack Fuller, Roger Krupp, Charles Lyon

**Recurring Cast:** *Victor Gook:* Art Van Harvey; *Sade Gook:* Bernardine Flynn; *Rush Gook:* Bill Idelson, Johnny Coons, Sid Koss; *Uncle Fletcher:* Clarence Hartzell, Merrill Mael; *Chuck Brainfeeble:* Carl Kroenke; *Dottie Brainfeeble:* Ruth Perrott; *Russell Miller:* David Whitehouse, Johnny Coons; *Roy Delfeeno:* Forrest Lewis, Norman Gottschalk; *Dwight Twentysixer:* Cliff Soubier; *Mayor Geetcham:* Hugh Studebaker; *Rishigan Fihigan:* Hugh Studebaker; *Blue-Tooth Johnson:* Leonard Smith; *Art McConnell:* Jack Culbertson; *Sweet Corn McBlock:* Jack Culbertson; *Mrs. Belker:* Dolly Day; *Mrs. Harris:* Dolly Day; *Harry Dean:* Johnny Coons; *Smelly Clark:* Johnny Coons; *Mervyn S. Sprawl:* Johnny Coons; *L.J. Gertner:* Johnny Coons; *Cracky Otto:* Johnny Coons; *Orville Wheeney:* Johnny Coons

**Sponsors:** Sustained (1932–34; 1937, NBC; 1941, MBS); Procter & Gamble Company, for Crisco shortening (1934–45, with fleeting exceptions); F.W. Fitch Company, for Fitch shampoo (1946)

**On the Air:** June 29, 1932–December 7, 1945, NBC, CBS, NBC Blue, MBS between 8:30 A.M. and 11 P.M. Eastern Time, almost continuous, often airing on two or three webs concurrently in complete-in-a-quarter-hour sketches four to five days (or nights) weekly; June 27–September 19, 1946, MBS, Thursday, 8:30–9:00 P.M. (reconfigured into a half-hour sitcom)

# Chapter Notes

## Introduction

1. Erik Barnouw, *A Tower in Babel: A History of Broadcasting in the United States to 1933* (second printing, pub. 1969); *The Golden Web: A History of Broadcasting in the United States 1933–1953* (pub. 1968); and *The Image Empire: A History of Broadcasting in the United States from 1953* (pub. 1970)—all three released by Oxford University Press, New York.

2. Alfred Balk, *The Rise of Radio: From Marconi through the Golden Age* (Jefferson, N.C.: McFarland, 2006), p. 160.

3. Gerald Nachman, *Raised on Radio: In Quest of The Lone Ranger, Jack Benny, Amos 'n' Andy, The Shadow, Mary Noble, The Great Gildersleeve, Fibber McGee and Molly, Bill Stern, Our Miss Brooks, Henry Aldrich, The Quiz Kids, Mr. First Nighter, Fred Allen, Vic and Sade, The Cisco Kid, Jack Armstrong, Arthur Godfrey, Bob and Ray, The Barbour Family, Henry Morgan, Joe Friday, and Other Lost Heroes from Radio's Heyday* (New York: Pantheon Books, 1998), p. 212.

4. J. Fred MacDonald, *Don't Touch That Dial!: Radio Programming in American Life from 1920 to 1960* (Chicago: Nelson-Hall, 1991), p. 135.

5. Ibid., p. 141.

6. Ibid., p. 145.

7. Ibid., p. 153.

8. *The Amos 'n' Andy Show* ran much longer than the list implies, but only a dozen years of its three decades aired as a sitcom. *Fibber McGee & Molly* and *The Great Gildersleeve* also ran in quarter-hour serialized installments, which weren't counted, and they and *The Jack Benny Program* aired lengthy repeats, which were not included either.

9. Harrison B. Summers, editor, *A Thirty-Year History of Programs Carried on National Radio Networks in the United States, 1926–1956* (New York: Arno Press and *The New York Times*, 1971).

## Chapter 1

1. Historiographer John Dunning disagrees with this in *Tune in Yesterday: The Ultimate Encyclopedia of Old-Time Radio, 1925–1976* (Englewood Cliffs, N.J.: Prentice-Hall, 1976), stating: "Original music, composed and conducted by Billy May, became one of radio's best-known themes" (p. 11).

2. At its inception, *The Adventures of Ozzie and Harriet* was titled *The Ozzie Nelson–Harriet Hilliard Show*, according to Jon Swartz and Robert Reinehr in *Handbook of Old-Time Radio: A Comprehensive Guide to Golden Age Radio Listening and Collecting* (Metuchen, N.J.: Scarecrow, 1993), p. 212.

3. John Dunning, *On the Air: The Encyclopedia of Old-Time Radio* (New York: Oxford University Press, 1998), p. 11.

4. Nelson included the song in the 1940 motion picture *Ozzie Nelson & His Orchestra*, along with a myriad of standards and a novelty number highlighting his own career: "Begin the Beguine," "Put on Your Old Grey Bonnet," "I've Got Those 'Oh What an Easy Job You've Got, All You Do Is Wave a Stick' Blues."

5. http://www.parabrisas.com/d_nelsono.php and http://en.wikipedia.org/wiki/Ozzie_Nelson.

6. On June 24, 1953, her father died in a Des Moines hotel in which he had been a resident for the previous six weeks, suggesting little change in his lifestyle as the years rolled by. Her mother passed in Los Angeles on August 1, 1971.

7. One historiographer disagrees with IMDb's speculation that *The Campus Mystery* was Harriet Hilliard's first film (she was identified by Hilliard before she arrived in Hollywood). Writing in *Tune in Yesterday* (p. 9), John Dunning advises that she premiered as an uncredited dancer in the short Paramount film *Musical Justice* (which was released in 1931, not 1932 as indicated), starring Rudy Vallee. Although nothing is impossible, it begs the question: If Ozzie Nelson was seeking a female vocalist, how did Hilliard impress him there if he didn't hear her sing?

8. Chuck Schaden, *Speaking of Radio* (Nostalgia Digest Press, 2003), p. 329.

9. When Joe Penner left in 1935, Robert "Believe It or Not" Ripley inherited the timeslot. Nelson and Hilliard continued performing with him.

10. Coincidentally, their long-running family broadcast series debuted on the same day nine years after they married—October 8, 1944.

11. Schaden, p. 334.

12. http://en.wikipedia.org/wiki/Ricky_Nelson.

13. http://www.museum.tv/archives/etv/N/htmlN/nelsonozzie/nelsonozzie.htm.

14. Dunning, 1998, pp. 11–12.

15. Lucille Ball would accomplish a similar feat a few years afterward at CBS.

16. Their contract allowed the couple to share the same bed on-camera, the first TV couple to occupy a double bed until *The Brady Bunch* arrived on ABC in 1969, 17 years after the Nelsons broke the barrier.

17. The deal was a good one for ABC, too, which was formed only a few years before. The struggling chain needed proven talent that wasn't about to defect to the competition—the well-entrenched and more affluent CBS and NBC. Securing the Nelsons for 10 years helped ABC project an image as a viable, stable alternative to its rivals.

18. Movie critic Leonard Maltin remembers this slightly differently in *The Great American Broadcast* (New York: Penguin, 1997): "Ozzie Nelson actually put his family into a theatrical feature film ... to prove to the powers

that be that they could play themselves successfully on TV" (p. 298).

19. *http://imdb.com/name/nm0625651/bio.*

20. Nachman, p. 234.

## Chapter 2

1. General Foods Corporation's origins date to 1895, although the name wasn't established until 1929. Through mergers and acquisitions it added brand names beyond Jell-O, like Maxwell House, Postum, Post, Baker's, Log Cabin, Calumet, Gaines, Oscar Mayer and dozens more. In 1985 General Foods Corporation was acquired by Philip Morris Companies Inc. for $5.6 billion, the largest non-oil acquisition in history. Three years later Philip Morris purchased Kraft Inc. for $12.9 billion. In 1989 Phillip Morris combined Kraft and General Foods, forming Kraft General Foods. The entity was renamed Kraft Foods Inc. in 1995, with General Foods assigned to brand status. In 2000 Philip Morris bought Nabisco Holdings, integrating its brands into the Kraft Foods conglomerate.

2. By 1942 Ezra Stone coveted the film role he played on radio and was bitterly disappointed that the studio signed Jimmy Lydon for the part instead, noted John Dunning in *Tune in Yesterday: The Ultimate Encyclopedia of Old-Time Radio, 1925–1976* (Englewood Cliffs, N.J.: Prentice-Hall, 1976, p. 24).

3. Ezra Stone, the most durable of radio's Henrys, was far too old to play the 16-year-old on television. When the series left the home screens for the last time in 1953 he was 35. Maintaining the proper high-pitched voice inflection, he got away with it on radio until he was 33 before he left the show forever. But he would hardly have passed as a mid-teen to video viewers.

4. Casting for the television adaptation erupted into a huge controversy when actress Jean Muir, a 20-year veteran of radio and motion pictures, was hired for the part of Mrs. Aldrich for the 1950–51 season. Right-wing factions protested vehemently, condemning her for perceived communist sympathies. Her name appeared in *Red Channels*, a publication citing alleged leftist atrocities of numerous public figures. As a result, sponsor General Foods Corporation and advertising agency Young and Rubicam canceled the first installment of *The Aldrich Family* for the new TV season. Muir was promptly dismissed, without opportunity to defend herself. Before a Congressional committee afterward she testified that she wasn't and had never been a communist. "But the truth didn't really matter.... The accusations alone had been enough virtually to destroy her career," wrote Tim Brooks and Earle Marsh in *The Complete Directory to Prime Time Network TV Shows, 1946–Present* (Ballantine, 1988, p. 23).

5. Alfred Balk, *The Rise of Radio, from Marconi Through the Golden Age* (McFarland, 2006), p. 164.

6. Jim Harmon, *The Great Radio Comedians* (Garden City, N.Y.: Doubleday, 1970), pp. 93–94.

7. Stone managed to incorporate his life's passion into meeting his military obligations. He acted in and directed several U.S. Army special service productions while on his tour with Uncle Sam.

8. Gerald Nachman, *Raised on Radio: In Quest of The Lone Ranger, Jack Benny, Amos 'n' Andy, The Shadow, Mary Noble, The Great Gildersleeve, Fibber McGee and Molly, Bill Stern, Our Miss Brooks, Henry Aldrich, The Quiz Kids, Mr. First Nighter, Fred Allen, Vic and Sade, The Cisco Kid, Jack Armstrong, Arthur Godfrey, Bob and Ray, The Barbour Family, Henry Morgan, Joe Friday, and Other Lost Heroes from Radio's Heyday* (New York: Pantheon Books, 1998), p. 213.

9. John Trotwood Moore and Austin P. Foster, *Tennessee, The Volunteer State, 1769–1923*, Volume 3 (Chicago: S.J. Clarke Publishing, 1923).

## Chapter 3

1. *http://www.tvparty.com/50amosl.html.*

2. John Dunning, *On the Air: The Encyclopedia of Old-Time Radio* (New York: Oxford University Press, 1998), p. 32.

3. Erik Barnouw, *A Tower in Babel: A History of Broadcasting in the United States to 1933* (New York: Oxford University Press, 1966), pp. 229–230.

4. Gerald Nachman, *Raised on Radio: In Quest of The Lone Ranger, Jack Benny, Amos 'n' Andy, The Shadow, Mary Noble, The Great Gildersleeve, Fibber McGee and Molly, Bill Stern, Our Miss Brooks, Henry Aldrich, The Quiz Kids, Mr. First Nighter, Fred Allen, Vic and Sade, The Cisco Kid, Jack Armstrong, Arthur Godfrey, Bob and Ray, The Barbour Family, Henry Morgan, Joe Friday, and Other Lost Heroes from Radio's Heyday* (New York: Pantheon Books, 1998), p. 68.

5. By comparison, the 2004 Super Bowl earned a rating of 44.2.

6. *http://en.wikipedia.org/wiki/Amos_'n'_Andy.*

7. Elizabeth McLeod, *The Original Amos 'n' Andy: Freeman Gosden, Charles Correll and the 1928–1943 Radio Serial* (Jefferson, N.C.: McFarland, 2005), p. 30.

8. *http://www.tvparty.com/50amosl.html.*

9. McLeod, p. 57.

10. Irna Phillips, who would create the first pure soap opera for WGN in 1930, would run into similar troubles with some of the same individuals a couple of years afterward as she attempted to send *Painted Dreams* to the nation as a network feature. She did so anyway by changing the title of the show to *Today's Children,* modifying the characters' names and moving to Chicago rival station WMAQ, which shared her dramatic feature with the country via NBC.

11. After a two-week hiatus at WGN, *Sam 'n' Henry* resumed over the *Tribune's* powerful outlet, with WGN staff novelty team Henry Moeller and Hal Gilles as the namesake figures. Ironically, they, too, were alumni of the Bren Company. Gosden had instructed them both in speaking African-American dialect.

12. The duo tried out several combinations of monikers until settling on one. After giving up *Sam 'n' Henry* they considered *Jim 'n' Charley* and *Tom 'n' Henry* before picking *Amos 'n' Andy.* Gosden noted that Amos was derived from the telephone book and "had a nice biblical ring." Correll said Andy sounded "pleasant, round, and juicy," like the roly-poly fellow portraying him.

13. *http://www.tvparty.com/50amosl.html.*

14. Adapted from Judith C. Waller, *Radio: The Fifth Estate* (New York: Houghton Mifflin, 1946), pp. 18–19.

15. McLeod, p. 89.

16. McLeod, p. 142.

17. Ibid., p. 143.

18. Ibid., pp. 144, 145.

19. Jim Harmon, *The Great Radio Comedians* (Garden City, N.Y.: Doubleday, 1970), pp. 70, 71, 72–73.

20. Nachman, pp. 276, 277, 278.

21. *http://www.museum.tv/archives/etv/A/htmlA/amosnandy/amosnandy.htm.*

22. Jim Cox, "The Top 40: What were the longest running aural network series on the air?," *SPERDVAC Radiogram,* September 2006, pp. 8–9, 14.

23. *http://www.museum.tv/archives/etv/A/htmlA/amosnandy/amosnandy.htm.*

24. Jim Cox, *Music Radio: The Great Performers and Programs of the 1920s through Early 1960s* (Jefferson, N.C.: McFarland, 2005), pp. 152, 153.

25. Harmon, p. 86.

## Chapter 4

1. The reader's attention is called to Appendix A, however, in which virtually all of the generally accepted radio sitcoms have been identified.

2. Mr. Waldo Weatherbee, principal of Riverdale High School in *Archie Andrews*, was purportedly a copy of Earl McLeod, principal of Haverhill High School. Jughead Jones was patterned after a student named Skinny Linehan. The Haverhill librarian, Elizabeth Tuck, was the inspiration for Riverdale's Miss Grundy, Archie's teacher. Several other characters were based on living figures in the Massachusetts high school.

3. Established in November 1939, MLJ Magazines was named for its trio of founding partners—Maurice Coyne, Louis Silberkleit and John Goldwater.

4. Adapted from a personal communication with the author on July 2, 2006, and used by permission.

5. Hal (Harlan) Stone, *Aw ... Relax, Archie! Re-laxx!: When Radio Was "King" I Was Once a "Prince" but Ended Up a "Jughead"* (Sedona, AZ: Bygone Days Press, 2003), pp. 163–164, 192.

6. Stone, p. 183.

7. Pop Tate's Chocklit Shoppe was patterned after three commercial enterprises that high school students frequented in the 1930s in Haverhill, Massachusetts: the Tuscarora on Winter Street, the Chocolate Shop and Crown Confectionery, both on Merrimack Street. This is the city where Bob Montana, the cartoonist who originated Archie Andrews, lived during some of his adolescent years, and upon which he based his stories.

8. *http://www.archiecomics.com/acpaco_offices/inside_scoop/inside_scoop_6.html.*

9. *http://scoop.diamondgalleries.com/scoop_article.asp?ai=645&si=124.*

## Chapter 5

1. John Dunning, *Tune in Yesterday: The Ultimate Encyclopedia of Old-Time Radio, 1925–1976* (Englewood Cliffs, N.J.: Prentice-Hall, 1976), pp. 52–53.

2. http://en.wikipedia.org/wiki/Fanny_Brice.

3. Jim Harmon, *The Great Radio Comedians* (Garden City, N.Y.: Doubleday, 1970), pp. 1–2.

4. Dunning, 1976, pp. 51–52.

5. Leonard Maltin, *The Great American Broadcast: A Celebration of Radio's Golden Age* (New York: Penguin Putnam, 1997), p. 243.

6. Alfred Balk, *The Rise of Radio: From Marconi Through the Golden Age* (Jefferson, N.C.: McFarland, 2006), p. 162.

7. Frank Morgan belonged to a prominent family of thespians. His brother was stage and movie actor Ralph Morgan, whose daughter (Frank's niece) was Claudia Morgan, not only a stage actress but soap opera queen of NBC and CBS's *The Right to Happiness*, where she was Carolyn Allen Walker Kramer Nelson MacDonald, "the most married heroine in daytime radio" (1942–60), and star of *The Adventures of the Thin Man*, where she was leading lady Nora Charles on all four radio webs (1941–50).

8. While Fanny Brice and company shifted to CBS in the fall of 1944, the debuting *Frank Morgan Show*, a comedy-variety half-hour, with comedienne Cass Daley

and Robert Young as host, remained at NBC. Both series were sponsored by General Foods Corporation.

9. Harmon, 1970, p. 18.

10. Ibid., p. 21.

11. Writer Jess Oppenheimer reports this situation differently in chapter 17 (*My Favorite Husband*): "Fanny Brice flung a fit in May 1948 and stormed off the air after being asked to accept a salary cut of $2,500 weekly from the $5,500 she was getting." According to Oppenheimer, for the first time in a dozen years he was suddenly out of work following Ms. Brice's decision. This presumably also would have curtailed the income of various actors, writers, musicians and production personnel.

12. Others were Bud Abbott and Lou Costello, Jack Benny, Edgar Bergen and Charlie McCarthy, and Stan Laurel and Oliver Hardy.

13. *http://en.wikipedia.org/wiki/Fanny_Brice.*

14. Maltin, pp. 216–217.

## Chapter 6

1. Gerald Nachman, *Raised on Radio: In Quest of The Lone Ranger, Jack Benny, Amos 'n' Andy, The Shadow, Mary Noble, The Great Gildersleeve, Fibber McGee and Molly, Bill Stern, Our Miss Brooks, Henry Aldrich, The Quiz Kids, Mr. First Nighter, Fred Allen, Vic and Sade, The Cisco Kid, Jack Armstrong, Arthur Godfrey, Bob and Ray, The Barbour Family, Henry Morgan, Joe Friday, and Other Lost Heroes from Radio's Heyday* (New York: Pantheon Books, 1998), p. 277.

2. Ibid., p. 239.

3. In a widely reported parallel incident, a five-year-old girl interrupted a church service she was attending in that era by belting out, "Somebody bawl fo' Beulah?" The congregation guffawed.

4. There are numerous indications that "Beulah" even received letters from black GIs proposing marriage.

5. Several vintage radio historiographers who are typically reliable on such matters have incorrectly intimated that *The Great Gildersleeve* introduced the radio spinoff to the ether. While that show was an early example of the form, at least two daytime serials with links to existing narratives were already airing: *The Right to Happiness* premiered on October 16, 1939, and was an outgrowth of *The Guiding Light*. *Bright Horizon*, a derivative of *Big Sister*, launched as a new drama on August 25, 1941, and had broadcast a week's worth of episodes by the time *The Great Gildersleeve* arrived.

6. Marlin Hurt and Phil Leslie shared the same professional agent, Ken Dillon.

7. Hollywood publicists embellished Hattie McDaniel's legacy upon the release of *Gone with the Wind* to paint her dad as a Baptist minister, according to Jill Watts' contemporary biography of the legendary performer. Although numerous scholars maintain that her birthplace was Wichita, Kansas, Watts—with corroborating data—proclaims that McDaniel was a Denver native instead.

8. *http://members.aol.com/ttelracs/Hattie.htm.*

9. A few sources intimate that McDaniel appeared in over 300 films, although she only received screen credits for about 80. She is known to have sung many times with choral groups onscreen, for which she was uncredited.

10. Prior to the high profile emphasis on Civil Rights in the 1950s and 1960s, filmmakers faced a major hurdle when they wished to cast Negroes in conventional movies. How could blacks and whites appear in realistic situations or even believably *be* in the same place at the same time interacting with one another? Such things seldom oc-

curred in real life; thereby, without placing a Negro in a servile post, the setting would be patently rejected by an audience acutely aware that the prevailing environment embraced a strictly segregated society.

11. *http://www.imdb.com/name/nm0567408/bio.*

12. *http://www.members.aol.com/ttelracs/Hattie.htm.*

13. So identified was McDaniel with "mammy" roles that she inspired the human "Mammy" character in the Tom and Jerry cartoons. The screen figure was best recalled for exuberantly shouting *"Thomas!"*

14. In *The Little Colonel*, for instance, released in 1935, black servants were depicted as longing for a return to the Old South, something more progressive blacks could hardly abide.

15. J. Fred MacDonald, *Don't Touch That Dial!: Radio Programming in American Life from 1920 to 1960* (Chicago: Nelson-Hall, 1991), pp. 101–102.

16. Nachman, p. 293.

17. MacDonald, p. 366.

18. According to *Making Waves: The 50 Greatest Women in Radio and Television*, edited by Jacci Duncan (Kansas City: Andrews McMeel, 2001), despite the progress toward racial equality in the 1950s, when the professional society of American Women in Radio and Television marked its half-century anniversary in 2001 it asked its membership to elect the 50 greatest women in the history of broadcasting. Together they found no African American women in radio worthy of citing, and but two blacks in television—Diahann Carroll and Oprah Winfrey.

19. Examples of daytime serials following this pattern include *Aunt Jenny's Real Life Stories, Front Page Farrell, Modern Romances*, and, later, *Best Seller* and *Whispering Streets*. At one point the famous evening detective sleuth *Mr. Keen, Tracer of Lost Persons* also meted out quarter-hour doses in five-part mysteries per week.

20. Nachman, p. 240.

21. As previously mentioned, at least one report claims the McDaniel episodes were filmed but never screened. Most authorities do not support that position, however.

22. After the radio and television show's cancellation, the networks, as well as independent television producers, afraid of being accused of perpetuating racial stereotypes, stopped casting blacks in their shows almost entirely for 15 years. The next series starring a black woman was *Julia* in 1968, featuring Diahann Carroll. Between 1953 and 1968 only two Negroes, Nat King Cole and Bill Cosby, starred in national TV series. However, in 1961 the sitcom *Hazel* premiered on television, derived from a comic strip created by Ted Key. While *Hazel* proffered essentially the same format as *Beulah*, the video series continued for five seasons without protests because it cast the housekeeper as a white woman, played by Shirley Booth. By the early 1970s, blacks appeared in about a third of all TV commercials and in many continuing features. NBC-TV's *The Flip Wilson Show* (1970–74), headlined by a black comedian, enjoyed widespread acceptance.

23. Taken from communications the author received from Stuart Lubin on April 13 and 15, 2006. Used by permission.

## Chapter 7

1. *http://rinkworks.com/movies/m/blondie.1938.shtml.*

2. "Blondie's Father," *Time*, May 9, 1949.

3. Lawrence Van Gelder, "Chic Young, Creator of 'Blondie,' Dead," *The New York Times*, March 16, 1973, p. 44.

4. *http://rinkworks.com/movies/m/blondie.1938.shtml.*

5. *http://www.polarblairsden.com/blondiearthurlake01. html.*

6. *http:www.polarblairsden.com/blondieearthurlake 01.html.*

## Chapter 8

1. "The Little Man Who Wasn't There." Music and lyrics by Harold Adamson and Bernie Hanighen.

2. John Dunning, *Tune in Yesterday: The Ultimate Encyclopedia of Old-Time Radio, 1925–1976* (Englewood Cliffs, N.J.: Prentice-Hall, 1976), p. 171.

3. A number of radio historians have mistakenly applied several variations and combinations of his true moniker (that appears in U.S. Census Bureau records) to identify him (e.g., Friederich Poggenburg), all of them being incorrect.

4. *http://www.imdb.com/name/nm0306908/bio.*

5. *http://en.wikipedia.org/wiki/Duffy's_Tavern.*

6. Tim Brooks and Earle Marsh, *The Complete Director to Prime Time Network TV Shows, 1946–Present*, 4th edition (New York: Ballantine Books, 1988).

7. Alex McNeil, *Total Television: The Comprehensive Guide to Programming from 1948 to the Present*, 4th edition (New York: Penguin Books, 1996), p. 241.

8. The unique moniker was based on an actual establishment located on New York's West 40th Street, Duffy's Radio Tavern.

9. *http://www.audio-classics.com/mgduffystavern.html.*

10. For its treatment of a Negro figure (Eddie Green), the series won a coveted George Foster Peabody Award. Other than Eddie (Rochester) Anderson on *The Jack Benny Program*, at that juncture Green was the only continuing black male character in a radio comedy.

11. *http://www.audio-classics.com/mgduffystavern.html.*

12. Quoted in Leonard Maltin, *The Great American Broadcast: A Celebration of Radio's Golden Age* (New York: Penguin Putnam, 1997), pp. 173–174.

13. The show had already uprooted once, moving everybody from New York to Hollywood when a sponsor had insisted, in 1943, that they relocate. A major benefit was in more easily acquiring a prolific number of venerated icons residing on the West Coast.

14. *http://www.audio-classics.com/mgduffystavern.html.*

15. John Dunning, *On the Air: The Encyclopedia of Old-Time Radio* (New York: Oxford University Press, 1998), p. 212.

16. *http://www.audio-classics.com/mgduffystavern.html.*

17. Maltin, p. 284.

18. Gardner had taken considerable pride in Abe Burrows' accomplishments on Broadway, among them collaborating with Jo Swerling in adapting various short stories by Damon Runyon to create the book for the musical smash hit *Guys and Dolls*. In fact, Burrows traced his aptitude for creating the *Guys and Dolls* street characters to his *Duffy's Tavern* days, populated by "Damon Runyon types."

## Chapter 9

1. John Dunning, *On the Air: The Encyclopedia of Old-Time Radio* (New York: Oxford University Press, 1998), p. 243.

2. *http://www.museum.tv/archives/etv/F/htmlF/father knows/fatherknows.htm.*

3. Gerald Nachman, *Raised on Radio: In Quest of The Lone Ranger, Jack Benny, Amos 'n' Andy, The Shadow, Mary Noble, The Great Gildersleeve, Fibber McGee and Molly, Bill*

Stern, Our Miss Brooks, Henry Aldrich, The Quiz Kids, Mr. First Nighter, Fred Allen, Vic and Sade, The Cisco Kid, Jack Armstrong, Arthur Godfrey, Bob and Ray, The Barbour Family, Henry Morgan, Joe Friday, and Other Lost Heroes from Radio's Heyday (New York: Pantheon Books, 1998), p. 216.

4. http://www.imdb.com/name/nm0336474/bio.

5. Included in the June 20, 2004, issue.

6. Steve Allen, "Dumbth": The Lost Art of Thinking (Amherst, N.Y.: Prometheus Books, 1998), p. 27.

7. Ibid., p. 28.

8. The New York Times, July 23, 1998, p. D20.

## Chapter 10

1. John Dunning, Tune in Yesterday: The Ultimate Encyclopedia of Old-Time Radio, 1925–1976 (Englewood Cliffs, N.J.: Prentice-Hall, 1976), p. 203.

2. Frank Buxton and Bill Owen, The Big Broadcast, 1920–1950, 2nd edition (Lanham, MD: Scarecrow Press, 1997), p. 79.

3. John Dunning, quoted by Alfred Balk in The Rise of Radio: From Marconi Through the Golden Age (Jefferson, N.C.: McFarland, 2006), p. 169.

4. Gerald Nachman, Raised on Radio: In Quest of The Lone Ranger, Jack Benny, Amos 'n' Andy, The Shadow, Mary Noble, The Great Gildersleeve, Fibber McGee and Molly, Bill Stern, Our Miss Brooks, Henry Aldrich, The Quiz Kids, Mr. First Nighter, Fred Allen, Vic and Sade, The Cisco Kid, Jack Armstrong, Arthur Godfrey, Bob and Ray, The Barbour Family, Henry Morgan, Joe Friday, and Other Lost Heroes from Radio's Heyday (New York: Pantheon Books, 1998), p. 84.

5. J. Fred MacDonald, Don't Touch That Dial!: Radio Programming in American Life from 1920 to 1960 (Chicago: Nelson-Hall, 1991), p. 135.

6. Arthur Frank Wertheim, Radio Comedy (New York: Oxford University Press, 1979), pp. 217–218.

7. Ruggiero Leoncavallo wrote and composed Pagliacci about 1890. It was the first opera to be recorded in its entirety (1907) and is the 14th most frequently performed opera in North America.

8. Raymond William Stedman, The Serials: Suspense and Drama by Installment (Norman, OK: The University of Oklahoma Press, 1971), pp. 226–227.

9. The dates and origination points were supplied by the McGee show biographers, Charles Stumpf and Tom Price. They conflict with another usually reliable source, The Third Revised Ultimate History of Network Radio Programming and Guide to All Circulating Shows. The latter volume indicates that Smackout was beamed over CBS and not merely a local Chicago station on March 2, 1931, and was aired four to five times weekly to October 31, 1931. It transferred to NBC on November 3 and persisted two to six times weekly on that web to August 3, 1935, more than two years beyond the dates ascribed by Stumpf and Price.

10. Charles Stumpf and Tom Price, Heavenly Days!: The Story of Fibber McGee and Molly (Waynesville, N.C.: The World of Yesterday, 1987), p. 55.

11. Yet another mirthful couple in a similar vein arrived on the afternoon airwaves in the spring of 1938, initially on NBC and later on CBS. Matthew and Winfred Wilbur, hero and heroine of the daytime soap Your Family and Mine, closely paralleled Lorenzo and Belle and Fibber and Molly. He fooled with gadgets and inventing several of the useless type (Lorenzo and Fibber made over), while she was practical, helping keep their heads above water during the lean times. The Wilburs' symbolic difference from the other couples was that they had kids ages

17 and 12 who were greatly affected by their father's worthless scheming. Their serial lasted two years.

12. Quoted in Leonard Maltin, The Great American Broadcast: A Celebration of Radio's Golden Age (New York: Penguin Putnam, 1997), p. 186.

13. Adapted from Jim Cox, Music Radio: The Great Performers and Programs of the 1920s through Early 1960s (Jefferson, N.C.: McFarland, 2005), pp. 210–211.

14. For more discussion on radio formats that combined mixed elements into variety broadcasts, including the pacing of music comedy series, the reader is referred to Music Radio by this author, giving special focus to pp. 209–211. "Did Billy Mills even have an orchestra?" is considered there.

15. George Burns, with David Fisher, All My Best Friends (New York: Putnam, 1989), p. 128.

16. Maltin, p. 204.

17. Balk, p. 162.

18. Irene Heinstein, old.time.radio@oldradio.net, August 12, 2006.

19. Stumpf and Price, p. 205.

20. Stumpf and Price, p. 227.

21. MacDonald, p. 138.

## Chapter 11

1. http://en.wikipedia.org/wiki/George_Burns.

2. Gerald Nachman, Raised on Radio: In Quest of The Lone Ranger, Jack Benny, Amos 'n' Andy, The Shadow, Mary Noble, The Great Gildersleeve, Fibber McGee and Molly, Bill Stern, Our Miss Brooks, Henry Aldrich, The Quiz Kids, Mr. First Nighter, Fred Allen, Vic and Sade, The Cisco Kid, Jack Armstrong, Arthur Godfrey, Bob and Ray, The Barbour Family, Henry Morgan, Joe Friday, and Other Lost Heroes from Radio's Heyday (New York: Pantheon Books, 1998), p. 76.

3. As time progressed, several alterations occurred in casting the TV show. Hal March was followed by John Brown, Fred Clark and Larry Keating as Harry Morton. The announcer, Bill Goodwin, was succeeded by Harry Von Zell in the show's second year. Ronnie Burns, son of the stars, appeared as himself from 1955 to 1958.

4. George Burns, with David Fisher, All My Best Friends (New York: G.P. Putnam's, 1989), pp. 86–87.

5. Leonard Maltin, The Great American Broadcast: A Celebration of Radio's Golden Age (New York: Penguin Putnam, 1997), p. 172.

6. Some other walk-ons during the televised sequences included Jack Benny, Mary Livingstone, Robert Easton, Jill St. John, Gerald Mohr, Ronald Reagan, Marion Ross, Robert Cummings and Francis X. Bushman.

7. http://en.wikipedia.org/wiki/George_Burns.

8. George Burns, Gracie, a Love Story (New York: Penguin Books, 1988), pp. 305–306.

9. http://en.wikipedia.org/wiki/George_Burns.

10. Nachman, p. 78.

11. Ibid., p. 80.

## Chapter 12

1. The similitude didn't stop there. In 1942, bearing a striking resemblance to Today's Children, Lonely Women premiered on the NBC airwaves, introduced there by Irna Phillips. When it ceased broadcasting in 1943, she folded its characters back into Today's Children, making a comeback.

2. Jim Harmon, The Great Radio Comedians (Garden City, N.Y.: Doubleday, 1970), pp. 23, 31.

3. Beulah, the McGees' maid, was the second character in *Fibber McGee & Molly* to be developed into a separate feature. *Beulah* debuted on CBS on July 2, 1945, as a weekly half-hour sitcom before settling into a weeknight quarter-hour in 1947, where it ran to 1954.

4. Gerald Nachman, *Raised on Radio: In Quest of The Lone Ranger, Jack Benny, Amos 'n' Andy, The Shadow, Mary Noble, The Great Gildersleeve, Fibber McGee and Molly, Bill Stern, Our Miss Brooks, Henry Aldrich, The Quiz Kids, Mr. First Nighter, Fred Allen, Vic and Sade, The Cisco Kid, Jack Armstrong, Arthur Godfrey, Bob and Ray, The Barbour Family, Henry Morgan, Joe Friday, and Other Lost Heroes from Radio's Heyday* (New York: Pantheon Books, 1998), p. 228.

5. http://www.ethomsen.com/gildy/name.html.

6. http://en.wikipedia.org/wiki/The_Great_Gildersleeve.

7. The show *Honest Harold* is sometimes interchangeably referred to as *The Harold Peary Show*, signifying not only his starring role but his ownership of the series.

8. John Dunning, *On the Air: The Encyclopedia of Old-Time Radio* (New York: Oxford University Press, 1998), p. 327.

9. Nachman, p. 226.

10. http://www.ethomsen.com/gildy/peary.html.

11. Rival web CBS began the late-evening strip format on June 21, 1954. It added a quarter-hour five-night-a-week serialized *Mr. Keen, Tracer of Lost Persons* at 10 P.M. That sleuth was already heard in a longstanding Friday night crime drama; both series ran concurrently. The episodic configuration lasted to January 14, 1955, when it was withdrawn. CBS generally tended to fill its vacant late-evening time periods after that with lesser known orchestras in 15-minute doses.

12. http://www.ethomsen.com/gildy/television.html.

13. http://en.wikipedia.org/wiki/The_Great_Gildersleeve.

14. http://www.imdb.com/title/tt0047735/.

15. "Gildersleeve's Ex-Wife in Another Jam," *The Los Angeles Times*, July 11, 1946.

16. "Gildersleeve's Ex-Wife Fined," *The Los Angeles Times*, October 5, 1946.

17. *The Lima (Ohio) News*, June 6, 1937, p. 32.

## Chapter 13

1. Luther F. Sies, *Encyclopedia of American Radio, 1920–1960* (Jefferson, N.C.: McFarland, 2000), p. 286.

2. Jack Benny and Joan Benny, *Sunday Nights at Seven: The Jack Benny Story* (New York: Warner Books, 1990), pp. 75–76.

3. http://www.museum.tv/archives/etv/B/htmlB/bennyjack/bennyjack.htm.

4. Benny and Benny, p. 72.

5. Benny and Benny, p. 94.

6. http://www.museum.tv/archives/etv/B/htmlB/bennyjack/bennyjack.htm.

7. Benny and Benny, p. 78.

8. http://en.wikipedia.org/wiki/Jack_Benny.

9. In addition to Jack Benny, also plucked from NBC and added to CBS's roster in those same talent raids masterminded by William S. Paley were *The Adventures of Ozzie and Harriet*, Edgar Bergen and Charlie McCarthy, George Burns and Gracie Allen, Harold Peary (who originated *The Great Gildersleeve*) and Red Skelton, plus Bing Crosby and Groucho Marx from ABC. The lightning speed with which the CBS head carried out his moves against his competition was dubbed "Paley's Comet" by industry insiders.

10. Jim Cox, *Say Goodnight, Gracie: The Last Years of Network Radio* (Jefferson, N.C.: McFarland, 2002), p. 86.

11. *Variety*, January 9, 1946, p. 7.

12. David Halberstam, *The Fifties* (New York: Villard Books, 1993), pp. 202–203.

13. Ibid., p. 203.

14. Thomas A. DeLong, *Radio Stars: An Illustrated Biographical Dictionary of 953 Performers, 1920 through 1960* (Jefferson, N.C.: McFarland, 1996), p. 30.

15. Others included on the commemorative postage stamps were Bud Abbott and Lou Costello; Edgar Bergen and Charlie McCarthy; Fannie Brice; and Stan Laurel and Oliver Hardy.

## Chapter 14

1. http://www.museum.tv/archives/etv/L/htmlL/lifeofriley/lifeofriley.htm.

2. Gerald Nachman, *Raised on Radio: In Quest of The Lone Ranger, Jack Benny, Amos 'n' Andy, The Shadow, Mary Noble, The Great Gildersleeve, Fibber McGee and Molly, Bill Stern, Our Miss Brooks, Henry Aldrich, The Quiz Kids, Mr. First Nighter, Fred Allen, Vic and Sade, The Cisco Kid, Jack Armstrong, Arthur Godfrey, Bob and Ray, The Barbour Family, Henry Morgan, Joe Friday, and Other Lost Heroes from Radio's Heyday* (New York: Pantheon Books, 1998), p. 246.

3. Brecher, 92, was still living as of 2006.

4. Several sources credit Groucho Marx for his involvement, although Wikipedia maintains that the non-performing Marx brother, Gummo, was a major participant in developing the original Riley model.

5. http://en.wikipedia.org/wiki/Life_of_Riley.

6. Alex McNeil, *Total Television: The Comprehensive Guide to Programming from 1948 to the Present* 4th edition (New York: Penguin Books, 1996), p. 479.

7. Editors of TV Guide, *TV Guide: Guide to TV* (New York: Barnes & Noble Books, 2004), p. 367.

8. Nachman, p. 248.

9. A slightly altered inference from that given here is delineated at http://www.phrases.org.uk/bulletin_board/40/messages/516.html. Many other suppositions likely abound.

10. http://en.wikipedia.org/wiki/Life_of_Riley and http://www.jameswhitcombriley.com/the_life_of_riley.htm.

11. http://www.geocities.com/alcus2/riley.html.

12. William Bendix is sometimes mistakenly identified as a descendant of maestro and violinist Max Bendix, but that is not the case; his dad was an altogether different artist.

13. The film's identity has long been lost to history. Ms. Walker appeared in 167 motion pictures from her debut in 1909 to her retirement in 1934, 18 of which were released in 1911, the year of William Bendix's small contribution.

14. A few sources intimate that Bendix went beyond being a bat boy to become a minor league player. This hasn't been corroborated, however. The story may have been repeated and embellished over time; at least one report claims he played in the majors, a statement that appears to have little foundation.

## Chapter 15

1. J. Fred MacDonald, *Don't Touch That Dial!: Radio Programming in American Life from 1920 to 1960* (Chicago: Nelson-Hall, 1991), p. 98.

2. John Dunning, *Tune in Yesterday: The Ultimate Encyclopedia of Old-Time Radio, 1925–1976* (Englewood Cliffs, N.J.: Prentice-Hall, 1976), p. 359.

3. Alfred Balk, *The Rise of Radio: From Marconi Through the Golden Age* (Jefferson, N.C.: McFarland, 2006), p. 272.

## Chapter 16

1. http://www.imdb.com/name/nm0869429/bio.
2. Many Sepahrdic Jews lived in the Ottoman Empire for hundreds of years after they were expelled from Spain.
3. In the televersion there was also a Mrs. J.R. Boone Sr., played by Isabel Randolph.

## Chapter 17

1. Jess Oppenheimer, with Gregg Oppenheimer *Laughs, Luck ... and Lucy: How I Came to Create the Most Popular Sitcom of All Time* (Syracuse, N.Y.: University of Syracuse Press, 1996), p. 115.
2. Ibid., p. 117.
3. Ibid., p. 119.
4. Ibid., pp. 119–121.
5. Gerald Nachman, *Raised on Radio: In Quest of The Lone Ranger, Jack Benny, Amos 'n' Andy, The Shadow, Mary Noble, The Great Gildersleeve, Fibber McGee and Molly, Bill Stern, Our Miss Brooks, Henry Aldrich, The Quiz Kids, Mr. First Nighter, Fred Allen, Vic and Sade, The Cisco Kid, Jack Armstrong, Arthur Godfrey, Bob and Ray, The Barbour Family, Henry Morgan, Joe Friday, and Other Lost Heroes from Radio's Heyday* (New York: Pantheon Books, 1998), p. 92.

## Chapter 18

1. Jay Hickerson, *The Third Ultimate History of Network Radio Programming and Guide to All Circulating Shows* (Hamden, CT: Presto Print II, 2005).
2. Gloria Grahame was of royalty. Her father's family descended from King Edward III through John of Gaunt; her mother's came from the Scottish Kings of the Hebrides. Grahame wed four times and divorced all her husbands. Cy Howard was her third mate.
3. At least one media historian, Gerald Nachman, insisted that men were drawn to the show by "Wilson's sexy nasal voice and the sparky-sounding Lewis" *Raised on Radio* (New York: Pantheon, 1998), p. 91.
4. Interestingly, in a sitcom (*Meet Millie*) displaying similar proclivities that arrived on the air while this one was still running, the broad there—Millie Bronson—was a secretary to an investment counselor. It seemed more than a little coincidental that the range of occupations was so limited on like-minded shows. In Millie's case, however, her boss was already married; instead, she pursued his son, Johnny Boone, Jr., as a potential spouse.
5. *The Phil Harris–Alice Faye Show* in 1947–48, its second season on the air, reached the ratings summit by surpassing *My Friend Irma's* showing of 18.1 that season, its first year. No other new sitcom was close to those numbers. In 1948–49, *Irma* surpassed all such features, at 21.5; *A Day in the Life of Dennis Day* was second at 17.7; *Harris-Faye* was third with 16.1. By 1949–50, *Irma* held at 20.8, while *Life with Luigi*, in its second season, improved to 16.4. All others introduced in that era trailed significantly.
6. Elliot Lewis's professional accomplishments in radio are recognized no fewer than 42 times in the index of John Dunning's text *On the Air: The Encyclopedia of Old-Time Radio* (New York: Oxford University Press, 1998).
7. In 1959, following his and Cathy's divorce, Elliott

Lewis remarried, again wedding another busy actress, Mary Jane Croft. She was divorced from her first spouse, Jack Zoeller. Elliott Lewis and Mary Jane Croft remained married to each other until his death from cardiac arrest on May 23, 1990.
8. Ackerman earned impressive credentials in the broadcasting industry. Shortly after he became executive producer and vice president in charge of network programming for CBS in 1948, he relocated to Hollywood. From 1949 to 1951 he was the web's vice president and director of TV and radio; from 1951 to 1955 he was vice president in charge of TV programming in Hollywood; and from 1956 to 1957 he was executive director of special productions for CBS-TV. At least one wag theorized that Mary Shipp got the job of replacing Cathy Lewis on *My Friend Irma* in 1953 because she was married to the boss at the time.
9. Elinor and Harry Ackerman raised three sons of their own and were still married to each other at the time of his death after three decades. Three years later, in 1994, she gave his personal papers to the Dartmouth College Library at New Hanover, New Hampshire, to form the Harry Ackerman Collection. He had earned a bachelor's degree there in 1935.
10. The charmed life of entertainer Gale Gordon, son of Gloria Gordon and Charles Aldrich, is extensively detailed in the chapter on *Our Miss Brooks* in this volume.
11. Such allegations were never proved in the majority of cases, although many broadcasting careers were wrecked by the accusations. A gripping account of the effect of blacklisting on the professional careers and private lives of entertainers is presented in Rita Morley Harvey's text *Those Wonderful, Terrible Years: George Heller and the American Federation of Television and Radio Artists* (Carbondale: Southern Illinois University Press, 1996).
12. Cancer was a factor in the deaths of Frances Elena Farmer, Margaret Hayes (nee Florette Regina Ottenheimer) and Leif Erickson (nee William Anderson). Erickson did not remarry. Farmer remarried twice, divorcing once more, while Hayes remarried once and divorced again.

## Chapter 19

1. This theme was used throughout the radio run and for the first three seasons of the televersion. The opening music was replaced in the final video season (1955–56) with "Whistling Bells," by Farlan I. Myers.
2. Gerald Nachman, *Raised on Radio: In Quest of The Lone Ranger, Jack Benny, Amos 'n' Andy, The Shadow, Mary Noble, The Great Gildersleeve, Fibber McGee and Molly, Bill Stern, Our Miss Brooks, Henry Aldrich, The Quiz Kids, Mr. First Nighter, Fred Allen, Vic and Sade, The Cisco Kid, Jack Armstrong, Arthur Godfrey, Bob and Ray, The Barbour Family, Henry Morgan, Joe Friday, and Other Lost Heroes from Radio's Heyday* (New York: Pantheon Books, 1998), p. 218.
3. She maintained a lifelong habit of hiding her true age, although her family certified that she was 82 at the time of her death in 1990. Source: http://www.imdb.com/name/nm0000781/bio.
4. The child obviously experienced some insecurity in her early life. Her parents, Charles Peter and Lucille Quedens, split up when she was a youngster, undoubtedly causing significant sadness for her. Much later she confessed that she ultimately required counseling after perceiving that her mother was "so much more beautiful" than she was. She was raised by her mother and some aunts who supported her early expressions of interest in the theater.

5. Eve Arden's new name was derived from a combination of factors, she told radio interviewer Chuck Schaden in 1975: she read a book whose heroine was named Eve, and was applying Elizabeth Arden cosmetics at the time. Ordered by producer Lee Shubert of the *Ziegfeld Follies* to create a moniker that would fit on the marquee, she offered "Eve Arden." He liked it and it stuck permanently.

6. *http://en.wikipedia.org/wiki/Eve_Arden*.

7. *http://www.imdb.com/name/nm0000781/bio*.

8. In the fall of 1955, the video incarnation switched locales, while the radio manifestation continued unabated. On TV Madison High School was razed to make way for a new highway (in reality, to juice up faltering ratings). Miss Brooks and Mr. Conklin found employment at Mrs. Nestor's private elementary school. He was again the principal, while she was a teacher. Some new cast members were introduced, though most of the familiar figures were still around. Ratings continued to plummet, and the televersion was withdrawn in the spring of 1956. Two decades later Arden said that when the show switched from a public to private school and high to grammar school, "It never recovered. That was really the reason we went off the air."

9. *Our Miss Brooks* was the introduction of a long line of spinsters on TV, soon followed by Sally Rogers (Rose Marie) on *The Dick Van Dyke Show* and Jane Hathaway (Nancy Kulp) on *The Beverly Hillbillies*.

10. Sources put Arden's 1952 salary from *Our Miss Brooks* at $200,000 annually, a hefty sum in that era. The schools that legitimately pursued her as a teacher could hardly have afforded her.

11. Arden was married to Ned Bergen from 1939 to 1947. They divorced. On August 24, 1952, she wed actor Brooks West. They had one child by birth, Douglas Brooks West, born in September 1954, and the couple adopted two girls and a boy. Arden was still married to West at the time of his death on February 7, 1984. She never remarried.

12. The production opened and closed at the Eugene ONeill Theatre in New York City on February 22, 1983.

13. *http://www.imdb.com/name/nm0000781/bio*.

14. Even though he was never a headline radio star, sources claim Gale Gordon was the highest paid actor in Hollywood radio by 1933, nearly a decade before he began to acquire the roles that were to distinguish him throughout his life.

15. Gordon had 30 minutes in the "live" broadcast days to get from CBS's *Our Miss Brooks* to NBC's *Harris-Faye* program. The two studios were situated two blocks from each other in Hollywood, not a tremendous distance; yet some of his mock stress could have been for real as he hustled from one venue to the other.

16. Gordon's bellow-and-bluster was apparently only an act. "Off stage," maintained the *We Love Lucy* newsletter a few weeks after his death in 1995, "he was one of the sweetest, gentlest men to walk the earth."

17. Lucy wanted Gale Gordon and Bea Benaderet to appear as Fred and Ethel Mertz in *I Love Lucy*. Desi selected William Frawley as Fred after Frawley allegedly interjected himself into the deliberations. The show's original director, Marc Daniels, picked Vivian Vance for the part of Ethel. Such developments intimate that Lucy didn't carry the authority at the time that she earned once the show became a smash hit, although sources acknowledge that Benaderet was already under contract to *Burns and Allen* for the part of Blanche Morton.

18. *Life with Lucy* vanished abruptly because those behind the return of Ball to the small screen apparently didn't consider that a 75-year-old lady could no longer perform the physical antics that made her so funny when *I Love Lucy* debuted 35 years before. While her name was a big draw, the show couldn't simply rest on that alone.

19. The couple also appeared together on episodes of *Death Valley Days*.

20. John Dunning, *On the Air: The Encyclopedia of Old-Time Radio* (New York: Oxford University Press, 1998), p. 529.

21. *http://en.wikipedia.org/wiki/Jeff_Chandler_(actor)* and *http://www.imdb.com/name/nm0001996/bio*.

22. Lemond's late wife, Barbara Brewster, who died June 21, 2005, was the surviving member of the infamous "Brewster Twins" of the late 1930s. Twentieth Century–Fox identified them as "the Most Beautiful Twins in America." The Lemonds met when Barbara was performing with the USO in the South Pacific. They were married 58 years.

23. Nachman, p. 220.

## Chapter 20

1. John Dunning, *Tune in Yesterday: The Ultimate Encyclopedia of Old-Time Radio, 1925–1976* (Englewood Cliffs, N.J.: Prentice-Hall, 1976), p. 480.

2. John Dunning, *On the Air: The Encyclopedia of Old-Time Radio* (New York: Oxford University Press, 1998), p. 543.

3. *Variety*, June 4, 1947, p. 27.

4. Frank Buxton and Bill Owen, *The Big Broadcast, 1920–1950* 2nd edition. (Lanham, MD: Scarecrow Press, 1997), pp. 81–82.

5. Quoted in Thomas A. DeLong, *Radio Stars: An Illustrated Biographical Dictionary of 953 Performers, 1920 through 1960* (Jefferson, N.C.: McFarland, 1996), p. 93.

6. Gerald Nachman, *Raised on Radio: In Quest of The Lone Ranger, Jack Benny, Amos 'n' Andy, The Shadow, Mary Noble, The Great Gildersleeve, Fibber McGee and Molly, Bill Stern, Our Miss Brooks, Henry Aldrich, The Quiz Kids, Mr. First Nighter, Fred Allen, Vic and Sade, The Cisco Kid, Jack Armstrong, Arthur Godfrey, Bob and Ray, The Barbour Family, Henry Morgan, Joe Friday, and Other Lost Heroes from Radio's Heyday* (New York: Pantheon Books, 1998), p. 82.

7. Nachman, p. 81.

8. From an appearance before a convention of the Society to Preserve and Encourage Radio Drama, Variety and Comedy (SPERDVAC), quoted in Leonard Maltin, *The Great American Broadcast: A Celebration of Radio's Golden Age* (New York: Penguin Putnam, 1997), p. 178.

9. *http://en.wikipedia.org/wiki/Alice_Faye*.

10. Ibid.

11. *http://imdb.com/name/nm0269647/bio*.

12. *The New York Times*, May 11, 1998, p. A15.

13. Ibid.

# Bibliography

In addition to the published works listed here, an abundance of websites were also explored. Many are identified within the Chapter Notes. Extensive investigations into copious periodical issues were conducted, too. Especially useful were the following publications: *Advertising Age*, *The Airwaves* (of the Chattanooga Old-Time Radio Club), *Billboard*, *Broadcasting*, *The Chicago Daily News*, *The Chicago Tribune*, *The Illustrated Press* (of the Old Time Radio Club), *The Los Angeles Times*, *The New York Daily Mirror*, *The New York Times*, *Newsweek*, *Nostalgia Digest*, *Radio Guide*, *Radio Life*, *Radio Mirror* (and its extended monikers), *Radio Recall* (of the Washington Old Time Radio Club), *Radiogram* (of the Society to Preserve and Encourage Radio Drama, Variety and Comedy), *Time*, *TV Guide*, *USA Today*, *Variety* and *The Washington Post*.

Allen, Steve. *"Dumbth": The Lost Art of Thinking.* Amherst, N.Y.: Prometheus, 1998.

Balk, Alfred. *The Rise of Radio, from Marconi Through the Golden Age.* Jefferson, N.C.: McFarland, 2006.

Barnouw, Erik. *A Tower in Babel: A History of Broadcasting in the United States, Vol. I—to 1933.* New York: Oxford, 1966.

_____. *The Golden Web: A History of Broadcasting in the United States, Vol. II—1933 to 1953.* New York: Oxford, 1968.

_____. *The Image Empire: A History of Broadcasting in the United States, Vol. III—from 1953.* New York: Oxford, 1970.

Benny, Jack, and Joan Benny. *Sunday Nights at Seven: The Jack Benny Story.* New York: Warner Books, 1990.

Berard, Jeanette M., and Klaudia Englund. *Radio Series Scripts, 1930–2001: A Catalog of the American Radio Archives Collection.* Jefferson, N.C.: McFarland, 2006.

Bresee, Frank, and Bobb Lynes. *Radio's Golden Years: A Visual Guide to the Shows and the Stars.* Hollywood: Frank Bresee Productions, 1998.

Brooks, Tim, and Earle Marsh. *The Complete Directory to Prime Time Network TV Shows, 1946–Present*, 4th ed. New York: Ballantine, 1988.

Burns, George, with David Fisher. *All My Best Friends.* New York: Putnam, 1989.

_____. *Gracie, a Love Story.* New York: Penguin, 1988.

Buxton, Frank, and Bill Owen. *The Big Broadcast, 1920–1950*, 2nd ed. Lanham, MD: Scarecrow, 1997.

Campbell, Robert. *The Golden Years of Broadcasting: A Celebration of the First 50 Years of Radio and TV on NBC.* New York: Scribner, 1976.

Chase, Francis, Jr. *Sound and Fury: An Informal History of Broadcasting.* New York: Harper, 1942.

Cox, Jim. *Confessions of a Moonlight Writer.* Brentwood, TN: JM Publications, 1982.

_____. *The Daytime Serials of Television, 1946–1960.* Jefferson, N.C.: McFarland, 2006.

_____. *Frank and Anne Hummert's Radio Factory: The Programs and Personalities of Broadcasting's Most Prolific Producers.* Jefferson, N.C.: McFarland, 2003.

_____. *The Great Radio Audience Participation Shows: Seventeen Programs from the 1940s and 1950s.* Jefferson, N.C.: McFarland, 2001.

_____. *The Great Radio Soap Operas.* Jefferson, N.C.: McFarland, 1999.

_____. *Historical Dictionary of American Radio Soap Operas.* Lanham, MD: Scarecrow, 2005.

_____. *Mr. Keen, Tracer of Lost Persons: A Complete History and Episode Log of Radio's Most Durable Detective.* Jefferson, N.C.: McFarland, 2004.

_____. *Music Radio: The Great Performers and Programs of the 1920s through Early 1960s.* Jefferson, N.C.: McFarland, 2005.

_____. *Radio Crime Fighters: Over 300 Programs from the Golden Age.* Jefferson, N.C.: McFarland, 2002.

_____. *Radio Speakers: Narrators, News Junkies, Sports Jockeys, Tattletales, Tipsters, Toastmasters and Coffee Klatch Couples Who Verbalized the Jargon of the Aural Ether from the 1920s to the 1980s—A Biographical Dictionary.* Jefferson, N.C.: McFarland, 2007.

_____. *Say Goodnight, Gracie: The Last Years of Network Radio.* Jefferson, N.C.: McFarland, 2002.

DeLong, Thomas A. *Radio Stars: An Illustrated Biographical Dictionary of 953 Performers, 1920 through 1960.* Jefferson, N.C.: McFarland, 1996.

Duncan, Jacci, ed. *Making Waves: The 50 Greatest Women in Radio and Television.* Kansas City: Andrews McMeel, 2001.

Dunning, John. *On the Air: The Encyclopedia of Old-Time Radio.* New York: Oxford University Press, 1998.

_____. *Tune in Yesterday: The Ultimate Encyclopedia of Old-Time Radio, 1925–1976.* Englewood Cliffs, N.J.: Prentice-Hall, 1976.

Editors of TV Guide. *TV Guide: Guide to TV.* New York: Barnes & Noble, 2004.

Finkelstein, Norman H. *Sounds in the Air: The Golden Age of Radio.* New York: Scribner, 1993.

Fox, Ken, and Maitland McDonagh, eds. *TV Guide Film and Video Companion, 2004.* New York: Barnes & Noble, 2003.

Goldin, J. David. *The Golden Age of Radio: The Standard Reference Work of Radio Programs and Radio Performers of the Past.* Sandy Hook, CT: Radio Yesteryear, 2000.

Halberstam, David. *The Fifties.* New York: Villard, 1993.

Harmon, Jim. *The Great Radio Comedians.* Garden City, N.Y.: Doubleday, 1970.

Hart, Dennis. *Monitor: The Last Great Radio Show.* San Jose, CA: Writers Club, 2002.

Harvey, Rita Morley. *Those Wonderful, Terrible Years: George Heller and the American Federation of Television and Radio Artists.* Carbondale: Southern Illinois University Press, 1996.

Hickerson, Jay. *Necrology of Radio Personalities.* Hamden, CT: Jay Hickerson, 1996. Plus supplements 1–5: 1997, 1998, 1999, 2000, 2002.

_____. *The Third Revised Ultimate History of Network Radio Programming and Guide to All Circulating Shows.* Hamden, CT: Presto Print II, 2005.

Hyatt, Wesley. *The Encyclopedia of Daytime Television: Everything You Ever Wanted to Know About Daytime TV but Didn't Know Where to Look! From American Bandstand, As the World Turns, and Bugs Bunny, to Meet the Press, The Price Is Right, and Wide World of Sports, the Rich History of Daytime Television in All Its Glory!* New York: Billboard, 1997.

Lackmann, Ron. *Remember Radio.* New York: Putnam, 1970.

_____. *Same Time ... Same Station: An A-Z Guide to Radio from Jack Benny to Howard Stern.* New York: Facts on File, 1996.

*The Lima* (Ohio) *News,* June 6, 1937, p. 32.

MacDonald, J. Fred. *Don't Touch That Dial!: Radio Programming in American Life from 1920 to 1960.* Chicago: Nelson-Hall, 1991.

Maltin, Leonard. *The Great American Broadcast: A Celebration of Radio's Golden Age.* New York: Penguin Putnam, 1997.

McLeod, Elizabeth. *The Original Amos 'n' Andy: Freeman Gosden, Charles Correll and the 1928–1943 Radio Serial.* Jefferson, N.C.: McFarland, 2005.

McNeil, Alex. *Total Television: The Comprehensive Guide to Programming from 1948 to the Present,* 4th ed. New York: Penguin Books, 1996.

Moore, John Trotwood, and Austin P. Foster. *Tennessee, the Volunteer State, 1769–1923,* vol. 3. Chicago: S.J. Clarke Publishing, 1923.

Mott, Robert L. *Radio Sound Effects: Who Did It, and How, in the Era of Live Broadcasting.* Jefferson, N.C.: McFarland, 1993.

Nachman, Gerald. *Raised on Radio: In Quest of The Lone Ranger, Jack Benny, Amos 'n' Andy, The Shadow, Mary Noble, The Great Gildersleeve, Fibber McGee and Molly, Bill Stern, Our Miss Brooks, Henry Aldrich, The Quiz Kids, Mr. First Nighter, Fred Allen, Vic and Sade, The Cisco Kid, Jack Armstrong, Arthur Godfrey, Bob and Ray, The Barbour Family, Henry Morgan, Joe Friday, and Other Lost Heroes from Radio's Heyday.* New York: Pantheon, 1998.

Oppenheimer, Jess, with Gregg Oppenheimer. *Laughs, Luck ... and Lucy: How I Came to Create the Most Popular Sitcom of All Time.* Syracuse, N.Y.: University of Syracuse Press, 1996.

Paulson, Roger C. *Archives of the Airwaves,* vol. 1. Boalsburg, PA: Bear Manor, 2005.

_____. *Archives of the Airwaves,* vol. 2. Boalsburg, PA: Bear Manor, 2005.

Poindexter, Ray. *Golden Throats and Silver Tongues: The Radio Announcers.* Conway, AR: River Road, 1978.

Robinson, Marc. *Brought to You in Living Color: 75 Years of Great Moments in Television & Radio from NBC.* New York: Wiley, 2002.

Schaden, Chuck. *Speaking of Radio: Chuck Schaden's Conversations with the Stars of the Golden Age of Radio.* Morton Grove, IL: Nostalgia Digest, 2003.

Settel, Irving. *A Pictorial History of Radio,* 2nd ed. New York: Grosset & Dunlap, 1967.

Siegel, Susan, and David S. Siegel. *A Resource Guide to the Golden Age of Radio: Special Collections, Bibliography and the Internet.* Yorktown Heights, N.Y.: Book Hunter, 2006.

Sies, Luther F. *Encyclopedia of American Radio, 1920–1960.* Jefferson, N.C.: McFarland, 2000.

Slide, Anthony. *Great Radio Personalities in Historic Photographs.* Vestal, N.Y.: Vestal, 1982.

Smith, Sally Bedell. *In All His Glory: The Life of William S. Paley, the Legendary Tycoon and His Brilliant Circle.* New York: Simon and Schuster, 1990.

Stedman, Raymond William. *The Serials: Suspense and Drama by Installment.* Norman: University of Oklahoma Press, 1971.

Sterling, Christopher H., and John M. Kittross. *Stay Tuned: A Concise History of American Broadcasting,* 2nd ed. Belmont, CA: Wadsworth, 1990.

Stone, Hal (Harlan). *Aw ... Relax, Archie! Re-laxx!: When Radio Was "King" I Was Once a "Prince" but Ended Up a "Jughead."* Sedona, AZ: Bygone Days Press, 2003.

Stumpf, Charles, and Tom Price. *Heavenly Days!: The Story of Fibber McGee and Molly.* Waynesville, N.C.: The World of Yesterday, 1987.

Summers, Harrison B., ed. *A Thirty-Year History of Programs Carried on National Radio Networks in the United States, 1926–1956.* New York: Arno Press and *The New York Times,* 1971.

Swartz, Jon D., and Robert C. Reinehr. *Handbook of Old-Time Radio: A Comprehensive Guide to Golden Age Radio Listening and Collecting.* Metuchen, N.J.: Scarecrow, 1993.

Terrace, Vincent. *Radio Programs, 1924–1984: A Catalog of Over 1800 Shows.* Jefferson, N.C.: McFarland, 1999.

Waller, Judith C. *Radio: The Fifth Estate.* New York: Houghton Mifflin, 1946.

Wertheim, Arthur Frank. *Radio Comedy.* New York: Oxford, 1979.

Wolfe, Charles Hull. *Modern Radio Advertising.* New York: Printer's Ink, 1949.

# Index